The Palgrave Handbook of Gender, Media and Communication in the Middle East and North Africa

Loubna H. Skalli • Nahed Eltantawy
Editors

The Palgrave Handbook of Gender, Media and Communication in the Middle East and North Africa

palgrave
macmillan

Editors
Loubna H. Skalli
Washington Program
University of California
Washington, DC, USA

Nahed Eltantawy
Nido R. Qubein School of
Communication
High Point University
High Point, NC, USA

ISBN 978-3-031-11979-8   ISBN 978-3-031-11980-4   (eBook)
https://doi.org/10.1007/978-3-031-11980-4

Cover illustration: Alistair Laming / Alamy Stock Photo

This Palgrave Macmillan imprint is published by the registered company Springer Nature Switzerland AG.
The registered company address is: Gewerbestrasse 11, 6330 Cham, Switzerland

ACKNOWLEDGMENTS

We would like to thank our contributors for their hard work and patience throughout the stages of preparation and publication of this handbook. Their dedication to this project has been remarkable despite the contextual and health challenges imposed by the Covid-19 pandemic.

We appreciate all you have done.

We thank our Palgrave editor, Camille Davies, for giving this project her full support and attention from start to finish. We also acknowledge Samriddhi Pandey and the entire editing and production team for their professionalism. Our thanks go to Salwa Mansuri, our research assistant, for her dedication to this project.

We acknowledge, with gratitude, the love and support of our respective families. A project such as this has taken time away from being with our dear ones.

We appreciate your understanding and flexibility.

CONTENTS

NOTES ON CONTRIBUTORS

Reman Abdel All is vice dean for Environmental Affairs and a member of the Department of Political Science at Suez Canal University. Before her present position, Dr. Reman was the post-graduate studies coordinator of the Faculty of Commerce at Suez Canal University. She is interested in research related to international politics, Africa, environmental studies, and women, and political participation.

Hadeel Abdelhameed is a Konrad-Adenauer-Stiftung e.V. research fellow in Iraqi gender politics, electoral and political issues, and a non-residential fellow at Lancaster University's Richardson Institute in Iraqi women's activism and de-sectarianization. She received her PhD from La Trobe University in Iraqi Theatre about War and Gender Politics in 2019. Her research interests center around the Iraqi issues of women's political representation and gender performance, women activism and social movements, gender roles in electoral and political processes, and cultural productions related to gender politics and war in Iraq. Dr. Abdelhameed has had his research published in Cambridge Core, the *Journal of Contemporary Iraq & the Arab World*, AIIA, KAS, and MDPI.

Angie Abdelmonem is a faculty associate in Arizona State University's School for the Future of Innovation in Society. Her research centers on the sexual harassment movement, gender, and sexual violence, and NGOs and social movements in Egypt.

Amel Al Ariqi is originally from Yemen, where she worked as a journalist and managing editor at the *Yemen Times*. She traveled to many of the region's media hubs in Lebanon, Egypt, and Jordan where she gained a deep understanding of the media landscape. Now living in the United Kingdom, she works as the assistant team manager for the Rory Peck Trust, a charity supporting freelance journalists globally. Amel has been a visiting lecturer at the London College of Communication and was a journalism fellow at the Reuters Institute for the Study of Journalism at Oxford University in 2008/2009.

Benjamin Ale-Ebrahim (he/him) is a PhD candidate in sociocultural anthropology at Indiana University, Bloomington. His research uses ethnographic methods to study how the internet and social media platforms shape the experiences of LGBTQ+ Arabs, Muslims, and Middle Eastern people in managing issues of identity, privacy, and self-expression. He has conducted research in Morocco and the United States and has previously worked as a research intern at the Social Media Collective at Microsoft Research.

Ruba Ali Al-Hassani is a postdoctoral research associate at Lancaster University and Project SEPAD in the United Kingdom and is completing her PhD at Osgoode Hall Law School, Canada. Her doctoral research relies on digital sociology to study state sovereignty, while her wider research explores interdisciplinary approaches to Iraqi studies, law, transitional justice, crime, social control, and social movements. Ruba has taught at York University and Trent University. She holds a BSc in Psychology and Sociology, an MA in Criminology, and an LLM in Transitional Justice.

Ghyath Alkinani is Lecturer in Comparative Literature at the University of Kufa, Iraq. He received his PhD from the University of Arkansas in Comparative Literature and Cultural Studies. His research interests are Iraqi and American fiction, decolonizing war trauma narrative, and comparative literature.

Fatima Alsalem holds a PhD in Mass Communication from Indiana University Bloomington in the United States and is working as Associate Professor of Mass Communication at Kuwait University. Alsalem has had many research articles published on social media in Kuwait and women's political participation in numerous international and Arab academic journals.

Rafiah Al Talei is the editor-in-chief for Sada in Carnegie's Middle East Program, where her research focuses on civil rights, women's issues, and political developments in the Gulf. She has over 25 years of experience in Omani and international media networks and most recently held the position of senior producer in the Public Liberties and Human Rights Centre at Al Jazeera Media Network. Al Talei has held fellowships at Stanford University, Syracuse University, and the National Endowment for Democracy. She has conducted research on women's issues with Freedom House and with the International Council for Research and Exchange (IREX). She is a former candidate for parliament in Oman (Majlis Al-Shura).

Zayer Baazaoui is a teacher of French and Francophone Studies at St. Paul's School in Concord, New Hampshire. Zayer holds a PhD in Literary, Cultural, and Linguistic Studies from the University of Miami.

Sarah Benamara is an Algerian-American scholar based out of New England. She studied political science with a passion for MENA women's issues at Wellesley College, where she initially started exploring the issue of domestic violence in Algeria. She is in the process of obtaining a JD from Boston College

Law School. Previously, she worked as a strategy consultant for public sector institutions in the GCC region.

Michela Cerruti DEA, is a MAS candidate in International Strategy and Leadership at the Graduate Institute in Geneva. She collaborates as a research consultant with the charitable organization "Syria Reporting Center" based in Berlin. Her PhD research project is dedicated to study female movements in Syria before and during the conflict. She has had a book chapter published in *Women Rising: In and Beyond the Arab Spring.*

Nahed Eltantawy (she/her) is Professor of Journalism and Women and Gender Studies and associate dean at the Nido R. Qubein School of Communication, High Point University. Her research focuses on women and gender studies, media representation, social media activism, and critical and cultural studies. Her work has been published in various books and peer-reviewed journals, including *Feminist Media Studies, International Journal of Communication,* and *Communication and Critical/Cultural Studies.* Eltantawy has presented her research at various national and international academic conferences and conventions. She has also been an invited conference speaker at various universities, including the Columbia Journalism School in New York, the University of Toronto, and the University of Southern California Annenberg School for Communication and Journalism. She is a recipient of two Fulbright awards. She can be followed on Twitter at @ntantawy or contacted at neltanta@highpoint.edu.

Itir Erhart studied philosophy and Western languages and literatures at Bogaziçi University, Istanbul. She completed her MPhil in Philosophy at the University of Cambridge. Since 2001 she has been teaching and researching gender, human rights, sports, social movements, and civil society at Istanbul Bilgi University. She is the co-founder of Adım Adım (Step by Step), a volunteer-based organization that promotes charitable giving through the sponsorship of athletes in local sports events. Itir also co-founded Açık Açık, a platform that unites donors with NGOs that respect the rights of donors.

Hande Eslen-Ziya is Professor of Sociology at the University of Stavanger and director of the Populism, Anti-Gender, and Democracy Research Group. She holds a PhD in Sociology from the Polish Academy of Sciences, Warsaw, Poland, and an MA in Social Psychology from Bogazici University, Istanbul Turkey. She also has a Gender Specialization from Central European University, Budapest, Hungary. She has an established interest in gender and social inequalities and she is working on an edited book with Dr. Alberta Giorgi on *Populism and Science in Europe.* Dr. Eslen-Ziya has also co-edited the book titled *The Aesthetics of Global Protest: Visual Culture and Communication.*

Zoe Hurley is the Assistant Dean for Student Affairs in the College of Communications and Media Sciences at Zayed University, Dubai, United Arab Emirates. She holds her PhD from Lancaster University, United Kingdom, and her thesis focused on issues of Arab women's empowerment through social media. Zoe teaches undergraduate courses in social media and her research develops feminist theorizing of microcelebrities, participatory cultures, and the post-digital condition.

Haala Hweio is an adjunct professor at Dominican University in River Forest, Illinois. She holds a doctorate from Northern Illinois University in comparative politics and biopolitics with a special focus on the Middle East and North Africa. She also holds a master's degree in International Relations from Sussex University in the United Kingdom and a bachelor's degree in Political Science from Garyounis University in Benghazi, Libya. Her main research interests include gender dynamics, political Islam, and state-society relations in the Middle East and North Africa.

Senni Jyrkiäinen is a social anthropologist who holds her PhD in Social and Cultural Anthropology at the University of Helsinki in 2019. Her PhD dissertation examined the technologically mediated navigation of desires for love and marriage in post-2011 Egypt through a focus on the usage of smartphones and other digital communication tools amongst young people in Alexandria, Egypt. Primarily focused on contemporary Egypt, her research interests include technologically mediated communication, social media, gender, youth, and mobility. Jyrkiäinen works in Finland and focuses on digital participation.

Magdalena Karolak is Associate Professor of Humanities and Social Sciences at Zayed University (ZU), UAE. She received her PhD in Linguistics, MA in Political Science, MA in Latin American Studies, and BA in French Language. Before working at ZU, Dr. Karolak held assistant professor positions in Bahrain and Saudi Arabia. In 2014–15, she was an American Political Science Association MENA Fellow. Her research interests include transformations of societies in the MENA region and comparative linguistics. Dr. Karolak has had more than 50 journal articles and book chapters published on the shifting gender relations, social media, culture and identity, and political system transformations in the MENA countries. She is the author of three scholarly monographs.

Tamara Kharroub is a senior research fellow and the deputy executive director of Arab Center Washington DC, based in Washington DC in the United States. Her research work focuses on political communications and digital rights in the Arab world including digital authoritarianism, cyber geopolitics, disinformation, surveillance, identity politics, women's rights, the role of media and communication technology in the political process, and the Palestinian context. She holds a PhD from Indiana University Bloomington and an MA from the University of Westminster and is the recipient of several awards and fellowships including Fulbright.

alma aamiry-khasawnih is an assistant professor in the Department of Women's, Gender, & Sexuality Studies and an affiliate faculty of the African American Studies Department at The College of New Jersey. She researches access to the street in post-colonial and settler-colonial nation-states as a site of understanding and articulating access to citizenship. alma's research projects examine ephemeral visual culture production (graffiti, murals, and other forms of street/public art) as stand-alone material objects that orient, disorient, and reorient feminist debates on social political-cultural movements within urban geographies and the phenomenology of erasure, cooptation, and resistance. alma is invested in examining how urban beautification projects and cleansing public spaces are part of authoritarian visual culture and politics of respectability that aims at policing minoritized bodies in public spaces.

Amany Ahmed Khodair chairs the Department of Political Science and vice dean for Environmental Affairs at The British University in Egypt, since September 2016. She joined The British University in Egypt in 2011 as a part-time Professor in Political Science. Before her present position, Professor Khodair was the vice dean for Environmental Affairs and the head of the Political Science Department at Suez Canal University. She was also the English section coordinator of the Faculty of Commerce at Suez Canal University. In 1994, Professor Khodair was a visiting post-doctorate researcher at Rutgers State University, New Jersey, United States. She is interested in research related to media and politics, communication and public opinion, public administration and public policy, and women and political participation.

Lilia Labidi is a professor at the University of Tunis and an anthropologist and psychoanalyst, holding doctorates from the University of Paris VII. She is the co-founder of several Tunisian NGOs, is the author of numerous books and articles on the Arab world, and has held positions at the Institute for Advanced Study (Princeton), Woodrow Wilson Center (Washington, DC), American University in Cairo, Yale University, Swedish Collegium, and National University of Singapore. She has organized several documentary exhibitions on women's movements in Tunisia and has presented happenings and installations on political violence.

Einat Lachover is an associate professor at Sapir Academic College, Israel. Her work is dedicated to the critical analysis of the encounters between gender and a broad range of media forms and contexts. She has had her research published in international journals, such as *Communication Theory, Journalism, International* the *Journal of Communication, Communication Culture and Critique, Feminist Media Studies,* the *Journal of Children and Media,* the *Journal of Media and Religion, European Journal of Women's Studies,* the *Journal of Gender Studies, Israel Affairs,* NASHIM, and the *Journal of Israeli History.*

Brinda J. Mehta is the Germaine Thompson Professor of Francophone Studies and Professor of Women's, Gender, and Sexuality Studies at Mills College in Oakland, California, where she teaches postcolonial Anglophone and Francophone literature and transnational feminist thought. She is the author of five books and over 65 articles on postcolonial feminist literature. She is working on her sixth project, The Wounds of War and Conflict in Contemporary South Asian Women's Writings.

Noha Mellor is Professor in Media at the University of Sharjah, UAE, and a visiting professor at Bournemouth University, United Kingdom. She is the author of several books about Arab media, including The Making of Arab News (2005), Modern Arab Journalism (2007), Arab Media (2011), Reporting the MENA Region (2015), and Voice of the Muslim Brotherhood (2017), and she has recently co-edited the first comprehensive Handbook on Arab Media (2021).

Cristina Moreno Almeida is a British Academy postdoctoral research fellow in the Department of Digital Humanities at King's College London. Her research is about creative cultures in North Africa and the Middle East at the intersection of aesthetics, politics, and media. She has had her research published extensively on rap music, the politics of resistance, multimodal digital culture, participation, and creativity. Her first book is titled *Rap Beyond Resistance: Staging Power in Contemporary Morocco* (Palgrave Macmillan, 2017).

Lynn Mounzer is a researcher and consultant specializing in female economic participation and entrepreneurship. Lynn has worked with think tanks, non-profits, and fintech start-ups to increase women's labor force participation and entrepreneurship. She is the Lead Research Analyst at the Wilson Center working on the MEP-SCW project focused on identifying the missing links between low women economic participation and entrepreneurship and financial and digital inclusion, and existing laws in the Middle East and North Africa (MENA) region. Dr. Mounzer is also the founder of GenDev Consulting, a consulting firm that helps organizations foster opportunities for female economic inclusion and female entrepreneurship based on her PhD research on female entrepreneurship in the MENA region. Through her work at GenDev, she designed and led workshops and research on female economic participation, entrepreneurship, and other topics.

Loubna H. Skalli is a visiting professor at the University of California Washington Program, Washington, DC. She is a scholar-practitioner with subject area expertise in the politics of development, youth, gender, and communication. She taught at numerous universities in Morocco and the United States, including the American University's School of International Service and the George Washington University's Elliott School of International Affairs. She is the author, co-author, and editor of over 30 peer-reviewed journal articles, book chapters, and books. She is also the editor of the book series *Communication, Culture and Gender in the Middle East and North Africa* (Palgrave Macmillan) and *Gender and Activism* (Rowman & Littlefield). As a practitioner, she consulted with numerous intern/national development organizations and agencies including USAID, World Bank, U.S. Department of Labor, FHI 360, U.S. Department of State, the Global Fund for Women, and Counterpart International. She is a recipient of two Fulbright Fellowships. She received her

BA from Mohammed V University in Rabat, Morocco; her MA in Social/ Cultural Anthropology from Essex University, United Kingdom; and her PhD in International Communication from the Pennsylvania State University.

Mona Tajali is Associate Professor of International Relations and Women's, Gender, and Sexuality Studies at Agnes Scott College in Atlanta, Georgia. Her areas of expertise are gender and politics, human rights, and social movements in Muslim countries. Her book, *Women's Political Representation in Iran and Turkey: Demanding a Seat at the Table* (2022), investigates how religious and cultural norms, attitudes, institutional structures, and voter behavior affect the representation of women and the quality of democracy in Muslim contexts, with a comparative focus on Iran and Turkey. She has had her research published in both academic and popular outlets, including the *Middle East Journal; Politics & Gender;* the *Journal of Women, Politics & Policy; The Conversation; Jadaliyya;* and *The Nation.*

Leila Tayeb is a humanities research fellow at NYU, Abu Dhabi, and a performance studies scholar focused on contemporary Libya. Her interdisciplinary research uses performance ethnography and unconventional archives to explore the politics of cultural performance and the performativity of political life. Her in-progress first book project explores how sound practices in Libyan daily life became sites of political contestation between militias and civilians during the years after 2011.

Willow F. Williamson has a PhD in International Relations from American University. Her research focuses on the relationships between gender, identity, creativity, and communication in foreign policy. She has written book chapters and articles on women's empowerment and public diplomacy, improvisation and public diplomacy, creativity and research, and technology and public diplomacy. She has also composed music for award-winning films, TV, theater, and dance. She is a career member of the U.S. State Department Foreign Service. The views expressed in this article are her own and do not represent the views of the U.S. Department of State.

Polly Withers is a Leverhulme Early Career Research Fellow at the LSE Middle East Centre and a visiting fellow at the LSE Department of Media and Communications, where she researches issues related to gender, and feminism, popular culture, and global media and communications.

LIST OF FIGURES

LIST OF IMAGES

LIST OF TABLES

CHAPTER 1

Introduction to Gender, Media, and Communication in MENA

Loubna H. Skalli

The relationship between gender and communication in the Middle East and North Africa (MENA) is evolving through tensions and contradictions. *The Palgrave Handbook of Gender, Media and Communication in the Middle East and North Africa* is the first volume of its kind to provide a probing analysis of this complex relationship within one of the most dynamic regions of the world. Authors in this volume situate their case studies in a variety of political, economic, and social-cultural settings to provide a grounded, original, and balanced examination of the numerous ways gender and communication intersect, shape, and inform each other.

Over the last few decades alone, the region has seen the fall of a few dictators (Tunisia's Zine El Abidine Ben Ali, Libya's Muammar Qaddafi, Egypt's Hosni Mubarak, and Iraq's Saddam Hussein) whose oppressive apparatuses of surveillance and control reached far and deep into all aspects of gender experiences, knowledge production, information flows, and media production. Yet, it is under these same regimes, and many other authoritarian variants throughout the region, that the media and information ecosystems have undergone considerable transformations, while debates about gender identities, sexualities, and expectations have become more intensely entangled in these transformations. Regimes of oppression are not immune to change or even convulsions. As the late bell hooks wisely put it, oppression and marginality are the ultimate "site of radical possibility, a space of resistance" (hooks 1990). The 2011 democratic

L. H. Skalli (✉)
Hemodan, VA, USA
e-mail: lhanna@ucdc.edu

© The Author(s), under exclusive license to Springer Nature Switzerland AG 2023
L. H. Skalli, N. Eltantawy (eds.), *The Palgrave Handbook of Gender, Media and Communication in the Middle East and North Africa*, https://doi.org/10.1007/978-3-031-11980-4_1

1

uprisings across MENA have confirmed precisely this reality, and foregrounded its gendered dimensions.

The combined processes of modernization, education, economic development, and globalization have impacted citizens' relationships to their national institutions and regimes of power. They have also reshaped their overall communication habits, uses of information and communication technologies (ICTs), and attitudes toward media production and consumption. These transformations are unquestionably mediated by varying national policies and resources in the region, as well as by differences in gender needs and aspirations, age, class, ethnic, and racial identities. Nonetheless, the transformations are real, evolving, and perhaps even irreversible in some areas.

For a region whose size of the youth population is among the largest in the world, young men and women are reportedly spending an average of five hours a day on social media. By the end of 2020, nearly 80% of the young turned to social media as their primary source of news at a time when Algeria, Egypt, and Morocco stood as the ninth-largest markets for Facebook in the world (Radcliffe & Abuhmaid, 2021). The same report indicates that Libya, the United Arab Emirates, and Qatar were among the countries with the highest levels of reach for Facebook, relative to the population while Iraq, Saudi Arabia, and Egypt were among the 13 largest markets for Snapchat worldwide (Wan, 2021). Smartphone penetration is advancing at a dizzying speed in every country in MENA while mobile data consumption is projected to increase more than fivefold by 2025. Schools of communication and media studies are seeing an unprecedented growth and demand in many countries which are also witnessing the narrowing of the gender gap in these educational institutions and programs (Tweissi, 2015; Ziani et al., 2018). Today, television screens have more female newscasters and program hosts, while magazines and newspaper rooms boast more female journalists and reporters (Mellor, 2019).

Yet, in a region where conservative forces retain their stronghold on the definition of gender roles, relations, and norms, the processes of transformation described above do not systematically translate into the deepening or broadening of gender justice. The strength of the countries' political will to push their national development toward twenty-first-century competitiveness, finds no parallel in promoting gender equity and equality. Gender biases and discrimination have proven enduring and resilient, while patriarchal backlash continues to jeopardize advances in women's rights and the rights of non-binary gender identities. Recent and protracted conflicts compounded with the devastating Covid-19 pandemic have further complicated the safety and rights of women, girls, and sexual minorities in the region.

The relationship between gender and communication is, therefore, deeply shaped and informed by all these tensions and contradictions. While more girls are attending communication classrooms and more women are working in media organizations and newsrooms, they continue to experience "simultaneous sticky floors and glass ceilings": they continue to be "tethered" to their domestic responsibilities while their careers are constrained by limited opportunities for leadership and ownership, decision-making or promotions in the media sectors (Melki & Hitti, 2021). Likewise, as access to digital technologies is growing among women in MENA, newer forms of patriarchal intimidations are emerging and pervasive gender-based violence still threatens to curtail their online and on the ground presence (Erhaim, 2020).

Further, gender inequities and distortions are still pervasive in the content of both public and commercial media, in the amount and quality of information in news, featured articles, television programming, or coverage of political leadership and socio-economic accomplishments. Media's construction of sexual identities is still constrained by binaries and biases. While masculinities continue to be largely built around ideas of violence and virility, economic independence and career achievements, femininities are confined within frames of appearances and adornments, vulnerabilities, and fragilities. Non-binary identities are either vilified or altogether unacknowledged.

The Palgrave Handbook of Gender, Media, and Communication in the Middle East and North Africa is driven by the scholarly ambition to *both* capture these enduring contradictions and acknowledge the disruptions taking place despite them. The Handbook does so by providing an authoritative and up-to-date engagement with the critical debates, research methods, and ongoing reflections on how gender and communication intersect with the economic, social, political, and cultural fabrics of the countries in the region. Contributors to the Handbook are established and rising scholars who bring together their various disciplinary expertise and fresh data to contextualize the complex ways gender and communication intersect through media institutions, technologies, and the practices of everyday life. They contextualize these intersections within specific localities to examine how gender is constructed and communicated in the following six broad areas: political action, activism and civic engagement, the articulation of identities and sexualities, the incidence of online and on the ground violence, investments in business and social entrepreneurship, and the production of artistic and cultural products. The sections of this Handbook are premised on the following definitions of gender, communication, and media.

First, gender and gender identities are socially constructed, rather than biologically determined. Social institutions typically confine gender within a reductionist binary framework that determines and assesses what male/masculinity and female/femininity are and ought to be. This normative construction of gender rests on a fundamentally asymmetrical distribution of power, desirability, freedoms, opportunities, and rewards. Asymmetries rank and reward masculinities and femininities according to their level of (masculine) authority and toxicity and (feminine) docility and domesticity. Finally, the hierarchical construction of gender tolerates the existence of no identities or sexualities beyond the binary framework. This Handbook uses gender beyond the binary and restrictive meanings of the term precisely because of the inequities, injustices, and exclusions that are permitted by the orthodoxy.

Second, contributors to the Handbook understand that debates about women and gender in MENA have always evoked deep passions, anxieties, and uncertainties reflected in the countries' institutions, policies, and discourses. The Handbook is deliberate in its use of gender and women. Despite the relatively greater academic interest in gender dynamics in the region, there still is a tendency to reduce gender to women-only analysis, especially in research on media and communication. While a few of the Handbook's chapters focus exclusively on women's uses of communication, others approach gender beyond merely "women's issues" to examine the full range of gender identities, sexualities, and expressions. Chapters also reflect on the myriad ways in which femininities, masculinities, and non-binary identities are constructed, debated, and communicated through cultural spaces, and other mediated and digitized forms of expression.

Third, the Handbook is also premised on the understanding that gender influences practically every aspect of our communication needs and priorities, identity performances, and practices. As media scholars clearly put it

> when conjoined, 'gender and communication' create a powerful alchemy that encompasses interpersonal relationality, systems of judgment, modes of becoming, performative contexts, means of identity, degrees of mobility in place and space, types of power over one's body, and sources of self-determination (Goins et al., 2021).

We understand that acts of communication are fundamentally about people's generation of meaning in various forms and spaces and through numerous channels and media, both old and new. At the same time, the communication tools and platforms we choose, as well as the media contents and frames we construct, play a critical role in our definitions, experiences, and understanding of gender. Put simply, gender and communication intersect, shape, and inform each other at all levels of our being and doing. This is an important dynamic to underscore particularly within environments where gender expectations and performances are strictly monitored and policed along with citizen's communication practices and platforms. Therefore, communication by, about, and between genders in MENA tends to acquire exaggerated meanings and implications. The gendered access to and uses of information technologies also tend to be politicized and turned into sites of power struggles, control, contention, and resistance. The uniqueness of this Handbook is its conscious effort to capture this complex relationship between gender and communication within environments that seek to restrict their meaning and freedoms.

Fourth, the Handbook has moved debates on gender and media beyond simplistic or reductionist frames of analyses to complicate gender uses of social media and digital technologies outside the dual frames of unbridled triumphalism or disenchantment. Contributors to the Handbook understand that it is critical to interrogate the gray spaces where optimism and pessimism coexist, and to expose how zones of empowerment are tested and/or restrained by forces of repression and (self) censorship. As chapters in this volume show, women directors and filmmakers are not only challenging gender injustices and hierarchies of power; they are also complicit in reproducing and reinscribing some of them in their artistic productions. Digital technologies and social media are not only creating liberating spaces for the Lesbian, Gay, Bisexual, Transgender, and Queer (LGBTQ) communities in MENA to connect and commiserate. Rather, digital technologies and media spaces, as some chapters demonstrate, are also heightening the vulnerabilities of these communities by exposing them to online forms of violence that have tragic real-life consequences, ranging from suicide to loss of livelihoods. Similar arguments are made in the case of digital technologies and entrepreneurship. While ICTs have been enablers in engendering entrepreneurship and supporting women's self-employment opportunities, they have done so within environments where differences in class, social capital, and educational attainments undercut the promises of technology.

Further, this Handbook is also premised on the understanding that a rigorous examination of gender and communication demands recognition of how these articulate with their specific localities, regional trends, and global forces. The Handbook delivers fascinating case studies that extend beyond the few countries about which a disproportionate amount of (English) scholarship exists (Egypt, Jordan, Morocco, Tunisia, and Lebanon). Contributors reflect on gender and communication in Yemen, Oman, Syria, Turkey, Israel, Libya, and other countries typically marginalized in research on gender and communication in MENA. Discussions are anchored in these countries' complicated postcolonial histories and contemporary (post) revolutionary realities. This socio-political, temporal, and economic grounding acknowledges significant commonalities and differences within the MENA region, but also tapers off the irrational enthusiasm of the Arab Spring liberation narratives and the gloomy predictions of post-revolutionary times. What emerges is a nuanced understanding of how gender and communication are politicized within their specific localities as well as in relation to global forces, discourses, and practices.

Finally, this Handbook is premised on the value of cross and interdisciplinary approaches to assessing complex phenomena, environments, and relationships. Research on gender and communication in MENA remains fairly limited despite the remarkable surge of publications after the so-called Arab Spring. That which exists tends to be institutionally based in single academic disciplines which rarely talk to each other (women and gender studies, communication studies, cultural studies, Queer and Lesbian studies, anthropology, and political science). This Handbook provides a unique space for cross-disciplinary dialogue on the intersections of gender and communication given the complexity of forces, institutions, and actors that shape these intersections. This approach makes this Handbook rich, timely, and pertinent in covering many familiar and first-time explored topics in a single volume.

The Handbook is organized in six thematic sections each introduced by a concise overview of major debates, conceptual frameworks, and research methodologies. The first section of the Handbook, *Gender Identities and Sexualities,* delves into the complicated and shifting connections between communication, gender, identities, and sexualities in MENA. Authors are driven here by the intellectual desire to explore the kind of empowerment spaces and opportunities digital technologies and/or traditional communication tools facilitate, permit, or inhibit. This line of inquiry has produced fascinating insights into the different articulations of gender and (non-conforming) sexual identities in and through a variety of cultural/media products and social media spaces including Facebook, Instagram, and Twitter. Some chapters examine contested gender performances and the conflicting roles social media play in the lives of LGBTQ individuals and communities in contemporary Morocco and Tunisia. Others examine the politics and violence of representation of gendered and sexual identities within environments that legitimate homophobia and heteropatriarchy. Despite pervasive biases, violences, and heteronormative discourses on gender and sexualities, chapters suggest that media platforms and digital spaces are increasingly exposing competing and shifting definitions of masculinities and femininities, and communicating the struggles of individuals who do not conform to heterosexual and binary gender norms.

In the second section of the Handbook, *Gender and Activism*, the authors broaden the meaning of politics beyond formal political institutions and processes to include a wide range of meaningful political activities and impactful interventions. They use a variety of settings to assess if and how digital technologies and social media have contributed to gendering activism and civic engagement, political discourses, and cultures. Chapters here include the examination of media uses by Turkish activists following the Gezi protests and the performance of motherhood as a mobilizational strategy for advancing human rights in post-Saddam Hussein Iraq. Other chapters examine the uses of digital technologies in pre-and post-Syrian conflict to document the traumas of displacement and the combined oppression of conflict, patriarchy, and reductionist discourses of victimhood. Insights from this section provide unique perspective on the implications of digital technologies for gender and generational relationships within movements for social and political change.

In the third section of the Handbook, *The Gender of Politics*, researchers assess continuities and ruptures in media's frames of representation of political candidates and their campaigns, political participation in national legislative bodies, and other political positions. As women's movements and rights groups throughout MENA continue to press for the gendering of political institutions, spaces, and leadership roles, questions about the role of old and new media remain current, critical, and pressing. Chapters in this section on Libya, Iran, Egypt, Oman, and Israel provide a basis for interrogating this critical role of media prior to, during, and since the recent uprisings. The authors introduce new contexts for exploring the intersections between politics, women, gender, and media; and share insights on how these intersections can be simultaneously empowering and constraining. The significant consensus among contributors is that the gendering of public spheres and political action in MENA is a slow and complicated process that demands vigilance about the communication means, modes, and tools utilized by various actors in society.

Section four of the Handbook on *Gender-based Violence* (GBV) is one of the original contributions of this volume. While the vexing issue of violence has been on the agenda of human rights activists within and outside MENA, and even if the topic has attracted relatively more academic attention in recent years, no volume has produced a multi-country examination of the communication dimensions of GBV. Researchers in this volume examine how violence is defined and experienced by its survivors in their personal and professional lives and in their intimate and public spaces of interaction. Chapters discuss how GBV is rooted in the patriarchal histories of the countries and their institutions as well as in the ongoing conflicts and continuing militarization of societies. In all these cases, contributors rely on original interviews with survivors of GBV and analyze their social media presences to underscore not only stories of traumas but also narratives of defiance and determination to break the cycle of violence, silence, and state complicity in this. Chapters also underscore the opportunities digital technologies create for new forms of activism around GBV and some of the legal breakthroughs resulting from the combined online/ offline activism. However, contributors caution against the rise of novel forms of violence and patriarchal policing facilitated by the new technologies despite the promising trends they facilitate.

Another original contribution of this Handbook is the section focusing on the rarely researched linkages between gender, communication, and entrepreneurship in MENA. Here, authors acknowledge that while women entrepreneurs have been gradually receiving some scholarly and policy attention in recent years, significant disciplinary divisions continue to limit the breadth of the research focus and methods. Specifically, most of the existing research on entrepreneurship in MENA is conducted within the business and economic frameworks of analysis and visibly less so within gender or feminist epistemologies.

While existing scholarship is rich and insightful, chapters in this section seek to fill in important gaps by contextualizing the intersection between gender, communication, and entrepreneurship within specific localities including Bahrain, Lebanon, the United Arab Emirates, and Jordan. Authors assess the institutional as well as technological realities that shape gender and entrepreneurship to demonstrate areas of improvement and development. Finally, the section makes another interesting contribution by exploring the gender dimension of social entrepreneurship -an area that has remained under-researched in the scholarship on MENA.

The section of the Handbook titled, *Gender and Expressive Cultures*, delves into the creative world of cultural and artistic production to examine how gender impacts and is impacted by various expressive forms and spaces. Contributors here, some of whom are artists themselves, reflect on the intersections between gender and popular cultures, visual and street art, music, theater, performances, literary works, and numerous other mediated contents. They do so to reveal ways in which cultural/artistic spaces and practices are structured by gender dynamics, hierarchies of power, struggles and processes of contestation, and subversion. Contributors situate us in a variety of countries (Tunisia, Morocco, Algeria, Iraq, Palestine, and Egypt) to provide fascinating insights into how these dynamics work within specific localities and in relation to global cultural flows and influences. What emerges from this section is a rich analysis of the dynamic cultural and artistic scenes that reflect significant gender, age, class, religious, and racial differences in MENA.

The editors of *The Palgrave Handbook of Gender, Media, and Communication in the Middle East and North Africa* intend the volume to be a useful and accessible resource for college students, academics, researchers, and all individuals interested in the politics of gender and communication in MENA. Given the interdisciplinary nature of the Handbook and the wide range of thematic areas and theoretical frameworks it covers, we expect this volume to contribute to a broad selection of fields of study and academic programs. Contributions in this Handbook are original publications that rely on recent data collected to reflect the dynamic realities of MENA societies and the complex ways gender and communication intersect. While the chapters are theoretically informed and empirically robust, we have decided to communicate results of the research in an accessible and engaging way that appeals to a wider readership.

One of the ambitions of the Handbook is to bring together a wide range of scholarly perspectives on a region that is remarkably diverse in its cultures, faiths, languages, political economies, and technological infrastructures. Studying gender and communication within a diverse and dynamic region is a project that comes with varying levels of challenges. We have consciously and relentlessly tried to respect diversity in representation and disciplinary traditions by seeking contributions *from* and *about* every single country in MENA, especially those about which there is limited research on gender and communication (Iraq, Yemen, Oman, Syria, Libya, Saudi Arabia). We have made every effort to be inclusive of voices and perspectives by reaching out to both established and emerging scholars who have interest and expertise in media, communication, women, and gender in MENA.

Some of the contributors to this volume are located within the region, but the majority are based in European, American, or Australian academic institutions. Different locations provide researchers with varying levels of support and resources for their research and publications. We understand that the researchers from MENA are typically constrained by resources and occasional concerns with freedom in collecting data. We also understand and respect the fact that many researchers from the region typically conduct research and publish in other languages than English. We are tremendously grateful to our contributors for all the time and efforts they have put in sharing their invaluable insights. The Handbook is stronger and better with their voices.

REFERENCES

Erhaim, Z. (2020, July 9). Women Activists in the Middle East face Online Bullying and Sexual Harassment. *Open Democracy*. https://www.opendemocracy.net/en/north-africa-west-asia/women-activists-middle-east-face-online-bullying-and-sexual-harassment/

Goins, M. N., McAlister, J. F., & Alexander, B. K. (2021). *The Routledge Handbook of Gender and Communication*. Routledge.

Melki, J., & Hitti, E. (2021). The Domestic Tethering of Lebanese and Arab Women Journalists and News Managers. *Journalism Practice, 15*(3), 288–307. https://doi.org/10.1080/17512786.2020.1715822

Mellor, N. (2019). The (in)visibility of Arab Women in Political Journalism. In C. Carter, L. Steiner, & S. Allan (Eds.), *Journalism, Gender and Power*. Routledge.

Radcliffe & Ahuhmaid. (2021). How the Middle East used social media in 2020. New Media Academy file:///C:/Users/lskal/Downloads/SSRN-id3826011.pdf

Tweissi, B. (2015). *Teaching Journalism in the Arab World: Challenges and Lost Opportunities*. Retrieved from http://www.al-fanarmedia.org/2015/06/teachingjournalism-in-the-arab-world-challenges-and-lost-opportunities/

Ziani, A. K., Elareshi, M., Alrashid, M., & Al-Jaber, K. (2018). Journalism Education in the GCC Region: University Students' and Professionalism Perspectives. *Journal of Communication Media Watch, 9*(1), 52–68.

PART I

Introduction: Gendered Identities and Sexualities

Questions about gender and identities (cultural, political, and religious) have a long history in MENA. The violence of the colonial histories in the region and the struggles of post-/colonial nation building have all triggered deep anxieties and intense debates about the constituents of Middle Eastern identities. Globalization has not only revived many such anxieties but further heightened the competing demands over identities as these continue to negotiate the tensions between traditions and (post)modernities, as well as local realities and global forces. The body of literature that engages with identity politics and concerns across MENA is impressive in both its breadth and depth of analysis. However, research into sexual identities and individuals who do not conform to heterosexual and binary gender norms remains very limited. Work that has examined sexualities has focused on the ways patriarchal institutions regulate and restrict sexual behavior and desire, as well as the monitoring, policing, and disciplining of the female body in the Muslim/Arab public and private spheres. The groundbreaking work of Samar Habib on female sexuality, homosexuality in Islam, and queer identities is a major contribution to and departure from this tradition of research.

Habib's work, including *Female Homosexuality in the Middle East* (2012) and *Islam and Homosexuality* (2010), provides a historical grounding for understanding dis-/continuities in dominant discourses and attitudes towards queer identities and homosexuality in MENA. In doing so, she has opened a space for defining homosexuality, queer identities, and homophobia in the contemporary contexts of the region and within its contradictory conservative and progressive ideological currents. Drawing on these and other insights, recent researchers are increasingly turning their attention to the emergence of LGBTQ activist communities in countries such as Morocco, Egypt, Jordan, Sudan, Lebanon, and Palestine (Alessi et al., 2021; Khalid, 2015; Magued, 2021; Nasser-Eddin et al., 2018). This line of research seeks to assess the nature and scope of the region's LGBTQ trans-/national networks, the specificities of their cultural and social movements, as well as the impact these are likely to have on furthering the rights of the sexual minorities.

This section of the handbook engages with the construction and expression of gender and (non-conforming) sexual identities in and through mediated forms (films, documentary, press) and social media spaces (Facebook, Twitter, etc.). The questions the chapters address are related to the politics and violence of representation of gendered and sexual identities in authoritarian regimes; the reproduction of homophobic, heteropatriarchal, and heteronormative discourses in and through media, public, and digital spaces; the competing and shifting definitions of masculinities and femininities in the varying contexts of MENA; and the struggles of minority identities to survive the threats of repressive cultural, religious, and legal constraints. The chapters provide new directions for research in these areas and fascinating ways of thinking about gender and sexual identities in the age of social media and digital technologies.

Benjamin Ale-Ebrahim's chapter on "Making Visible the Unseen Queer" takes Morocco as a case study for shedding light on the cost of being a member of the sexual minorities and the risks and challenges of creating a safe space for interaction. He demonstrates how online dating spaces, such as Grindr and PlanetRomeo, create simultaneous processes of empowerment and vulnerability for the gays, bisexual, and queer men in the country. Through a close analysis of an outing campaign targeting these sexual minorities, Ebrahim complicates our understanding of "safe spaces" and the promises of digital intimacies. Social media may create possibilities for sexual minorities to have a space of interaction and communication; however, they can also empower "homophobic vigilantes to 'hunt' gay men" and other sexual minorities. The outing campaigns in Morocco cost the members of the sexual minorities their safety, livelihoods, mental health, family relations, and friendships.

Similar challenges and risks are highlighted in Zayer Baazaoui's chapter on "Queer Resistance and Activism" which he traces through his analysis of the 2017 documentary *Upon the Shadow*. The context for exploring these issues is Tunisia and the focus is on the daily struggles of a group of young queer people in a conservative society. The documentary, according to Baazaoui, conveys a degree of realism as well as "authenticity" of the sexually marginalized and ostracized community. Yet, it is precisely their marginalization and vulnerability which creates a sense of community among the group of young men, fuels their solidarity and gives direction to their activism.

The chapter by Senni Jyrkiäinen provides a different angle of analysis on how social media and digital technologies are reshaping how young people express their sense of "self and loyalty to traditional institutions" and experience love and intimate desire. Drawing on ethnographic fieldwork and digital ethnography in post-Hosni Mubarak Egypt, Jyrkiäinen examines the different ways young people present their individualities on Facebook, express their intimate actions, and position themselves towards family and community. Digital spaces, she contends, allow for the coexistence of both the "connective and more individualistic aspects of the self" and the articulation of the self in relation to their Egyptianness, Islamic heritage, and global cultural trends.

In the case of Saudi Arabia, significant shifts in the definition of and demands on gendered identities are taking place under the leadership of Mohammed bin Salman. Magdalena Karolak's chapter examines how Bin Salman's ambitious modernist vision of the kingdom is at odds with the traditional gender roles and expectations. The push for women's greater participation in the country's economic development is neither based on the rights-based approach nor the gender justice platform. Yet, such utilitarian perspective on the "new modern woman" is riddled with tensions and contradiction even if it has the potential to create new empowerment spaces for the articulation of new identities. Karolak's chapter captures these dynamics of change and tensions through a discourse analysis of select Saudi newspapers.

In a similar fashion, Amel Al Ariqi chapter turns to the analysis of media content to reflect on how gender relations and power struggles play out in contemporary war-torn Yemen. Alariqi's discussion of the egregious production and circulation of gender biases by the Yemeni media are enduring acts of representational violence that validate and normalize gender-based violence in society.

Although Al Ariqi chapter on Yemen warns us about the resilience of patriarchal institutions and their constraining definitions of gender roles, identities, and norms. The chapters in this section are a reminder about the complex and changing environments in which gender and sexual identities are forged and expressed in MENA. Taken together, the chapters invite more research in the ways in which digital spaces and technologies are mediating the expression of identities, sexualities, intimacies, as well as real and imagined selves in the dynamic contexts of MENA.

REFERENCES

Alessi, E. J., Greenfield, B., Kahn, S., & Woolner, L. (2021). (Ir)reconcilable identities: Stories of religion and faith for sexual and gender minority refugees who fled from the Middle East, North Africa, and Asia to the European Union. *Psychology of Religion and Spirituality, 13*(2), 175–183.

Habib, S. (2010). *Islam and Homosexuality*. Praeger.

Habib, S. (2012). *Female Sexuality in the Middle East: Histories and Representation*. Routledge.

Khalid, M. (2015). The Peripheries of Gender and Sexuality in the 'Arab Spring'. *Mediterranean Politics, 20*(2), 161–177.

Magued, S. (2021). The Egyptian LGBT's Transnational Cyber-Advocacy in a Restrictive Context. *Mediterranean Politics* (pp. 1–10).

Nasser-Eddin, N., Abu-Assab, N., & Greatrick, A. (2018). Reconceptualizing and Contextualizing Sexual Rights in the MENA Region: Beyond LGBTQI Categories. *Gender and Development, 26*(1), 173–189.

CHAPTER 2

Loving Daughters, Devoted Sons and Kissing Protestors Online: Navigating Intimacy and Multiple Aspects of the Self Among Young Facebook Users in Egypt

Senni Jyrkiäinen

INTRODUCTION

Every year on March 21, many of the Egyptian Facebook walls I follow are filled with virtual flower bouquets, beautiful family photos, *ād'iyya* (invocations) and congratulatory messages directed at mothers. According to my observations, love for one's mother is shown around every Egyptian Mother's Day in many creative ways on Facebook, also including the sharing of Arabic songs, the use of religious phrases that highlight the high status of mothers in Egypt and the publishing of status updates in which young Facebook users express their love and appreciation towards their mothers.

On the Mother's Day in 2015, some of my Facebook friends, including 21-year-old language student Zahra, took part in an online social awareness campaign. The campaign, launched by UN Women, was called *Give Mom Back Her Name*. According to the organisers, its idea was to give Egyptian mothers 'their names back in public fora' (UNRIC, 2015) and to express that 'women are individuals' (Jakubczyk, 2015), as there is a practice among men in Egypt of not telling their mother's name in public to protect it from potential ridicule and disrespect. Some of my Facebook friends, including young men and

S. Jyrkiäinen (✉)
Helsinki, Finland

© The Author(s), under exclusive license to Springer Nature Switzerland AG 2023
L. H. Skalli, N. Eltantawy (eds.), *The Palgrave Handbook of Gender, Media and Communication in the Middle East and North Africa*,
https://doi.org/10.1007/978-3-031-11980-4_2

women from Alexandria, shared the campaign video on their walls, some of them writing their mother's name along the post and commenting on the campaign either in Arabic or English. Their Facebook audiences reacted to the posts with likes and comments.

The case is an illustrative example of how Alexandrian students and graduates use Facebook in class-specific ways to navigate their roles as loving sons and daughters but also as socially aware modern Egyptians. It indicates how young people as desiring modern subjects use Facebook[1] as a tool for intimate selving—'the process of becoming a self in intimate relationships'—and how Facebook serves as a versatile platform where the notions of connective and more individualistic aspects of the self are processed side by side (Joseph, 1999, p. ix). As such, the case highlights some themes of this chapter, including the exposure of intimate emotions and desires outside the privacy of the home, class-specific debates around the modern family and the emergence of virtual social spaces that escape the division between the familial and the public.[2]

Over the last years, the usage of social media platforms has become an integral part of the social lives of Egyptian university students, and it has affected the ways in which people articulate affection, navigate intimate desires and maintain relationships. Besides participating on Facebook in the celebration of family-oriented events, such as the Mother's Day or weddings, I have followed how young Egyptians also take part in Facebook events that seem to promote more individualistic desires, such as the National Kissing Day—an online event that I will discuss later—and how they use Facebook to find love, to flirt and to privately chat through the Messenger. The online events that I discuss have not come without disagreements. Their analysis reveals differences concerning gender, family and religion.

By employing an ethnographic approach, I try to understand how young people used Facebook as an intimate and emotional technology to shape multiple notions of the self, both as connective kins and desiring individuals. My focus is on young, university-educated Egyptians who were as versed in socialising on online platforms as in the numerous cafés of the city. As such, my focus is not on young Egyptians in general but on a limited segment of people, who had social, cultural and financial means to engage themselves with urban leisure and digital technologies. Similarly to Walter Armbrust (1999), I observed that

---

[1] I regard Facebook as part of a digital communicative milieu that consists of Internet- and mobile-based platforms, such as email, instant messaging, webcam and social networking sites (see Madianou & Miller, 2012). I observed that my interlocutors used Facebook and their other social media accounts through multiple devices, including mobile phones, laptops, tablets and desktop computers. Due to its portability, the mobile phone was used in communication day and night and as a personal, password-protected tool, it provided its users with more privacy than desktop computers, for instance.

[2] Intimacy, as many anthropologists have underlined, is an ambiguous concept. In some studies, it is closely linked with sexuality (see, e.g., Giddens, 1992), while in some others, it is understood more broadly. In this chapter, I discuss intimacy as deeply linked to the process of subject formation (see Sehlikoglu & Zengin, 2015).

the ideals they had were associated with certain attitudes and hopes relating with modernity and an ideology of national identity that aims at balancing local Egyptian, classical Islamic and—I would add—global cultural referents.

My fieldwork in Alexandria was inspired by the earlier work in feminist anthropology on intimate relationships and subjecthood. I draw on Sherine Hafez's (2011) idea of subjecthood as rhizomatic and multiple as well as on anthropologist Suad Joseph's notion of intimate relationality as a foundational framework in which 'notions of relational selfhood that exist side by side with individualist and other notions of self in the same society and even within the same person' (Joseph, 1999, p. 2). I discuss young Egyptian Facebook users as desiring subjects, whose subject positions 'never entirely belong to the individuals who identify with them because they are the result not only of personal fantasies', as Henrietta Moore importantly suggests (Moore, 2011, p. 58). Much like Moore, Joseph discusses both desire and personhood as 'relationally embedded' (Joseph, 2005, p. 101), discussing how relational selfhood coexists side by side with individualist notions of self in the Lebanese context (1999). Then again, Hafez pays attention to the rhizomatic nature and heterogeneity of the modern subject. She writes:

> *Desiring modern subjects lie at the nexus of ambivalence, contradiction, and hetero-geneity in discourses of modernity. Consequently, subjecthood can never be truly cap-tured as a single subject position in which the self undergoes a consistent and uniform journey of self-fashioning. Desire is an important point of departure for capturing subjectivity in its intensity and acts as the driving force creating the impetus for its very being.* (Hafez, 2011, p. 12)

Besides drawing on the contributions of feminist anthropology on the closely related topics of subjecthood and agency (Hafez, 2011; Joseph, 1999; Moore, 2011; Ortner, 2005; Sehlikoglu, 2015), this chapter is inspired by anthropological studies on gender and communication in the MENA region and elsewhere. In many anthropological studies of Arab-majority countries, intimate relationships and the display of affects have been examined mostly within the family realm (Joseph, 1999), but in recent years anthropologists have suggested that intimacy should also be discussed outside the home (Kreil, 2016). Moreover, while researchers in feminist anthropology and other feminist fields have debated the dichotomy between the feminine (affective) domestic and the masculine (instrumental) public for decades, anthropologists, including Farha Ghannam (2002), have stressed the need to re-evaluate the division. My ethnographic data supports the need to critically discuss spatial dichotomies and the articulation of emotions and intimate desires as private and domestic matters (see Illouz, 2007).

While youths in the MENA have been actively studied as revolutionary citizens, online activists and political actors (e.g., Allmann, 2014; Armbrust, 2011; el Ghobashy, 2011; Herrera, 2014; Onodera, 2015), more research is needed to understand how young people manage their intimate relationships and desires on digital platforms. With my focus on the gender- and class-specific ways of shaping multiple aspects of the self among young Facebook users, this chapter seeks to contribute to the discussion on the linkages between gender, intimacy and new media in the MENA.

Next, I introduce the ethnographic approach that I have used and then I move on to discuss youth in the urban and digital context. In the section that follows I explore how young people navigated different familial and non-familial roles on Facebook, noticing that Facebook is a social platform, where making spatial separations between kins and friends can be problematic. I continue the discussion by drawing attention to a Facebook event called the National Kissing Day. Through the event, I analyse Facebook as a test site for intimate desires that were closely linked with different visions of modernity. I conclude this chapter by reflecting what kind of desires young Egyptians have been capable of pursuing by means of engaging themselves with new social platforms.

Ethnographic Approach

This chapter is based on ten months of ethnographic fieldwork in post-revolutionary Egypt between the years of 2011 and 2014 as well as on more recent, shorter encounters with my interlocutors as well as digital ethnography.[3] The fieldwork, related to my PhD research, took place mostly in Alexandria, which is Egypt's second-largest city, located on the southern coast of the Mediterranean. I conducted there most of my fieldwork among university students and graduates between the winter of 2013 and the spring of 2014, periodically interrupted by serious political instability. Due to its popularity, my focus in virtual environments was on Facebook, where I interacted with my Egyptian interlocutors and those of their family members, who were active on Facebook. Those young Alexandrians, who participated in my research, used Facebook through various electronic communication devices, including personal, password-protected mobile phones, laptops and tablets and as well as desktop computers that were shared by people living in the same household.

While doing fieldwork, I used ethnographic methods, including participant observation, informal interviews and focus group techniques. During my fieldwork in Alexandria, I acted as a visiting researcher at the Bibliotheca Alexandrina, and I was kindly given the chance to organise various kinds of activities for students at the library, including workshops. Therefore, I got an opportunity to co-operate with more than a hundred local students and graduates, some of whom I met only at the library events, while others I befriended and am still in contact with. I also found participants in the research in other places in the city

---

[3] After leaving Alexandria in spring 2014, I have made short trips to Egypt, but I have also met some of the interlocutors mentioned in this article outside Egypt, most recently in 2021. Besides my post-2011 PhD fieldwork in Lower Egypt, I have conducted fieldwork in Upper Egypt in winter 2008.

popular among the young, including cafés and a moderately priced private language centre on the eastern side of the city.

My data include nearly 40 interviews with young men and women, ten interviews with the mothers of the young women interlocutors as well as interviews with experts, such as a social media expert, a marketing professional in a multinational phone company and cybercafé employees. All my young interviewees had a Facebook account. Dozens of young men and women gave me the permission to follow their personal Facebook profiles (some had two and I could follow both), which helped me study social interaction in the virtual environment and communicate with them via Facebook Messenger.

Despite my interest in digital communication, my focus was not on new technologies per se. Rather, my attention was directed to the interweaving of digital technologies with intimate social life and its physical dimensions (see Pink et al., 2016). As I analyse communication through Facebook as interwoven with offline forms of social life and with non-digital ways of communication, I have applied an approach that is not media-centric (Pink et al., 2016). In the context of my research, I found Jenna Burrell's strategy for locating ethnographic research beneficial, given my view of digital technologies as inseparable from the social environments in which they are used. The field site is thus regarded 'as a network composed of fixed and moving points including spaces, people, and objects' rather than a bounded space (Burrell, 2009, p. 189).

Cafés, shopping centres and other urban spaces were as important to my study as online environments. Instead of being a separate social space, Facebook appeared as a continuation of other social spaces, such as the café. I quickly learned that Facebook was a common topic of discussion and a source of gossips in the meetings of young Alexandrians. In a café that offered a free WLAN connection, my interlocutors talked with other patrons, while also using their smartphones to communicate with their non-present friends on Facebook Messenger and other applications. During the gatherings, smartphones were used to take pictures that were sometimes later shared on Facebook. Once everybody had left the café and returned home, it was typical for the students to stay connected with each other through Facebook Messenger and to communicate late into the night.

As my online and urban research sites were connected in many ways, I regard digital ethnography as part of the larger ethnographic approach, similar to Sarah Pink (2013). Given the overlapping nature of virtual and physical spaces in my study, I looked at the field site as a network, which is a continuous space without proximity in a physical sense (Burrell, 2009). 'Continuity does not imply homogeneity or unity; it implies connection' (Burrell, 2009, p. 190). Moreover, as digital ethnography requires no physical travel, I understand it as temporally flexible (see also Pink et al., 2016). I stayed for a total of ten months in Egypt between the years 2011 and 2014, but my research project lasted until 2019 and I continued monitoring Facebook profiles and events, such as the Mother's Day campaign in 2015. I have kept in touch with many interlocutors mostly through WhatsApp and Facebook Messenger up to now.

To sum up, my analysis draws on my fieldwork in Egypt, in which young people easily blended their digital participation with other elements of their social lives. Thus, choosing to focus on the use of Facebook without understanding the everyday lives that the students led alongside their use of Facebook and other social media platforms would not have been productive.

In this chapter, my focus is on university students and recent graduates, educated either in public or private schools and universities. Instead of concentrating on a strictly defined age group in my research, my focus was on 20-something technologically adept men and women who were not married and had no children of their own. When speaking with them about social classes, most of them said they were 'normal'. As public-school graduates and ordinary microbus passengers, they associated themselves with the broad idea of the middle class, while the few ones with expensive private education and private cars saw themselves as privileged. Most of the interlocutors came from Muslim families. Besides the Alexandrian participants, some of my interlocutors lived in Cairo, where I visited from time to time and where I spent some time in late 2011. As some interlocutors live nowadays *barra* (outside Egypt), I have met with them in several countries after returning from Egypt back to Finland.

On the following pages, I introduce Rahma, Zahra, Huda, Ahmed, Karim, Mustafa and some other young persons, who were among the nearly 40 young interviewees and among those, with whom I spent time actively both online and offline. All the names I use are pseudonyms.

URBAN YOUTH AND THE DIGITAL AGE

'Facebook and Twitter are like Umm Kulthum and Fairouz. You usually love one of them', university graduate Rahma (aged 26) told me in May 2013, comparing social networking services to the two famous Arab singers, when we were having breakfast at the Bibliotheca Alexandrina and enjoying the magnificent view of the Mediterranean. Rahma, like all my young interlocutors, was a Facebook user but as a young intellectual, she was also following Twitter, which she and her friends understood more as an elite platform.[4]

By the time of my fieldwork, consumption of mobile technologies and social media had become an integral part of the lifestyles of Alexandrian university students. Social media was a usual topic of discussion in those Alexandrian

---

[4] By 2021, some interlocutors have joined and become more active on other social media platforms, such as TikTok, Snapchat or Instagram. Yet, many are active on Facebook too. Moreover, since my 2014 departure from Egypt, monthly data packages have become more widespread among my Egyptian interlocutors and mobile voice-calling applications have largely replaced expensive phone calls that were a constant headache for students during the time of my fieldwork in Alexandria.

cafés, where the youth gathered, often simultaneously using social media through their mobile devices.

The waterfront of Alexandria and the city centre around the Raml station are full of traditional *'ahāwī* (coffee houses) and new, trendy cafés. My interlocutors also spent time in shopping centres, university campuses and open-air spaces. The Qait Bey citadel and the seafront promenade were popular meeting spots especially among those students who could not afford hanging out in cafés. Spaces related to studying, such as universities, private language centres and private study centres, were also central spaces regarding peer relations. By the time of my fieldwork, mobile technologies had become widespread, and cybercafés had lost their importance among the better-off segments of the Alexandrian youth. Some shopping centres, such as San Stefano, and hypermarkets, including Carrefour, appeared to me as exclusive spaces where young people could experience with what Anouk de Koning (2009) has discussed as '"First World" lifestyles'. Yet only a very limited number of Egyptians can afford shopping in these cosmopolitan spaces. Also many of my interlocutors had to settle for visiting these spaces without buying much or anything.

In the city of Alexandria, youthful aspirations for modernity often appeared as acts of balancing available global and local elements (cf. Spronk, 2009), in relation to class-specific ideas of desirable ways of life. Anthropologist Ted Swedenburg regards youth as a social and cultural category, 'a transitional phase between childhood and adulthood that, in its contemporary form, is a product of modernity' (Swedenburg, 2007, p. n.p.). Importantly, the period of youth has been greatly extended in Egypt, especially because married life must often wait due to heavy financial obligations and lack of jobs, for instance (Swedenburg, 2007; Herrera, 2010). New technologies and other products of modernity, including the emerging urban youth culture, have contributed to this prolonged period (Swedenburg, 2007). For young Alexandrians, aspirations for modernity seemed to be linked with material issues, like living in style, but also with a new emotional culture. My interlocutors described themselves as modern Egyptians, who contrasted their educated selves, romantic ideals and emotional skills with 'backward' people whose ideas on family life were 'retarded'.[5]

Those young people, who participated in my research, are part of Egypt's 'wired youth', which is widely known for its active, partly digitally mediated participation in the 2011 uprising (Herrera, 2014, p. 5). They grew up under President Mubarak's long rule and experienced the so-called Arab Spring and its aftermaths. Especially during the most turbulent months of my fieldwork in 2013, it was difficult for the youth to organise social gatherings or study sessions in the city. Demonstrations, clashes, fencing of public spaces and finally a night-time curfew limited the mobility of most young Alexandrians but especially of women, as families considered the streets as unsafe spaces. After a night-time curfew and state of emergency were declared in Egypt in August

---

[5] On a discourse of modernity and *takhalluf* (backwardness; retardation), see Massad (2007).

2013, the importance of social media as a medium for communication only grew.

In their childhood, the research participants, born in the late 1980s and early 1990s, experienced Egypt's gradual shift into the digital age. In the 1990s, computers were a rarity and telecommunication technologies were not widespread, but the situation started to change after the millennium when three telecommunications services providers, including Egyptian Mobinil (nowadays Orange), British Vodafone and Emirati-based Etisalat, built mobile networks in Egypt.

Facebook was founded in the US in 2004 by some Harvard College students and it soon started spreading to various countries. During one of my talks with 26-year-old, private-sector employee Mustafa in 2013, he told me that he heard about Facebook for the first time in 2007 through an Egyptian friend who lived in Europe. Back then, she had introduced Facebook to Mustafa, explaining that 'there is something cool called Facebook' and urging him to try it. Mustafa, at that time 20 years old, had joined what Egyptians often call 'FB' and liked it. Mustafa said to me that when he joined Facebook, most people around him had no understanding of what Facebook is. As an affluent young man with mastery of foreign languages and in possession of other forms of cosmopolitan capital, he was able to join early.

Among my interlocutors, most students were not as privileged as Mustafa. 23-year-old Ahmed, for example, had attended a poor public school in his childhood and had to wait several years longer than Mustafa to get his first personal mobile phone. Whereas Mustafa had his first cell phone at the beginning of the new millennium, Ahmed got his in 2007.

When I entered Alexandria in 2013, there were 16 million Egyptian Facebook users, of which the majority, 12 million, were users below 30 years (eMarketing Egypt, 2013). Within the youth segment I spent time with, 'everybody' was using Facebook, or this is what my interlocutors used to say, when describing the central role of Facebook in their social lives.

Facebook has retained its popularity among Egyptians into the 2020s. By 2021, none of my key informants had left Facebook. One phenomenon that both Ahmed and Zahra had noticed in their social circles, and wanted to point out to me in our private message exchanges on WhatsApp in 2021, was the growing number of 'old people' on Facebook. In recent years the number of Egyptian Facebook users has been generally on the rise but, as Zahra and Ahmed underlined, in the 2020s the range of applications used has also become more diverse. Instagram, for example, is gaining popularity among the youth.[6]

---

[6] The total number of users accounted for 18 per cent of Egypt's population, the total number of Egyptians being 88 million. In 2020, Egypt population hit 100 million and as the number of Facebook users reached 40 million, the total amount of users already reached 40 per cent of the entire population. Young users still consisted the majority, the number of users above 34 years being 28 per cent (NapoleonCat Stats, 2020).

Two Facebook Accounts: Ways to Navigate Multiple Aspects of the Self

Due to the socio-economic status of the segments of the youth I studied, I knew lots of Alexandrian families where not only the young generation but also some members of the older generation had found their way to Facebook. This had led to the situation in which Facebook had become a versatile tool, serving as a space where family ties and peer relations as well as informal and more formal connections were nurtured simultaneously. Some of the mothers I knew had the habit of befriending their daughters' friends on Facebook, complimenting their profile pictures and keeping in touch with messages.

Having mothers, fathers, brothers and other family members on Facebook made it possible for the young Facebook users to nurture their family ties and to show their love through Facebook, as I have discussed at the beginning of this chapter. However, the mixing of different social categories and generations sometimes appeared as tricky for those students who did not want to share too detailed information with their family and relatives about their social lives and relationships outside the home. As my interlocutors pointed out, in offline contexts parents, relatives and older people in general could not directly see with whom their daughters, sons and young relatives spent time on campus, in cafés or other semi-public spaces. However, on Facebook, depending on privacy settings, they could quickly learn a lot about the young person's social life through checking her or his list of friends, looking at the pictures posted and following communication on the Facebook wall. The openness of the Facebook wall can be adjusted by the user (see Lushetich, 2014) and yet, in many cases I saw that the intended limitations of privacy did not work as planned, which led to unwanted information leakages. As several anthropological accounts of young people in contemporary Egypt and elsewhere in the MENA show, there often exist two social spaces, such as 'familial' and 'public social' (de Koning, 2009, p. 114), or 'home' and 'away from home' (Scalco, 2016, p. 327), whose boundaries, while not necessarily strict, are preferably maintained when possible. Among my Alexandrians interlocutors, many felt that on Facebook these two social spaces were constantly overlapping and sometimes causing trouble. The dilemma was how to manage multiple aspects of the intimate, emotional self on one platform, as a 'good' and 'polite' daughter and as a young woman who goes out with friends and dates someone, for instance.

Zahra, the language student introduced in the beginning of this chapter, was one of those female interlocutors who had both her friends and family on Facebook and found it problematic. Her solution was to maintain separate accounts so that she had one account for her family and another one for friends. On the account made for friends Zahra actively posted pictures of her *shilla*; a group of friends, consisting of young Alexandrian women and men. On her family account Zahra shared pictures of her family and relatives, while refraining from sharing pictures of mixed-gender social activities or anything else that could cause conflicts with the family. When we discussed recent changes in

Facebook usage via WhatsApp in autumn 2021, she pointed out that Facebook's popularity had increased among older age groups. Thus, the need for two separate accounts had not vanished and Zahra still maintained two accounts in the 2020s. Yet she logged in to her 'family account' rather seldom, while being very active on the account that is for her 'friends'.

Some other Facebook users, including university graduate Huda, had just one Facebook account. Similarly to Zahra, she had many relatives on Facebook besides her friends. Once, when I was sitting with her and her friends in a trendy and expensive café, she told me an incident that took place during her student years. As a student, Huda used to spend time in mixed-gender groups and date someone. Her relatives, who are more conservative and do not approve hanging out with boys, did not know about Huda's relationship before they found it out through Facebook. One of Huda's friends had posted pictures where Huda sits with her boyfriend, arms on each other's shoulders.

Huda found it regrettable that because of a camera phone and Facebook, some intimate aspects of her life became suddenly exposed to her relatives living hundreds of kilometres away from Alexandria (see more on this case and impression management in Jyrkiäinen, 2016). Huda explained that after the incident she learned that it was important to utilise the option to limit the visibility of her posts and to regulate how much content each Facebook friend could see on her Facebook wall.

Young men also pointed out to me issues that they needed to consider when acting on social media platforms. People were eager to post pictures on Facebook and yet there were many issues that younger brothers did not want their older brothers to see, or young men did not want to share with their sisters or other family members. For example, some young men who smoked cigarettes did not do it in front of their parents out of respect. Thus, some felt that pictures displaying smoking should not be visible to them on Facebook either.

As Facebook's design has developed over the years, users have been equipped with more tools to manage their privacy. Facebook makes it easy to tag people in pictures and status updates, but Facebook also allows its users to change the privacy settings to require approval before these tags appear on the user's timeline. Moreover, the user can decide who can see her or his posts. To elaborate on how Facebook's policies and design are shaping the platform's culture and behaviour of its users, I draw on Adrienne Massanari's (2017) term 'platform politics'. She introduces the concept in her article that discusses how Reddit's design, algorithm and platform politics implicitly support toxic, anti-feminist technocultures.

While Facebook is aware of the social consequences of its design and offers some solutions, the participants in my research felt that the solutions available to users are only partially working. In her article on Facebook and heartbreak Ilana Gershon (2011) describes how US students often felt ambivalent about the ways information circulates on the network. She points out that from the beginning, Facebook users have regarded shifts in Facebook's design controversial whenever they have influenced on how information flows on the social networking site. Similarly, Alexandrian students often pointed out to me problems that can be seen as linked with the platform's politics, including problems like unintended presentation of posted information. As Facebook's design did not provide young Egyptians with sufficient tools to manage different aspects of the self, they sometimes resorted to creative solutions such as having two separate accounts.

Test Site for Intimate Desires

In the beginning of my chapter, I described the virtual celebration of the Egyptian Mother's Day. Besides family-oriented events, such as the Mother's Day or weddings, I observed that there were many other events on Facebook that many of my interlocutors preferably kept in the 'away from home' category (Scalco, 2016, p. 327). In summer 2013, in the midst of political turmoil, I saw a Facebook event called National Kissing Day planned for August 30. The idea behind the international Kissing Day is that couples would kiss on the street or other public spaces (on a kissing protest in Ankara, see Sehlikoglu, 2015). Alexandrian Facebook users soon launched their own event 'National Kissing Day in Alex', promoting it as a 'day of love'. This event gained some popularity among my Alexandrian Facebook friends.

Having experienced the 2011 political uprising and the June 2013 protests, Karim, a recent university graduate, was in the mood for more reform. He clicked the 'attending' button to show his support for the event. After all Karim had no girlfriend and felt that in his social circles young women and men had very limited opportunities for romance. When we talked about the Kissing Day, he suggested that as Egypt was becoming more 'global' and the understanding of religion was changing, intimacy should be next in line. He predicted, although jokingly, to a group of friends in August 2013 that 'there is going to be another revolution, the revolution of kissing'.

Besides Karim and other Facebook users, who took part in the event virtually, there were others who opposed it on the basis of a certain interpretation of religion, seeking to create a competing thread of discussion about the morality of public kissing (cf. Madianou & Miller, 2012). Among the counter-responses, there were the launching of a Facebook page 'Milion [sic] No for National Kissing Day' and a Facebook event 'National Forgiveness Day' for August 30. On the page, there was a text in English saying, 'Sorry National Kissing Day I'm a Muslim' and on the event page, there was a *du'ā'* (invocation) on asking for forgiveness with a picture of an open Quran.

August 30 came but neither I nor my friends living in Alexandria witnessed any public kissing (see also Egypt Independent, 2013). Karim, who had clicked 'attending', did not participate outside Facebook either. Except some young kissing couples on the seafront late in the evening, it was rare to see such a public show of affection in Alexandria. Instead of the kissing revolution that Karim had been joking about, a political protest, organised by ex-President

Mursi's supporters, took place on the streets on that day. Although kissing couples did not suddenly fill the streets of Alexandria, thousands of young people had announced on Facebook that they would be 'attending' the event.

Noticing the 'revolutionary' idea of the event, clicking 'attending' can be seen as a daring act and as an expression of intimate desires not matching with the dominant moral codes of behaviour. Not surprisingly, the majority of attendees were men. All the young woman students to whom I talked stressed that they were aware of the public moral gaze that was directed at them as unmarried, young women, both on those virtual platforms, where they had accounts under their real names, and in the city.

As the kissing day events were 'public' and the responses were visible to all Facebook users, the virtual attendance evokes questions about the changing culture of privacy (cf. Sehlikoglu, 2015). As anthropologist Susanne Dahlgren (2010) points out, public propriety cannot be understood without paying attention to the contextual character of *adāb* (proper comportment). 'What is proper in one context might be improper in another' (Dahlgren, 2010, p. 4).

The ones, who found the event improper, argued on Facebook that they opposed it on the basis of religion and family values, the 'dignity' of sisters in particular. However, it would be incorrect to portray those 'attending' the event as detached from religion or family values. Karim and most of the people I spoke to found that the deep values linked with religion and family were inseparable from their sense of selfhood. By returning to Hafez's (2011) idea of desiring modern subjects at the nexus of contradiction and ambivalence, it can be understood that this foundation was not shaken by the fact that, in their everyday lives, they skilfully negotiated, re-evaluated and twisted religious and family norms.

The Kissing Day debate illustrates well how contradictions are an essential part of the discourses of modernity. Friends like Karim often portrayed themselves as enlightened and progressive people, differentiating themselves from people with 'backward' ideas who are bound to traditions and conservatism. Yet, when it comes to the opposing parties, their perceptions of themselves as modern actors were hardly different. It is not surprising that both parties had written the titles of their Facebook events and their central arguments—for example, 'Sorry National Kissing Day I'm a Muslim'—in English. I observed that among Alexandrian university students, knowledge of English was a class marker and a sign of refinement, strongly linked with the possession of cosmopolitan capital (cf. de Koning, 2009, p. 62). Those, who could not speak English, were sometimes referred as 'ignorant people' from 'free schools' (cf. de Koning, 2009, p. 62).

Thus, the ability to participate in online debates, where participants often switched from Egyptian Arabic often written in Latin letters to classical Arabic or English, or even to identify oneself with the themes of these debates, can be seen as a rather class-specific issue, given that acquiring the needed cultural capital and knowledge requires years of training (see Bourdieu, 1986). Moreover, it is important to look at the Kissing Day debate in a larger context, namely that of the so-called 'family crisis' (see Hasso, 2011; Kholoussy, 2010). To contextualise the current online debates, a look at historian Hanan Kholoussy's sociohistorical overview of the so-called 'marriage crisis' in the early twentieth century is needed to keep in mind that while the debates on sisters' dignity and the morality of premarital intimacy now partly take place on online platforms, the discourses surrounding the modern Egyptian family are nothing new. As such, the current debate can be seen as what Kholoussy calls 'a middle-class urban phenomenon' (Kholoussy, 2010, p. 2).

Conclusion

In this ethnographic article, I have focused on discussing how Facebook as an intimate and emotional technology enabled the shaping of multiple notions of the self among young Egyptian social media users. As a social space that was neither familial nor extra-familial, but a mix of both, Facebook enabled the simultaneous shaping of multiple notions of selves so that young people were able to operate as connective selves who expressed their love to their mothers on Facebook's public arenas, while they were also able to imagine the shaping of other more individualist aspects of the self as kissing protestors.

As a number of anthropologists have pointed out, instead of hailing all the novel prospects that new technologies may offer, people are often keen to realise their old desires by means of new technologies (Horst & Miller, 2006). '[T]he technology is used initially with reference to desires that are historically well established, but remain unfulfilled because of the limitations of previous technologies' (Horst & Miller, 2006, pp. 6–7). Similarly, the young partici-pants in my study were willing to utilise Facebook's versatility, noticing its potential in serving as a space where family ties and peer relations as well as informal and more formal connections could be nurtured simultaneously.

Noticing that people's social networks on Facebook were closely linked with their offline social networks, Facebook appeared as part of a larger social milieu. Yet, whereas in offline contexts young people usually communicated with peo-ple belonging to different categories, including family members, friends, lov-ers, neighbours and relatives, separately in different social spaces, such as home, university, café or home street, on the user's Facebook wall, there were typically people present from all these categories. Indeed, the blurring of the boundaries between familial and public social spheres was the feature that made Facebook different from other platforms of social interaction. Thus, young women, in particular, but men too, had to think about ways to manage the presence of their family members and relatives through creative solutions, such as main-taining two separate accounts. This allowed them to fulfil, on the one hand, expectations that they had as connective yet modern kins and, on the other hand, to navigate the more individualistic aspects of the self and desires that they felt could not be voiced in social spaces linked to the family. To draw on Sherry Ortner's (1996) idea of agency, young people found ways to act with skill and intention to navigate the complexity of desires.

While Facebook did not appear as an alternative reality where people could operate separately from other social environments, Facebook offered young people opportunities to negotiate and test the conventional boundaries of intimacy. Moreover, Facebook made emotional selving a public process. Young people as desiring modern selves exposed intimate desires (such as kissing in public) and family matters (mother's name) outside the privacy of the home. Intimate actions that were unthinkable, or at least very unusual, in other public spaces were imaginable on Facebook.

As Hafez has suggested, 'a focus on the production of desire as embedded in wider imbrications of colonialism, nationalism, and projects of modernization, secularization, and Islamization captures the complex range of subject positions among desiring subjects' (Hafez, 2011). Inspired by Hafez's idea of desires as a departure point for capturing subjectivity, I have discussed how young Alexandrians shaped multiple notions of the self in an environment, where aspirations for modernity appeared not only in material but also in emotional forms. Along with the expression of emotions on the Facebook wall, a new kind of publicity stepped in, hinting that new arenas of communication are not meaningless to those who, as desiring modern subjects, look for tools and platforms to navigate the joys and complexities of intimate relations.

REFERENCES

Allmann, K. (2014). Mobile Revolution: Toward a History of Technology, Telephony and Political Activism in Egypt. *CyberOrient, 8*(2), 46. Retrieved November 05, 2018, from http://www.cyberorient.net/article.do?articleId=9145

Armbrust, W. (1999). Bourgeois Leisure and Media Fantasies. In D. Eickelman & J. Anderson (Eds.), *New Media in the Muslim World: The Emerging Public Sphere* (pp. 102–128). Indiana University Press.

Armbrust, W. (2011, February 23). The Revolution against Neoliberalism. Jadaliyya. Retrieved May 03, 2021, from http://www.jadaliyya.com/pages/index/717/the-revolution-against-neoliberalism-.

Bourdieu, P. (1986). The Forms of Capital. In J. G. Richardson, Handbook of Theory and Research for the Sociology of Education (pp. 241–258). : Greenwood Publishing Group, Inc.

Burrell, J. (2009, May). The Field Site as a Network: A Strategy for Locating Ethnographic Research. *Field Methods, 21*, 181–199.

Dahlgren, S. (2010). *Contesting Realities: The Public Sphere and Morality in Southern Yemen.* Syracuse University Press.

de Koning, A. (2009). *Global Dreams: Class, Gender, and Public Space in Cosmopolitan Cairo.* The American University in Cairo Press.

Egypt Independent. (2013, August 13). *Egypt's Invitation to National Kissing Day.* Retrieved May 28, 2018, from Egypt Independent. http://www.egyptindependent.com/egypt-s-invitation-national-kissing-day

el Ghobashy, M. (2011). The Praxis of the Egyptian Revolution. Middle East Research and Information Project, 258. Retrieved May 03, 2021, from http://www.merip.org/mer/mer258/praxis-egyptian-revolution

eMarketing Egypt. (2013). *eMarketing Egypt Online Competitiveness Intelligence Report*. Retrieved October 29, 2018, from eMarketing Egypt. www.emarketing-egypt.com

Gershon, I. (2011). Un-Friend My Heart: Facebook, Promiscuity, and Heartbreak in a Neoliberal Age. *Anthropological Quarterly, 84*(4), 865–894.

Ghannam, F. (2002). *Remaking the Modern: Space, Relocation, and the Politics of Identity in a Global Cairo*. University of California Press.

Giddens, A. (1992). *The Transformation of Intimacy: Sexuality, Love, and Eroticism in Modern Societies*. Stanford University Press.

Hafez, S. (2011). *An Islam of Her Own: Reconsidering Religion and Secularism in Women's Islamic Movements*. The American University in Cairo Press.

Hasso, F. (2011). *Consuming Desires: Family Crisis and the State in the Middle East*. The American University in Cairo Press.

Herrera, L. (2010). Young Egyptians' Quest for Jobs and Justice. In A. Bayat & L. Herrera (Eds.), *Being Young and Muslim: New Cultural Politics in the Global South and North* (pp. 127–144). Oxford University Press.

Herrera, L. (2014). *Revolution in the Age of Social Media: The Egyptian Popular Insurrection and the Internet*. Verso.

Horst, H. A., & Miller, D. (2006). *The Cell Phone: An Anthropology of Communication*. Berg.

Illouz, E. (2007). *Cold Intimacies: The Making of Emotional Capitalism*. Polity Press.

Jakubczyk, A. (2015, April 5). Watch Arab Men Talk About an Unspeakable Taboo: Mom's Name. *TakePart*. Retrieved from http://www.takepart.com/video/2015/04/05/give-mom-back-her-name.

Joseph, S. (1999). *Intimate Selving in Arab Families: Gender, Self, and Identity*. Syracuse University Press.

Joseph, S. (2005). Learning Desire: Relational Pedagogies and the Desiring Female Subject in Lebanon. *Journal of Middle East Women's Studies, 1*(1), 79–109.

Jyrkiäinen, S. (2016). Online Presentation of Gendered Selves among Young Women in Egypt. *Middle East Journal of Culture and Communication, 9*, 182–198.

Kholoussy, H. (2010). *For Better, For Worse. The Marriage Crisis that Made Modern Egypt*. The American University in Cairo Press.

Kreil, A. (2016). Territories of Desire: A Geography of Competing Intimacies in Cairo. *Journal of Middle East Women's Studies, 12*(2), 166–180.

Lushetich, N. (2014). The Performative Constitution of Liberal Totalitarianism on Facebook. In B. Chow & A. Manglod (Eds.), *Žižek and Performance* (pp. 94–109). Palgrave Macmillan.

Madianou, M., & Miller, D. (2012). *Migration and New Media: Transnational Families and Polymedia*. Routledge.

Massad, J. (2007). *Desiring Arabs*. The University of Chicago Press.

Massanari, A. (2017). #Gamergate and the Fappening: How Reddit's Algorithm, Governance, and Culture Support Toxic Technocultures. *New Media & Society, 19*(3), 329–346.

Moore, H. (2011). *Still Life: Hopes, Desires and Satisfactions*. Polity Press.

NapoleonCat Stats. (2020). *Facebook Users in Egypt*. Retrieved from https://napoleon-cat.com/stats/facebook-users-in-egypt/2020/01

Onodera, H. (2015). *Being a Young Activist in the Late Mubarak Era: An Ethnography of Political Engagement in Egypt*. (P. o. 24, Ed.) Helsinki: Unigrafia.

Ortner, S. (1996). *Making Gender: The Politics and Erotics of Culture*. Beacon Press.

Ortner, S. (2005). Subjectivity and Cultural Critique. *Anthropological Theory,* 5(1), 31–52.

Pink, S. (2013). *Doing Visual Ethnography.* SAGE Publications.

Pink, S., Horst, H., Postill, J., Hjorth, L., Lewis, T., & Tacchi, J. (2016). *Digital Ethnography: Principles and Practice.* SAGE Publications.

Scalco, P. (2016). The Politics of Chastity: Marriageability and Reproductive Rights in Turkey. *Social Anthropology, 24*(3), 324–337.

Sehlikoglu, S. (2015). The Daring Mahrem: Changing Dynamics of Public Sexuality in Turkey. In G. Ozyegin (Ed.), *Gender and Sexuality in Muslim Cultures* (pp. 235–252). Ashgate Publishing.

Sehlikoglu, S., & Zengin, A. (2015, Autumn). Introduction: Why Revisit Intimacy? *The Cambridge. Journal of Anthropology, 33*(2), 20–25.

Spronk, R. (2009). Media and the Therapeutic Ethos of Romantic Love in Middle-Class Nairobi. In J. Cole & L. M. Thomas (Eds.), *Love in Africa* (pp. 181–203). The University of Chicago Press.

Swedenburg, T. (2007). *Imagined Youths.* Retrieved April 03, 2018, from Middle East Research and Information Project. http://www.merip.org/mer/mer245/imagined-youths

UNRIC. (2015, April 01). *Celebrate Your Mother – Give Her Back Her Name.* Retrieved December 17, 2018, from UNRIC: https://www.unric.org/en/latest-un-buzz/29719-celebrate-your-mother-give-her-back-her-name

Making Visible the Unseen Queer: Gay Dating Apps and Ideologies of Truthmaking in an Outing Campaign in Morocco

Benjamin Ale-Ebrahim

Grindr, the world's most popular dating app designed for same-sex desiring men, markets itself as "a safe space where you can discover, navigate, and get zero feet away from the queer world around you" (Grindr, 2021). Alongside other popular gay apps like PlanetRomeo and Hornet, Grindr appeals to its users with the promise that, by downloading the app, they will be put in contact with an unseen world of men-seeking-men that exists around them—in their neighborhood, their city, their community—through the means of its location-based chat services. These apps seek to make visible a world of male same-sex desire that is otherwise hidden beneath the surface of everyday life. Users are encouraged to connect with other queer men in a specific geographic area by creating a profile, browsing a grid of nearby users, and exchanging texts and images in conversation with other users. As queer media studies scholar Shaka McGlotten writes, Grindr is designed as a space for cultivating virtual intimacy among men, encouraging its users to "channel [their] desires into chat, dates, relationships, sex, and networking. But something emerges in the space of everyday practice. It can't be this easy, and it's not" (2013: 126).

What happens when gay dating apps do not function as the "safe spaces" for queer male intimacy they are designed to be? How do app users respond when the promise of making visible the desires of nearby queer men not only allows

B. Ale-Ebrahim (✉)
Department of Anthropology, Indiana University, Bloomington, IN, USA
e-mail: baleebr@iu.edu

31

L. H. Skalli, N. Eltantawy (eds.), *The Palgrave Handbook of Gender, Media and Communication in the Middle East and North Africa*,
https://doi.org/10.1007/978-3-031-11980-4_3

for emotional and sexual connection among men but also unwanted exposure and violence? In recent years, location-based gay dating apps like Grindr, Hornet, and PlanetRomeo have been deployed as tools for homophobic vigilantes to "hunt" gay men in order to expose their sexual orientation, to shame gay men in front of their families and friends, and to commit homophobic acts of violence. In Russia, for example, criminal gangs are known to create fake profiles on gay dating apps, luring unsuspecting men into meeting them only to extort these men for bribes under the threat of exposure or violence (Carroll, 2019). In Egypt, undercover police officers have used fake profiles on gay dating apps in order to arrest gay men under charges of "debauchery" and "sexual deviance" (Trew, 2017). In South Korea, screenshots from gay dating apps have been used as evidence in military trials implicating active-duty soldiers of illegal same-sex acts (Gitzen, 2021).

In this chapter, I analyze a campaign targeting gay, bisexual, and queer men in Morocco in which young women create fake profiles on Grindr and PlanetRomeo in order to expose or "out" local men presumed to be gay. These young women take screenshots of texts and images they have received from other dating app users and upload them to large private groups on Facebook. This is done with the intent of shaming men presumed to have engaged in same-sex sexual activity—a crime punishable by up to three years in prison in Morocco (IRBC, 2013).[1] In addition to facing potential criminal punishment on the basis of their sexuality, many Moroccan gay men experience abuse and violence from the police, neighbors, and family when they are perceived to challenge local heteronormative expectations of proper gendered behavior (Ale-Ebrahim, 2019). The screenshots at the center of this outing campaign are presented as evidence of criminal activity, moral deviance, and shameful queer desire. I discuss how images and texts shared on Grindr and PlanetRomeo are invested with meaning as transparent indicators of same-sex desire by multiple actors within Moroccan social media networks. I then discuss how queer social media users in Morocco and abroad respond to this outing campaign, seeking to maintain Grindr and PlanetRomeo as "safe spaces" for queer men by promoting strategies of increased skepticism toward other users on these platforms, encouraging temporary abstention from using these apps, and appealing for greater online content moderation. I argue that the design features of location-based gay dating apps like Grindr and PlanetRomeo allow for the possibility of both desirable connection and unwanted exposure for queer men in Morocco, challenging the misconception that these apps function as uncomplicated "safe spaces" for queer intimacy and community building. Multiple actors in Moroccan social media networks, working alongside the

---

[1] Article 489 of the Moroccan Penal Code, which criminalizes "lewd or unnatural acts with a person of the same sex," represents a direct inheritance from the penal code of the colonial French Protectorate in Morocco (1912–56). For additional context on the history of the criminalization of same-sex sexuality in Morocco and the Arab world in general, see Hayes (2000), El-Rouayheb (2009), Massad (2007), and Provencher (2017).

design of the apps themselves, "entextualize" (Bauman & Briggs, 1990) images and text messages shared on gay dating apps as transparent indicators of same-sex desire, a "media ideology" (Gershon, 2010) that presents risks for gay app users in Morocco. Maintaining one's safety as a queer dating app user requires a great deal of labor and strategy, especially in a context like Morocco where unwanted exposure of a non-normative sexual orientation can result in serious negative consequences.

"I Feel Bad for Some Faggots, But I Don't Really Care": Sofia Talouni and the Call to Expose

On April 13, 2020, over three weeks into Morocco's first nationwide lockdown as a response to the COVID-19 pandemic, a popular Instagram influencer known as Sofia Talouni (@naoufalmoussa) began a live-streaming broadcast for her 602,000 followers. Talouni, a queer individual who has identified as both transgender and gay and who uses she/her and he/him pronouns, is a Moroccan expatriate living in Turkey. By early 2020, she had gained a large social media following, "using her platform to talk crudely about sex and to entertain her followers in an insolent and confrontational manner in vulgar Moroccan Arabic" (Alami, 2020). Over 90,000 viewers consistently tuned in to her live-streaming broadcasts on Instagram. She often asked her followers to share their personal secrets with her on her Instagram live streams, soliciting photos or screenshots from them as fodder for gossip about the hypocritical behavior she observed in Moroccan society.

Talouni's April 13 broadcast began relatively normally when she invited one of her followers, a young man from a large city in northern Morocco, to join her Instagram live stream. This interaction soon became a confrontation when Talouni pressured the young man to publicly identify himself as gay and threatened to post "revealing photos showing him with another gay man" if he did not comply (Alami, 2020). After he persistently refused to identify himself as gay despite increasing pressure from Talouni, she then displayed a photo for her viewers of what appeared to be the young man lounging at a pool with an older bearded European man, presenting the photo as undeniable evidence of his homosexuality. Simply by displaying this image to her viewers on Instagram, Talouni succeeded in outing the young man as gay in front of tens of thousands of people. This incident prompted many of Talouni's followers to report her account to Instagram, flagging this act of coerced exposure as a violation of the platform's community guidelines against hate speech and blackmail (Instagram, 2021).

Having been reported and her account flagged, Talouni angrily broadcast another livestream that same night to respond to growing threats against her message and platform. In later social media posts, Talouni claimed that her intent with this second livestream was to bring gay men "closer to the main-stream society" in Morocco by encouraging her followers to "think of gay people as the man or woman next door and to stop the negative fantasy of who gay people are, how they look like and how they live" (Greenhalgh & Al-Khal, 2020). Despite her claims, this second Instagram broadcast reinforces misogynistic, homophobic, and transphobic rhetoric in Morocco that glorifies hegemonic heteromasculinity at the expense of non-normative gender expression and same-sex sexuality. Talouni plays upon long-standing anxieties in Moroccan society about receptive anal sex, associating this act with a passive and effeminate persona that is at odds with normative ideologies of Moroccan masculinity that privilege a dominant and independent sense of self (Rebucini, 2013; Gouyon, 2018).

Talouni begins her second Instagram broadcast by stating, in colloquial Moroccan Arabic, "I feel bad for some *loubiyat* [derogatory term for gay men, roughly equivalent to 'faggots' in English], but I don't really care." She goes on to encourage her female audience to download gay dating apps like Grindr and PlanetRomeo as tools to discover a salacious underworld of same-sex desire in their immediate geographical vicinity:

> Listen up, girls: Open the App Store, you'll type [in the search bar] 'gay apps.' There are three that are famous—memorize their names, girls!—PlanetRomeo, Grindr, and Hornet. These are the three apps. All you women, girls, those who wear hijab who say 'there is no husband like mine [on these apps],' the mother who says 'my son is the best' and curses and swears about homosexuals like me, who says 'my husband is much more masculine than you, Sofia, you *loubia*.' You, wearing hijab who think that you've got it all when you're in a relationship with a handsome bearded man, this is your chance! ... [Open the app] and when you are asked to put in your type [sexual position], don't select *'actif'* [top]. Select *'passif'* [bottom] or both [vers]. *Passif* is the person who gets fucked, like me... These apps show you the people near you, 100 meters, 200 meters, even one meter away in the living room, because you are together at home [in COVID lockdown]. It might show your husband who is in the bedroom, or your son who is in the toilet or something, maybe your boyfriend who lives in the next building, maybe your cousin who lives just two blocks away from you, maybe your uncle... You'll discover wrongdoing [*l-munkar*]! That's what you wanted—to discover faggots [*loubiyat*]! ... You'll discover the truth. Let me know what you've found tomorrow: who has found her husband, her boyfriend, her fiancé, her brother, her father. Even if you find your father or brother, do not confront them! When the quarantine ends, go out and do whatever you want. When he speaks with you about it, tell him: here is the evidence! Shut up, dad! Shut up, brother! Shut up, fiancé! Shut up, husband! You have sex and I suffer. I can also have sex and do what I want.

Here, Talouni presents gay dating apps like Grindr and PlanetRomeo as a means of exposing the hypocrisy of masculine-presenting men (e.g., men with beards, those who are married or dating women) seeking same-sex encounters online while maintaining the privileges of heteronormative masculinity in their offline lives. Talouni gives detailed instructions for how women can easily create fake profiles on gay apps like Grindr, posing as gay men in order to solicit compromising information about the same-sex desires of their male relatives and neighbors for future use in blackmail and intimidation. Talouni presents this as a quasi-feminist act, encouraging her female followers to arm themselves with an archive of digital evidence depicting the shameful homosexual desires of the men in their immediate social circles as a way to counteract potential future criticism of their own sexuality and relationships.

Talouni's call was taken up by dozens of Moroccan women who began to share screenshots of photos and text messages they had solicited from local profiles on PlanetRomeo, Grindr, and Hornet. These women created several private Facebook pages to share the screenshots they had taken from gay apps, seeking to publicize the shameful and criminal desires of men in their communities. According to local Moroccan social media reports and international news coverage, over 100 men were forcibly outed as a result of these women's actions (Alami, 2020). Dozens of men were kicked out of their homes in the middle of the first wave of the COVID pandemic (Greenspan, 2020) while over 50 lost their jobs and at least 4 individuals died by suicide after their photos were made public online.

Multiple actors within Moroccan social media networks frame digital images and text messages as transparent indicators of same-sex desire, investing screenshots with meaning as powerful tools to expose the true hidden queerness of local men throughout Morocco. In the Instagram broadcast that started this outing campaign, Talouni displays a digital photograph, obtained from an unknown source, as supposedly undeniable proof of a young man's homosexual orientation. Despite his own protests and persistent refusal to identify himself as gay, Talouni succeeds in outing him to an audience of tens of thousands by displaying a photograph of him lounging in a pool in close physical proximity to an older shirtless man. What is important in constructing the young man's gay identity in this moment is not his own words but rather the publicly displayed photograph; it is framed as physical evidence of the man's true hidden desires, a more trustworthy indicator of his inner homosexual nature and of his enduring internal feelings than his own verbal testimony in this moment. The image speaks for itself, functioning as a potent encapsulation of the young man's same-sex desires, challenging his own verbalized denial of any homosexual or queer orientation. Truth about the man's sexual orientation is constructed with reference to external physical evidence, in the form of a digital photograph, rather than through his own embodied and verbalized speech.

This strategy of truth making by reference to external physical evidence resonates with sociolinguist Gregory Matoesian's argument about how the United States legal system privileges tape recordings over verbal testimony in courtroom trials (2001). Matoesian argues that when recorded speech on tape is in conflict with a witness's verbal testimony, an attorney will "strategically [adopt] the footing of mere nonspeaking relayer of speech on tape" in order to "let the tape speak for itself" as a "perfect icon—a mirror image—of the speech it seeks to represent" (Matoesian, 2001: 146). Through this strategy, the attorney frames the tape as a more reliable narrator of the past events in question than the fallible memory of the witness's verbal testimony (146). In other words, the tape is represented as a more faithful rendering of the words it documents than the witness's spoken rephrasal of these words, constituting the most minimal "intertextual gap" (Briggs & Bauman, 1992: 149) between the original context of the recorded speech and its replication in the courtroom, and therefore closer to the unedited truth. Popular understandings of the affordances of tape-recording technology contribute to this ideological hierarchy of legal evidence, since American courtroom audiences understand the tape recorder as a technology designed to capture and exactly replicate sound.

Similarly, Sofia Talouni works to frame the digital screenshot as a more faithful representation of the young man's true sexual orientation than his own spoken words. In the face of conflicting evidence regarding the man's sexuality, Talouni presents the digital photograph as incontrovertible proof of the young man's true inner nature as a gay man. The photograph serves as tangible, visible, external evidence of an otherwise hidden and internal aspect of the man's identity that he seeks to deny with his words. Like a courtroom attorney simply pressing "play" on an audiotape recording, Talouni takes up the footing of "mere nonspeaking relayer" of the image's message, encouraging her audience to let the photograph "speak for itself" as a transparent indicator of the man's past homosexual acts and his ongoing same-sex desires (Matoesian, 2001: 146). Her audience seems to be convinced by the photograph as a true representation of homosexual desire. Art historian and philosopher Scott Walden argues that photographs are commonly understood as "transparent pictures," a means of representing the world that is capable of capturing reality more objectively than other media like painting, drawing, or verbal description (Walden, 2005). This is because photographs are created through the means of a technological apparatus (the refraction of light through a camera lens onto film) that supposedly operates outside the realm of human subjectivity and fallibility. In other words, photographs are understood to create minimal "intertextual gaps" (Briggs & Bauman, 1992) between a past event and its replication, while verbal speech is seen to create maximal gaps, leaving more room for deception, dishonesty, and inaccuracy.

Despite the fact that numerous technologies exist that allow photo manipulation and editing, Talouni minimizes these aspects of photography for her viewers in this moment in order to influence how her audience understands this image. Just as the tape recording is not actually as objective as it seems, since a courtroom attorney engages in numerous hidden decisions about "which texts to play, what the voices on the tape will say, and how to interpret those voices" in order to "[control] the contextualization and recontextualization of discourse" (Matoesian, 2001:146), Talouni does not discuss where this image comes from, does not present it as evidence whose meaning is up for debate, and does not seek to question the young man about what he might have been doing in this photo other than fulfilling his shameful same-sex desires. She simply presents the image as transparent proof that the man is lying about his sexuality, daring him to deny what appears to be the objective truth represented in this image of him sitting in a pool, suggestively close to an older bearded man drinking a fruity cocktail.

Like Talouni herself, the women who respond to her call to create fake profiles on gay dating apps also interact with digital images and text messages as transparent indicators of hidden same-sex desire. After collecting screenshots of gay dating app users in their local vicinity, they share these uncensored images in large private Facebook groups with tens of thousands of followers. They leave minimal comments on each screenshot, uploading dozens in bulk, often simply writing things like "I installed the application and this is who I found" or "by God, you can't trust anyone this handsome anymore [smiling emojis] all of these guys are faggots [laughing emoji, facepalm emoji]" ("*wallah, ma baqi ntiq f-shi had zwin* [emoji] *hadu kolhum loubia* [emoji]")! The members of this group laugh at the men they discover on Grindr and other gay apps, expressing how shocked they are to find so many faggots [*loubiyat*] in their local neighborhood when they downloaded the app. In one post, a woman shares a screenshot of a conversation she had with another Grindr user in which she discovers that they are both women who downloaded the app after hearing about it in Talouni's broadcast. They laugh about how they had hoped to discover whether their ex-boyfriends were secretly gay, using the app to "expose the faggots [*zawamil*] among the guys in our neighborhood" [*kan-qilb ʿala zawamil dyal oulad derbna*].

By sharing photos of conventionally attractive Moroccan men with handsome bearded faces and muscular bodies, these women intend to humiliate and shame men who might otherwise pass for straight by exposing their same-sex desires in a public Facebook group with thousands of members. They project a homosexual identity onto these men simply by referencing the fact that their images were found on same-sex dating apps, making an assumption that these images reveal a hidden truth about these men's supposedly-effeminate gender identity and queer sexual orientation that is at odds with their external masculine appearance. Here, again, these women are operating under the assumption that an image can speak for itself as obvious and unquestionable evidence of the desires of the men who appear in the image. The only information they present about these images is that they are screenshots taken from a gay dating app. Like Talouni's presentation of the photograph as clear evidence of the young man's internal desires in her Instagram live broadcast, the women who post these screenshots on Facebook presume a strong and transparent link between a visual digital artifact and the hidden queer subjectivity of the gay dating app user it depicts. Regardless of whether the men in these images would identify themselves as gay, bisexual, or queer, these images function as unquestionable evidence of the men's homosexuality since they originate from a platform that is designed explicitly to facilitate male same-sex encounters.

The fact that Talouni and these women engage with images and text shared on gay dating apps as transparent indicators of same-sex desire and therefore queer subjectivity is not surprising, since this is an ideology built in to the design of the apps themselves. Gay dating apps like Grindr and PlanetRomeo are designed to operate as technologies through which the expression of male same-sex desire is transformed into visible queer subjectivity, a media ideology that Talouni and her followers weaponize in order to expose same-sex desiring men in their local communities. The designers and corporations behind apps like Grindr and PlanetRomeo promote their platforms as sites where queer men can connect with one another through the mediated exchange of digital artifacts, including photographs, text messages, videos, and demographic information. Grindr promotes itself as "the largest social networking app for gay, bi, trans, and queer people" (Grindr, 2021) while PlanetRomeo describes itself as "an open-minded and friendly home for every gay, bi, and trans person" (PlanetRomeo, 2021). There is some slippage here between same-sex desire and queer subjectivity: gay apps are designed under the assumption that their users are men who would identify themselves as queer. In other words, these apps encode sexuality as an identity category rather than, for example, "loose affective, experiential, or affinal ties" (McGlotten, 2013: 6) among men-seeking-men. To express male same-sex desire through these apps is thus made to represent an externalization of an enduring internal sexual identity, foreclosing alternative possibilities for men like Talouni's interviewee who resist categorizing themselves as gay, bisexual, or queer.

As digital media researcher John Cheney-Lippold writes, there is a gap between how identity functions in virtual spaces like Grindr and how internet users understand their own sense of self (2017: 179). Online identity operates through an algorithmic logic, such that "who we are is what our data is made to say about us" (xii). Individual internet users have a limited amount of agency to know and determine how their identity functions online. Online identity operates as a Bayesian inference, a dynamic statistical probability calculated by an algorithm that draws on ever greater amounts of data to assign an internet user to a temporarily-assigned category or "measurable type" (9–10). Cheney-Lippold argues that these categories are "algorithmic caricatures" of offline social identities like gender, race, and sexuality (10). An internet user's online "gender" does not have a straightforward and transparent correlation to that user's offline sense of gender identity; instead, "a user is a 'man' according to how closely 'his' data stacks up to preexisting models of 'man,'" categories which can and do change constantly (19). Algorithmic systems rely on the messiness and confusion between a measurable type and an offline social category. People trust algorithms because they are commonly framed as an objective technological means of observing large sets of data that are outside and above the realm of human understanding. This media ideology can result in real-world violence when there is a large discrepancy between an algorithmic category and offline identity, such as when drone strikes are ordered on a bus full of schoolchildren in Yemen because they fit the algorithmic profile of terrorists (39–40).

Political theorist Louise Amoore summarizes this point by arguing that algorithms offer their own new forms of defining the truth about an individual internet user's identity (2020: 6–7). Rather than crafting identity from within a Foucauldian technology of the self rooted in self-ownership and expertise (Foucault, 1988), algorithms function according to their own terms, determining the limits of identity and selfhood by "[condensing] multiple potential futures to a single output" (5). Internet users therefore have much less control over their online identity than they would like to think. Individual internet users are only one node in a vast network of actors working to determine the truth about who they are, what they like, and what they might do next. What matters to social media platforms and their algorithmic infrastructures is condensing large amounts of user data to a single actionable output, such as presenting a user with a targeted advertisement or a link they are likely to click. Within the algorithmic systems that structure socialization on social media platforms, pinpointing a user's true offline identity matters much less than assigning them to an actionable category based on the data they upload and circulate.

In this case, Grindr and PlanetRomeo are designed as virtual spaces to mediate male same-sex desire in specific geographic locations. They market themselves as specifically queer spaces in order to attract their target demographic, setting themselves apart from other social media platforms and dating apps as sites exclusively designed for the expression of male same-sex desire. As a result, any user who downloads these apps and uses them to connect with nearby users is—quite literally, within the algorithmic logics of app design—declaring themselves visible and identifiable as a queer man in a specific geographic area. Images and text circulated on these apps function as real, material proof of homosexual desire, even more real and trustworthy than one's own conscious conception of oneself (McGlotten, 2013: 7–8). Ideally, these externalized and materialized instantiations of otherwise unseen same-sex desires would be visible only to other queer men. However, there is always the risk that unwanted audiences could see these digital artifacts and use them to expose male app users as deviant criminals deserving of ridicule and shame, as we see in this case. Since these apps encourage the external manifestation of same-sex desire through the means of uploading digital photos and sharing text-based conversations, and because it is relatively simple to circulate these digital artifacts outside their original context through creating and sharing screenshots, they can be weaponized rather easily to expose same-sex desiring Moroccan men against their will.

"Please, Instagram, Do Something!": Strategies of Responding to Sofia Talouni on Social Media

In the wake of Sofia Talouni's April 13 livestreams, a number of social media users and LGBTQ activist organizations around the world rushed to condemn her actions, promoting strategic responses to minimize the harm she had caused dozens of Moroccan men who were outed in this campaign. These responses sought to remake Grindr, PlanetRomeo, and other gay dating apps commonly used in Morocco as "safe spaces" for queer men again. In order to achieve this goal, one wave of responses sought to publicize the fact that many young women had begun to create fake profiles on these apps in order to expose local gay men. This awareness campaign worked within the ideological framework of the digital image as a transparent representation of queer subjectivity. These actions encouraged queer men to be very careful about what information they shared on gay apps, to be skeptical of other users, and, if possible, to temporarily suspend using these apps until fake accounts could be identified and removed. Another wave of responses appealed to Instagram, Facebook, and Grindr as queer-friendly corporations and governance structures, seeking a greater degree of content moderation and intervention on the part of these platforms to suspend Talouni's account, close down the harassing women's Facebook groups, and alert Grindr users about the ongoing outing campaign.

Among the first responses to the outing campaign were posts from Moroccan social media users seeking to spread awareness of the ongoing events among gay dating app users in Morocco. On April 14, a day after Talouni's broadcast, Association Akaliyat released an emergency alert on Facebook, encouraging gay men in Morocco not to share any photos on gay apps, to delete their app accounts, and to warn their friends to do the same. By April 15, individual gay Moroccans began sharing and reposting warnings for other gay Moroccans, especially users of dating apps like Grindr, PlanetRomeo, and Hornet. These posts encouraged gay men to "remove their pictures [from dating apps] and not use [the apps] for a while." Other Instagram users created their own original content to spread awareness of the outing campaign, including an openly gay Moroccan comic artist known as @fagouta. On April 16, he posted an illustration to his Instagram account depicting a young man with a hood on his head in the shape of the Grindr logo, tied to a wooden post flying the Moroccan flag. Angry onlookers take photos of him, calling him a *loubia* [faggot] as they attempt to burn him at the stake. The words "Stop Queer Hunting" appear to the left of the young man, while the encouraging phrase "stay safe kings!!" appears alongside the hashtag #OutedinGrindr at the bottom of the image. This illustration captures a sense of fear and victimization that many gay Moroccans experienced as a result of the outing campaign, as if they were being hunted and strung up by angry mobs taking photos of them and humiliating them in public. The message to "stay safe" indicates that @fagouta directs this image at his fellow Moroccan queers, and in the comments he encourages anyone whose identity has been exposed to reach out to him and, if they feel comfortable, to "talk to the press about it."

This call to "talk to the press" was echoed by many other social media users, appealing to the international LGBTQ community to spread the word in various global media outlets about the ongoing situation in Morocco. In an April 16 Reddit post to the r/lgbt subreddit, a large online community for LGBTQ people with over 484,000 members from around the world, a Moroccan man asks for help in "covering this issue" from voices outside Morocco, saying "many lives are on stake (*sic*) and many queer individuals are facing hard times because of this" and "we have to make our message reach the social media outlets these attacks are being presented on and as individuals we have no power." Here we see the threats facing Moroccan users of gay dating apps framed as an issue affecting a global queer community. Social media users work to facilitate the circulation of information both within Morocco—prompting individual users of gay dating apps to take specific steps to mitigate their personal risks—and outside Morocco—invoking the political and economic power of thousands of queer individuals from around the world to put pressure on Facebook, Instagram, Grindr, and other powerful global institutions to take action against Talouni and her followers.

Adam Eli, a New York-based activist and writer, was among the first major international figures to begin sharing information about the outing campaign in Morocco. Eli is the founder of Voices4, a global queer activist organization that played an important role in first publicizing information about the "gay concentration camps" set up in Chechnya in 2017 (Weiss, 2017). On April 16, he shared an edited version of Sofia Talouni's broadcast with his 71,000 followers on Instagram. In this post, he asks his followers to "head over to @naoufalmoussa and REPORT her," arguing that, because of her actions, "young people are being outed and kicked out of their homes DURING the #COVID19 lockdown with nowhere to go." Eli's call to report Talouni's account to Instagram echoes similar posts shared by Moroccan Instagram users; both Eli and Moroccan Instagram users ask their followers to report the account by providing her handle @naoufalmoussa and argue that Talouni's call to create fake gay dating profiles directly resulted in increased danger for queer Moroccans. Other social media users make similar appeals against the women's Facebook groups, asking individual Facebook users to report these groups for violating prohibitions on "harassment" and "intimidation" on the platform.

Alongside these calls for individual social media users to report Sofia Talouni and the women's Facebook groups, other voices spoke directly to the administrators of social media platforms, supporting increased content moderation and greater levels of intervention from the platforms themselves (Gillespie, 2018). On April 14, after receiving numerous reports of the outing campaign from users and LGBTQ activist organizations, Grindr released an alert to all of its users in Morocco warning them that "outing campaigns are currently underway" and asking them not to share photos or information with unknown persons. The alert goes on to warn Moroccan Grindr users that "outing campaigns are underway following hate speech against the LGBT+ community in Morocco," referencing Talouni without naming her specifically. Users who are seeking further support and assistance are instructed to contact L'Union Féministe Libre (UFL), a feminist NGO based in Rabat that offers LGBTQ-affirming counseling services and maintains an online mapping and reporting initiative for hate crimes and gender-based violence in Morocco called Manchoufouch (Skalli, 2014). In a statement to the media, a Grindr spokesperson asserted that "the safety and security of our users is a core value and as such we are deeply committed to creating a safe online environment for all of our users. As we learned of the troubling reports in Morocco, we responded quickly with warning messages in both the Moroccan dialect of Arabic and French to let our users know to take extra caution at this time" (Greenspan, 2020). This action was praised by Moroccan LGBTQ organization Association Akaliyat in an April 14 Facebook post as well as in an April 15 Instagram post from a gay Moroccan user, who wrote approvingly that "Grindr is here to help." PlanetRomeo also took swift action after being made aware of the outings in reports from users and activist organizations. PlanetRomeo founder and CEO Jens Schmidt released a statement claiming that the company was "shocked when we were contacted by the LGBT group in Morocco. We took immediate action by sending a security message to all our 41,000 users in Morocco, we blocked all profiles created from the time this person addressed her users, and contacted Facebook to have the group page taken offline" (Greenspan, 2020).

In an open letter released on multiple social media platforms in English, French, and Arabic, eight Moroccan LGBTQ organizations called upon both individual social media users as well as social networking platforms to take action to prevent further outings as a result of Sofia Talouni's April 13 post. In this letter, the organizations condemn Talouni for "[exposing] the identities of Moroccan queer people" and ask individual social media users to "contact the concerned authorities to instantly suspend the Instagram account Naoufalmoussa pending review. Then, ban him/her from the platform due to the policy of hate/speech and violence." The letter ends with an assertion that "Instagram has to hold him/her [Talouni] accountable for the violence and harm he/she has caused to the LGBTQA community in Morocco." These specific calls to action are notable because they speak to a shared ideology among Moroccan queer activist organizations that specific digital media artifacts, such as the photo shared by Talouni in her Instagram live broadcast or the screenshots shared on the women's Facebook pages, constitute truthful evidence of one's queer identity. Talouni's account must be taken down because mere exposure of these apps and the images they contain is all it takes for queer men to be outed and condemned.

This statement also frames Instagram as an "authority" that must take action to "hold [Talouni] accountable" for posts shared on this platform. As a mediator of sensitive information and images originating from gay dating apps, and due to the lack of legal protection for Moroccan queer individuals, these organizations call upon Instagram as a queer-friendly corporation to step in and accept the moral responsibility to protect its queer Moroccan users by upholding their rights to privacy, dignity, and physical safety. These rights can only be achieved, the letter argues, by deactivating Talouni's account and therefore limiting her capacity to publicize more personal information about queer Moroccan individuals. This provides further evidence that all of the actors involved in this situation, queer and homophobic alike, understand images and texts shared on gay dating apps as a technological means of authentically and transparently expressing a queer subjectivity. Male same-sex desiring app users, queer activists in Morocco and abroad, and homophobic female social media users all interact with digital media artifacts created from data shared on gay dating apps as texts which can speak for themselves (Matoesian, 2001: 146), as images that can effectively communicate queer subjectivity with minimal explanation or contextualization.

All of the responses to Sofia Talouni's broadcast and the women's Facebook pages, from grassroots awareness campaigns within gay Moroccan networks to international media coverage, work within an ideological framework that understands screenshots captured from gay dating apps as iconic representations of otherwise hidden queer subjectivity. Because screenshots are commonly understood to be a technology that captures digital data both perfectly and exactly, and since Grindr, PlanetRomeo, Hornet, and other gay dating apps are designed to operate with an understanding of the images and text shared on these platforms as visible manifestations of queer subjectivity, screenshots of data shared on these platforms are granted a great deal of ontological weight in the construction of truth about one's sexual orientation. These images are more believable and trustworthy than voiced words about one's sexual identity since they represent the most perfect replication, with minimal "intertextual gaps" (Briggs & Bauman, 1992), of one's sexual desire as made visible and tangible on these apps. Screenshots of gay dating apps are potent manifestations of same-sex desire made real and visible, immediately understandable, and easily shared.

In order to uphold the safety of the men who use gay dating apps in Morocco, these powerful images must be carefully managed. Queer activists argue that those who publicize them with malicious and homophobic intent must be stopped and silenced. Upholding the anonymity and invisibility of the unseen world of same-sex desire that these apps make visible is the only way to maintain the privacy of the men who use them. Once a screenshot is shared and seen by others, a man cannot say anything convincing to successfully deny the ostensibly-objective reality of his internal queer identity as represented in the image. Recognizing the power of digital images and text messages shared on gay dating apps as transparent indicators of queer identity, Moroccan LGBTQ activist organizations and individual social media users attempt to limit who can view these images by seeking to shut down the largest platforms on which they are being shared. In other words, they seek to interrupt an intertextual chain of image circulation at critical distribution points by silencing Talouni and the women's groups on Facebook; they hope to prevent more screenshots from moving out of their original, relatively private context (the supposedly all-queer, all-male "safe spaces" of gay dating apps) by interrupting their chain of transmission into unsafe public venues like Talouni's live broadcasts or the women's Facebook groups.

"WE ARE IN THIS TOGETHER": CONCLUSIONS
AND IMPLICATIONS OF THE SOFIA TALOUNI AFFAIR

On April 17, four days after her initial livestream broadcast, Instagram finally deactivated Sofia Talouni's account. Despite the fact that Talouni soon created secondary accounts on Instagram, Facebook, and other platforms, gay Moroccan social media users and activists celebrated Instagram's decision as a victory. In a follow up to his initial post warning queer Moroccans about the outing campaign, gay Moroccan comic artist @fagouta shared an image of the same shirtless young man wearing a hood shaped like the Grindr logo. Instead of being shamed and burned at the stake, however, this image depicts the young man reaching out a hand to accept support from a diverse group of young people, with the text "we are in this together" above him. The caption to this post praises the actions taken by social media users and activists in Morocco and abroad, expressing pride in "every single person who helped take down Sofia's platform." The artist then reminds his readers of the damage that has already been done, saying "our main focus should be on the victims and supporting them." On Facebook, meanwhile, it took over a month before the private groups created to share screenshots were finally deactivated and the posts removed.

In addition to this story receiving coverage from major international news outlets including the New York Times and BBC News as well as gay-focused publications like Pink News, The Advocate, and TÊTU, this outing campaign shaped how queer activists and social media users in the wider North African region conceptualize online data privacy and their relationship with gay dating apps. In neighboring Algeria, for example, queer activist organization Alouen announced on April 20 that they had collaborated with Grindr to send an alert to all Grindr users in Algeria warning them of the possibility of a similar outing campaign, encouraging users to "avoid sending personal information and photos to unknown persons" for the near future. Two weeks later on May 4, Kasbah Tal'fin, a queer activist organization based in the city of Agadir in southern Morocco, shared a Facebook post in Moroccan Arabic warning LGBTQ social media users that "in order for each of us to use and enjoy all the features offered by social networking websites and applications, we must first know the risks that they can present to our personal lives and to the information and data they use." This outing campaign has had a profound effect on how queer activist organizations across North Africa strategize digital risk, making it clear that upholding online data privacy should be an important aspect of their broader work moving forward. The success of the campaigns on Grindr and PlanetRomeo to alert their Moroccan users to the ongoing outings have provided models for other North African queer activists to cooperate with the administrators of gay dating apps in order to uphold the safety of the local queer communities they serve.

The Sofia Talouni affair indicates that social networking platforms promote an ideological stance toward truthmaking and identity construction that privileges external digital manifestations of one's internal same-sex desires over other forms of self-representation. Digital images and text document one's presence on gay dating apps and thus act as a transparent indicator of otherwise unseen same-sex desire. It "speaks for itself" (Matoesian, 2001) as a form of evidence, produced from within the technological field of algorithmic identity construction that lies at the core of gay dating app design. The digital image is understood as a more faithful representation of one's true sexual identity than one's own words since the data it captures functions on social media platforms as the externalization and materialization of one's innermost desires. Queer social media users and homophobes alike work within this ideology, shaping how they seek out local same-sex desiring men for the purposes of queer connection or malicious exposure. Digital images are therefore powerful tools that can be used both for queer connection and the expression of one's truest internal desires, as imagined by Grindr and its ideal users, as well as for unwanted exposure, moral condemnation, and violent repression, as Talouni and her female audiences use them in this outing campaign.

Activists also work within this media ideology, promoting strategies of concealment and obfuscation rather than more familiar gay activist strategies of visibility and "coming out" that have been developed in the United States and other Global North countries. Moroccan activists understand that gay dating apps are only "safe spaces" for queer self-expression to the extent that they remain inaccessible and invisible to a homophobic general public. By seeking to silence those who expose these apps, they work to limit who can capture, share, and redeploy the potent identity-producing data that is created and shared through these platforms. Because social networking technologies like Facebook, Instagram, Grindr, and others are generally designed to encourage the sharing of more data, promoting more connection and more visibility, achieving this activist strategy of concealment is exceedingly difficult. It requires a great deal of individual and grassroots communal labor to ensure the safety-in-concealment of queer social media users, striking the right balance between enough visibility to connect with other queer app users but not enough to be exposed to homophobic violence.

Faced with the threat of unwanted public exposure from a misguided member of their own community, Morocco's LGBTQ populations joined together to issue a collective response to the violence targeting men who use gay dating apps. They successfully lobbied transnational queer activist networks and journalists to amplify their requests for content moderation on social media platforms such as Grindr, PlanetRomeo, Instagram, and Facebook. The tragic events of April 2020, spawned the publication of *L'amour fait loi* (Pascual, 2020), an urgent call to action against shame and homophobia written from the perspective of queer and feminist activists based in Morocco and its diaspora abroad. It is clear that queer social media users and activist organizations in Morocco and the wider North African region are increasingly conscious of the risks and dangers presented by social networking technologies. This consciousness will shape how they use these technologies, how they seek to connect with each other, and how they promote strategies of media use to maintain the safety and confidentiality of queer people living in the region. The Talouni affair has prompted a definitive shift in how regional activists think about social networking platforms in popular discourse and practice, from imagining these platforms as a means of connection and communication to potentially dangerous technologies for data extraction and unwanted loss of privacy.

REFERENCES

Alami, A. (2020). Dozens of Gay Men Are Outed in Morocco as Photos Are Spread Online. *New York Times.* Published April 26. Accessed May 3, 2020, from https://www.nytimes.com/2020/04/26/world/middleeast/gay-morocco-outing.html.

Ale-Ebrahim, B. (2019). 'Your Chance to Make Your Voice Heard': Akaliyat Magazine and the Creation of a Queer Community in Morocco. *Journal of Global Initiatives, 14*(2), 85–104.

Amoore, L. (2020). *Cloud Ethics: Algorithms and the Attributes of Ourselves and Others.* Duke University Press.

Bauman, R., & Briggs, C. L. (1990). Poetics and Performance as Critical Perspectives on Language and Social Life. *Annual Review of Anthropology, 19,* 59–88.

Briggs, C., & Bauman, R. (1992). Genre, Intertextuality, and Social Power. *Journal of Linguistic Anthropology, 2*(2), 131–172.

Carroll, O. (2019). Gay Hunters: How Criminal Gangs Lure Men on Dating Apps Before Extorting Cash and Beating Them. *The Independent.* Published April 14. Accessed May 2, 2020, from https://www.independent.co.uk/news/world/europe/gay-hunters-russia-moscow-apps-gangs-homophobia-a8865376.html.

Cheney-Lippold, J. (2017). *We Are Data: Algorithms and the Making of Our Digital Selves.* NYU Press.

El-Rouayheb, K. (2009). *Before Homosexuality in the Arab World, 1500-1800.* University of Chicago Press.

Foucault, M. (1988). In L. H. Martin, H. Gutman, & P. H. Hutton (Eds.), *Technologies of the Self: A Seminar with Michel Foucault.* University of Massachusetts Press.

Gershon, I. (2010). Breaking Up is Hard to Do: Media Switching and Media Ideologies. *Journal of Linguistic Anthropology, 20*(2), 389–405.

Gillespie, T. (2018). *Custodians of the Internet: Platforms, Content Moderation, and the Hidden Decisions That Shape Social Media.* Yale University Press.

Gitzen, T. (2021). The Limits of Family: Military Law and Sex Panics in Contemporary South Korea. *Positions, 29*(3), 607–632.

Gouyon, M. (2018). *'Ana Loubia': Ethnographie des homosexualités masculines à Casablanca.* Éditions du croquant.

Greenhalgh, H., & Al-Khal, A. (2020). Morocco Instagram Influencer Apologises for Role in Outing of Gay Men. *Yahoo News.* Published May 13. Accessed April 23, 2021, from https://www.yahoo.com/lifestyle/morocco-instagram-influencer-apologises-role-164914071.html.

Greenspan, R. E. (2020). Gay men in Morocco Say They Are 'Living in Constant Fright' After an Influencer's Video Sparked a Trend of People Using Dating Apps to Out Them. *Insider.* Published April 17. Accessed May 3, 2020, from https://www.insider.com/moroccan-instagram-influencer-moussa-gay-men-outed-adam-eli-2020-4.

Grindr. (2021). *About us.* Accessed April 23, 2021, from https://www.grindr.com/about/.

Hayes, J. (2000). *Queer Nations: Marginal Sexualities in the Maghreb.* University of Chicago Press.

Immigration and Refugee Board of Canada (IRBC). (2013). Morocco: Situation of Sexual Minorities, Including Treatment by the Authorities and Society; The Application of Article 489 of the Penal Code and Cases with Convictions for Homosexuality; State Protection and Support Services (2010-October 2013). Published October 28. Accessed April 23, 2021, from https://www.refworld.org/docid/53732cbf4.html.

Instagram. (2021). *Community Guidelines.* Accessed April 23, 2021, from https://www.facebook.com/help/instagram/477434105621119.

Massad, J. A. (2007). *Desiring Arabs.* University of Chicago Press.

Matoesian, G. M. (2001). *Law and the Language of Identity: Discourse in the William Kennedy Smith Rape Trial.* Oxford University Press.

McGlotten, S. (2013). *Virtual Intimacies: Media, Affect, and Queer Sociality.* SUNY Press.

Pascual, P. (Ed.). (2020). *L'amour fait loi.* Éditions le Sélénite.

PlanetRomeo. (2021). *About.* Accessed May 5, 2021, from https://www.planetromeo.com/en/about/.

Provencher, D. (2017). *Queer Maghrebi French: Language, Temporalities.* Liverpool University Press.

Rebucini, G. (2013). Hegemonic Masculinities and 'Sexualities' Among Men in Morocco: Between Local Configurations and the Globalization of Gender and Sexual Categories. *Cahiers d'études africaines, 209-210*(1), 387–415.

Skalli, L. H. (2014). Young Women and Social Media Against Sexual Harassment in North Africa. *The Journal of North African Studies, 19*(2), 244–258.

Trew, B. (2017). 'We Are Being Hunted': Why LGBTQ Egyptians Are Living in Fear. *The Daily Beast.* Published October 26. Accessed May 2, 2020, from https://www.thedailybeast.com/we-are-being-hunted-why-lgbtq-egyptians-are-living-in-fear.

Walden, S. (2005). Objectivity in Photography. *British Journal of Aesthetics, 45*(3), 258–272.

Weiss, S. (2017). This Group of New Yorkers Is Fighting for LGBTQ People In Chechnya. *Refinery29.* Published September 28. Accessed May 3, 2020, from https://www.refinery29.com/en-us/2017/09/174383/voices-4-chechnya-lgbtq-activism.

CHAPTER 4

Queer Resistance and Activism in *Upon the Shadow*

Zayer Baazaoui

Introduction

This chapter closely examines how queer subjectivities are presented on the silver screen through *Upon the Shadow* (2017), a documentary of Nada Mezni Hfaeidh, a young Tunisian film director, known for the audacity of the subjects treated in her films such as relationships before marriage and sex in her film *Hekayet tounsiya* (2011). *Upon the Shadow* is produced by Leyth Production, a Tunisian-based film production company. It talks about a group of young queer people who found themselves in the home of Amina Sboui, the famous Tunisian activist, and the former member of the radical feminist group FEMEN. Media, particularly cinema, have sparked and fueled debates around queer issues in the MENA region for the past two decades. In fact, unlike literary texts, artistic media and visual productions manage to attract a wider audience, given that they are more readily accessible to a large section of the population. Media have thus become a very primordial cultural domain in the dissemination of knowledge and reflections on several aspects of contemporary society, including issues and discussions of LGBTQ identities. This field is then, as shown by Gray (2009), "the primary site of production for social knowledge [regarding] LGBTQ identities" (1165). The development of these new media forms shows not only the courage of the producers but also the bravery of the young people who play queer roles, especially in the context of

Z. Baazaoui (✉)
St. Paul's School, Concord, NH, USA
e-mail: zayerbaz@miami.edu

L. H. Skalli, N. Eltantawy (eds.), *The Palgrave Handbook of Gender, Media and Communication in the Middle East and North Africa*,
https://doi.org/10.1007/978-3-031-11980-4_4

the MENA region. In this context, Christopher Pullen states in the preface to his *Queer Youth and Media Cultures* collection (2014):

> Queer youth are enablers of future progress concerning bravery, integrity, thoughtfulness and commitment. Through the media as a representational and performative landscape, the apparition of queer youth, whether as gay, lesbian, bisexual, transgender, intersex or androgynous, establishes a new foundation, one that addresses a wide world of interested parties who can learn about personal feeling, and profound commitment to being themselves. (xv)

The role of these media is thus twofold. On the one hand, they educate and inform society about current discussions around taboo questions of underrepresented identities, and on the other hand, they are the means by which queer people explore their subjectivities in order to accomplish this journey of discovery and self-acceptance.

Upon the Shadow has generated various debates and polemics which were sometimes aggressive and intense and made the headlines of local newspapers for weeks. It has also been the subject of much debate in Tunisian society and more widely around the world due to its participation in several film festivals. Its first broadcast in the Arab world was at the Carthage Film Festival in Tunisia (Les Journées cinématographiques de Carthage).

The queer persons in *Upon the Shadow* have been rejected by their families because of their sexual orientation and are taking refuge in Amina's house. In this documentary, we witness real moments of the daily lives of these young people who try to navigate in solidarity their own society with its violence, homophobia, and rejection.

Queer Subjectivities and Family: Negotiating Home

Research about young queers' lives within the family shows that they are mainly subject to homophobic behavior in their home of origin, which leads them to seek an "alternative" family where they feel safer, included, and emotionally supported (Weston, 1991; Weeks et al., 2001).

Documentaries are distinguished from fictional films by their veridical aspect, which aims to present facts of society (Rothman, 1997). That is why Bill Nichols talks about the "status of documentary film as evidence from the world" and the "status of documentary as discourse about the world" (1991, ix–x). Despite the studies (Trinh, 1993) that negotiate the real, truthful, and documentational nature of documentaries, they always present a certain approach to reality that eventually incorporate aesthetic additions necessary for the creation of a complete plot, as well as for the sake of understandability and the need for a coherent argument. These realities are presented, as Fuchs and Holmlund thoroughly explain in their introduction to the book *Between the Sheets, In the Streets, Queer, Lesbian, Gay Documentary* (1997), as "profilmic events and experiences," through which "we realize that documentaries do exist, in rhetorical and political dimensions" (3–4). These documentaries are therefore very involved and invested in the culture of the society they choose to analyze.

Having said that, Nada Mezni Hafaiedh's documentary explores the realities of the Tunisian queer community's lived experience in their native country. These realities shed light on the real dynamics of marginalized subjects in the region. The cast consists mainly of Amina Sboui (queer activist), Sandra Neifer (transgender woman), Ramy Ayari (gay), Atef Pucci (gay/transvestite), Ayoub Moumene (gay), and some other secondary characters.

Upon the Shadow opens with a *mise en scene* on the beach in the suburbs of Tunis on the cliffs of Sidi Bou Said. This *mise en scene* consists of the shadow of a person whose gender is unknown. From this shadow that moves, jumps, and runs on the beach, a progressive close-up shows us Amina who appears little by little in the background of the camera's shot. The *mise en scene* is an essential cinematographic tool for understanding the style of the film, and it provides a complex and meaningful site that illuminates an argument or an idea. It supports the idea that the film is both a documentary work and an aesthetic one too.

Most of the *mises en scene* take place on the beach, mainly with Amina, but also sometimes with the other young queer people living with her. These *mises en scene* are generally a statement or comments and personal explanations about the life of each individual in question, but also about the life of the LGBTQ community in general. Therefore, they illustrate certain realities in order to explain them, but above all, to give voice to these young people so that they may express themselves from a personal point of view.

After this entry, we go directly to the second scene where we see Amina at home in her bed, and the filmmaker's camera enters her private space as it was to wake her up. The camera begins to scan the entire room and zooms in on the open closet. When Amina gets up, she heads toward the window, the camera following her, and she begins to look at the horizon and the sea. These first two scenes put the viewer in the true depth of the story. They are loaded with meaning and images. When framed in a significative perspective, the shadow, the beach, the waves, the sea, the closet, the bed, the window, and the horizon often constitute allegories of queerness.

We later learn that the house where Amina lives serves as a refuge for other queer people who have been rejected by their families. All these young people together see this house as a new possibility to protect themselves from the difficult living conditions in a society that does not accept them. This society is violent and aggressive, as Amina explains at the very beginning of the film. She says that society imposes and assigns certain rules that must be followed in order to feel included: "Mom taught me good manners in her way…No not in her way but in the society manners. How people perceive good manners. [For] Example 'Don't go with guys.' 'Don't wear tight pants.' 'No lipstick.' 'No short skirt.' 'No bare back.' 'No sexy clothes.' 'At the beach swim with a t-shirt.' For her if I obey all these rules… I will be the example of the perfect girl. It is not even for me… It is for the society. And of course, to find Mr. Right so I can hide my bad reputation."

When she says these words, we see that the camera zooms in on Amina's face. Her facial expressions are highlighted, and we see the bitterness and sadness that emanate from her visage. From this, we understand that Amina's family of origin is trying to impose on her a lifestyle that certainly should not go beyond the limits of what is deemed normative. Similarly, when these young people publicly display their non-normative sexual orientations, they are forced to leave their family home, for challenging standards always exacts a price for the transgressor. As we see in the documentary, everyone has a backstory: a story of social rejection but also of familial abandonment. The two go hand-in-hand.

The family home is generally associated with security, compassion, and a deep awareness of and sympathy for other's suffering (Duncan, 1996; Moran & Skeggs, 2004; Valentine et al., 2003). This is the place where people should normally feel safe and be authentic with their feelings and sexual orientations (Rapport & Dawson, 1998). However, research on the life of homosexual people in the family home has shown the difficult, sometimes violent, conditions in which they live. They are indeed mainly and exclusively exposed to normative heterosexuality and must follow normative gender roles. Atef, one of the queer persons living with Amina, says that the thing he can never forget is the day his father burned him with a cigarette because he was wearing a slightly feminine t-shirt. His father tore his t-shirt, hit him, and burned his chest with his cigarette. In this private family space, homosexual children are thus forced to hide their true feelings because they are constantly watched and surveilled (Valentine et al., 2003; Dunne et al., 2002; Prendergast et al., 2002). The young people in Amina's home are subject to rejections from the family home first, then from a society that does not accept them. This family rejection represents not only a "merely cultural" (Butler, 1997) form of oppression and exclusion, but also, above all, a destruction of the life of the homosexual person, who goes from depression (emotional, affective, and relational) to suicide, as is demonstrated in the end of the movie, when Atef tries to end his own life. The family home has expectations that are the result of normative patriarchal society.

Valentine et al. (2003, p. 484) explain that children are seen as the image of the family and that parents (or the family as a social institution) are responsible for the image that their children will give/expose to the community. A queer person can thus be considered a parenting failure and can therefore damage the image and reputation of her family. This is why, for example, Amina talks about rules of good behavior and morals that her mother imposed on her when she was a child. The family home is the first and essential site where the child is forced to follow a pattern coded by normative notions of sexuality and gender. In this context, Arnett (1997) explains that the evolution of the child within the family goes through traditional and normative transitions, namely education, work, and then marriage and reproduction. Children in possession of a non-normative identity, sexually and socially speaking, encounter resistance and refusal from the family. This forces them to leave the parental home in order to emancipate themselves and live away from parental pressure. Amina and all the other young queers have followed this same trajectory.

Going to live in Amina's house is a necessity, not a choice. Staying at Amina's and sleeping in the street seem to be the only two possible alternatives, upon rejection from the family home. These young queer people gather in Amina's house because they feel safe in some ways and have a roof over their head. At the very beginning of the documentary, Ramy confesses to Amina that she is the only person he can turn to after his family rejected him. "You are the only person who is left for me, since my family pushed me out." And throughout the film, each character speaks in an individual *mise en scene* to confess the pain, sadness, and experience of familial rejection. Toward the end of the film, Amina at the edge of the beach sums up a bit of the others' experience in these words: "My friends have found themselves in a situation where I am the only one who opens the door to them…I didn't choose that all my friends are rejected from the society."

The family is a locus of social relationships and is ultimately an extension of society and public space. The family gaze, as conceived by David Morgan (2011) in his study that rethinks family practices through time, space, the body, emotions, and ethics, follows queer people even when they decide to leave their parental home. Consequently, this family gaze turns into a societal gaze. Negotiating queerness remains a very sensitive subject within the family and the parental home, and most often leads to total rejection. By leaving the familial home, the queer person confronts the public space and all its challenges.

Negotiating Public Space and Creating Queer Alternative Sites

Pursuing the perspective of the negotiation of the queer person's entourage, this essay is now shifting to the exploration of public space. "Queer bodies disturb the city as they navigate it" (Khouri, 2015, 99) and their visibility would represent a frontal threat to the heterosexual patriarchal regime. Due to their vulnerability, queer persons find it difficult to navigate public space and establish relationships and interactions with other people. "Their essential fluidity, precarity and vulnerability resemble a flamboyant challenge to familiarity, certainty and mass agreement. They interact with the rigidity of concrete structures around them to create crucial emotional and intellectual conversations – on both internal and external levels – about their identities and performances, and their relationship to the public space they are navigating" (Khouri, 2015, 99).

Richardson (1998, 2000) shows that non-normative subjects are marginalized in both private and public spaces and argues that if there is a tolerance for queer minorities it is "constructed largely on the condition that they remain in the private sphere and do not seek public recognition" (Richardson, 1998, 89–90). Socio-economic capital is nonexistent and most of the young queer youth in *Upon the Shadow* are uneducated, in the sense of not having a university degree, and they find it difficult to integrate themselves into economic and social life. In a very emotional confession in front of the camera, Atef says that he feels guilty because he has not been able to achieve the wish of his mother, which is finishing his studies and getting a university degree. This confirms the idea that to have access to LGBTQ-friendly spaces, "having economic, cultural, and social capital" (Moussawi, 2018, 184) is required. The absence of socio-economic capital in the case of these young people makes their navigation of public space very difficult and aggressive. Moran and Skeggs (2004) effectively show that public urban space is a site of aggression and violence. It constitutes a danger for vulnerable people who have no form of privilege. Skeggs (1999) adds that the public sphere is constructed and established to accommodate heterosexual people exclusively. This becomes particularly complicated when the queer person is distinguished by physical traits which expose him/her/they as a non-normative person who does not conform to the standards of masculinity/femininity (Skeggs, 2001). Add to all of this that generally the public sphere is governed by male presence.

The assaults are more violent. They take place in full public on the street in the case of Amina and her friends, as the presence of the different bodily and physical non-normativities (Lesbian, transgender, gay) constitutes a real menace to the divisions mentioned above. The queer youth group is attacked by a stranger while they are walking peacefully on the street. ("You're not ashamed! I will kick your fucking ass." A stranger screams in minute 11.) Their non-normativity disturbs society and heteropatriarchal public space. Most of these queer persons are trying to create alternatives to survive aggression in the public space and family rejection. These alternatives are essentially places where queer subjects go to let off steam.

Accompanied by her female friend, Amina visits a mausoleum several times where she performs Sufi rituals in a traditional Sufi atmosphere. These ritual performances are known for their purifying and releasing effect. It is as if Amina is going to free her body so that she might rid herself of social pressure, rejection, and vulnerability.

It is also clear that the queer body takes refuge in the sea. The film reaching its end on the beach is only a confirmation of the complex rapport that queer persons have with society and the possibility of creating other alternatives, even temporary ones, like somehow being free in the sea. In this same context, Nouri Gana explains the importance of these alternative places for the rejected and marginalized people because they give them the possibility to explore and to reconcile with their marginalities. By studying the films of Tunisian cineaste Nouri Bouzid, Gana asserts that the sea/beach is a "liminal space outside social norms" (2017, 184) which symbolizes "anathema to traditionalism, piety, and the patriarchal order writ large" (2017, 185).

In her book *Sex and the Citadel: Intimate Life in a changing Arab World* (2013), Shereen El Feki asks if the region's new generation, which desires political freedom and went out into the streets demanding political and social change, would be able to initiate a conversation around freedom of sexual practices. She answered in the negative, because according to the interviews and research she had done, she realized that young queers insisted on the importance of the family and its expectations. Most of them are forced to remain invisible while leading two lives, one normative and visible, the other non-normative and invisible. She also concludes that not only does the family have expectations but also society and its neoliberal economy oblige them to follow the roles of normative gender. And as Khouri (2015) asserts, "the city is an extension of [the] family house and neighborhood. The duality exists in both in very similar dynamics. The good and the bad, the allowed and the prohibited, [the] anxieties" (Khouri, 114). However, the importance of breaking the rules and challenging heterosexual patriarchy should not be overlooked. By going out in the streets and knowing what awaits them, these young queers participate directly or indirectly in change. And at the very least, their doing so creates debate around questions of sexual difference and non-normativity, as well as the presence of the queer body. In this same context, Khouri insists on the participation of queer women in the public sphere. It is true that her study is based on a performance that she has set up with other queer women to express their frustration with the public space and to take a place within patriarchal society, but this applies to the contexts of the documentary studied here insofar as "queer women's struggles cannot be untangled from the struggle of women in the everyday" and that the "bodies [they] carry in public are bodies perceived as belonging to the realm of the private, and [...] are reminded of that every time [they] step out of [their] houses" (2015, 100). Going out and facing society would therefore be resistance and activism.

RESISTANCE AND ACTIVISM

The film can be viewed as engaging in a form of awareness spread. Indeed, it represents different aspects of society with a cast and a management team completely from Tunisia. I insist on this point because generally films addressing the question of LGBTQ narratives in the Maghreb or in the Middle East are produced by Westerners and in the West (Lagabrielle, 2013). Generally, Western filmmakers present them as subjects of exotic homoerotic desire who are torn between a conservative cultural milieu and a Eurocentric gaze which according to them recalls the days of colonialism.

The awareness spread I am talking about here is one that forces debate around taboo topics, which gives minorities the opportunity to express themselves through an artistic production that is accessible to the general public. This film can (and has already) create debates on the question of the place of sexual minorities in the region. The debates thus go beyond the framework of the movie theater. Bruce Brasell explains it well when he says, "Queer audiences and queer filmmakers collaborate to produce a queer discourse, one which exists not only during the film viewing process but which also circulates outside in the streets of the lesbian and gay community" (1996).

This study focuses mainly on Amina's activism in the documentary because it is a work that shows queer young people's real engagement in society. The fact that these young people go out on their own to challenge society and defend their right to exist is not only strong evidence of their courage in the first place, but it also shows their awareness of the importance of speaking up on behalf of their community. "Additionally, the act of performing our stories by ourselves in public communicated a political statement reclaiming agency, taking charge of our own self-narratives, rejecting victimization and stereotypical portrayals of our bodies, and granting the performance a level of truthfulness that otherwise would not have been possible," argues Khouri (2015, 99) in this same context.

In 2013, Amina Sboui writes in English "Fuck Your Morals" on her body and publishes her first topless provocative image on Facebook and entered then a new phase in her activism. E. Butler says, "With her first image, 'Fuck Your Morals,' Sboui purposefully transgressed one of the most important cultural proscriptions for Arab women, including Tunisians, by creating and disseminating a topless photograph of herself" (2017, 132).

In March 2013, during the protest movement following the assassination of Tunisian leftist politician Chokri Belaïd and the resignation of the Tunisian government, Amina Sboui posted on Facebook a photograph of herself topless. In Arabic, she paints the following phrase on her chest "My body is mine and not the source of anybody's honor." Amina knows the pressure imposed on the female body (whether it be normative or not) and thus decided to use this same body to counter and transgress the codes imposed by heteropatriarchal society: "The messages she writes and her toplessness work together to explode the social and cultural codification that still dictates how women may present their bodies" (E. Butler, 2017, 135). These actions sparked an intense controversy in Tunisia and in the world. She was threatened with death by Salafists, and her family kidnapped and sequestered her for more than three weeks in Kairouan (E. Butler, 2017). She then managed to escape her family home. Soon after, on May 19, she was arrested for tagging the wall of a cemetery in Kairouan the meeting place of the congress of the *Ansar al-Sharia*, a group of very extremist Islamists. Shortly afterward, she was detained in jail and accused of desecration of a cemetery and possession of a self-defense aerosol, for which she incurred a total of two and a half years in prison.

On May 29, three FEMEN activists, two French and one German, were arrested in Tunis after a support action for Amina. Inna Shevchenko, leader of FEMEN in Paris, explains that this was their first action in the Arab world (E. Butler, 2017).

The indictment chamber of Sousse ordered Amina's release on August 1. After getting out of prison, she posed for a photo shoot while holding a Molotov cocktail in her hand. She announced on August 20, 2013, in the newspaper *Al Huffington Post* that she had left the FEMEN group. She explained that her departure stemmed from the fact that FEMEN is an "Islamophobic" movement and that she is also skeptical about their sources of funding. In an interview with the *Huffpost*, Amina basically explains that the management of this organization is not transparent and lacks clarity on many of its actions and financial resources:

> I don't know how the movement is financed. I asked Inna several times, but I didn't get a clear answer. I don't want to be in a movement supported by dubious money. What if it is financed by Israel? I want to know. And then, I don't want my name to be associated with an Islamophobic organization. I did not appreciate the action taken by the girls shouting "Amina Akbar, Femen Akbar" in front of the Tunisian embassy in France, or when they burned the black Tawhid flag in front of a mosque in Paris. These actions offended many Muslims and many of my friends. We must respect everyone's religion. (2013)

She later got a student visa and scholarship with the help of the Tunisian Association of Democratic Women and Amnesty International and went to study in Paris. She was able to finish high school and got her baccalaureate (high school diploma). However, she did not finish her university studies and she does not hold a university degree. On the occasion of International Women's Day (March 8, 2014), she protested completely naked in Paris with six other feminist activists from the Arab world. She has been repeatedly shirtless or totally naked on social networks, mainly Facebook. Although she still uses FEMEN's provocative approach as a template for her activism, she did not participate in certain actions, such as their imitation of the Muslim prayer in front of the Tunisian Embassy in Paris. When asked if she is aware that public opinion found her actions to be shocking, or that they even alienated the moderates and educated people, she responded that the "aggression" of heteropatriarchal mentality in Tunisia is so powerful that it requires a radical reaction, that the traditional methods of feminists are not enough anymore and that what she did forced a debate at the very minimum. In this same context, E. Butler affirms that "Sboui uses the inherent politicism of her female body to make claims about her agency. These assertions disrupt expectations of male social and physical control over women's bodies" (2017, 134).

This power imposed by heterocentrist institutions (family, society, politically manipulated religion, etc.) when it becomes an over-power, can provoke a revolt among those subjected to it. This was the case with Amina, who reacted to the extreme power with yet another form of extreme power. What Amina did is a form of resistance, despite the criticisms one might level against her, such as the fact that she is in contact with foreign organizations. These images, the poses, and the written texts show the will and the resistance of a woman who wants to get rid of the pressures of the gender roles society assigns:

Her body language indicates her attempts to assert her status as a subject. The same hands that wrote "Fuck your morals" underscore that message with their gesture. Sboui's full frontal pose and return of the viewer's gaze convey a directness that disrupts her construction as a passive sex object. It is Sboui's articulation of her authority to mark or display her own body that constitutes a claim to subjecthood, particularly through specific textual messages that use first- and second-person pronouns, thereby personalizing her statements. (E. Butler, 2017, 135)

All of these actions are not intervention and assistance from foreign organizations, although we can see some of these types of interventions in the documentary. This is seen at the very beginning of the film (min13), when a French editor calls Amina via Skype to remind her of book's submission deadline. This editor mentions that her publishing house provided Amina with everything, including the rent payment for the villa in Sidi Bou Said where she lives with her queer friends. The Frenchwoman reminds her that "time is money." One can eventually think here of Joseph Massad's work on the Gay International and the Arab world.

Joseph Massad's "The Gay International and the Arab World" (2002) argues that, in a time when activism for LGBTQ rights became a synonym of a society's evolution and a way to show how democracy develops in a country, international organizations that advocate and defend homosexuals hide an urgent missionary mission, to liberate Arabs and Muslims from the "oppression under which they allegedly live by transforming them from practitioners of same-sex contact into subjects who identify as homosexual and gay" (362). These organizations are what Massad calls the Gay International. He names, for instance, the International Lesbian and Gay Association (ILGA) and the International Gay and Lesbian Human Rights Commission (IGLHRC), which are mainly run by white Western males. The discourse of the Gay International is an orientalist discourse that imposes the production of homosexuals (gays, lesbians) "where they do not exist" (363). As a student of Edward Said, Massad's starting point are the concepts of Orientalism, and thus, Otherization. Those "Others" (all the non-Western subjects) cannot represent themselves, so another, a Western subject, should represent them and speak for them.

According to Massad, "the Gay International and a small minority of Arab same-sex practitioners who adopt its epistemology" (374) use what he calls an "incitement to discourse." Using this notion borrowed from Foucault, Massad explains that both the Gay International and these Arab minorities have incited this orientalist discourse since the early 1980s when they started to universalize and impose their vision of a gay identity. We note in this context that this "other Westerner" is very present in the figure of the French editor who pays Amina to write a book on the lives of young queer people in Tunisia.

According to Massad, by inciting both the people and the politics of MENA countries to accept a Western binary epistemology, this orientalist discourse protects only a very minor part of the population. This minority belongs to the wealthier segments of society that have already adopted a Western identity

(373). Massad criticizes them because of their collusion with the Gay International. He addresses this issue of the Gay International and how it negatively influences Arabs' sexuality by forcing it to be only heterosexual or less homosexual. While Massad's argument is strong, it is crucial that we should not eradicate or overlook all the activism that Amina works to do. But, first, one should realize that activism such as Amina's has a real affect on real people in the real world in which they are. Moreover, Massad has a tendency of conceiving the Muslim-Arab world as an autonomous entity which it is of course not anymore, as globalization is evidently everywhere. Based on some aspects of fluid sexuality in the MENA region, he goes on to often "invent" what could be seen as another orientalist fantasy: that of a world open and tolerant to "deviant" sexualities, which it is absolutely not. Samar Habib, in an interview published by *Sawt al Niswa*, rightfully corrects such misconception in very firm terms: "We [in the Arab-Muslim world] have had our own brand of homophobia long before there were Western colonial impositions and conceptual migrations of that kind" (sawtalniswa.com/article/317). Finally, while Amina is very active in civil society, she does not fall into the social class category that Massad focuses on in his essay, neither do her friends. They all come from lower-middle-class or even poor families, and they are not all educated. At the start of the documentary, Amina takes care of a street boy and goes to the aid of his mother, whose husband is abusing her. She says after bringing the aggressed women and her son to stay with her and save her from the violence of the husband: "For me, good manners are not about [leaving] a poor [person] starving. It's about how much you're able to give to others. It ain't about how much you're willing to give to yourself, the image of the perfect girl so at the end you find 10 guys willing to marry you." Furthermore, the Tunisian Association of Democratic Women's (the major feminist association in Tunisia which was founded in 1989) intervention at the end of the film shows how proud these women are of Amina and of her courage. The Democratic Women have insisted that Amina exercises her activism and dedication to sexual freedom during a very difficult time. Indeed, she is leading women's rights in Tunisia into a new phase. "In that period, Amina manifested with a lot of courage. For me it's a very courageous move, and even an activist one concerning the future of women in this society," says one of the Democratic Women.

"My friends have found themselves in a situation where I am the only one who opens the door to them. We were forced to stay together. We fight, we make peace, we laugh, we cry. I didn't choose that all my friends are rejected from the society. I could have had other normal friends. But, unfortunately in Tunisia because of our families and the police we found ourselves locked up all together. At the end we help and love each other." Amina sums up remarkably the situation of sexual minorities in these words. Queer youth are clearly rejected by family, society, and the state. This is not an "orientalist" ideological invention: this is a fact, and a lived, existential one. The only way for them to resist is to remain united, and to find allies. When a public and safe space for queer living will be established and protected (legally, institutionally, culturally), there will be plenty of time for discussing the regional specificities of sexual freedom, including queer one, and gender equality, and finding localized models of socio-sexual identities.

This is also why, at the end of the documentary, Amina and her comrades decide to launch an awareness campaign to help women who are assaulted and who are victims of violence. It is true that the campaign does not exclusively concern homosexuals; but because these young queers know very well what it means to be rejected and harassed on a daily basis for the simple reason of being different, they are very aware of the social injustices that others face as well. The awareness campaign "deals with rejected people from the society. They will express themselves freely about what they've been through. We want to push women to talk about their suffering," explains Amina in the documentary.

All of that having been said, one can point at orientalist aspects in the documentary, whether it is artistically speaking (such as the visits to places of Sufi rituals) or through the relationships that Amina has with the French publishing house. However, these aspects cannot and should not hide the main point of this whole story, namely the resistance and the daily fight that Amina leads. On the contrary, this activism creates alliances and builds cross-border networks, thus developing regional movements that incorporate others' experiences in order to find solutions in the fight against queerphobia.

The dream of Amina and her friends should not be suppressed, because asking for equality, dignity, and recognition of the rights of all people regardless of sexual orientation is a right that everyone must fight to have and have established. Amina eloquently says at the end of the documentary: "I dream of a world without racism, without sexism, without homophobia, without xenophobia. I dream of a world full of unlimited love, music, peace. A world that respects ... Freedom, dignity and social justice." And for that, the fight must go on and this youth must not throw in the towel. Indeed, it must fight the shadow in addition to the *invisibilization* of queer people that heteropatriarchal society imposes.

At the end of the documentary these young queers, who are joined by activists from the Tunisian Association of Democratic Women, say it all: "I love life. I want to live free and with my head held high. Shadows, I won't shut up, words disturbing me, and ideas are killing each other. I won't shut up; time will come, and I will blow up. France has put Act 230 since 1913, France has changed this act in its constitution. How much time and victims do we need to change this law? [...] Let's not forget that in our country today, homosexuals are thrown into prison and deprived of their rights where they are tortured by the police and prisoners. No one chooses the color of his hair, nor his size or shape. Defend dignity, equality, freedom, and justice, defend humanity."[1] Most of the MENA countries inherited strict laws against homosexuality from the

---

[1] These are the words of both the queer young group and the women of the Tunisian Association of Democratic Women who each spoke a little at the very end of the documentary.

French or British colonial systems of justice, which have persisted unchanged ever since, as explained in the above-mentioned quote by the different members of this small community of queers and other women activists.

It is important nowadays to have activist movements in the Global South because such experiences can help to improve the situation of homosexual Arabs in a way divergent from the agenda of the Gay International. To this regard, Lila Abu-Lughod rightfully states: "we need to look closely at what we are supporting (and what we are not) and to think carefully about why. How should we manage the complicated politics and ethics of finding ourselves in agreement with those with whom we normally disagree" (2002, 787). In other words, it is undoubtedly relevant to speak up and defend all the rights of minority subjects, but without being guided by neocolonial foreign impositions such as the Gay International. Understanding, in its socio-cultural context, the cause we defend and support, as Abu-Lughod says, helps to avoid falling into orientalist traps.

Law, like culture, is changeable, transformable, and evolutionary: it can and should change, but the path seems to be long and complicated. Activism and resistance are then vitally indispensable.

In their report of the year 2018, OutRight Action International, with the support of The Arab Foundation for Freedoms and Equality, affirms that in spite of its many challenges:

> we have seen enormous advances in the MENA region in LGBTIQ organizing and rights in recent years. Activists always find a way, even in the hardest places. We wrote this report to show a different kind of activism. The activism described in this report shows that progress is slow, but MENA activists have created original strategies to overcome seemingly insurmountable odds. Instead of seeing the MENA region as 'stuck', this report demonstrates the opposite. There's so much to learn about resilience, coalition-building and art for social change from LGBTIQ activists in MENA (2018, 1).

Amina and her friends showed exemplary courage. Amina's activism journey in particular should be highlighted. Talking about this activism is the least we can do in order to adequately acknowledge the daily suffering of queer people in the region. In the same perspective of hiding and *invisibilizing* queer youth, the resilience and activism of these young people are often overlooked or demonized, as explained in the report: "However, the complex realities of LGBTQ people, including resilience, activism, and hard-fought legal and social progress remains largely neglected" (2018, 3).

Like cultural and artistic productions (novels, films, documentaries, etc.), doing activism on the ground is a key aspect to not only understand the situation of sexual minorities but also (and above all) to combat the heteropatriarchal regime in place and to work toward new possibilities. Thus, being inspired by other experiences or being in contact with Western foreign organizations must not be condemned and qualified as orientalist but must be understood in a transnational context in movement. Human beings are dynamic agents in the stimulation and transfer of "social remittances" at global and local levels. By "social remittances" sociologist Peggy Levitt means "the ideas, behaviors, identities, and social capital that flow from host-to sending-country communities" (2001, 54). Transnationalism should be understood thus as a process of sharing ideas, cultures, and behaviors. The transnational can be practiced locally, without the need to cross the borders; this is what Amina and her queer friends do. Globalization, in its general sense, has made transnationalism spread everywhere. According to Lionnet and Shi (2005), "the transnational, therefore, is not bound by the binary of the local and the global and can occur in national, local, or global spaces across different and multiple spatialities and temporalities" (2005, 6). Instead of thinking of Amina and her friends as being westernized, we should rather see them as transnational subjects who "want to get ahead rather than just get by. They do not change because they have to, but because they want to learn and benefit from the new world around them. They creatively add and combine what they observe with their existing ideas and practices, thereby expanding and extending their cultural repertoire" (Levitt, 2001, 57). Sexuality and gender belong to the cultural repertoire of people and nations. To defend the rights of minor groups is to recognize their existence and to admit that they are part of a whole called the nation.

When we talk about sexuality and human rights, we think immediately about body. The latter, because it is the source of each one's sexual performance, contains feelings and affections. Even in its oppressed forms, the body produces and discharges feelings. The affect of these marginal subjects matters. Activism, human rights, and normative or non-normative sexuality create affects because they participate in the emancipation of the human body. The values of sharing and proximity generated by the different forms of resistance and activism create affect. Sara Ahmed (2010) emphasizes the notion of happiness because it "shapes what coheres as a world" (2010, 2). By opening up to the others, by actively participating in activism on LGBTQ rights, by adapting methods inspired by transnational movements, there is an intensifying feeling of happiness. "Happiness becomes, then, a way of maximizing your potential of getting what you want, as well as being what you want to get" (Ahmed, 2010, 10). This feeling of happiness can ultimately be produced and assembled by looking at and analyzing the achievements of other transnational experiences. "We can even anticipate an affect without being retrospective insofar as objects might acquire the value of proximities that are not derived from our own experience" (2010, 28). This feeling of happiness is very noticeable in the documentary, which, despite the repressive context and the daily challenges, has an ending that is not sad and carries a charge of hope. Furthermore, the settings of the final scene contain an open-endedness, symbolized by the sea. We know that solidarity and resistance have created this feeling of joy. Queer people in the MENA region do not want to be portrayed only as victims anymore. Just because it is by definition a visual medium, engaged queer or queer-related cinema has no choice but to make the queer body visible and this is the way it is by itself objectively a form of activism. And queer subjectivities are not condemned to invisibility forever.

CONCLUSION

The documentary ends by closely observing civil society's investment in understanding the issue and the activism of queer youth and some women in the defense of their rights to liberty and non-exclusion from society because of their difference. This confirms that things change over time. It is now invalid to talk about Gay International and foreign interventions when all these concepts previously considered to be "Western," became known throughout the world (transnationalism, globalization, etc.). Indeed, technology, social networks, and media in general are accessible everywhere now, and facilitate the voyage of all these concepts, allowing the creation of a kind of transnational connection which is far from being a Western imposition despite (and one cannot hide nor deny it) the persistence of the orientalist perception in approaching the question. Moreover, almost all the laws that criminalize homosexuality in the MENA region are inherited from the colonial regimes (French and British). The French imposed laws against sodomy or same-sex relationships in countries like Morocco, Tunisia, Algeria, and Lebanon in the late 1800s and early 1900s. The British themselves created and implemented the Indian Penal Code in their protectorates across the region in 1861. The constitutions of these countries changed after independence, but these laws have not changed. On the contrary, and with the rise of fascism in government today, the dominance of the right and the far right, and the supposed reliance on religious discourse, the situation of sexual minorities is unfortunately not as rosy as one might wish. The documentary *Upon the Shadow* is the perfect example.

REFERENCES

Abu Lughod, L. (2002). Do Muslim women really need saving? Anthropological Reflections on Cultural Relativism and Its Others. *American Anthropologist, 104*(3), 783–790.

Ahmed, S. (2010). *The Promise of Happiness.* Duke UP.

Arnett, J. J. (1997). Young People's Conceptions of the Transition to Adulthood. *Youth and Society, 29*(1), 3–21.

Brasell, R. B. (1996). The Queer as Producer: Benjamin, Brecht, and The Making of 'Monsters. *Jump Cut, 40,* 47–54.

Butler, J. (1997). Merely Cultural. *Social Text, 52*(53), 265–277.

Butler, A. M. E. (2017). Fuck Your Morals: The Body Activism of Amina Sboui. In N. G. Yaqub & R. Quawas (Eds.), *Bad Girls of the Arab World* (pp. 131–145). University of Texas Press.

Duncan, N. (Ed.). (1996). *Bodyspace: Destabilizing Geographies of Gender and Sexuality.* Routledge.

Dunne, G., Predergast, S., & Telford, D. (2002). Young, Gay, Homeless and Invisible: A Growing Population? *Culture, Health and Sexuality, 4*(1), 103–115.

El-Feki, S. (2013). *Sex and the Citadel: Intimate Life in a Changing Arab World.* Pantheon Books.

Fuchs, C., & Holmlund, C. (1997). *Between the Sheets, in the Streets Queer, Lesbian, Gay Documentary.* University of Minnesota Press.

Gana, N. (2017). Sons of a Beach: The Politics of Bastardy in the Cinema of Nouri Bouzid. *Cultural Politics, 13*(2), 177–193.

Girijashanker, S., & David, W. L. (2018). *Activism and Resilience: LGBTQ Progress in the Middle East and North Africa. Case Studies from Jordan, Lebanon, Morocco and Tunisia* (pp. 1–65). OutRight Action International.

Gray, M. L. (2009). Negotiating Identities/Queering Desires: Coming Out Online and the Remediation of the Coming-Out Story. *Journal of Computer-Mediated Communication, 14,* 1162–1189.

Khouri, A. (2015). No Matter Where I Go. In *Queer Dramaturgies: International Perspectives on Where Performance Leads Queer* (pp. 98–115). Palgrave Macmillan.

Lagabrielle, R. (2013). Maghrébinité et homosexualité. A propos du long-métrage Le Fil (Mehdi Ben Attia, 2010). in Scènes des genres au Maghreb, edited by Claudia Gronemann and Wilfried Pasquier. *Francopolyphonies, 11,* 305–323.

Levitt, P. (2001). *The Transnational Villagers.* University of California Press.

Lionnet, F., & Shi, S. (2005). *Minor Transnationalism.* Duke University Press.

Massad, J. (2002). Re-Orienting Desire: The Gay International and the Arab World. *Public Culture, 14*(2), 361–386.

Moran, L. J., & Skeggs, B. (2004). *Sexuality and the Politics of Violence and Safety.* Routledge.

Morgan, D. (2011). *Rethinking Family Practices.* Palgrave Macmillan.

Moussawi, G. (2018). Queer Exceptionalism and Exclusion: Cosmopolitanism and Inequalities in 'Gay-Friendly' Beirut. *The Sociological Review, 66*(1), 174–190.

Nichols, B. (1991). *Representing Reality: Issues and Concepts in Documentary.* Indiana University Press.

Predergast, S., Dunne, G., & Telford, D. (2002). A Light at the End of the Tunnel? Experiences of Leaving Home of Two Contrasting Groups of Young Lesbian, Gay and Bisexual People. *Youth and Policy, 75,* 42–61.

Pullen, C. (2014). *Queer Youth and Media Cultures.* Palgrave Macmillan.

Rapport, N., Dawson, A. ed. (1998) Migrants of Identity: Perceptions of 'Home' in a World of Movement. .

Richardson, D. (1998). Sexuality and Citizenship. *Sociology, 32*(1), 83–100.

Richardson, D. (2000). *Rethinking Sexuality.* Sage.

Rothman, W. (1997). *Documentary Film Classics.* Cambridge University Press.

Skeggs, B. (1999). Matter out of Place: Visibility and Sexualities in Leisure Spaces. *Leisure Studies, 18,* 213–232.

Skeggs, B. (2001). The Toilet Paper: Femininity, Class and Miss-Recognition. Women's Studies International. *Forum, 24*(3-4), 295–307.

Trinh, T. M. (1993). The Totalizing Quest of Meaning. In Theorizing Documentary (Ed.), *Michael Renov.* Routledge.

Valentine, G., Skelton, T., & Butler, R. (2003). Coming Out and Outcomes: Negotiating Lesbian and Gay Identities with, and in, the Family. *Environment and Planning D: Society and Space, 21,* 479–499.

Weeks, J., Heaphy, B., & Donovan, C. (2001). *Same-Sex Intimacies: Families of Choice and Other Life Experiments.* Routledge.

Weston, K. (1991). *Families We Choose: Lesbians, Gays.* Columbia University Press.

CHAPTER 5

Saudi Women in the Mohammed bin Salman Era: Examining the Paradigm Shift

Magdalena Karolak

INTRODUCTION

The Kingdom of Saudi Arabia has been undergoing profound social changes in recent years. These are related to the attempts at diversifying the economy and activating the local workforce to limit the dependence on oil and expatriates and, raising the local families' incomes through employment. Such a shift marks a gradual withdrawal from the rentier model (Luciani & Beblawi, 1987) that Gulf Cooperation Council (GCC) economies[1] have implemented. In the past, relying heavily on oil profits for development, the local rulers engaged in distributing oil surplus among citizens in the form of free services and subsidies (Hertog, 2010, p. 4). Recent economic constraints due mainly to falling oil prices and current demographic pressures linked to a rapid population growth called for a holistic strategy to transform the GCC economies and societies. As in the near future the likely dwindling oil wealth will have to be divided among a larger population, there will be considerable pressure on states' budgets to maintain the same level of social welfare (Gause, 1997, p. 67) or rethink the

---

[1] Gulf Cooperation Council countries include Bahrain, Qatar, Kuwait, Oman, Saudi Arabia, and the United Arab Emirates.

M. Karolak (✉)
Zayed University, Dubai, UAE

L. H. Skalli, N. Eltantawy (eds.), *The Palgrave Handbook of Gender, Media and Communication in the Middle East and North Africa*, https://doi.org/10.1007/978-3-031-11980-4_5

current fiscal policy, in particular taxation. These demographic considerations are combined with a long-term need for economic diversification and gradual shift away from oil dependency (World Bank, 2004, p. 42). The drive toward greater sustainability requires substantial economic contributions from members of society. However, within a rentier context, the majority of citizens display "low societal capacities" (Hertog, 2010, p. 5), which translate into low productivity and high expectations from state resources. In the past, national workers would be easily absorbed in the public sector where their jobs would be secured indefinitely. At present, nationals must look for jobs in the private sector as the public sector is already saturated. This poses a problem for GCC labor market since foreign workers, who dominate the private sector, potentially offer better skills, and have lower wage expectations (Kapiszewski, 2006, p. 13). Within this context, Saudi Arabia, the most populous of the GCC countries with more than 20 million nationals (General Authority for Statistics, 2016), faces profound challenges. Close to 60% of its population is below 25 years old, and relative poverty among nationals, while the rates are not officially disclosed, was acknowledged to exist (United Nations, 2017, p. 5). In addition, the minimum wage of Saudi national workers that was set initially to 3000 SAR, and increased to 4000 SAR in 2020, is too low for a family to live comfortably on one income. The transition of women from household duties into the workforce is deemed necessary to support the country's economy as well as to make citizens take charge of their own earnings and reduce various state subsidies. In the current economic climate, the Saudi authorities have had to move away from the conservative readings of the gender roles that limited women's access to the labor market, banking, and transportation. Indeed, the recent changes related to the female status and led by the Crown Prince Mohammed bin Salman, are not a simple continuation but rather a significant break with the established norms and, most importantly, mark the royal family taking a firm lead and upper hand on the religious establishment.

The aim of this chapter is to assess the dynamics of gender representation in Saudi Arabia in the aftermath of the sweeping reforms carried out under the watch of Mohammed bin Salman (MBS), the de facto ruler of Saudi Arabia. His rule marks a sharp turn in the modern history of the kingdom with a reversal from conservative readings and application of conservative social norms to an era of transformation and economic reforms in which full participation of women is required. Consequently, women's contributions are now expected and praised, unlike in the past, when gender segregation prevented women from achieving their full potential and their empowerment was considered unnecessary in a rentier economic climate. To boost the female presence in the public sphere, women were appointed to governmental posts and allowed to participate in the limited political processes taking place in the kingdom. The aim of this chapter is to assess how the Saudi media communicate these new messages about women's changing roles in the society. Through a discourse analysis of selected Saudi newspapers, we uncover the frames that promote female participation in the society. Ultimately, through the analysis of such constructs in the media, we assess extent to which they mark a new dawn for Saudi women.

Women's Status in KSA: A Historical Overview

Over the years, the Saudi authorities have promoted some incremental reforms of the status of women. Given the special role of the religious establishment in supporting the legitimacy of Al Saud, reforms usually took into account the opinion of the clergy to keep a balance of power. Under the rule of King Abdullah (r. 2005–2015), the political decisions concerning women begun to "indicate a deviation between the religious establishment and clerical elite on the one hand, and the political decision-making apparatus of the state on the other" (Al Heis, 2011). Before the reign of King Abdullah, it was King Faisal bin Abdulaziz Al Saud (1906–1975) who is known for his role as reformer in the area of women's status. His policies opened doors to female formal education that did not exist until 1960 (Al Rawaf & Simmons, 1991, p. 287). Since the king's decision initially met a fierce opposition of the religious establishment, female education was put under its supervision. Al Rasheed believes that at that time the state was too weak to implement the reform without the religious backing (2013, p. 90), thus this arrangement kept the balance of power. Indeed, the Department of Religious Guidance approved women's curricula until 2002, while the Ministry of Education oversaw men's education. Access to education for both genders sealed the segregation of public spaces with special facilities built for female only institutions; the latter being tightly separated from the surroundings. Starting with education, the segregation was subsequently extended to other public spaces (van Geel, 2012, p. 63). The clergy ensured education would prepare women for their family roles and jobs deemed appropriate for the female nature (Hamdan, 2005, p. 44). As a result, the contents of women's and men's educational curricula differed. Women were prohibited from studying subjects deemed contrary to their nature, such as architecture, pharmacy studies, and engineering, while greater emphasis was put on Islamic studies (Wilson & Graham, 1994, p. 243). When initiating reforms, however, the approval of the religious establishment was necessary to overcome the opposition to the idea of women leaving the house to study present also among ordinary people (Lacey, 1981, p. 364). The approval of ulama to open up education to women, while ensuring physical gender segregation as well as separation of contents taught to men and women, is illustrative of the approach of the religious establishment toward gender issues. Their strong opposition to promotion of ideas of gender equality caused, among others, the withdrawal of the Saudi delegation from the conference of United Nations Population and Development in Cairo in 1994 due to disapproval of topics on the agenda. For the same reasons, Saudi Arabia did not send a delegation for the UN conference on women held in Beijing in 1995. The growing pressure of the fundamentalists in the wake of the 1991 US operation in Iraq led to attacks on women and further demands to confine them to the households and administer harsh punishments for breaking the established order (Wilson & Graham, 1994, p. 249).

The tragic events of 9/11 brought a shift to the balance of power on the side of the government. Abdullah, whose influence as crown prince grew after King Fahd suffered a stroke in 1995, purged the religious establishment from approximately 2000 preachers and reduced the weight of the inflammatory discourse in educational materials (Kéchichian, 2012, p. 43). The government got the upper hand over ulama. With regard to women, the shift of power was cemented by transferring the control over female education to the Ministry of Education in 2002. The public debate that ensued after deaths of female students, prevented by religious police from being rescued from a school fire, helped the government accomplish this reform. The step opened up the study of scientific disciplines from which women were barred before.

After formally ascending the throne in 2005, women's status became "one of the primary items on [King Abdullah's] reform agenda" (Freedom House, 2012). His policies concerned increasing participation of women in the public sphere as well as encouraging their contribution in the economy. Within the first area of reforms, the king appointed Norah Al Faiz to the post of deputy minister for education in 2009, the first Saudi woman to hold a ministerial position; and in 2013 he appointed women to serve in the Majlis al-Shūra (Consultative Assembly). In addition, in 2011 he extended the suffrage rights to enable women to participate in municipal council elections starting from 2015, which resulted in 20 women being elected. Saudi women became visible on the international scene when they competed for the first time in the Olympics in 2012. These changes were accompanied by a growing visibility of women in the media starting from mid-2006 (Sakr, 2008). Secondly, King Abdullah pushed further women's tertiary education opportunities. He included female students in the King Abdullah Scholarship Program established in 2005. The program sponsors students to complete their degrees abroad in order to meet the needs of the labor market in the Kingdom of Saudi Arabia. In addition, the establishment of King Abdullah University of Science and Technology (KAUST) marked a new dawn on Saudi education given its commitment to academic excellence and extensive funds for research but also by its unique mores. The institution is co-educational, the first of its kind in Saudi Arabia, and it allowed women to drive on its campus, while it was still forbidden for them to do so in the kingdom overall. The push for female education was accompanied by inclusion of women in the economy. In 2013, the first legal anti-violence law was promulgated, protecting of women and children from physical, psychological, or sexual abuse.

MBS AND WOMEN

Nonetheless, the reforms of King Abdullah were still short of full-scale impact on women's status. Doumato (2001) pointed out that the literal application of the Koran and Sunna and the existing tribal customs have severely limited opportunities for Saudi women in the society in the past 60 years. Indeed, the social changes prompted by the adoption of modern technologies caused an even more stringent control of women. For instance, the local custom of women being accompanied by a male guardian in the neighborhood became formalized into a bureaucratic procedure that forced women to produce permissions of their closest male relatives to perform public sphere tasks such as traveling outside of the country alone or getting a certain type of medical treatments. The custom of keeping women apart from unrelated men was turned into a gender division of public areas and workspaces that prevented women from operating any form of a vehicle for transportation[2] or working in mixed-gender environment. The downsides of the gender inequality inscribed in the Saudi legal system and social structure were multiple: the limitations caused by the guardianship system, narrow opportunities for women's careers, the rampant abuses caused by the lack of a codified personal and family code as well as the lack of a codified penal code, to name a few.

The subsequent changes that transformed the lives of the Saudi women carried out by MBS came as a surprise given the fact that the current ruler, King Salman (r. 2015–), was seen as aligned with the hardline conservatives in the kingdom, unlike the late King Abdullah, who was seen as a reformer (McDowall, 2015). The sheer extent of the reforms is impressive. The crown prince oversaw the creation of ambitious plans of transformation of Saudi Arabia known as Vision 2030 that were unveiled in 2016. They are based on three themes, namely, a vibrant society, a strong economy, and an ambitious nation (Vision 2030, n.d.). To achieve a strong economy, the vision emphasizes growth and diversification of the economy as well as an increase in employment rates among the nationals. The latter ought to increase to 40% from an initial number of just below 20% (Clyde & Co LLP, 2020). Activating women's potential directly supports this goal and was swiftly accomplished through a series of decrees promulgated after MBS took de facto power in 2017. To implement his reforms, he initiated a purge among the royal family, wealthy businessmen, critical clergy, and any opponents, on a scale that was unseen ever before. This cemented his rule and allowed him to conduct the reforms with no opponents in sight as well as served as a lesson to those who may have thought of opposing him in the future. In this manner, MBS was able to force reforms related to the female status with no opposition from the clergy who were so far a major impediment to such changes as they could undermine the legitimacy of the ruling family declaring them un-Islamic. Already in 2016, the power of the religious police, the Commission for the Promotion of Virtue and Prevention of Vice, was undermined. The final acknowledgment of the primacy of the crown price came in 2019 when a prominent Salafi cleric who was not eliminated during the purge, publicly apologized for the past "mistakes" related to the extremist readings of Islam that were pushed onto the Saudi society (Ismail,

---

[2] Despite this limitation, the first Saudi female pilot graduated in 2004.

2019, June 4), and thus openly approved the reforms already promulgated by MBS.

Right after consolidating his grip on power, the crown prince made a number of substantial changes. In 2018, Saudi women obtained the right to drive, which removed a major impediment to their entry into the labor market. In the past, women's work depended on their ability to hire and pay a driver or have a male family member take them to work, which often made their work not feasible or not worth it given the high fees for transportation that would reduce their earnings. The same year, just ahead of the lifting of the ban on women's driving, saw the promulgation of an anti-harassment law that criminalizes any verbal and physical harassment attempts and, in any form, whether in person or online. In 2017, women were allowed to enter national stadiums as spectators, even though the audience sectors were gender segregated. In 2018, they were allowed to watch football games live. In addition, various tournaments with female competitors have taken place in Saudi Arabia since. In 2018, women were permitted to open their own businesses and bank accounts without the guardian's approval. In 2019, MBS promulgated laws permitting even greater mobility to women, including the right to obtain a passport and travel abroad without a male relative's permission. In addition, they also obtained the right to register the births of their children, and marriages, live apart from their husbands, and obtain family records. Women also received standard employment discrimination protections and started being recruited in a variety of sectors that previously were restricted to men simply because there were no positions for women open in the past. A *Women in the Workplace* initiative launched in 2019 ought to make women comfortable in the workspaces by providing them separate areas if they wish to avail them and guarantee equal payment for the same work as men. These changes have transformed Saudi women's opportunities by increasing female employment, spurring their business activity, and allowing mobility. Women's participation in the labor force increased from 17.7% to 25.9% in 2020 (General Authority for Statistics, 2020). Nonetheless, obvious barriers exist to female empowerment such as discriminatory citizenship laws, as well as remaining restrictions to the guardianship system such as not being able to marry, leave prison or a domestic violence shelter without the consent of their male guardians.

REPRESENTATION OF SAUDI WOMEN IN THE MEDIA

This chapter explores how Saudi newspapers portray women in the aftermath of these sweeping changes initiated by MBS. As mentioned previously, these changes in the public and private spheres are not accidental but are a conscious attempt to transform the Saudi society and economy; and women's participation is a must to achieve these goals. The state is thus using women as instruments to the centrally planned national development initiatives. However, despite the large gains in women's status experienced in the Gulf region, many converging and diverging trends and outcomes relating to the position of women still remain. Conversely, women's representation in the public across the Gulf—as strategically framed by the local Gulf officials and media—is also now transforming, formulating women's embedded positionality and image as part of a broader state agency agenda. More particularly, the state is rapidly yet cautiously advancing women's multiple roles in all aspects of public sphere, including in areas that were previously limited to men: young leaders, soldiers, educators, sportswomen, fighters, and pilots. Therefore, women in the Gulf are symbolically emerging as the new ideological "instruments" of the state-led campaign to construct the multilayered vision of the nation-state building agendas and potentially to contribute to this construction and its direction.

The representation of women by the media, that are in the case of Saudi Arabia by default connected to the state, must adhere to certain codes in order to convey the intended message to the audiences. Studies about the representation of Muslim women in Muslim countries conducted previously concluded, for instance, that there is a direct link between nationalism and gender, in which "the purity of the nation's women is identified with the purity of the nation itself" (Timmerman, 2000, p. 18). Consequently, Saudi women must resist Westernization in order to uphold the nation's values, and the Saudi press should thus reflect these responsibilities of women in their portrayals. Nonetheless, Kurdi (2014) demonstrated that the Saudi press, particularly female Saudi journalists, addressed women's issues, such as women's victimization at home, work, and school, and the prohibitions against them driving, which hindered their lives in the past. Their articles must be balanced, as they have to comply with social norms due to censorship and social pressure, but they do report on both the privations of women and unfair practices toward them. Among the examples cited by Kurdi is an article about a woman whose family members refused to drive her to work, citing mixing with unrelated men in the workplace as a reason, but who were keen to drive her there when she offered to pay them for doing so. With regard to female role models presented in the Saudi press, Kurdi discovered that "the perfect role models for Saudi women should find a balance and hold on to their traditions and culture. Also, they must be educated and independent women in that they have demonstrated they can make their own decisions and choices" (p. 113). Nonetheless, Saudi press reports on the recent changes to the female status very positively. The progression of female political rights in the kingdom was analyzed by Karolak and Guta (2020) who concluded that Saudi media celebrated the municipal elections and hailed women's participation in them as a historical victory for women's rights in the kingdom, while Western newspapers presented mixed views.

Methodology

So far there have been no in-depth studies that analyze the image of Saudi women projected after the reforms initiated by MBS. This study is thus the first to analyze the topic. It applies content analysis to the articles published in three

Saudi daily newspapers, namely, *Okaz*, *Arab News*, and *Al Riyadh*. The choices are dictated by their circulation numbers,[3] but also by their characteristics. *Okaz* is published in Jeddah, a less restrictive part of the kingdom, and is considered a somehow independent voice (Kurdi, 2014, p. 20). *Al Riyadh* originated in the capital, that is in the conservative part of the kingdom, and is regarded as being under the influence of the crown prince. *Arab News* is the largest English language daily in the kingdom. Such a comparative approach can reveal how these different dailies frame the roles and images of Saudi women while fulfilling the overarching needs of the state. The intended audiences may also play a role since the English language news will no doubt target the international audiences and expatriates in the kingdom.

The analysis focuses on the content published between August 2020 and December 2020. This timeframe was dictated by the accessibility of the search engine on the webpage of the dailies. Articled beyond these days were not accessible. However, the collected material is large and deemed sufficient in volume and topic coverage.

In order to reveal these portrayals, framing analysis was applied to the newspaper content. Framing researchers argue that media discourse is presented in a "set of interpretive packages" that serve as the central organizing idea of any news story's frames (D'Angelo, 2002; Entman, 1993, 2007; Pan & Kosicki, 1993; Scheufele, 1999). Framing analysis thus enables us to deconstruct the "interpretive packages" embedded in media texts. In terms of media frames, these organizing ideas or frames can be thought of as themes that "[connect] different semantic elements of a story (e.g., descriptions of an action or an actor, quotes of sources, and background information) into a coherent whole" (Pan & Kosicki, 1993, p. 59). Frames, as cognitive constructs, are thus organizational devices that enable audiences to process information such that it fits into a prior established system, fill in the missing information from previously established frames, and process and comprehend information presented to them through the media. Information remains neutral and meaningless until some frame has been applied to it. Entman (1993, p. 52) explains further that "to frame is to select some aspects of a perceived reality and make them more salient in a communicating text, in such a way as to promote a particular problem definition, casual interpretation, moral evaluation, and/or treatment recommendation for the item described". He further states that framing essentially involves selection and salience. Finally, exclusion becomes an important element in framing because the way in which an issue is ignored or disguised somehow reinforces attributes of insignificance or unworthiness, which are never neutral.

[3] While the exact numbers are difficult to obtain, the following rankings offer some insights: https://industryarabic.com/arabic-newspapers/; https://carnegieendowment.org/files/New_Chart.pdf

DATA ANALYSIS

In order to uncover the articles about Saudi women, a search was performed on the website of each of the newspapers with the keywords: "women" and its singular, as well as "Saudi", both in Arabic and in English. The search uncovered 65 articles published in *Al Riyadh*, 106 articles written in *Arab News*, and 20 articles from *Okaz*. As mentioned previously, the timeframe for the search was dictated by the limitations of the search engines on the newspapers' websites. However, the extracted volume of articles is very large with a total of 191 articles and deemed sufficient to provide enough data for the analysis to accomplish the aim of this research. The articles were read over, and once the material was grouped thematically, frames were extracted. The linguistic analysis of English language data was accomplished using the Voyant Tools.[4]

Arab News

The 106 articles published in *Arab News* were processed and divided into three main frames, namely, the profiles of Saudi women in top leadership positions (25 entries), Saudi women breaking into new areas of economic and social activity (38 entries), the support of Saudi Arab authorities to female empowerment (31 entries) and miscellaneous articles, among others, such as those mentioning prizes awarded to women or having female empowerment as one of the areas of progress among others.

The first theme focused on the achievements of women in multiple areas, among others, politics, museums, medicine, sports, and innovation, in which they hold positions of directors, chairs, representatives in political and social organizations, or researchers. These portraits of Saudi female high achievers ought to inform the audiences about such high posts being awarded to women and not only men, creating an image of inclusivity in the kingdom as well as showing Saudi women being capable to reach the top leadership positions at home and abroad through their work. The women's profiles are accompanied by photos. None of the women donned a niqab (full face covering), two were not covered at all and wore Western clothing, one had a covering that exposed most of her hair, and seven wore the hijab but a colorful one. The remaining ones wore the traditional black abayas and veils. Such images that are in an English language publication echo the recent statements from the Saudi authorities that the traditional black abaya and hijab were not compulsory to wear in the kingdom even among nationals as modest clothing of any color was sufficient. The most frequent words in the corpus after exclusion of the keywords "women" and "Saudi Arabia" were: university (52); society (32); G20 (29); degree (27); member (27); board (25); leadership (24); years (24); development (23); Dr. (23); and education (23). Many of the women were

---

[4] Voyant Tools is an open-source, web-based application for performing text analysis (https://voyant-tools.org/).

PhD or Master holders, and their educational background as well as years of experience were highlighted. In addition, their roles in the society were stressed as community leaders in the development of the country.

The second frame encountered in *Arab News* details women's breakthroughs in various areas where they managed to achieve success as entrepreneurs or by entering into what was considered until now male public sphere. The areas include sports, industry, science, engineering, music, IT, STEM, and even taking job usually performed by expatriates such as welcome and pilgrim service in the Grand Mosque. Three articles presented foreign women's achievements in modeling, golf, and law, stressing their connection to Saudi Arabia through their previous residence and formative experiences in the kingdom. Most frequent words in the corpus after removing redundant entries were those related to the word "women" (275), golf (84); sports/sport (40+25); international (48); team (45); work (42); news (36); time (35); new (34); military (33); country (31); national (31); cybersecurity (29); support (28); tournament (28); and music (25). Due to the timeframe, the sample had a large coverage of female participation in sports events in the kingdom and abroad such as golf tournaments and football matches. The female achievements were also framed in terms of novelty of the areas in which they can perform and achieve. Their exceptional accomplishments were presented in terms of support to the national development. Most of the images accompanying such news about the participation of Saudi women in competitions showed women wearing sport attires and not the traditional abayas. In addition, some had their hair completely uncovered or covered in a fashionable and sporty manner. Furthermore, some other articles presenting the breakthrough of Saudi fashion designers and engineers featured them uncovered and wearing makeup. The achievements of women were also highlighted by the position of the word "women" in text. They were collocated in sentences with expressions such as "make history", "first", "contributions to the country", "diversity and inclusion", "central role", "growing number", "increase in employment", "science", "economy", "industry", "opportunity", "work hard/in all fields", "skills/craft", and "goals/dream". All in all, the articles celebrated women having innovative ideas, overcoming obstacles to reach for their dreams, and becoming "sheroes" (female heroes). These achievements would not be possible without the active role of the Saudi authorities to support them.

The third frame details specifically the efforts of the Saudi authorities in empowering women. The last thematic sample stressed women (total of 349 mentions of women/female) in the context of: G20 (63); percent (59); work/-ing (78); development (45); economic (37); gender (37); social (37); new (35); empowerment (33); program (33); and support (31). The last three terms highlight the efforts of the Saudi authorities, while "percentage" refers to the women's participation in various sectors and their opinions about the changes. In addition, the stress is put on work and the holistic development of the Saudi economy and society. The word "women" was placed in sentences along the expressions "private sector", "companies", "own a house", "hire", "equal", "reform, "law", and "encourage". Remaining articles that were not classified to any of the frames spoke of women's achievements such as a Guinness Record or an Oscar nomination, both achieved by Saudi women. The sentiment analysis reveals the use of highly positive words throughout all three frames and the articles do not discuss any challenges. The only article in the whole sample that could mention a problematic situation relates to the trial of Loujain Al-Hathloul, a vocal social activist who was sentenced to jail; however, it stresses the reduction of her initial sentence and her path toward "rehabilitation" as positive steps.

Al Riyadh

The focus of the publications by *Al Riyadh* differs in focus from *Arab News*. 39 articles describe the efforts of the rulers directly and/or Saudi Arabia as a country to empower women. Ten articles urge the audiences to change attitudes with regard to certain social issues related to women, while 12 articles detail the path of Saudi women to overcome challenges and achieve success in the professional world focusing on personal experiences of selected women.

The first frame celebrates the wise Saudi leadership and their commitment to empowering Saudi women. Multiple titles connect directly the king to the reforms, among others, "The era of King Salman … a time for empowering women", "King Salman and the Saudi women", "The King: A reform journey to empower women and support their participation in national development". Other articles highlight the link between the country and its achievements: "The kingdom and supporting women's aspirations" or "The Kingdom's vision increases women's participation in the workforce to 30%". Finally, Saudi Arabia is shown as an international model in empowerment: "The United Nations adopts a Saudi project that supports the international response to the impact of Corona on women." The articles praise reforms related to women's status and their impact on the society and use very positive terms, such as: "The accession of Saudi women to the highest positions, to say the least, is a historic victory for them, which was achieved thanks to the belief and support of the wise leadership in the role of Saudi women in the national work process and in the march of Saudi society towards progress and prosperity" (*Al Riyadh*, October 25, 2020). The connection between female empowerment and the country's needs in terms of development and progress is often made, with women called on to share the responsibility for the kingdom and future generations. In this manner, their empowerment is presented as playing a vital role in the country's future. Apart from relating the extent of the reforms connecting them to the king but also to MBS, as the leader of Vision 2030 project, some articles stressed the real value of the reforms: "The Kingdom has proven to everyone 'in reality' not 'in words', that the Saudi women's empowerment programs and their participation in the development and reform journey are not a luxury or a beautiful decoration to embellish the country's external appearance" (*Al Riyadh*, October 25, 2020). Finally, some writers reflected on how the reforms help equalize opportunity for all women: "There is no doubt that the personal and family circumstances of each woman differ from the circumstances of others, and what distinguishes generous support and empowerment decisions is that they have greatly reduced those differences that were difficult to overcome" and reminded the audiences about the plights of women in the recent past that they did not deserve: "Before those great decisions that are equitable for women's rights; After the death of her father or her husband [...], the woman would turn perhaps into a subordinate at the mercy of a man who might seek revenge against her deceased good guardian by taking revenge on her, so he withholds his written consent to her work regardless of her academic rank, as for travel to complete studies or complete a business deal related to her work [...]" (*Al Riyadh*, October 31, 2020).

The second frame relates challenges stemming from bureaucratic procedures, gender segregation, and related attitudes. Interestingly, these articles exposed at times the discrimination that exists within the state structures such as the study abroad scholarship program that offers more disciplines to male students than to the female applicants. Another article highlighted that some employees display old mentality rigidly and lack critical thinking, which stands in the way of Saudi women's success: "If the competent employee knew what it means for a person to be a student at the University of California and Massachusetts Institute of Technology, he would have been supportive [...]" (*Al Riyadh*, August 19, 2020). In another article, a negative stereotype of Saudi women in the Western media depicted as interested in luxury goods and shopping and not having a career is countered with the historical accounts of Muslim women in the army and the recent appointments of Saudi women to serve in the armed forces. Finally, worth mentioning is a real story of the interviewee who described how she could not find a job and started to deliver items on order. Even though delivery services were done by men, due to the arising need, she found it as an opportunity to take on such assignments, delivering solely to female customers (*Al Riyadh*, December 5, 2020).

Lastly, the articles encouraging social change tackled issues considered problematic in the Saudi society such as violence against women (5 articles), depriving women of inheritance (1), Islam's support for the women's status in society (2), lack of proper understanding of women's capabilities in sports (1), and industry (1). The authors discussed, for instance, the causes of violence such as psychological disorders that perpetrators are affected with, the fact that violence is learned by the perpetrator as a child through socialization in the family; and men's attempts at cementing the patriarchal supremacy through violence. In all of the articles, they acknowledged the existence of problems and wrong attitudes and stressed the need to raise awareness of the phenomenon and of the damages it causes for the whole society.

Okaz

The articles from *Okaz* are the smallest in number. This may be due to its search engine having more limitations than the other two newspapers analyzed. Another reason could be that *Okaz* publishes occasionally a separate publication titled *Saudiyat* (Saudi women) that comprises only articles on the subject of women. However, this magazine was not published during the timeframe of this study. Similarly to the previous dailies, *Okaz* showcases female breakthroughs in new areas (seven articles) such as music, digital crime investigation, military healthcare, fashion design entrepreneurship, or public prosecution. Some of these articles were interviews in which Saudi women were asked about their opinions on the progress of women's status in the kingdom. While they thanked the authorities for bringing about these substantial changes, some also encouraged other women to take part in the opportunities: "Nothing is impossible for any Saudi man or Saudi woman, and therefore I send a message to everyone that we work with all effort, sincerity and dedication to serve the soil of this country, and strive hard to make our wise leadership plans succeed and complete the march to achieve the vision of our dear kingdom" and "My demands today are not to the responsible authorities, but rather to the woman herself, as she must work to exercise all her powers and expend her energy in building a social, knowledge and scientific ground for next generations." Four articles explained the importance of women's contributions to the Saudi society, for example, one article stated: "Empowering women is not a luxury, but rather an imperative that reflects its impact on society, its economy and culture" (*Okaz*, September 23, 2020). The same article also stressed that these changes are supported by Islam: "the adoption of legislation approved by the teachings of Islam [...] such as revoking guardianship, preventing the marriage of minors, organizing an alimony fund for divorced women, and adopting an anti-harassment law". Four subsequent articles focused on the progress of women in specific regions of the country and women's work was highlighted as a major contributor to the regional development. The remaining five articles relate different topics, however, one of them is especially interesting as it provides a lengthy account of the discussion about the women's right to marry without the consent of the guardian, which is still not allowed in Saudi Arabia. The article quotes a female member of the Shura Council: "The principle in Sharia is that every sane adult has the right to be independent in disposing of all his affairs. Women in Sharia are fully competent and able to act in all their affairs. [...] On this basis, [having] guardianship over her in marriage is contrary to the original [prescriptions of Islam]." All in all, *Okaz* presents some similarities with *Al Riyadh*, stressing the link between female empowerment and the growth of the country, as well as presenting profiles of women who are high achievers. It also differs in the way that it offered fewer articles that were focused on the role of the authorities in these changes (two articles); however, it presented regional coverage and brought up a discussion over the controversial issue of marriage.

DISCUSSION AND CONCLUSION

The data analysis shows that Saudi dailies have created a new type of state feminist discourse and framed the progress of female empowerment in specific terms. To begin with, all the dailies stress the link between the wisdom of the Saudi authorities and their vision, and the achievements of the reforms accomplished so far. For *Arab News* and *Al Riyadh*, those are the major frames with 31 and 39 articles, respectively. This proportion is especially high for *Al Riyadh* as they constitute more than half of all the articles in the sample (65 total). *Okaz* had a lower proportion of such articles focusing solely on the link between women's rights to the Saudi king and crown prince (two articles), but they were often mentioned as a detail among its articles. Overall, such articles aim to strengthen the legitimacy of the rulers among the Saudi citizens but also, when it comes to those written in English, improve the image of the country and its leadership abroad. The latter was especially tarnished by the assassination of Jamal Khashoggi and the war in Yemen. This may help explain why overall the English language *Arab News* had the highest proportion of articles on the subject of women among the three newspapers. In addition, Saudi Arabia strives to be not only acknowledged for its reforms but also seen as a model for other countries, and that was highlighted in the context of G20. Furthermore, the Arabic language dailies emphasize the link between the decisions made by the authorities to empower women and vital needs of the country. As such, the audiences are made aware that the recent changes were not made haphazardly, but they serve a specific purpose. Without these reforms the country will cease to grow. In this manner, those who may have been opposed to the recent decisions of the authorities are made aware of the reasons behind them and that they could not be stopped, otherwise the country's future would be in danger. Four articles in *Okaz* specifically point out the economic gains of various regions within Saudi that occurred when women started to take various jobs.

The second main topic relates to Saudi women breaking into new areas of economic and social activity: 38 articles in *Arab News*, 7 articles in *Okaz*, and 12 in *Al Riyadh*. In addition, *Arab News* presented profiles of prominent Saudi women in top leadership positions (25 entries) to familiarize the readers with these high achievers. Overall, such articles play a very important role of highlighting the capabilities of women and also making the audiences used to women being appointed or reaching high positions by themselves. Consequently, the resistance to women playing major roles in the Saudi society will be reduced. The articles also motivate women further showing them examples of those who have achieved success through their hard work and zeal. This is especially visible in the articles of *Al Riyadh* where some women detailed the challenges that they had to overcome to reach further but, ultimately, they were successful thanks to their perseverance. Finally, one of the main frames of *Al Riyadh* was based on ten articles urging the audiences to change their attitudes with regard to certain social issues related to women. Those articles provided detailed explanations why some detrimental attitudes continue in the Saudi society, and explain their negative effects not only on individuals, but also on the country overall. Having such in-depth analysis may help people change their behavior or seek counseling in specialized centers.

All in all, the articles provide a very positive account of the recent changes. They paint the picture of Saudi Arabia as a country of progress that other countries may take as an example and one that thanks to these reforms will achieve prosperity for the generations to come. Very few articles directly mention issues that may be controversial and cast a shadow over the rulers such as the trial of Loujain Al-Hathloul that was related only in the *Arab News*. Similarly, only *Okaz* referred to the still existing impediment to female empowerment, namely, the requirement for guardian's approval to marry. Interestingly, this change has not been made so far since it is not considered a priority for the country's development and has no direct link to the economy, while other reforms implemented so far are directly or indirectly related to the women's ability to work. All in all, since the tone of the publications is positive and as expected refrains from criticism, it is not clear either what is the percentage of the Saudi female population that got empowered through the recent reforms or what exactly are the impediments to empowering the whole population.

The newspaper analysis testifies also to the fact that the ruling family has firmly gotten the upper hand over the ulama. Such deep transformation of the Saudi society was possible after taking full control over the clerics. In addition, thanks to the reforms, MBS has gathered large support among the mostly youthful Saudi population, and this is unlikely to change. The religious voices must support the changes, or they will be silenced. To rule out any opposition based on religious grounds, some articles in *Al Riyadh* and *Okaz* also stress that Islam supports such changes, and the previous interpretations of Sharia were not accurate, hence indirectly hinting that nobody should oppose the changes to women's status using Islam as an excuse to do so.

Saudi Arabia entered the era of progressive state feminism reforms. The data analyzed testifies to the fact that Saudi authorities are the ones leading the process of female empowerment and women are invited to partake in this process to the extent pre-defined by the leadership. They are not, however, given their own initiative to push for further reforms by themselves but to become "partners" in development following Vision 2030 created by the crown prince. Saudi Arabia faces major economic challenges due to its over-reliance on oil and foreign workforce. The female participation in the society and the economy is thus a necessity not a simple giveaway of the rulers. In this process, women's rights are instrumentalized to serve the needs of the country. While the newspapers analyzed in this chapter did give women a voice through interviews and the economic progress achieved thanks to activating the female half of the Saudi population is highlighted, this is a top-to-down process. Consequently, women's voices may not always be taken into account during policy making and the policies may ultimately serve the economy but not women or not all women. All in all, those who break away from the well-defined paths of empowerment and seek to lead their own campaigns, are punished (Al Rasheed, 2020, p. 234).

REFERENCES

Al Heis, A. (2011). *Women Participation in Saudi Arabia's Political Arena*. Retrieved February 13, 2013, from http://studies.aljazeera.net/ResourceGallery/media/Documents/2011/11/27/20111127125151908734Women%20Participation%20in%20Saudi%20Arabias%2 0Political%20Arena.pdf.

Al Rasheed, M. (2013). *A Most Masculine State: Gender, Politics and Religion in Saudi Arabia*. Cambridge University Press.

Al Rasheed, M. (2020). *The Son King: Reform and Repression in Saudi Arabia*. Oxford University Press.

Al Rawaf, H. S., & Simmons, C. (1991). The Education of Women in Saudi Arabia. *Comparative Education, 27*(3), 287–295.

Clyde & Co LLP. (2020). *Saudi Arabia Promoting Women in the Workforce: 2020 Each for Equal - the Decade Ahead to Vision 2030*. Accessed December 20, 2021, from https://www.lexology.com/library/detail.aspx?g=b9608695-ed74-46f3-aa55-04f32702eb3f

D'Angelo, P. (2002). News framing as a Multiparadigmatic Research Program: A Response to Entman. *Journal of Communication, 52*(4), 870–888.

Doumato, E. A. (2001). Between Breadwinner and Domestic Icon? In J. Souad & S. Slyomovics (Eds.), *Women and Power in the Middle East* (pp. 166–182). University of Pennsylvania Press.

Entman, M. R. (1993). Framing: Towards a Clarification of a Fractured Paradigm. *Journal of Communication, 43*(4), 51–58.

Entman, M. R. (2007). Framing bias: Media in the Distribution of Power. *Journal of Communication, 57*(1), 163–173.

Freedom House. (2012). *Countries at the Crossroads 2012: Saudi Arabia*. Retrieved February 13, 2013, from www.freedomhouse.org/report/countries-crossroads/2012/saudi-arabia

Gause, F. G., III. (1997). The Political Economy on National Security in the GCC. In G. G. Sick & L. G. Potter (Eds.), *Essays in Politics, Economy, Security, and Religion*. St. Martin's Press.

General Authority for Statistics. (2016). *Population in Saudi Arabia by Gender, Age, Nationality (Saudi/Non-Saudi) - Mid 2016 A.D.* Accessed January 12, 2021, from https://www.stats.gov.sa/en/5305

General Authority for Statistics. (2020). *Labor Market Statistics Q1,2020*. Accessed January 3, 2021, from https://www.stats.gov.sa/sites/default/files/labor_market_statistics_q12020_en_1.pdf

Hamdan, A. (2005). Women and Education in Saudi Arabia: Challenges and Achievements. *International Education Journal, 6*(1), 42–64.

Hertog, S. (2010). The Sociology of the Gulf Rentier Systems: Societies of Intermediaries. *Comparative Studies in Society and History, 52*(2), 1–37.

Ismail, R. (2019, June 4). How is MBS's Consolidation of Power Affecting Saudi Clerics in the Opposition? Monkey Cage, The Washington Post. Accessed January 2, 2021, from https://www.washingtonpost.com/politics/2019/06/04/how-is-mohammads-consolidation-power-affecting-oppositional-saudi-clerics/

Kapiszewski, A. (2006). *Arab Versus Asian Migrant Workers in the GCC Country. Paper presented at the United Nations Expert Group Meeting on International Migration and Development in the Arab Region*. Challenges and Opportunities. Beirut.

Karolak, M., & Guta, H. (2020). Saudi Women as decision Makers: Analyzing the Image of the Female Political Participation in Saudi Arabia. *Hawwa, 18*(1), 75–95.

Kéchichian, J. A. (2012). *Legal and Political Reforms in Sa'udi Arabia.* Routledge.

Kurdi, E. (2014). *Women in the Saudi Press. Dissertation Cardiff School of English.* Communication and Philosophy, Cardiff University.

Lacey, R. (1981). *The Kingdom: Arabia and the House of Sa'ud.* Harcourt Brace Jovanovich.

Luciani, G., & Beblawi, H. (1987). *The Rentier State.* Croom Helm.

McDowall, A. (2015, February 3). Saudi Arabia's New King Might Be Turning Away from Modern Reforms. Business Insider. Accessed December 14, 2019, from https://www.businessinsider.com/r-sacking-two-reformers-and-handing-out-cash-new-saudi-king-signals-approach-2015-2

Pan, Z., & Kosicki, G. (1993). Framing Analysis: An Approach to News Discourse. *Political Communication, 10*(1), 55–75.

Sakr, N. (2008). Women and Media in Saudi Arabia: Rhetoric, Reductionism and Realities. *British Journal of Middle Eastern Studies, 35*(3), 385–404.

Scheufele, D. A. (1999). Framing as a Theory of Media Effects. *Journal of Communication, 49*(1), 103–122.

Timmerman, C. (2000). Muslim Women and Nationalism: The Power of the Image. *Current Sociology, 48*(4), 15–27.

United Nations. (2017). *Report of the Special Rapporteur on Extreme Poverty and Human Rights on His Mission to Saudi Arabia.* Accessed January 10, 2021, from https://chrgj.org/wp-content/uploads/2018/02/Saudi-Arabia-report-poverty-alston.pdf

van Geel, A. (2012). Whither the Saudi Woman? Gender Mixing, Empowerment and Modernity. In R. Meijer & P. Aarts (Eds.), *Saudi Arabia Between Conservatism, Accommodation and Reform.* Netherlands Institute of International Relations 'Clingendael'.

Vision 2030. (n.d.). Accessed January 3, 2021, from https://www.vision2030.gov.sa/en/vision/themes

Wilson, P. W., & Graham, D. F. (1994). *Saudi Arabia: The Coming Storm.* M. E. Sharpe, Inc..

World Bank. (2004). *Unlocking the Employment Potential in the Middle East and North Africa: Toward a New Social Contract. MENA Development Report.* The World Bank.

PART II

Introduction: Gender and Activism

Perhaps no area of research on MENA has attracted as much scholarly attention over the last few years as activism and ICTs have. Across disciplines, researchers have used a variety of theoretical frameworks and research designs to assess the extent to which digital technologies and social media have contributed to redefining activism and civic engagement, reshaping political discourses and cultures, or transforming communication practices and information ecosystems across the region (Eltantawy & Wiest, 2011; DeVriese, 2016).

The gendered nature of the 2011 democratic uprisings has unquestionably invigorated debates on the role gender plays in the organization, unfolding, and outcomes of social movements for democratic change. These questions have been the focus of an already interesting body of research produced prior to the uprisings (for a review, see Pratt, 2020). However, the questions have since acquired a new sense of urgency and complexity. The emergence of a new generation of young political actors in MENA, the visibility of their leadership roles in practically all the protest movements, and advances in and greater access to digital technologies have all renewed interest in the gender dimension of activism (Radsch & Khamis, 2013; Gheytanchi & Moghadam, 2014).

In the early years of the uprisings, considerable attention went into documenting women's resourcefulness and ingenuity in negotiating patriarchy and authoritarianism through online and on-the-ground activism. This provided a basis for establishing historical continuities and transformations in women's movements throughout the MENA region. The research also focused on unique and distinct developments in gender and generational activism that help debunk the long-held Orientalist perceptions of MENA as a stagnant region and its women as passive observers of their own subjugation (Stephan & Charrad, 2020, Ventura, 2017).

Gradually, academic focus has broadened beyond the immediate dynamics of the Arab uprisings to attend to other forms of activism and other continuing or emerging struggles where gender continues to play a critical role in the lives of MENA citizens. Scholars are, for example, exploring the mobilization of digital technologies to end gender-based violence (see the part on GBV in this

handbook), the rights of LGBTQ and other oppressed communities, the gendered impact of conflicts, and struggles with loss, displacement, and uncertainties in refugee camps. The chapters in this part cover many such vexing issues
and seek to assess how digital technologies play a role in the new forms of
activism around contemporary challenges.

Hadeel Abdelhameed and Ghyath Alkinani's chapter delivers a fascinating
reflection on motherhood and activism in post-Saddam Hussein Iraq. The
authors focus on the figure of the grieving mother-turned activist, whose voice
of protest is increasingly imposing itself on the Iraqi political landscape.
Drawing on theories of gender performativity of mothering, the authors make
a compelling case for the effectiveness of this mode of communication and
activism to demand justice for murdered Iraqi sons and daughters. Iraq is also
the focus of Ruba Ali Al-Hassani's chapter that examines the *Tishreen* Movement
(October Movement). For Al-Hassani, although *Tishreen* erupted in 2019 in
response to specific demands, the movement is but a new chapter in a long
tradition of mobilization for gender justice in Iraq. The chapter not only highlights the gender dimension of the movement but contextualizes the struggles
within the broader geopolitical forces that have shaped the lives and realities of
contemporary Iraqi people.

The chapters by Michela Cerruti and Noha Mellor take us to Syria to reflect
on another context of conflict, trauma, and struggles for resistance. Cerruti's
chapter provides a rare perspective on Syrian women's intentional use of the
blogsphere prior to and after the recent revolution. This approach allows her
to humanize the bloggers in a society about which misconceptions prevent us
from understanding the complex lives and concerns of ordinary citizens. One
of these concerns discussed in the chapter is "Deconstructing "Sex," honour,
and patriarchism in the Middle East," as one of the bloggers put it.

Noha Mellor's chapter complements the analysis of Cerruti's in that it takes
us to the world of Syrian refugees, whose number has reached nearly six million
worldwide since the conflict broke out a decade ago ("Syrian Refugees Appeal"
2021). Mellor's focus is specifically on Syrian displaced women with the aim to
explore how and if they exercise their agency despite the dominating narratives
of victimhood and misery. Without undermining the traumas of displacement
and the horrors of gender-based violence many refugees endure, Mellor highlights how educated and tech-savvy refugee women are mobilizing digital technologies to contest the combined oppressions of conflict, gender hierarchies,
and essentializing discourses of victimhood. The chapter argues that this brand
of activism draws on a long tradition of Syrian feminist movement and highlights contemporary refugee context to discuss how activists are fighting
today's oblivion both online and in the new environments in which refugees live.

Connections between generations of feminists and activists are the focus of
Hande Eslen-Ziya and Itir Erhart's chapter on the Gezi protests that erupted
in 2013. Here, the authors bring attention to Turkish women's activism during
the Gezi protests to discuss the unique transformations taking place in Turkish

feminist movements. Given the strategies, tools, and organizational skills demonstrated by contemporary Turkish activists, the authors contend that the Gezi protests mark a turning point in the history of Turkish feminism: while it united diverse feminist groups, it also launched what can be seen as the fourth wave of feminism in Turkey.

Intergenerational activism is the focus of Angie Abdelmonem's chapter on Egypt. Here the author delves into Egyptian women's induction into the now global #MeToo movement and ways activists have adopted and adapted their strategies to meet the specific realities of Egyptian people. Abdelmonem provides an informative overview of Egyptian women's history of digital activism against sexual harassment while highlighting the Egyptian state's imposed constraints and challenges on the movement. She also sheds light on the increasingly gendered character of this movement against violence.

An interesting consensus seems to emerge from this part despite the unique contexts the authors choose for discussing gender, media, and activism. The oppressive contexts of MENA and the egregious violations of human rights continue to press citizens to innovate in their modes of contestation and methods of protest. The chapters in this part have contextualized the powerful words of the late bell hooks when she defined oppression and marginality as the ultimate "site of radical possibility, a space of resistance" (hooks, 1990). The uses of digital technologies and activism for gender justice in MENA are precisely about creating radical possibilities despite the numerous contextual constraints.

References

DeVriese, L. (2016). Genie out of the Bottle: Social Media and the Expansion of the Public Sphere in the Arab Gulf. *Nidaba, 1*(1), 72–82. Eltantawy, N., & Wiest, J. B. (2011). Social Media in the Egyptian Revolution: Reconsidering Resource Mobilization Theory. *International Journal of Communication, 5*, 1207–1224.

Gheytanchi, E., & Moghadam, V. N. (2014). Women, Social Protests, and the New Media Activism in the Middle East and North Africa. *International Review of Modern Sociology*, 1–26.

Göksel, O. (2018). Eurocentrism Awakened: The Arab Uprisings and the Search for a "Modern" Middle East. In Işıksal, H. & Göksel, O. (Eds.). *Turkey's Relations with the Middle East* (pp. 33–51). Springer.

Hooks, bell. (1990). *Marginality as a site of resistance*. http://pzacad.pitzer.edu/~mma/teaching/MS80/readings/hooks.pdf

Pratt, N. (2020). *Embodying Geopolitics: Generations of Women's Activism in Egypt, Jordan, and Lebanon*. University of California Press.

Stephan, R., & Charrad, M. M. (Eds.). (2020). *Women Rising: In and Beyond the Arab Spring*. NYU Press.

Ventura, L. (2017). The "Arab Spring" and Orientalist Stereotypes: The Role of Orientalism in the Narration of the Revolts in the Arab world. *Interventions*, 19(2), 282–297.

Zahrae, F., & Alaoui, C. (2015). The Arab Spring Between the Streets and the Tweets. In K. E. Tassie & S. M. B. Givens (Eds.). *Women of Color and Social Media Multitasking: Blogs, Timelines, Feeds, and Community* (pp. 35–68). Lexington Books.

CHAPTER 6

Mothering the Protest: Gender Performativity as a Communication Mechanism in the Iraqi Protest Movement

Hadeel Abdelhameed and Ghyath Alkinani

In a recent popular video in Iraqi (social) media (Al-Tagheer Channel a, 2021), an old woman dressed in traditional black *abayah* walks across a security barrier of armed policemen, leading a group of young protesters and planning to set up a sit-in tent in front of the Karbala Courthouse. The woman was Samira al-Wazni, mother of the late activist and protester Ihab al-Wazni who was assassinated on May 9, 2021. Rather than mourning her loss privately, Al-Wazni, like a growing number of bereaved mothers after the October protest movement in Iraq, assumed an unprecedented gender role, the activist mother. Al-Wazni's walk embodied the transformation of individual grief into a form of public political activism. Mutating from the role of a mother of one murdered individual, she moved into a political role of mothering, that is, protecting, emotionally supporting, and leading protesters. As she surpassed the police

H. Abdelhameed (✉)
La Trobe University, Melbourne, VIC, Australia

Bundoora, VIC, Australia
e-mail: h.abdelhameed@latrobe.edu.au

G. Alkinani
Kufa, Iraq

University of Kufa, Kufa, Iraq
e-mail: ghyathm.alkinani@uokufa.edu

L. H. Skalli, N. Eltantawy (eds.), *The Palgrave Handbook of Gender, Media and Communication in the Middle East and North Africa*, https://doi.org/10.1007/978-3-031-11980-4_6

barrier, the bereaved mother continued shaming the policemen and their leaders:

> My son's blood is so precious, it is not cheap. You all witnessed what happened, you are all supported by militias. Today, I am going to set up my tent. You all know who used the silencer to kill my son. You are all cowards. (Al-Tagheer Channel a, 2021)

Recognizing her right to be enraged, the policemen were silent, humiliated, and ashamed. After passing the security barrier, a press conference was held in front of the courthouse (Al-Tagheer Channel b, 2021). Al-Wazni waved with her *sheila* (took off her traditional headscarf of old Iraqi women[1]), addressing Ayatollah Al-Sistani and other religious, tribal, and societal leaders of Iraq. Symbolically gesturing to the responsibility of these patriarchs of the Iraqi community to step up and bring justice to her son and all other protesters who were killed by pro-government militias during and after the 2019 protest movement.

It was not a unique phenomenon to see a bereaved mother, such as Al-Wazni, publicly articulating her personal grief and rage. Months before this incident, another Iraqi mother, Shahlaa' Younis (henceforth called "Um Muhanned," or mother of Muhanned), was afflicted by the murder of her son in Al-Najaf, a nearby city with similar religious symbolic value for Shi'a Muslims. The calamities of these mothers and the way they publicly responded to them are interesting case studies; they show how mothers can perform stereotypical gender roles to communicate their political communication and resist the patriarchal order around them.

While Al-Wazni's case is a case of assassination in which the real murderer is not disclosed and the whole militia-backed regime is accused of; the case of Um Muhanned is more specific. Rather than making accusations against a relatively insignificant militia member (Samira al-Wazni vocalised her accusations against a prominent member of Hizbullah al-Iraq militia named Qassem Muslah. The latter was released after two weeks of arrest for lacking evidence of his culpability in the murder of al-Wazni's son and other activists) (France 24, 2021), Um Muhanned is attacking one significant patriarch of the corrupt political regime for the killing of her son Muhanned al-Qaisy, transforming the personal trauma of a bereaved mother into a political campaign for justice which makes her case a more interesting subject of this chapter.

---

[1] The intended meaning in this traditional gesture is that there are no *real* men around (especially among those that she addressees) so she does not need to wear her headscarf anymore, not before those men step up to do their duties. The expected masculine response for this move is for those who assume real masculine power to re-veil the women (or ask her to do so herself) promising to fulfill her demands. See: Salaam Smeisim, "Sirr al-Sheila al-Iraqiyah (the Secret of the Iraqi Traditional Headscarf). *AsraarMedia*. 9 Feb. 2019. Web. رس "الشيلة" العراقية (asrarmedia.com)

This chapter argues that mother activism is a form of gender communication that is generated through the traditional gender performativity of mothering. It focuses on an Iraqi mother activist who has become a public figure after waging a public campaign to bring to justice the murderers of her son Muhanned al-Qaisi. Shahlaa' Yonis, mostly known by her maternal relationship to the murdered son Muhanned (*Um Muhhanned* or Muhanned's mother), communicates her gender identity through the stance of a bereaved mother demanding justice for her son who was killed during the anti-government protests in October 2019. Being a bereaved mother granted Um Muhanned a space of freedom to openly vocalize her clear accusations of a prominent cleric and political figure, Muqtada Al-Sadr, for killing her son and his armless friends in the demonstrations' zone in Najaf (a Southern province in Iraq). This mother activist communicated her activism through the normalized patriarchal motherhood model (the caregiver and emotional mother). Instead of delimiting her activism to this essential and emotional mechanism of motherhood, Um Muhanned performed a sophisticated paradigm of mothering. Her claims were based on her experiential knowledge of bereavement, however, she showed a logical, and an argumentative persona of a citizen who knows what she wants and aims at a clear target; that is bringing Al-Sadr to the court. Though she went through several phases of grief, Um Muhanned was finally able to articulate her claims for justice with a reasoning language and a confident posture when she appeared in media outlets.

Applying Natalie Wilson's concept of "activist mothering" (2010), this book chapter interprets mothers' bodies in protests and/or public appearances as embodied activism. Gender communication, here, goes beyond and above the grammar and signs of the social movement, instead the (gendered) bodies become the means of communication.

Practicing stereotypical gender performativity (such as mothering) as a means of political activism is not widely explored in the Arabic social movement studies. With the popularity of literature that investigates women's experiences in the Iraqi protests and the Arab Spring,[2] the scholarship that examines women's non-liberal involvement in the protest so far remains lacking. There is insufficient research on domestic gender performativity that challenges the dominant socio-political norms in Iraq, post 2003. In general, studying gender performativity as part of gender communication is sparse as Elizabeth Bell and Daniel Blaeuer argue that "the [...], body of any act of communication—its relationality, dynamics, historical and cultural embeddedness, and emergent

---

[2] This term should be reconsidered when analyzing the social movements that took place in MENA during the second decade of the twenty-first century. When thinking about intersectionality, the reference to the Arab Spring/Uprising as being exclusively "Arabic" excludes the indigenous people such as Amazigh and other nationalities such as Kurds. It is understandable that Arabs are the socio-political denominator in MENA, however there are other ethnicities, and minorities that took part in the uprising.

quality—is refigured as absent" (2006, p. 10) from the academic work on gender communication.

Seeking to address this lacuna in literature, this chapter investigates the gender communication of embodied mothering activism. Having this in mind, the chapter attempts to answer this question: how far can stereotypical gender roles, such as mothering go to pose a challenge to a dominant masculine/ patriarchal culture? Second, rather than examining the linguistic activism of the Iraqi protest and its relation to gender communication, the chapter focuses on the enactment of the process of mothering the protests that redefined the binary of private-public space, reshaping the mothering experience and the political activism as well. In order to closely examine the embodied activism of mothering, Um Muhanned's case will be critically analyzed in the third section of the chapter. It shows the transformation of her activism from pure embodiment of emotionality of anger and woe to a more logical and argumentative citizen protester. Finally, the chapter concludes by arguing that mothers' activism in Iraq has revolutionized the concept and practice of mothering as well as the political act itself.

THE DATA COLLECTION

In order to map the transformational process of Um Muhanned's activism, the chapter draws on a systematic analysis of YouTube videos about this mother activist. The first video is a documentary film about her that was published on the Al-Sharqiyah Tube on April 28, 2020, nearly two months after Muhanned's murder (https://www.youtube.com/watch?v=SFZ6wJ0JppU&t=1051s).

The second video is a personal video of Um Muhanned and her daughters that was uploaded on Homeland-وطن channel. It was made available on YouTube on May 24, 2020, three months after her son's murder (https://www.youtube.com/watch?v=O2OfJ8x-43c). The last one is her latest appearance in media, which was a 32-minute interview in one of the most popular TV shows in Iraq: *Al-Basheer Show* (https://www.youtube.com/watch?v=hIo_agEQnkY). This video was uploaded on March 20, 2021. It has so far reached 1,636,543 views, with 24,049 comments (September 30, 2021). The time of uploading these videos is significant as it facilitates tracing the changes in her activism endeavor in accordance with the time span. Since the publication of this last interview, Um Muhanned has not appeared publicly again. Attempts to reach her for comment failed due to security reasons and out of respect for her choice, the data analysis was limited to materials available online for the public. Since Um Muhanned does not have any personal accounts on social media, these videos can be considered primary resources. There are other secondary resources used as well.

The Theoretical Framework

Before delving into the politics of motherhood, an overview of the "performance turn" in gender communication studies is important. It will show how poststructuralism facilitated the shift of communication channels from the tools of language and sign to the realm of physicality and corporeality, and later it centralized gender performativity to be the means of communication. Hence, to understand how the socially and traditionally structured gender role of mothering can embed anti-government views and activism, decoding how gender can communicate with its surroundings should be examined first.

The "Performance Turn" and "Gender Performativity" in Communication Studies

Since the second half of the twentieth century, scholars of communication studies have increasingly sought to understand how the human body can embody and generate reciprocal communication. The impact of poststructural theorists and philosophers such as John. L. Austin (1960s), Michel Foucault (1970s, 1980s), and Jacques Derrida (1980s) catalyzed critical engagements with communication studies to examine how body performativity has affected (and is influenced by) the nature and scope of communication, power relations, and identity politics. At the core of poststructural communication theory is the emphasis that discursive practices fashion the identity and behavior and that the power lies in the individual subject qua the agency of action. The interest in human physicality suggests limitless possibilities for cultural communication and transformation, simply because the body is investigated, beyond its biological dimension, as a complex matrix of social, political, and cultural boundaries.

This reconceptualization of the human body necessitated a "performance turn" across the communication discipline (Langellier, 1999 and 2001; Krolokke & Sorensen, 2006; Yep, 2004 and 2020; Calafell, 2020). The turn marked an intellectual shift from thinking in terms of structured systems and powers into more complex, heterogeneous, and diverse sites and agencies of communication (Krolokke & Sorensen, 2006: 21). The intersectionality of the corporeal performance with social markers such as (to name some) gender, sexuality, race, class, age, ethnicity, and (dis)ability has introduced a plethora of possibilities for communication methodologies through the human body. Hence, the human physicality becomes the key operator and producer of communication, the body becomes the site of power that goes beyond and above language, sign, and social context to engender meaning and establish connection.

It is widely argued that the "performance turn" started when J. L. Austin attracted attention to the performativity of the language (Mangion, 2011; Yep, 2020; Krolokke & Sorensen, 2006; Bell & Blaeuer, 2006). In his lecture *How to Do Things with Words* (1962), Austin included "performative sentences" and "performative utterances" that act once they are uttered (such as: I hereby announce you man and wife) to explain that "the issuing of the utterance is the performing of an action" (1962: 11). Austin considered the description "performative" a cognitive and a constructive term in understanding speech acts (1962: 11). Austin's theory claimed that language is an "embodied enactment" (Krolokke & Sorensen, 2006: 38), the embodiment of the language means that words/utterances act and that means they are powerful, the power of language exists in its ability to perform or embody performance.

Based on Austin's hypothesis, Jacques Derrida's theory of citationality (1988) emphasized the reiteration of languages, and that every human language is "always and already quoted and quotable" (Bell & Blaeuer, 2006: 12). However, for Derrida, the power of performative language besides being repetitive is that it can be performed in endless spatial and temporal contexts (1988: 60). As the power of performative language lies in its recycling reiteration, it will produce reiterated performances in diversity of contexts.

In a parallel vein, Michel Foucault's series of lectures (1970s, 1980s) introduced biopolitics as a means of power control over the body. He examined how human bodies operate and interact within discursive regimes of structured systems that dictate how a human should act/perform. Foucault referred to this systemization of human existence as a "simultaneous process of subjectification and embodiment" (Krolokke & Sorensen, 2006: 34). Further, Foucault reconceptualized spatial contexts (physical and heterotopic) as sites where systematic power is exercised and knowledge is (re)produced.

As per the paragraphs above, the "performance turn" laid more focus on the centrality of the human body in generating communication. The "performance turn" considered bodily activities as "embodied communicative practice[s]" (Krolokke & Sorensen, 2006, p. 34) that are constituted by already-established cultural and societal regimes. Our human physicality is inseparable from other agencies of communication such as language, signs, and societal norms, and our (reiterated) corporeal performativity and behavior are products as well as reflections of a network of power relations.

To this hitherto philosophical interpretation of physicality and articulation, the gender theorist and philosopher Judith Butler (1990s) introduced gender and sexuality (later on ethnicity) as agencies of performative communication. Gender performativity, for Butler, is a "regulatory social practice" (1993, p. 6) that communicates through repetitious quotidian activities. The repetition of gender roles is a centerpiece of Butler's theory as it emphasizes the sociocultural and political boundaries that structure and maintain gender roles. Performing arts and theater becomes a logical threshold to engage with Butler's interpretation of gender communication through bodily performativity. Butler exemplifies gender norms by saying:

> The act that one does, the act that one performs, is, in a sense, an act that has been going on before one arrived on the scene. Hence, gender is an act which has been rehearsed, much as a script survives the particular actors who make use of it,

but which requires individual actors in order to be actualized and reproduced as reality once again. (1988, p. 526)

The gendered bodies interplay and operate within the social matrix in a discursive societal discourse and rhetoric. Bodies which perform their gender, as Butler sees them, are constructed by social, cultural, and political powers and they interact in locative (physical/heterotopic) and temporal spaces; hence they are communicative because they produce and preserve effects (Butler, 1990, 1993). The discursive nature of gender practices is a production of the normalization of roles, and norms that are accepted and expected by any social structure, family, community, society, and the nation. Gender performativity is a reiterated enactment of societal gender norms and practices. It is a "stylized citational practice" (1999, p. 5). Performance of gender is installed on the human body by the societal and cultural "bio-power" (1999, p. 6). Gender performativity means that the body communicates through its stereotypical roles and norms, it establishes channels of communication by emphasizing gender binaries. Finally, the communication produced by gender performativity constitutes the identity (public and private), the community, and the society.

MOTHERING ACTIVISM: MOTHERING VERSUS MOTHERHOOD

Motherhood is a discursive gendered practice rather than an identity, it is constructed by traditional and cultural norms that categorize women as unconditional caregivers, and self-sacrifice figures. Practicing motherhood, as any other gender performativity, is based on repetitive acts that are normalized and regulated by patriarchal societies. In this aspect, Butler's concept of subjectivity as performance can be applied on motherhood to be a form of "performativity [that] is not a singular act but always a reiteration of a norm or set of norms, and to the extent that it acquires an act-like status in the present, it conceals or dissimulates the conventions of which it is a repetition" (1993, p. 12). When talking about being mothers, this personal and exclusive experience is dominated and framed by social criteria of a "bad" and/or "good" mothering. Ideal and romanticized paradigms of motherhood usually dictate the concept and the practice of mothering which is anticipated to meet established cultural and societal expectations; that is to meet patriarchal expectations.

In this aspect, O'Reilly asserts that motherhood as an ideological construct is disempowering for women (2010, p. 17). Further, some feminist critics such as Adrienne Rich (1986) established a binary between motherhood and mothering. Rich argues that the terminology of motherhood is a reference to the institutionalization process of mothering, this process is dominated and controlled by sexist societies and patriarchy. Motherhood, Rich continues, is a male-invented set of standards that regulates women's potentials of productivity and maternity. Mothering, on the other hand, is the latent apport of women to their productive powers and their offspring, it is a natural connection that is free from any type of ideologies (1986, p. 33).

Andrea O'Reilly expands on Rich's demarcation between motherhood and mothering. O'Reilly contends that motherhood is "a cultural practice that is continuously redesigned in response to changing economic and societal factors" (2016, p. 16), and as long as this patriarchal paradigm is structured, it is capable of being reconstructed and restructured and even demolished. Alexis Jetter, Annelise Orleck, and Diana Taylor consider motherhood an inseparable concept and practice from the national power relation, as they put it that although being a mother is a personal experience, it is "a social institution, shaped and tied to the ideology of the nuclear family" (1997, p. 5). Not only that, even with the most romanticized and idealized representations of mothering, it is considered a politicized notion. Limiting motherhood to self-sacrifice and devotion normalizes traditional and cultural portrayal of mothering in different eras generating specific forms of motherhood that "regulates acceptable behavior, restricts expressions, and designates appropriate spaces for action" (2016, pp. 16–7).

If motherhood is the "natural" set of expectations, and the ready-made gendered-identity that dominant patriarchy sets up for women, mothering is the reproductive, positive performance that redefines and politicizes that identity. Unlike motherhood, mothering is a role, rather than an identity. It is played with love, affection, and dedication that is why it is practiced outside ideologies and/or patriarchy; O'Reilly believes that mothering "matters, and it is central to the lives of women who are mothers" (2016, p. 1). While O'Reilly believes that mothering is the counter-discourse of patriarchal motherhood, O'Brien Hallstein sees that mothering is an agency of empowerment for women (2010). Maternal agency, as O'Brien Hallstein argues, is the dynamic of change that springs from "mothering practices" and "efforts to challenge and act against aspects of institutionalized motherhood that constrain and limit women's lives and power as mothers" (2010, p. 698). Achieving this powerful stance is connected to mothers' autonomy, independence, and the ability to control their lives inside and outside the domestic and private sphere.

Mother Activists: Strategizing Essentialism and Emotionalism

Mother activists deconstruct the social and cultural role of mothers who are confined to the private domain and whose voices are illegitimate to be heard in the public sphere.[3] The deconstruction comes through a sophisticated process of redefining the institution of patriarchal motherhood that regulated the essentials of being a mother such as caregiving, emotionality, and dependence. Mothers who are politically active instrumentalize the maternal status (biologi-

---

[3] It is important to clarify the term "public" which will be currently used in this chapter. The "public" is often used as a descriptor for numerous articulations of the term in different contexts. In this chapter, it could refer to a place—physical, virtual, and heterotopic (domestic)—to population and public opinion, and to political affairs and issues.

cal and traditional), and their personal experiences to lobby for a designated political right. Mother activists do care about their children but their concerns are manifested outside the patriarchal paradigm that determines that "care" should be practiced within the domestic sphere.

Their activism to lay claims for their children (or futuristic generations) shows care, dedication, and self-sacrifice; it follows the "normative motherhood" (O'Reilly, 2016, p. 122) by prioritizing their children's well-being. However, the manifestation of care is practiced in the public and is related to political issues; hence they breach the masculine sphere through claiming the public spaces and through engaging with politics. Meghan Gibbons provides a more nuanced description of mother activists by saying that those mothers are "manipulating the maternal paradigm that was supposed to control them" (2010, p. 256), so they defy patriarchy through the same "maternal obligations assigned to them" (255–256) by the patriarchal state or the religious establishment. Mothering through political protest is a performance of good mothering but it deconstructs the motherhood identity imposed by patriarchy. The gender performativity as mother activists re-conceptualizes their traditional role as domestic caregivers and reshapes political activism as well. Mothering performativity relocates its spatial dimension from the private and domestic space to the public space.

Most, if not all, mother activists are involved in political activism due to personal experiences of injustice against their children. This experiential knowledge of iniquitous acts is catalyzed by emotional drives (grief, mourning, anger, etc.). Following their essential mothering characteristics of being emotional, those mothers base their political activism around their legitimate feelings of care, fear, and love. The emotions of mother activists are situated at the heart of their political activism. There is a form of reciprocity of activism and emotions that shape their political experiences as they politicize their emotions. More specifically, these maternal emotions spur a transformative mothering identity that is able to create a sophisticated mothering paradigm that can operate within the "rational" masculinized public sphere of politics and the "emotional" feminine private sphere of mothering. Gibbons asserts that this linkage between "rationality" and "emotionality" is a "counter" approach adapted by mothers against the "competition, individuality, and exclusive rationality of the traditional politics" of the public domain (2010, p. 258).

This unprecedented model of politics has been referred to with a coined terminology that might look paradoxical such as "the politics of the heart" (Orielly, 2016), "the politics of grief" (DiQuinzio, 2006), or "the labour of loss" (Damousi, 1999), and others that intersect politics, civil rights, and mothering. Problematizing the situation of the "passionate" nature of mothers within the "ruthless" climate of politics has critically engaged several feminists who claimed that mothering can be practiced outside the essentiality and emotionality of motherhood. Mothers are capable of performing the role of activists as citizens rather than as mothers. Natalie Wilson (2010) introduces the term "activists mothering" that describes mothers who go beyond the strategies of maternal essentialism and/or emotionalism and consider their mothering as a "launch point rather than a base" (233). Activist mothering, according to Wilson, is an endeavor of political activism when mothers do not follow the grammar and stance of traditional mothering that align with the public expectations of mothers' personae as "caring, soft-spoken, and domestic" rather they perform to be reasonable, argumentative, outspoken, and confident (233). They practice activism as citizens, who lay claims to justice, rather than as mothers (or women), though they foreground their mothering as the reason behind their taking to streets, they utilize the same language and performance of other (male) citizens-protesters. Mothers who are politically active in grassroots movements are fully aware that mothering is not apolitical, private, or personal experience. Caring about children encompasses spaces (private or public), ages (infant, young, old), needs (physical, emotional, mental, social, environmental), and delivering mode (traditional, non-traditional). Hence, finding women/mothers who practice their mothering outside the patriarchal and societal expectations is seen as outside the epistemology of motherhood (O'Reilly, 2004). In the dominant patriarchal order "good" mothers should be physically tied to their children at home, the physical attachment means an attentive mother who is based in the domestic realm where her children are.

This type of physical connection has been utilized as a counter mechanism to prove mothers' relativity to their children. While motherhood institutionalized mothering through domesticating their physicality and limiting their mothering to the physical presence at home, activist mothering as Natalie Wilson suggests, also centralizes mothers' bodies but in the public space. Wilson contends that activist mothering is an "embodied activism" that is delivered through the emphasis of the centralization of the mothers' bodies in the public spaces and work as substitution for their children's (absent, tortured, disappeared, abused, imprisoned, dead) bodies. They physically embody the attachment with their children through their physical visibility in the public space to show that "injustices are not abstract wrongs that hurt a particular nation but literal wounds that injure living, breathing bodies" (Wilson, 2016, p. 236). The presence of mothers' bodies in the public spaces signifies a public embodiment of the personal, thus a politicization of the personal. The corporeal enactment of mothers-activists signifies their bodies as "the power to demand attention" (Gibbons, 2010, p. 262).

In fact, to watch mothers' bodies move, cluster, walk, orate (vis-à-vis or virtually), and vocalize for justice in public is to watch these bodies out of (state's, patriarchal, societal, motherhood institution's) control. Once the body is free, so to speak, it subverts stereotypicality. And that what happens with Um Muhanned, the grief-stricken Iraqi mother whose loss of her young son during the anti-government protest in Najaf/Iraq galvanized a daring, loud-spoken, and confident form of mothering through the persona of the mother activist Um Muhanned.

Um Muhanned's mother activism can be situated within a previous phenomenon of mother activism which is the *Madres de la Plaza de Mayo* (mothers of the Plaza de Mayo) in Argentina during the 1970s. During the dictatorship of the military junta regime in the 1970s and 1980s, many Argentine women gathered in the *Plaza de Mayo,* a central city square in Buenos Aires, Argentina to protest the forced disappearance of their sons by the dictatorship regime. Because of their symbolic status as mothers, they were the only group that "was able to publicly decry the violence of the era without being largely silenced" (Gibbons 253). Their gender and social identity as mothers enabled these women to articulate and embody activist discourse that others could not perform because of the repressive regime. Their mother activism reinvigorated the socially and ideologically constructed identity of motherhood that disempowered women and subjugated them to the patriarchal regime. Indeed, women in patriarchal systems "are not meant to be active citizens but symbolic ones" (Wilson 239). Similarly, but in a different historical and socio-political context, Um Muhanned and other Iraqi mother activists seek to find forms and means of articulation and embodiment of protest and revolutionary politics.

What Happened in Al-Sadrain Square?

On February 3, 2020, a group of masked people attacked the camps of Al-Kufa University's student protests which were located in front of the university; the attackers started to spread among the protesters and forced them to leave the place. The protesters refused to do so, and a big fight erupted in the place. Despite that, the protesters managed to stay in their places. The Governor of Al-Najaf announced that the protesters should gather all in Al-Sadrain square, the designated location for the protests where police protection for the protests is set up, and that they should restrict themselves to the square. He assured them that he will provide a police force to protect them from any outside attacks. Two days after, on the 5th of February, followers of Muqtada al-Sadr (a cleric, religious, and political leader of al-Sadrists semi-party and militia) called themselves the blue hats and attacked Al-Sadrain square at 4 pm (Abu Zeed, 2020). The university students in the square called other students from outside the square to join them and help them to fight back against the blue hats. The blue hats used live ammunition, 7 students were killed and nearly 130 were injured (MEMO.com/2020). Muhanned Al-Qaisi, a 22-year-old student, was one of those who were murdered on that day. Unlike previous acts of violence against the protestors that were attributed to "unknown fire" or a "third-party" attackers, "the blue hats" group was clearly responsible for this one (MEMO.com/2020).

Muhanned's mother has been ever since the murder of her son quite vocal and articulate in naming Al-Sadr as the first responsible person for the death of her son. This has been the first time that Al-Sadr is openly accused of such a crime in public by an individual citizen. Having one of the strongest militia groups and the largest parliamentary bloc, al-Sadr has been above criticism and beyond comparison to fellow politicians, let alone ordinary citizens. Holding accountability for the murder of young armless protesters, including Muhanned, would definitely be embarrassing. However, being a woman, specifically being a mother, is the very reason Um Muhanned enjoyed this minimal space of freedom to accuse and embarrass this political and religious patriarch in public. Interestingly, the word patriarch in the previous sentence is not simply an accusation, for the man has continuously used the very word *Hukooma abawiyah* حكومة ابوية (patriarchal government) as the key description for his political project (arabic.rt. 2018). Al-Sadr's patriarchal role has been evident in many instances when he assumes the role of teaching Iraqis (be they politicians or protesters) a lesson like a father punishing his son to teach him a lesson. In this famous interview, he states that what he (read: his militia groups) has done is *jarrat Ithin* جرة اذن (pinching their ears) as if he was a father punishing his son for bad behavior.

Um Muhanned's significant role has been standing up to face this patriarchy from within. Importantly, she has not broken the agreed upon codes of her society or religion. Unlike other active women protesters, she could not be shushed for being accused of being liberal, or being used by external powers for a certain agenda. Her cause was very clear one. Her personality and calamity can hardly be shushed or silenced for any pretext.

Shielded by his special position above the law, Al-Sadr has not spoken about the case in public, ignoring the case was his main strategy to marginalize the woman and her call for justice. The only response he has given to the case was calling for evidence for the claims of his responsibility of the murder of Muhanned and the other protesters. His followers have threatened Um Muhanned to provide that evidence or stop her campaign. However, she has spoken countless times repeating what everyone knows about the incident, but what very few people can dare to talk about in public. In a symbolic act of challenging the established patriarchal system from within, she has visited the shrine/grave of Muhammad Sadiq Al-Sadr, father of Muqtada al-Sadr in a gesture of further embarrassing the patriarch.

UM MUHANNED: FROM THE PERSONAL GRIEF TO THE PUBLIC CALL FOR JUSTICE

Since February 2020, Um Muhanned has become a familiar face in Iraqi media outlets, and social media channels. Despite the fact that she does not have personal accounts on social media, many supporters of her case shared footage and photos of her on social media channels. Aiming at disclosing the murder of her son, Um Muhanned shared her activism with media outlets; she accepted invitations to TV shows (*Al-Basheer Show*) and to be part of a documentary about her son Muhanned produced by Al-Sharqiyah Channel. Ironically, many haters and skeptics of her intentions also did the same. They circulated many montaged talks of her to emphasize their claims that she is a pawn for foreign forces that try to subvert the political process in Iraq, and that she is a hysterical woman that should be discredited for her public grieving.

Um Muhanned has been criticized for sharing her personal calamity in public, that she should have quietly retreated to her domestic domain and privately practiced her mourning. In fact, Um Muhanned mourned her dead son within her private space (home), and followed the traditional Aza'a عزاء, and the burial ceremonies مراسيم الدفن والجنازة. Natalie Wilson argues that private mourning "fits into motherhood as an institution in which the selfless mother is to efface herself (and her body) in order to live her life through and for her [other] children" (2010, p. 236). That grieving is allowed as long as it is exercised within the private sphere; it was accepted to see her wailing and loudly crying for the loss of her son, or to hear her clear and open accusations of the corrupt state and the militia-backed government that failed to provide protection to the armless young protesters. The first footage showed Um Muhanned crying over the coffin of her son, surrounded by Muhanned's friends, she was beating on her chest and saying loudly:

> I swear by God, I will never let your blood go unnoticed, I will avenge for your murder by my voice. I do not have weapons, as they do, I will use my voice. By my son's blood and my voice, I will avenge his murder. By my voice, I will shame them all and will shame those who protect them. (Al-Sharqiyah Tube, 2020)

Here, Um Muhanned uses shaming, a tactic used by men mostly to subjugate women in patriarchal systems, to subvert the system itself. It was condoned to hear her loud voice decrying the state's violence and claiming for justice, and to see her authorizing herself to mouth about politics and security issues, simply because her bereavement permitted her grievances. Driven by her emotions of anger and loss, Um Muhanned was galvanized to continue what her son died for. Mothers' emotions become sites of power when they are correctly directed, as O'Reilly suggests that emotionalism can be "an effective practice of resistance and protest if it is employed strategically and situated as a political rather than a sentiment" (2016, p. 123). Seeking to keep Muhanned's protesting legacy, Um Muhanned shifted the power of her emotions toward political activism, her grief was heading toward a second stage. Um Muhanned started to join the protest every Wednesday, the weekday when Muhanned was murdered, and at the same spot (Al-Sadrain square in Al-Najaf) to take part in the protest. She appeared in full black clothes and *abayah* holding in her hands a big photo of Muhanned framed with flowers and a strip of battery-fairy lights. She was accompanied by her husband and four daughters. When Muhanned's friends saw her coming, they welcomed her by chanting "Today, the square (we) felt peaceful when we saw you among us" (Al-Sharqiyah, 2020).

Um Muhanned walked slowly toward the same spot where Muhanned was murdered, she looked quiet, and she seemed in control of her tears. To apply Natalie Wilson's model of "activist mothering" (232), the following criteria of activist mothering can be highlighted in the case of Um Muhanned. First, visiting the place where her son was murdered is "a performance of any normal mum," she performed the role of the bereft mother who seeks the continuation of her late son's legacy. Second, going to Al-Sadrain square and taking part in the protest was to emphasize that "the personal is political" (232), being a mother protester expands the concept and practice of Iraqi women's participation in the social movement post 2003, it disrupted discursive discourses of patriarchy and of political activism. Third, the physical presence of Um Muhanned is an "embodied activism" (232) where her gendered body, the mother, is centralized as a corporeal means of protest.

Under the antagonistic environment against the protests and protesters, Um Muhanned was shielded by her cultural and traditional role of mothering, she played on the religious model of a devout, self-sacrificing Muslim mother dedicated to her family. Her appearance (in the public spaces or via media outlets) is of a hijabi woman who follows the modest dress code of Al-Najaf city, usually carrying Muhanned's framed photo in her hands and wearing a long necklace with an icon of his photo. Having Muhanned's photos with her when she walks into the protests' zone signifies the embodiment of her grief while giving the (spiritual) presence of Muhanned among his peers. Wilson says that when mother activists use visual representations of their disappeared, dead, hurt children it is to say that there are "far more bodies than those specifically involved in the protest need to be taken into account" (235–6). Hence, her performative body has been able to communicate to the public that it was not only Muhanned who was dead, she is also a lifeless body "I am a speaking dead" (Al-Basheer Show, 2021) as she says in her latest appearance in a popular TV show. She foregrounded her woe to expand on the concept and practice of mothering. Being a primary school principal, she followed an Iraqi educational and upbringing tradition to punish a troubling child. In May 2020, she visited the shrine-grave of Muhammed Sadiq Al-Sadr, the late father of Muqtada, and one of the Iraqi prominent religious and political Shia' figures of the 1990s. Um Muhanned appeared sitting on the ground with her three daughters, she was holding Muhanned's photo in her hands, and facing the shrine where a big photo of Grand Ayatollah Al-Sadr is situated. She said:

> I am here today not to pay respect of the Ziyara/visiting rituals. I am here today to complain and to reproach what your son Muqtada did to my son, to other young people, and to Iraq. Look at what he calls his project to reform Iraq! Answer me, what is the reason behind the murder of my son? Your son, Muqtada, said what he did to the protesters is pinching their ears to be disciplined. Do you agree with that? Look at my son, why is this youth resting under the ground? I am here to complain against Muqtada, the one who deprived me from my sole son. (Homeland, 2020)

Here Um Muhanned is using what Wilson calls the "every-mom stance" (Wilson, 2010, p. 239), she plays the role of a mother/educator who approaches the parent of an abusive child, a bully. When she addresses Al-Sadr the father, she purposefully uses and repeats the two words "your son" and "my son." Situating her traditional status as a mother/parent in a parallel position of the Grand Al-Sadr's status as a father/parent is to embarrass Muqtada and the patriarchal discourse behind him. By indulging the binary of your son/my son, with the late Al-Sadr, she demystifies the constructed gap of (religio-political) status between herself and a major patriarch of the system, subverting the ideology behind that gap. Like any other mother, she wanted to disclose the wrongdoer who despite his high-profile is acting "childishly" and irresponsibly. Some critics in mothering and motherhood studies argue that the public use of emotionalism strategy might risk the legitimization of mother's activism as being too sentimental and/or illogical (DiQuinzio, 2006; Moravec, 2007).

However, others consider that the public enactment of mother's grief, that is, politicizing their emotions as quite logical because they refuse the idea that their grief should have a temporal limit, or a private sphere (Wilson, 2010; Gibbons, 2010; Mantoan, 2018). By engaging the public with her visit through sharing the YouTube link (https://www.youtube.com/watch?v=O2OfJ8x-43c), her recorded visit went viral on the internet https://www.youtube.com/watch?v=O2OfJ8x-43c, Um Muhanned combined the private/public spheres by deconstructing the binaries between the two spaces. She has created a public base that is aware of her activism, the stages and steps that she is taking to reach her aim of bringing murderers to justice. Judith Butler asserts that "[m]any people think that grief is privatizing, that it returns us to a solitary situation and is, in that sense, depoliticizing. But I think it furnishes a sense of political community of a complex order, and it does this first of all by bringing to the fore the relational ties that have implications for theorizing fundamental dependency and ethical responsibility" (2004, p. 22). Um Muhanned's public grief in front of Al-Sadr's grave is her mothering strategy to highlight the absence of the government's responsibility toward its people, to lament the void created by the silent judicial and official apparatuses to the continuous process of murdering armless protesters. The materialization of Um Muhanned on the Grand Al-Sadr's door is in itself an embodiment of activism. She is performing her gender role to embody communication through her physicality of mothering, as Wilson suggests that bodies of mother activists "deployed as a visible reminder of injustice, grief, and injury, both through the living, present bodies of protestors [...] and through the pictorial/oral reminders of those bodies killed/injured" (2010, p. 246). Hence, the transformation of the personal to the public and the public to the personal (as she is filming her personal enactment of the visit) was an essential tactic of Um Muhanned's activism, because including the "virtual" public astutely shows that her grief is a justifiable base to air her grievance. However, Um Muhanned's activism was not chained to airing her mothering grief; she extended this form by going beyond emotionality. She took emotionality as the base for further actions, she filed a lawsuit in Al-Najaf Court in May 2020 against Muqtada Al-Sadr (Salim, 2020).

Natalie Wilson's model of mothering activism suggests that "activist mother often instigated their activism through reference to their role as mothers, but they did not tend to use this status as the entire grounding for their aims" (2010, p. 234). Such mother activists refused to submit to the stereotypical role of bereaved mother activists who base their activism around "compliant" language, voice, or embodiment. Instead, they decided to lay claims by being activists, not mother activists. That exactly applied to Um Muhanned. In her recent appearance on *Al-Basheer Show* (2021), she looked very calm, logical, strategic, and argumentative. Unsurprisingly, she did not shed tears when she recounted the incident of her son's murder. In her black clothes, hijab and *abayah*, she looked very confident and doubtless about her goal, unlike the documentary that was filmed a year before in which she failed to continue her sentences, recurrently bursting into tears.

In this show, Um Muhanned presented a new trope of mother activism. She called upon Muqtada to "appear in public and to swear by God that he did not ask his followers to murder the young protesters in Al-Sadrain square (Al-Basheer Show, 2021). She referred to him by his first name "Muqtada" without titles or formal references. This form of trivialization and demystification of his status and grandeur as she affirms is "to strip him away of the sanctity that he wraps himself with" (Al-Basheer Show, 2021) and to instigate him to respond back in public. Through her calling him "Muqtada," Um Muhanned wanted to say that bereaved mothers and their murdered sons deserve more attention and respect than what the official discourse is showing (or not showing). Her appearance this time materializes an activist rather than a mother activist, though she started by narrating Muhanned's story, but she took it from there to emphasize that she is going to continue what Muhanned and his murdered friends were asking for. She is going to be the mouthpiece of those young protesters and all murdered protesters "I am the mother of revolutionaries and protesters" (Al-Basheer Show, 2021). In the documentary about her story, Murtadha, Muhanned's close friend, says that after the murder of Muhanned, his mother continued to participate in the protest with them:

> We did not feel that Muhanned was not with us, on the contrary, she did all his activities. Her voice becomes more powerful. She showed strength and resilience, and on many occasions she said that "Muhanned's blood gives me strength". Because of her presence among us, we become stronger. Um Muhanned now is the conservator of our revolution, if this revolution stops for any reason, with Um Muhanned's presence, it will not come to an end. Because we will stay resilient due to her resilience. Um Muhanned is a temporal interval that changed our perception of the revolution. (Al-Sharqiyah Channel, 2020)

Um Muhanned, "the conservator" of the Iraqi anti-government protest insisted that she will continue protesting, not only to bring Muqtada to court, but to support the claims of the protesters, to achieve justice for nearly 700 young people who were murdered in the demonstrations. She is bold enough to emphasize that they are not dead, they were murdered. When she was asked about the lawsuit she had against Muqtada, she calmly answered:

I trust the Iraqi Judicial system, but I cannot deny that it is controlled by the corrupt elite. I used to go to court with my husband. The judges and investigators show sympathy and understanding for our case, but at the same time they postponed the case under different excuses. I am going to ask for international bodies to intervene in order to achieve justice. (Al-Basheer Show, 2021)

As per her speech above, Um Muhanned is not acting because of emotionality anymore, she is going beyond the "irrationality" of emotions, she is a citizen who ceaselessly asks for her right and other mothers' rights of bringing the murderers of their sons to justice, and to achieve the protesters' demands. Living in inhospitable and hostile climate, Um Muhanned received endless threats, intimidation gestures, open and clear threats of assassination. Despite all that, she proved herself to be linguistically and logically capable of expressing her demands, to continue appearing in the protest zones, and in media outlets. It is true that the essentialist notion of mothering granted Um Muhanned her public voice, but she expanded on the practice of mother activism. She is the, as Murtadha says, the "conservator" of the revolution.

Conclusion

This chapter used the performance turn in communication and gender theories to develop a theoretical framework of how mothering as a gender discursive practice has been galvanizing a sophisticated form of activism. Mother activists remodeled the patriarchal paradigm of motherhood and of political activism itself by providing their own model that is based on essentialism (caregiving) and emotionalism (grief and anger).

However, mother activism is as heterogeneous and contextual as feminism, and attributing emotionalism to women/mothers' activism has been problematized by many feminist scholars. This book chapter is based on Natalie Wilson's model of "activist mothering". The model argues for the capability of mother activists to utilize their emotions and essentials as a ground point for their activism, but they decide to continue their activism as citizens rather than limiting themselves to being mothers. This chapter analyzes a case study from Iraq; Um Muhanned who was able to embody activism and communicate with her hostile environment through her activist mothering. She showed that gender communication can be realized and reached through body performativity. Her appearance in the demonstration zones and on media outlets signifies her body as a tool of communication and a medium of resilience.

If the "Mothers of the Plaza de Mayo in Argentina" and other places in the world succeeded in turning their personal grievances into a public movement, the case of Um Muhanned, Um Ihab, and other Iraqi mothers traumatized by the loss of their children have not yet crystallized into a well-organized mother activist movement.

Women, mothers in particular, usually occupy an intricate positionality in times of wars and political upheavals like in the geopolitical context of Iraq.

However, what gives this woman and other Iraqi mothers the right to do what she does in standing up for justice and naming those to blame for her loss is a combination of contextual and identity-related factors that helped her assume her mother activist role. The great momentum and support the protest movement was building at the time of the murder of her son gave Um Muhanned a platform to transform her individual grief into public rage. The woman's relationship to the protesters was reciprocal. On the one hand her "mothering" role was necessary for providing a sense of purpose and meaning to their rather abstract demands. Instead of the general slogan of *Nureed Watan* (we want a country/homeland), their demands now are specific: they want justice for their murdered friends. On the other hand, their presence and support was crucial to Um Muhanned who finds in them a reminder of her son as well as a protective shield that enables her to launch her campaign for justice.

However, history and other peoples' experiences teach us that revolutions and great socio-political movements do not continue because of one heroic action or specific conservator(s) no matter how articulate and powerful they were. The case of Um Muhanned shows that patriarchal systems are not that solid as they present themselves to be and that an articulate, willful mother activist can undermine the system gravely. Um Muhanned's communication tactics to subvert the system from within its conventional sphere prove to be rhetorically successful. However, unlike the *Madres de la Plaza de Mayo* movement in Argentina, the mother activists in Iraq have not yet moved from their individual campaigns into nation-wide organized political action. Without the individual cases of Um Muhanned, Um Ihab, and other mothers of victims of the system in Iraq organizing in mother activist groups or political movements/organizations, the voice of Iraqi mothers would not be heard and their demands would not be met.

REFERENCES

Abu Zeed, A. (2020). Who Are Sadr's Blue Hats in Iraq and What Side Are They On?. Al-Monitor. https://www.al-monitor.com/originals

Al-Basheer Show. (2021, March 20). اللقاء الكامل مع والدة الشهيد شو القيسي | البشير شو الجمهورية. [Video]. YouTube. https://www.youtube.com/watch?v=hIo_agEQnkY&t=1440s

Al-Sharqiyah Tube. (2020, April 28). المرأة المثالية | أم الشهيد محند وميض القيسي. [video]. YouTube. https://www.youtube.com/watch?v=SFZ6wJ0JppU&t=1163s.

Al-Tagheer Channel a. (2021, June 21). الوزني من الاعتصام في كربلاء. شاهد لحظة منع ام الشهيد. [Video]. YouTube. https://www.youtube.com/watch?v=QQ8abbLZzRo

Al-Tagheer Channel b. (2021, June 21). "شيلها" وتناشد تربي الوزني ايهاب الشهيد والدة.. شاهد السيستاني. [Video]. YouTube. https://www.youtube.com/watch?v=Di6__7Yv0-M

Arabic. Rt. (2018). الصدر يلتقي العامري لتشكيل "حكومة أبوية" على وجه السرعة. https://arabic.rt.com/middle_east/

Austin, J. L. (1962). *How to do Things with Words* (2nd ed.). Cambridge, MA: Harvard University Press.

Bell, E., & Blaeuer, D. (2006). Performing Gender and Interpersonal Communication Research. In B. J. Dow & J. T. Wood (Eds.), *The SAGE Handbook of Gender and Communication* (pp. 9–24). SAGE Publication.

Butler, J. (1988). Performative Acts and Gender Constitution: An Essay in Phenomenology and Feminist Thought. *Theatre Journal, 40*, 519–531.

Butler, J. (1993). *Bodies that Matter: On the Discursive Limits of "Sex.".* Routledge.

Butler, J. (1999). *Gender Trouble: Feminism and the Subversion of Identity.* Routledge. (Originally published 1990).

Butler, J. (2004). *Precarious Life: The Powers of Mourning and Violence.* Verso.

Calafell, B. M. (2020). The Critical Performative Turn in Intercultural Communication. *Journal of Intercultural Communication Research., 49*, 410. https://doi.org/1 0.1080/17475759.2020.1740292

Damousi, J. (1999). *The Labour of Loss: Mourning, Memory and Wartime Bereavement in Australia.* Cambridge University Press.

Derrida, J. (1988). *Limited Inc.* Northwest University.

DiQuinzio, P. (2006). The Politics of the Mothers Movement in the United States: Possibilities and Pitfalls. *Journal of the Association for Research on Mothering, 8*(1-2), 55–71.

Foucault, M. (2008). *The Birth of Biopolitics Lectures at the Collège De France, 1978–1979.* UK: Palgrave Macmillan..

France 24, Iraq Frees Pro-Iran Commander Arrested Over Activist Murder. Iraq frees pro-Iran commander arrested over activist murder - France 24

Gibbons, M. (2010). Political Motherhood in the United States and Argentina. In F. Jocelyn & R. P. Pageen (Eds.), *Mothers Who Deliver Feminist Interventions in Public and Interpersonal Discourse* (pp. 253–278). Suny Press.

Homeland- 2020) وطن, May 24). مقتدى من مجزرة النجف.[Video]. YouTube. https://www.youtube.com/watch?v=O2OfJ8x-43c ام الشهيد محمد القيسي تشكو في مرقد السيد الشهيد محمد الصدر على ما فعله إبنه

Jetter, A., Orleck, A., & Taylor, D. (1997). *The Politics of Motherhood: Activist Voices from Left to Right.* University Press of New England.

Krolokke, C., & Sorensen, A. S. (2006). *Gender Communication Theories and Analyses: From Silence to Performance.* Sage Publications Ltd.

Langellier, K. M. (1999). Personal Narrative, Performance, Performativity: Two or Three Things I Know for Sure. *Text and Performance Quarterly, 19*, 125–144.

Mangion, C. (2011). *Philosophical Approaches to Communication.* Intellect Books.

Mantoan, L. (2018). *War as Performance: Conflicts in Iraq and Political Theatricality.* Macmillan Palgrave.

MEMO. (2020). Iraq's Sadr Dissolves Own 'Blue Hats' Unit Accused of Killing Protesters. Middle East Monitor. https://www.middleeastmonitor. com/20200213-iraqs-sadr-dissolves-own-blue-hats-unit-accused-of-killing-protesters/

Moravec, M. (2007). Another Mother for Peace: Reconsidering Maternalist Peace Rhetoric from an Historical Perspective, 1967–2007. *Journal of the Motherhood Initiative, 1*(1), 9–29.

O'Brien Hallstein, D. (2010). Maternal Agency. In A. O'Reilly (Ed.), *Encyclopedia of Motherhood* (pp. 698–699). SAGE Publications, Inc.

O'Reilly, A. (2010). Outlaw(ing) Motherhood: A Theory and Politics of Maternal Empowerment for the Twenty-first Century. *Hecate., 36*(1/2), 17–29.

O'Reilly, A. (Ed.). (2004). *Mother Outlaws: Theories and Practices of Empowered Mothering.* Women's Press.

O'Reilly, A. (2016). *Matricentric Feminism Theory, Activism, and Practice.* Demeter Press.

Rich, A. (1986). *Of Woman Born: Motherhood as Experience and Institution* (2nd ed.). W.W. Norton.

Salim, Z. (2020). ام محمد: عراقية تحول مقتل ابنها الى قضية رأي عام /Um Muhanned: An Iraqi Transfers the Murder of her Son to a Public Issue. العربي الجديد / *The New Arab.* https://www.alaraby.co.uk/

Wilson, N. (2010). From Gestation to Delivery: The Embodied Activist Mothering of Cindy Sheehan and Jenifer Schumaker. In J. F. Stitt & P. R. Powell (Eds.), *Mothers Who Deliver: Feminist Interventions in Public and Interpersonal Discourse* (pp. 231–252). Suny Press.

Yep, G. A. (2020). Towards a Performative Turn in Intercultural Communication. *Journal of Intercultural Communication Research., 49,* 484. https://doi.org/10.1080/17475759.2020.1802325

CHAPTER 7

Iraq's October Revolution: Between Structures of Patriarchy and Emotion

Ruba Ali Al-Hassani

7.1 INTRODUCTION

In front of a women's rights organization tent at Tahrir Square, a protesting girl was asked, 'What are your demands?' She replied, 'We do not have demands, rather rights ... and rights are not demanded, but wrestled' (Yassine, 2021).

Iraq's *Tishreen* [October] Revolution emerged in 2019 as a culmination of years of grassroots mobilization. This protest movement combined various social, political, and economic issues—corruption, ethno-confessional consociationalism, foreign intervention, and impunity—pointing to the structural roots of Iraq's woes. Protestors have called for the dismantling of political structures to rebuild the country with transparency, accountability, and democratic governance. In the early protest days, videos of girls breaking out of their schools to join protests went viral. They challenged school principals who tried to contain them, 'freed' students from other schools which were allegedly locked down for their safety and marched together to protest squares (Yassine, 2020a). They wanted to join their male counterparts in protesting a socio-political system and to belong to a collective whose central slogan has been نريد وطن 'We Want a Homeland'. While the protest movement's primary demands have not been gender specific, many have argued that 'the revolution was female, heart and soul' (Mansour, 2021).

R. Ali Al-Hassani
Lancaster University, Lancaster, UK
email: r.alial-hassani@lancaster.ac.uk

© The Author(s), under exclusive license to Springer Nature Switzerland AG 2023
L. H. Skalli, N. Eltantawy (eds.), *The Palgrave Handbook of Gender, Media and Communication in the Middle East and North Africa*,
https://doi.org/10.1007/978-3-031-11980-4_7

To offer a comprehensive understanding of power relations and gender dynamics in Iraq, this chapter takes a structuralist approach to examine the intersection between women's and men's struggles against institutionalized patriarchy. The first section borrows from bell hooks' feminist theory to examine traditional and NGOized patriarchal structures in Iraq. The second section examines Theodore Kemper's structural theory of emotions. The third section examines how protestors have expressed themselves—whether in cyberspace or physical public spaces—and what their emotional expressions tell us about the movement and gender dynamics. Exploring the intersection of women's and men's struggles against institutionalized patriarchy can offer a comprehensive understanding of power relations and gender dynamics in Iraq.

7.2   Defining the Patriarchy

7.2.1   Structuralism

Zahra Ali (2018, p. 261) categorizes Iraqi women's activism into four general trends: Human Rights Feminism, Islamist Activism, Muslim Feminism, and Leftist and Radical Feminism. She bases these categories on how activists situate themselves within local social culture(s), international legal and human rights norms, religious institutions, and personal relations. Iraqi women activists realize their footing in society depends on larger socio-political structures, which impact both women and men. bell hooks' feminist theory may help us situate Iraqi women's activism within the context of the October Revolution.

According to bell hooks, feminism started as a movement to end sexist oppression, but would be better defined as the movement to end sexism, sexist exploitation, and oppression without neglecting other forms of oppression, such as racism, classism, imperialism, and others' (hooks, 1984, p. viii). She identifies the patriarchy as a socio-political system, where

> males are inherently dominating, superior to everything and everyone deemed weak, especially females, and endowed with the right to dominate and rule over the weak and to maintain that dominance through various forms of psychological terrorism and violence. (ibid., p. 26)

hooks' notion of patriarchy is reminiscent of Kimberlé Crenshaw's 'intersectionality' (Biana, 2020, p. 14) as it points to 'interlocking webs of oppression' (hooks, 1984, p. 31) and Crenshaw stresses 'the intersectionality of race and sex that both play roles in the systems of discrimination' (Crenshaw, 2015, p. 139). In an ethnoconfessionally pluralistic Iraq, intersectionality is crucial. There's a discrepancy in experience between Yazidi and Muslim women; displaced and non-displaced people; Muslim women and men; Afro-Iraqi men and fair-skinned men; and so on. Intersectionality helps expose the various forms of socio-political discrimination. hooks condemns the legacy of liberal feminism, which has made women's liberation synonymous with gaining social equality with men (hooks, 1984, p. 67). Excluding men from feminist mobilization reinforces sexism and implicates that women's empowerment comes at men's expense. Approaching the patriarchy from a non-intersectional and anti-male angle isolates men and women in their struggles and denies them cross-gender solidarity within socioeconomic classes or ethnic groups. Therefore, hooks posits that the feminist movement must clarify an antisexism, not anti-male, stance. Such clarity reminds people that both men and women 'have been socialized from birth on to accept sexist thought and action' (ibid., p. viii). Like women, men are socialized into passively accepting sexist ideology. As Joy Justice points, 'There is the perspective that men oppress women. And there is the perspective that people are people, and we are all hurt by rigid sex roles' (hooks, 2004, p. 32). hooks argues that patriarchal ideology brainwashes men to believe their domination of women is beneficial when it is not. It has boys and men believing in a masculinity that denies them access to full emotional well-being. Relative to women, men thus lack the emotional intelligence necessary for their personal and social fulfillment. Sara Ahmed notes that this 'Psychological patriarchy' is a valuing system that defines 'masculinity' and 'femininity', exalting half of our human traits while devaluing the other (Ahmed, 2004, p. 36). Both men and women participate in it. Men are constantly concerned with the contradiction between the notion of masculinity they have been taught and their inability to live up to that unrealistic notion. They are alienated, frustrated, and insecure and direct their aggression—a privilege afforded to them by the patriarchal system—toward women and girls. Their capacity to assert control over their female counterparts is neither rewarding nor fulfilling.

Therefore, the crisis facing men is not the crisis of masculinity, rather the crisis of patriarchal masculinity (ibid., p. 36). As long as men equate violent domination and abuse of women with privilege, they do not realize the patriarchy's damage to themselves and others, and do not rebel against it. Acknowledging this male suffering does not negate or diminish male responsibility for the exploitation of women or male enjoyment of gender-based privileges. Male oppression of women and male suffering from a sexist system can coexist as two connected realities. hooks argues that men who actively struggle against this sexism have a place in the feminist movement. They are women's comrades as feminism is 'for everybody' and what Sara Ahmed calls '...a sensible reaction to the injustices of the world' (hooks, 2004; Mehra, 2017).

bell hooks' definitions of patriarchy and feminism were initially rooted in a Western experience but later expanded to identify the 'imperialist white-supremacist capitalist patriarchy' (Biana, 2020, p. 20). The following discussion explores how 'NGOized' notions of patriarchy and feminist mobilization in post-2003 Iraq contrast with bell hooks'.

7.2.2   Intervention

In contrast to bell hooks' notions of patriarchy and feminism is their 'NGOization'. Islah Jad developed the term 'NGOization' to describe the professionalization, bureaucratization, and institutionalization of social movements in the 'Third World' as they adopt the form of nongovernmental organizations (NGOs). Jad posits that the multiplication of foreign-funded NGOs significantly reshapes women's civil society activism on the ground (Ali, 2021, p. 6). She also posits that the rights-focused agenda of international women's NGOs and civil society organizations have led to the rapid proliferation of issue-oriented groups, de-politicization, and de-contextualization of women's activism. Consequently, women's rights organizations do not situate issues-focused efforts within a wider political, social, and economic context (Jad, 2004). When women's rights groups convert continued gender inequality from a structural problem into an individual affair, they segregate women's rights from men's rights. This prevents cross-gender mobilization on a radical level to challenge oppressive social and political systems. In Iraq, such systems have existed both before and after 2003.

The US-led invasion of Iraq in 2003 led to the intended militarization and disintegration of state institutions. With the US establishment of consociational governance (Dodge, 2020) or *muhasassa ta'ifiyya*, ethnosectarian discrimination became institutionalized as policy. Relying on an ethnosectarian and party quota, this system boosts unelected politicians into power, denying the public their votes, and disempowering them. While Iraqis feel unrepresented by the political process, minorities are especially alienated. Maya Mikdashi (2018, p. 3) argues that colonial legacies influence consociational governance to further colonial rule. Consociationalism enables and maintains corruption. Corruption deepens inequality as it relies on exploitation through mechanisms that allow a party to establish privilege and power through the hoarding of opportunities (Al-Hassani, 2020a). Corruption in Iraq has placed it at 162 on the World Corruption Index (Worth, 2020; Country Data: Iraq, 2020). Political corruption has left many Iraqis in poverty and without basic services, such as sustainable health care, consistent electricity, and clean water (Aboulenein & Levinson, 2020; Agence, 2020; Iraq: Water Crisis in Basra, 2019; Kullab, 2021). Besides the lack of basic public services, there is a great lack of opportunities, and an increase in gendered corruption like sextortion, where sex rather than money is the currency of bribery (Bettinger-Lopez, 2018). Due to its exploitative nature, the corrupt consociational system is gendered.

Maya Mikdashi (2018) describes this system as 'sextarian'. Mikdashi argues that the intersection between sectarian and sexual differences as two types of political difference is the foundation of this consociational mode of governance. Sex and sect are biopolitical categories 'defined at birth and categorized, quantified, and managed through state law and institutions at the level of the individual (citizen, non-citizen) and at the level of populations (sexes, sects, citizenry)' (ibid., p. 3). Sex and sect are mutually constitutive modes of political difference; articulated and operated together to form the legal infrastructure of 'biopolitical citizenship' (ibid., p. 2). In a country like Iraq, sect and citizenship are inherited patrilineally (ibid.). Sectarian consociationalism is, therefore, designed by ethnic, religious, and sexual difference. Not only do political parties rely on blackmail and sabotage each other's efforts, but they also target independent politicians, especially women. In the 2018 election cycle, sexual blackmail targeted women candidates to force them out of the electoral race and deny women an equal footing in politics (Al-Hassani, 2020a; Bajec, 2019). This also impacted male constituents opposed to the status quo who would have voted for these women candidates. Such blackmail and other methods that stall the state-building process lead to what Sa'ad Salloum calls the 'no-state project' (Taher, 2017).

The no-state project is a direct result of the intended militarization of society and state institutions. Data on reported violence shows a direct link between the proliferation of firearms in Iraq, high crime rates, poverty, and violence against women (Fayaq Abdul Wahab et al., 2021). This correlation indicates that women's and men's struggles are interconnected, since violence against women increases when male perpetrators are less socially powerful or are under significant social stress. As a result, Iraqi citizens, regardless of gender or sex, feel alienated from political state structures as well as from their society and own agency. This alienation is exacerbated by the political elite's paternalism.

7.2.3   Paternalism

Paternalism is a mode of patriarchal governance pervasive in Iraq. This involves the unelected government's limitations on constituents' freedoms and autonomy in the name of protecting their interests and maintaining the peace. The paternalist here is only concerned with state power and coercion. The paternalistic imagination here assumes a homogeneous, obeying population that contributes to social and political submission to the 'higher' will of the leader. This leads to the absence of individual willpower and alienation of citizens, denying their social identities (Al-Haidari, 2016). Households and society replicate this system where men assume leadership roles, expecting submission from women (ibid.). This socio-political system instills emotional instability, fear, helplessness, and anger in individuals to control them, and demonizes those who rise against it (ibid.).

The paternalistic ruling elite in Iraq oscillate between underestimating and overestimating the October Revolution (Nathmi, 2020). They underestimate the protest movement, assuming it will fade away over time, and overestimate it by claiming it has the power to destroy Iraqi society and threaten national security. The political elite posit that protestors lack agency, are manipulated by foreign parties, and are 'Jokers' (after the American film) hell bent on destruction (Al-Hassani & Shea, 2021). This paternalistic interpretation denying protestors' agency has nurtured the rise of conspiracy theories around the October

Revolution and incited violence against activists and protestors to silence them (Al-Hassani, 2021a). In response, Iraq's protests—like other social movements—are 'cauldrons of emotion at the boil' (Kemper, 2001, p. 72). Emotions arising from real, lived experience fuel protests. The ruling elite may not understand the dynamics of a leaderless October Revolution (Al-Anbar, 2020) as they assume it must have paternalistic leadership, and not be fueled by collective emotion. The next section examines the Sociology of emotion around social and political movements. This will help clarify the protest movement and the camaraderie in mobilization between men and women.

7.3   Emotion in Social Movements

Emotion is a constituent part of all social phenomena. Norman Denzin defines emotion as a

> lived, believed-in, situated, temporally embodied experience that radiates through a person's stream of consciousness, is felt in and runs through his body, and, in the process of being lived, plunges the person and his associates into a wholly new and transformed reality—the reality of a world that is being constituted by the emotional experience. (1984, p. 66)

According to Eduardo Bericat (2016), the Sociology of emotions studies the social nature of emotions and the emotional nature of social reality. Central to the Sociology of emotions is the fact that most emotions are experienced, carry meaning, emerge from, and are shared in social relations (ibid., p. 4). There is a fundamental distinction between subjective, internal emotional experience, and emotional expression which manifests externally and involves another individual (ibid.). Both are crucial in the study of social structures and processes. James Jasper (2014, p. 348) notes four major categories of emotions that people share: (a) reactions to others' actions; (b) feelings arising from their own actions; (c) feelings arising from our long-term affective and moral commitments; and (d) medium-term moods, such as excitement, hope, or resignation. Therefore, understanding emotions means understanding the situation around which emotions emerge and the social relations producing it.

Bericat (2016, p. 13) outlines three types of social emotions: (a) interactional, (b) group and collective, and (c) climates and cultures. Interactional emotions are emotional dispositions and processes emerging from social interactions and related to the positions that actors occupy in social structures. Individuals experience and express collective emotions as members in social situations. Emotional climates and cultures are transient or lasting emotional states rooted in a society or social group's characteristics. There are five theoretical approaches to the interpretation and study of social emotions: Cultural Theories, Symbolic Interactionist Theories, Ritual Theories, Structural Theories, and Exchange Theories. This chapter examines Theodore Kemper's structural theory.

Kemper (1978) outlines that emotions can be structural, situational, or anticipatory, and centers his analysis on two fundamental relational dimensions—power and status. Structural emotions are based on one's position in hierarchies of power and status; situational emotions are based on changes in power and status during interactions; and anticipatory emotions are based on the power and status expected, considering hierarchical positionality. Fear and anger are central emotions in power-infused relations, while shame and pride are central emotions in status-infused relations (Kemper, 1987, p. 275). The compelling force of these four key emotions allows for a system of social control (Bericat, 2016, p. 12).

Fear constitutes a broad emotional family composed of feelings like worry, anxiety, panic, terror, and horror that differ in content and intensity. Kemper (2001, p. 65) posits that fear and anxiety increase when one's own power decreases and the other's increases because this may cause potential risks. Sara Ahmed (2017, p. 65) suggests that fear 'is linked to the "passing by" of the object, even if the absence of the object in fear creates a different impression from the impression it creates in anxiety'. Fear has a temporal dimension; the object feared is both present and provokes an anticipated future pain or injury. According to Ahmed (ibid., p. 67), objects of fear substitute each other over time. For Iraqi men and women, the object of fear shifts consistently from the domestic to the public; from financial to physical insecurity; from government and nongovernment violence. Women's fear in public spaces is especially shaped by an inability to secure an undisputed right to occupy them, especially after the US invaded Iraq (Mallick, 2010). Fear of 'the world' as a scene of future injury works as violence in the present, shaping women's bodies and how they inhabit space (Ahmed, 2017). In Iraq, men are more likely to take up public space, despite fears of murder and/or forced disappearances, and to express anger openly without the gendered repercussions women face (Al-Hassani, 2021a).

Perceived or actual injury, insult, betrayal, or injustice often trigger anger. Anger is triggered by, and activates, power discrepancies as hostility or aggression toward an 'other' deemed responsible for negative and/or unjustified outcomes such as loss of power or status (Bericat, 2016; Jasper, 2014; Kemper, 1990). Bericat (2016, p. 12) identifies four forms of anger: frustration (with undesirable outcomes), resentment (of outcomes that benefit others), reproach (blaming others), and anger (for undesirable outcomes blamed on others). Anger, rage, and indignation are moral emotions often provoked by injustice and prevalent in social movements. Because anger provokes aggression, it is deemed masculine; women are expected to repress it. Society assigns different emotions to each gender whereby men may express aggressive emotions like anger to assert one's rights and statuses while women must display passive weakness and self-deprecating emotions like fear or sadness (Bericat, 2016; Jasper, 2014). With gendered expectations, conservative Iraqis discouraged women and girls from participating in protests, and Iraqi media denied them the platform afforded to men activists. Women's emotions—and those of other vulnerable social groups—are stereotyped in ways that blunt their challenges to the status quo. Their emotions arising from socio-political conditions are used to interpret their expressions narrowly and critically 'as always either being on the edge of excess, or already excessive' (Jasper & Owens, 2014, p. 535). When women and girls challenge social norms, conservatives shame them.

Shame is a '"public" emotion arising from exposure to disapproving others', arises from a negative judgment of one's core identity, and is therefore a 'painful, disruptive emotion' (Tangney et al., 2011, p. 707). Shame is also a mechanism which society employs in the 'othering' process; protecting social norms by shunning those who deviate from them. In a collectivist society like Iraq, public shaming is common. When women joined protests, conservatives claimed that a woman's voice is a عورة or flaw that must be silenced (Al-Hassani, 2020b). When a school official tried to shame a girl, she said بعد لا تقول بنية وولد، هاي راحت بعد 'Stop saying "boy" and "girl"; this [language] is dated' (Yassine, 2020a, 2020b). Male protestors and activists supported their female counterparts by chanting صوتج ثورة 'Your voice is a revolution', which turned into a viral hashtag on social media, and by carrying signs that said صوتج مفتاح لكل ثورة 'Your voice is the key to every revolution'. At the Tahrir Square tunnel entrance are the words شماغج والحُمرة محلّيات الثورة 'Your yashmagh and lipstick beautify the revolution'. The kuffiya/yashmagh (also known as 'keffiyeh' elsewhere), is a man's traditional headdress and a symbol of resistance throughout the Middle East. Using it to mask their faces from security forces, militias, and their families, Iraqi women protestors felt empowered. Despite various attempts to shame women and deter them from joining protests, women were active and proudly celebrated participants.

Like shame, pride is a social emotion that arises from evaluating oneself from an external perspective. This mechanism of social self-assessment involves three steps: 'imagining how we appear to the other'; 'imagining how the other judges this appearance'; and 'a response based on what we think of this judgment in the form of a feeling such as pride or shame' (Bericat, 2016, p. 12). Pride and shame are 'opposing pairs of emotions' and 'moral batteries' because people are motivated to avoid one and are attracted to the other (Jasper & Owens, 2014, p. 537). As Iraqi women and girl protestors moved away from shame, they grew prouder in their bodies and voices. Words like أنت ثورة 'You are revolution' instilled pride in them. Pride and shame are central to politics as unacknowledged shame leads directly to anger, insult, and aggression at individual, collective, and even national levels (Jasper & Owens, 2014; Scheff, 1994). They emerge from secure bonds which produce solidarity and insecure bonds which produce alienation.

Fares Nathmi (2020) posits that Iraq's patriarchal polite elite aim to control society by reshaping its fabric into a more militarized one steeped in misogyny, corruption, and hatred. They alienate people politically and socially, antagonizing and humiliating them through oppressive policies and the lack of public services. By triggering fear, anger, and hatred, politicians and non-state armed groups want to bring out the worst in people (ibid.). In Iraqi collectivist culture—shaped by the people's relationship with family and religion first, and by their relationship to the state, its institutions, and laws second—this is especially distressing (Taher & Sbayyeh, 2020). The October Revolution is a societal response to systemic efforts of alienation (Al-Hassani, 2020c; Taher & Sbayyeh, 2020).

While insecure bonds produce alienation, secure bonds produce pride, hope, and optimism. Pride emerges when status is accorded for an attainment or achievement. Optimism or hope emerges in anticipation of positive change in power or status (Kemper, 2001, p. 79). Solidarity and belonging emerge out of secure bonds where trust is shared between actors holding equal power and status or are willing to share it. The October Revolution's rallying cry—نريد وطن 'We Want a Homeland'—reflected a deep, collective desire for belonging which is a fundamental human need, involving love, pride, and joy (Al-Hassani, 2020c; Jasper & Owens, 2014; Scheff, 1994). Group identification builds affective commitments that persist, often long after the group itself dissolves (Jasper & Owens, 2014, p. 531). Negative shared emotions can sometimes strengthen positive reciprocal emotions. Common in protests, fear and anxiety can create a sense of collectivity and motivate collective actions (Eyerman, 2005, p. 43). Indeed, the violent efforts to silence protestors and activists in Iraq (Al-Hassani, 2021a) have inadvertently created a strong sense of solidarity and protectiveness among them, regardless of individual identity (Al-Hassani, 2021a, 2021b). Lacking ethnosectarian or gendered connotations, the movement's slogan has brought people together from different socioeconomic classes and given Iraqis a newfound sense of unity and solidarity (Taher & Sbayyeh, 2020). Such emotions have helped recruit people into the movement and maintained secure bonds between them (Jasper & Owens, 2014). Unlike the patriarchy that has denied male access to full emotional well-being, the October Revolution has allowed men, women, and other genders a full range of emotions. The following section discusses how these emotions and the movement's demands have been expressed in physical and cyberspace.

7.4   Mobilized Expression in Public and Virtual Spaces

Emotional displays can reassure or threaten audiences. Protestors can restrain their emotions in a 'cool' style expected of them or they are labeled irrational, disorganized, and/or malicious. Critics and opposition have consistently attempted to disqualify protestors from having public voices and taking up public space by falsely accusing them of malicious intent and violently targeting them (Al-Hassani, 2021a). Nevertheless, the October Revolution has empowered young men, and especially women, to reclaim public space.

7.4.1   Expression in Public Space

'Place matters to emotions in several ways, extending political struggles to new arenas' (Jasper & Owens, 2014, p. 539). Places or physical spaces stimulate and carry cultural meanings that are entwined with emotions; structure activities that take place in them; and provide space for secure bonding and internal solidarity (ibid.). Iraq's October Revolution, mobilization, and expression have a direct connection to public spaces. Targeted by snipers in October 2019, protestors took reference to a mountain where Muslims were stationed during a battle in 625 ACE. As some fighters abandoned the mountain, the battle was lost. This reference carried similar meaning to Baghdad's protestors: abandoning the base meant endangering the protest movement (Taher & Sbayyeh, 2020, p. 79). When protestors lost control of the building months later to militia affiliates, collective disappointment was clear. Today, Tahrir Square—where the building stands—remains a symbol of the movement. As a protestor said, ساحة التحرير تخلّينا نحلم 'Tahrir Square allows us to dream'.

Baghdad's Tahrir Square and Nasiriyah's Habbouby Square are the October Revolution's most significant protest sites. The first is notable for its Liberty Monument by sculptor Jawad Selim and the latter is where poet Muhammad Sa'īd al-Habbouby's statue stands. The Monument tells the story of the 1958 Revolution that ended the British mandate in Iraq. It depicts colonialist oppression, followed by liberation and images of prosperity. Meanwhile, at Habbouby Square stands a statue of its namesake, known for leading cultural and military campaigns against British colonialism in 1914. Physical symbols of revolution resonated a message to those gathered around them. When the government-imposed curfews and closed bridges to prevent gatherings, families took to the streets and surrounded protestors at Tahrir Square. Floods of more protestors protected the families and square's periphery, blocked entrances, and shielded them from the reach of state forces' tear gas. Circles of solidarity formed within and around Tahrir Square, marking a defining moment for the October Revolution.

Killed on the front lines by tear gas grenades was Safaa' al-Sarray, who became an icon of the revolution. Rather than naming him after his father, as is traditional in a patriarchal society, protestors named al-Sarray after his mother, dubbing him 'son of Thanwa'. This was unconventional and signaled a shift in ideology—a challenge to a patriarchal system that erases a mother's role as a source of tribal leadership. 'Son of Thanwa' has since been a moniker commonly ascribed to fallen protestors and activists, many of whom now go by their mothers' names (Al-Hassani, 2020b). Mothers were also present on scene along with younger women, providing logistical support and nurture. It may have been the presence of mothers, and families who later withdrew to protect children from escalating state violence, that factored into women's sense of safety at protest squares. Several women's rights organizations and activists state that no cases of sexual harassment have been reported in protest spaces (Omar, 2019; Yassine, 2020a, 2020b). Instead, women protestors have described respectful treatment and warm welcome (Omar, 2019; Shawki, 2020).

While the revolution was the culminating point of years of grassroots mobilization, it was triggered by state violence against women higher education graduates who protested unemployment. This incident triggered widespread outrage and mass protests which women and girls joined in large numbers to reclaim public spaces and demand dignified living. Women's participation rose from 14% in the 2015 protests to over 40% in the 2019 October Revolution (Jabar, 2018, p. 24; Odeh, 2021). The October Revolution has allowed women to reclaim public spaces in unprecedented ways and male comrades to engage on a different emotional level. A 'porousness of feeling' was possible whereby men and women could absorb each other's emotions through direct interaction and secure bonds (Reeser & Gottzén, 2018).

Protest squares have allowed protesting women and men from different socioeconomic classes to redefine norms around social hierarchies, uniting them in the face of state and non-state violence. Men and women experienced a newfound sense of solidarity as they provided free services at protest sites—from health and food services to legal and social education. Women activists played a vital role in launching revolution-focused media: *Tuktuk Newspaper* and *al-Musaawaat* Journal. Some women medics tended to injured protestors and faced live fire on the front lines. A woman medic told men who wanted to protect her اللي يجرالكم يجرالي 'Whatever happens to you [men] happens to me'. Women and men allowed each other self-expression beyond traditional gender roles and celebrated their unified presence. A popular protest chant was a cheerful, rhythmic address to the homeland, oscillating between 'Here are your youth' and 'Here, are your daughters, homeland'. هاية شبابك يا وطن هايه، هاي بناتك يا وطن هايه. Young men and women flooded the streets in celebration, بغيرتج ثورة صوتج أختي مو عورة، زم تتحامى بهالجهرة، على جبل أحد صعدي ونادي 'My sister, your voice is not a flaw. Men seek protection in your face [visual presence]. Climb Mount Uhud and bravely scream "revolution"'. Such metaphorical imagery was common in protestors' expression.

Bushra al-Rawi and Mohammed Al-Azzawi (2019, 2020) note two stylistic expressions common among protestors' slogans, chants, and signs: witty colloquial, and symbolic-heavy Classical Arabic. Regardless of style, protest slogans, signs, and chants steer away from sectarianism and focus on the political elite's guilt (ibid. 2019; ibid. 2020). Symbolic imagery plays a significant role in Iraqi culture, where a حسجة' hascha' employs a combination of metaphors, similes, or analogies, as well as satire and sarcasm to send an implicit message (Taher & Sbayyeh, 2020). Haschas are especially prevalent in Southern Iraq. In Thi Qar, protestors sent veiled threats to political parties about burning down their offices by referring to cold weather and a need for warmth (Taher & Sbayyeh, 2020, p. 82). Militia leader and politician Muqtada al-Sadr warned protestors of an 'ear tug' إذن جرّة or not-so-slight injury. Indeed, al-Sadr's militia has been violent against protestors and activists in Nasiriyah, where the revolution has been especially tenacious (Al-Hassani & Shea, 2021). There is a great discrepancy between protestors' and the government's expressions; while protestors relied on metaphorical imagery and other forms of expression, the political elite used basic, declarative statements of no emotional value (Taher & Sbayyeh, 2020, p. 82). Protestors' devotion to the movement, expressed in chants like نموت عشرة، نموت ميّة، أنا قافل عالقضية 'Whether we die by the tens or hundreds,

I'm committed to this cause' did not meet a parallel devotion from the political elite. Poignant expressions like this drew great attention from supporters and critics alike.

Marked by poignant slogans like نريد وطن 'We Want a Homeland' and آخذ حقي نازل 'I'm Going Out to Take Back My Rights', the movement is relatable and inclusive. It had no paternal protest leader, and no one could be credited for coining slogans and hashtags. Therefore, state forces and non-state armed groups' violence was both indiscriminate and discriminate (Al-Hassani, 2021a). Among the assassinated women activists were Huda Khutheir, Zahra Karlusy, Jenan al-Shahmani, Reham Yacoub, and Anwar Jassem, who have become icons of the movement. Militias kidnapped women activists like Saba al-Mahdawi and Mari Mohammed, releasing them later (Al-Hassani, 2020b). The murder of activists Sarah Taleb, Hussein Adel al-Madani, and their child in a home invasion triggered protests in Basra. As physical violence escalated, people resorted more heavily to online engagement and mobilization to amplify their stories to foreign audiences.

7.4.2   Expression in Virtual Spaces

According to literature on emotional expression in cyberspace, there is no conclusive empirical evidence that it is less emotional than face-to-face communication (Kivran-Swaine & Naaman, 2014). In fact, studies have showed that virtual engagement shows more explicit emotional communication and that the desire to share emotions is a primary driver for blogging and social media engagement (ibid., p. 424). While online engagement can be performative to reach an audience, it remains an interaction-based mechanism with emotional exchanges as with face-to-face ones (ibid., p. 427). Online engagement elicits social sharing; people share more experiences where strong emotions are involved (Garcia et al., 2014, p. 404; Rimé, 2009). While Iraqi women and girls have long used pseudonyms and anonymous profile images to protect their identities online, they have been more vocal than men in criticizing social norms. Women have been subject to cyber-bullying and blackmailing which had failed to silence them over the long term. Cyberspace has created a parallel Iraqi society where women, not men, were leaders of social discourse (Barbarani, 2021; Fatah, 2019).

The widespread use of hashtags helped evolve this online engagement with the October Revolution. The hashtag بناتك_يا_وطن# addressed the homeland with 'Your daughters'—present and proud. This proud moment of women's cyber presence faced a campaign of shame and defamation that replaced 'daughters' with 'whores' عاهراتك_يا_وطن#. Muqtada al-Sadr incited this defamation campaign by falsely accusing male and female protestors of lewd behavior at protest sites and camps (Barbarani, 2020). This was an intended character assassination of the movement, painting it as a danger to society's family values. Al-Sadr had supported the protests in its earlier stages and fluctuated in his support until this moment. Some women activists had rejected the participation of al-Sadr's affiliates in the protests for their conservative views toward women. Others had welcomed them, citing this as an opportune moment for those men to reconsider their misogynistic views through 'porousness of feeling' and the formation of secure bonds (Ali, 2020, p. 83; Reeser & Gottzén, 2018). When al-Sadr called for the segregation of the sexes, male and female protestors criticized his 'dated', 'misogynistic' views, and shared on social media images of them fraternizing at protest sites. They also arranged the country's largest women marches across several cities and governorates, including the most conservative ones (Barbarani, 2020).

The protest movement was not launched to specifically advocate for women's rights. However, it has consistently demanded an end to abusive and oppressive politics that targeted women and men. Among the hashtags that 'trended' was #أنقذوا_الأيزيديات_المختطفات Save Kidnapped Yazidi Women. A non-Yazidi, feminist group in Basra launched the hashtag campaign (Hasan, 2021). Activists took up this cause as part of the wider protest movement because they both point to the greater issue: a patriarchal, oppressive system (ibid.). Activists connect government corruption and ineptitude with its inability to prevent, and failure to respond to, the *Daesh* genocide and sexual slavery of Yazidi women, 2000 of whom are still missing (ibid.).

Over a year into the movement, over one thousand protestors have been murdered and tens of activists assassinated, leading to a new hashtag campaign that calls for an end to impunity (Al-Hassani, 2021a). The viral hashtags ask, 'Who killed me?' #من_قتلني and point to systemic impunity #الإفلات_من_العقاب (Nitti, 2021). This campaign emerged after the assassination of activist Ehab al Wazni in Basra, whose mother wanted to camp and demonstrate outside police headquarters to demand accountability. The image of an elderly woman defiantly protesting while multiple police officers tore down her tent turned her into the revolution's new icon with a hashtag named after her #أم_ايهاب_ثورة Ehab's Mother's Revolution. Soon after, other mothers whose activist sons were assassinated joined her in solidarity, with videos of them circulating on social media. A hashtag emerged in celebration of these mothers, #لبوات_العراق_سند_الثورة 'Iraq's Lionesses Buttress the Revolution'. Lionizing these women drew from symbolic and artful imagery that have played a significant role in protest expressions, and portrayals of gender relations.

7.4.3 Artistic Expression

In contrast with their aggressors in state- and non-state forces who relied on violence to incite fear and helplessness, protestors focused on rights, equality, and intellectual discourse, presenting themselves as a cultured, promising future for a better Iraq. Artists took to protest, influencing collective expression. Musical expressions during mass protests prompted support from prominent musicians who released songs that became protest anthems. One song connected public spaces to the movement. الجسر والساحة الوطن عالي جناحه بين 'Between the bridge and square, the nation's wings soar high'. Another fused a folk children's song about climbing a mountain حچنچلي بچنچلي into hip hop with altered lyrics about climbing Tahrir Square's Mount Uhud. Another song emphasized protestors' bravery and defiance of death by describing them as kissing tear gas and embracing their killers. Other songs used politicians' controversial statements in mockery and rejection. The core artistic expressions of the movement transcended through cyberspace to Iraqis in the diaspora, drawing greater solidarity. Seta Hagopian—a widely admired woman Iraqi musician—came out of decades-long retirement and released a song to support the protests. Only one song focused on Iraqi women, but various others had verses that glorified women's mobilization. Protestors played music even in conservative cities' protest sites, like Najaf and Karbala, where it was unprecedented for men and women to fraternize, let alone with music.

Apart from music, protestors expressed themselves using graffiti, graphic art, mixed media, and cartoons. Protestors transformed the Tahrir Square tunnel into an art gallery with murals and graffiti art. One mural said in English, 'We have a love story with streets'. Art prominently portrayed tuk-tuks, which had become symbolic to the movement. Until the October Revolution, the rickshaw or tuk-tuk in Baghdad was often considered the humbler ride of the underclass compared to taxis (Salim & Berger, 2019). When state- and non-state forces used violence against protestors, tuk-tuk drivers were the first on scene to rush the injured to hospitals, refusing payment (ibid.). Art emerging from the protests celebrated them. While tuk-tuks were a Baghdadi symbol of the movement, a more universal one was that of the empowered, defiant woman.

The Iraqi women's art movement includes two kinds: contemplative and contemporary (Yassine, 2021). Contemplative art focuses on women's internal reflections and ownership of the self and body, which may include trauma or identity conflict. Contemporary art revolves around immediate developments and events (ibid.). Contemporary art exploded in Iraq in recent years and grew more popular with the October Revolution. Such art has been prevalent in public protest spaces and cyberspace. This art portrayed women in various roles—medics, nurturers, and revolutionaries. Digital art expanded the forms of expression further. One poignant piece portrays a masked male protestor in an oil barrel with a tear gas grenade flying past him. On the barrel are the words in English, 'Do You See Me Now'. This reflects protestors' desperate desire for the world to hear and see them. It points to the belief among many Iraqis that their oil—not their stories—seems to matter on the world stage. Another poignant digital piece is of a masked girl in her school uniform, standing above crowds of protestors and waving Iraq's flag. Another piece portrayed a woman's image split vertically, with one half dressed traditionally, and the other in protest garb, masked, and holding a sign that says 'Separating religion from the state is better than separating men from women'. One man's art at the Tahrir tunnel portrays a woman's profile with the word طخ 'screw it' next to it, expressing apathy and defiance of social norms. This art may effectively summarize the protests' collective emotion toward structural patriarchy and oppression.

7.5 Conclusion

To offer a comprehensive understanding of power relations and gender dynamics in Iraq's October Revolution, this chapter discussed the intersection between women's and men's struggles against institutionalized patriarchy. The discussion relied on a structuralist approach, therefore borrowing from bell hooks' definition of patriarchy and Theodore Kemper's structuralist theory of emotion. The October Revolution has allowed both men and women a full range of emotions—from fear and anger to pride, belonging, and solidarity, which they have communicated in physical and cyberspace through chants, hashtags campaigns, and artistic expressions. Some militia and party leaders have described public squares as 'the kitchen of the nation', especially blaming women for 'cooking up change' alongside men (Mansour, 2021). Exploring emotional communication has allowed us to untangle the complex relations between social context and emotional expression. Although this chapter did not discuss LGBTQIA gender dynamics, they fit into this intersectional discussion. The most significant outcome of the protest movement is the emergence of a collective sense of confidence and the belief that people can bring about change, despite violent crackdown (Taher & Sbayyeh, 2020). This belief resonated in a poetic chant that Reham Yacoub had written and recited in protests before her assassination. In it, she identifies protestors as the proactive, passionate, patriotic, heroic sovereign (Yassine, 2020a, 2020b) and repeatedly asks hypocritical aggressors with إنت منو؟ 'who are you?' Beyond the grave, those words—coming from a woman and repeated by men today—continue to taunt those illegitimately assuming power in a patriarchal, oppressive system.

References

Aboulenein, A., & Levinson, R. (2020). Iraq's Healthcare System Is in Crisis. Patients Are Suffering. *Reuters.* Available at: https://www.reuters.com/investigates/special-report/iraqhealth/?fbclid=IwAR0L6iryGOJq8pMlYEcUfLVZHpZqPXS58ZCrROlLFno2xl1dxs4vQ8-vqaA. Accessed June 12, 2021.

Agence, F.-P. (2020). Poverty, Resentment of Corruption Among Engines of Continuing Protests in Iraq. *The Arab Weekly.* Available at: https://thearabweekly.com/poverty-resentmentcorruption-among-engines-continuing-protests-iraq. Accessed June 12, 2021.

Ahmed, S. (2004). *The Cultural Politics of Emotion* (2nd ed.). Edinburgh University Press.

Ahmed, S. (2017). *Living a Feminist Life.* Duke University Press.

Al-Anbar, A. (2020). Al-Iraq: Al-Abawiyyah fi Khitab al-Sultah. *Middle East Online.* Available at: https://tinyurl.com/b43nwb57. Accessed June 4, 2021.

Al-Azzawi, M., & Al-Rawi, B. (2019). Shi'ārāt al-Mutathāherīn al-Iraqiyīn al-Mutālibah bil Islāh: Dirāsah Semiyā'iyah. Dirasat: Human and Social Sciences, 46(3).

Al-Haidari, I. (2016). Al-Haymanah al-Abawiyyah al-Thukūriyya fi al-Mujtama' wal Sultah. Al Jadeed Magazine. Available at: https://tinyurl.com/b43nwb57. Accessed June 4, 2021.

Al-Hassani, R. A. (2020a). Corruption and Exploitation of Gender in Iraq (Part I of III). *Inside Arabia*. Available at: https://insidearabia.com/corruption-and-exploitation-of-gender-in-iraqpart-i-of-iii/.

Al-Hassani, R. A. (2020b). Maintaining the Feminist Spring of Iraq's October Revolution (Part III of III). *Inside Arabia*. Available at: https://insidearabia.com/maintaining-the-feministspring-of-iraqs-october-revolution-part-iii-of-iii/.

Al-Hassani, R. A. (2020c). The Seeds and Blossoming of Iraq's October Spring. *Zenith Magazine*, 72–74. Available at: https://tinyurl.com/b43nwb57.

Al-Hassani, R. A. (2021a). *Free Speech Under Threat in Iraq*. TIMEP. Available at: https://timep.org/commentary/analysis/free-speech-under-threat-in-iraq/.

Al-Hassani, R. A. (2021b). Iraq Protests Battle for State Sovereignty. *Tahrir Institute for Middle East Policy*. Available at: https://timep.org/commentary/analysis/iraq-protests-battle-forstate-sovereignty/.

Al-Hassani, R. A., & Shea, J. (2021). Hate Speech, Social Media and Political Violence in Iraq: Virtual Civil Society and Upheaval. *Tahrir Institute for Middle East Policy*. Available at: https://timep.org/commentary/analysis/hate-speech-social-media-and-political-violence-iniraq-virtual-civil-society-and-upheaval/.

Ali, Z. (2018). *Women and Gender in Iraq: Between Nation-Building and Fragmentation*. Cambridge University Press (Cambridge Middle East Studies). https://doi.org/10.1017/9781108120517

Ali, Z. (2020). Feminist Activism and the Protest Movement in Iraq. In F. Nathmi (Ed.), *Al Suluk al-Ihtijaji fi Al-Iraq: Al-Dinamiyat al-Fardiyyah wal Ijtima'iya* (pp. 61–90). Al Rafidain Publishers.

Ali, Z. (2021). From Recognition to Redistribution? Protest Movements in Iraq in the Age of "New Civil Society". *Journal of Intervention and Statebuilding, 0*(0), 1–15. https://doi.org/10.1080/17502977.2021.1886794.

Al-Rawi, B., & Al-Azzawi, M. (2020). The Intertexuality and Reference in the Slogans of the Iraqi Demonstrators: A Semiotic Study. In F. Nathmi (Ed.), Al-Suluk al-Ihtijaji fi Al-Iraq: Al Dinamiyat al-Fardiyyah wal Ijtima'iya (pp. 167–201). Al-Rafidain Publishers.

Bajec, A. (2019). Scores of Iraqi Women Victim to Online Sexual Blackmail. *The New Arab*. Available at: http://english.alaraby.co.uk/analysis/iraqi-women-victim-online-sexualblackmail. Accessed June 12, 2021.

Barbarani, S. (2020) Hundreds of Iraqi Women Challenge al-Sadr's Call for Segregation. *Al Jazeera News*. Available at: https://www.aljazeera.com/news/2020/2/14/hundreds-of-iraqiwomen-challenge-al-sadrs-call-for-segregation. Accessed July 1, 2021.

Barbarani, S. (2021). Three Iraqi Women Explain How and Why They Stay Anonymous Online. *Rest of World*. Available at: https://restofworld.org/2021/three-iraqi-women-explain-how-andwhy-they-stay-anonymous-online/. Accessed July 12, 2021.

Bericat, E. (2016). The Sociology of Emotions: Four Decades of Progress. *Current Sociology, 64*(3), 491–513. https://doi.org/10.1177/0011392115588355

Bettinger-Lopez, C. (2018). Corruption and Gender Inequality in the Age of #MeToo. *Council on Foreign Relations*. Available at: https://www.cfr.org/blog/corruption-and-gender-inequalityage-metoo. Accessed June 12, 2021.

Biana, H. T. (2020). Extending Bell Hooks' Feminist Theory. *Journal of International Women's Studies, 21*(1), 13–29.

Country Data: Iraq. (2020). *Transparency.org*. Available at: https://www.transparency.org/en/countries/iraq. Accessed June 12, 2021.

Crenshaw, K. (2015). Demarginalizing the Intersection of Race and Sex: A Black Feminist Critique of Antidiscrimination Doctrine, Feminist Theory and Antiracist Politics. *University of Chicago Legal Forum, 1989*(1), 139–167.

Denzin, N. K. (1984). *On Understanding Emotion*. Transaction Publishers.

Dodge, T. (2020). Iraq's Informal Consociationalism and Its Problems. *Studies in Ethnicity and Nationalism, 20*(2), 145–152. https://doi.org/10.1111/sena.12330

Eyerman, R. (2005). How Social Movements Move: Emotions and Social Movements. In H. Flam & D. King (Eds.), *Emotions and Social Movements* (pp. 41–56). Routledge.

Fatah, L. (2019). In 'Virtual Civil Society', Iraqi Women Are the Leaders. *Middle East Eye*. Available at: http://www.middleeasteye.net/opinion/virtual-civil-society-iraqi-women-areleaders. Accessed June 3, 2021.

Fayaq Abdul Wahab, E. et al. (2021). The Correlation Between the Proliferation of Small Arms and Light Weapons in Iraq and Rates of Violence Against Women. *WILPF*. Available at: https://www.wilpf.org/portfolio-items/the-correlation-between-the-proliferation-of-smallarms-and-light-weapons-in-iraq-and-rates-of-violence-against-women/. Accessed May 25, 2021.

Garcia, D., Garas, A., & Schweitzer, F. (2014). Modeling Collective Emotions in Online Social Systems. In C. von Scheve & M. Salmela (Eds.), *Collective Emotions: Perspectives from Psychology, Philosophy, and Sociology* (pp. 389–406). Oxford University Press.

Hasan, S. (2021). 'I Demand Justice': How Iraqi Female Activists Are Taking a Stand for Yazidi Women. *The New Arab*. Available at: https://english.alaraby.co.uk/analysis/iraqi-femaleactivists-take-stand-yazidi-women. Accessed June 10, 2021.

Hooks, B. (1984). *Feminist Theory: From Margin to Center*. Pluto Press.

Hooks, B. (2004). *The Will to Change: Men, Masculinity, and Love*. Atria Books.

Iraq: Water Crisis in Basra. (2019). *Human Rights Watch*. Available at: https://www.hrw.org/news/2019/07/22/iraq-water-crisis-basra. Accessed June 12, 2021.

Jabar, F. A. (2018). *The Iraqi Protest Movement: From Identity Politics to Issue Politics*. LSE Middle East Centre. Available at: http://www.lse.ac.uk/middle-eastcentre/publications/paper-series. Accessed May 5, 2020.

Jad, I. (2004). The NGO-isation of Arab Women's Movements. *IDS Bulletin, 35*(4), 34–42. https://doi.org/10.1111/j.1759-5436.2004.tb00153.x

Jasper, J. M. (2014). Emotions, Sociology, and Protest. In C. von Scheve & M. Salmela (Eds.), *Collective Emotions: Perspectives from Psychology, Philosophy, and Sociology* (pp. 341–355). Oxford University Press.

Jasper, J., & Owens, L. (2014). Social Movements and Emotions. In J. E. Stets & J. H. Turner (Eds.), *Handbook of the Sociology of Emotions* (Vol. II, pp. 529–548). Springer.

Kemper, T. D. (1978). *A Social Interactional Theory of Emotions*. Wiley.

Kemper, T. D. (1987). How Many Emotions Are There? Wedding the Social and Autonomic Components. *American Journal of Sociology, 93*(2), 263–289. https://doi.org/10.1086/228745

Kemper, T. D. (1990). *Research Agendas in the Sociology of Emotions*. SUNY Press.

Kemper, T. D. (2001). A Structural Approach to Social Movement Emotions. In J. Goodwin, J. M. Jasper, & F. Polletta (Eds.), *Passionate Politics: Emotions and Social Movements* (pp. 58–73). University of Chicago Press.

Kivran-Swaine, F., & Naaman, M. (2014). Gender and Social Sharing of Emotions in Large-Scale Social Awareness Streams. In C. von Scheve & M. Salmela (Eds.),

Collective Emotions: Perspectives from Psychology, Philosophy, and Sociology (pp. 422–436). Oxford University Press.

Kullab, S. (2021). Power Outages Hit Iraq Amid Scorching Temperatures. *Associated Press*. Available at: https://apnews.com/article/middle-east-iraq-power-outages-government-andpolitics-business-3447f9ff3c75357d306bf47dfe8f398b. Accessed July 5, 2021.

Mallick, H. (2010). Remembering a 'very good' Iraqi girl. *The Toronto Star*. Available at: https://www.thestar.com/opinion/editorialopinion/2010/12/21/mallick_remembering_a_very_good_iraqi_girl.html. Accessed June 21, 2021.

Mansour, A. (2021). Iraq: Protesters Die Demanding a Homeland. Daraj. Available at: https://daraj.com/en/72927/. Accessed June 3, 2021.

Mehra, N. J. (2017). Sara Ahmed: Notes from a Feminist Killjoy. Guernica. Available at: https://www.guernicamag.com/sara-ahmed-the-personal-is-institutional/. Accessed June 8, 2021.

Mikdashi, M. (2018). Sextarianism: Notes on Studying the Lebanese State. In A. Ghazal & J. Hanssen (Eds.), *The Oxford Handbook of Contemporary Middle Eastern and North African History*. Oxford University Press. https://doi.org/10.1093/oxfordhb/9780199672530.013.24

Nathmi, F. (2020). Psychologia al-Sultah listinzāf al-Hirāk al-Thawri al-Tishreeni. Al-Mada Paper. Available at: https://almadapaper.net//view.php?cat=224250. Accessed June 6, 2021.

Nitti, S. (2021). 'Who Killed Me?': Iraq's Protest Movement Reignites Amid Targeted Killings and Impunity. *The New Arab*. Available at: https://english.alaraby.co.uk/analysis/who-killed-meiraqs-protest-movement-reignites. Accessed June 15, 2021.

Odeh, S. (2021). Can a Revolution Succeed Without Women's Mobilization? *Women's Voices: Hamzat Wasl*. Available at: https://www.youtube.com/watch?v=IhTuRTIRdmw.

Omar, O. (2019). The Fearless Women at the Fore of Iraq's Protests. *The Arab Weekly*. Available at: https://thearabweekly.com/fearless-women-fore-iraqs-protests. Accessed June 29, 2021.

Reeser, T. W., & Gottzén, L. (2018). Masculinity and Affect: New Possibilities, New Agendas. *NORMA, 13*(3–4), 145–157. https://doi.org/10.1080/18902138.2018.1528722

Rimé, B. (2009). Emotion Elicits the Social Sharing of Emotion: Theory and Empirical Review. *Emotion Review, 1*(1), 60–85. https://doi.org/10.1177/1754073908097189

Salim, M., & Berger, M. (2019). The humble three-wheeled tuk-tuk has become the symbol of Iraq's uprising. *The Washington Post*. Available at: https://www.washingtonpost.com/world/2019/11/01/why-humble-tuk-tuk-has-becomesymbol-iraqs-uprising/. Accessed July 3, 2021.

Scheff, T. J. (1994). *Bloody Revenge: Emotions, Nationalism, And War*. Westview Press.

Shawki, A. (2020). Al-Mar'ah al-Iraqiyyah fi Sahāt al-Ihtijāj. Deutsche Welle Arabic. Available at: https://tinyurl.com/b43nwb57. Accessed June 30, 2021.

Taher, A. (2017). Psychologiya al-Ihtijāj: Qirā'ah fi al-Ihtijāj al-Madani fi al-Iraq Ba'd 31 Tammūz 2015. Research Gate. Available at: https://tinyurl.com/b43nwb57. Accessed June 14, 2021.

Taher, A., & Sbayyeh, A. (2020). Ihtijājāt Tishreen al-Awwal 2019: "Sirā" al-Khitābāt li Rasm Masār al-Amaliyya al-Siyāsiyya. Hiwār al-Fikr, pp. 74–84.

Tangney, J. P., Stuewig, J., & Hafez, L. (2011). Shame, Guilt and Remorse: Implications for Offender Populations. *The Journal of Forensic Psychiatry & Psychology, 22*(5), 706–723. https://doi.org/10.1080/14789949.2011.617541

Worth, R. F. (2020). Inside the Iraqi Kleptocracy. The New York Times. Available at: https://www.nytimes.com/2020/07/29/magazine/iraq-corruption.html. Accessed June 12, 2021.

Yassine, D. (2020a) Al-Shāri' Shāri'na: Thā'irāt al-Iraq wa'Isti'ādat al-Fadhā' al-Umūmi. JEEM. Available at: https://jeem.me/de/node/348. Accessed May 31, 2021.

Yassine, D. (2020b, August 23). Reham Yacoub: Bintuka Ya Watan. Assafir Al-Arabi. Available at: https://tinyurl.com/b43nwb57. Accessed June 4, 2021.

Yassine, D. (2021, February 25). Al-Neasawiyya wa Harakat al-Ibdā' al-Fanni fi al-Iraq. Assafir Al-Arabi. Available at: https://tinyurl.com/b43nwb57. Accessed June 3, 2021.

CHAPTER 8

Blogging in Pre-war Syria: Female Voices from Within an Authoritarian Regime and Patriarchal Society

Michela Cerruti

The further I write, the more solid the articulation of myself and my identity becomes, as if the text and I have some bizarre relationship that allows us to grow together [...]. (Maysaloon, 2008)

In the Arab world, blogging is not a recent phenomenon. A rich literature has developed since 2006 (see, e.g., Elting et al., 2009; Taki, 2011) analyzing the local specificities of this phenomenon. Blogs as forms of communication, new media, and political counter-spaces have been explored with particular attention to the connections between cyberactivism and censorship. Similarly, the interpenetration between gender, sexuality, religiosity, and weblogs in the Middle East and North Africa's blogospheres has been extensively investigated. Several contributions (see Amir-Ebrahimi, 2008; Sreberby & Khiabany, 2010; Cerruti, 2020) have analyzed how female bloggers have been using their cyber diaries to express personal opinions, reveal intimate emotions or convey information globally.

This chapter wants to deconstruct the pre-revolutionary Syrian blogosphere, as intended by the Syrian female blogger Maysaloon in her post "Deconstructing 'Sex,' Honour and Patriarchism in the Middle East" (Maysaloon, 2007). The aim is to understand how it was used as an alternative stage to promote new

M. Cerruti (✉)
Neuchatel, Switzerland
e-mail: michela.cerruti@graduateinstitute.ch

127

L. H. Skalli, N. Eltantawy (eds.), *The Palgrave Handbook of Gender, Media and Communication in the Middle East and North Africa*, https://doi.org/10.1007/978-3-031-11980-4_8

forms of female visibilities and communication interchanges between male and female bloggers.

The stories narrated in the posts by two female bloggers (Maysaloon, and Dania, *blogger of My Chaos*) will be used as primary sources toward "understanding social life" (Plummer 2001). Through the creativity, the intimacy, and the human dimension expressed in these stories, it will also be possible to trace the motivations that brought them to blog from within an authoritarian regime and a patriarchal society.

According to Maha Taki, in Syria and Lebanon, people blog to communicate their ideas and "make changes in society for social development" (Taki, 2011). In the case of Maysaloon and Dania, understanding "their motivations through a content/textual analysis […]" (Taki, 2011), reveals their intention to create new forms of female militantism. This contribution will focus on their activist efforts in creating a narrative that could go beyond national contexts to "broadening the scope of their [feminist] interventions" (Skalli, 2006).

In Syria, on the verge of the war, the only feminist activism legally recognized by the government was the one carried on by the "state feminism" represented essentially by the General Women's Union (GWU). Several other feminist groups were fully operative in the field, supporting women and children in need. The Syrian Law on Associations restricted their right to circulate their gender empowerment messages. Some of these female groups were illegal also because they were proselytizing for conversion to Islam. Groups led by Imams and Sheikhas trained in the Sheikh al-Bouti religious complex were highly active in recruiting followers. The women they converted could be easily seen in the offline public space as they were displaying their religiosity by wearing manteaux and headscarves with specific colors (beige, blue, and black).

This chapter will examine three main aspects of the Syrian female blogosphere prior to the civil war: The Syrian blogosphere 2008–2011 as mainly a male cluster, the choice of blogging in English, and two different forms of activism. This selection will highlight how blogs represented a hybrid way to carry on female activism that promotes female visibility and empowerment by bypassing the regime restrictions.

THE SYRIAN BLOGOSPHERE 2008–2011: A MALE CLUSTER[1]

The blogosphere is a collection of weblogs, a cluster of posts often classified in unchronological order. Bloggers decide how they want to blog (anonymously or nominatively), in which form they want to communicate (using intimate posts, creating a site of news), and the type of content they want to produce (exclusively textual, with multimedia elements, hyperlinks). Readers can leave comments at the end of each note and eventually open a debate. In general,

[1] This contribution stems from a portion of my doctoral fieldwork that, between 2008 and 2011, has been devoted to the study of the Syrian female blogosphere.

bloggers utilize the virtual public space to request new visibility forms while connecting locally and globally.

From a methodological standpoint, blogs provide researchers an opportunity to access data despite the spatio-temporal constraints their geographic location can impose. The data they access is already formatted, classified chronologically, and related to subjects within specific contexts. The posts can be considered fundamental primary sources in understanding local social dynamics. The exchanges between female and male bloggers in the section dedicated to the comments are to be read as new forms of social interactions in a context of a patriarchal and segregating society. To better understand the conflictual nature of these social relations in the virtual public space, an interpretive approach to blogs (observations and semi-structured interviews with bloggers) was chosen. As Nilüfer Göle states in her "Islam in Public: New Visibilities and New Imaginaries," "Approaching the public sphere as a social imaginary [...] emphasizes its dynamic aspect, as an ongoing process, a creation of significations and practices rather than an 'imagined' and 'preestablished' frame" (Göle, 2002). In this perspective, blogs allow the analysis of the virtual public space as a constantly changing space where women could unveil their practices and highlight the non-Western modernity that the female bloggers introduced into their patriarchal society.

The analysis of the online public sphere prior to the Syrian conflict has revealed that Dania and Maysaloon represented a minority within a space vastly dominated by male presence. Blogging was socially considered a privilege conceded to men. Data produced by Harvard University's Berkman Center for Internet and Society (Elting et al., 2009) confirmed that the Syrian public space was a mainly male cluster (87% of male bloggers versus only 13% of female bloggers). It also observed that other online daily activities, such as the "Couch Surfing" where the members share hospitality in the common intent of sharing social and cultural values, remained an absolute male prerogative (99.8% of hosts are men). If studies underscore that most online activities in the first decade of 2000 were carried on by men, it is also proved that male bloggers were actively engaged in observing the female part of the Syrian blogosphere and that they often interacted with the female bloggers.

An excellent example of the interest men devoted to the female part of the blogosphere is shown in comments left by male bloggers under the posts of Maysaloon and Dania. Their comments, interestingly, were on topics generally considered feminine. On August 26, 2009, for example, Anonymous, who describes himself as "[...] a Muslim male and a feminist sympathizer," engaged in a lengthy discussion on what being empowered as a woman meant at that moment in Syria. Their exchanges continued through several exchanges, touching many interesting points (Maysaloon, 2007). Maysaloon's long and detailed answers instilled in Anonymous the interest in answering in an equally complex and pointed manner.

In the case of Dania, topics are even more controversial, such as homosexuality (Dania, 2008b), about which she received seven comments from men, prompted by the nature of the topic. The blogger had concluded her intervention by supporting new laws to include rights for the homosexuals:

> According to all human laws, homosexuals JUST LIKE heterosexuals have the right of freedom of expression, of believe, of having sexual relationships, of marriege, of equal treatment, of BLOOD DONATION!!!!, of not having or beeing forced into hiding a part of who they are, so how come some laws in the middle east, like the Syrian law ban these human rights on the basis of sexual orientations instead of promoting them!!!!
>
> I mean seriously... how ridiculous that sounds? Read it carefully, and think about it for a minute... (Dania, 2008b)

She received several comments from Syrian men opposing her views even though she had brought evidence supporting her statements in her post. One of the men, anasqtiesh, said: "maaan!! usually I enjoy reading the comments on this topic more than the posts themselves ... it's hilarious. a study said that introducing people to hard evidence contradicting a belief they have would very likely back fire and make them cling to it even more. dania, i totally agree with u, but i'm not gonna bother and argue the point with anyone. Cheers."

The male appreciation of female posts in the Syrian blogosphere also came in the form of a direct post written by one of the most active male bloggers, Abu Fares, in 2008. In his intervention, he advocated for the interest expressed by other men in their comments and the subsequent frequency with which they answered female blogs. He described his personal interest in the posts of some female bloggers (e.g., Mariyah and Dania) and dedicated his intervention to the relationship between female and male bloggers explaining that he liked following these female bloggers' posts because these were "exciting" posts. He stated that women were skilled writers, and their comments were subtle and passionate. More specifically, he said:

> "[...] Among the exciting blogs I am regularly reading now are those of three beautiful ladies. You cannot fault me for liking women more than men. As a matter of fact, I do not like men at all except to watch a football game with or as drinking buddies. Mariyah pervaded our senses like a gentle zephyr impregnated with scents of jasmine and magnolia. As a reader, I find her one of the most exciting and talented writers on the Syrian blogosphere. [...] Then there is Dania, who calls her blog My Chaos. In fact, she is not chaotic at all; sensitive perhaps, candid and fervent in defending her right to be free is what the reader will find in and between the lines of her hyper and intelligent post". (Abu Fares, 2008)

He then summarized his thoughts by saying that ultimately female bloggers "use their writings as contrasting samples to the new breed of mainstream Syrian blogs" (Abu Fares 2008). In the comments to this post, other male bloggers publicly and openly confirmed that even if women were still a minority in the blogosphere, the quality of the communication offered by them, when compared to the posts widely spread by men, was to be admired.

BLOGGING IN ENGLISH: A FEMALE WAY TO ESCAPE THE LIMITS OF A NON-INCLUSIVE SOCIETY

It is crucial to understand in which language the bloggers decided to blog and why to study how Syrian women used their weblogs to overcome the constraints of their patriarchal society and articulate their forms of social and political activism globally. In Syria, as in many other Muslim contexts, vertical social emancipation has over the years, affected mainly the urban, social, and intellectual elite, which had always prided itself on a particular liberal spirit. The space that Information technologies have opened to women was incomparably considerable. From the privacy of their homes and anonymity of the Internet, and by using English instead of Arabic, they have been able to evade the restrictions of their nation-state through the global connections they have created in the virtual public space.

In their posts, Maysaloon and Dania clearly expressed their pride in their Arabic culture and Syrian nationality. However, they decided to blog in English in an effort to send their messages beyond the Arab blogosphere. They belonged to the so-called Levantine blogosphere. In the Berkman study by Elting and his colleagues (2009), the researchers explained that the Levantine blogosphere comprises bloggers geographically located in the so-called Levant, specifically in the eastern Mediterranean and Iraq. The authors maintained that those who blog in this group "frequently use English in addition to or instead of Arabic. They are joined in this section of the network, which connects to the US and international blogosphere, by 'bridge bloggers' from other Arab countries, who write mainly in English" (Elting et al., 2009).

Similar points are made by other scholars who focused on the choice of English in the Middle Eastern blogsphere. In her study of weblogs and blogger in Lebanon and Syria, and Jordan, Maha Taki reports the considerations of an anonymous blogger who states: "I think that in the Middle East, there is almost never honest talk about politics. People are afraid to say things openly. On blogs they can say almost whatever they like. I see blogs from Syria where they say all sorts of terrible (but true) things about the al-Asad family in English that they could never say in Arabic online or in person. It lets people tell the truth openly with less fear than other media forms" (Taki, 2005).

Analysis of these blogs shows the dangers incurred by bloggers in pre-war Syria and will illustrate how blogging in English might have helped online activists escape the regime's repression. In addition, the language chosen for blogging is a matter of identity and willingness to send the message as further as possible in the virtual public sphere. This perspective is shared by Sarah Jurkiewicz, who reflects on the publicness in the Lebanese blogosphere. In her 2011 analysis of the language used by Lebanese bloggers, she goes beyond the link to "foreign language"/"escape from censorship" to highlight the communicative dimension of the linguistic preference. She explains how "the English-language bloggers describe it as 'natural' to post in English, saying that this is the internet language and allows their blogs to be read more internationally. The bloggers writing in Arabic mainly want to target a Lebanese or Arab audience. But choice of audience is only one part of the story. Those who blog in Arabic often describe this as a political choice" (Jurkiewicz, 2011). She continues by commenting on the political and identity aspects of the language chosen among English, Arabic, or French to blog in the Lebanese virtual public space. Here again, the experiences of Maysaloon and Dania seem to match Jurkiewicz's analysis.

By reading Maysaloon and Dania's posts, it seems clear that they used English instead of Arabic to send their messages as widely as possible in an effort to advocate for their ideals. Most of the time, they did not seem willing to admit that they actively wanted to create a bridge with the West. Still, the reality is that they reached readers worldwide by expressing their feelings in the modern *koine*. Here is how Maysaloon in 2008 answered the question "Who I Wrote for and Why in English": "I write mainly for myself, that is, I wish to put down somewhere my reflections and thoughts on what is happening in the Arab world. This amazing part of humanity has offered and continues to offer so much that is meaningful to the world. […]" (Maysaloon, 2008).

The blogger continued by explaining that she was more comfortable expressing her feelings in English than in Arabic because of the schools she attended. In other words, English was part of her identity. In one of the comments, she highlighted that she did not want to build a bridge but simply felt better by blogging in English. As some followers told her, though, she was actually building a bridge between Western and non-Western cultures because her messages were a way to communicate her traditions even to Westerners, which could be considered a good reason not to write in Arabic.

DIFFERENT FORMS OF ACTIVISM: FEMALE VOICES FROM WITHIN THE AUTHORITARIAN REGIME AND PATRIARCHY

With the beginning of the Revolution in 2010, many websites got banned by the authorities. The censorship intensified especially in May 2011, when the Syrian Electronic Army, a group of hackers linked to the President, surfaced online. Since 2011, this Internet Army targets dissidents and political opposition web pages, blogs, Western political and human rights websites, as well as government websites in the Middle East, Europe, and the United States. States (Helmi, 2011).

Internet control and repression have a long tradition in Syria. Before the war, censorship of the online spaces was already extensive and aggressive. The Syrian President, Bashar al-Assad, became the President of the Syrian Computer Company when his brother Basil died. The modern image the young Assad had spread around brought many to think he could be the change Syria needed toward a more democratic regime. During an interview he granted to an Egyptian magazine in 1997, he explained that he considered the Internet an "open Arab medium that uses advanced technology to convey our position"

(Zisser, 2006). Moreover, in the inaugural Presidential speech, he reiterated the importance of information institutions and information technologies (Al-Assad, 2000). In 2007, the government blocked Facebook (to lift the ban in 2011) as it represented a threat to political power. Web users living in the country were censored, persecuted, and sometimes arrested for what they expressed online. The Syrian Center for Media and Freedom of Expression highlighted that 225 websites had been blocked in 2009 and that citizens had been arrested. They had to face the secret services and were subsequently sent to prison for having sent private e-mails that had been tracked down by selective control of the online post (Syrian Center for Media and Freedom of Expression, 2009).

Regardless of the risk they ran, Syrians between 2008 and 2009 blogged mainly about domestic issues and were quite critical toward their political leaders (Elting et al., 2009). All the female bloggers followed by the author over the years wrote extensively about Syria, and 50% of them expressed clear-cut opinions regarding Syrian politics and the government. In most cases, these women complained about the governmental censorship and their risk of being persecuted because of their points of view.

According to some bloggers, this lack of freedom of expression was one of the reasons that has pushed them to blog anonymously. Their experience in the censored Syrian blogosphere resembled the one narrated by Masserat Ebrahimi. She claimed that the posts were considered a form of civil disobedience in Iran and a substantial danger to the religious-political power. While the impact of online female activism through blogs seemed to remain poor on offline life, these women and youth, and minority groups defied the Islamic Republic and its patriarchal social conventions. In her study of the Iranian blogsphere, the author focused on how Iranian women blogged by using a "pseudonym or a constructed identity such as a false name and surname" (Amir-Ebrahimi, 2008) to protect themselves from censorship and dishonor. According to Amir-Ebrahimi, others decided from the beginning to make their voices heard by writing under their real name to legitimize their points of view (Amir-Ebrahimi, 2008).

In the case of Syrian bloggers, Maysaloon decided to give no details about her life and identity while Dania accepted the risk of opening up to the readers. By posting her name, profession (working for an NGO), and city from where she blogged (Damascus), she showed that she had decided to express her feelings openly even if this meant that she could easily be identified and tracked down. Regardless of their attitude toward anonymous, both bloggers were rather vocal in their social and religious activism.

Dania sought a tool to spread her modernizing secular feminist ideals. She was the product of a secular society. The tones of critics, notably in terms of women's and human rights used in her posts, were straightforward. Her activism was centered on gender justice, human rights, freedom of expression, and freedom of speech.

In a 2008 post, she freely condemned the so-called honor crimes and how this cultural and religious tradition impacted women's lives in the country. Later, in November 2008, she addressed the problem of an inevitable religious awakening both offline and online in a post called "Religious Fever." Answering comments on this post, she had no problems reminding her readers that the State should be secular and stated:

> 'Sharia' which is unfortunately applied in Syria, is promoting for death penalty, unfair laws for women…and can you imagine killing people for having sexual relationship without marriage, cutting the arms of the thieve…I lived and been raised in a Muslim family, I drank Islamic culture with milk in my childhood 'private schools', and I say NO, a big NO to applying a law created by one religion and force every one- even if they were non-Muslim to live under this law. Religions when practiced should be a personal matter and should not affect the social, legal, and political life, but unfortunately religions won't allow (Dania, 2008a).

In 2008, as mentioned before, she also touched on the very delicate topic of homosexuality in Syria. In the post entitled "Homosexuals in Syria, the ignorant ignoring of a right of existence," she explained why there is nothing "abnormal" in belonging to the LBGTQ minority, then stated that all the human beings deserve to experience the same type of rights.

It seems clear Dania had a convincing way to make her voice be heard, even if her values did not correspond to what most of her countrymen believed in. By blogging about homosexuality, she did not only give space to a disregarded fight for the rights of a minority but also opened up a channel of communication with other male and female bloggers on the topic. In this perspective, it was interesting to read the answer she got from those who were always very active like Abu Fares. In response to her post, he confirmed he did not share her perspective, but liked how she opened up communication lines, saying:

Dania, I'm very glad to read this post of yours. The most important thing is to keep all communication channels open between us Syrians of different beliefs and principles.

> Your article is more in line (as a matter of principle of freedom of speech and expression) with my attitude than the prohibitive, preaching and hateful tone of an increasing number of Syrian blogs. For standing up to your belief you have my full support. And, by the way … I totally disagree with your point of view, but that's another story. (Abu Fares, in Dania, 2008b)

Dania, through her attentive, brave, and straightforward narrative, contributed to shaping the online public sphere as an inclusive and gender-respectful space where women and men could be socially and politically freed and empowered. She never withdrew from a debate, and her showing respect for everybody's opinions received appreciation and mutual respect.

Maysaloon, conversely, declared herself in a certain way anti-feminist and looked for a space to freely preach her religious values as an Islamic feminist.

Like many other Islamic feminist activists, the blogger challenged the values of secular female activism by embracing a militantism that negotiated women's rights and religious values. Extensive literature has focused on the juxtaposition of the terms "feminism" and "Islam" and the push toward this form of activism (see, e.g., Wadud, 1999; Mir-Hosseini, 2002; Badran, 2009; Wadud, 2013). In other words, these religious activists believe that women's rights are already embedded in the Islamic religion and that what is missing is an interpretation faithful to the original Qur'anic message. In this sense, Islamic feminists have been calling in several Muslim countries for new *ijtihad* (individual independent analysis of the Islamic legal sources such as Qur'an, Hadiths, and in general of the existing Fiqh) and for a less patriarchal codification of the Islamic legislation.

With Maysaloon's blog, we are exposed to the practice of the 2.0 Islamic feminist activism. Anna Piela's work on Muslim Women Online (Piela, 2011) clearly describes the relationship between faith and virtual public space and how Muslim women, through different identities and values, manage to gender the blogosphere in which they blog substantially. Through the life stories narrated by the bloggers, the dialogues between them as well as their conflictual virtual encounters, Piela deconstructs different forms of Muslim religiosity 2.0. to shed light on this gendered virtual public space while giving voice to a kaleidoscopic group of Muslim women.

In the case of Maysaloon's posts, we could see the growth she made in her religiosity. On October 30, 2007, as mentioned, she wrote a post regarding the ideas of patriarchy and feminism entitled "Deconstructing 'Sex,' 'Honour' and Patriarchism in the Middle East." She stated: "[...] My argument would be that what we call a 'patriarchal society' is in fact a truly 'unjust' society which preys on its weaker members and both males and females have in fact been complicit in these injustices" (Maysaloon, 2007).

She then added that according to her point of view:

[...] Traditional conceptions of sex and gender have to be recognized and realigned not as victim and perpetrator, but as something which recognizes the different and complementary roles they play in constructing society. Sex too, needs to be destigmatized not by utilizing a 'libertine' approach of what some call 'free love', but in fact legalizing it in the sense that traditional obstacles to concepts such as 'marriage' and 'divorce' are turned into legal contracts which are respected by all [...] (Maysaloon, 2007).

In her quest for more rights, in the "non-liberal" way, she aligns with the requests generally made by Islamic activists to recognize more freedom for women in full compliance with the rules of reinterpreted Islamic texts. Her path into active proselytism for a religious life changed over the years, and it became even more evident in 2009 when she wrote a post entitled "Why I Am an Anti-feminist." Here she explained how her convictions developed with the experiences she went through over time.

[…] I am an ardent anti-feminist, though it is not a position that I came suddenly but rather through my experience, and especially over the past two years, which has solidified my view of this perspective as causing more harm than good. […] There are points of view in feminism which I should, and in fact I do agree with, but the agreement is coincidental and not incidental. […] My perspective on relations between sexes is defined Islamically. When I say Islamically that means that I use the Qur'an and the prophetic sunnah as a guideline. […] (Maysaloon, 2009).

Maysaloon's posts changed from expressing an interest in religion to acts of convincing her readers to re-embrace Islam. Her engagement is in line with the religious commitment of the *da'wah* (invitation), which was often preached by female Imams in female religious study groups and secretive meetings organized in urban contexts in Syria. Her engagement to invite people to return to religion in 2010 went even further as she wrote a post entitled: "A Word on Religious Bigotry." Here she explained why she reached her conversion to Islam by stating:

[…] Living alone for so long, immersed in one's own thought and books, can lead to the construction of an internal world which is beautiful in its preciseness, order and logic. This world, contrasted with the foolishness that surrounds us, becomes an ideal to which all is compared. […] My own studies and investigations have always been about finding the rustic heart, the simple beauty, that the first Muslims found in the Qur'an, and of the experiential path to become nearer to the divine. I was never interested in dogma, stale instructions and blind imitation (Maysaloon, 2010).

Her belief is that Islam should be intended as a path toward personal growth, a discipline of the *nafs* (the soul) instead of acts of bigotry. She reminded the readers that ultimately the Islamic religion "[…] is an inward faith, it's about doing right regardless of those who oppose it, and of being more concerned with your own failings and problems than of those in people surrounding you" (Maysaloon, 2010).

Overall, the analysis of Maysaloon's and Dania's narratives shows that they do not really belong to the percentage of Syrian bloggers who expressed an apparent dissent toward the regime. Their political neutrality is probably one of the reasons for which they seemed only partially concerned about, and spared by, censorship. They were more interested in opening communication channels between men and women inside and outside the Syrian blogosphere, even by discussing sensitive social issues. Their direct engagement in raising people's awareness about their social activism in the virtual space generally received a positive feedback from other bloggers. The number of comments under their posts (in general between 7 and 24 comments) confirms the attention their postings elicited.

Conclusions

The Syrian blogosphere has dramatically changed In Syria since the outbreak of the conflict. The proto-female engagement online to emancipate women and protect children has been overcome by the offline conditions of gender-based violence, displacement, and forced migration. Indeed, according to a study carried out by the United States Institute of Peace, PeaceTech Initiative in 2014, "Syria's has been the most socially mediated civil conflict in history. An exceptional amount of what the outside world knows—or thinks it knows—about Syria's nearly three-year-old conflict has come from videos, analysis, and commentary circulated through social networks" (Lynch et al., 2014). The online public space has therefore been fundamental to showing the gravity of the offline conflict.

Since the beginning of the conflict, Syrian bloggers have also focused their cyberactivism on overcoming governmental censorship. In Syria, like in other Arab contexts, the bloggers have also devoted their online activism to challenging the regime's political status quo and the interference of foreign powers in the Syrian political affairs. Fahmi (2009) has demonstrated how virtual public sphere had influenced the urban public space by transporting new forms of protest from the online to the offline. During the uprising, Syrian young bloggers, women, and Islamic militants have used the new open networks to send a flow of images and information from the blogosphere to the offline public spaces to weaken the regime.

In general, many of the bloggers who in the pre-war were actively carrying on their social, cultural, and political fights online stopped blogging. Similarly, due to the war and the consequently higher levels of online censorship, Dania is no longer blogging, at least under the name we know. After almost three years of silence, she left a last post on her blog in August 2012 where she confessed:

> [...]What's the point of those bullets being shot out of the helicopter over my roof? Back to blogging, it could be a good attempt to regain control back, the little bit I managed to keep from myself. I promise myself I will post this as soon as I and the electricity are back! Peace! (Dania, 2012).

Maysaloon, on the other hand, stopped blogging for some time and then went back to her online activity. On July 11, 2016, she wrote a post entitled "Baby Steps," where she confided that:

> I've forgotten what it's like to blog. The clue should have come to me from the name, a blog is a 'weblog', and it's supposed to be a place where I ponder my thoughts about what's going on. At some point I lost sight of that, and the resulting paralysis has gone from weeks to months to years. I'll have to take baby steps again, to relearn things that I once knew and start applying them again (Maysaloon, 2016a).

In general, her posts between 2011 and 2019 have substantially changed. Her blogging has become more nostalgic, showing solitude and pain for the losses she and the country had to experience. Posts about Islam as the main topic stopped in 2011 even if she still mentioned the religion randomly. For example, in her 2017 post "Just want to be" (Maysaloon, 2017), she even mentioned the need of being respected if she decided to drink openly without the presence of people judging her. In general, the focus of her posts moved to considerations regarding displaced people and refugees, damages of historic cities such as Aleppo and the futility of a war that can resemble a civil conflict (Maysaloon, 2016b). She also somehow criticized the political leadership involved in the destruction of Syria. In December 2019, though, she decided that her blog was on a "hiatus [at least] for the moment." She explained that too many emotions had been devolved in commenting on the war, and she needed a break.

Ultimately, this contribution highlights how the current blogosphere has been created by the pre-war active online engagement of women like Dania and Maysaloon. If today, after ten years of conflict, non-Syrians can understand what is happening in the country, it is because the online public sphere has been shaped and nourished by the female proto-rebels who chose blogging as a tool to spread the values of their activism. Theirs were fights that were not aimed to destabilize the country. They were devoted to opening channels in which the freedom of speech and expression was respected and developed regardless of the social structure and political power in the country.

Thanks to the stories of Maysaloon and Dania, this chapter offers a rare opportunity to access the historical moment of rupture in the Syrian female blogosphere when the old socio-political system was challenged in Syria and the new chaos became the reality of the country.

REFERENCES

Abu Fares, abufares said…the World According to a tartoussi. (2008). *Secular Shivers and Religious Fever*. Accessed December 2008, from https://abufares.wordpress.com/page/5/.

Al-Assad, B. (2000). President Bashar Al-Assad: Inaugural Address. Speech Delivered by Bashar al-Assad on his Inauguration as President of Syria in 2000. Accessed March 2008, from https://al-bab.com/documents-section/president-bashar-al-assad-inaugural-address.

Amir-Ebrahimi, M. (2008). Transgression in Narration: The lives of Iranian Women in Cyberspace. *Journal of Middle East Women's Studies, 4*(3), 89–118. muse.jhu.edu/article/245155

Badran, M. (2009). Feminism in Islam: Secular and religious convergences. London: Oneworld. Chicago

Cerruti, M. (2020). 21. Half Syrian Sufi Blogger: Faith and Activism in the Virtual Public Space. In R. Stephan & M. Charrad (Ed.), *Women Rising: In and Beyond the Arab Spring* (pp. 198–203). New York, USA: New York University Press. https://doi.org/10.18574/nyu/9781479846641.003.0022

Dania, My Chaos. (2008a). *Religious Fever*. http://myfog-dania.blogspot.com/
Dania, My Chaos. (2008b). *Homosexuals in Syria, the Ignorant Ignoring of a Right of Existence*. http://myfog-dania.blogspot.com/
Dania, My Chaos. (2012). *Pre 3 Km*. http://myfog-dania.blogspot.com/
Elting, B., Keely, J., & Faris, R., (2009). Mapping the Arabic Blogosphere: Politics, Culture and Dissent. In *Internet & Democracy Case Study Series*. The Berkman Center for Internet & Society at Harvard University. Accessed January 2010, from https://cyber.harvard.edu/sites/cyber.harvard.edu/files/Mapping_the_Arabic_Blogosphere_0.pdf.
Fahmi, S. W. (2009). Bloggers' Street Movement and the Right to the City. (Re)claiming Cairo's Real and Virtual "Spaces of Freedom.". *Environment and Urbanization, 21*(1), 89–107. https://doi.org/10.1177/0956247809103006
Göle, N. (2002). Islam in Public: New Visibilities and New Imaginaries. *Public Culture, 14*(1), 173–190.
Helmi, N. (2011). *The Emergence of Open and Organized Pro-Government Cyber Attacks in the Middle East: The Case of the Syrian Electronic Army*. OpenNet Initiative. Accessed May 2021, from https://opennet.net/emergence-open-and-organized-pro-government-cyber-attacks-middle-east-case-syrian-electronic-army.
Jurkiewicz, S. (2011). Of Islands and Windows: Publicness in the Lebanese Blogosphere. *Oriente Moderno, 91*(1), 139–155. http://www.jstor.org/stable/23253711.
Lynch, M., Freelon, D., & Aday, S., (2014). Syria's Socially Mediated Civil War. In Blogs and Bullet III. United States Institute of Peace. Accessed May 15, 2021, from https://www.alnap.org/system/files/content/resource/files/main/142-pw91-syrias-socially-mediated-civil-war.pdf.
Maysaloon, Commenting on the Arab World: Its History, Culture and Politics. (2007). *Deconstructing "Sex," "Honour" and Patriarchism in the Middle East*. Accessed March 2008, from http://www.maysaloon.org.
Maysaloon, Commenting on the Arab World: Its History, Culture and Politics. (2008, December). *Who I wrote for and why in English*. http://www.maysaloon.org. Accessed October 2008.
Maysaloon, Commenting on the Arab World: Its History, Culture and Politics. (2009). *Why I am an Anti-Feminist*. Accessed March 2010, from http://www.maysaloon.org.
Maysaloon, Commenting on the Arab World: Its History, Culture and Politics. (2010). *A Word on Religious Bigotry*. Accessed December 2010, from http://www.maysaloon.org.
Maysaloon, Commenting on the Arab World: Its History, Culture and Politics. (2016a). Baby Steps. Accessed January 2020, from http://www.maysaloon.org.
Maysaloon, Commenting on the Arab World: Its History, Culture and Politics. (2016b). *Enjoy the Show*. Accessed January 2020, from https://www.maysaloon.org/2016/12/enjoy-show.html.
Maysaloon, Commenting on the Arab World: Its History, Culture and Politics. (2017). Just Want to "Be". Accessed January 2020, from http://www.maysaloon.org/2017/01/just-want-to-be.html.
Mir-Hosseini, Z. (2002). Debating Women: Gender and the Public Sphere in Post-Revolutionary Iran. In A. Sajoo (Ed.), *Civil Society in Comparative Muslim Contexts* (pp. 95–122). I.B. Tauris & Institute of Ismaili Studies.
Piela, A. (2011). *Muslim Women Online: Faith and Identity in Virtual Space*. Routledge.
Plummer, K. (2001). *Documents of Life 2: An Invitation to a Critical Humanism*. Sage.

Skalli, H. L. (2006). Communicating Gender in the Public Sphere: Women and Information Technologies in the MENA. *Journal of Middle East Women's Studies, 2*(2), 35–59. Accessed March 2008. https://doi.org/10.2979/mew.2006.2.2.35

Sreberny, A., & Khiabany, G. (2010). *Blogistan: The Internet and Politics in Iran.* I.B. Tauris.

Syrian Center for Media and Freedom of Expression. (2009). Accessed March 2011, from http://scmsy.org/?page=category&category_id=23&num_page=2&lang=en.

Taki, M. (2005). Human Rights Watch "False Freedom Online Censorship in the Middle East and North Africa" (2005). Weblogs, Bloggers and the Blogosphere in Lebanon, Syria and Jordan: An Exploration. Dissertation Submitted in Fulfilment of the Requirements for the M.A. Degree in Communications, University of Westminster, London, 2005. Accessed online: https://www.hrw.org/report/2005/11/14/false-freedom/online-censorship-middle-east-and-north-africa#_ftn250

Taki, M. (2011). Why Bloggers Blog in Lebanon and Syria? Methodological Considerations, Oriente Moderno, Nuova serie, Anno 91, Nr. 1, Between Everyday Life And Political Revolution: The Social Web In The Middle East (2011), pp. 91–103, Istituto per l'Oriente C. A. Nallino.

Wadud, A. (1999). *Quran and Woman: Rereading the Sacred Text from a Woman's Perspective.* Oxford University Press.

Wadud, A. (2013). *Inside the Gender Jihad: Women's Reform in Islam.* Oneworld Publications.

Zisser, E. (2006). *Commanding Syria: Bashar Al-Assad and the First Years in Power* (p. 31). I. B. Tauris.

CHAPTER 9

Syrian Women in the Digital Sphere

Noha Mellor

Keywords Digital sphere • Digital media • Empowerment • Media activism • Syrian women

INTRODUCTION

The Syrian civil war is one of the most important global conflicts since the 2011 Arab uprisings. This is primarily because it has become a proxy war between the USA and its Gulf allies on the one hand, and Bashar al-Assad, Russia, and Iran, on the other. The Western nations which have become entangled in this proxy war, justify their interventions by declaring their motives are to help minorities, in a similar way to the international discourses of the nineteenth century, when European powers declared their intentions were to protect the Catholics and Alawi or the Protestant minorities in the Levant. Now, Russia, however, 'wants to be the protector of all these minorities' in the current conflict (Al-Azm, 2014).

The number of Syrian refugees who have fled the country as a consequence of this protracted conflict is estimated at well over six million, and an equivalent number of Syrians have been displaced within Syria. The majority of Syrian refugees are hosted by Lebanon, Turkey, and Jordan, while oil-rich countries such as Qatar, Saudi Arabia, Kuwait, and Bahrain have not taken in any refugees, on the grounds that hundreds of thousands of professional Syrians already

N. Mellor (✉)
College of Communication, University of Sharjah, Sharjah, United Arab Emirates
e-mail: nmellor@sharjah.ac.ae

© The Author(s), under exclusive license to Springer Nature Switzerland AG 2023
L. H. Skalli, N. Eltantawy (eds.), *The Palgrave Handbook of Gender, Media and Communication in the Middle East and North Africa,*
https://doi.org/10.1007/978-3-031-11980-4_9

reside and work in these countries. Of those Syrian refugees who have managed to reach European shores, only 1% have been offered residency, notably in Germany, Sweden, and Denmark. The USA accepted only 12,000 refugees, while Canada accepted 40,000; other countries, including Russia, Japan, Singapore, and South Korea, offered no settlement places for Syrian refugees (Asaf, 2017, p. 3).

Keeping the focus on those displaced Syrians, this chapter sheds light on displaced Syrian women by moving away from their stereotypical representations as passive victims, to shed new light on their active agency. Syrian women have endured the worst consequences of the war and conflict in Syria and the refugee camps: they have been exposed to rape, sexual violence, assault, and kidnapping, sometimes within their homes or in detention (Asaf, 2017, p. 6). It is necessary to define 'displacement' before proceeding. I use the term 'displaced' to refer to refugees who have fled Syria, and moved to neighbouring countries such as Jordan, Lebanon, and Turkey, or to Europe. I also use this term to refer to internally displaced women who were forced to leave their communities in the government-controlled territories. This is to acknowledge the intricate positioning of those women who have been pushed outside their communities, even though they remain within the borders of Syria.

The focus of the chapter revolves around displaced Syrian women who have found a new tool for visibility and empowerment in activism. Displaced Syrian women have arguably found new opportunities to challenge traditional norms, voice their concerns, and launch their campaigns on digital media which can be defined as a tool of empowerment. Digital media here is considered a new tool of discursive power characterised as the ability to amplify and maintain certain discourses about women's rights; on the other hand, as I argue, these women have faced several challenges, particularly when it comes to contesting gender hierarchies.

Drawing on Gerson and Peiss' (1985) framework which acknowledges gender relations in terms of the processes of boundaries, negotiations, and consciousness, the chapter provides examples of Syrian female activists who have marked their presence as spokeswomen or media professionals in the numerous initiatives funded by Western donors. The chapter begins with a brief overview of Syrian feminist activism, demonstrating how the 2011 uprisings have created new avenues for Syrian women's activism. The chapter then juxtaposes the opportunities afforded to these women with the challenges they face in the digital space. The analysis is based on different forms of evidence including female media activists' reflection on their situation, and their interpretations of the challenges they face. This form of reflection is treated as mediated accounts communicating Syrian women's authorial voices which ultimately create a narrative path for the readers to navigate.

Syrian Women's Activism: An Overview

The modern Syrian feminist movement dates back to 1946, when women in Syria demonstrated against veiling which resulted in the unveiling of most urban women; by 1949, women obtained the right to vote (Kelly & Breslin, 2010). When the Ba'ath Party took over in 1963, it declared its commitment to women's rights. The Party banned civil society associations as well as political parties and activities, including women's associations, unless they were affiliated with the Ba'ath Party and serving the party's goals. The Women's Union was launched in 1967 to lead the feminist debate in Syria, but its aims were closely aligned with the Ba'ath Party's targets, and confined to eradicating illiteracy and establishing nursery schools. The Union was led by an elite group of women from the party's community (Al-Jarmani, 2017, p. 10). The Women's Union was effectively incorporated into the Ba'ath Party in 1968. The Party proposed equal rights for women in the 1973 constitution, but Shari'a laws remained intact and unchallenged, especially after independent women's associations ceased operations, and new state associations emerged aligned with the Ba'ath Party's ideology (Keddie, 2007, p. 138).

When Bashar al-Assad came to power following his father's death in 2000, women in Syria regarded this as an opportunity to modernise the work of feminism, but they soon found that their work would be subject to the guardianship of the President's wife, Asma al-Assad, who supported selected organisations such as the Syrian Commission for Family Affairs, the *Mawred* Foundation, and the Rural Development Unit. Asma al-Assad, Syria's 'First Lady', created the largest state-organised trust, which controlled more than 80 per cent of the funds for civil society groups within Syria. The trust was dominated by middle-class women, who arguably influenced the interests of civil society work according to their own interests; notably, Asma al-Assad was represented by Western media and politicians as a symbol of a modern Arab woman (Sukarieh, 2015). Women's associations were mostly occupied with literacy programmes under al-Assad's regime, doing little to combat the patriarchal culture in society or male superiority in the political sphere (Habib, 2018, p. 4). Organisations that attempted to work independently with funding from abroad (such as Syrian Women for Social Development) were often accused of working according to foreign agenda (Al-Jarmani, 2017). Women's literacy increased, and they gained access to the labour market—although many professional women came from the elite class, they were encouraged to stay at home once they had children.

Syria ratified the Convention on the Elimination of All Forms of Discrimination against Women (CEDAW) in 2003, but it has maintained reservations about several provisions. The incompatibility of some provisions with Shari'a laws, for instance, as well as objections to the provision concerning women's right to pass on their nationality to their children. The Syrian government also objected to the provision regarding women's freedom of movement, generally refusing to commit to ending discrimination against women as defined by CEDAW; other reservations related to women's rights during marriage, and penalties for adultery (Kelly & Breslin, 2010, p. 463). The reservation about women's right to pass on their nationality to their children has also greatly affected the Palestinian population in Syria, as well as Iraqi refugees who fled to Syria after 2003. Patriarchal restrictive norms have led to the maintenance of women's exposure to gender-based violence, whether at home or in a public space. Domestic violence is common throughout Syria, as is spousal rape—neither is unlawful (Kelly & Breslin, 2010, p. 460). The problems are exacerbated for women in rural areas, who have no links with women's associations in the capital and other urban centres; they have limited awareness of their rights, including property rights. Islamist groups tend to insist on aligning Syrian laws with (their interpretations of) Shari'a laws, resulting in fewer rights for women in marriage, divorce, working outside the home without spousal permission, and equal inheritance (Kelly & Breslin, 2010, p. 461).

Before the 2011 uprising, Syrian women's representation in parliament used to be higher than that in many Arab states, but they had limited presence in other sectors such as the judiciary (Kelly & Breslin, 2010). Women's participation in political life remained restricted, partially because of economic instability and partially because of the strength of Islamist discourses. These political and economic factors forced the government to refrain from reforming personal status laws—with a few exceptions such as setting the minimum age of marriage for women at 17 (Keddie, 2007, p. 138). Syrian women have generally been subject to legal discrimination, with their freedom of movement curtailed, custody of their children denied, and ability to pass on citizenship to their children under Syrian law. Women cannot travel without their husbands' approval whereas men can move freely, while adult women who marry without their guardians' consent (a father or a male relative) are subject to the authority of the guardian to annul the marriage. Syrian women also have limited financial rights within marriage (Shackle, 2017); similar to their counterparts in several Arab countries, they have also been subject to so-called honour killings, usually at the hands of male relatives (Habib, 2018, p. 2). The penalty for honour killings tends to be far more lenient than for other types of murder; in addition, Syria does not have legislation that outlaws gender discrimination (Shackle, 2017). Syrian laws and constitutions, in theory, grant women the opportunity for equal participation in the political sphere, similar to many other Arab states; in reality, however, women are usually restricted by traditions, norms, and societal and familial boundaries.

Following the outbreak of protests in March 2011, Syrian women volunteered to work as first aid assistants and took on other logistical roles such as transporting food and medicine. This resulted in them becoming targets of harassment and detention by the regime (Habib, 2018, p. 5). The secret service persecution of women activists during the 2011 uprising forced male relatives to march with women in their demonstrations in order to protect them, and to arrange other protests calling for the release of female prisoners (Al-Jarmani, 2017). It is important to note, however, that the persecution of

Syrian women's activities began well before 2011—for instance, a Syrian blogger, Tal al-Mallohi, was detained in 2009 on the charge that she had disclosed state secrets on her blog; since then, al-Mallohi has been kept in detention, although a Syrian court ordered her release at the end of 2014 (Committee to Protect Journalists, n.d.).

There have been more than 210 civic groupings set up, both outside and in Syria since 2011, in the territories out of the government's control, as an alternative to coherent collective action. The overall aim for such groupings in Syria was to aid protestors by facilitating the transport of food and medicine. Another important way in which they worked was coordinating a news service to post as much information and as many photographs as possible on Facebook pages; several women who took videos and photographs of protests were shot dead while recording their news material, including the activist Bayan Rihan (Al-Jarmani, 2017, p. 22). Female activists who still reside in Syria, face political and familial obstacles to their participation in civil society; for instance, Mona Muhammad, a member of Raqqa City Council, said that she was forced to leave her activist work and sit at home because of family pressure aimed at restricting her work and movement beyond the home (Nassar, 2021). There are several other organisations which have been established outside Syria such as in Turkey, Sweden, and France, in addition to the numerous women's groups launched in Syria in the regions outside the regime's control (Nassar, 2021). There were many women who were active in joining the protests in the early days of the 2011 uprisings, but the deteriorating security situation following the war quickly quenched women's hopes. The journalist Samar Yazbek (cited in Shackle, 2017) said:

The war became extremely violent, and women's rights became a secondary issue. But despite the horrifying intensity of the war, there are still women activists working to create life and maintain a civil society, both within the heart of the war and as refugees.

Yazbek, who resides in Paris, became one of the leading Syrian activists in the diaspora, winning the Penn Pinter prize, and using the prize money to launch her *Women Now for Development* movement, one of the numerous associations set up by Syrian women activists outside Syria.

The Syrian feminist movement in diaspora according to one such feminist, however, has not yet been able to articulate a coherent identity or a distinctly feminist perspective. Movements such as these suffer from discrepancies between the flashy slogans and contradictory practices, which only reinforce patriarchal mentalities, and eventually lead to fragmentation and division among Syrian feminist groups; many members approach feminist work primarily as a gateway to earning money (Nassar, 2021). The traditional norms that confine women to the domestic sphere are among the obstacles to women's activism; even those who fled to Turkey have faced additional hurdles, including command of the Turkish language, the Turks' stereotypical image of Syrians as less educated and less skilled, and the fact that Syrian refugees in Turkey tend to self-isolate within their communities (Syrian Dialogue Centre, 2018). A survey of Syrian women about their views of women's activist networks indicated that a large percentage of the target group was not satisfied with the number of relevant associations or programmes, as many of them did not address the needs of women. A number of respondents pointed to the tendency of many such associations turning to certain segments of the population or geographical locations; many activities were not widely publicised or were limited to the needs of their donors and supporters, thereby limiting the opportunities of empowerment available to Syrian women (Syrian Dialogue Centre, 2018).

The following section briefly reflects on the concept of empowerment, demonstrating its manifestations in the work of Syrian women who have joined Western-funded NGOs and media outlets as media activists.

OPPORTUNITIES

It is hard to define, let alone measure, the concept of empowerment. Naila Kabeer (1999, p. 437) defines the concept as 'a process of change', entailing three interconnected dimensions: resources, agency, and achievement and outcomes. Resources refer to social relationships—the allocation and access to resources are contingent on societal rules that regulate the distribution of power. Agency is the ability to define and pursue goals, including negotiations and bargaining to reach them. Gerson and Peiss (1985) provide another conceptual framework that acknowledges this process of change resting on three pillars: boundaries, negotiations, and consciousness. Boundaries include physical, social, and ideological limitations that regulate gender relations and the distribution of power, both between men and women and even between women, thus constraining the behaviour of each gender group. Negotiation refers to the process of challenging or conversely supporting existing power relations, including women's bargaining for privileges and resources, while consciousness refers to women's experiences through interaction with other gender groups (Gerson & Peiss, 1985, p. 318). There is no clear articulation which has emerged, however, of what this process of empowerment looks like, or how it could differ according to specific geopolitical and cultural contexts such as the Arab region; either way, it inevitably has an impact on women's access to resources. This critical awareness of context and its boundaries enables women to trigger changes in, or to negotiate with, their circumstances in order to overcome obstacles to gaining fair access to resources (Kieffer, 1984). Zimmerman (1995, p. 583) distinguishes between the empowering process and the empowered outcome: the former refers to the process that facilitates the empowerment of communities or organisations, while the latter refers to the consequences of this process. The process of psychological empowerment could manifest itself in involving Syrian women in the development of new professional practices (Zimmerman, 1995, p. 584). The outcome of this process can be measured qualitatively, for instance, by documenting the increasing visibility of Syrian women in their professional fields.

The following sections focus on Syrian women activists who have joined the numerous Western-funded NGOs set up after 2011. Women's empowerment is tracked here through the opportunities that exist for women to pursue, given the freedom of choice available to them; as many of these women have been assigned work as media professionals, it is apt to consider the opportunities afforded to them to move within institutions across various countries, particularly Turkey, Jordan, and Europe. If the liberal feminist approach argues for women's inclusion in the labour market as a sign of equality between the sexes, a post-modernist view of feminism acknowledges that women might use social restrictions to negotiate their way into new fields or reconstitute boundaries within such fields. Here, women's access to work and decision-making posts can be measured, as well as questioning specific constraints on women in accessing certain professions and (or) how they negotiate their routes into such professions in order to enforce a new politics of power distribution within the field. Syrian women engage in the process of negotiation to challenge gender roles within organisations as I argue below. Women have been accepted as media activists and reporters, although they still engage in the process of negotiation to show that they are capable of delivering a 'male' performance, particularly in field reporting (see, e.g. Mellor, 2012).

Syrian Women as Media Activists

Digital media has played a pivotal role in circulating news and information from Syria which was not accessible to international media outlets; this also helped to shift the public agenda to enable Syrian communities to debate topics previously confined to the private space. This means that those involved in circulating such reports on alternative platforms may have contributed to setting the news agenda in legacy media, although the latter still has the power to frame the news in the desired way (Jungherr et al., 2019, p. 407). New power to influence mainstream media is termed discursive power or 'the ability of contributors to political communication spaces to introduce, amplify, and maintain topics, frames, and speakers that come to dominate political discourse' (Jungherr et al., 2019, p. 406). This discursive power is a pivotal factor in the Arab region, characterised as it is by the increasing digital literacy of its young people under the age of 24, who constitute 50 per cent of the region's population. Youths aged between 15 and 24 make up more than 21 per cent of the Syrian population; internet penetration is around 47 per cent, while social media penetration sits at about 35 per cent. One Syrian journalist residing in Germany, Youmna Al-Demashqi, praised social media for empowering Syrian women to challenge long-held social restrictions limiting their participation in public debate:

I know a lot of women who have become more powerful and have the courage now to debate with men even virtually on *Facebook* [...] *Facebook* has created a lot of space for me to express my opinions and I am no longer afraid of defamation (cited in WDR, n.d.).

There were many Syrian regions which were not in the control of the government after 2011, allowing opposition and anti-government media outlets to proliferate, mainly supported by international, particularly European, donors (Mellor, 2021, pp. 417–8). Syrians longed for new outlets to satisfy their need for information regarding the extent of the uprisings, or, as one Syrian journalist put it, 'before the [uprising] the media was of no importance to people; now people are reading and discussing the news and commenting on it from all sides' (cited in *BBC Media Action*, 2012, p. 2). According to a survey of the active media in Syria since 2011, there were 343 such organisations in Syria: many faced closure because of the withdrawal of donor funding. The lack of transparency in donors' funding strategies arguably resulted in 'unhelpful competition between the different newspapers' and it was, therefore, difficult 'to foster cohesion and a spirit of solidarity under these conditions' (Mellor, 2021, p. 421). Displaced Syrians have also formed networks on new social media sites, circulating news about the situation in Syria. The Democratic Union Party (PYD) in Syria exerted control over three provinces in 2014, extending its control of the media sector in these provinces, and requiring media institutions or media activists to seek licences through their media councils (Syrian Journalists Association, 2017, p. 14).

A need existed for more publicity for such organisations with the increasing number of NGOs and associations emerging in and outside Syria after 2011, especially to indicate that they were mostly funded by Western donors. This meant that many NGO staff found themselves performing journalistic work, and acting as 'unintentional journalists' (Spyksma, 2019), thus creating news hubs about their work in Syria and among Syrian refugees. Military operations on the ground provided opportunities for some women to work as military reporters such as Maysa al-Mahmoud (cited in Syrian Journalists Association, 2017, p. 12), who moved between Idlib and Aleppo, and worked as a media officer for armed factions. She said:

There is a presence of female media workers in media institutions in the Syrian north, but they are few and lack work experience. They do not exceed 20 workers between activists and journalists. Five of them at least are in Idlib province. The main reason they are few and that women do not consider working in the media sector is the Islamist armed factions, most importantly *al-Nusra* Front, which tracks down media workers and arrests them.

Another female professional, Souad Khabieh, talked about the acute need to document protests and other activities in Syria, and to communicate this information to journalists outside Syria; many women found themselves preparing reports and news material without prior training in journalism or documentation (Al-Jarmani, 2017, p. 23). London-based Zaina Erhaim (2018, p. 72) saw an overlap between media activism and journalism to help fellow Syrians, and regarded 'documenting and recording current events' as a duty:

Some [Syrian journalists] who initially rose and documented the revolution are still working as journalists inside Syria [...]; some are seeking fame, which is dangerous in war zones; others hope that, through journalism, they will help to stop the powerful from manipulating reality and rewriting history.

Female journalists such as Erhaim have contributed their skills to train budding journalists in Syria, drawing on their cultural awareness to build capacity and to increase the number of Syrians on the ground who can document events happening there. Women like Erhaim arguably aim to foster solidarity with Syrians inside their homeland and in diaspora communities while maintaining a sense of 'hybrid identity' or an identity 'that is neither wholly of the homeland nor exclusively reflective of the hostland' (Brinkerhoff, 2009, p. 14). These women still struggle, however, to negotiate their position in their professional fields. Erhaim (2018, p. 76) for instance, commented that:

> Despite all the sacrifices made by what many call 'Syrian media activists', they are still being treated unequally. They are not considered actual journalists by most, if not all, international media outlets. We are told this is because they are not 'objective' or 'neutral'. What does 'objective' mean in the Syrian context? Does being 'objective' when covering Syria mean giving voice to a war criminal and his propaganda, and allowing the regime to justify their bombing of civilian areas, schools and hospitals? I do not believe the BBC, for example, would remain impartial to a latter-day Hitler who laid siege to their homeland or a neighbouring country.

CHALLENGES

On the other hand, Syrian women in the field of activism as media and communication professionals have faced several challenges. The most important of these relate to negotiations of boundaries within the field. Boundaries refer here to division and hierarchy within the media and communication field. This boundary-setting includes efforts on the part of female media professionals to negotiate and ascertain their belonging to a global field of professionals with specialised knowledge (Carlson, 2015, p. 10). The boundaries of the field have arguably shifted as a result of disparate group access with the emergence of numerous Syrian media outlets and NGOs outside Syria, staffed by budding Syrian journalists. Syrian women have not managed to shift boundaries, however, within the regional or global media field such as in Europe, where thousands of women now reside. These Syrian women have attracted considerable attention in the Western media, although their agency should be measured not only by their ability to 'produce output', but also by their ability to be 'noticed and granted an authority to do so consistently' (Robinson, 2015, p. 162).

The *Syrian Female Journalists Network* (SFJN) was launched in the Netherlands in 2013, as a non-profit organisation aiming to connect the media and the Syrian feminist movement. The organisation also aimed to empower women journalists to apply for leading positions in media institutions and work towards enhancing women's representation in the media (Khalaf, 2016). The

SFJN published a study about the status of Syrian women and media discourses on women for the period between 2011 and 2015 (Khalaf, 2016). The study documents the lack of opportunities for female journalists to reach senior positions in the emerging Syrian media, whether in or outside Syria, as institutions tended to be led by men, especially in the print media. The rise of armed groups has placed further immense pressure on female journalists, even so-called moderate groups, as they tend to limit female journalists' mobility unless they are accompanied by male relatives. There are some media outlets in Syria which have asserted that they can only publish certain material online relating to women because of the censorship they face offline at the hands of such armed groups (Khalaf, 2016). Photographs of women published in many emerging Syrian media publications also tend to feature mostly Sunni women as passive victims rather than activists on the ground (Khalaf, 2016). One female journalist and activist in Daraa said that she joined a revolutionary media organisation but was abused by her employer who had no media experience, but his activist work afforded him the necessary support to set up a media organisation. She stated that her salary was withheld because she 'refused to be friends' with her employer. She could not complain about him, fearing his 'revenge', and eventually quit her job (Syrian Journalists Association, 2017, pp. 10–11).

Examples abound of the online harassment to which Syrian women have been subjected: one Syrian journalist resident in Turkey removed her veil but kept her *Facebook* profile picture veiled. When she shared a recent photograph of herself at a family event, she was taken aback by the digital campaign against her, insulting her honour and morals for removing her veil (WDR, n.d.); other journalists such as Yaqeen Baido, were subjected to harsh online harassment after they denied the presence of revolutionary Syrian media, which prompted the SFJN to issue a petition on *change.org* pleading for solidarity with Baido (https://bit.ly/3hj4MaC). A Syrian journalist, Dina Bataish from *Step News Agency* who resides in Jordan, received numerous insulting comments on social media, accusing her of intentionally offending Jordanian society after she posted the details of a harassment incident she suffered there. Following the comments directed against her, Dina refrained from writing about any topics related to Jordan, lest she faced expulsion to Syria (Othman, n.d.). Melia Aydmouni, a founding member of the SFJN, believes that digital media has contributed to creating a space for women to express themselves, but it has also exposed women to digital harassment and bullying (WDR, n.d.).

These women cannot genuinely participate in decision-making in media institutions as they are rarely employed in managerial or editorial positions, save for *Al-Jeen* broadcasting, according to the journalist Chirine Ibrahim (Syrian Journalists Association, 2017, p. 15). Staff create images and symbols in newsrooms that reinforce gender divisions and such 'images, symbols, and forms of consciousness function ideologically to help to naturalize relations of power' (Chafetz, 2006, p. 182). Male journalists may refer to their training and knowledge of the craft of journalism, while female journalists often refer to their innate ability to show compassion in their reporting. This division could eventually play a key role in hiring, maintaining, and promoting female journalists. A practical need exists, however, to hire Syrian female journalists in order to meet the demands of Western media donors, and to reflect a progressive image of new and emerging outlets, both in and outside Syria.

In summary, there have been many Syrian women who have joined the numerous Western-funded institutions as media activists or field reporters post-2011, but they have faced the risk of being characterised as single-issue reporters, who report on matters only related to Syria, or representatives of interest groups. They often lack opportunities to report on other issues outside the Syrian conflict, and their wages are lower than their Western counterparts. This is reminiscent of the situation in the so-called refugee research industry from which Western researchers draw on Syrian researchers such as those who reside in Lebanon, in return for low wages and without genuine opportunities for permanent contracts or shared authorship (Sukarieh & Tannock, 2019).

CONCLUSION

The above discussion sheds light on displaced Syrian women who have found a new tool of discursive power in the digital media after 2011. Women's (re-) negotiation of their boundaries and roles has inevitably become transnational, following the displacement of millions of Syrians, resulting in many activities now being led in the global digital sphere. These women have managed to deploy digital media to challenge offline gender hierarchy, while they have struggled to contest this hierarchy within their professional communities, both in and outside Syria.

The digital space, on a positive note, has created a new avenue for Syrian women specifically, and Arab women generally, to question the patriarchal order. For instance, numerous social media accounts have raised awareness in Egypt, shedding light on cases of sexual assault that used to be covered up in public debates (BBC, 2020). In Kuwait, women joined the hashtag #Lan_asket, a social media campaign aiming to prevent harassment against women. The campaign featured dozens of testimonies from women who were victims of harassment or assault (Al-Jazeera English, 2021). In Yemen, too, the hashtag #We are all_Marwa_Al-Bayti was trending on social media in November 2020 in reference to Yemeni wife Al-Bayti, who died after her husband burned her in front of her children (Al-Qudsi, 2021); and, in March 2021, another social media campaign was launched, demanding revenge against a man who kidnapped a Yemeni girl, Asmaa Ramzi Hashem.

REFERENCES

Al-Azm, S. J. (2014, August 18). Syria in Revolt. Understanding the Unthinkable War. *Boston Review*. www.bostonreview.net/world/sadik-al-azm-syria-in-revolt

Al-Jarmani, A. A. (2017, December). Trends in the Feminist Movement in Light of the Arab Spring Revolutions (in Arabic). *Arab Reform Initiative.* https://docs. euromedwomen.foundation/files/ermwf-documents/7443_3.230.trendsoffeminis minthearabspringuprisings-thesyrianexperience.pdf

Al-Jazeera English. (2021, February 9). Women in Kuwait Launch Online Campaign Against Harassment. https://www.aljazeera.com/news/2021/2/9/anti-harassment-campaign-led-by-women-in-kuwait-gains-traction

Al-Qudsi, Z. (2021, April). Users of Social Networking Sites in Yemen Take the Right of Those Who Have Been Let Down by the Law. *Open Democracy.* https://bit. ly/3AgYUWe

Asaf, Y. (2017). Syrian Women and the Refugee Crisis: Surviving the Conflict, Building Peace, and Taking New Gender Roles. *Social Sciences, 6,* 110. https://doi. org/10.3390/socsci6030110

BBC. (2020, October 26). *Egypt sex Attacks Fuel "Feminist Revolution".* BBC. https:// www.bbc.co.uk/news/world-middle-east-54643463

Brinkerhoff, J. M. (2009). *Digital Diasporas. Identity and Transnational Engagement.* Cambridge University Press.

Carlson, M. (2015). Introduction: The many Boundaries of Journalism. In M. Carlson & S. C. Lewis (Eds.), *Boundaries of Journalism. Professionalism, Practices and Participation* (pp. 1–18). Routledge.

Chafetz, J. S. (2006). *Handbook of the Sociology of Gender.* Springer.

Committee to Protect Journalists. (n.d.). *Tal al-Mallohi Imprisoned.* https://cpj.org/ data/people/tal-al-mallohi/

Erhaim, Z. (2018). War on Your Doorsteps: Journalism and Activism. In A. Joumaa & K. Ramadan (Eds.), *Journalism in Times of War* (pp. 71–82). Doha.

Gerson, J. M., & Peiss, K. (1985). Boundaries, Negotiation, Consciousness: Reconceptualizing Gender Relations. *Social Problems, 32*(4), 317–331.

Habib, N. (2018). *Gender Role Changes and Their Impacts on Syrian Women Refugees in Berlin in Light of the Syrian Crisis,* WZB Discussion Paper, No. SP VI 2018–101, Wissenschaftszentrum Berlin für Sozialforschung (WZB), Berlin.

Jungherr, A., Posegga, O., & An, J. (2019). Discursive Power in Contemporary Media Systems: A Comparative Framework. *The International Journal of Press/Politics, 24*(4), 404–425.

Kabeer, N. (1999). Resources, Agency, Achievements: Reflections on the Measurement of Women's Empowerment. *Development and Change, 30*(3), 435–464.

Keddie, N. R. (2007). *Women in the Middle East.* Princeton University Press.

Kelly, S., & Breslin, J. (Eds.). (2010). *Women's Rights in the Middle East and North Africa.* Freedom House & Rowman and Littlefield.

Khalaf, R. (2016). *Women in Emerging Syrian Media. A Critical Discourse Analysis (2011–2016).* Female Journalists Network.

Kieffer, C. H. (1984). Citizen Empowerment: A Developmental Perspective. *Prevention in Human Services, 3,* 9–36.

Mellor, N. (2012). Hearts of Steel. *Feminist Media Studies, 12*(2), 180–194.

Mellor, N. (2021). The Syrian Press and Online Media: A driver of Arabism. In N. Miladi & N. Mellor (Eds.), *Routledge Handbook of Arab Media* (pp. 417–427). Routledge.

Nassar, A. (2021, February 28). The Syrian Feminist Movement Summarizes the Stages of the Revolution in Its Ten Years' (in Arabic). *Syria Direct.* https://bit.ly/3yuND3t

Othman, R. (n.d.). Feminist Freedom of Expression on Social Media' (in Arabic), Syrian Female Journalists Network. https://bit.ly/3jO4IS2

Robinson, S. (2015). Redrawing Borders from Within: Commenting on News Stories as Boundary Work. In M. Carlson & S. C. Lewis (Eds.), *Boundaries of Journalism. Professionalism, Practices and Participation* (pp. 152–168). Routledge.

Shackle, S. (2017, August 7). Syrian Feminists: "This Is the Chance the War Gave Us –to Empower Women". *The Guardian.* https://www.theguardian.com/global-development-professionals-network/2017/aug/07/syrian-feminists-chance-the-war-gave-us-to-empower-women

Spyksma, H. (2019). Unintentional Journalists. *Journalism Studies, 20*(1), 1–21. https://doi.org/10.1080/1461670X.2017.1351885

Sukarieh, M. (2015). The First Lady Phenomenon: Elites, States, and the Contradictory Politics of Women's Empowerment in the Neoliberal Arab World. *Comparative Studies of South Asia, Africa and the Middle East, 35*(3), 575–587. https://doi.org/10.1215/1089201X-3426421

Sukarieh, M., & Tannock, S. (2019). Subcontracting Academia: Alienation, Exploitation and Disillusionment in the UK Overseas Syrian Refugee Research Industry. *Antipode: A Radical Journal of Geography, 51*(2), 664–680.

Syrian Dialogue Centre. (2018). The Social Role of Syrian Women (in Arabic). 27 May 2018. Syria Dialogue Centre. https://bit.ly/2U4AzDF

Syrian Journalists Association. (2017). Female Journalists in Syria. *Reality and Challenges.* https://drive.google.com/file/d/0BxbX_uxZ3yqWT2EyXzcwSjgx-alk/view?resourcekey=0-yHD_7fTF9kWEH07Rqq5h9Q

WDR. (n.d.). *Women's Challenges in Light of the Development of social media' (in Arabic).* https://www1.wdr.de/nachrichten/wdrforyou/arabisch/doku-arabisch/kolumne-frauen-soziale-netzwerke-ar-100.html

Zimmerman, M. A. (1995). Psychological Empowerment: Issues and Illustrations. *American Journal of Community Psychology, 23*(5), 581–599.

CHAPTER 10

Following in Gezi's Steps: Women's Activism After the Gezi Protests

Hande Eslen-Ziya and Itir Erhart

This is just the beginning, the struggle continues.
Gezi Park Protests, 2013

INTRODUCTION

"This is just the beginning, the struggle continues" was a slogan that was chanted during the Gezi Protests. The protests started as a reaction to government policies infringing upon the civil liberties of secular groups affecting various gender, ethnic, religious, and class groups differently (Arat, 2013). These protests turned into a mass upheaval when bulldozers started to cut down trees in Gezi Park to build a shopping mall, without valid permission from the court. The people who demonstrated against this illegal destruction were confronted with police brutality. On the night of May 29, 2013, the protesters were removed from Gezi Park by the police. The protests, with no centralized leadership, generated many different interest groups and unusual alliances voicing their demands (Eslen-Ziya & Erhart, 2015). Women's groups were one of the most visible and vocal among them. Soon, the protests turned into a

H. Eslen-Ziya (✉)
Stavanger, Norway
e-mail: hande.eslen-ziya@uis.no

I. Erhart
Istanbul, Turkey
e-mail: itir.erhart@bilgi.edu.tr

L. H. Skalli, N. Eltantawy (eds.), *The Palgrave Handbook of Gender, Media and Communication in the Middle East and North Africa*, https://doi.org/10.1007/978-3-031-11980-4_10

155

unification of all groups that were against the totalitarian leadership, authoritarianism, patriarchal rule, and urban policies of the AKP (Justice and Development Party) and of President Erdoğan, Prime Minister at the time. Environmentalists, LGBTI (Lesbian, Gay, Bi-sexual, Transgender, and Intersex), Kurdish, feminist, socialist, and anti-capitalist Muslim groups joined forces and resisted together (Konda, 2014: 18–19). The movement continued with 'neighborhood forums' operating according to the principles of direct democracy and anti-government discourse.

The women's groups that took part in the protests questioned the patriarchal governmental policies and practices as well as the totalitarian leadership style of President Erdoğan. They lobbied and tweeted to change it (Eslen-Ziya & Erhart, 2015). They did this via non-violent protests, press releases, and forming online networking channels to communicate their messages. The women's protests became a reaction to the AKP government and its policies that would limit women's sexual and reproductive rights.

The Gezi Park uprising demonstrates a unique phenomenon in Turkish politics where group alliances of diverse groups with different political, social, and cultural backgrounds were established. By using social movements and resource mobilization theories, this chapter attempts to show that the women and women's organizations in these protests gendered the public sphere through their feminist slogans and chants, which brought about an alternative leadership model that distinguished itself from other feminist movements within the history of the Turkish Republic. To illustrate this, the chapter examines two questions: How do the Gezi Protests help us theorize transformations in the women's movements in Turkey? What was the mechanism of political mobilization used by the women and women's organizations in the campaigns following the Gezi Protests? To illustrate the second question, women's activism and women's demands for revoking proposed changes in the Turkish Penal Code will be studied. To address these questions, this chapter first displays women's activism during the Gezi Protests as a form of social movement. It argues that the Gezi Park movement's most distinguishing feature was its post-heroic, multi-leader, and, in some instances, leaderless, non-hierarchical configuration (Eslen-Ziya & Erhart, 2015). The authors show that, when coupled with the use of new media technologies (mainly Twitter and Facebook) and alternative forms of organizing, this new configuration produces a new wave of feminism.

METHODOLOGY

The data presented in this chapter was gathered throughout June 2014 when the End Violence Platform reacted to proposed changes to the Turkish Penal Code (TCK) and worked to raise awareness. The End Violence Platform, founded in 2011, represented the efforts mobilized for the new anti-violence law. It was an attempt to facilitate the advocacy process, increase networking between women's organizations, and establish relations with the media and better organize advocacy efforts around the law.[1]

The data was collected via manual searches using keywords through an advanced Twitter Search—the search function available on the Twitter website. The data set includes the tweets, posts, and posters using the hashtags #*TCK should be revoked* ('TCK should be revoked') and #*alleged penalty increase, in essence 'impunity'* ('alleged penalty increase', in essence 'impunity') as well as posts on the Facebook pages of these organizations supporting the End Violence Platform. The data set also includes advertisements placed in daily newspapers by the platform as well as TV appearances and interviews given by the representatives. Letters sent to politicians were also analyzed. The research team also followed the discussions on the bill on the Turkish Parliament's live-streaming channel.[2] The chapter drew on Charmaz's (2001) grounded theory approach to identify thematic codes for analyzing this data set. As a result, authors developed a conceptual understanding of the rich empirical data. Alongside line-by-line coding, they used focused coding to help comprehend the data. Once the codes were combined under code families, the authors came up with the most salient categories. These categories became the backbone of the analyses where they discussed how the new form of leadership and way of organizing inspired by Gezi is reflected in the reactions against the bill.

THEORETICAL FRAMEWORK

Social movements, defined as "collective organized actions to bring about or resist change by means of various historically conditioned strategies" (West & Blumberg, 1991: 4), seek to form a collective identity. Such identities set via "conflictual relations with clearly identified opponents…are linked by dense informal networks" (Della Porta & Diani, 2006: 20). As Zald and McCarthy (1987) state, the social movements that start as reactions to repressive political conditions have the goal to mobilize the masses and to create a favorable change. According to Ganz (2010), social movements emerge because of the efforts of purposeful actors, either individuals or organizations, with the goal to assert new public values, form new relationships, and mobilize political, economic, and cultural power and translate these values into action.

The female presence and resistance at the Gezi Protests fulfill the criteria applied to contemporary social movements in several ways. First, they are drawn from a population that shares a sense of grievance, providing a potential source of collective identity; second, their activities are intended to disrupt the established social orders. They also operate outside conventional forms of political participation, and their goal is to shift the existing distribution of power. The women protesters at Gezi exercised influence in empowering and

---

[1] http://www.wwhr.org/platforms/ Accessed (22.01.2021).
[2] http://www.trt.net.tr/anasayfa/canli.aspx?y=tv&k=trt3tbmmtv. Accessed (22.01.2021).

advancing the position of women and challenging the dominant patriarchal norms within society (Bretherton, 2003).

This research is unique as it takes concepts such as collective action and performance to a different dimension, one that has not been adequately explored in social movement theory previously. The action repertoire here will bring together humor, sarcasm, and demands in tweets and Facebook posts that were previously marginalized by social movement theory. Social movement theory emphasizes established political institutions and power at the expense of those not considered to be 'powerful' (Tarrow, 1998). However, the integration of these performances as a political tool and as a means of expression will enable the understanding of new political actors and spaces as well as claims.

As Jenkins (1983) argues, resource mobilization theory emphasizes the significance of outside contributions. Hence, social movements are organized and developed when social activists make use of the available resources around them. According to Eltantawy and Wiest (2011), resources such as time, money, organizational skills, and certain social or political opportunities are important for the success of social movements. In this case, it was the use of social media. The Gezi Protests were organized mainly via online channels due to their speed, relative freedom, and ease of usage, and online social activism was the main strategy employed by the women activists during the Gezi Protests and continued afterward.

According to Kellner (2002), online social activism and social media create new grounds for political struggle for voices and groups excluded from the mainstream media, which increases the potential for the involvement of additional oppositional groups' (i.e., other groups with similar aims). Consequently, social media provides an alternative for expressing the views of less privileged groups and organizing their movements in a participatory and non-hierarchical fashion (Wasserman, 2007; Al-Rawi, 2014). This freedom allows for the creation of a new public sphere (Lister et al., 2003), which Benkler (2006) called the networked public sphere. It is within this sphere that boycotts, protests, and demonstrations are initiated (Eltantawy & Wiest, 2011; Gouws & Hassim, 2011; Langman, 2005). In Egypt, Bahrain, and Kuwait, for instance, social media were used to mobilize, advocate, and coordinate political movements (Hamdy, 2009; Al-Rawi, 2014). These were achieved, according to Hamdy (2009), via the powerful impact of blogs in influencing media, which in return, influenced a larger public. Before showing how the networked public sphere created by the women's groups during the Gezi Protests continues to exist, this chapter will first discuss the history of the women's movements in Turkey.

THEORIZING TRANSFORMATIONS IN THE WOMEN'S MOVEMENTS

In the history of the Turkish Republic, there have been four periods when major improvements were made to the status of women. The early years of the Republic mark the first period when a new political thought and a new form of politico-moral order were introduced. In the mid-1920s, *laïcité* was introduced with the goal of dislocating the sacred order and instituting a new system of politics based on secularism in Turkey (Mardin, 1991; Berkes, 1998 and recently Diner & Toktaş, 2010; Eslen-Ziya & Korkut, 2010). During this period, the beginning of the modernization process started with the process of eliminating the Islamic political order in Turkey, which is when legal changes to the status of women came into effect. Polygamy was outlawed, and Islamic courts were abolished in favor of secular institutions, and women were granted equal rights in matters of divorce and child custody.

Though the modernization process itself is an important point in the history of the Turkish Republic and women's movements, the kind of secularism introduced and the position of women within the Republic and their form of feminism was top-down (Turam, 2008; Eslen-Ziya & Korkut, 2010). Turam refers to it as 'state feminism' (2008: 478). State feminism, also called Kemalist feminism, indicates the way women's rights were acquired. In Turkey, it was a top-down process of acquisition of rights, whereby women were targeted by the state during the process of modernization and treated "as a symbol and tool of modernization and Westernization" (Arat, 1994: 78). Despite these progressive legislative developments, women were assigned to traditional gender roles, and they were seen, defined, and expected to behave as the mothers of the next generation.

An alternative branch within the feminist movement, liberal feminism, came up with the idea of objecting to the patriarchal state discourse in the mid-1980s. Liberal feminism achieved significant gains for women and paved the way for various legal reforms to the status of women during the European Union (EU) accession process (which was later abandoned). For instance, the first widespread campaign of the new feminist movement targeted domestic violence, sexual harassment, and sexual violence. Hence, it was in the 1980s that women's groups started questioning the rights and duties assigned to them by the state and lobbied and networked to change these during the EU accession process (Eslen-Ziya 2012 and 2013). The motto of the era was "personal is political" (Tekeli, 1990: 33). This new feminist movement brought the private sphere and women's human rights violations in Turkey to public attention for the first time. This chapter considers that, in the early 2000s, both the emergence of a new feminist movement and the state's willingness to take part in EU accession talks, mark the beginning of the second period of feminism in Turkey, when major legal amendments regarding gender equality were achieved.

As argued by Eslen-Ziya (2013), the EU accession process enabled civil society to develop and created spaces for political participation which, in turn, gave women's groups the opportunity to influence policymaking. In Turkey, women's rights activists used the Europeanization process as a tool for achieving legislative changes (Eslen-Ziya, 2007), especially in the Turkish civil and penal code amendments that constituted a major step toward gender equality and protection of the sexual and bodily rights of women and girls. The

Europeanization process further improved gender equality, freedom of association and assembly and child protection, freedom of the press, thought, and expression. The amendments to the Turkish Constitution obliged the Turkish state to take all necessary measures to promote gender equality. Family courts have been established, employment laws amended, and there were new programs for tackling domestic violence and improving the access of girls to education. These changes were the result of a very effective campaign by a broad-based women's movement.

The women's movement in the early years of the Republic was composed of middle-class, secular, straight Turkish women (and excluded Islamist, Kurdish or LGBTI) women. As Çaha (2011: 438) argues, the "history of the women's movement in Turkey was strictly confined to a holistic approach and the movement was initiated largely by the middle-class". In the 1990s, however, a new wave in the women's movement emerged in Turkey that split feminism with challenges from the Islamist, Kurdish nationalist, and the LGBTI movements. Each of these groups had diverse worldviews with respect to the causes of and solutions to women's problems (Diner & Toktaş, 2010: 42). The independent Kurdish women's movement, which became visible in the 1990s, was part of this new wave of the feminist movement. Kurdish feminists were critical of, both the state and its assimilation policies and of the patriarchal Kurdish society—especially, the men of the Kurdish political movement who did not treat them as equals. Kurdish feminists also disapproved of Turkish feminism, which had been ignoring the Kurdish question and the problems of Kurdish women who lived in conflict zones in Turkey (Çaha, 2011). Kurdish feminists tried to draw attention to the dual exploitation they experienced as Kurdish women, both "in the patriarchal tribal system dominant in Kurdish culture and the imperialist system that the centralist Turkish state has imposed on the Kurdish people" (Diner & Toktaş, 2010: 42).

Islamist feminists fought for their right to be observant Muslims and women. They successfully mobilized university students to achieve the right to wear a *hijab* in the public sphere, especially in public offices and at universities. During their struggle with the patriarchal and secular state, they also expressed their discontent with Kemalist feminists who mostly saw *hijab*-wearing women as subjects bowing to a backward social order (Marshall, 2008). LGBTI feminist groups, on the other hand, focused almost solely on the problems the LGBTI community faces in Turkey, that is, discrimination, violence, and the lack of laws (Ilkkaracan, 2014). Transgender sex workers gained some visibility in the 1990s in their fight against police violence, yet rights around sexual orientation and sexual identity and advocacy for anti-discrimination provisions had not received support from other feminist groups.

Although Kemalist feminists, Liberal feminists, Islamist feminists, LGBTI feminist groups, and Kurdish feminists occasionally agreed with one another on social and political issues (like violence against women) and influenced each other, they mostly functioned as separate groups. There was solidarity between certain fractions, but not all of them were ready to accommodate each other

(Arat, 1998: 128), and they remained divergent on a wide range of women's issues. However, joined voices began to rise in the mid-2000s, when EU membership hopes waned and the European Union's force started to diminish, and the Turkish government started freely expressing and implementing its patriarchal discourse. In what follows, this chapter discusses this period, feminist groups' reactions to it, and why women's activism during and after the Gezi Protests can be said to mark the fourth wave of feminism in Turkey.

WOMEN'S ACTIVISM AT GEZI

Women's groups were reacting to the ruling AKP's attempts to push conservative gender norms by restricting women's choices. The target of the protests was often President Erdoğan who defined women in terms of their reproductive, homemaking, and nurturing functions, referred to them as his sisters, and asked them to have three children to secure the future of Turkey. Erdoğan also attacked abortion and cesarean births and referred to them as plots to stall Turkey's economic growth and a conspiracy to wipe the Turkish nation off the world stage (Eslen-Ziya, 2013).

> I am a Prime Minister who opposes caesarean births, and I know all this is being done on purpose. I know these are steps taken to prevent this country's population from growing further. I see abortion as murder, and I call upon those circles and members of the media who oppose my comments … I say every abortion is an Uludere … we are preparing the abortion legislation and we will pass it. (Hürriyet Daily News, 2012)[3]

With this analogy between abortion and an air strike by the Turkish military that killed 34 civilians in Uludere (a district on the Iraqi border) on December 2011, Erdoğan was asserting that abortion is murder, and thus unacceptable. On a similar note, Recep Akdağ, the Minister of Health at the time, stated that all women, including rape victims, should bear their children.[4] The Mayor of Ankara, Melih Gökçek,[5] further suggested that a woman should "kill herself before she considers abortion".

These attempts by the ruling party to regulate women's bodies and sexual encounters led to a public reaction. As Eslen-Ziya's (2013) analysis shows, the government's plans to politicize reproductive health and rights triggered major reactions from women's organizations and groups. The "My Body, My Choice"

---

[3] Hürriyet Daily News, 'Abortion sparks raging debate in Turkey'. 28 May 2012. Available at: http://www.hurriyetdailynews.com/abortion-sparks-raging%20debate.aspx?pageID=238&nid=21740 [accessed 25 April 2017].

[4] Radikal, 'Bakan o sözlerine açıklama getirdi'. 31 May 2012. Available at: http://www.radikal.com.tr/politika/bakan_o_sozlerine_aciklama_getirdi-1089678 [accessed 27 April 2017].

[5] Haberturk, 'Cocugun ne sucu var., anasi kendisini öldürsün'. 6 June 2012. Available at: http://www.haberturk.com/polemik/haber/747352-cocugun-ne-sucu-var-anasi-kendisini-oldursun- Accessed (20.01.2021).

campaign and some of the campaigns condemning Erdoğan, Arınç, and Gökçek for their sexist remarks also invited the participants to gather in and around Taksim to show their discontent. For instance, on June 10, 2012, a group met in Taksim and protested Gökçek and what feminist groups called his invitation to suicide. It was not until the Gezi Park protests, however, that tens of thousands actually took to the streets and protested together to express their discontent. After the brutal eviction of the park by the police, the anti-government protests grew in scope, size, and intensity and brought many different interest groups, including Kurds, LGBTI, anti-capitalist Muslims, socialists, and feminists' groups together.

During the protests and the two-week occupation of the park, women's groups expressed their discontent with the government by criticizing the way it casts women as mothers, sisters, and wives and protested against the implementation of social policies like banning abortion and limiting women's sexual and reproductive rights. They also challenged the patriarchal norms within society and re-claimed the public sphere, which is mostly populated by men. Inside the urban utopia, Gezi Park, they re-claimed ownership of their bodies as well as sexualities and freedom. Posters carried by women's activists read 'We will give birth on the way to Gezi' and 'We don't owe men or the state any children'. The slogans were accompanied by highly physical acts like marching, singing, chanting, and dancing. The body is a means of transmitting values and ideas but also a means of challenging and recreating them, and thus, in their embodied acts, the protesters externalized and performed their traumatic memories of discrimination and oppression. In Taylor's words, a performative shift took place where the antecedent—the dominant discourse that turned these activist women into de-sexualized 'ladies' and 'sisters'—was not erased but rather preserved and highlighted (Taylor, 2002 and 2003).

Solidarity Among Women's Groups

Feminist groups that dwelled in the harassment-free park during the occupation also organized a march to condemn secularist harassment targeting women in headscarves inside the park. This action was one of the milestones exemplifying solidarity among women. They wanted to show that they did not want a patriarch who would decide what women could and could not wear in public. On the posters they asked the patriarchs to get their 'hands off their bodies, headscarves and identities'. The protest was a condemnation of the discourses endorsed by the government. In this way, occupants of the urban utopia were calling out for alternative leadership.

This solidarity at Gezi is significant in that it signals the unification of Kemalist, Liberal, Islamist, LGBTI, and Kurdish feminists. It indicates that women themselves now see wearing the headscarf as a human rights issue and no longer a symbol of a backward social order. Similarly, slogans like 'someone attacking the veil cannot be human' or 'someone who attacks the veil is not one of us' uttered during these protests mark an important moment within Turkish feminist history: solidarity against the oppressive state. As feminist activist Nilgün Yurdalan observes:

> A woman coming to be harassed or attacked because of her headscarf is a very serious matter. In a situation like this, it is necessary to catch the attacker imme- diately. It was very important that the march was joined by women from different areas of society, whether they are secular, feminist, or socialist. (Eslen-Ziya & Erhart, 2015: 11)

For the Kurdish feminists, the elimination of patriarchal oppression of the female body has been an important field of struggle (Çaha, 2011: 446). The protests organized by the women at Gezi were against the patriarchal order of the ruling party and the Prime Minister's authoritarian discourse. Inside Gezi Park, the demonstrators created an alternative space: a harassment, rape, dis- crimination, murder, and 'Prime Minister'-free zone. The model of leadership they proposed for this utopic space was egalitarian, democratic, civil, and all- inclusive, where all voices would be allowed and heard. Collective empower- ment, social change/justice, and participative and linear decision-making structures (Porter & Daniel, 2007) were the key components of this new model.

A year after the protests, it was apparent how the general dynamics of the Gezi resistance, referred to by the activists as the *Gezi Spirit*, transferred to the outside world. The ways in which these women's activists employed all-inclusive strategies for the Gezi Protests will be discussed in the next section.

A YEAR AFTER GEZI: THE TURKISH PENAL CODE (TCK) REFORMS

In 2014, the umbrella organization End Violence Platform (with 270 women's groups and organizations) got started. Most were also members of the *Kadın Platformu* (Women's Platform), which is a coalition of about 256 local, national, and international organizations and NGOs fighting for equality and against violence. Both platforms are still active and are very diverse, bringing together organizations with various visions and missions (member groups include Flying Broom Women's Communication and Research Association, LGBTI Peace Initiative, Kayseri Women's Solidarity Association, Confederation of Public Workers Union, Equality Monitoring Women's Group, Women in Foreign Policy, and Confederation of Revolutionary Workers Unions).[6] The platforms aim to raise awareness and create public opinion around women's rights through online and offline campaigns, joined action and press releases. Their previous campaigns focused on issues like electoral gender quotas,

---

[6]The original names (respectively) are *Uçan Süpürge Kadin İletisim ve Araştırma Derneği*, LGBTI *Barış Girişimi*, *Kayseri Kadın Dayanışma Derneği*, *Birleşik Kamu İşçileri Konfederasyonu*, *Eşitlik İzleme Kadın Grubu*, *Dış Politikada Kadınlar*, and *Devrimci İşçi Sendikaları Konfederasyonu*.

domestic violence, and violence against the LGBTI community. This time, they demanded that the bill making changes to the TCK be revoked.

President Erdoğan had announced the bill in question at a press conference on May 11, 2014, arguing that it would help eliminate crimes against women and children:

> He who raises a hand to women raises a hand to humanity. He who raises a hand to a child, who subjects a child to violence, has sunk below humanity. This bill we are almost done preparing will be one that seriously increases the penalties in this issue. (Tahaoğlu, 2014)

However, as soon as the proposed amendments were published, the bill was severely criticized by the End Violence Platform. The spokesperson for the platform, attorney Hülya Gülbahar, objected to the section of the proposed changes that increased prison sentences for consensual sexual acts between youths aged 15–18. They argued that the proposed change threatened young women and men, as well as their parents, with long periods of incarceration.

On June 4, lawyers from the End Violence Platform published a declaration[7] stating that they were aware that investigation and prosecution authorities tended to safeguard the offender in sexual violence crimes. As such, they argued that the increase in penalties would not provide an outcome in favor of the victims but strengthen sexist mechanisms. They emphasized that sex crimes could only be eliminated by enforcing the current Penal Code.

They further discussed how sexual intercourse between adolescents at the ages of 15–18 and forced marriages under legal age are equated.[8] For them, consensual sex between youths and underage and forced marriages were two separate issues, and perceptual confusion by society and the judiciary must be avoided and child marriages regulated with a special penal code article. In Turkey, though the minimum age of marriage is 17, the civil code allows for marriage at the age of 16 with the consent of the court in 'exceptional circumstances' like sexual assault and rape. In addition, even younger girls were being forced to marry older men illegally through religious marriages. According to the Hacettepe University Institute of Population Studies (2008), 39.7% of married women report that they were 18 or younger and had not given consent when they got married. Legally equating these forced early marriages with consensual sex between two young adults was one of End Violence Platform's main concerns.

The current TCK does not include special or preventive regulations against early marriages (nor did the draft contain any regulations about this topic). While sexual abuse crimes committed against children by adults were always kept on the agenda for populism purposes, marriages between underage girls

---

[7] http://kadinkoalisyonu.org/siddete-son-platformu/ Accessed (22.01.2021).

[8] Mor Çatı, 'Views on Amendment of Articles 102, 103, 104 & 105 of Draft Turkish Penal Code (TPC)'. Available at: https://www.morcati.org.tr/en/home/264-views-on-amendment-of-articles-102-103-104-105-of-draft-turkish-penal-code-tpc [accessed 27 April 2017].

and older men were overlooked by the government.[9] The End Violence Platform reacted to the bill with the hashtags #*sözdecezaarttirimiozdecezasizlik* ('alleged penalty increase', in essence 'impunity') and #*TCK should be revoked* ('the penal code should be revoked').

CAMPAIGNING ONLINE AND OFFLINE

The End Violence Platform's reaction against the changes to the TCK revealed a certain lobbying strategy. They used both social media and traditional means of communication (sending letters to the authorities, placing advertisements in daily newspapers, publishing informative articles, and making TV show appearances) as complementary ways to increase the effectiveness and the scope of the campaign. In this section, the strategies employed by women's groups and their demands will be discussed in detail.

Women's organizations and activists first and foremost wanted to facilitate discussion about the proposed changes to the TCK and raise public awareness about the bill. To do this, they explained why the proposed changes fell short of meeting the objective, that is, deterring crime against women and children. Hülya Gülbahar frequently appeared on TV programs and stated the requests of women's organizations while at the same time explaining why the proposed changes, instead of solving the current social problems, would create new ones. She also invited the viewers to tweet using the campaign's hashtags. Many women's organizations like *Eşitiz Kadın Grubu* (All Equal Women's Group), *Mor Manşetler* (Purple Headlines), and *Abbasağa Kadın* (*Abbasağa* Women)[10] sent out tweets informing their followers about these TV programs and reminded them of the hashtags:

> @esitiz:Lawyer @hlyglbahar will talk about the demands of 270 #women's organizations tonight at 19:20 @HaberturkTV #TCK should be revoked @AbbasagaKadin @MorMansetler[11]
> Lawyer @hlyglbahar will explain why 270 women's organizations want #TCK to be revoked. Today, 19:20 @HaberturkTV #TCK should be revoked @hukuk_haberleri @sivilalan.[12]

Such an approach is significant because it reflects a double or even triple informative system in which the tweet itself becomes a way of disseminating intelligence about another information source (in this case, television). These

---

[9] Mor Çatı, 'Views on Amendment of Articles 102, 103, 104 & 105 of Draft Turkish Penal Code (TPC)'. Available at: https://www.morcati.org.tr/en/home/264-views-on-amendment-of-articles-102-103-104-105-of-draft-turkish-penal-code-tpc [accessed 27 April 2017].

[10] *Abbasağa* is one of the neighborhoods where regular forums are hosted to keep the demands of the Gezi protesters alive.

[11] '@esitiz:Av @hlyglbahar buaksam 19:20de @HaberturkTV de 270 #kadin orgutunun #tck-gericekilsin talebini konusacak @AbbasagaKadin @MorMansetler'.

[12] '@esitiz:Av @hlyglbahar buaksam 19:20de @HaberturkTV de 270 #kadin orgutunun #tck-gericekilsin talebini konusacak @AbbasagaKadin @MorMansetler'.

tweets also reflect the common position of women's organizations developed through frequent meetings and mail exchanges. This unified approach to information dissemination and empowering the less 'powerful' groups exemplifies strategies employed in contemporary social movements (Tarrow, 1998). Furthermore, the integration of old and new political tools serves to express understanding of new realms.

The arguments of women's groups were backed by the statements from professional organizations like the Child Psychiatry Association and Turkish Medical Association. In their arguments, these organizations outlined the problems that might have occurred if the government had proceeded with the planned draft. This chapter suggests that women's activists used such support to increase the credibility of their arguments when reaching out to the general public:

> Child Psychiatry Association warns against TCK #TCK should be revoked #thenewsexualabusebilldraft.[13]
>
> @ttborgtr Turkish Medical Association's warning: The proposed changes to sexual crimes law do not protect the victims.[14]

As resource mobilization theory would argue, by using outside contributions (in this case expert opinion), they increased their chances of disseminating their message and widening their support network. Furthermore, by using Twitter to direct their followers to certain TV programs, they not only helped their followers to be further informed, but also invited TV viewers to use Twitter and actively support their campaigns. This, in return, increased the visibility of their cause.

The End Violence Platform's demands can be summarized in three categories: first, there should be no statute of limitations for sexual crimes; second, the government must ban child marriages; third, the government should redraft the law after consulting women's organizations:

> #TCK should be revoked. There can't be a statute of limitations period for sexual crimes. #sozdecezaartirimiozdecezasizlik[15]
>
> @earmutcu The TCK which does not problematize early marriages but sees a potential for crime in flirting peers should be revoked. TCK should be revoked.[16]
>
> The changes to sexual crimes law drafted without consulting any NGO should be revoked. #sozdecezaartirimiozdecezasizlik TCK should be revoked.[17]

---

[13] '*Çocuk Psikiyatrisi Derneği TCK'ya karşı uyarı yayınladı TCK #TCKGeriCekilsin #yenicinselis tismaryasatasarısı*'.

[14] '*@ttborgtr TTB uyarıyor! Cinsel Saldırılarla ilgili yeni kanun düzenlemesi mağdurları korumuyor http://bit.ly/1kG08QI#TCKGeriCekilsin*'.

[15] '*#TCKGeriCekilsin Cinsel suçlarda zaman aşımı olmaz! #sozdecezaartirimiozdecezasizlik*'.

[16] '*@earmutcu Çocuk yaşta evlilikleri sorun etmeyip akranlar arası ilişkileri potansiyel suç olarak gören #TCKGeriCekilsin*'.

[17] '*Tek bir STK'ya danışılmadan hazırlanan yasal düzenleme #sozdecezaartirimiozdecezasizlik #TCKGeriCekilsin*'.

#TCKGeriCekilsin! TCK should be re-drafted after consulting women's and children's NGOs @ailebakanligi [picture, Ministry for Family Affairs and Social Politics].[18]

In the next section, the expression of these demands through women's online and offline activism will be presented. These demands included objecting to the draft TCK, explaining and raising awareness about the proposed bill, and condemning the proposed reduction of sentences for incest. The analysis will so show how the *Gezi Spirit* was kept alive in women's activism around TCK.

'WE OBJECT' ('*İTIRAZ EDIYORUZ*')

The End Violence Platform prepared and circulated posters with a common slogan: 'We object'. On these posters, various problems (reduced sentences for rape and sexual abuse, a proposed 'cure' for assailants, and the separation between 'attack' and 'abuse' in cases of sexual crimes against children) were criticized. The objection was that all these would lead to potential reduction of offenders' sentences and harsher sentences for teenagers engaging in consensual sexual intercourse. The End Violence Platform tried to make it clear that the proposed amendments, if implemented, would not protect children and women, nor deter attacks on them. The platform also underlined that, instead of solving social problems like forced early marriages, the amendment would further the AKP's conservative agenda. The posters were widely circulated on Twitter along with the hashtags #*TCK should be revoked* and #*sözdecezaarttirimiozdecezasizlik*. Some users also included their own messages and personal objections:

Get your hands off flirting teenagers and put them on rapists who marry children #alleged penalty increase, in essence 'impunity'.[19] (June 5)

#TCK should be revoked. The #alleged penalty increase will benefit the rapists and child molesters.[20] (June 10)

#TCK should be revoked. Sex is not a crime; sexual assault is not a psychological condition.[21] (June 10)

The TCK which does not deal with child marriages but considers affairs between peers, potential crime should be revoked #TCK should be revoked.[22] (June 11)

---

[18] '*#TCKGeriCekilsin! Kadın/Çocuk STK'larıyla tartışılıp yeniden düzenlensin.* @ailebakanligi *pic.twitter.com/zn5SM5ECny*'.

[19] '*Flirt eden gençlerle değil çocuklarla evlenen tecavüzcülerle uğraşın* #sözdecezaarttirimiozdecezasizlik'.

[20] '*#TCKGeriCekilsin Cinsel suçlara ceza artırımı değil cezasızlık getirecek bu tasarı sadece tecavüzcüler ve çocuk istismarcılarına yarayacak!*'.

[21] '*#TCKGeriCekilsin Seks suç değildir; cinsel istismar psikolojik bozukluk değildir*'.

[22] '*Çocuk yaşta evlilikleri sorun etmeyip akranlar arası ilişkileri potansiyel suç olarak gören* #TCKGeriCekilsin'.

They also started a Twitter campaign inviting users to tweet #*TCK should be revoked* on June 6 between 4 and 5 pm:

#TCK should be revoked. Start clicking! Today, 4–5 pm.[23] (June 6)

This was an attempt to make #*TCKshouldberevoked* a trending topic on Twitter. To further mobilize their resources, on June 10, 2014, they placed an advertisement in the mainstream daily Hürriyet.[24] This action exemplifies how social media and traditional media were used simultaneously to disseminate information and raise awareness. Their cause was supported by women parliamentary members and a single male parliamentarian, Hasip Kaplan of HDP (People's Democratic Party). The group also invited other parliamentarians to support this cause:

HDP Women's 4th general assembly opens with chants of "Women exist" TCK should be revoked #HDP.[25]

#TCK should be revoked. The omnibus bill being discussed at the parliament today will turn not only TCK but the whole legal system upside down. CHP, HDP, MHP [the other opposition parties] revoke the bill![26]

#TCK should be revoked @HasipKAPLAN gave an excellent talk on the omnibus bill at the parliament.[27]

While the previous tweets were sent out to ask for the support of the opposition parties, many users also tagged the Ministry for Family Affairs and Social Politics in their tweets in an attempt to mobilize them and get their attention before the proposal was debated in parliament. Then-President Gül was also tagged in some of the tweets and asked to veto the proposed changes. Women's groups further wrote a letter to Gül explaining their stance in detail and repeating their demands.[28] Some of the activists sent out tweets saying, 'our eyes are on the Parliament'. These activists tweeted the link to the live-streaming web page for Parliament and asked their followers to log in and watch the developments:

---

[23] '*#TCKGeriCekilsin Bugün 16.00–17.00 arası pamuk eller klavyeye! TCK tasarisi geri çekilsin!*'.
[24] Hürriyet. Available at: http://www.hurriyet.com.tr/gundem/26580958.asp [accessed 27 April 2017].
[25] '*HDP Kadın meclisi 4. genel kurulu "kadınlar vardır" ezgileri ile başlamak üzere #tckgericekilsin #HDP*'.
[26] '*TBMM.de tartışılan yeni torba yasa sadece TCK.yı değil, yargı sistemini de alt üst edecek. CHP, HDP, MHP tasarıyı reddedin!*'.
[27] '*#TCKGeriCekilsin az önce @HasipKAPLAN torba yasayı sorgulayan iyi bir konuşma yaptı TBMM*'.
[28] Bianet, '270 Kadın Örgütünden Cumhurbaşkanına Çağrı'. Available at: http://bianet.org/bianet/kadin/156586-270-kadin-orgutunden-cumhurbaskanina-cagri [accessed 27 April 2017].

The proposed bill on sexual crimes is being discussed at the parliament. WE'RE WATCHING http://www.tbmmtv.gov.tr/ TCK should be revoked.[29]

"Don't Touch My Child Body" ("*Çocuk Bedenime Dokunma*")

The posters and the messages shared on social media platforms (Facebook, Twitter), also objected to the proposed reduction of sentences for incest (Images 10.1 and 10.2):

> In the proposed bill, a FATHER who has sexual intercourse with his 15-year-old daughter will be sentenced to 12–23 years imprisonment. If the daughter is 16, he will be sentenced to 6–15 years! #donottouchmychildbody.[30]

Image 10.1 "Wake Up, I cannot Sleep" #donottouchmychildbody ('*Uyan, Ben Uyuyamıyorum #çocukbedenimedokunma*'—this image has been shared widely during the campaign to raise awareness.)

Image 10.2 "Will it go unpunished?" #donottouchmychildbody ('*Cezasız mı kalacak? #çocukbedenimedokunma*'—this image has been shared widely during the campaign to raise awareness.)

---

[29] '*TBMM'DE Cinsel Suçlar Yasa Tasarısı görüşülüyor! İZLİYORUZ! http://www.tbmmtv.gov.tr/ #yenicinselistismaryasatasarısı #TCKGeriCekilsin*'.

[30] '*Yeni Cinsel İstismar Yasa Tasarısı'na göre bir babanın 15 yaşındaki kızıyla cinsel ilişki kurması sonucu alacağı ceza 12–23 yıl iken, kızı 16 yaşında ise cezası 6–15 yıl olacaktır! #çocukbedenimedokunma*'.

These messages all reflected the general distrust in the legal system:

Who are you trying to protect now? RT @ifkfeminist: #TCK should be revoked (June 6).[31]

The protesters alleged that the supposed penalty increase was in fact a plot by the ruling party to protect the actual criminals and promote further conservatism. The solution they proposed involved revoking the bill and re-amending the code under the consultancy of leaders of non-governmental organizations in a way that would deter crimes against women, children, and LGBTI persons.

FOLLOWING GEZI'S FOOTSTEPS

Some of the tweets using the TCK-related hashtags included further democratic demands voiced during and following the Gezi Protests:

#DonotforgetSoma[32] #DonotforgetGezi #SaveTurkmen[33]
#Donotforgetthenorthernforests[34] #TCKshouldberevoked
#Taketothestreetsforanimals #Wehavewagedwar against pedophilia[35]
(June 17)

These tweets suggest that gender equality would only be possible in a world where everyone's rights were protected, including the rights of animals and the environment. The implication is that speciesism no longer echoes the debates about post-humanism and ecological feminism that were co-hosted by environmentalists and women's rights groups at Gezi Park. This unification of democratic demands that depict the Gezi Protests, in fact, characterizes a new era of feminism in Turkey.

CONCLUSION

By using social movements and resource mobilization theories, this chapter revealed that women and women's organizations gendered the public sphere through their feminist slogans and chants during the Gezi Park Protests. This gendering brought about an alternative, post-heroic, and even leaderless

---

[31] *'Kimi korumaya çalışıyorsunuz? RT @ifkfeminist: #TCKGeriCekilsin*
[32] Notes: Soma refers to the mining disaster in the town of Soma which claimed the lives of 301 workers.
[33] This hashtag refers to the Turkmen population in Iraq, which was at risk.
[34] This hashtag refers to the developmental projects, specifically the third suspension bridge over the Bosporus, which would have led to the destruction of the forests north of Istanbul.
[35] *'#SOMAUNUTULMAMALI #GeziyiUnutma #SaveTurkmen #KuzeyOrmanlarınıUnutma#t ckgericekilsin #HayvanlarİcinSokağaCık #pedofilesavasactik'*.

leadership model (Eslen-Ziya & Erhart, 2015) that distinguished itself from other feminist movements in the history of the Turkish Republic. For this reason, Gezi marks the beginning of the fourth wave of the feminist movement in Turkey, since it forged a broad alliance between feminist groups and created a new form of leadership and way of organizing.

This chapter answered the following questions: How do the Gezi Protests help us theorize transformations in the women's movements in Turkey? What were the mechanisms of political mobilization used by women and women's organizations in the campaigns regarding changes in women's rights following the Gezi Protests? As the chapter demonstrated, the protests that started as a sit-in at Gezi Park, mark a new era in the Turkish feminist movement, one in which women from all walks of life and backgrounds (Kemalist, Kurdish, Islamist, LGBTI, Liberal) were unified.

The mechanisms of political mobilization that the women's groups used were both social media platforms and traditional means of communication (sending letters to the authorities, placing advertisements in daily newspapers, publishing informative articles, and making TV show appearances). The chapter demonstrated that these means were used as complements to increase the effectiveness and the scope of the campaign. It argued that a few years after the protests, the *Gezi Spirit* was transferred to the outside world and the feminist utopia created inside the park became more and more visible in women's activism. This fact was evident in the End Violence Platform's demands to revoke the proposed changes to the Turkish Penal Code (TCK).

When compared to the historical feminist movements in the Turkish Republic, a major change is observed. The new wave is all-inclusive. Women's groups in their social media campaigns showed that gender equality cannot be achieved unless everyone's rights, including the rights of animals and the environment, are protected and no group is marginalized. Hence, the unification of democratic demands, which was the most significant message of the Gezi movement, marks the new era of Turkish feminism. Another important marker of this new era is the bottom-up nature of the movement using social media platforms. As Pearce observes, Gezi protesters "depended on this handy, accessible, and inexpensive medium, with accompanying tools such as mobile telephones, to communicate efficiently and broadly" (Pearce, 2014: 3). Seeing the efficiency of online campaigning during Gezi, women's groups took almost all their activism to online platforms—creating hashtags, developing strategies to make their messages trending topics, tagging politicians and journalists in their tweets to get their attention and to mobilize them. Whether these transformations could have happened without Gezi, solely with the help of new information technologies (mainly Twitter) is a valid question that remains unanswered. But as shown in this chapter, Twitter empowered the protesters. Various feminist (and other) groups could have come together without Gezi; however, sharing the same urban space (with its own library, child-care center, kitchen, and garden) and resisting together against the same 'enemy' accelerated the process.

Further research should investigate how the failed coup attempt on July 15, 2016, and the state of emergency subsequently declared (and extended three times following the incident) will shape women's activism and civil society in Turkey in the coming years. Under emergency powers granted to the current government, hundreds of non-governmental organizations and associations were closed for alleged links to terrorist organizations and threats to national security. More than 100,000 state employees (including soldiers, police officers, academics, health care workers, and teachers) have been dismissed. Several news outlets have been shut down. And yet, to this day, women's groups have remained vocal in their criticisms of the government and of human rights violations.

Acknowledgments Thanks to the members of the End Violence Platform for their continuous fight for women's rights in Turkey. We would like to thank the anonymous reviews received on this paper. Our sincere gratitude goes to editors, whose suggestions were exceptionally useful for the revisions.

REFERENCES

Al-Rawi, A. (2014). Framing the Online Women's Movements in the Arab world. *Information, Communication & Society, 17*(9), 1147–1161.

Arat, Z. (1994). Kemalism and Turkish Women. *Women and Politics, 14*(4), 57–80.

Arat, Y. (1998). Feminists, Islamists and Political Change in Turkey. *Political Psychology, 19*(1), 117–131.

Arat, Y. (2013). Violence, Resistance and Gezi Park. *International Journal of Middle East Studies, 45*(4), 807–809.

Benkler, Y. (2006). *The Wealth of Networks: How Social Production Transforms Markets and Freedoms.* Yale University Press.

Berkes, N. (1964/1998). *The Development of Secularism in Turkey.* Hurst & Company.

Bretherton, C. (2003). Movements, Networks, Hierarchies: A Gender Perspective on Global Environmental Governance. *Global Environmental Politics, 3*(2), 103–118.

Çaha, Ö. (2011). The Kurdish Women's Movement: A Third-Wave Feminism Within the Turkish Context. *Turkish Studies, 12*(3), 435–449.

Charmaz, K. (2001). Qualitative Interviewing and Grounded Theory Analysis. In J. F. Gubrium & J. A. Holstein (Eds.), *Handbook of Interview Research: Context and Method* (pp. 675–694). Sage.

Della Porta, D., & Diani, M. (2006). *Social Movements: An Introduction.* Blackwell.

Diner, Ç., & Toktaş, Ş. (2010). Waves of Feminism in Turkey: Kemalist, Islamist and Kurdish Women's Movements in an Era of Globalization. *Journal of Balkan and Near Eastern Studies, 12*(1), 41–57.

Eltantawy, N., & Wiest, J. B. (2011). Social Media in the Egyptian Revolution: Reconsidering Resource Mobilization Theory. *International Journal of Communication, 5*, 1207–1224.

Eslen-Ziya, H. (2012). The Role of Women's Activism in the Amendments of the Turkish Penal Code: A Success Story. *Journal of Sociological Research, 15*(1), 119–149.

Eslen-Ziya, H. (2013). Social Media and Turkish Feminism: New Resources for Social Activism. From Veiling to Blogging: Women and Media in the Middle East. *Special Issue of Feminist Media Studies, 13*(5), 860–870.

Eslen-Ziya, H., & Erhart, I. (2015). Towards Post-Heroic Leadership: A Case Study of Gezi's Collaborating Multiple Leaders. Special Issue: Leadership and Authority in a Crises-Constructing World. *Leadership, 11*(4), 471–488.

Eslen-Ziya, H., & Korkut, U. (2010). Political Religion and Politicized Women in Turkey: Hegemonic Republicanism Revisited. *Totalitarian Movements and Political Religions (Renamed Politics, Religion and Ideology), 11*(3–4), 311–326.

Ganz, M. (2010). Leading Change: Leadership, Organization, and Social Movements. In N. Nitin & K. Rakesh (Eds.), *The Handbook of Leadership Theory and Practice* (pp. 509–550). Harvard Business Review Press.

Hacettepe University Institute of Population Studies. (2008). *2008 Turkey Demographic and Health Survey.* Hacettepe University Institute of Population Studies, T.R. Ministry of Development and TÜBİTAK, Ankara, Turkey. Accessed January 22, 2021, from http://www.hips.hacettepe.edu.tr/TNSA2008-AnaRapor.pdf.

Hamdy, N. (2009). Arab Citizen Journalism in Action: Challenging Mainstream Media, Authorities and Media Laws. *Westminster Papers in Communication and Culture, 6*(1), 92–112.

Ilkkaracan, P. (2014). Democratization in Turkey from a Gender Perspective. In C. Rodriguez, A. Avalos, & H. Yilmaz (Eds.), *Turkey's Democratization Process* (pp. 154–176). Routledge.

Jenkins, J. C. (1983). Resource Mobilization Theory and the Study of Social Movements. *Annual Review of Sociology, 9*, 527–553.

Kellner, D. (2002). Globalization, Techno-Politics and Revolution. In J. Foran (Ed.), *The Future of Revolutions* (pp. 180–190). Zed Books.

Konda. (2014). *Konda Gezi Raporu, Electronic Version.* Accessed January 22, 2021, from http://konda.com.tr/en/raporlar/KONDA_Gezi_Report.pdf

Langman, L. (2005). From Virtual Public Spheres to Global Justice: A Critical Theory of Interworked Social Movements. *Sociological Theory, 23*(1), 42–74.

Lister, M., Dovey, J., Giddings, S., Grant, I., & Kelly, K. (2003). *New Media: A Critical Introduction.* Routledge.

Mardin, Ş. (1991). The Just and the Unjust. *Daedalus/Religion and Politics, 120*(3), 113–129.

Pearce, S. C. (2014). Producing culture in Taksim. In V. S. Öğütle & E. Göker (Eds.), *Gezi and Sociology: Facing the Object, Constructing the Object.* Istanbul, Turkey.

Porter, N., & Daniel, J. (2007). Developing Transformational Leaders: Theory to Practice. In J. Lau Chin & B. Lott (Eds.), *Women and Leadership: Transforming Visions and Diverse Voices* (pp. 245–263). Blackwell.

Tahaoğlu, Ç. (2014, 5 June). 243 Women's Organizations Object to Sexual Crimes Bill, Bianet. Accessed April 28, 2017, from http://bianet.org/english/women/156224-243-women-s-organizations-object-to-sexual-crimes-bill.

Tarrow, S. (1998). *Power in Movement.* Cambridge University Press.

Taylor, D. (2002). "You are Here": The DNA of Performance. *The Drama Review, 46*(1), 149–169.

Taylor, D. (2003). *The Archive and the Repertoire: Performing Cultural Memory in the Americas.* Duke University Press.

Tekeli, Ş. (1990). 1980'ler Türkiye'sinde kadınlar. In Ş. Tekeli (Ed.), *1980'ler Türkiye'sinde Kadın Bakış Açısından Kadınlar.* İstanbul.

Turam, B. (2008). Turkish Women Divided by Politics: Secularist Activism Versus Pious Non-Resistance. *International Feminist Journal of Politics, 10*(4), 475–494.

Wasserman, H. (2007). Is a New Worldwide Web Possible? An Explorative Comparison of the Use of ICTs by two South African Social Movements. *African Studies Review, 50*(1), 109–131.

West, G., & Blumberg, R. (1991). Reconstructing Social Protest from a Feminist Perspective. In G. West & R. L. Blumberg (Eds.), *Women and Social Protest* (pp. 3–36). Oxford University Press.

Zald, M., & McCarthy, D. (Eds.). (1987). *Social Movements in an Organizational Society*. Transaction.

CHAPTER 11

Egypt's #MeToo in the Shadow of Revolution: Digital Activism and the Demobilization of the Sexual Harassment Movement

Angie Abdelmonem

In March 2018, Egyptian-American journalist Mona el-Tahawy questioned in a New York Times op-ed whether Egypt was experiencing its #MeToo moment when 23-year-old Rania Fahmy won a criminal case against her sexual harasser in the Qena Criminal Court (El-Tahawy, 2018). Over 2018 and 2019, Egyptian and international media coverage highlighted how women were using the #MeToo hashtag to speak out against sexual harassment, as well as the perils of doing so and the way the movement was falling short (Eltantawy, 2019). Except for Fahmy's high-profile case, and that of Gehad el-Rawy in the same year, #MeToo mostly limped along in Egypt until June 30, 2020, when poet and activist Sabah Khodir posted an image on Instagram of a young man, Ahmed Bassam Zaky, accused by a fellow student at the American University in Cairo (AUC) of sexual harassment. Her post inspired AUC student Nadeen Ashraf to create a new Instagram account she called @assaultpolice to provide a forum for the growing number of accusations leveled against Zaky and to call for an investigation into a 2014 gang rape that took place at the Fairmont Hotel. More testimonies emerged under the hashtags #NotOnlyAhmedZaki, #ScandalizetheHarasser, and #ListentoEgyptianWomen'sVoices. Because of this new flurry of activity, @assaultpolice's work was lauded as advancing Egypt's #MeToo movement.

A. Abdelmonem (✉)
Arizona State University, Tempe, AZ, USA
e-mail: angie.abdelmonem@asu.edu

175

L. H. Skalli, N. Eltantawy (eds.), *The Palgrave Handbook of Gender, Media and Communication in the Middle East and North Africa,*
https://doi.org/10.1007/978-3-031-11980-4_11

Yet the work of #MeToo online activists was made possible by earlier activism. Following the January 25, 2011 revolution, anti-sexual harassment initiatives expanded and flourished. This itself came after decades of political cooptation and the NGOization and fragmentation of civil society, in which sexual violence work targeted private sphere issues, such as domestic violence, rape, and female genital cutting/mutilation (Al-Ali, 2000; Jad, 2003; Tadros, 2015). With the revolution, a new generation of activists shifted the focus to violence that women faced in the public sphere.[1] Groups such as HarassMap, Harakat Bassma (Imprint Movement), Ded el-Taharrush (Anti-Sexual Harassment Movement), Shoft Ta7rosh (I Saw Harassment), OpAntiSH, and others deployed a multiplicity of techniques to confront the problem of sexual harassment. These initiatives operated within a context of diminished state oversight, which provided political opportunities for grassroots activism untenable prior to and since the revolution. Like the current #MeToo activism, these earlier activists used social media and crowdmapping to provide alternative spaces of testimony. Unlike the current #MeToo activism, however, they were also able to exploit digital media to mobilize large swaths of volunteers in on-the-ground campaigns and push out new conceptual frames of gendered norms and sexual violence. Since 2014, there has been an active state effort to coopt the movement, leading to its subsequent demobilization.

This chapter examines earlier and current forms of digital activism to combat sexual harassment in Egypt. It argues that the country's #MeToo social media hashtag activism is limited in scope, resulting from ongoing processes of the movement's demobilization and the Egyptian state's attempt to control the narrative and put an end to civil society activism on the issue. Such digital activism, however, represents activist/citizen efforts to keep attention focused on sexual harassment, which remains a pervasive social problem in Egypt. Drawing on data collected over four periods (pre-dissertation field work 2012, dissertation field work 2013–2014, post-dissertation field work follow-up 2015, and post-doctoral research 2019), including participant observation and 11 interviews with eight activists and civil society professionals, this chapter provides a detailed examination of the history of this activism, with attention to the role of technology, and the processes of its decline.

ICTs AND SOCIAL MOVEMENTS: THEORETICAL CONSIDERATIONS

Since their emergence in the early-to-mid 2000s, social media forums like Twitter and Facebook, blog sites, crowdmapping, and even widescale use of SMS have been critical features of social and political movements. Scholars drawing on social movement theorizing have explored the complex ways in

---

[1] Interview, GIZ Project Manager and coordinator of the Network of Women's Rights Organizations in Egypt, June 2019.

which such information and communication technologies (ICTs), deployed in a multiplicity of sociopolitical contexts, bolster the ability of various actors to mobilize resources, exploit political opportunities, frame messages, and engage in contentious politics (Eltantawy & Wiest, 2011; Khamis, 2011; Lim, 2012; ElSayed & Rizzo, 2014; Tadros, 2015; Kassem, 2017). Writing about protests to challenge authoritarian power in China, Cai and Zhou (2016) state that ICTs "can reduce participation costs, promote collective identity, create communities, facilitate the diffusion of protest activities, and help attract international attention and support" (733). Aouragh and Alexander (2011), however, argue for the need to distinguish between Internet-based technologies as both spaces and tools of dissidence (1345). As a space, the Internet serves as a means through which actors may frame discourses and cultivate subjectivities to build critical mass, while as a tool it provides one approach to action and mobilization (Aouragh & Alexander, 2011, 1347–1349). The authors are cautious about over-prescribing the impact of ICT use, arguing that the Egyptian revolution built on a long history of pro-democratic protest, such that when the Egyptian state shut down satellite communications activists continued to mobilize without ICTs. Cai and Zhou similarly examine how authoritarian regimes balance controls over ICTs, noting the state is itself a user and that ICTs are central to their economic functioning, but that they heavily regulate citizen use to prevent threats to regime (732–736). Their analysis illustrates how ICT use exists between episodes of guarded tolerance and strict constraints, such that the effects of ICT use are tied to prevailing political conditions.

Building on this, I argue that ICTs remain one of the last spaces and tools through which activists may try to keep movements alive in periods of demobilization when state repression limits political opportunities for mobilization, framing, and contention. While the last decade of research has demonstrated how ICTs have become central elements of social movement emergence and expansion, here I seek to broaden this theorizing to examine ICT use when a movement declines due to strict political controls on civil society activism. Tarrow (2011) examines demobilization as part of the overall cycle of conflict and contention (201–206). He discusses how movements may be initiated by innovation, how opportunities vary for "early risers" versus "late comers," and that as movements continue, different actors may pursue different goals, take on differential risks, and break into factions in ways that reduces popular participation (203–205). In Egypt, ICT use helped build the anti-sexual harassment movement prior to and during the revolution. The political opportunities emerging from the breakdown of order during the revolution paved the way for ICT innovation that expanded the movement. The post-revolutionary clamp-down disrupted cycles of contention with respect to anti-sexual harassment work as demobilization processes were forced on activists, who otherwise might have continued to engage in contentious political action. Critical elements of demobilization include the disappearance of popular protests from the streets and institutionalization as activists begin to compromise with political leaders. Tarrow argues that government repression restabilizes relations between sociopolitical actors with some reforms following (2011, 209). With respect to sexual harassment in Egypt, restabilization has reproduced a prevailing status quo that activists sought to transform, and reforms implemented by the state are largely cosmetic. ICT use in Egypt's current #MeToo moment demonstrates that, despite demobilization, anti-sexual harassment activists continue to engage in a politics of care—Internet spaces and tools serve as a popular pressure release mechanism as continuous low levels of social media reporting *and* periodic bursts of expanded activity show that underlying problems continue to fester. ICTs allow activists to cautiously ride the wave of state repression, keeping the issue of sexual harassment alive in the popular consciousness, even if they are not framing discourses to rouse public contention until political conditions shift and opportunities emerge for new forms of mobilization.

ANTI-SEXUAL HARASSMENT ACTIVISM IN EGYPT, 2005–2013

Activism to combat sexual harassment in Egypt emerged in late 2005. Media technologies were an important part of its growth and expansion, if not in its founding. Following on the heels of a short-lived attempt by activists to combat politically-motivated sexual assault earlier that year (El-Mahdi, 2010), the Egyptian Center for Women's Rights (ECWR), an NGO working on women's political participation, began a program to address the street sexual harassment problem. The initial goal of ECWR's program was to promote societal change to end the problem of everyday forms of sexual harassment. In November, ECWR's then International Relations Specialist and volunteers began working to gauge the scope of the problem.[2] Over the course of 2006, they collected surveys, held information sessions on university campuses and at cultural centers, conducted focus groups, produced pamphlets and videos in collaboration with NGO partners, and raised awareness through mass media outlets, in which ECWR director Nehad Abul Komsan appeared on a number of talk shows (Rizzo et al., 2012; Rizzo, 2014). ECWR's International Relations Specialist was in frequent discussions with political bloggers, including Wael Abbas and Nermine Edris, following a high-profile incident of mass sexual harassment

---

[2] Activist names are withheld to protect their safety. In some cases, activists have requested full anonymity, including not using former titles. I have retained the use of ECWR's director's name as she is a public figure, having briefly served as former Secretary-General to the reconstituted National Council for Women under the interim government in 2012 (https://ecwronline.org/?page_id=8663).

during the 2006 Eid el-Adhah holiday in downtown Cairo.[3] In this early work, ECWR activists engaged in contentiously defining sexual harassment in ways that clashed with popular wisdom, and they sought to foment collective action, but not in ways that made demands of state entities. In 2007, ECWR received UNFPA funding for their program, which they named "Making Our Streets Safe for Everyone" (also called "Safe Streets" by staff), precipitating a shift to a policy-oriented approach. They hired program staff, expanded research, produced reports, wrote draft legislation for a sexual harassment law, and developed a teacher training program aimed at prevention at an early age (FIDH, 2014; Rizzo et al., 2012). In 2008, they published "Clouds in Egypt's Sky," the first report to define and describe the scope of sexual harassment in Egypt, which they followed up with a 2009 report on the legal gaps across the Middle East (Hassan et al., 2008; Abul Komsan, 2009). Some scholars have raised concerns about ECWR's early effort targeting sociocultural norms (Abu Lughod, 2011, Amar, 2011), arguing they inadvertently advanced the security state's agenda of targeting young working-class men and engaged in commercializing rights work by accepting corporate sponsorships to promote a proposed crowdmapping platform.

However, ECWR's "cultural" approach infused the later work of the popular social initiative, HarassMap, which was formed in late 2010 by ECWR's International Relations Specialist and "Safe Streets" Program Manager (Abdelmonem, 2015; Abdelmonem & Galan, 2017).[4] Both left ECWR in 2009, concerned that ECWR's growing policy orientation was slowing down mobilizational efforts. Before that, though, the tech group NiJel approached them about implementing the Ushahidi crowdmapping platform to address sexual harassment in Egypt (Young, 2014; Skalli, 2014; Grove, 2015). Between 2009 and 2010, HarassMap's four co-founders developed the platform and explored options for deploying it and other programming both formally and informally as an unregistered community-based effort. In October, they went live with their platform and immediately received hundreds of reports and emails from people across Cairo and other cities in Egypt interested in volunteering.[5] Crowdmapping offered a way to raise public awareness of sexual harassment, but HarassMap's co-founders wanted their new initiative to do the work that the Egyptian government had prevented NGOized civil society from doing to that point, which was to mobilize the community.

---

[3] Interview, HarassMap co-founder, January 2014; Personal conversation, HarassMap co-founder, October 2021.

[4] These two former ECWR staff members brought on two colleagues to join them in founding HarassMap.

[5] There are no published analyses on the class dimensions of Egyptian anti-sexual harassment activism. Based on my participant observation data, HarassMap had outreach teams formed by residents of various neighborhoods that loosely reference upper, middle, or lower class, from elite Zamalek to the 'ashwai'yaat (slums) of Manshiyet Nasr. They had teams across major urban cities and smaller, rural towns—one of their more active captains, whom I spoke with at multiple trainings, was a middle-aged woman from the conservative, Upper Egyptian, rural town of Sohag.

Bystander intervention and volunteerism were two important features of anti-sexual harassment activism as it evolved following the January 25, 2011 revolution. HarassMap had held a single volunteers' meeting a month prior to the 18 days of activism that resulted in Hosni Mubarak's February 11 ouster. Those 18 days were widely reported to be sexual harassment free (Langohr, 2013), though one case highlighted (and, perhaps, foreshadowed) a different reality. CBS correspondent Lara Logan was raped by a mob in the Tahrir Square protests on the day Mubarak stepped down (Replogle, 2011). At the women's day march on March 8, activists and protestors were also sexually harassed and 17 women were arrested, and forced to undergo virginity testing, including Samira Ibrahim, which the military under then Field Marshal Abdel Fattah el-Sisi defended (Hafez, 2014b). Politicized sexual violence against women (VAW) continued throughout 2011 and 2012, including the infamous Blue Bra Girl incident, in which soldiers were caught on video stomping on a woman's exposed chest (Hafez, 2014a, 2014b). By late 2012, the case of Yasmine el-Baramawy highlighted a new phenomenon of mob assault in protest settings, in which women were singled out, surrounded by concentric rings of men, then assaulted and raped—this became known as the Circles of Hell (Langohr, 2013). Much of this violence was believed to be organized and backed by the state, as had occurred with Black Wednesday.[6] In early 2012, new groups emerged to address protest sexual violence and everyday street sexual harassment, and they did so by mobilizing swaths of volunteers to intervene and to encourage others to do the same.

Online-only groups harnessed the power of social media to encourage people to name and shame their harassers, such as Ifdah Mutaharrish (Scandalize the Harasser). Online-offline groups comprised of volunteers worked to intervene in sexual harassment incidents either directly or to encourage bystanders to do so. Harakat Bassma, Ded el-Taharrush, and Shoft Ta7rosh were prominent groups focused on everyday sexual harassment. Harakat Bassma became known for its highly regimented patrols of neighborhood streets and metro stations, and Shoft Ta7rosh similarly became known for its work in crowd conditions, particularly during the Eid celebrations (Tadros, 2014, 2015). Ded el-Taharrush engaged in similar patrol work, and like HarassMap, they also took a bystander intervention approach, speaking to people in the street to convince them to stand up against sexual harassment, while also circulating photos of harassers. Groups such as Operation Anti-Sexual Harassment (OpAntiSH) and Tahrir Bodyguard emerged to specifically address sexual

---

[6] There has been wide belief that Tahrir sexual violence was perpetrated by state-hired *baltigiyya*, or thugs (Amar, 2011; Langohr, 2013), but a Nazra program director countered this, noting, "Everyone was saying it's the MB [Muslim Brotherhood] and it's politically commissioned. No, I'm sorry, from what we've seen it's not politically commissioned. It's the average man on the street and it is a cultural epidemic and it's been getting worse because of the constant state of impunity…" (Interview, February 2014).

violence in protest settings, pulling women out of the Circles of Hell (Galan, 2016). Though they operated offline, they all utilized digital technologies in specific ways to organize work and raise awareness not only about sexual harassment but also about the gendered nature of the problem.

Digital Activism to Combat Sexual Harassment

Technological activism to combat street/public sexual harassment in Egypt gained international attention through HarassMap's innovative work with crowdmapping (Skalli, 2014; Grove, 2015; Young, 2014). Though HarassMap was founded before the revolution, they operated in the context of the revolutionary period. In that political moment, when police had retreated from the streets and government oversight of civil society had decreased (El-Meehy, 2017), HarassMap's digital activism allowed them to bridge online and offline spaces and served as a model for the expansion of the movement. Powered by web 2.0 interactive technology, HarassMap's Ushahidi crowdmap provided a means for individuals to submit a report of sexual harassment, via the web interface or SMS, and pin the location of an incident on a map. HarassMap's co-founders launched their platform to create a forum for Egyptian women and girls to discuss their experiences and, more importantly, receive information on legal and psychological services. Offline, HarassMap's early plans included targeting map "hotspots" for community outreach, to convince bystanders to speak up against sexual harassment in affected neighborhoods. Problems with map reporting, such as map pins that didn't correspond to locational information in reports and insufficient numbers of reports, quickly made it clear that map hotspots were problematic. HarassMap's co-founders understood that sexual harassment existed everywhere, even if the public didn't report. Their strategy shifted from targeting map hotpots to conducting outreach campaigns in volunteers' home neighborhoods. HarassMap's community outreach program evolved to training volunteers to become "community captains," who recruited other volunteers to join their neighborhood teams. Once or twice a month, they would conduct outreach events to convince friends and neighbors to speak out against sexual harassment. Map reports became a subsidiary tool for captains—they could pull reports before an outreach event to show bystanders what others in their communities had experienced, but map reports did not guide outreach work.

Beyond crowdmapping, HarassMap and other anti-sexual harassment initiatives actively engaged with social media to receive reports, push out information, and organize on-the-ground meetings and events. In lieu of creating and maintaining a website, Facebook and Twitter became the two primary platforms in use between 2012 and 2014. Most of the prominent groups had Facebook followers numbering in the tens to hundreds of thousands (OpAntiSH 36 k; Bassma 38 k; Shoft Ta7rosh 53 k, HarassMap 71 k, Ded el-Taharrush 211 k). A former HarassMap Director of Marketing and Communications noted that "social media is wonderful because its free, accessible, and social...it's about interaction, which is important if you are trying to change mindsets."[7] A Ded el-Taharrush co-founder also stated:

> We don't have a website, we don't have an app... but we have a Facebook page and our Facebook page today is 120,000 likes...which is huge because when you post something you can see that it's seen by 10,000 people for one post... you can influence people. Social media is important, really we started on social media and we communicate from social media, we're getting people on the ground from social media and when we have an event, we need volunteers, we see a lot of volunteer requests from social media.[8]

Social media allowed groups to post images from community events, festivals, street patrols, public meetings, press conferences, and university outreach days. It allowed groups to respond to and engage with members of the public. Groups put out calls for volunteers through social media. HarassMap's community outreach teams organized their own community Facebook pages where they promoted work in their neighborhoods or cities (if outside of Cairo). Social media was also the primary venue through which most of the major anti-sexual harassment awareness campaigns were organized, including the 2013 joint "salahha fi dimaghak" (Get it Right) campaign and HarassMap's 2014 "mish sakta" (I am Not Silent) and 2015 "mutaharrish mugrim" (The Harasser is a Criminal) campaigns.[9] Moreover, Twitter analytics allowed groups to analyze the reach of their campaigns. For instance, during "salahha fi dimaghak," organizers were able to monitor the campaign's geographic distribution, top tweets, the number of potential impressions (numbering close to 15 million at the campaign's peak), and major influencers. Social media was and arguably still is the most critical tool for anti-sexual harassment activism in Egypt.

THE DEMOBILIZATION OF THE ANTI-SEXUAL HARASSMENT MOVEMENT, 2014 AND BEYOND

The year 2014 witnessed a number of crucial events for sexual harassment activism in Egypt. In March, an incident of mass sexual harassment targeting a young woman on the Cairo University campus, caught on video and circulated via social media, sparked a massive public outcry that led interim President Adly Mansour to approve a new penal code law, Article 306, illegalizing sexual harassment (Abdelmonem & Galan, 2017; LOC, 2014). On June 7, at President Abdel Fattah el-Sisi's inauguration celebration in Tahrir Square, Shoft Ta7rosh reported that at least six women had been sexually harassed and assaulted, though the actual number may have been higher, with at least one caught on video (Langohr, 2014; Taha, 2014). On his second day in office, Sisi

---

[7] Interview, HarassMap Director Marketing and Communications, April 2014.

[8] Interview, Ded el-Taharrush co-founder, April 2014.

[9] "Salahha fi dimaghak" was a collaborative effort by HarassMap, Tahrir Bodyguard, OpAntiSH, Nazra for Feminist Studies, and the Egyptian Initiative for Personal Rights (EIPR).

ordered the Ministry of Interior, which had created an internal VAW unit and later a sexual harassment hotline, to crack down on the problem, and a few days later he formed a ministerial committee that included individuals from the National Council for Women, Al Azhar, and the Coptic Church to develop a plan for increasing public security for women (Begum, 2014; Saleh, 2014). On Sisi's third day in office, he visited a survivor of the inauguration day mass assault in the hospital, vowing a strict implementation of the law to put a stop to sexual harassment (ABCNews, 2014; Egyptian Streets, 2014). Some activists criticized Sisi for using the hospital visit as propaganda, and HarassMap's former Community Outreach Director noted sexual harassment to be Sisi's "favorite social cause" (Mada Masr, 2014).[10] However, government efforts in this year sparked some hope that the state would seriously address the sexual harassment problem and renewed calls for a national strategy to combat violence against women in Egypt (Nazra, 2014; Langohr, 2014).

It is important to note here that following the July 2013 deposal of Muslim Brotherhood President Mohamed Morsi and over the span of the next several years, the state implemented a number of new laws designed to coopt or suppress opposition. In November 2013, Mansour approved Law 107, the "Protest Law," which made public organizing without a permit illegal (Hamzawy, 2016). The Ministry of Social Solidarity set a deadline for all independent initiatives and organizations working on social justice causes to formally register as NGOs by November 2014, under Law 84 of 2002 ("The NGO Law"), or face shut down and even jail time (HRW, 2014). Throughout 2014, activists had heard of upcoming amendments to the NGO law, sparking fears that it would be worse than the 2002 law. By the end of the year, Bassma submitted their registration paperwork Other initiatives chose not to. HarassMap had in 2012 incubated with the NGO Nahdat el-Mahrousa to gain legal status, but by 2016 had also submitted their own formal application for NGO registration.

In 2015, the Egyptian state was able to use the pretext of the Protest Law to curb what had been a flourishing of community-based/oriented street activism to combat sexual harassment, setting the stage for their (forced) demobilization. Groups like Bassma and Ded el-Taharrush had, from the beginning, worked closely with police units before implementing street patrols and outreach events. According to a Bassma co-founder, they wanted to assure police they were not usurping law enforcement work but simply aiding an already strapped police force (Tadros, 2014).[11] However, in 2015 four members of Bassma were taken into custody, accused by local residents of protesting while conducting an outreach campaign in the Imbaba neighborhood.[12] Bassma's co-founder explained that they had sought the right permissions from the Ministry of Interior's VAW unit and had already conducted similar campaigns

---

[10] Interview, HarassMap Director of Community Outreach, October 2015.
[11] Interview, Bassma co-founder, February 2014.
[12] Interview, Bassma co-founder, March 2019.

in the neighborhoods of Ezbet el-Hagana and Manshiyet Nasr, but through a miscommunication, the police station in Imbaba was not notified. Eventually, however, the VAW unit began to deny Bassma's permit requests. HarassMap had never sought permits nor tried working with police until after the state began to use the Protest Law to target street activism—the Community Outreach Director noted how the VAW unit created "complications" with their requests and stopped responding to them, such that scheduled outreach days had to be canceled.[13] Ded el-Taharrush, which also never sought formal permissions though they would notify the VAW unit of their activities, did not try after the October 2014 Eid holiday. They chose not to register and, because of the Protest Law and the targeting of activists in this period (Abuzaid, 2019), decided the safety of their volunteers was paramount.[14] Through 2015 and into 2016, there was a slow decline as the state's attempt to reign in volunteer-based initiatives had its desired effect—for the safety of volunteers and staff, initiatives had no choice but to cease mobilizing in the streets.

At this time, there was what HarassMap's Community Outreach Director noted to be a new divide emerging, between work in the streets and in institutions.[15] As permits for community outreach dwindled, anti-sexual harassment activists focused on programs in institutional settings, particularly university campuses (Galan & Abdelmonem, 2022). Through its Safe Areas unit, HarassMap had already established a presence on a number of campuses beginning in 2013 and had attempted to implement programs in secondary schools in partnership with the NGO Safe Kids. The mass sexual harassment incident at Cairo University set off a flurry of campus activism by civil society activists, students, and faculty. Maha el-Said, Chair of the English Department, and Hoda el-Sadda, faculty in the same department and co-founder of the Women and Memory Forum, invited faculty, students, and activists from HarassMap, Bassma, and Nazra to a new working group that evolved into an anti-sexual harassment unit on campus, tasked with developing policy and procedures for dealing with campus sexual harassment cases.[16] Given political shifts underway, campuses became the primary focus of work over the course of 2015 to 2016. Bassma and Ded el-Taharrush engaged in university activism, but by 2016 both had folded under the political pressure and HarassMap remained the only major anti-sexual harassment initiative still working. In this period and through 2020, HarassMap continued to partner with Cairo University and were the leading civil society group providing training to students and faculty about university policies and reporting procedures. Their work expanded to Helwan, Alexandria, Tanta, Beni Suef, Menoufiyya, and other universities (Galan & Abdelmonem, 2022). In addition to universities, HarassMap's Safe Areas unit focused on small businesses and corporates. Between 2013 and 2015, they

[13] Interview, HarassMap Director of Community Outreach, October 2015.
[14] Interview, Ded el-Taharrush co-founder, March 2019.
[15] Interview, HarassMap Director of Community Outreach, October 2015.
[16] Interview, Hoda El-Sadda, August 2019.

formed partnerships with microbus drivers, street kiosk owners, street cart vendors, shop/restaurant owners (Om Dahab; Eish we Melh), and cultural centers (Townhouse Gallery), as well as larger corporates and institutions (Uber, Egypro Construction, Insanya, Education for Employment Network, the British Council), as part of an effort to change "street culture" through a filter down effect.[17] Moreover, between 2018 and 2019, HarassMap received funding from the Canadian International Development Research Center to refocus efforts on crowdmapping and to develop a platform more user-friendly than Ushahidi, but through an expanded global effort that they could centrally manage to provide the IT assistance that small groups often needed but did not always consistently receive.

Beyond the Egyptian state's efforts to drive anti-sexual harassment initiatives out of the streets and the resulting institutionalization of the movement, between 2016 and 2019 it also sought to minimize the scale of the problem and coopt institutional work, particularly that in universities. In 2017, the government's National Council for Women commissioned a new study that was widely blasted by women's rights activists across the country for noting that only 9.6% of Egyptian women surveyed indicated they had been sexually harassed—a number that informed the NCW's National Strategy for the Empowerment of Women by 2030 (NCW, 2017). This was in response to two separate 2013 studies: Thomson Reuters, which ranked Egypt as the worst of 22 Arab states to be a woman, and UN Women, which found 99.3% of women surveyed in Egypt reported they had been sexually harassed (Boros, 2013; El-Deeb, 2013). Those reports followed ECWR's 2008 study, which similarly found the numbers of women reporting they had been sexually harassed to be high—83% percent of Egyptian women and 98% of foreign women (Hassan et al., 2008). In an interview, NCW President Maya Morsi denounced the validity of the UN Women and Thomson Reuters reports, noting that if true, women and girls "would not be able to walk the streets" and that the country had "achieved relevant progress in terms of human development" (Egyptian Streets, 2017). Morsi's comments can be viewed as part of the state's effort to gain control over public discourse on sexual harassment, to assure women that its severity had been inflated but that the government had made strides in containing the problem—a legitimation strategy to assuage the public that the government was indeed serving its interest.[18] It goes hand in hand with efforts the NCW has made since 2018 to take over university anti-sexual harassment programs. In that year, HarassMap staff were called to a meeting with UNFPA, which had funded anti-sexual harassment programs in many universities. They were asked to sign on as a partner and it was suggested to them (informally) that if they wanted continued involvement in university anti-sexual harassment work, they would have to submit to the UNFPA's model, devised in

---

[17] Interview, HarassMap Safe Areas Operations Manager, April 2014.
[18] See Yefet and Lavie (2021) on legitimation strategies in authoritarian regimes.

collaboration with the NCW.[19] El-Sadda noted the NCW made similar efforts to take over Cairo University's anti-sexual harassment unit, but as it had begun as a faculty-run initiative they had escaped the NCW's control.[20] By 2018, however, the Egyptian state had managed to sideline activism and usurp the narrative on the sexual harassment problem, and by 2020 they had taken over campus activism.

#MeToo Resurgence of Anti-sexual Harassment Activism, from 2018

It is in the context of this post-revolutionary trajectory of demobilization that the current #MeToo (#AnaKaman) movement in Egypt must be understood. Given the near total shut down of anti-sexual harassment initiatives,[21] the state's effort to control the narrative around sexual harassment, and their targeting of human and women's rights activists, #MeToo was slow to take root in Egypt after the hashtag went viral around the globe in 2017. Throughout 2018, Egyptian media continued to highlight some cases of sexual harassment, assault, and rape, including the resignation of Bread and Freedom party head and one-time presidential candidate Khaled Ali after accusations of sexual harassment, the winning of a sexual harassment court case in February 2018 by Rania Fahmy (the "Upper Egyptian Girl") and another in September 2018 by Gehad el-Rawy, and the jailing of activist Amal Fathy on charges of spreading "fake news" for criticizing the government's handling of sexual harassment (BBC, 2018; El-Tahawy, 2018; Mada Masr, 2018). The hashtags #AnaKaman, and #AnaAydan circulated via social media, though unlike #MeToo in the West, "no major Arab woman celebrities or public figures joined the #MeToo movement apart from a few journalists" (Ghazal, 2020, 376). Women in Egypt and from across the Arab World, however, continued to spread their testimonies via #AnaKaman (Ghazal, 2020, 378–380). El-Tahawy (2018), however, noted early on that, "It's tempting to call this Egypt's #MeToo moment. But it may prove just another example of Egyptian women speaking out against sexual violence," clearly cautioning that accountability at the state level would likely not follow. In March 2019, university student Zeina Dessouky started the Instagram account @CatcallsofCairo, modeled after @CatcallsofNYC to offer Egyptian women another venue, in the vein of HarassMap's crowdmap and the Facebook pages of all former anti-sexual harassment initiatives, to tell their stories of sexual harassment (Farouk, 2019). The years 2018–2019,

[19] Personal communication, HarassMap staff member, February 2022. This staff member noted that the model promoted by NCW and its UNFPA partner involved a conceptual shift away from "anti-sexual harassment" to the broader "anti-violence against women (VAW)," highlighting the NCW's effort to minimize attention on sexual harassment and absorb it as one element of a larger VAW effort.

[20] Interview, Hoda El-Sadda, August 2019.

[21] HarassMap was an exception. They continued to work until June 2020, when they finally canceled their NGO registration.

however, witnessed little activism that made the social and political waves of the initiatives born in the revolutionary period.

In June 2020, the founding of the Instagram account @assaultpolice instigated a new flurry of online anti-sexual harassment activism—hailed as Egypt's actual #MeToo moment and a "digital feminist revolution" (Khairat, 2020). Founded by 22-year-old AUC student Nadeen Ashraf, the account was created to publicize the numerous cases of sexual harassment and assault committed by university student Ahmed Bassam Zaki. The page quickly garnered more than 170 K followers in its first two months and more than 50 women provided testimony of their experiences. It is important to note that initial posts were in English and "targeted the AUC community" (Marzouk & Vanderveen, 2021, 6), but once translated into Arabic, this precipitated the widespread growth in followers, though which segments of Egyptian society were following is not clear. Within a week, however, authorities had arrested Zaki and by April 2021 he had been convicted and sentenced to eight years in prison (Mustafa, 2021; Walsh, 2020). At the end of July 2018, @assaultpolice expanded beyond Zaki's case to highlight a 2014 incident that had taken place in Cairo's Fairmont Hotel, in which an 18-year-old woman alleged that several young men had drugged and gang-raped her (Samir, 2020). Unlike in Zaki's case, after the names of seven young men associated with the incident were released through an anonymous Twitter account, the backlash against @assaultpolice was swift, including death threats against prominent members that forced them to delete all posts related to the matter (Samir, 2020).[22] While four men were eventually held in pre-trial detention (others underwent investigation), by May 2021 Egypt's attorney general moved to close the case, citing a lack of evidence (Egypt Today, 2021a). Three key witnesses had also been held in pre-trial detention, which Mada Masr (2021) argued "marked a turning point" that "paved the way for the case to ultimately be shelved." Despite the Fairmont backlash, Zaki's case sparked the approval of a new law, Article 113, protecting the identities of sexual violence survivors during pre-trial investigations (LOC, 2020). In 2021, the government also amended Article 306 to increase penalties for sexual harassment offenses (EgyptToday, 2021b). While the online activism of @assaultpolice may be credited with continuing to raise awareness of the problem and perhaps serving as the impetus for the approval of Article 113 (Marzouk & Vanderveen, 2021), and while it has generated attention and excitement about renewed possibilities for combatting sexual harassment and assault, it is important to also understand the constraints on activism in the current moment and what that means with respect to future possibilities.

---

[22] There are important and complex class dimensions with respect to the Fairmont case—according to one report, the multiple individuals involved hailed from families who "wield pervasive influence within the Egyptian state administrations, and reaches those most sheltered in the pillars of the ruling system, both politically and economically" (El Ammar, 2020). However, Zaki's wealthy, upper-class status did not afford him the same protections as perpetrators in the Fairmont case.

In the political climate in which Egypt's #MeToo has ensued, online space is the primary (if not the only) mode through which anti-sexual harassment activism has continued. Activists have not been able to leverage online spaces to mobilize the public in grassroots/on-the-ground efforts. Prior to the revolution, women's rights advocacy organizations operated in a tightly regulated and internationalized NGOized space influenced by decades of governance feminism and populated by upper-middle-class professional women, many of whom were lawyers and doctors (Abdelmonem, 2020; Jad, 2003).[23] Their work was policy-oriented, focusing on research, improving the law, raising women's awareness of their legal rights, and helping women access basic services (Abdelmonem, 2020; Al-Ali, 2000; Tadros, 2016). After ECWR began its anti-sexual harassment program, tensions internal to that organization emerged around policy-orientated work, as pushed by Abul Komsan, and the desire to engage in new and transformative efforts to change social perceptions, as envisioned by ECWR's International Relations Specialist, Program Manager, and their volunteers, resulting in HarassMap's founding.[24] Revolutionary-period initiatives broke away from policy-oriented work, though many formed cooperative relationships with various NGOs. The flourishing of street anti-sexual harassment activism after January 25 was, in part, a reaction to strict controls the state had over civil society work and top-down change advocated for by professionalized classes, which a HarassMap co-founder argued to be ineffective in the context of state cooptation and repression.[25] To this, the revolution provided the political opportunity for a strategic shift in who could engage in sexual violence activism and how it unfolded, allowing initiatives to pursue bottom-up approaches while eschewing a reliance on the state (Tadros, 2015). Concerned youth from cities and towns across Egypt flocked to anti-sexual harassment work, joining the initiatives and massively expanding their efforts. These youth came from a range of class backgrounds, though organizers were often middle-to-upper-middle-class university students or early career professionals—most on both sides had no experience in civil society work (Abdelmonem & Galan, 2017). On the ground grassroots activities, mediated in/by online spaces, were critical for fomenting the transformations activists hoped to inspire. Post-2015, state cooptation and repression has made it impossible (and dangerous) for #MeToo activists to take to the streets to mobilize the public. Within this larger context, online spaces remain the only place for activists to continue to remind the public that sexual harassment remains a serious problem.

Yet even that has been limited. Missing in today's #MeToo hashtag era are the large-scale online awareness campaigns that were a significant feature of

---

[23] Halley et al. (2006) define governance feminism as the "installation of feminists and feminist ideas in actual legal-institutional power," referring to the way in which feminists working inside political institutions have helped to produce policy and practice.

[24] Interview, HarassMap co-founder, March 2012.

[25] Interview, HarassMap co-founder, March 2012.

anti-sexual harassment work in the revolutionary period. Sexual harassment understood as *taharrush* was a widely contested idea; frame alignment was crucial to revolutionary-period work; that is, getting the public to agree that the behaviors associated with street harassment were *taharrush* rather than *muakasa*, or flirtation, and reshaping entrenched patriarchal gendered norms (Abdelmonem, 2015). HarassMap's 2011 "Why Does He Harass?" campaign sought to debunk gendered myths around sexual harassment. This was followed by the 2013 joint "Get it Right" campaign to define and establish the difference between *taharrush* and *ightasab* (rape), as well as to challenge gendered norms that women like to be harassed/flirted with. HarassMap's 2014 "I Will Not Be Silent" campaign urged bystanders to speak up to help women facing sexual harassment and the "We Need a Policy" campaign called on schools and universities to develop zero-tolerance policies and procedures. Their 2015 "The Harasser is a Criminal" campaign encouraged bystanders to stand up to harassers, and "It's Harassment and Not Flirtation" campaign challenged continued use of *muakasa* (still) in popular lingo.[26] These campaigns brought together activists, artists, marketing professionals, and media consultants, many of whom offered their services pro bono or at reduced rates given their commitment to the cause, and they bridged social media with physical public spaces and in some cases mass media. The campaigns were designed to confront and reshape public discourses and cultural perceptions that sexual harassment was a real problem, that women needed to be believed, and that citizens (and not just the state) had a responsibility to create safe public spaces. Some of this persists with @assaultpolice's effort at providing messages of why sexual harassment exists, addressing power imbalances, showing care and support for survivors, calling for bystander help and urging the resharing of stories, offering information on legal services, and outing offenders—all while also supporting rather challenging government efforts to address the problem (Marzouk & Vanderveen, 2021). These efforts build on more than a decade of work that preceded it, but they do not engage in intentional processes of (re) framing perception and praxis.

However, media coverage, youth activists' ongoing ICT use, and subsequent bursts of public reporting/outcry demonstrate that sexual harassment remains a persistent problem that has yet to be adequately addressed, whether at the political/legal or societal levels. The protest law, the approval of two separate updates to the draconian NGO law, the denial of permits for community activities, and the arrests and/or imprisonment of prominent human and women's rights defenders and outspoken youth activists have been made worse under Sisi's regime by the passage of additional laws, including Law 180, Law 175, and amendments to Law 58 of 1937 regulating the spread of false information via mass and social media (LOC, 2019)—the same set of laws used to prosecute Fathy for her denunciation of the government for failing to deal with

---

[26] See Abdelmonem (2015) for discussion on *taharrush*, *muakasa*, and *ightasab* in Egyptian anti-sexual harassment activism.

sexual harassment. A new law targeting social media pages with over 5000 followers, allowing the state to shut down such accounts, was also passed in 2018
(Reuters, 2018). Not only has the Egyptian state successfully managed to erase
vibrant street activism fomented by the revolution thereby making vital offline
anti-sexual harassment work untenable, it has now sought to target the spaces
and tools offered by ICTs, limiting even more what activists can say via (or do
with) online forums. However, as Cai and Zhou have noted for the Chinese
case, it isn't possible for the Egyptian state to completely shut down Internet
communications, with its own vision of a digitalized future (IDSC, 2021).
Despite the clamp down, ICTs minimally allow activists to continue to show
support and cultivate care for survivors of sexual harassment who continue to
report testimonies.[27] ICT use allows concerned youth to engage in some
amount of non-politicized activism and makes it possible for them to refocus
attention on the problem of sexual harassment until political tides shift and
mobilization for more expanded online and offline work once again becomes
tenable. While the successes and possibilities of #MeToo anti-sexual harassment activism leave much room for debate and continued exploration, activists
are deploying ICTs to keep the issue alive for a population that continues to
experience the effects of sexual harassment.

CONCLUSION

Digital technology has played a critical role in the fight against sexual harassment in Egypt, allowing activists to open public debate, provide survivors
spaces of testimony, and mobilize everyday people to take action in their neighborhoods. In the pre-revolutionary period, mass media, social media platforms,
and political blogs made it possible for activists to confront what had been to
that point a highly taboo topic, paving the way for activism to flourish. During
the revolutionary period, given the political opportunities afforded by the
breakdown in the political process, social media served as the vehicle for a massive expansion in activism, allowing activists to incite public action and reframe
popular conceptions of the problem. Since the end of the revolution, social
media has continued to play a vital role in demonstrating that, despite state
efforts to end or coopt activism and take control of the narrative around sexual
harassment, Egyptians cannot and will not be silenced. Egypt's #MeToo digital
activism has shown that sexual harassment remains a widely pervasive problem
in the country and that citizens have the will and desire to take action in the
absence of adequate state measures. The last more than 15 years of anti-sexual
harassment activism highlights the possibilities in fomenting widespread social
and political shifts when citizens and civil society are provided the space and

---

[27] Though HarassMap shut down in 2020, their crowdmap remains open. Between 2010 and
today, their map has received less than 2000 reports. Nine of those were submitted between
January and December 2021. No hard numbers are available for reports submitted to any initiative
via social media.

tools to engage in the processes of change. This long history of pre-and-post revolutionary activism, both online and offline, makes clear that the story of Egyptians combatting sexual harassment is far from over.

REFERENCES

ABC News. (2014, June 11). *Egypt's President Visits Woman Assaulted During his Victory Celebration.* Last Accessed November 3, 2021. https://abcnews.go.com/blogs/politics/2014/06/egypts-president-visits-woman-assaulted-during-his-victory-celebration.

Abdelmonem, A. (2015). Reconceptualizing Sexual Harassment in Egypt: A Longitudinal Assessment of el-Taharrush el-Ginsy in Arabic Online Forums and Anti-Sexual Harassment Activism. *Kohl: Journal of Gender and Body Research, 1*(1), 23–41.

Abdelmonem, A. (2020). Disciplining Bystanders: (Anti)Carcerality, Ethics, and the Docile Subject in HarassMap's 'The Harasser is a Criminal' Media Campaign in Egypt. *Feminist Media Studies, Onlinefirst, 22,* 238. https://doi.org/10.1080/14680777.2020.1785911

Abdelmonem, A., & Galan, S. (2017). Action-Oriented Responses to Sexual Harassment: The Cases of HarassMap and WenDo. *Journal of Middle East Women's Studies, 13*(1), 156–167.

Abul Komsan, N. (2009, December 13–14). *Sexual Harassment in the Arab Region: Cultural Challenges and Legal Gaps.* ECWR. Last Accessed November 7, 2021. https://egypt.unfpa.org/sites/default/files/pub-pdf/8655f498-85a0-434c-9396-bfa3b390f63e.pdf.

Abuzaid, R. A. (2019). 'Foreign Funding' Case No. 173/2011: The Implications of State Encroachment on the Feminist Community in Egypt. *Journal of Middle East Women's Studies, 15*(2), 237–243.

Al-Ali, N. (2000). *Secularism, Gender and the State in the Middle East: The Egyptian Women's Movement.* Cambridge University Press.

Amar, P. (2011). Turning the Gendered Politics of the Security State Inside Out? *International Feminist Journal of Politics, 13*(3), 299–328.

Aouragh, M., & Alexander, A. (2011). The Egyptian Experience: Sense and Nonsense of the Revolution. *International Journal of Communication, 5,* 1344–1358.

BBC News. (2018, December 31). Amal Fathy: Egypt Court Imposes Jail Term Over Harassment Video. Last Accessed November 3, 2021. https://www.bbc.com/news/world-middle-east-46720727.

Begum, R. (2014, June 15). How Egypt Can Turn the Tide on Sexual Assault. *Mada Masr.* Last Accessed November 3, 2021. https://www.madamasr.com/en/2014/06/15/opinion/society/how-egypt-can-turn-the-tide-on-sexual-assault/.

Boros, C. (2013, November 12). POLL-Egypt is Worst Arab State for Women, Comoros Best. *Thomson Reuters News Foundation.* Last Accessed November 3, 2021. https://news.trust.org/item/20131108170910-qacvu/?source=spotlight-writaw.

Cai, Y., & Zhou, T. (2016). New Information Communication Technologies and Social Protest in China. *Asian Survey, 56*(4), 731–753.

Egypt Today. (2021a, May 11). *Egypt's Attorney General Says 'Fairmont Gangrape' Lawsuit Cannot Be Filed Due to Lack of Evidence*. Last Accessed November 3, 2021. https://www.egypttoday.com/Article/1/103831/Egypt's-Attorney-General-says-Fairmont-gangrape-lawsuit-cannot-be-filed.

Egypt Today. (2021b, July 12). *Egyptian House Approves Draft Law Toughening Penalty of Sexual Harassment*. Last Accessed November 4, 2021. https://www.egypttoday.com/Article/1/105972/Egyptian-House-approves-draft-law-toughening-penalty-of-sexual-harassment.

Egyptian Streets. (2014, June 11). *Egypt's President Sisi Visits Victims of Brutal Sexual Assault*. Last Accessed November 3, 2021. https://egyptianstreets.com/2014/06/11/egypts-president-sisi-visits-victims-of-brutal-sexual-assault/.

Egyptian Streets. (2017, November 14). *Sexual Harassment Rate in Egypt Is Only 9.6 Percent: Head of National Council for Women*. Last Accessed November 3, 2021. https://egyptianstreets.com/2017/11/14/sexual-harassment-rate-in-egypt-is-only-9-6-percent-head-of-national-council-for-women/.

El Ammar, M. (2020, September 22). *The 'Fairmont' Case: Sexual Violence and Class Immunity*. Daraj. Last Accessed January 26, 2022. https://daraj.com/en/55598/.

El-Deeb, B. (2013). Study on the Ways and Methods to Eliminate Sexual Harassment in Egypt: Results/Outcomes and Recommendations. *UN Women*. Last Accessed November 3, 2021. https://s3-eu-west-1.amazonaws.com/harassmap/media/uploaded-files/287_Summaryreport_eng_low-1.pdf.

El-Mahdi, R. (2010). Does Political Islam Impede Gender-Based Mobilization? The Case of Egypt. *Totalitarian Movements and Political Religions, 11*(3–4), 379–396.

El-Meehy, A. (2017). *Islamist and Non-Islamist Local Activism: Comparative Reflections from Egypt's Popular Committees*. Middle East Studies Political Science Project. https://pomeps.org/islamist-and-non-islamic-local-activism-comparative-reflections-from-egypts-popular-committees.

ElSayed, H., & Rizzo, H. (2014). *Media, Political Opportunity and the Anti-Sexual Harassment Campaign in Post-2011 Egypt*. Unpublished manuscript.

El-Tahawy, M. (2018, March 13). A #MeToo Moment for Egypt? Maybe. *New York Times*. Last Accessed November 3, 2021. https://www.nytimes.com/2018/03/13/opinion/egypt-metoo-email-girl.html.

Eltantawy, N. (2019, November 18). In Egypt, the Me Too Movement Is Falling Short. *Fair Observer*. Last Accessed November 5, 2021. https://www.fairobserver.com/culture/me-too-movement-sexual-harassment-egypt-middle-east-womens-rights-news-61521/.

Eltantawy, N., & Wiest, J. B. (2011). Social Media in the Egyptian Revolution: Reconsidering Resource Mobilization Theory. *International Journal of Communication, 5*, 1207–1224.

Farouk, A. (2019, December 26). We Chat With Zeina Dessouky, the 19 Year-Old Who Created a Platform for Girls to Share Stories of Their Harassment. *Teen Times*. Last Accessed November 3, 2021. https://teenntimes.com/2019/12/26/we-chat-with-zeina-dessouky-the-19-year-old-who-created-a-platform-for-girls-to-share-stories-of-their-harassment/.

FIDH, Nazra for Feminist Studies, New Women Foundation, & Uprising of Women in the Arab World. (2014). *Egypt: Keeping Women Out. Sexual Violence Against Women in the Public Sphere*. Joint Report. Accessed January 29, 2015. https://www.fidh.org/IMG/pdf/egypt_women_final_english.pdf.

Galan, S. (2016). Beyond the Logic of State Protection: Feminist Self-Defense in Cairo After the January 25 Revolution. *Kohl: Journal of Gender and Body Research, 2*(1), 71–89.

Galan, S., & Abdelmonem, A. (2022). From the Streets to the Campus: Youth Activism Against Sexual Harassment in Educational Institutions in January 25th Revolution Egypt. In C. L. Lovin & I. Rivers (Eds.), *Young People Shaping Democratic Politics: Interrogation Inclusion, Mobilising Education.* Palgrave. Forthcoming.

Ghazal, R. T. (2020). #AnaKaman–MeToo in the Arab World: A Journalist's Account. In *The Routledge Handbook of the Politics of the #MeToo Movement.* Taylor & Francis.

Grove, N. (2015). The Cartographic Ambiguities of HarassMap: Crowdmapping Security and Sexual Violence in Egypt. *Security Dialogue, 46*(4), 345–364.

Hafez, S. (2014a). Bodies that Protest: The Girl in the Blue Bra, Sexuality, and State Violence in Revolutionary Egypt. *Signs, The Journal of Women in Culture and Society, 40*(1), 20–28.

Hafez, S. (2014b). The Revolution Shall Not Pass Through Women's Bodies: Egypt, Uprising and Gender Politics. *Journal of North African Studies, 19*(2), 172–185.

Halley, J., Kotiswaran, P., Shamir, H., & Thomas, C. (2006). Rape at Rome: Feminist Interventions in the Criminalization of Sex-Related Violence in Positive International Law. *Michigan Journal of International Law, 30*(1), 1–123.

Hamzawy, A. (2016, November 24). *Egypt's Anti-Protest Law: Legalizing Authoritarianism.* Al-Jazeera. Last Accessed November 7, 2021. https://www.aljazeera.com/features/2016/11/24/egypts-anti-protest-law-legalising-authoritarianism.

Hassan, R., Qomsan, N. A., & Shoukry, A. (2008). Clouds in Egypt's Sky: Sexual Harassment, from Verbal Harassment to Rape–a Sociological Study. ECWR Report. Accessed January 19, 2015. http://egypt.unfpa.org/Images/Publication/2010_03/6eeeb05a-3040-42d2-9e1c-2bd2e1ac8cac.pdf.

Human Rights Watch. (2014, August 30). *Egypt: Dissolution Ultimatum for Independent Groups.* Last Accessed November 3, 2021. https://www.hrw.org/news/2014/08/30/egypt-dissolution-ultimatum-independent-groups#.

Information and Decision Support Center (The Egyptian Cabinet). (2021, May 3). *Egypt Digitalization in Alignment with Egypt Vision 2030 for SDGS.* Last Accessed January 26, 2022. https://idsc.gov.eg/Upload/DocumentLibrary/Attachment_A/4798/3%20-%20EGYPT%20DIGITALIZATION.pdf.

Jad, I. (2003). *The NGOization of Arab Women's Movements.* Al-Raida, 38–47. http://www.alraidajournal.com/index.php/ALRJ/article/view/442.

Kassem, N. (2017). Transformation or Just More Information: Social Media Use and Perceived Opportunities for Mobilizing Change in Post-Revolution Egypt. In M. Friedrichsen & Y. Kamalipour (Eds.), *Digital Transformation in Journalism and News Media: Media Management, Media Convergence and Globalization.* Springer.

Khairat, F. (2020, September 20). Meet Assault Police's Nadeen Ashraf: The Student Behind Egypt's Anti-Harassment Revolution. *Egyptian Streets.* Last Accessed November 3, 2021. https://egyptianstreets.com/2020/09/20/meet-nadeen-ashraf-the-student-behind-egypts-anti-harrassment-social-media-revolution/.

Khamis, S. (2011). The Transformation Egyptian Media Landscape: Changes, Challenges, and Comparative Perspectives. *International Journal of Communication, 5*, 1159–1177.

Langohr, V. (2013). 'This is Our Square': Fighting Sexual Assault at Cairo Protests. *Middle East Report, 238*(Fall), 18–35.

Langohr, V. (2014, July 7). New President, old Pattern of Sexual Violence in Egypt. *Middle East Report*. http://www.merip.org/mero/mero070714.

Library of Congress (LOC). (2014, June 19). *Egypt: Rape and Sexual Assault Suspects Referred to Criminal Court*. Last Accessed November 3, 2021. https://www.loc.gov/item/global-legal-monitor/2014-06-19/egypt-rape-and-sexual-assault-suspects-referred-to-criminal-court/.

Library of Congress (LOC). (2019, April). *Initiatives to Counter Fake News in Selected Countries*. Last Accessed November 3, 2021. https://irp.fas.org/eprint/lloc-fake-news.pdf.

Library of Congress (LOC). (2020, September 8). *Egypt: Parliament Approves Draft Law Concealing the Identity of Victims of Sexual Violence Crimes during the Pretrial Investigative Stage*. Last Accessed November 3, 2021. https://www.loc.gov/item/global-legal-monitor/2020-09-08/egypt-parliament-approves-draft-law-concealing-the-identity-of-victims-of-sexual-violence-crimes-during-the-pretrial-investigative-stage/.

Lim, M. (2012). Clicks, Cabs, and Coffee Houses: Social Media and Oppositional Movements in Egypt, 2004–2011. *Journal of Communication, 62*(2), 231–248.

Lughod, A. (2011). The Active Social Life of 'Muslim Women's Rights': A Plea for Ethnography, Not Polemic, With Cases from Egypt and Palestine. *Journal of Middle East Women's Studies, 6*(1), 1–45.

Mada Masr. (2014, June 11). *Sisi Visits Tahrir Square Mob Sexual Assault Victim in Hospital*. Last Accessed November 3, 2021. https://www.madamasr.com/en/2014/06/11/news/u/sisi-visits-tahrir-square-mob-sexual-assault-victim-in-hospital/.

Mada Masr. (2018, September 12). 2-Year Prison Sentence for Man Accused of Sexual Harassment Over Eid. Last Accessed November 3, 2021. https://www.madamasr.com/en/2018/09/12/news/u/2-year-prison-sentence-for-man-accused-of-sexual-harassment-over-eid/.

Mada Masr. (2021, September 2). Witnesses Arrested and Intimidated: How the Fairmont Rape Case Fell Apart. Last Accessed November 3, 2021. https://www.madamasr.com/en/2021/09/02/feature/politics/witnesses-arrested-and-intimidated-how-the-fairmont-rape-case-fell-apart/.

Marzouk, A., & Vanderveen, G. (2021). Fighting Sexual Violence in Egypt on Social Media: A Visual Essay on Assault Police. *Global Public Health*, Onlinefirst. https://doi.org/10.1080/17441692.2021.1991972.

Mustafa, O. (2021, April 11). Ahmed Bassam Zaki Sentenced to 8 Years in Prison for Sexual Assault. *Egyptian Streets*. Last Accessed November 3, 2021. https://egyptianstreets.com/2021/04/11/ahmed-bassam-zaki-sentenced-to-8-years-in-prison-for-sexual-assault/.

National Council for Women. (2017, March). *National Strategy for the Empowerment of Egyptian Women 2030*. Last Accessed November 3, 2021. http://ncw.gov.eg/wp-content/uploads/2018/02/final-version-national-strategy-for-the-empowerment-of-egyptian-women-2030.pdf.

Nazra For Feminist Studies. (2014, June 9). Joint Statement: The Mob-sexual Assaults and Gang Rapes in Tahrir Square During the Celebrations of the Inauguration of the New Egyptian President is Sufficient Proof for the Inefficiency of the Recent Legal Amendments to Combat these Crimes. Last Accessed November 3, 2021. https://nazra.org/en/2014/06/mob-sexual-assaults-and-gang-rapes-tahrir-square-during-celebrations-inauguration-new.

Replogle, E. (2011). Reference Groups, Mob Mentality, and Bystander Intervention: A Sociological Analysis of the Lara Logan Case. *Sociological Forum, 26*(4), 796–805.

Reuters. (2018, July 17). *Egypt Targets Social Media with New Law.* Last Accessed January 26, 2022. https://www.reuters.com/article/us-egypt-politics/egypt-targets-social-media-with-new-law-idUSKBN1K722C.

Rizzo, H. (2014). The Role of Women's Rights Organizations in Promoting Masculine Responsibility: The Anti-Sexual Harassment Campaign in Egypt. *Cairo Papers in Social Science, 33*(1), 102–129.

Rizzo, H., Price, A. M., & Meyer, K. (2012). Anti-Sexual Harassment Campaign in Egypt. *Mobilization, 17*(4), 457–475.

Saleh, Y. (2014, June 10). Egypt's Sisi Tells Interior Minister to Fight Sexual Harassment. *Reuters.* Last Accessed November 3, 2021. https://www.reuters.com/article/us-egypt-sisi-harassment/egypts-sisi-tells-interior-minister-to-fight-sexual-harassment-idUSKBN0EL17J20140610.

Samir, N. (2020, August 13). The Infamous Fairmont Incident: What We Know So Far. *Daily News Egypt.* Last Accessed November 3, 2021. https://dailyfeed.dailynewsegypt.com/2020/08/13/the-infamous-fairmont-incident-what-we-know-so-far/.

Skalli, L. H. (2014). Young Women and Social Media Against Sexual Harassment. *Journal of North African Studies, 19*(2), 244–258.

Tadros, M. (2014). Reclaiming the Streets for Women's Dignity: Effective Initiatives in the Struggle Against Gender-Based Violence in Between Egypt's Two Revolutions. *Institute for Development Studies*, Evidence Report #48: Empowerment of Women and Girls, January 2014, Accessed December 20, 2014. http://www.wluml.org/sites/wluml.org/files/Tadors%20Reclaiming%20the%20Streets.pdf.

Tadros, M. (2015). Contentious and Prefigurative Politics: Vigilante Groups' Struggle against Sexual Violence in Egypt (2011–2013). *Development and Change, 46*(6), 1345–1368.

Tadros, M. (2016). *Resistance, Revolt, and Gender Justice in Egypt.* Syracuse University Press.

Taha, R. M. (2014, June 9). Sexual Assault Reported in Tahrir Square During Al-Sisi's Inauguration: Anti-Harassment Group. *Dailey News Egypt.* Last Accessed November 3, 2021. https://dailynewsegypt.com/2014/06/09/sexual-assault-reported-tahrir-square-al-sisis-inauguration-anti-harassment-group/.

Tarrow, S. (2011). *Power in Movement: Social Movements and Contentious Politics* (3rd ed.).

Walsh, D. (2020). The 22-Year-Old Force Behind Egypt's Growing #MeToo Movement. *New York Times*, October 2, 2020. Last Accessed November 3, 2021. https://www.nytimes.com/2020/10/02/world/middleeast/egypt-metoo-sexual-harassment-ashraf.html.

Yefet, B., & Lavie, L. (2021). Legitimation in Post-Revolutionary Egypt: Al-Sisi and the Renewal of Authoritarianism. *Digest of Middle East Studies, 30*(3), 170–185.

Young, C. (2014). HarassMap: Using Crowdsourcing Data to Map Sexual Harassment in Egypt. *Technology Innovation Management Review.* Accessed January 17, 2015. http://timreview.ca/sites/default/files/article_PDF/Young_TIMReview_March2014.pdf.

PART III

Introduction: The Gender of Politics

Academic interest in gender, women, communication, and politics in MENA has produced a fascinating, though fairly modest, body of research. A review of this literature suggests that while earlier questions and methodologies remained anchored within quasi-strict disciplinary lines, interesting developments have emerged since the democratic uprisings of 2011. Prior to the uprisings, most research was conducted by political scientists interested in defining the structural, institutional, and socio-cultural obstacles constraining women's participation in legislative bodies. Questions asked revolved around women's voting rights, (Islamist) party politics and parliamentary representation (Ben Shitrit, 2016), Islamic teachings on women's political role, as well as the adoption and effectiveness of the quota system in advancing women's leadership in national legislature (Moghadam, 1970; Dahlerup, 1970).

Although the dominant political system across MENA is recognized as authoritarian, the recognition of significant brands of authoritarianism has determined the spaces and scope of women's political participation. This explains why most of the earlier research examined these questions in a few countries (Morocco, Tunisia, Lebanon, Jordan, and Egypt) and only recently broadened the focus to include Syria, Oman, Yemen, Saudi Arabia, and Kuwait.

Since the 2011 democratic uprisings, more scholarly attention turned to the implications of political transitions for women's political participation and the impact of the uprisings on the gendering of politics. Some have explored gender and power dynamics within the legislative committees of national parliaments (Shalaby & Elimam, 2020), while others turned to gender analysis to explore links between political identities and intersectionality to examine the electability of female candidates (Kao & Benstead, 2021).

The contribution of communication scholars and gender analysis to these areas of research has produced further insights at the thematic and theoretical levels and innovations in the research methodologies. The main questions addressed by researchers, writing in both Arabic and English, relied on content analysis of national print and broadcast media to highlight the framing practices that produce (mis)representations of political women. Also central to these contributions are questions about the role of ICTs in gendering the public sphere, the gendering of politics, redefinition of political action, and the political spaces women occupy, including those facilitated by digital technologies (Khiabany & Sreberny, 2004; Skalli, 2006, 2014). Researchers have also used Gaye Tuchman's theory of "symbolic annihilation" to examine media construction of female political leadership (Skalli, 2011), while others have focused on public perception to understand the connections between gender and the electability of women candidates (Baradei & Wafa, 2021).

Unsurprisingly, academic interest in gender, media, and politics intensified since the 2011 uprisings. Questions that have been tackled over the last decade range from women's political leadership during and since the uprisings to the political roles and spaces women occupy in the post-uprising regimes. Contributors in this part advance scholarly research on a wide range of issues and introduce new contexts for exploring the intersection between politics, women, gender, and media.

Haala Hweio's chapter provides a rare opportunity for understanding the political participation of women and their uses of media during and after the Gaddafi regime. Given the limited knowledge about women's political behavior in Libya, Hweio situates her discussion within the historical and political developments of the country while underscoring women's political participation in building modern-day Libya. Hweio's chapter highlights the steep cost of doing politics under a dictatorial regime and the determination of the brave women who seek to engender the political scene despite this cost. Ultimately, the chapter provides context for reflecting on the opportunities and challenges that the 2011 revolution raises for women's political action.

Amany Khodair and Reman Abdel All's chapter takes us to the unique context of the Covid-19 lockdown in Egypt and the first Parliamentary Elections (2020) that took place following the constitutional amendments of 2019. The researchers use this context to assess the effectiveness of social media for promoting the candidacy of women politicians in Egypt and shaping the political behavior of voters. Despite the heavy reliance of many Egyptians on Facebook as a source of political information, the researchers provide a nuanced assessment of the power and limitations of social media for political mobilization within a typically repressive context.

Rafiah Al Talei's contribution in this part focuses on media's coverage of political leadership and its impact on the gendered outcomes of political processes and participation in Oman. Al Talei uses a mixed method approach (in-depth interviews, content analysis of newspapers, and Twitter) to provide a probing analysis of the challenges Omani women politicians navigate to carve out a space for meaningful political action and engagement. In addition to the quasi-absence of a national strategy for promoting women's political participation, her chapter points to the pervasive gender biases in media's coverage of women's candidacy which continue to undermine their competence and capabilities.

These critical questions of media's roles in women's political lives are also examined in the following two chapters on Israel and Iran. Einat Lachover provides a probing analysis of Israeli women's magazines' portrayal of female politicians. Lachover analyzes three popular Israeli women's magazines and their main profile articles over the span of the past 15 years to highlight the complex and contradictory role that media plays in covering women parliamentary politicians. These contradictions, she argues, are a reflection and extension of the broader paradoxes towards gender issues one finds within the Israeli political and social discourses.

In the case of Iran, Mona Tajali presents a more promising role of media for the empowerment of female politicians despite the constraints of the Iranian theocratic state. Tajali's conclusion is based on a close analysis of the print edition of *Zanan* magazine and its online successor, *Zanan-e*. In this case, she contends, female politicians have succeeded to create a powerful space to debate their political concerns in ways that challenge the gender discriminatory attitudes of Iran's political and religious elites. Challenging these centers of power comes with a high cost including censorship, frequent episodes of closure of the magazine, and even threats to the politicians themselves.

Yet, Iran is not unique in imposing a high cost to women's political participation and intervention. As all the chapters in this part demonstrate, the gendering of public sphere and political action is a complicated process that demands women's determination, resilience, and continued innovation in the uses of old and traditional media. Given the entrenched gender biases in practically all national institutions as well as mainstream and commercial media, the chapters underscore why researchers and rights activists should remain vigilant about media uses and abuses.

REFERENCES

Baradei, L., & Wafa, D. (2021). Women in the Second Egyptian Parliament Post the Arab Spring: Do they think they Stand a Chance? *Journal of International Women's Studies, 14*(3).

Ben Shitrit, L. (2016). Authenticating Representation: Women's Quotas and Islamist Parties. *Politics and Gender*, 12(04), 781–806.

Dahlerup, D. (1970). Women in Arab Parliaments: Can Gender Quotas Contribute to Democratization?. *Al-Raida Journal*, 28–37.

Kao, K., & Benstead, L. (2021). Female Electability in the Arab World: The Advantages of Intersectionality. *Comparative Politics, 53*(3), 427–464.

Khiabany, G., & Sreberny, A. (2004). The Women's Press in Contemporary Iran: Engendering the Public Sphere. In N. Sakr (Eds.). *Women and Media in the Middle East: Power Through Self-Expression* (pp. 15–39). I.B. Tauris.

Lachover, E. (2017). Signs of Change in Media Representation of Women in Israeli Politics: Leading and Peripheral Women Contenders. *Journalism*, 18(4), 446–463.

Moghadam, V. (1970). Women, Politics, and Gender Quotas. *Al-Raida Journal*, 18–27.

Shalaby, M., & Elimam, L. (2020). Women in Legislative Committees in Arab Parliaments. *Comparative Politics, 53*(1), 139–167.

Skalli, L. H. (2006). Communicating Gender in the Public Sphere: Women and Information Technologies in MENA. *Journal of Middle East Women's Studies, 2*(2), 35–59.

Skalli, L. H. (2011). Constructing Female Leadership in the Middle East: The Gender of Politics in Moroccan Media. *Gender and Society, 25*(4), 473–495.

Skalli, L. H. (2014). Defying Marginality: Young Women's Politics and Social Media in MENA. In F. Nouraie-Simone (Ed) *On Shifting Ground; Muslim Women in the Global Era* (2nd Edition, pp. 31–51). CUNY: Feminist Press.

CHAPTER 12

Women and Politics in the Islamic Republic of Iran: The Role of Women's Magazines

Mona Tajali

Journalism in Iran is akin to tight-roping, walking a fine line to respect state regulations while seeking to reach an end point, with nearly no protection (Personal interview with Shahla Sherkat, June, 2015).

Scholarship on women's rights advocacy has been highlighting the diverse ways that local women's rights advocates engage with the state and its institutions. Such analysis has shed light on new and interesting ways that women make claims from and pressure the state, with the recognition that "feminists, like other political actors, cannot avoid the state" (Chappell, 2002, 3). Working within highly patriarchal and undemocratic state structures has made such engagements more challenging. However, women's rights advocates, as active agents, have often persisted by arriving at influential ways of protesting gender inequality and discrimination against women, while also garnering public support for their demands.

Women's magazines have historically provided an effective platform for advocates of women's rights to present their grievances, raise awareness of their concerns, and publicize their demands (Hendelman-Baavur, 2019; Siddiqui, 2014; Skalli, 2006a, 2006b; Zachs, 2014). This chapter offers a detailed analysis of how Iranian women have creatively and diplomatically used women's magazines to engage with Iran's theocratic regime on the demand to increase

M. Tajali (✉)
Agnes Scott College, Decatur, GA, USA
e-mail: mtajali@agnesscott.edu

201

L. H. Skalli, N. Eltantawy (eds.), *The Palgrave Handbook of Gender, Media and Communication in the Middle East and North Africa*, https://doi.org/10.1007/978-3-031-11980-4_12

women's access to political decision-making roles. By presenting an overview of widely circulated monthly *Zanan* (*Women*) and its successor magazine, *Zanan-e Emrooz* (*Today's Women*), it discusses these magazines' roles in carving out a space for debate and discussion of gender and politics within the Iranian public sphere since the 1979 revolution, with an outline of the various shifts that such discourses and publications have undergone throughout the past decades. The chapter demonstrates how these magazines, working within the confines of the theocratic state, challenged the gender discriminatory attitudes and behaviors of Iran's political and religious elites across the ideological spectrum. It also discusses the contexts in which despite women's efforts to articulate their demands diplomatically and in a way that resonates with the ruling elites, they nonetheless occasionally faced backlash from hard-liners, leading to magazine closures and other forms of censorship. The chapter sheds light on the role and agency of women who utilized print media as a medium to raise awareness and publicize women's concerns in formal politics while working from within a highly patriarchal and undemocratic context, in ways similar to other global contexts that are influenced by conservative gender thought.

METHODS AND REASONING FOR CASE SELECTION

Both *Zanan* and *Zanan-e Emrooz* started as monthly periodicals published in Persian to address key political, social, and economic aspects of women's rights in Iran, with frequent attention to gender-related global and regional debates and trends. While these magazines published articles about a plethora of women's rights concerns ranging from their family rights to equal access to employment, education, and more, this chapter mostly focuses on their coverage and advocacy around women's political rights and representation since *Zanan's* launch in 1992. This is because expansion of women's political representation has been a central demand of the Iranian women's movement given its potential to enable substantive representation of other women's rights concerns. Election periods usually witness an intensification of women's rights organizing for this demand. Iranian women's magazines have historically provided an important platform to publicize women's campaigns and help focus discussions on women's political candidacy and recruitment, which further facilitate content analysis and research as undertaken by this chapter. As a scholar who has been documenting women's organizing around the expansion of their political roles in Iran for the past decade and half (Tajali, 2022b), I often found myself referring to these publications to research women's struggles, strategies, and campaigns. To grasp a deeper understanding of women's pressuring efforts of the ruling elites, such content analysis is then complemented with personal interview data conducted in Persian with the magazines' managing editor, Shahla Sherkat, as well as various journalists, activists, and scholars who frequently contributed to the magazine during multiple field research trips to Iran from 2009 to 2016.

This research focuses its analysis on *Zanan* and *Zanan-e Emrooz* as opposed to other equally influential locally published women's magazines in Iran for several reasons. First, the magazines' managing editor, Shahla Sherkat, benefited from a successful career in journalistic coverage of women's rights concerns in Iran since at least the 1979 revolution, as discussed later. Given her decades-long experience in this field, Sherkat and her magazines offered a platform for the active Iranian women's rights movement, particularly those aligned with the reformist viewpoints on gender. Second, according to Sherkat and many other women's rights activists who I interviewed in Iran during field research, the magazines benefited from notable popularity. By 2015, for instance, *Zanan-e Emrooz's* circulation had reached 10,000 for its print format, and around 50,000 readers when adding its subscribers and online readers (Sherkat et al., 2015, 376). Lastly, and related to their popularity and publicizing Iranian women's rights concerns in print, both magazines faced backlash from some ruling elites in terms of suspensions and other forms of intimidation, further highlighting their political impact and the extent that their coverage of women's rights was deemed threatening by various forces of the theocratic regime.

The data gathered reveals the extent that these publications represented the demands of the larger Iranian women's rights movement, particularly of those allied with the reformist parties and groups. This proximity between women's rights advocates and the magazines' editors enabled *Zanan* and to some extent *Zanan*-e *Emrooz* to engage in pressuring and lobbying campaigns of particularly reformist political elites given their more amicable campaign promises on women's political rights in comparison to their conservative counterparts.[1] Their publications also helped raise public awareness about women's advocacy surrounding such concerns as well as the level of resistance and hostility toward women's political roles across the ideological spectrum apparent from both reformist and conservative factions.

The findings contribute to our greater understanding of grassroots women's activism and their strategic interactions with political elites in a theocracy. Unlike previous research that has largely focused on Iranian women's magazines' impact on the dichotomous discourses of modernity and tradition or secularism and Islamism in contemporary Iran (Hendelman-Baavur, 2019; Moghissi, 2016; Najmabadi, 2000), in this research, I rather emphasize

---

[1] While internal divisions have always existed in Iranian politics, a major one of the past decades has been between conservatives and reformists, or hard-liners and soft-liners (Keshavarzian, 2005). The conservatives tend to fiercely support the office of the Supreme Leader and the theocratic regime, often taking all measures necessary to maintain this political hegemony through the use of unelected institutions such as the Council of Guardians and the Islamic Revolutionary Guard Corps (IRGC). On the other hand, reformists and to some extent moderates (represented by former President Hassan Rouhani) advocate for gradual democratization of the political system through more pluralistic elections, better relations with the West, and greater social and political freedoms, including for women and youth.

women's organizing that moves beyond the religious and secular divide, drawing from both local and global discourses on women's political rights. Thus, while categorization of women activists and their publications according to their secular, reformist, or conservative stands may provide useful tools of analysis, it is important to note that these categories are fluid and ever shifting, with women as key actors in muddling these previously dominant paradigms (Najmabadi, 2000).[2]

WOMEN AND POLITICS IN IRAN

The 1979 Iranian Revolution accompanied important political and social shifts for the Iranian population, particularly for its women. Women are documented to have played a key role in toppling the Pahlavi monarchy through their active participation in student and other political groups and parties and marching in the streets alongside men (Nashat, 1980; Paidar, 1995). The founders of the Islamic Republic, particularly Ayatollah Khomeini, welcomed women's presence and declared their political participation, including voting, "an Islamic duty," marking a sharp departure from Khomeini's previous stance in 1963 when he vehemently opposed women's suffrage as un-Islamic under the Pahlavi regime (Hoodfar, 1999; Tajali, 2011, 2022b). Soon after the revolution, however, Iran's clerical establishment reversed many of the hard-won women's rights of the Pahlavi era, particularly in areas of family rights, and instead legislated policies that in effect treated women as second-class citizens. In the area of formal politics, women were barred from serving as judges and other decision-making posts that required religious training, such as *ijtihad* (independent reasoning). The post-revolutionary Iranian constitution also limited women's access to the office of presidency through the ambiguous criterion of *rijal*, which Iran's conservative-dominated institutions have thus far interpreted as referring to men, disallowing women to even become candidates for this popularly elected post, which many women and reformist clerics challenge (Tajali, 2011, 2022b; Taleghani, 1997a). Much of the restrictions placed on women's political and public roles were in accordance with the Islamic Republic's conservative gender ideology that prioritizes women's domestic duties as mothers and wives over their active participation in the public sphere, similar to other conservative religious political movements that exist across the globe (Arat, 2005; Bacchetta and Power, 2002; Ben Shitrit, 2016; Deeb, 2006; Schreiber, 2008; Tajali, 2015).

Iranian women, however, did not remain silent in the face of such restrictions. Just weeks after the coming to power of the Islamic regime, women poured into the streets on the eve of International Women's Day celebrations on 8 March 1979, protesting Ayatollah Khomeini's rapid Islamization efforts.

---

[2] Indeed, Iran's self-identified Islamic women have often advocated for the adoption of secular human rights standards, while many secular women activists have sought to address gender discrimination in Iran through reference to religious precepts.

"The protestors included young and old, rich and poor, veiled and unveiled" (Paidar, 1995, 234). While hard-liners and other vigilante groups violently attacked women protestors on numerous occasions, women continued to voice their opposition to the new regime's gender discriminatory policies both from within and outside state structures. Indeed, some of the revolutionary women who held strong religious tendencies and thus gained access to a few political decision-making positions in post-revolutionary Iran also vocalized their concerns about the ruling clergy's restrictive stance on women. For example, despite widespread opposition from conservative elites to women's active presence in the public sphere, women such as Maryam Behrouzi (an influential female preacher and one of Ayatollah Khomeini's only female students) and Zahra Rahnavard (a scholar, professor, and fierce revolutionary activist, and later wife of Prime Minister Mousavi) insisted on women's equal rights in political representation, education, and employment, which they justified using egalitarian interpretations of Islam (Paidar, 1995). Behrouzi, one of only four women elected to the first 270-seat parliament following the revolution, publicly expressed dismay at the anti-woman sentiment of some of her revolutionary male colleagues, arguing that like the women of early Islam described in Muslim texts, Muslim women have the right and the obligation to serve their country, both as mothers and as political leaders (Afshar, 2012). To foster women's political representation, she established the Zeinab Society (*Jameh Zeinab*), a women's party closely tied to the conservative faction.[3]

A close analysis of women and politics throughout the Islamic Republic's history reveals that there is a gap between the level of women's political interest and activism and their access to formal politics. Women's political representation in Iran has been among the lowest in the region (women's parliamentary presence is currently below 6%),[4] despite the fact that women constitute a highly politicized and mobilized section of the society as apparent by their high rates of voting, or involvement in voter recruitment or street protests, such as in the 2022 women-led 2022 protests against mandatory veiling as well as the 2009 Green Movement demonstrations, and civil society activism. Similar to other global contexts, a variety of factors hinder women's access to political decision-making, ranging from cultural and religious to institutional and structural. As I have extensively argued elsewhere, the religion of Islam, while a

---

[3] Although Behrouzi remained affiliated with the conservative faction until her death in 2012, she did not see a contradiction between her faith and women's public roles, and continuously fought for women's greater presence in Iran's elite politics. Her lobbying efforts eventually led to the nomination and appointment of post-revolutionary Iran's first (and until now) only female minister, Marzieh Vahid-Dastjerdi, in the cabinet of conservative President Mahmood Ahmadinejad, as later discussed (Tajali, 2015, 2017).

[4] Only a few countries across the Muslim region rank lower than Iran in terms of women's parliamentary presence, and those tend to be those that granted suffrage to women more recently. Most other countries have had notable rates of women's parliamentary representation largely thanks to gender quotas, or affirmative action measures that aim to guarantee a certain limit of women representatives or candidates (Hoodfar & Tajali, 2011; Inter-Parliamentary Union, 2020).

barrier to women's equal access to the public sphere according to Iran's conservative ideological stance on gender, is not the most important factor keeping women out of politics (Tajali, 2022b). Gender discriminatory attitudes or behaviors that often become institutionalized in formal political structures are particularly significant in hindering women's equal access to the political sphere.

Given the multitude of restrictions, Iranian women have to be prepared to take advantage of any political openings that present themselves in Iran's closed authoritarian context, such as the coming to power of sympathetic and moderate parties and elites, to advance their political rights and influence. For instance, the political openings of the reform era (1997–2005) under the presidency of Mohammad Khatami enabled greater organizing and activism of diverse groups of women, particularly secular women, on various aspects of women's rights, including women's political participation. During this era, women demonstrated their political might at the ballot box as they turned out in overwhelming numbers in support of reformist and more moderate voices that campaigned on women's rights. Thanks to women's support, the sixth post-revolutionary Iranian parliament (2000–2004) witnessed the election of a notable number of outspoken reformist women parliamentarians (Tajali, 2022a). Despite their low numbers, the women of this parliament formed an active parliamentary women's caucus that sought to address a number of women's rights concerns (Moghadam & Haghighatjoo, 2016; Tajali, 2022a). The number of registered women's NGOs also rose from 67 in 1997 to 480 in 2005 (Mir-Hosseini, 2006a), further highlighting women's agency and interest in addressing their own concerns from the grassroots in the theocratic state.

Women's advancements during the reform era were, however, short-lived since the coming to power of conservative forces and the election of President Mahmud Ahmadinejad (2005–2013) created a hostile environment for women's rights advocacy. Many women's NGOs and magazines were closed and the next three parliaments that followed the reformist-backed sixth parliament included token women members of parliament (MPs) who rarely challenged the regime's conservative stance on women (Tajali, 2020). The conservative hard-liners' little tolerance of feminist and outspoken voices on women's rights led to extensive crackdown on high-profile members of the Iranian women's rights movement, declaring them threats to national security and forcing much of women's organizing underground (Gheytanchi, 2008). Women's pressuring of political and religious elites continued to the extent possible, with Ahmadinejad, in politically expedient moves, at times siding with women to increase his appeal or to distinguish himself from more conservative forces (Shahrokni, 2009; Tajali, 2015, 2017, 2022b). For instance, after decades of women's organizing, Ahmadinejad publicly supported women's access to sports stadiums though his conservative colleagues banned women from attending them as spectators (Shahrokni, 2020), while he also dared to break the taboo on the appointment of a female minister in his cabinet, a move that no other post-revolutionary Iranian president, regardless of political ideology, has made to date.

In 2013, the landslide election of moderate President Rouhani re-energized Iranian women's rights advocates. Similar to the reformist era of the late 1990s, women took advantage of these openings to articulate and organize around their demands. These were done both in women's publications and magazines, but also on social media, despite the state's frequent filtering of such tools. This context even facilitated the launch of multiple campaigns ahead of the tenth parliamentary election to ensure a women-friendlier parliament.[5] Such efforts led to a record number of women registering for candidates and getting elected, reaching 5.9% female parliamentary presence, a record for post-revolutionary Iran. A majority of the women MPs of the tenth parliament (2016–2020) were backed by the reformists, and they replaced all the conservative female incumbents who had poor records on women's rights from the major cities.[6] Women in this parliament had closer links to the Iranian women's rights movement and thus acted critically on women's rights on various occasions. Their outspokenness against the undemocratic, corrupt, and discriminatory aspects of the state tested the patience of the conservative elites. Iran's hardliners, with the support of institutions that they had put in place to ensure preservation of power into the hands of a select few, namely, the Council of Guardians, succeeded in regaining control over the eleventh parliament (2020–2024) by rejecting the candidacy of many outspoken reformists, including incumbent MPs, or through harassment and interrogation of key officials, including high-profile Rouhani-era women politicians (Tajali, 2022a).[7] Consequently, the conservative-dominated eleventh parliament witnessed the election of token women MPs with conservative tendencies on women's rights and roles.

The election of President Ebrahim Raisi in summer of 2021 solidified conservative control over all branches of the government, furthering Iran's autocratic rule and limiting any meaningful competition among the different political factions (Chehabi, 2021). Similar to the women MPs elected in 2020, the few women in his cabinet, including his Vice President for Women's Affairs, are also backed by the conservative faction, functioning mostly as mouthpieces

---

[5] Women's rights activists, many of whom with secular tendencies, launched the Campaign to Change the Male-dominated Face of Parliament to facilitate the election of women who will represent women's interests. Reformist party women, on the other hand, lobbied their parties for a voluntary 30 percent women's quota to be applied to their nation-wide list of candidates, dubbed the *List of Hope* (*Omid*). These efforts notably increased women's access to the parliament (Tajali, 2022a).

[6] Tehran's thirty-member district is among the most politicized in Iran. In the 2016 parliamentary elections, all of the eight women candidates who were nominated by the reformist faction for this district entered the parliament. All conservative-backed women MPs who had been representing Tehran were voted out of office during that election.

[7] The founders of the Islamic Republic established unelected bodies to protect conservative clerical authority in the theocracy. Among them, the Council of Guardians is tasked with vetting candidates for the major elections, rejecting anyone with questionable allegiance to the regimes and its revolutionary ideals (Keshavarzian, 2005). This body is considered a major barrier to Iran's democratization efforts as it has been increasingly disqualifying reformists and moderates, in effect engineering election results (Samii, 2001).

for the political establishment rather than representing grassroots women's interests, as apparent by this office's silence in response to the 2022 women-led protests to mandatory veiling with the chants for 'woman, life, freedom.' With Iranian hardliners' dismissal of women's demands, women's rights concerns are not expected to receive much attention from within the state institutions, though women are expected to continue to publicize their discontents to the extent possible in women's magazines, journals, social media, the street, and other non-state platforms.

DIPLOMATIC CHALLENGES TO THE STATUS QUO: THE ROLE OF IRANIAN WOMEN'S MAGAZINES

A notable contradiction of the Islamic Republic of Iran throughout its more than four-decade rule has been women's active and growing presence in nearly all aspects of cultural and intellectual production, despite the regime's conservative gender ideology which manifests itself in discriminatory laws, regulations, and treatments (Najmabadi, 2000). Women's magazines have been at the forefront of such cultural and intellectual production, providing venues for debate and analysis of competing ideologies and discourses on gender and women's rights in an Islamic country. In Iran's case, the theocracy has particularly fostered debates and discussions on women's rights from within an Islamic framework. As scholars such as Ziba Mir-Hosseini (2006b) have previously argued, the Islamic Republic created its own antithesis by putting forth a hegemony of patriarchal interpretations of Islam and imposing anachronistic jurisprudential constructions of gender relations that many Muslims, particularly women, disagreed with. Some of the most effective challenges to the dominant state ideologies on gender and exposing the inequalities embedded in Iran's laws were launched by women from within state institutions, including some of its most prominent ideological apparatuses. For instance, two post-revolutionary women's periodicals, *Zanan* (Women) and *Huquq-e Zanan* (Women's rights), considered by many to be especially outspoken against Iran's gender discriminatory rulings were managed by two women who were previously editors of *Zan-e ruz* (Today's woman), a weekly published by Kayhan Institute. According to Afsaneh Najmabadi (2000), "this institute is possibly the most ideologically and viciously rigid Islamist cultural organization in Iran," whose publications continue to serve as the mouthpiece of the conservative establishment (29–30). The fact that "Islamist hardliners produce a lineage of feminist editors" speaks to the fluidity of Iranian political and ideological developments, as well women's agency in boldly highlighting women's rights concerns in conservative and patriarchal contexts (Najmabadi, 2000). While some of these editors rose from the ranks of revolutionary women who were mobilized and politicized by the revolution and its promises, today, their central stands on women's rights are indistinguishable from secular feminists. Indeed, the uniting of forces of pious and secular women in post-revolutionary Iran has contributed to the formation of a strong women's movement that is a major force of democratization and, thus, feared by the theocratic state (Hoodfar, 1999).

A large amount of scholarship on Iranian women's rights advocacy throughout the past decades has credited the role of women's magazines (Kian, 1997; Mir-Hosseini, 2006b; Najmabadi, 2000; Vakil, 2011). As noted above, many of these women's magazines used their pages to publicize a variety of women's issues, ranging from women's family rights to their equal access to the public sphere. Women's political roles has been among particularly controversial topics for these magazines to cover as advocacy for women's greater political participation and representation poses a threat to male dominance and authority in formal politics (Hoodfar & Tajali, 2011).[8] For this reason, women editors and journalists have been especially diplomatic in the articulation of their demands for women's expanded political influence in Iran. I define women's diplomatic pressuring as their strategic articulation of their demands for reform or enhancement of women's rights in a way that seeks to find resonance with the dominant ideology, often through reference to religious discourses (Tajali, 2015, 2022b).

A notable example of this is how Islamic women activists, some of whom with very strong linkages to the founders of the theocratic state, have been challenging the gender unequal interpretation of the constitutional criterion *rijal* for the office of presidency described above. Among them, *Payam-e Hajar* (Hajar's message), a weekly magazine, stands out as a vocal critique of the regime's discriminatory mandate on the presidency, despite having been edited by a high-profile Islamic activist. Azam Taleghani (1943–2019) was the daughter of Ayatollah Mahmoud Taleghani, a key Shi'i political and religious figure, and a former parliamentarian who served in the first several rounds of the Iranian parliament following the revolution given her revolutionary credentials. To help foster the new generation of Islamic women, Taleghani founded the Society of Muslim Women just months after the 1979 revolution with Ayatollah Khomeini's blessing, and established *Payam-e Hajar*.

For more than two decades, Taleghani used this magazine to express her opposition to the discriminatory rulings of the theocracy, often in line with secular feminists' demands, but through a religious framework made possible by her strong religious convictions and religious training (Kamvari, 2019).[9] In 1997, a presidential election year, she devoted an entire issue of *Payam-e Hajar* to an in-depth discussion of *rijal* as it pertains to women's access to the office of the presidency. To counter the stance that *rijal* references solely "men," Taleghani publicized her own interpretation of the term in the magazine based

---

[8] Indeed, throughout the world, male elites long resisted women's rights to elect and get elected in an effort to keep politics in the hands of a select few. These rights were only recognized thanks to women's extensive organizing (Hoodfar & Tajali, 2011).

[9] *Payam-e Hajar* was ordered closed by conservatives in 2000 alongside a number of other reformist publications. Despite this closure, Taleghani continued her activism and protests through the Society of Muslim Women and other reformist parties (Personal interview with a reformist party woman, 12 June 2011).

on her reading of the Quran by arguing that, "every time the term '*rijal*' appears in the Quran it is in reference to both genders and it simply means 'humans' in plural form" (Taleghani, 1997b). In her writing, she cited Quranic verses in which it would be impossible to interpret *rijal* as only men such as its usage in *Al-A'raf* (The Heights) in which occupants of hell and heaven are conversing with one another (Quran 7:46 and 48). Taleghani states that, "it is impossible that all those in hell and heaven are men. It has been our effort all this time to prove the point that *rijal* means men and women who are active in politics and society" (Taleghani, 1997b). In the same issue, Taleghani also interviewed a number of male religious scholars, such as Allameh Seyed Mohammad Hussein Tabatabaei and Ali Tahmasebi, both known scholars of Shi'i Islam, on their interpretation of the term, with the majority agreeing with Taleghani's understanding that *rijal* is a gender-neutral term, referring to persons with extraordinary character and religious authority. Akin to launching a campaign, Taleghani continued her challenges in that year by making the bold move (with seven other women) of registering to become a presidential candidate. Thus, 1997 marked the first time in Iranian history when women aspired to compete for the highest executive office. Despite her exceptional political experience and religious training, the conservative-dominated Council of Guardians rejected Taleghani's candidacy.

Contention over *rijal* has continued in Iranian print media, both in women's journals and more general news outlets. The popular women's monthly, *Zanan*, continued Taleghani's path in the run-up to the 2001 presidential elections with the article, "22 years conflict over 'rijal'," in which it also interviewed key Islamic and ley scholars on the topic, while noting its impact on women's political rights in Iran since 1979 (Karimi Mojadad, 2001). In the run up to the 2017 presidential elections, its successor *Zanan-e Emrooz* reflected on "Azam Taleghani's 20 years persistence on interpretation (*tafsir*) of 'political *rijal*'" since her initial campaign in 1997 (Shirafkan, 2017). Women politicians and party activists linked to the reformists have also penned important articles in more general newspapers. Massoumeh Ebtekar (2013), a long-term vice-president in reformist cabinets published about the "Capabilities of Rijal Women" in the daily *Bahar Newspaper* to highlight the fact that women in post-revolutionary Iran have also been acquiring exceptional religious and political qualifications that make them fit for the presidency. Despite these publications, the conservative-backed Council of Guardians has never qualified a woman to compete for this office, although increasing number of women—including Taleghani until her death in 2019—continued to register to become candidates and never ceased their protests (Esfandiari, 2017).[10]

---

[10] Following women's continued protests against their limited access to the office of president, the Council of Guardians in recent years has stated that gender is not a factor in their disqualification of candidates. However, women's rights advocates that I have interviewed are not convinced by this stance, and emphasize that only qualifying a woman would satisfy this demand given the notable number of qualified women who aspire for this office (Personal interviews, July 2015 and March 2016).

My interviews with Iranian women's rights activists across the ideological spectrum have revealed that women like Taleghani were well-positioned to diplomatically articulate their demands in a way that challenges the gender status quo of the theocratic regime. The women's strong religious convictions, commitment to revolution and its ideals, and at times personal ties with members of the ruling establishment greatly advantaged them in comparison to their secular counterparts to be able to publish, write, and even directly lobby key religious and political figures. Notably, despite women's proximity to the regime and their religious standing, the conservative forces still had little tolerance for highly critical women's publications, ordering their closures on various occasions. Indeed, in recent decades, a number of widely circulated women's magazines that sought to address women's rights have been either closed or their editors have been discouraged from continuing their publications, such as *Payam-e Hajar*, *Huquq-e Zanan* (Women's rights), *Zan* (Woman), and *Zanan* (Women).

Zanan magazine (re-named to *Zanan-e Emrooz* in 2014), and its managing editor, Shahla Sherkat, who similar to Taleghani gained the trust of the official state institutions soon after the revolution thanks to her religious background, has been able to provide a prominent platform for the Iranian women's movement. While a number of scholars declare Sherkat and her publications as instances of Islamic feminism in Iran (Mir-Hosseini, 2006b; Najmabadi, 2000; Paidar, 2001), Sherkat herself disagrees with the term arguing that she and many others like her resort to Islamic precepts given Iran's theocratic structure. In a personal interview, she prided herself on having mastered "the art of both respecting Iran's regulations while simultaneously seeking to make progress on women's rights" throughout her decades of journalism. She expressed remorse when the conservatives "unjustly banned" her magazine, but persisted in successful reversals of these decisions, while recognizing the precariousness of the environment she publishes in (Personal interviews, 2 July 2011 and 7 June 2015). Expectedly, the COVID-19 pandemic exacerbated the publishing abilities of many independent outlets in Iran, resulting in *Zanan-e Emrooz's* inability to publish regularly since late 2020.

Zanan and Zanan-e Emrooz

Shahla Sherkat launched *Zanan* in 1992, soon after she was fired from *Zan-e Ruz* (Today's woman) for "intensification of her modernist, Westernizing, and feminist tendencies" following ten years of editing this magazine in post-revolutionary Iran. Reminiscing about her earlier experiences in journalism, Sherkat writes, "the early women's magazines [namely *Rah-e Zeinab* (Zeinab's way) and *Zan-e ruz*] emphasized the narratives of the armed revolutionary Muslim woman" who protested corruption and Westernization. However, gradually, and thanks to the "phone calls and letters that *Zan-e Ruz* received from its readers" she became aware of the extent and significance of women's problems (Sherkat, 2003, 2009). From its modest beginnings, *Zanan* became one of Iran's most widely circulated women's magazines. According to Sherkat, the magazine's popularity was because of its coverage of key aspects of women's rights in the highly politicized and gendered context of theocratic Iran (Personal interview, 2 July 2011). A graduate of psychology, Sherkat had a keen interest to investigate gender relations, roles, and various forms of discrimination, with an eye on women's experiences and their perseverance to be present and active in a patriarchal society. *Zanan* made its readers aware of central women's rights concerns and their accomplishments in cinema, politics, sports, and more, without overly infuriating the mullahs.

That lasted, however, until 2008, when Sherkat was suddenly notified that the state had closed *Zanan* after 152 issues under the claim that the magazine was a "threat to the psychological security of the society as it showed Iranian women in a black light" (New York Times, 2008). The closure had occurred in a reactive move against many liberal and more progressive publications at a time when the conservative faction had become fearful of internally driven reformist forces. Despite the ban on her magazine, Sherkat continued to remain active in journalism, recognizing that these closures could give way to openings in Iran's unpredictable political context since control over some institutions at times swings from one faction to another, with the public continuously demanding greater freedom of expression and media. That opening presented itself following moderate Hassan Rouhani's election in 2013 and the appointment of "a more open Minister of Culture," when Sherkat was able to once again call herself a managing editor, this time of *Zanan-e Emrooz* (Today's women) launched in May 2014 (Personal interview, 7 June, 2015). Continuing *Zanan* magazine's legacy, this new women's monthly aimed "to make the government and women aware of and sensitive to gender discrimination (*tab'iz-e jensiyati*) and to empower women to use the best means available to rid themselves of submission and abuse," through within the restrictive parameters set by the regime (Sherkat et al., 2015, 377).

Significantly, although the launch of *Zanan-e Emrooz* coincided with notable decrease among a large section of the society's interest in print media thanks to their greater access to internet and satellite television, the women's rights concerns raised by the magazine continued to have political importance. While the magazine's re-appearance had created hope for Iranian women's rights advocates, Iran's hardliners showed sensitivity to the magazine soon after its initial launch. Merely three months following the publication of *Zanan-e Emrooz's* first issue, Sherkat was summoned to appear at Iran's Press Court to respond to charges of "promoting 'obsolete' feminist views and ideas that are un-Islamic" (Esfandiari, 2014). Many other conservative forces blamed the initial licensing of the magazine as a failure of the Rouhani administration for allowing Sherkat to once again publish given her "background and deviant views" (Esfandiari, 2014). The pressures from the hard-liners finally succeeded in the suspension of *Zanan-e Emrooz* in May 2015 after only eleven issues published.[11] However, in Iran's factional political struggles between conservatives and reformist forces (to which Sherkat is closer), this suspension was temporary with Sherkat resuming the publication in October 2015 thanks to her own pressures and support from official allies within the reformist camp, among them, the Vice President for Women's Affairs in President Rouhani's cabinet, Shahindokht Molaverdi (Personal interviews with Iranian women activists, March 2016). The harassment, interrogation, and even arrest of *Zanan-e Emrooz's* journalists and contributors however continued, with the magazine experiencing multiple suspensions within the past years.

One of *Zanan-e Emrooz's* suspensions occurred soon after the 2016 Iranian parliamentary elections in which a reformist-backed list of candidates, and nearly all of the women it had listed in major cities, were successful in entering the parliament. In the run up to the elections, *Zanan-e Emrooz* invited contributions and interviews with scholars and activists who worked on women's political representation for its fifteenth issue. Knowing of my research on gender and politics in Muslim contexts, Sherkat invited me to write an article on my comparative research on women's political participation and representation between Iran and Turkey. The issue also featured an interview with my co-author of a book on parliamentary gender quotas across the globe, anthropologist Homa Hoodfar, who is also an expert on the topic (Hoodfar & Tajali, 2011). The success of the reformist camp in the 2016 elections once again threatened the conservative forces' strong hold on power, while the entrance of outspoken reformist women to the parliament increased the likelihood that they would challenge the regime's gender status quo. These threats resulted in the conservatives targeting *Zanan-e Emrooz* personnel and its contributors. The night before her flight out of Iran to return home to Canada, Homa Hoodfar was arrested by Iran's hardliner Islamic Revolutionary Guard Corps (IRGC). After many interrogations, it became clear that IRGC was particularly sensitive to women's political rights and roles in the Islamic Republic, and thus had little tolerance for publications, campaigns, and efforts that aimed to expand women's access to formal politics.[12]

The repeated harassments and closures of Iranian women's magazines such as *Zanan* and *Zanan-e Emrooz* is indicative of their political impact and the extent that the conservatives fear such publications' ability to publicize women's demands and mobilize voters, jeopardizing conservatives' strong hold over power. The following section briefly outlines instances of how Sherkat's

---

[11] A reason for the hard-liners' rage against the magazine was its coverage of the increasing phenomenon of "white marriage" or co-habitation between unmarried couples. Sherkat publicly defended "covering a complicated reality in Iranian society that deserves objective analysis," dismissing the accusation that the magazine's coverage was promoting cohabitation instead of marriage. She also pointed to the fact that other magazines and publications had also written about this phenomenon with no repercussion (Personal interview, 7 June 2015).

[12] Homa Hoodfar was released from prison after six months thanks to an extensive international campaign that protested Iranian authorities' violation of her fundamental right to academic freedom.

magazines engaged with the theocratic regime and its institutions on the issue of women's political participation and representation, with attention to the discourses used, politicians targeted, and Iranian elites' responses to these publications.

DEMANDS FOR WOMEN IN POLITICS

Women's greater access to political office has been a central demand of the Iranian women's rights movements across the ideological spectrum. Expectedly, women's magazines have paid particular attention to this concern and have provided an important platform for discussion of women's political roles and rights in an Islamic society. In its early issues, *Zanan* addressed the topic by including contributions from renowned Islamic scholars, human rights lawyers, and activists discussing the reasons and justifications for women's political underrepresentation in Iran. Given Sherkat's own religious background, such discussions were largely from within an Islamic framework, with a women-centered re-reading of Islam. For instance, in its initial issues, *Zanan* invited the reformist cleric, Mohsen Saidzadeh (writing as Mina Yadegar Azadi), to write about the different religious readings on women's judgeship, which has been banned since the 1979 revolution.[13] In two different articles (featured in issues 4 and 5 of *Zanan*), Saidzadeh outlines the various clerical positions and justifications on this topic, highlighting the lack of clerical consensus in Shi'i Islam on whether women can serve as judges (Yadegar Azadi, 1992b, 1992c). In issue 8, Saidzadeh similarly tackles the issue of whether women can reach the level of *ijtihad* (independent reasoning), another form of authority to which women have very limited access in the Islamic Republic (Yadegar Azadi, 1992a). According to Ziba Mir-Hosseini, such publicizing of the clerical debates on women's rights and roles, while advocating for a reformist stance that encouraged a women-centered rereading of Islamic precepts contributed to *Zanan's* early success (Mir-Hosseini, 1999). The early clerical contributions quickly progressed into dialogues between religious scholars and secular feminists, such as Mehrangiz Kar, a human rights lawyer, in which the latter posed questions about the range of problems or discrimination that women face, justified through reference to Islam, to the former. The unfolding of such discussions in a widely circulated magazine contributed to the public's scrutiny of the Islamic Republic's gender policies. Coverage of women's political participation and representation in comparison with other Muslim countries also contributed to pressuring Iran's elites for their failure to grant women more roles in formal politics, such as in comparison to Pakistan and its twice successful

---

[13] Mohsen Saidzadeh was later defrocked for his writings and advocacy for women-centered re-readings of Islam, which argued that gender discriminatory practices and rulings in Islam are largely due to clerical mis-interpretations rather than God's divine will which he, like many reformists, believed is inherently egalitarian (Mir-Hosseini, 1999; Tajali, 2011).

election of Prime Minister Benazir Bhutto, who coincidentally had Iranian heritage (Tarighi, 2008).

Perhaps the most important tool that *Zanan* and its successor *Zanan-e Emrooz* used to engage with Iran's formal political institutions, particularly the legislative and the executive branches, was to use their journalistic access to these bodies to carefully document any bills, proposals, or laws under discussion relevant to women. In *Zanan*, Sherkat appointed Zahra Ebrahimi, a seasoned journalist, to prepare monthly reports on the happenings of the Iranian parliament related to women.[14] Ebrahimi's reports played a central role in introducing key parliamentarians to *Zanan's* readers, including many women's rights activist, thus enhancing the Iranian women's rights groups' ability to lobby and engage with their female representatives. Coverage of Iran's women MPs intensified during the sixth parliament (2000–2004), when a decision was made to create a parliamentary women's caucus. During this parliament's term, *Zanan* closely reported on the women MPs' activities and interviewed the most outspoken members. When the conservative faction intentionally disqualified most of the women MP incumbents from running for the seventh parliament, *Zanan's* reportage publicized the extent that women's issues were politicized and served as a battleground for factional politics (Tajali, 2022a). *Zanan's* coverage of the parliament continued whether reformist or conservative-backed women occupied the few seats of Iran's total 290-member parliament, and remains a regular feature of *Zanan-e Emrooz* when the magazine is in print. Raising awareness of the happenings of the Iranian parliament related to women's rights also assisted Iranian women's rights activists in their campaigning efforts whether through lobbying of its members on important bills or through campaigns near parliamentary elections to impact its composition (Personal interview with Iranian women activists, 2011 and 2015).

In addition to the parliament, *Zanan* and to a lesser extent *Zanan-e Emrooz*[15] have also engaged with the executive branch and other state institutions on the nomination and appointment of women to other high-level political posts. Political appointments can gain urgency for Iranian women advocates in the context of Iran's fiercely engineered and undemocratic elections which rarely reflect the will of the people, particularly of women. Such urgency rises when a president with reformist or moderate tendencies at least acknowledges

---

[14] Zahra Ebrahimi once commented that while her monthly reports on women in the parliament has helped create an archive of their efforts in *Zanan* that is useful for research and more, she also noted that "placing women under the microscope, merely because of their gender is not fair." "Many of the men, throughout their four-year parliamentary terms, come and go silently like regular employees while benefiting from all of the privileges of serving in the house of the people, but no one knows if they have done anything for their constituents. The actions of these men remain hidden from the public's gaze" (29).

[15] *Zanan-e Emrooz* was only launched after President Rouhani took office, while the magazine has also faced numerous hurdles in being permitted to publish. For these reasons, unlike *Zanan*, *Zanan-e Emrooz* has been much more cautious in targeting official institutions and politicians, including those from the reformist camp.

women's concerns in their campaigns, and is able to win an election, often with a landslide, as it occurred during elections of both Presidents Khatami and Rouhani. In such contexts, women's magazines like *Zanan* and *Zanan-e Emrooz* become especially active in publicizing women's rights concerns, while many of the magazine's contributors consider appointments of critical women to the cabinet as a key tactic to the expansion of women's political roles, and possibly representation of women's rights in the theocracy.

In this regard, Sherkat's magazines, when licensed to print, have played central roles in providing a larger platform for reformist candidates among their competitors, and in cases when they were victorious, have tactfully pushed for greater inclusion of women in formal politics. For instance, in 1997, *Zanan* devoted an issue to Mohammad Khatami as he was campaigning for office, inquiring about his stance on women's rights including on inclusion of women to his cabinet. When in an interview to *Zanan* he declared that "merit and not gender should determine appointment to politics" (Khatami, 1997), the magazine printed a series of articles, penned at times by feminist scholars and activists, on the debates and stereotypes around meritocracy, with attention to the public's perceptions on women in political leadership (Hafezian, 1997). In his first term in office, Khatami did not nominate any women as ministers, but did appoint Masoumeh Ebtekar as Vice-President on Environment and a few women as consultants, including reformist Zahra Shojaee on women's affairs. To many women's rights advocates, including *Zanan*, these appointments were not enough, signaling a missed opportunity from a sympathetic president.

In the run up to 2001 presidential elections, *Zanan* intensified its pressuring of Khatami who was running for re-election. Women's rights advocate and regular *Zanan* contributor, Noushin Tarighi, posed a direct question to Khatami on "Will women ministers finally happen?," by highlighting the fact that "Khatami's election in 1997 was made possible thanks to the exceptional voter turnout of women and youth who were energized by Khatami's promises. Were those promises made just to garner votes?" The article then continued with quotes from key women's rights scholars and advocates, justifying the need for a female minister in Iran's political context. Sociologist Zhaleh Shaditalab is for instance quoted as saying, "We have no need to beat around the bush (*ta'arof*) with Mr. Khatami. Whether he is the president or not, women should be in high-level decision-making. This is not a request but a necessity." Another advocate of women's rights states, "When 80 percent of the country's agriculture is done by women, why shouldn't a woman be considered as the minister of agriculture?" (Tarighi, 2001, 3, 6, 7). In the end, despite *Zanan's* strategic targeting of Khatami, he did not appoint any women to his cabinet as ministers, but only as vice-presidents or consultants that do not require parliamentary approval. Perhaps bowing to women's pressures, Khatami did establish a Center for Women's Participation (CWP) under the leadership of Zahra Shojaee, an advocate of women's rights with strong religious reformist tendencies, to consult him on women's issues. The closest thing to an official women's machinery, this office, including its name, function, and director, became a central focus of women's rights advocates and magazines.[16] In a later issue published following Khatami's landslide re-election in 2001, *Zanan* problematizes his failure to nominate a female minister as an indication of most political elites' discriminatory stance toward women, regardless of their ideological backing. The article titled, "Khatami says there is no obligation to appoint a female minister," publicized his remarks that "appointment of a female minister was too big of a political risk" for him to take, while it also included the voices of key reformist female and male politicians on the complications of women's access to the ministry in Iran's political context (Omidy, 2001, 10–11). This critical article of a sitting president and others like it helped *Zanan* establish its independence and its prioritization of women's issues over factional politics.

Following the election of conservative Mahmoud Ahmadinejad in 2005, *Zanan* once again publicized the demand for women's presence in the cabinet as ministers. Given that Ahmadinejad had never campaigned on this demand of the Iranian women's movement (unlike his predecessor), women expected less from him on his cabinet's composition. *Zanan's* Zahra Ebrahimi (2005) reported on the fact that "the ninth government also does not have a woman minister," while she also raised awareness about his conservative agenda on gender. As noted above, Ahmadinejad's election accompanied major restrictions on women's rights activism and media, and in 2008, as part of a larger attack on civil society, his administration revoked *Zanan's* license. This closure pushed much of women's rights campaigning and organizing underground. Thus, in 2009, *Zanan* was unable to cover the eruption of the Green Movement protests—in which women played central roles—to Ahmadinejad's contentious re-election, or all that occurred in its aftermath. This re-election and near-complete marginalization of reformists from the political landscape provided conservative women activists with a key opportunity to pressure their candidate on women's central demands, among them, women's greater political presence. As I have argued elsewhere (Tajali, 2015, 2017), the women's party, Zeinab Society, utilized the political upheavals of the 2009 popular uprisings to demand women ministers, to which Ahmadinejad, who was eager to establish his independence from more conservative forces, was responsive. Thus, post-revolutionary Iran's only female minister has been appointed during Ahmadinejad's presidency, thanks to decades of women's organizing and the unexpected political opportunities of the 2009 elections.

After six years of censorship, *Zanan-e Emrooz*, launched in 2014, continued to push for women's greater presence in formal politics, but in a more hostile political environment. According to Sherkat (Sherkat et. al., 2015), "because of redlines" the magazine "cannot publicly tackle some matters, but we discuss

---

[16] Following coming to power in 2005, conservative president Ahmadinejad changed the name of the Center for Women's Participation to the Center for Women and Family affairs and appointed women with poor records on women's rights to lead it, causing protests among many women's rights activists.

them (among the editors and other experts who write for the magazine), as an opportunity to address a previously forbidden issue may (later) arise" (376). Redlines—in journalism, code for the boundary between writing about an issue in acceptable and unacceptable ways—has resulted in much censorship, including self-censorship as journalists and editors have been forced to shy away from covering controversial topics in an effort to avoid closure or worse (Casey, 2008; Sherkat, 2003). Within the past years, the hard-liners' little tolerance for women's rights advocacy, as evident by frequent arrests of gender experts, or closure of women's magazines and organizations, has taken a toll on Sherkat's ability to truly push for change from within the system. Such challenges, coupled with scarcity of financial resources in a sanctioned and economically weak country, forced *Zanan-e Emrooz* to publish its issues quarterly as opposed to monthly as it had been for decades, with frequent irregularities. According to its website, *Zanan-e Emrooz's* latest issue (no. 45) was published in late 2020 as the country was battling a number of difficulties among them, the COVID-19 pandemic. Despite these limitations, as Sherkat (2009) once put it, "Anyone who did research on women's issues benefitted from hundreds of articles, stories and interviews that were featured" in her magazines. Indeed documenting the key happenings, debates, and discourses on women's rights has created a helpful archive for research and analysis, though such documentation is understandably limited and imperfect given Iran's closed authoritarian context and its sensitivity to gender issues. For instance, homosexuality or the rights of sexual minorities, a major taboo for a context such as Iran, is rarely addressed in any women's publications, though there is notable activism in these areas on behalf of women's rights advocates.

CONCLUSION

Throughout her career, Sherkat has been both praised for having mastered the ability to walk a fine line between respecting state regulations, while seeking to publicize women's rights concerns for many years, while also criticized for silencing the magazines' contributors by "using her red pen to remove some of the most important sentences of an article," as secular feminist lawyer and regular *Zanan* contributor, Shadi Sadr, shared in the magazine's 100th issue (2003, 99). This chapter demonstrated that her interest to work within such a precarious political context or to seek to publish on timely women's rights concerns within a theocracy that upholds a patriarchal gender ideology is an instance of women advocates engaging with the state (Chappell, 2002). As previous research has argued, seeking to publicize and address women's rights concerns in highly undemocratic and gender unequal state structures is challenging, though women's rights activists seek to persist in their activism and awareness-raising efforts. This chapter's findings highlight the important role that women's magazines and journals have played in diplomatic articulation of their demands from the theocratic state. Since many secular women activists were marginalized from Iranian print media given their ideological tendencies, a number of Islamic women, or those with religious convictions, such as Azam Taleghani, Ashraf Germizadegan, and Shahla Sherkat, made notable contributions to debates on women's rights and roles in Iranian society. This analysis also showcased the extent that these women were well-positioned to initiate many public discussions on women's rights, particularly on women's political participation and representation, given their religious tendencies. While arguably falling short of representing the voices of all women in Iran, these widely circulated magazines did help move these discussions forward thanks also to the input they received from their readers.

Using advocacy and lobbying around women's political rights, this chapter outlined the ways in which various women's magazines, particularly *Zanan* and *Zanan-e Emrooz*, have consistently strived to expand women's political roles in the Islamic Republic, while facing numerous challenges. This demand is central to women's rights advocates across the ideological spectrum, while women's greater access to political decision-making can greatly impact other aspects of women's rights. Analysis of women's writings and pressuring around women's political underrepresentation also sheds better light on women's maneuverings of the openings and constraints of their political context, and their perseverance of taking advantage of key opportunities that may arise while remaining vigilant during closures and crackdowns. With important political openings, such as the coming to power of sympathetic and moderate parties and elites, women's outspokenness and active lobbying of key political elites often increases on the pages of women's publications. However, with certain constraints such as the backlash of conservative forces against women's challenging of patriarchal norms in women's media, women activists are forced to resort to online forms of awareness raising, mobilization, and even street protests and strikes as we are witnessing as of this writing during the 2022 women-led protests in Iran. Knowing Iranian women, articulation of their demands will continue, whether in the streets, online, or with some openings, in print.

REFERENCES

Afshar, H. (2012). Competing Interets: Democracy, Islamification, and Women Politicians in Iran. In H. Afshar (Ed.), *Women and Fluid Identities: Strategic and Practical Pathways Selected by Women*. Palgrave Macmillan.

Arat, Y. (2005). *Rethinking Islam and Liberal Democracy: Islamist Women in Turkish Politics*. State University of New York Press. http://www.loc.gov/catdir/toc/ecip0420/2004017001.html.

Bacchetta, P., & Margaret Power. (2002). *Right-Wing Women: From Conservatives to Extremists Around the World*. Psychology Press.

Ben Shitrit, L. (2016). *Righteous Transgressions: Women's Activism on the Israeli and Palestinian Religious Right*. Princeton University Press. https://press.princeton.edu/titles/10629.html

Casey, M. (2008, February 10). *Influential Women's Magazine Silenced in Iran*. News. Women's ENews. https://womensenews.org/2008/02/influential-womens-magazine-silenced-in-iran/.

Chappell, L. A. (2002). *Gendering Government: Feminist Engagement with the State in Australia and Canada. Book, Whole.* UBC Press.

Chehabi, H. (2021). *Iran's Shrinking Political Society.* Organization. Wilson Center. https://www.wilsoncenter.org/article/irans-shrinking-political-society.

Deeb, L. (2006). *An Enchanted Modern: Gender and Public Piety in Shi'i Lebanon. Princeton Studies in Muslim Politics, Book, Whole.* Princeton University Press.

Ebrahimi, Z. (2005, July). *The Ninth Parliament also Does Not Have a Woman Minister (in Persian).* Zanan Magazine.

Ebtekar, M. (2013). Capabilities of 'Rijal' Women (in Persian). Bahar Newspaper, May 22, 2013, 129 edition.

Esfandiari, G. (2014). *Iranian Women's Monthly Under Pressure From Hard-Liners.* News. Radio Free Europe/Radio Liberty. https://www.rferl.org/a/iran-womens-monthly-under-pressure/26561137.html.

Esfandiari, G. (2017, April 19). *No Woman Has Ever Run For Iranian President. Will Azam Taleghani Be the First?* News. RadioFreeEurope/RadioLiberty. https://www.rferl.org/a/iran-taleghani-woman-president-election/28439661.html.

Gheytanchi, E. (2008). *Women's Rights Activists Are Not a Threat to Iran's National Security.* News. Huffpost. https://www.huffpost.com/entry/womens-rights-activists-a_b_87391.

Hafezian, M. H. (1997). *Are Women Truly Qualified? (in Persian).* Zanan Magazine.

Hendelman-Baavur, L. (2019). *Creating the Modern Iranian Woman: Popular Culture between Two Revolutions. The Global Middle East.* Cambridge University Press. https://doi.org/10.1017/9781108627993

Hoodfar, H. (1999). *The Women's Movement in Iran: Women at the Crossroads of Secularization and Islamization. Book, Whole.* Women Living Under Muslim Laws.

Hoodfar, H., & Tajali, M. (2011). *Electoral Politics: Making Quotas Work for Women. Book, Whole.* Women Living Under Muslim Laws (WLUML).

Inter-Parliamentary Union. (2020). *Women in National Parliaments.* Global Data on National Parliaments. https://data.ipu.org/women-ranking?month=6&year=2020.

Kamvari, N. (2019, October 31). *Azam Taleghani: The Link Between Secular and Religious Feminists in Iran (in Persian).* Blog. RadioZamaneh. https://www.radiozamaneh.com/471995.

Karimi Mojadad, R. (2001). *22 years Conflict Over 'Rijal' (in Persian).* Zanan Magazine.

Keshavarzian, A. (2005). Contestation without Democracy: Elite Fragmentation in Iran. In M. P. Posusney & M. P. Angrist (Eds.), *Authoritarianism in the Middle East: Regimes and Resistance* (pp. 63–90). Lynne Rienner Publishers, Inc. http://www.loc.gov/catdir/toc/ecip0511/2005011302.html

Khatami, S. M. (1997). *What does Khatami Say about Women? (in Persian).* Zanan Magazine.

Kian, A. (1997). Women and Politics in Post-Islamist Iran: The Gender Conscious Drive to Change. *British Journal of Middle Eastern Studies, 24*(1), 75–96.

Mir-Hosseini, Z. (1999). *Islam and Gender: The Religious Debate in Contemporary Iran. Princeton Studies in Muslim Politics, Book, Whole.* Princeton University Press.

Mir-Hosseini, Z. (2006a). Is Time on Iranian Women Protester's Side?

Mir-Hosseini, Z. (2006b). Muslim Women's Quest for Equality: Between Islamic Law and Feminism. *Critical Inquiry, 32*(4), 629–645. https://doi.org/10.1086/508085

Moghadam, V. M., & Haghighatjoo, F. (2016). Women and Political Leadership in an Authoritarian Context: A Case Study of the Sixth Parliament in the Islamic Republic of Iran. *Politics & Gender, 12*(1), 168–197. https://doi.org/10.1017/S1743923X15000598

Moghissi, H. (2016). *Populism and Feminism in Iran: Women's Struggle in a Male-Defined Revolutionary Movement.* Macmillan.

Najmabadi, A. (2000). (Un)Veiling Feminism. *Social Text, 18*(3_64), 29–45.

Nashat, G. (1980). Women in the Islamic Republic of Iran. *Iranian Studies, 13*(1/4), 165–194.

New York Times. (2008). Shutting Down Zanan. *New York Times,* February 7, 2008, sec. A.

Omidy, S. (2001). *Khatami: 'Selection of a Female Minister Is Not Necessary' (in Persian).* Zanan Magazine.

Paidar, P. (1995). *Women and the Political Process in Twentieth-Century Iran. Book, Whole.* Cambridge University Press.

Paidar, P. (2001). *Gender of Democracy: The Encounter between Feminism and Reformism in Contemporary Iran.* UNRISD.

Sadr, S. (2003). *From within the Society (in Persian).* Zanan Magazine.

Samii, A. W. (2001). Iran's Guardians Council as an Obstacle to Democracy. *Middle East Journal, 55*(4), 643–662.

Schreiber, R. (2008). *Righting Feminism: Conservative Women and American Politics.* Oxford University Press. https://doi.org/10.1093/acprof:oso/9780195331813.001.0001

Shahrokni, N. (2009). All the President's Women. *Middle East Report* 253 (Journal Article).

Shahrokni, N. (2020). *Women in Place: The Politics of Gender Segregation in Iran - Nazanin Shahrokni - Google Books.* University of California Press.

Sherkat, S. (2003). *One Hundred Lashes for a Forbidden Love (in Persian).* Zanan Magazine.

Sherkat, S. (2009). Telling the Stories of Iranian Women's Lives. Organization. Nieman Reports.https://niemanreports.org/articles/telling-the-stories-of-iranian-womens-lives/.

Sherkat, S., Shahrokni, N., & Hasso, F. (2015). Zanan-e Emrooz. *Journal of Middle East Women's Studies, 11*(3), 376–379.

Shirafkan, A. (2017). *Azam Taleghani's 20 Years Persistence on Interpretation (tafsir) of 'Political Rijal' (in Persian).* Zanan Magazine.

Siddiqui, N. (2014). Women's Magazines in Asian and Middle Eastern Countries. *South Asian Popular Culture, 12*(1), 29–40. https://doi.org/10.1080/1474668 9.2014.879423

Skalli, L. H. (2006a). *Through a Local Prism: Gender, Globalization, and Identity in Moroccan Women's Magazines.* Lexington Books.

Skalli, L. H. (2006b). Communicating Gender in the Public Sphere: Women and Information Technologies in the MENA. *Journal of Middle East Women's Studies, 2*(2), 35–59. https://doi.org/10.2979/MEW.2006.2.2.35

Tajali, M. (2011). Notions of Female Authority in Modern Shi'i Thought. *Religions, 2*(3), 449–468.

Tajali, M. (2015). Islamic Women's Groups and the Quest for Political Representation in Turkey and Iran. *The Middle East Journal, 69*(4), 563–581.

Tajali, M. (2017). Protesting Gender Discrimination from Within: Women's Political Representation on Behalf of Islamic Parties. *British Journal of Middle Eastern Studies, 44*(2), 176–193. https://doi.org/10.1080/13530194.2017.1281570

Tajali, M. (2020). *Women Politicians of Iran on Women's Rights: Critical Actors or Futile Figureheads? E-zine.* Jadaliyya. https://www.jadaliyya.com/Details/40788.

Tajali, M. (2022a). Women's Substantive Representation in the Islamic Republic of Iran: The Potential of Women Critical Actors. *Politics & Gender, 1–31,* 1. https://doi.org/10.1017/S1743923X21000416

Tajali, M. (2022b). *Women's Political Representation in Iran and Turkey: Demanding a Seat at the Table.* Edinburgh University Press.

Taleghani, A. (1997a). *Can a Woman Become President? (in Persian).* Payam-e Hajar.

Taleghani, A. (1997b). *Why Did I Become a Presidential Candidate? (in Persian).* Payam-e Hajar.

Tarighi, N. (2001, June). *Will Women Ministers Finally Happen? (in Persian).* Zanan Magazine.

Tarighi, N. (2008). *An Interview with Shahla Haeri: The Qualities and Mistakes of Benazir (in Persian).* Zanan Magazine.

Vakil, S. (2011). *Women and Politics in the Islamic Republic of Iran: Action and Reaction. Book, Whole.* Continuum.

Yadegar Azadi, M. (1992a). *Ijtihad and Women's Marja'iyat (in Persian).* Zanan Magazine.

Yadegar Azadi, M. (1992b). *Judgeship and Women (in Persian).* Zanan Magazine.

Yadegar Azadi, M. (1992c). *Women's Judgeship (in Persian).* Zanan Magazine.

Zachs, F. (2014). Cross-Glocalization: Syrian Women Immigrants and the Founding of Women's Magazines in Egypt. *Middle Eastern Studies, 50*(3), 353–369. https://doi.org/10.1080/00263206.2013.863757

CHAPTER 13

Omani Women in the Media: Navigating Political and Social Powers

Rafiah Al Talei

In Oman, media outlets influence gendered outcomes for political processes and participation. According to female candidates, state media coverage of elections is indicative of authorities' biases against female candidates, too. Given the cultural challenges Omani women face when running for office, media disregard for these hardships disproportionately impacts their campaign success. As such, Omani female politicians call for a quality new approach to media coverage of elections to elevate women's political participation.

Women remain underrepresented in Oman's' Majlis A'Shura—the state's only elected legislative body akin to a national council—due to the outsized influence of social factors. In the most recent election cycle, despite female candidates' attempted outreach to larger segments of the electorate, coverage by traditional media failed to generate social or cultural recognition of their ability to compete with men as leaders. Notably, Omani media is not only constrained by social taboos impeding women's access to leadership positions but also personal interpretations of written and unwritten rules related to women's political participation that continue to deprioritize female representation.

Generally, state media in Oman reflects non-sensitive gender discourses when discussing women's issues. While the media refrains from educating Omanis as to how gender plays a role in public life and politics, the same outlets reaffirm Oman's traditional values and gender roles. Furthermore, due to restrictive laws and media monopolies, independent media is virtually nonexistent in Oman. Though under current socio-political circumstances it is

R. Al Talei (✉)
Washington, DC, USA

L. H. Skalli, N. Eltantawy (eds.), *The Palgrave Handbook of Gender,
Media and Communication in the Middle East and North Africa*,
https://doi.org/10.1007/978-3-031-11980-4_13

223

impossible to predict if independent media would benefit the political campaigns of female candidates, its potential to affect outcomes is undeniable.[1]

Scholars such as Al-Lamki (2008), Al-Farsi (2009), and Al-Hayes (2010)[2] have found that media could influence Omanis' perspectives and voting behavior toward women; however, academics and policy makers have yet to acknowledge the entrenchment of cultural values in news outlets' handling of information. Existing research identifies the failure of Omani media to support women's candidacy and raise voters' awareness regarding women's political leadership. Furthermore, research has noted media framing of women's underrepresentation as a local issue—rather than national—that cannot be solved through public discussion. While scholars generally concur that societal and political gender inequality are challenges for Omani women, some studies go as far as to suggest the obligation for their improvement rests only on women (Al-Yahyai, 2011). This chapter finds that not only does Oman lack a national strategy for improving women's political participation and engagement but this challenge is underpinned by competing visions for women's political engagement. Furthermore, this disconnect is exacerbated by Oman's lack of a women's movement: public discussion of gender equality in leadership positions remains occasional and isolated.

Omani media laws and policies prohibit anti-propaganda to prevent the emergence of differences, criticism, and liberal opinions. Though national outlets do not directly deprecate female candidates, their owners seem disinterested in changing national discourses, despite widespread agreement that media could do more to change national prejudices—like those that relegate women to the private sphere or disavow their inability to lead communities or society. And while media outlets may acknowledge that Omani women running for office face gendered challenges, the media does not investigate either the social factors themselves or the state's laws and policies compounding these influences, ultimately reinforcing Oman's gender biases in electoral processes.

Through the lenses of gender, politics, and communication, this chapter explores how gender is articulated in Omani political media campaigns. It also examines how the media constructs profiles of male versus female candidates. Moreover, this chapter attempts to shape a framework for the role that media could play in establishing an empowering environment for women to enhance their representation in national politics. This chapter draws on in-depth interviews with five media professionals and five female politicians, in addition to media content analysis from the *Oman Newspaper* (Arabic), the *Oman Observer* (English), and social media (Twitter).

---

[1] For example, in Kuwaiti elections, women complained that media works against them. Some of the independent media in Kuwait are owned by powerful people opposing women's political leadership.

[2] For example, see Al-Farsi, S. (2009). *Evaluation of Omani women experience in Majlis A'Shura.* Nadwat AlMara'h Al-Omaniya, and Al-Hayes, A. (November 21, 2010), *The social challenges facing Omani women in the Shura elections: A field study on Omani voters' perspective.*

History of Women, the Media, and Politics in Oman

In the 1994 elections—the first in Oman's history where women could vote—two women won seats. But in the nearly 30 years since Oman became the first Gulf state to grant women the right to vote and hold office in 1994, women have yet to meaningfully enhance their representation in Majlis A'Shura (BBC, 2011). In the 2019 elections, again, only two women won Majlis A'Shura seats. Evidencing entrenchment of gender divides in Omani politics, of the 637 candidates running for office in 2019, only 40 were women, and only two of the 86 elected candidates were female (Times News Service, 2019). Municipally, 2011 marked new opportunities for women to participate in Oman's political processes, and while more women are winning more municipal seats than A'Shura seats, the proportion of women in elected representative roles remains roughly the same at both the national and sub-national level. Of the 86 seats in A'Shura council, two are held by women, while on the municipal level seven of the 202 seats are occupied by female politicians—under 4% in both arenas (Müller & Castelier, 2017).

Insufficient female representation is in no way unique to elected councils but a factor in Oman's appointed councils and high government positions, too. When the late Sultan Qaboos announced his last government in November of 2019, only 15 women were appointed to the 85-member state council (Oman Observer, 2019). Simultaneously, two women were named ministers—raising the number of female ministers to four (of 32 ministers)—in the Cabinet, a figure recently reduced to only three.[3] These government announcements and election results point to the sociocultural obstacles—hierarchy, lack of support inside decision-making institutions, prevalence of traditional tribal and religious perspectives—between Omani women and political representation, In many cases, election results seem to confirm and approve voting biases against women. Media, influenced by the same concepts, beliefs, and individuals, is unable to change Oman's gender discourse.

According to Freedom House, in Gulf countries, the status of political rights and civil liberties—in addition to democratic trends—majorly impact women's political participation regardless of the marginal differences in the freedom's measures and political space. The 2020 "Freedom in the World" report states that, both male and female citizens throughout the Gulf "lack the power to change their government democratically and have only limited rights to peaceful assembly and freedom of speech" (Freedom House, 2020). Restricted political and limited civil liberties space constrain the region's citizens from practicing their full political rights and demanding more extensive participation. Furthermore, the Polity IV project, measuring regional regime trends between 1945 and 2013, described Oman and all other Gulf states as autocracies (Marshall & Gurr, 2013). Ultimately, the restricted political environment

---

[3] Oman's Observer Daily: https://www.omanobserver.om/article/1104605/oman/royal-decree/his-majesty-issues-royal-decree-for-new-appointments 1

does not enable women to discuss—let alone confront—social or institutional barriers.

Though the constitution of Oman supports freedom of the press, Oman's Publication Law (49/84) and Cyber Crimes Law (12/2011) govern media and social media platforms (Ministry of Justice and Legal Affairs, 1984, 2011). The Press and Publication Cyber Crime laws allow the state to exercise control over visual, audio, and print media. Omani media audiences can be divided into two main categories: one believes traditional media does not reflect the people's needs or aspirations (largely youth), while the other (predominately older generations) supports the media's presentation of state policies. In its current form, Omani media is unable to compete with the youthful and agile citizen journalism, which operates quickly and interactively in the relative freedom of cyberspace. The gap between the two can hardly be missed by Omani citizens who hope to have a more professional and credible media apparatus. Furthermore, rising social media participation by Omanis (an increase of 11% between 2020 and 2021) may indicate Omani's readiness for freer and more representative press (Kemp, 2021).

For female candidates running in Oman's elections, state-owned media is seen as failing to promote women as leaders (Al Talei, personal communications, 2020). While both state and privately owned traditional Omani media outlets cover elections and encourage citizens to vote, the Ministry of Interior prohibits them from running political advertisements. Though this prohibition limits the reach of all campaigns, female candidates are disproportionately disadvantaged as male candidates can seek alternative public platforms—men's majlis, mosques, community committees, and other public fora—where social restrictions prevent women from mixing with males or even appearing. Given these taboos, women need to use a broad public platform to reach voters and change narratives, which media could provide.

But since women started participating in Oman's elections in 1994, there have been no changes to media's presentation of women in political processes. State and privately owned outlets cover elections by encouraging voters to vote equally for candidates, regardless of gender. Consistently, media turns a blind eye to the real issues preventing women from reaching leadership positions through elections and appointments. However, social media, and, in particular, Twitter, have introduced an alternative tool in the political campaign space—free from suffocating laws and bureaucratic oversight—these platforms hold potential to transform prevailing narratives limiting women's potential.

Collectively, the foundational scholars—Al-Farsi, Al-Hayes, Al-Lamki, and Al-Yahyai—investigating gender and politics in Oman stress the potential for media and mass communication outlets to educate Omanis about elections and women's participation, and recommend utilizing media in election campaigns. Nevertheless, these studies ignored the main factors—tribal and gender hierarchies, in addition to discriminatory laws and policies—that influence not only voting behaviors, but also media mindsets. While scholars called for utilizing media in election campaigns, they clearly meant that media should encourage voters to consider voting for women; however, scholars ignore the fact that doing this demands intense media investigation of the social and political factors currently limiting women's roles. And given the media's current status, all are difficult questions to interrogate.

As such, the problem is not with candidates who wish to campaign on traditional media outlets but with Omani media itself, which is not free nor does it have the desire to explore such freedoms. Bound to laws, interpretations, unwritten norms, and personal views, Omani media contributed to preventing women from reaching leadership position and winning elections.

In the 2019 A'Shura election, 40 women ran in a field of more than 600 candidates. Only two women won, representing two major cities in Oman: Matrah and Sohar, in a country where women represent 49%of the population (Times News Service, 2019). Reflecting the status quo of women in Oman, in 1994 women also won only two seats in Majlis A'Shura. While some female candidates[4] said that they encountered severe competition in the 2019 election because of their gender, in addition to other difficulties related to running their election campaigns, others said that media did not play a supportive role in women's candidacy and leadership. Since 2007, Omani candidates have been allowed to promote their candidacy with ten highly regulated public posters in their electoral districts (Al Bayan Daily, 2007). This is the only form of political promotion for new candidates, as they cannot advertise on or be interviewed by Oman Television and Radio. Meanwhile, current (predominately male) members of Majlis A'Shura can appear on state TV as the people's representative, subtly highlighting their bids for reelection. And though all candidates are allowed to use or rent venues like private halls and sports clubs fields, female candidate may face difficulties in securing access to these venues because of social and religious norms, especially when the most popular campaign site is a mosque.

STUDYING FEMALE CANDIDATES' ELECTION CAMPAIGNS

Under the restrictions from the Election law and the Publication and Press law, candidates, especially females, have to depend on personal efforts to meet voters and utilize their individual skills to gather support and momentum (Ministry of the Interior, 2007; Ministry of Justice and Legal Affairs, 1984). For this chapter, five female candidates were interviewed to investigate the difficulties they faced during their election campaigns in terms of communicating with voters and conveying political messages and agendas. While none of the candidates interviewed won their Majlis A'Shura campaigns, they are all experienced political communicators. Basma, a lawyer and political activist, ran in Bowshar, a district in the Muscat Governate. Sana, a sitting member of a municipal council representing al-Amerat, a district in the Muscat Governate, ran for the

---

[4] Interviews for this chapter were conducted in 2020 with Omani women who had run in the 2019 A'Shura elections.

second time. Khalsa, a school principal and head of women's association in Manah, in the Interior Governate approximately 180 kilometers west of Muscat, has run unsuccessfully in the 2011, 2015, and 2019 A'Shura elections. And, finally, Mahfooza, an educator and trainer, ran in Sama'el, in the Interior Governate approximately 150 kilometers west of Muscat.

According to female candidates in Oman's 2019 Majlis A'Shura election, canvassing in their neighborhoods was the preeminent communication tool to disseminate information about their electoral campaigns and candidacy. Second to door-to-door calls, the same candidates reported participation in public meetings and social media as the second most effective tools. Social media usage varied between the candidates with most relying on Twitter as a platform for announcements and others using it as a key tool to craft their political persona through engagement.[5] To a lesser extent, some female candidates also used YouTube[6] and Facebook.[7] Like their respective communication strategies, the design and size of the campaigns profiled varied as well. Several campaigns were well resourced and organized with campaign managers, teams, and focused committees, while several other profiled campaigns relied on the personal efforts of the female candidate alone with the support of one or two individuals.

RUNNING A CAMPAIGN AS A WOMAN IN OMAN

Dominated by tribal and social hierarchies, Omani's patriarchal society presents unique obstacles to female candidates. Reflecting on past campaigns, female candidates identified the ideal ticket as a male sheikh or a son of a sheikh from a prominent tribe (Sana, personal interview, 2021). Understanding the nature of Omani society, the female candidates interviewed recognized they must consult with tribal sheikhs, influential community members, and trusted relatives to consolidate widespread support essential to a successful campaign. Compared to their male peers, gaining this widespread support from the very outset of the campaign—rather than incrementally building a political presence through community outreach and political messaging—was an essential step to their candidacy as women, as it would set the precedent for the rest of the family and tribe's members to follow suit in showing their support. To competitors, this wide support base also communicates the seriousness of her campaign.

Given their unique backgrounds, candidates approached the process of consolidating familial and tribal support differently. For Khalsa, despite her role as head of her community's women's association, she first had to approach male members of her family, then close relatives, and, finally, powerful tribe

---

[5] See, for example: https://twitter.com/BasmaMubarak versus https://twitter.com/jokhaalil, between July and October 2019.

[6] For example, this video for Salema Al-Farsi, who has run three times in A'Shura elections: https://www.youtube.com/watch?v=8-n26rPyqF4

[7] See Basma Mubarak's Facebook page: https://www.facebook.com/basma.mubarak, and Khalsa's page: https://www.facebook.com/khalsa.altobi

members before announcing her candidacy publicly (Khalsa Al-Tobi, personal communication, 2020). Meanwhile, Mahfooza failed to gain support after neglecting to consult her tribe's powerful members or sheikhs, and attributes her 2019 loss to, among other factors, her tribe supporting another candidate (Mahfooza, personal communication, 2020). In all campaigns, the support of male relatives proved crucial. Other candidates interviewed shared stories of male relatives refusing to support their candidacy and demanding they withdraw from elections, ultimately when running without male support, these candidates were unable to win seats (R. Al Talei, personal communications, 2020).

Past garnering familial support, female candidates leveraged their existing community-oriented networks to promote their candidacy. In addition to publishing content on social media, most female candidates also distributed flyers, leaflets, and brochures to introduce themselves. In campaigns for the 2019 Majlis A'Shura elections, candidates' social media usage was broadly targeted toward youth and educated employees, leaving most voters—especially in remote villages and towns—absent from social media conversations.

Case Study: Despite Cultural Backlash, Basma Leverages Social Media

Basma's campaign depended chiefly on social media and reached a broad national audience (Basma, author interview, March 7, 2020). However, she failed to sufficiently influence voters in her district of Bowshar, in the heart of the capital city. Starting her campaign late,[8] Basma was nervous that she might not receive state approval as a candidate because of her participation in the 2011 protests and detention as a political prisoner afterwards. Even after the soft launch of her candidacy, Basma says it was difficult to consolidate support as "many of my friends thought that [state rejection of her candidacy] might happen; nevertheless, my name was among the final approved candidates, and I started my campaign" (Basma, author interview, March 7, 2020). But Basma was encouraged by the support she felt from younger Omanis on social media, and by the voluntary support of a professional team for her virtual campaign.

Basma's campaign team members volunteering to promote her platform and manage her campaign were "young and technology-oriented" (Basma, author interview, March 7, 2020). While the team conducted an expert campaign on social media, Basma's challenges arose from her lack of public speaking experience, cultural differences, and lack of familiarity with her district. At her friends' recommendations, Basma launched her campaign on her fame as a human rights defender and lawyer, in addition to her prominent role in the 2011 protests in Oman. While she was known as a lawyer in Bowshar, she had little interaction with community members prior to beginning her campaign (Basma, author interview, March 7, 2020). When visiting the district's villages

---

[8] While the official start of election campaigns is usually three months before election day, candidates usually start discussing their intentions to run up to a year in advance.

and towns Basma was fiercely challenged by other candidates attacks against her because she does not wear a hijab and because of her political imprisonment. Though professional women in Oman commonly forego the hijab, the residents of Bowshar were initially hesitant to elect a representative openly ignoring the traditional symbol—subsequently, her competitors weaponized this hesitancy.

To redirect what could become an appearance-based smear campaign, Basma and her team began a social media campaign emphasizing her ideas and agenda. While Basma described this digital campaign as the "most successful in Oman," and it certainly reached the country's youth, it was ineffective in influencing the district voters (Basma, author interview, March 7, 2020). Recognizing the limited capacity of Majlis A'Shura representatives to influencing policy making,[9] Basma promoted her platform as a broad national vision of what citizens should enjoy under the constitution. While Basma promoted an honest agenda in her platform, the goals were largely unrealistic.[10] Given the limited policy making tools available to Majlis A'Shura representatives, Basma's campaign struggled to establish realistic campaign promises without deceiving voters (Basma, author interview, March 7, 2020).

Despite messaging challenges, Basma's campaign became popular on social media by targeting nationally oriented messaging toward Omani youth (Basma, author interview, March 7, 2020). However, her social media popularity did not translate to votes in Bowshar district. Reflecting on her campaign, Basma's observations underscore the influence of patriarchal values in her loss. Despite founding a self-described model for a successful campaign, community leaders—who prevented her from meeting voters in public places like masjids—and competitors' agents—who fanned the religious and social arguments around her not wearing hijab—inhibited her ability to promote her platform (Basma, author interview, March 7, 2020). Like other female candidates, Basma faced not only competitors using financial power to influence voters and community but was also sometimes denied the opportunity to speak in the district's public fora because community leaders and tribal sheikhs were instructed to prevent her from talking to people.[11] To her authoritarian leaning opponents, Basma, as a young educated Omani lawyer, advocating for social justice, and with a history in the 2011 protests, threatened the status quo with her campaign.

Voters' comments and remarks on Basma's candidacy reflect the degree of influence of cultural values on voters' choices. For example, one video directed to her shows an individual calling for a "fatwa" to prevent women like her from

[9] See Royal Decree # 7/2021: https://qanoon.om/p/2021/rd2021007/, and for more information about the powers of Majlis A'Shura read: Regressing Council Powers in Oman: From Constitutional Rights to Codification: https://carnegieendowment.org/sada/84301

[10] See Basma's message to voters on October 2, 2019, regarding social justice and equality: https://twitter.com/BasmaMubarak/status/1180168651665752064?s=20

[11] For example, see Basma's October 7, 2019, apology to voters when her meeting venue was made unavailable:
https://twitter.com/BasmaMubarak/status/1181145483051503617?s=20

running, as it is "haram for women wearing no hijab to run" (Morshid, 2019). In another instance, a female voter claimed that Basma "does not represent us" because she does not adhere to Islamic teaching, mentioning that Basma tried to convince people that not wearing hijab has nothing to do with her candidacy but her meetings were full of male voters who might vote for her because she is not wearing a hijab, emphasizing that "we do not want votes in exchange to get naked" (Aljabria, 2019). Even after the election, arguments over Basma's appearance without the hijab continued, stressing that despite the reach of her campaign her difference from the average Omani woman factored into her loss.

As illustrated by Basma's reliance on social media outlets, Oman's female candidates ran their political campaigns without the support of the traditional media. While some of the female candidates interviewed think that media outlets sufficiently encouraged Omanis to vote for female candidates, others believed that media should have done more to support women's candidacies. Among the candidates calling for a more engaged media, some said that the promotion of women in leadership should be occasional and tied to electoral cycles, while others see securing political leadership roles for women as demanding constant action on behalf of media outlets.

Omani Media: Between Expectations and Reality

Preserving political and social gains in the hands of powerful male leaders is the unspoken goal of officials controlling both Omani media and politics. Despite Omani media showing no difference in the coverage of female and male candidates, this impartiality does not equate to equal treatment or balanced coverage. Men occupy the majority of elected and appointed government positions. Meanwhile, Omani women hold few leadership roles, for example, just two seats in A'Shura council and three in the Cabinet. However, Omani media outlets do not discuss this imbalance. According to female politicians and media practitioners, Oman's media has no role in constructing images of male and female candidates given restrictions by laws and elections' regulations. According to an editor of *Oman Newspaper* (Ar.), the Ministry of the Interior does not allow media outlets to interview candidates, highlight their agendas, or even discuss public events attached to campaigns (Khaled, author interview, January 28, 2021). As such, traditional media outlets carry just paid advertisements, consequently, covering campaigns of only well-financed candidates—typically men.

This explains the circumstances in which media outlets operate and points to the function of media in Oman's political system. These limitations affect not only journalists' performance but also impact candidates' opportunities to reach larger audiences. While this applies to both male and female candidates, it disproportionately restricts voter exposure to female candidates, as male candidates have relatively exclusive access to other public venues. Moreover, Oman's predominately male officials, male sitting members of elected and appointed councils, and male community leaders frequently appear in media outlets—reinforcing the stereotype that men are better leaders. Meanwhile, given the fewer female leaders, the opportunities to present diverse examples of women in leadership are rare. Finally, and perhaps most crucially, media outlets continue to treat this imbalance as the norm, rather than an urgent social issue.

Reflecting this indifference to the lack of media support for female candidates, other journalists confirmed that under state policies, media can play no substantial role in covering candidates' campaigns. A female anchor in a private radio said that the restrictions imposed on media during elections periods prevent them from playing the role they should, therefore, "there is no difference in presenting female and male candidates' images because it is not allowed to cover any of the candidates' activities, agendas, or any issues they focus on" (Jamila, author interview, February 7, 2021). Candidates, male and female, "can only depend on their personal efforts to reach out to voters" (Jamila, author interview, February 7, 2021).

Case Study: Salema Is Challenged By Traditional Media

Female candidates consider the policies promulgated by the Ministry of Interior regarding election coverage as biased against female candidates and describe the media coverage as weak. Given the disproportionate social and cultural challenges faced in campaigning, female candidates see the need for special treatment in election coverage. Salema, a three-time candidate for Majlis A'Shura, argues media "only focuses on encouraging people to vote, not teaching them how to choose the best candidates" (Salema, author interview, February 17, 2021). Expounding, Salema notes how the media's avoidance of discussing core social issues, such as the social and cultural difficulties female candidates face, paired with state restrictions on electoral coverage negatively affects female candidates, becoming a bias against them (Salema, author interview, February 17, 2021). Illustrating this, Salema highlights the lack of media coverage—due to the Ministry of the Interior moratoria on candidate coverage—of her leadership as the head of the women's association in her district or volunteer work, paired with the double standard of sitting male members of A'Shura council receiving media (though perhaps inadvertent) coverage during their reelection campaigns (Salema, author interview, February 17, 2021). Despite the policies governing media coverage of election campaigns, the Ministry of Interior tries to create fair campaign standards for all candidates, however, the imposed restrictions foster ignorance of how some candidates serve their community more than others (Salema, author interview, February 17, 2021).

Case Study: Sana Navigates Privately Owned Media

While most media outlets refrain from interviewing candidates, some privately owned channels offer candidates opportunities to pay for interview slots to speak directly to voters. The outlets circumnavigate Ministry of Interior restrictions by abstaining from direct discussion of the individual's candidacy, or, in some cases, obtaining approval from powerful government figures. Sana, a two-term representative in Muscat's al-Amerat district municipal council and a 2019 A'Shura candidate, shares that a private radio station approached her, and several other candidates, offering an interview as an advertisement service (Sana, author interview, February 27, 2021). While Sana ran out of time to take advantage of the opportunity, she noted that several other candidates were promoted through the radio station this way (Sana, author interview, February 27, 2021). As Sana ran her campaign, she notes that she and other female candidates received support from the Ministry of Social Development in the form of state-designed campaign posters—indirectly acknowledging the disproportionate challenges women face when running for office in Oman (Sana, author interview, February 27, 2021). This material support for female candidates points to preliminary government understanding of the barriers between Omani women and political office. Should traditional media outlets be empowered to cover the campaigns of Oman's female candidates, not only would they have the opportunity to display their qualifications and leadership skills but also traditional media would gain influence as an important tool in influencing Omani's views. Instead, Oman's traditional media outlets lose this opportunity to social media platforms, in addition to degrading their credibility and freeness.

REFLECTING ON GENDER IN TRADITIONAL VERSUS NEW MEDIA

While the media practitioners (journalists and anchors) interviewed agree that social media currently plays a more impactful role on candidates' campaigns than traditional media, Omani female candidates themselves diverged in their evaluations of the impact of social media; ranging between "huge" and "no difference." In interviews, all participants (candidates and media practitioners) generally agreed that traditional media and social media employ different tools to reach different audiences, while identifying that the main difference between the two types of public communications is speed. However, a journalist interviewed said that social media invades candidates' personal lives negatively affecting female candidates more—particularly those who have different lifestyle, such as "female candidates wearing no hijab"—when compared to "more conservative" traditional media (Omani journalist 1, author interview, February 2, 2021). For Omani women, among reasons that discourage them from seeking leadership roles, is the social pressure to protect their reputation from harm: entrenched traditional social values subject women outside of their home to verbal criticism and even harmful behaviors. In some extreme views, women who seek any public attention are seen to be jeopardizing not only their own reputations but that of their family as well. For example, one female candidate interviewed[12] was pressured by her family to suspend her campaign over taboos

[12] SH was interviewed in November 27, 2019 for my PhD research which was on women's political participation in Oman.

surrounding speaking publicly to strangers, especially males. For Omanis, social media is regarded as a space outside of the home, meaning female candidates can expect the same attacks and harmful speech from a large audience. Traditional media, when compared to social media, encourages more respect of a woman's reputation due to the common view of traditional media as guardian of society's traditions and values.

Other differences between Omani traditional media and social media can be found in traditional media's support for state authority (Omani journalist 2, author interview, February 5, 2021). Through this lens, traditional media's respect for Omani social and cultural values prevents these outlets from presenting newer gender discourses with respect to women in political leaderships (Omani journalist 2, author interview, February 5, 2021). Meanwhile, new media, like Twitter, "brings new and different ideas," people feel freer to express opinions that "support women and gender equality" (Omani journalist 2, author interview, February 5, 2021). Official restrictions on traditional media do not yet exist on social media; furthermore, younger and disenfranchised generations find opportunity to express their views on social media platforms. The current authority cannot allow free discussions or liberal ideas to invade its stronghold of the traditional media.

Media practitioners and candidates alike note both the freeness and speed of social media. Jamila, a radio anchor, emphasized this, saying "[candidates can] promote themselves freely," and directly communicate with voters (Jamila, author interview, February 7, 2021). And as one candidate emphasized, in Omani elections, social media is "more active, faster, and its outreach is huge" (Muna, author interview, February 2021). From the perspective of traditional print media, Khaled, the head of the local news department in *Oman Newspaper* (Ar.), sees a "clear difference" between traditional media outlets, like the one he belongs to, and social media platforms such as Twitter and Facebook. Khaled notes a "gap between" the performance of traditional and new media: a social media platform is controlled by the candidates; they can send the messages they want directly to the targeted audience (Khaled, author interview, January 28, 2021). However, as highlighted by other practitioners, "female candidates face challenges when using social media platforms," mostly backlash against female candidacy (Khaled, author interview, January 28, 2021). Despite the anonymity often associated with such slander on the internet, in Oman's patriarchal society, female candidates facing such bullying campaigns on social media are still seen as damaging not only their own reputation but that of their family too.

"Oman is not yet convinced yet that a woman could be a representative in elected councils" (Khaled, author interview, January 28, 2021). Confirming this point, Sana, the two-term representative interviewed for this chapter, shared that a poster with her image was vandalized in 2019 during her Majlis A'Shura campaign (Al Maashari, 2019, October 4). While female candidates are generally aware they may face such social resistance, Sana notes that some Omanis do not approve displaying women's pictures in public avenues, "they think it is against their culture and traditions" (Sana, author interview, February 27, 2021). Despite her experience with slander on social media and destruction of her campaign materials, Sana still sees positive impacts of social media for a candidate's campaign. In interviews, Sana mentioned a candidate in a rural area, who was previously unknown but by using social media "professionally" they won the elections (Sana, author interview, February 27, 2021).

But despite global attention on the role of social media in influencing opinions, some Omani women running for office argue its influence on public view is inconsequential. Khalsa, the three-time A'Shura candidate, and Mahfooza acknowledged the unique reach of social media when compared to traditional media, but see no unique impact on female or male candidates' campaigns (Khalsa, author interview, February 27, 2021; Mahfooza, author interview, February 9, 2021). For Omani women campaigning, "meeting people directly and being present at community events is the way to attract voters to a candidate," these candidates argued in interviews (Khalsa, author interview, February 27, 2021; Mahfooza, author interview, February 9, 2021).

Despite the advantages of social media in terms of freedom, speed, and reach, Oman's female candidates see better and more effective tools for influencing voter opinions, such as face-to-face meetings and prior community service. However, the candidates still believe traditional media should prioritize women's candidacy and women's political leadership in their news coverage. An official platform, friendly to society's values, culture, and tradition, would be the ideal place to present women as potential leaders and qualified representatives. Nevertheless, the fate of traditional media is in the hands of the Ministry of Information and the Ministry of Interior. And while the disadvantages for female candidates in Oman may seem like a "women's problem," it reflects the domination of the patriarchy over Omani politics and society.

Investigating Female Candidates' Challenges

Although all interviewees agree that female candidates face sets of challenges that media should tackle and investigate, they disagree on media efforts in investigating these challenges, whether in terms of frequency or depth. While female candidates say that discussion of election challenges is occasional and superficial, journalists defend their efforts under state restrictions.

Defending their efforts as journalists, Warda—a journalist closely following women's suffrage since 1993—and Jamila—a younger journalist—highlighted that traditional media investigated the challenges that face female candidates during the election campaigns and found that social factors are the most impactful to determine voter's choice. On the limited chances for female candidates to win in elections, Warda said, "challenges related to tribal and gender issues prevent women from winning" (Warda, author interview, February 2, 2021). From her own short-term investigation, Jamila concluded that there was "no evidence that laws and policies affect female candidates, they are mostly affected by social factors" (Jamila, author interview, February 7, 2021).

However, Jamila's investigation neglected to explore the motives, values, and cultural background of the male lawmakers dominating Oman's government. Other journalists, like Khaled and Muna, said that media efforts to investigate these influences are insufficient, while female candidates say that media "of course does not" investigate obstacles to female candidates' electoral bids. Caveating the lack of investigation, a journalist interviewed argued that investigative journalism requires an independent media—nonexistent in Oman—and notes the existing state-owned media cannot bring new ideas and discuss issues freely (Omani journalist 1, author interview, February 5, 2021). The official state media can only "emphasize the traditions and cultural values that are acceptable to society," attempting to walk a fine line satisfying both authorities and Oman's conservative society (Omani journalist 1, author interview, February 5, 2021).

THE ROLE OF MEDIA IN CREATING AN ENABLING ENVIRONMENT

On a global scale, journalists and female politicians agree that establishing an enabling environment for female candidates leads to a more equitable society. However, the Omani interviewees for this chapter disagree on the role of media coverage in creating this environment. Of the journalists interviewed, half said that the media realistically is powerless to show support for female candidates as the media is already doing so under the current restrictions or because they do not see individual journalists as having the power to confront the restrictions created by high-ranking officials. Warda, for example, stated that media "did its role … nothing more to do" (Warda, author interview, February 2, 2021). Warda's deflection of responsibility from the media underscores Omani society's restrictive interpretation of women's roles, and consistent religious discourse emphasizing traditional gender roles—a situation not unique to just Oman but framing the realities of many women globally. Others in the media community, like Khaled, put the responsibility for changing discourse on women and say, "changing stereotypes is a mission on women's shoulders" (Khaled, author interview, January 28, 2021). Meanwhile, other journalists like Muna see a significant role for traditional media in changing stereotypes and negative perspectives, calling for media to discuss the "untold truth about society diminishing the role of women to house chores and raising children, undermining their skills, and doubting their strength" (Muna, author interview, February 7, 2021). Stressing the media's potential to create an empowering environment for female candidates, Jamila called for the media to educate the public on women's political participation, "improving women's images generally, while authorities should grant more freedom for media to perform as it should" (Jamila, author interview, February 7, 2021). Another journalist noted that an environment allowing fair competition between female and male candidates will only come "from deep belief that men and women are equal regardless of social considerations," and called for a recentering of "expertise and qualifications in voting" (Omani journalist 1, author interview, February 5, 2021).

Perhaps, traditional media's coverage of women, gender issues, and female leadership should not be limited to the election season. In interviews, Salema wondered, "why media does not interview female candidates, who have experience, like me, after the elections and investigate what went wrong in the elections and discuss how female candidates were treated" (Salema, author interview, February 27, 2021). If male and female candidates were given equal opportunities to discuss their electoral experiences, female candidates could have outsized benefits. Furthermore, by focusing on the stories of successful women—in politics, culture, and society broadly—outside of election season, the media could better prepare Omani society for the participation of women candidates in the next political cycle. These positive appearances would make a difference in Omani's perceptions of women's political leadership (Khalsa, author interview, February 27, 2021). Ultimately, both journalists and female politicians realize the importance of press freedom in eradicating gender biases and promoting free and fair elections.

MEDIA CONTENT ANALYSIS

Between July and November 2019, *Oman Newspaper* (Ar.) (14 Arabic articles) and *Oman Observer* (seven English articles) published 21 articles covering women and the election cycle. These pieces, focused on women's participation in the elections and the coverage of the elections in general, were published as news stories, opinion articles, and interviews. Five articles celebrated Oman's Women's Day, October 17, highlighting the state's achievements and efforts toward the empowerment and advancement of women. Four were news stories and coverage of major events during the election period—such as training workshops on election laws and regulations, election day coverage, results of the elections, and the official visit of a female delegation visit to the State council (where the head of the council talked about Oman's government support for women in all fields). Below, I discuss a selection of six articles as examples of traditional media's coverage of elections and women's candidacy.

These articles capture the performance of traditional media outlets and the journalists in Oman. While most journalists interviewed described their work to promote women's candidacies sufficient, the examples here highlight the lackluster effort, showing that journalists could have asked better questions to more directly address the obstacles confronting female candidates. The examples displayed in this section indicate that despite state restrictions, Omani journalists could do more to challenge the status quo simply by practicing professional journalism. However, as most journalists shirk the blame by putting it on the authorities' shoulders, this illustrates how Omani women's challenges are deeper than just official restrictions—originating in the core beliefs and values of the journalists (and Omanis) themselves. The six following articles include an interview with a female politician, two opinion articles written by female candidates, two news stories, and an opinion article written by a famous male journalist. These six articles capture the discussion around women's candidacy and leadership in Omani media, and how these traditional media outlets reflect and influence public opinion.

Article Case Studies

1. **An Interview with Shukur-al Ghammari**

   An interview with Shukur al-Ghammari, one of the first two women to win seats in Oman's elected council and serve two terms in Majlis A'Shura (1994–1999), focused on Shukur as an example for a successful woman (Al Samsamiyah, 2019). The interview frames Shukur as a woman who had the opportunity to win in Oman's first election women could participate in without discussing the difficulties and challenges she faced during her election campaign or her service. The blasé account presented the mere participation of female candidates as an indicator of equal opportunity in Omani society. However, the journalist failed to ask substantive questions, like, why since 1994, women have been unable to improve their representation in the elected councils or in the Cabinet.

2. **Aziza al-Habsi's Opinion Piece**

   Aziza al-Habsi, a two-time losing A'Shura candidate, stresses in an election-day article (October 27, 2019) that women face several problems in their campaigns such as political money, tribalism, and counter-campaigns from other candidates (Al-Habsi, 2019). As both a former candidate and journalist, Aziza observes that all the attention that female candidates receive during the election period vanishes after the election. As other female candidates remarked, Aziza shares in her opinion piece that Omani women are left alone to face entrenched social and cultural values that oppose women's political leadership. Arguing that state authorities should pay more attention to women's challenges, Aziza identifies connections between women's challenges and the nation's main challenges, such as the unemployment crisis. Of the articles analyzed, this is the only piece—perhaps because of the author's unique experience—to engage in deep discussion of the hardships facing female candidates and suggest improvements to the political and social order.

3. **Tahera al-Lawati's Opinion Piece**

   Tahera al-Lawati, one of the two women to win seats in the 2019 election, published an opinion piece after election results were announced (Al-Lawati, 2019). In her piece, al-Lawati shares that she expected four to five female candidates to have won their electoral bids because of their well-organized campaigns and their dedication. However, al-Lawati repeatedly states, "women cannot win without men's votes," meaning women cannot rely on female voters alone. Al-Lawati ends her article with a powerful sentence—"men remain the cornerstone of women's success in various life fields"—a sentence designed to satisfy mainstream readers who uphold the prevailing social views and values. Al-Lawati's piece exhibits the type of argument typically published in traditional media—reaffirming the social hierarchy rooted in the patriarchal system.

4. **News Story: Journalists' Workshop**

   Oman Daily's published two news stories regarding electoral workshops. An October journalists' workshop focused on instructing journalists on the value and importance of elections, the legal regulations controlling media in elections, and the impact of the visual material on covering the elections (Al-Riyami, 2019, October 6). The published news story was very technical, describing the opening ceremony, speeches, and main sessions, without highlighting a problem or focus that the workshop had been designed to address. The article made no mention of covering candidates' campaigns, succeeding in traditional media's efforts to avoid campaigns and that discussing them would show biases toward candidates—even if that means ignoring the dynamics between campaigns, which ultimately affect election outcomes.

5. **News Story: Female Candidates' Campaign Workshop**

   The second workshop run by the Ministry of Social Development targeted female candidates with skills training for running effective political campaigns (*Oman Daily*, 2019, July 28). As with the journalists' workshop, the newspaper presented this event technically, without focusing on the unique factors precipitating a workshop of this nature for female—and not male—candidates. The story superficially identified women's needs for this workshop as "limited and humble representation," attributed to "a number of challenges preventing women from impactful participation." Overall, both workshops and their coverage in the traditional media emphasized to participants the importance of respecting laws, regulations, and social values. Although the workshops' aims were to help the target audience to improve their performance in the electoral season, as captured by the conservative media, the main messaging to the audiences was to respect state and social norms.

6. **Protecting Preeminent Social Views: Ali al-Mattani**

   Around the election season, the English-language *Oman Observer* published articles and news stories focused on the opportunities given to Omani women to compete and participate "equally" in the elections. Ali al-Mattani's article is not only an exemplar reflection of the discourse surrounding women in Oman's traditional media outlets but captures the domineering social narrative as well (Al-Mattani, 2019, November 6). Al-Mattani, a prominent Omani journalist, promotes a discourse that exonerates all parties of responsibility while blaming women for failing to secure votes. While al-Mattani's article itself is full of unanswered and false arguments, it also represents the dominant public opinion. For example, though al-Mattani acknowledges that women, "despite enjoying equal rights" are still "marginalized," he does not investigate the reasons behind women's marginalization. And while arguing, "the open space they were given in the country is unable to bring them to the centerstage," al-Mattani does not discuss why this "open space given to them" could not bring women to the center. Furthermore, al-Mattani describes quota systems as "an artificial method to empower women which may not give desired results." Finally, al-Mattani captures the essence of discussion around women's political participation: blaming women for electoral losses, placing responsibility on society and women, and diverting attention from government's complicity in the challenges facing Omani women.

CONCLUSION

Many candidates created Twitter, Facebook, and YouTube accounts during the election period, and most were active only during the campaign season between July and October 2019. Both female candidates and media professionals saw using social media as more effective in reaching voters, especially when candidates invested time and effort in these communications. However, some candidates refrained from creating accounts, relying on just direct outreach. All candidates interviewed preferred social media over traditional media outlets as a medium because of the platforms' freedom and self-control aspects. However, the candidates noted that though the instant reactions of social media could be an indicator of candidates' popularity, this was not proven true for female candidates.

Analysis of social media comments demonstrates the articulation of both gender and power relations in Oman's electoral process. Male candidates do not face criticism regarding their appearance, nor their personal behavior or leadership skills, and least of all questioning of their adherence to Islamic teachings. Social media analysis reflects the general assumption that women are less capable of leadership, and that voters will require them to represent social values more directly and emphatically than their male counterparts.

Oman's traditional media outlets do not play significant roles for political campaigns during election period. According to the rules and instructions of both the Ministries of Interior and Information, media cannot show any biases toward candidates or parties. Journalists describe this policy as fair and equal toward all candidates and justify this instruction from the authorities as aimed at leveling the playing field. However, female candidates, recognizing the significance of equal opportunity, see media's impartiality as support for the dominant culture: one that supports male leadership, emphasizes male mentality, and protects the hierarchy of the social patriarchy above all else.

Moreover, female candidates suggest that even under current restrictions and limitations, traditional media can engage in more meaningful discussion of women's political participation and gender issues. By simply broadening the period to discuss women's issues beyond the elections period, the traditional media can change national narratives and discourses surrounding women's fight for enhanced representation and leadership in a very traditional society. Women's campaigns are not inhibited by perceptions or access alone, rather female candidates describe tribalism and the use of money in exchange for votes as major factors limiting women's success in electoral bids—and influencing the freeness of Oman's elections overall. Furthermore, interviewees described harsh competition between candidates—perhaps worse for male candidates—as fostering coercive financial and tribal politics in addition to toxic masculinity. However, when male candidates noticed a female as a threat, they would weaponize every tool in their retinue in her direction.

As for the media's role in covering and highlighting female candidates' hardships, journalists and female candidates agree that media is either impartial or reaffirming gender stereotypes by highlighting the importance of preserving and respecting society's values, culture, and traditions. On the contrary, media could play a counterproductive, negative, role by broadcasting opinions that women "alone" can fix their problems and overcome challenges. Oman's media, while encouraging voters to elect women, does not offer convincing reasons or investigate the social constructions that deter women from seeking leadership positions.

However, both journalists and female candidates agree that if media is freed from restricting laws and policies, it could play a significant role in transforming social stereotypes. Even under current circumstances, traditional media can be more productive by setting a long-term agenda to include enhancing women's political participation and leadership while highlighting women's qualifications in other fields. Media, instead of focusing on just male figures as qualified leaders, should challenge Omani's often patriarchal mentality and present competent female figures, so voters see males and females as equal partners and competitors.

REFERENCES

Abumorshid. [@abumorshid]. (2019, October 19). *What Is the Candidate's Answer?* [Tweet]. Twitter. Retrieved from https://twitter.com/abumorshid/status/1185608888340619265

Al Bayan Daily (Arabic). (2007, August 17). Oman Allows the Publication of Electoral Propaganda Posters. (Arabic). *Al Bayan Daily.* Retrieved from https://www.albayan.ae/one-world/2007-08-17-1.781929

Al Maashari, S. [@sana_almaashari]. (2019, October 4). *To Everyone Who Rejected the Uncivilized Way of Exercising My Legitimate Right in the Electoral Process, I Say Thank You #Oman_forall (Arabic).* [Tweet]. Twitter. Retrieved from https://twitter.com/sana_almaashari/status/1180282756875608064

Al Samsamiyah, N. (2019) 'Distinguished Presence of Omani Women in the Shura Council Since the Second Term.'(Arabic). *Oman Daily.* Retrieved from https://www.omandaily.om/%D8%A7%D9%84%D9%85%D9%86%D9%88%D8%B9%D8%A7%D8%AA/%D8%AD%D8%B6%D9%80%D9%88%D8%B1-%D9%85%D9%85%D9%8A%D9%80%D8%B2-%D9%84%D9%84%D9%85%D9%80%D8%B1%D8%A3%D8%A9-%D8%A7%D9%84%D8%B9%D9%85%D8%A7%D9%86%D9%8A%D9%80%D8%A9-%D9%81%D9%8A-%D9%85%D8%AC%D9%84%D8%B3

Al-Farsi, S. (2009). *Evaluation of Omani Women Experience in Majlis A'Shura. Nadwat AlMara'h Al-Omaniya* (pp. 208–261). Ministry of Social Development.

Al-Habsi, A. (2019, October 27). The Accepted Feminist Bet in A'Shura. (Arabic). *Oman Daily*. Retrieved from https://www.omandaily.om/%D8%A3%D8%B9%D 9%85%D8%AF%D8%A9/%D8%A7%D9%84%D8%B1%D9%87%D8%A7%D9%86- %D8%A7%D9%84%D9%86%D8%B3%D9%88%D9%8A-%D8%A7%D9%84%D9%85% D9%82%D8%A8%D9%88%D9%84-%D9%81%D9%8A-%D8%A7%D9%84%D8%B4 %D9%88%D8%B1%D9%89

Al-Hayes, A. (2010, November 21). *The Social Challenges Facing Omani Women in the Shura Elections: A Field Study on Omani Voters' Perspective*. Retrieved from website of professor Abdullwahab Jawdat Al-Hayes http://elhyes-abdelwahab.blogspot. com/2010/

Aljabria, H. M. [@hajoooor111]. (2019, October 15). *#The_Oman_we_want to promote #Basma…* [Tweet]. Twitter. Retrieved from https://twitter.com/ hajoooor111/status/1184187400098058241

Al-Lamky, S. (2008). *The Citizens Perspective Towards the Experience of Shura in Sultanate Oman: A Field Study. Not Published-Graduate Research*. Sultan Qaboos University.

Al-Lawati, T. (2019, November 4). Nabad al-dar: Women in the Shura Council. (Arabic). *Oman Daily*. Retrieved from https://www.omandaily.om/%D8%A3%D8 %B9%D9%85%D8%AF%D8%A9/%D8%A7%D9%84%D8%B1%D9%87%D8% A7%D9%86-%D8%A7%D9%84%D9%86%D8%B3%D9%88%D9%8A-%D8%A7%D9% 84%D9%85%D9%82%D8%A8%D9%88%D9%84-%D9%81%D9%8A-%D8%A7%D 9%84%D8%B4%D9%88%D8%B1%D9%89

Al-Mattani, A. (2019, November 6). Why Women Could Not Make to It? *Oman Daily Observer*. Retrieved from https://www.omanobserver.om/article/21518/ Opinion/why-women-could-not-make-to-it

Al-Riyami, B. (2019, October 6). A Training Seminar Discussing the Role of the Media in Covering the A'Shura Election. (Arabic). *Oman Daily*. Retrieved from https://www. omandaily.om/%D8%B9%D9%8F%D9%85%D8%A7%D9%86%20%D8%A7%D9%84 %D9%8A%D9%88%D9%85/%D8%AD%D9%84%D9%82%D8%A9- %D8%AA%D8%AF%D8%B1%D9%8A%D8%A8%D9%8A%D8%A9- %D8%AA%D9%86%D8%A7%D9%82%D8%B4-%D8%AF%D9%88%D8%B1-%D8%A7% D9%84%D8%A5%D8%B9%D9%84%D8%A7%D9%85-%D9%81%D9%8A- %D8%AA%D8%BA%D8%B7%D9%8A

Al-Yahyai, S. (2011). *Omani Women's Rights Between Legislations and Social Practices and Values*. Retrieved from www.academia.edu: http://www.academia. edu/8741170/Omani_womens_rights_between_legislation_and_prectise

BBC. (2011). Q&A: Elections to Oman's Consultative Council https://www.bbc.com/ news/world-middle-east-15288960

Freedom House. (2020). Freedom in the World 2020: A Leaderless Struggle for Democracy. *Freedom House*. Retrieved from https://freedomhouse.org/report/ freedom-world/2020/leaderless-struggle-democracy

Kemp, S. (2021, February 12). Digital 2021: Oman. *Datareportal*. Retrieved from https://datareportal.com/reports/digital-2021-oman

Marshall, M. and Gurr, R. (2013) Polity IV Project: Political Regime Characteristics and Transitions, 1800-2013. *Systemic Peace*. Retrieved from https://www.systemic-peace.org/polity/polity4.htm

Ministry of Justice and Legal Affairs. (1984). *Royal Decree No. 49/1984 Issuing the Press and Publications Law. (Arabic)*. Ministry of Justice and Legal Affairs. Retrieved from https://mjla.gov.om/legislation/laws/details.aspx?id=22

Ministry of Justice and Legal Affairs. (2011). *Royal Decree No. 12/2011Promulgating the Law on Combatting Information Technnology Crimes. (Arabic)*. Ministry of Justice and Legal Affairs. Retrieved from https://mjla.gov.om/legislation/laws/details.aspx?id=152

Ministry of the Interior. (2007). Ministry of the Interior: Ministerial Resolution No. 102/2007 to Make an Amendmant to the Regulations for the Elections of A'Shura Council. *Qanoon.om*. Retrieved from https://qanoon.om/p/2007/interior 20070102/

Müller Q. and Castelier S. (2017, January 13). Omani Elections: Women Making Small Leaps in Politics. *Middle East Eye*. Retrieved from https://www.middleeasteye.net/features/omani-elections-women-making-small-leaps-politics

Oman Daily. (2019, July 28). (Arabic). A Training Program to Build the Capacity of Women in Managing the Electoral Process. *Oman Daily*. Retrieved from https://www.omandaily.om/%D8%B9%D9%8F%D9%85%D8%A7%D9%86%20%D8%A7%D9%84%D9%8A%D9%88%D9%85/%D8%A8%D8%B1%D9%86%D8%A7%D9%85%D8%AC-%D8%AA%D8%AF%D8%B1%D9%8A%D8%A8%D9%8A-%D9%84%D8%A8%D9%86%D8%A7%D8%A1-%D9%82%D8%AF%D8%B1%D8%A7%D8%AA-%D8%A7%D9%84%D9%85%D8%B1%D8%A3%D8%A9-%D9%81%D9%8A-%D8%A5%D8%AF

Times News Service. (2019, October 28). Final Results of Elections Declared in Oman. *Times of Oman*. Retrieved from https://libraryguides.vu.edu.au/apa-referencing/7Newspapers

The Intersection of Politics, Gender, and Media: Female Politicians in Popular Israeli Women's Magazines

Einat Lachover

Women in Israel have made great strides in many spheres of life—political, social, legal, economic, and cultural. However, true gender equality remains a distant vision, especially regarding political and economic power. There appears to be a gap between the status of Israeli women in basic human development indicators (such as health, education, and workforce participation) and their status in more complex indicators of empowerment and influence (Itzkovitch-Malka, 2021; Tzameret-Kertcher et al., 2020).

Despite this gap, the feminist scene is gaining a foothold in Israel in the third millennium (Fogiel-Bijaoui, 2016; Itzkovitch-Malka, 2021). Within this feminist climate, and as Israeli parliamentary elections focus increasingly on candidates' personalities (Rahat, 2019; Ribke, 2015), Israeli female politicians are seeking exposure in popular media outlets for women. In this process, they manage complex campaigns around gender that are based on their estimates of the current political gender climate so they can capitalize on feminism for political gain (e.g., Halevi, 2012; Lachover, 2014).

In the past, popular women's magazines were not highly regarded in Israel. This assessment was based on the cultural dichotomy between the public and private spheres (Herzog, 2000). Israeli women politicians were absent from women's magazines in an effort to move away from traditional definitions of

E. Lachover (✉)
Sapir Academic College, D.N Hof Ashkelon, Israel
e-mail: einatl@mail.sapir.ac.il

© The Author(s), under exclusive license to Springer Nature Switzerland AG 2023
L. H. Skalli, N. Eltantawy (eds.), *The Palgrave Handbook of Gender, Media and Communication in the Middle East and North Africa*,
https://doi.org/10.1007/978-3-031-11980-4_14

245

femininity and enhance their image as professionals. Hence, even though popular women's magazines were founded early in Israel's history, only one cover in almost five decades of their publication presented a woman politician. On January 2, 1995, Limor Livnat, a Rightist Israeli parliament member, appeared on the cover of *La'isha* (*For the woman*), Israel's oldest and most popular women's magazine, a short time before she became a minister. However, since 2005 and more prominently in the last decade, Israeli women politicians have been showing up regularly in local women's magazines. This development may reflect the magazines' acknowledgment of the emerging local feminist climate and the increasing appreciation of popular Israeli women's magazines. A landmark in this new trend occurred in the 2009 parliamentary elections, when Tzipi Livni—the head of a major party in Israel—became the first female politician to be a contender for the office of Israeli prime minister (Greenwald & Lehman-Wilzig, 2019).[1] In response to a crusade opposing her leadership, Livni led a gender-based campaign that included appearing in a popular women's magazine (Halevi, 2012; Lachover, 2014).

In an international context, two recent examples of women in power appearing on the cover of a women's magazine reveal the persistent cultural tension between women in power and femininity. They also reveal the double-edged sword of women politicians using popular media platforms and feminist messages in the process of self-branding. The first is Sanna Marin, Prime Minister of Finland, who appeared in October 2020 on the front cover of a local popular women's magazine wearing a trouser suit with no top beneath it and found herself at the center of a debate over sexism. The second is Kamala Harris, the first woman of color elected vice-president of the United States, whose appearance in January 2021 on the front cover of *Vogue* embroiled the magazine in a "whitewashing" controversy.

The current article draws on the argument that media both reflects and constructs political reality. But it also draws on models that maintain that media is heavily influenced by political processes, with political players striving to exert influence over media coverage. Below, I briefly discuss these theses and the emergence of feminist discourse in popular women's magazines. Then, I present Israel's gendered socio-political context. This is followed by the findings of this study, which are derived from an interpretive analysis of both textual and visual aspects of 17 front covers and the main profile articles accompanying them. The covers represent a variety of Israeli women parliamentary politicians in three popular Israeli women's magazines between 2005 and 2021. The first two magazines are *La'isha* and *At* ("you" in the feminine form)—the two oldest and largest-circulation women's magazines in Israel; and the third is *Lady Globes*—a women's career magazine. The chapter's conclusion underscores, first, the relationship between the thesis of gendered mediation and the agency of women politicians, and, second, the role of

---

[1] Golda Meier, the only Israeli woman prime minister (1969–1974) was appointed without running for the office.

political and civic discourse in popular women's magazines. I will explore these conclusions in the Israeli cultural context.

MEDIATED REPRESENTATIONS OF GENDER AND POLITICS

Despite progress women have made in the political arena, the political sphere continues to be dominated by men. As of the beginning of 2021, women still remain underrepresented in politics. Global averages show that women account for only 22 percent of elected national parliamentarians (Inter-Parliamentary Union, 2020). Of more than 190 countries in the world, only 12 have a woman as the head of government (president or prime minister) (Paxton et al., 2021).

Since the late 1990s, Israel has seen a substantial increase in the political representation of women in both the parliament (Knesset) and the cabinet. Following the 2021 elections, 35 women were elected to serve in the 24th Knesset (29 percent). Despite this improvement, the empowerment of Israeli women has not yet been consolidated into effective policy gains (Itzkovitch-Malka, 2021). Deeper analysis of women's participation in parliamentary work shows that a female politician has never been appointed minister of defense or minister of finance, two of the most important positions in Israel. Only one woman has served as the head of the parliament, and there has been no improvement in the percentage of women who have served as the head of the parliament committees. In local politics, women's underrepresentation is even more pronounced: only 14 of 250 heads of local or regional municipalities elected in 2018 and only 16 percent of the members of local municipalities elected the same year are female (Itzkovitch-Malka, 2021).

The media has been considered one of the major influences working against the entrance of women into politics (Jalalazi, 2013; Norris & Inglerhart, 2008). The contexts of personalized politics and "celebrity politics" have a specific impact on media coverage of female political leaders. Political personalization is a process in which the political weight of the individual politician actor's traits increases over time while the focus on the political party and ideology decreases (Rahat, 2019). Updated comparative studies show that the political system in Israel has undergone a particularly extreme process of personalization compared to similar developments in other established democracies (Rahat, 2019). Celebrity politics is constituted by a transformation of politics, including its popularization, personalization, and spectacularization (Van Zoonen, 2006: 289). Feminist media scholars argue that these trends of political personalization and celebrity politics present a complex and often unfavorable arena for women because of their inbuilt and extreme polarization of femininity and politics (Van Krieken, 2019; Van Zoonen, 2006).

Studies, including recent investigations on the representation of women politicians in the media, typically adopt the longstanding thesis of gendered mediation (Tuchman, 1978). This thesis holds that both qualitative and quantitative gendered characteristics can be found in the coverage of these women. In other words, women in politics are marginalized by the media: they receive less coverage than their male counterparts and are portrayed in a gender stereo-typical fashion (e.g., Harp & Bachmann, 2018; Ross, 2014). Nevertheless, in recent years, research has also noted change in the attitude of the media, par-ticularly from the quantitative standpoint (e.g., Goodyear-Grant, 2013; Hayes & Lawless, 2013). These studies indicate that the disparity between media coverage of women politicians and their male counterparts is decreasing, with some even finding higher profile coverage for women than for men (e.g., Goodyear-Grant, 2013; Meeks, 2012).

Consequently, a main concern of feminist media studies focusing on repre-sentation of women politicians is how media coverage reinforces gender stereo-typing of women leaders (Campus, 2013). This coverage confronts the common cultural premise of the mismatch between qualities traditionally asso-ciated with women and those traditionally associated with leadership. Western scholars indicate that the news media often highlight feminine personal traits, as well as the lack of experience, expertise, and qualifications relevant to the world of politics. Inordinate attention is paid to women politicians' appearance and age. They are also referred to by their first name and are photographed in the private sphere rather than in professional environments (e.g., Lee, 2021; Ross, 2014). Considering that voters rely heavily on the news media for politi-cal information, the gendered nature of political coverage is perceived to have an impact on women's electoral success and the potential to derail their politi-cal careers (e.g., Ette, 2021; Lee, 2021).

However, recent investigations also point to a change in qualitative aspects of media representation of women in politics (e.g., Campus, 2013; Goodyear-Grant, 2013; Lachover, 2017). For example, a few studies point to more con-spicuous gender similarities at the top, suggesting that coverage of leading figures is less stereotypically gendered than reported in past studies and even borders on gender blindness (e.g., Campus, 2013; Lachover, 2017). In addi-tion, studies argue that certain women politicians have significant influence over the structuring of their gendered portrayal (Goodyear-Grant, 2013; Lachover, 2017). On occasion, women politicians may make strategic use of hegemonic cultural norms to promote what they perceive as a positive gen-dered image. They de-emphasize their femininity (e.g., through their attire) while at the same time playing it up to soften their image (Lachover, 2017).

Over the years, research on gender and the mediated political sphere has examined mainstream news media that are directed mainly at men, with more recent research focused increasingly on online platforms (Bystrom, 2021). In contrast, the current study focuses on a specific mediated public discourse directed mostly at women: that is, popular women's magazines. It follows the emerging coverage of Israeli women politicians in this arena.

POPULAR WOMEN'S MAGAZINES AT A FEMINIST ZEITGEIST

Women's magazines are a remarkably resilient media form (Duffy 2013). They have remained popular across time and space despite significant economic and industry challenges, particularly with the "digital revolution" (Favaro & Gill, 2018).

For many years, liberal feminist criticism condemned how women's magazines perpetuated and disseminated gender identity. Starting in the early 1980s, however, this was gradually replaced by neo-Marxist perception of popular women's magazines as a site of political negotiations between domination and submission (Gough-Yates, 2003; Winship, 1987). Like those studies, the current study recognizes women's magazines as a highly flexible and diverse form.

Nowadays, this ambivalence stands out in the context of recent widespread interest in feminism in Anglo-American popular culture, which is notably promoted by women's magazines (Favaro & Gill, 2018). The interest in "emergent feminisms" is accompanied by a lively debate on their ideological authenticity, raising questions about the potential for radical social transformation of popular spheres like commercial women's magazines (Keller & Ryan, 2018). However, the commodification of feminist ideas clashes with feminism's transformational politics (Harvey, 2020). This global feminist trend has yet to be studied in the Israeli context, but there are signs that it is penetrating the local popular media in general and popular women's magazines in particular. For example, after a long period of near silence in Israeli women's magazines about violence against women, *La'isha* in recent years has published three special issues on the issue.

Despite the decline in the news industry of the first decade of the twenty-first century, the sector of women's magazines seemed to be safe. However, many iconic women's magazines disappeared from print in the second decade of the century, continuing their publications online only; and many have had to reinvent themselves to adapt to the digital world (Rodrigues Cardoso & Cardoso, 2021). Israeli women's print magazines, like much of Israel's print journalism, have seen a drop in readership because of the growing popularity of digital magazines, particularly since 2015 (S. Goldstein, personal communication, January 28, 2019). *La'isha* remains the most popular women's print magazine in Israel, and, moreover, is the most widely circulated magazine of any type in the country (Mann & Lev-On, 2015). In September 2021, *At* moved to a digital version only; and in mid-2020, *Lady Globes* was shut down for economic reasons.

THE ISRAELI GENDERED SOCIO-POLITICAL CONTEXT

In terms of economic, scientific, and technological criteria, Israel is a post-industrial nation with a high per capita income and a high rating on the Human Development Index (UNDP, 2015). Yet, while the country is experiencing some rising trends of individualization, it is also increasingly conservative, family oriented, and militaristic. The prevailing paradigm in Israel categorizes women first and foremost as wives and mothers, denying them the opportunity to make political claims based on equality and justice (Fogiel-Bijaoui, 2016; Itzkovitch-Malka, 2021). Despite this patriarchal structure, Israel's feminist scene is gaining in strength, and feminist voices have crystallized into a strong social force that cannot be ignored (Fogiel-Bijaoui, 2016; Itzkovitch-Malka, 2021). Women in Israel are not well organized enough to have a substantial political voice in shaping policy, and women's organizations lack interest in formal politics. Most feminist action occurs outside the realms of formal politics, making it easier for leaders to disregard feminist considerations when outlining policy (Itzkovitch-Malka, 2021).

An interesting development to underscore is that since 2003, women in parliament have been represented not merely in left-wing parties, as has been the case thus far, but in parties across the entire political spectrum as well. Exceptions to this are the ultra-Orthodox Jewish parties and some Arab Islamic parties that continue to completely exclude women (Itzkovitch-Malka, 2021).

Given this context—change in the media representation of women politicians, the emerging role of women's magazines in promoting feminist ideas, and the new trend of women politicians appearing on local women's magazine covers—the present study examines how Israeli women politicians have been represented in popular Israeli women's magazines over the past 15 years.

Methodology for this Study

The current study is based on 17 issues from the three main Israeli women's magazines. *La'Isha*, the most popular Israeli women's magazine, began publication close to the establishment of the State of Israel in 1947. *At*, its closest competitor, was founded in 1967. *At*, and especially *La'Isha*, had a self-declared national mission: to construct the identity of the Israeli woman in a new and developing society (Herzog, 2000; Lachover, 2019). For example, *La'isha* established prominent national women-oriented rituals, including a national beauty contest, which still takes place annually, and the national homemaker contest, and introduced Mother's Day into the Israeli public sphere (Herzog, 2000). The third women's magazine in this study is *Lady Globes*, a women's monthly founded in 1989 as an insert to the daily Israeli financial newspaper *Globes*. It sought to interest businesswomen or the wives of businessmen. All three magazines are primarily economic projects designed to attract as broad a readership as possible and to focus on "feel-good" contextual content (Gough-Yates, 2003). However, no data exists that might provide insight into the professional or marketing characteristics of the magazines and the profile of the magazines' readers. There is indication that at least *La'isha* is also consumed by a minority of men. However, the magazine's trial to dedicate a regular section to men did not last (Hovav, 2021).

The figures on the cover pages of Israeli women's magazines, as in other Western women's magazines (Rodrigues Cardoso & Cardoso, 2021), often present an idealized representation to which the magazine's buyers should aspire and are usually celebrity figures. The cover of the magazine is a hybrid field of analysis, situated between marketing, culture, and journalism. Given the status of magazines as cultural objects, scholarly research on magazine covers has been one of the most prolific paths of analysis (Johnson & Prijatel, 2013).

The research corpus focuses on front covers featuring women politicians and the main profile articles that accompany them.[2] It includes five Israeli women politicians who appeared on the magazines' covers more than once between 2005 (the year that Israeli women politicians began to appear regularly on women's magazines covers) and 2020. Following the rise of personal politics in Israel, which weakened the parties, politics have increasingly become an inter-personal game; and, as a result, individual politicians often change their party (Rahat, 2019). Despite this, the five politicians in this study represent different political orientations. Ayelet Shaked (four issues) and Orly Levy-Abekasis (two issues) can be identified as representatives of right-wing politics; Stav Shaffir (two issues) and Merav Michaeli (three issues) can be identified as left-wing politicians; and Zipi Livni (six issues) can be identified as representing the center. While they vary in their political power, they all had some prominent status in Israeli politics for a period of time.

This study builds on understanding journalism as a cultural process and embraces the notion, based in cultural studies scholarship, that meaning in journalistic texts is constructed intertextually and dialogically (Kitch, 2006: 96). Specifically, the study employs the well-established cultural-critical approach to journalism research that examines media content by means of critical discourse analysis (CDA), as developed by van Dijk (1988). CDA is commonly used in studies of journalistic texts, and women's magazines in particular (e.g., McRobbie, 2000; Winship, 1987). CDA is used to examine the structures and serial nature of the arguments and narratives, as well as the cultural meanings they reflect and imply (Gill, 2007). Data analysis for this study focused on the hidden messages in the text by extracting the narratives, myths, and silences. It integrated two levels of analysis: textual and intertextual. On the former, I analyzed the linguistic-rhetorical and visual elements of the text that reflect and generate hidden messages. I especially looked for the choice of words and structures of arguments located in the headlines, which play a crucial role in framing the news. The intertextual level involved a comparative analysis of the text in relation to widespread myths and ideologies. In particular, I attempted to identify value judgments around power relations regarding gender. This attempt was to locate not only the common myths and ideologies but also the contradictory and unique voices that digress from or offer a challenge to the text's main voice.

---

[2] The corpus was documented manually in a public library. As the magazines' covers lead to the main articles of the issue, the profile articles that accompany the covers were easily identified.

FINDINGS

The analysis paints the complex gender picture of dialectic flux within current Israeli society: the propensity for change versus the propensity to preserve the status quo. On the one hand, in contrast to media representation of women politicians in the past, the five politicians are represented in Israeli popular women's magazines as distinct and empowered political figures, almost as feminist figures. On the other hand, this is often balanced through a stereotypical feminine visual representation.

BREAKING GENDERED STEREOTYPES: DETERMINED POLITICAL FIGHTERS

All five women politicians, whether in leading or secondary roles, are represented in the women's magazines as strong and competent political figures. Because the Israeli political sphere is still considered a masculine one (Itzkovitch-Malka, 2021), such a representation breaks the gendered dichotomy between the "woman's world" and the world of politics (Fogiel-Bijaoui, 2016) and frames the women politicians as relevant and influential politicians. In other words, Israeli women's magazines reflect an effort to demonstrate qualities and behaviors in women consistent with those expected from (male) politicians, especially in terms of gaining power. In this way, they seem to shrink the distance between the political figure and the "normative" woman.

In this study, the most conspicuous image of the women politicians is their self-determination to achieve political power, traditionally considered a masculine quality. This is emphasized in the case of Tzipi Livni, the most powerful female politician in Israel since Golda Meir (Israeli Prime Minister, 1969–1974). Livni served in high-ranking positions such as Minister of Foreign Affairs and Minister of Justice and was the first female vice prime minister. In 2005, Livni was chosen by *Lady Globes* magazine as the most influential Israeli woman (*Lady Globes*, September 2005). This issue presented her as an ideological and principled politician "who is not deterred by difficulties," emphasizing her determination. In the years following 2005, all three of the women's magazines being studied framed Livni as a real alternative leader to Prime Minister Benjamin Netanyahu. The magazines' covers emphasize her determination to become Israel's state leader and, moreover, her willingness to engage in direct confrontation on her way to leadership: "I will give Bibi [Netanyahu] a fight" (*Lady Globes*, July 2008); "I will become a prime minister. Period" (*La'Isha*, February 2009); "Her way. What caused Zipi Livni to take off the gloves and to confront Binyamin Netanyahu with full power?" (*At*, January 2015).

The frame of determination to achieve power also characterizes the other women politicians, who are less senior than Livni: for example, Ayelet Shaked and Stav Shaffir, a young politician who started her political career in her 20s. Both were presented not only as talented politicians but as powerful figures as well: "The law minister [Shaked] came to conquer" (*Lady Globes*, September

2015); "[Shaffir] leaped to the top of the labor party […]. An interview of victory" (*Lady Globes*, February 2015); "Shaked will do anything to become the Minister of Justice in the next government" (*At*, March 2019). These examples expose the militarized rhetoric that characterizes Israeli journalism (Marciano & Yadlin, 2021) and resonate with masculine values. Shaffir's representation on *At*'s cover in August 2018 also clearly demonstrates this, with descriptions of "a militant interview" and claims that she "fights all frontiers."

The theme of determination is less conspicuous in the representation of the two other women politicians, Orly Levi-Abekasis and Merav Michaeli. The two represent a growing worldwide trend of the transition of celebrities from mass media and entertainment industries into politics, blending entertainment, news, and politics (Ribke, 2015). Levi-Abekasis was a local commercial model and hosted a lifestyle television program, while Michaeli was a news anchor and TV presenter. Levi-Abekasis and Michaeli were first covered in a more personal way, an approach that is often demonstrated in past studies of Israeli women politicians (e.g., Halevi, 2012; Lemish, 2004). Levi-Abekasis' first appearance on a women's magazine cover (*Lady Globes*, February 2013) emphasizes her relationship with her father David Levi, a senior Likud Party figure and former Minister of Foreign Affairs, and her emotional rather than ideological motivations. Similarly, Michaeli's first cover also focuses on her personal relationship status (*At*, April 2018).

Despite this personal focus, the women's magazines avoided framing Levi-Abekasis and Michaeli through their entertainment past or judging them on their physical attributes. Moreover, within two to three years, their representation had evolved into a frame of determined politicians. For example, *At* quotes Levi-Abekasis stating that "I will not return to a situation in which I have a boss," and claims, "She knows the game rules well and she knows where she is heading" (*At* October 2016). It also describes Michaeli as "a black panther" (*At* November 2020).

A FEMINIST IMAGE AS A POLITICAL ASSET

With the emerging representation of empowered women politicians in Israeli women's magazines, a feminist image has become an essential element in coverage. While absent in the first decade of the millennium, feminism has gradually appeared in these magazines even if it done in a rather implicit way.

This is seen clearly when analyzing the coverage of Zipi Livni, the most veteran Israeli woman politician, from 2005 to 2015. In the early years, magazines featured her image mainly within a professional context, while headlines and sub-headlines failed to refer directly to issues on the status of women or women's rights. These pro-feminist issues were embedded within the articles. However, beginning with her candidacy for prime minister in 2008 and throughout her campaign in 2009, Livni intentionally focused on gender issues (Gedalya Herzog & Shamir, 2011; Halevi, 2012), and explicit feminist representation trickled down to her image in the women's magazines. She herself refers to her own process within the feminist project and her own feminist identity. She is depicted as someone who denied the issue of gender in the past but became empowered through meeting with women voters: "Time and again I hear the same things from women—you have given me strength. I began to understand my part as a woman in this campaign, and I feel it big time [...] I became a feminist, I did not start as one" (*La'Isha*, February 2, 2009). This message has been repeated over the years (e.g., *At*, 2015).

Analyzing Ayelet Shaked's feminist image also illustrates the development of feminist discourse in Israeli women's magazines. Shaked's early representation reveals her taking what could be seen as a misogynistic stance because of the emphasis on her blaming her women colleagues: "The women politicians exploited my sayings cynically and politically [...]. The women were the attackers" (*Lady Globes*, September 2015, p. 50). But in 2017, *Lady Globes'* headlines give her a feminist slant—albeit a conservative liberal one—by presenting her plan to lead a legislation to incorporate women as directors (*Lady Globes*, October 2017). Moreover, in 2018, *At's* issue celebrating Israel's Independence Day dedicates its cover to Shaked, explicitly quoting her saying: "I think I am a feminist model." One could argue that the wording of the headline suggests the magazine does not agree with Shaked's self-declaration. Indeed, Shaked's feminist image on this festive cover led to a critical campaign of the Israeli Task Force Against Human Trafficking. The organization condemned Shaked's misappropriation of the feminist project, as she had not supported the legislative efforts in parliament to forbid women trafficking. The organization reused *At's* cover for its feminist campaign, but added the provocative question: "So why do you abandon women in trafficking?" Both Livni and Shaked are typically identified in the Israeli public sphere with traditional masculine agendas (politics and security issues). Therefore, their representation within a feminist discourse is meaningful.

Analysis of Livni's and Shaked's feminist images in Israeli women's magazines demonstrates an evolving liberal feminism representation that better suits a popular arena. In contrast, Michaeli's feminist representation is clear and conspicuous and suggests a radical message. Michaeli connects to feminist issues that are considered extremely sensitive in the Israeli public sphere, such as the legal status of marriage in Israel (which is based on a religious and not a civil law). However, the magazines soften her radical views on such issues by also focusing on her personal life. For example, the kicker of the item on a 2016 cover of *Lady Globe*, whose design uses a small font, offers a direct, radical quote of Michaeli: "Marriage as a juridical institute should be cancelled." The main title, however, promises a broader glance at her life: "On the paradox of power, the exposure, the relationships, sexuality and leadership. An interview with the leader of the Zionist faction" (*Lady Globes*, October 2016).

SOFTENING POLITICS THROUGH STEREOTYPICAL FEMININE APPEARANCE

Women's magazines are a visual medium where the visual representation of the women politicians plays a meaningful role in analysis. The above analysis shows that the textual messages in the headlines break stereotypical gender representation and feature women politicians as powerful and feminist figures. However, their visual depiction is more stereotypically feminine. The magazines emphasize their femininity through a variety of means, such as full presentation of their bodies, "feminine" gestures, crossed and exposed legs, long and loose hair styles, full smiles, and feminine clothing.

These strategies are not surprising given the role the female image plays in media news in general, often serving to attract readers' attention by depicting emotion, drama, and sexuality (Gallagher, 2005). However, in this context, the visual element also functions to soften women politicians' harsh and sometimes radical image. In other words, the stereotypical feminine appearance reapproves the distance between what is considered the political figure and the "normative" woman.

A prominent example of this practice can be seen in the 2009 cover of *Lady Globe* featuring Livni. In most cases, Livni, as the highest ranked woman politician, has not been photographed in positions that could be construed as particularly feminine or masculine. Most magazine covers present her in "power dressing" outfits—a common visual device for women working in politics (Young, 2011). Livni typically presents a balanced look, with minimal makeup, simple and conservative gold jewelry, and her light-colored hair worn at shoulder length. The *Lady Globes* cover in December 2009—as she was competing for state leadership—was thus striking (*Lady Globes*, December 2009), depicting her in a stereotypically feminine manner. The text on the cover describes her as a determined woman politician, stating, "Zipi Livni is not afraid of being arrested abroad." This refers to the option of her being arrested for war crimes, given that Livni was the Justice Minister at that time. However, the cover's photograph diminishes her power by presenting her as a seductive woman. Livni is wearing tight black pants and the sleeves of her form-fitting top are gathered and puffy at the shoulders, giving her a doll-like appearance. She looks as if she is leaning back against the table behind her. The fingertips of one hand are resting on the table and her other hand is raised behind her head, touching her hair. Her head is tilted to the side, and she is looking straight ahead with an expression that conveys amazement and surprise. Her mouth is partially open. Other photographs of her in this article also convey excessive femininity and reveal insecurity and embarrassment.

A similar example of this softening strategy through feminine appearance can be seen in Shaked's "feminist" cover of *At* in 2018, mentioned above. While the cover's rhetoric presents her as a "feminist model," her image evokes a fashion model. She wears an embroidered multi-colored jacket made of silk, cut close to her figure, with an extremely high collar. Her hands hold her waist, calling attention to the shape of her body. She wears a noticeable amount of make-up and expensive-looking earrings, and smiles widely with perfect teeth. Her long dark hair is very prominent. Her whole look reflects an ultra-feminized appearance and prestige.

These regressive sexiest visual images of Livni and Shaked might reflect what Alison Harvey (2020) identifies as a widespread global trend where strong female characters comply with the standards of idealized beauty to satisfy the male gaze. Given that both Livni and Shaked are not only veteran politicians but also employ public relations professionals, these covers must be seen as a gendered strategy. Since women who strive for leadership are considered unfeminine (Jamieson, 1995), they might use a gendered feminine image as a way to soften their public image among potential voters. Similarly, Goodyear-Grant (2013) argues that women politicians around the world occasionally consciously seek gendered coverage to strengthen their visibility and public approval. An example of this trend is the former Republican vice-presidential candidate Sara Palin's presentation of herself as a "hocky mom," which contributed to her stereotypical gendered media representation.

Confronting conflicting gender expectations—femininity versus professionalism—can lead women politicians to adopt a strategy of blurring femininity, as revealed by Michaeli's covers. Michaeli appears in black clothes only, and she completes her look by pulling her black hair into a long pony-tail, using only light makeup, and wearing no jewelry or other feminized accessories. This strategy of blurring femininity became Michaeli's trademark, adopted to face the challenge of her previous image as a celebrity figure. The women's magazines adhered to this strategy, despite their being considered a feminine sphere. This is most noticeable when we compare these images to Michaeli's cover published in *At* in 2010, a short time before she officially joined Israeli politics. In this cover photo, her hair is styled in an updo and her makeup (pink lipstick and long mascara) is conspicuous. This, combined with her big smile and fluffy sleeves, gives her a feminine and sweet look.

DISCUSSION AND CONCLUSION

The current requirements of popular and celebrity politics interrogate the intersection of politics, gender, and media. In this study, I examined this link within a specific media site directed at women: popular women's magazines in Israel. These magazines participate in the current global feminist discourse emerging within popular media. Following the new trend of women politicians appearing on magazine covers, I sought to examine the characteristics of the representation of women politicians in Israel's popular women's magazines over the last 15 years.

My findings join recent media representation studies that point to a change in how women politicians are portrayed in the media, focusing on the qualitative aspects of the coverage (e.g., Campus, 2013; Goodyear-Grant, 2013; Lachover, 2017). I find that Israeli women politicians are not, as past studies have found, represented stereotypically (e.g., Lee, 2021; Ross, 2014), but rather shown as distinct political figures that are often feminists. The idea that patriarchal forces have weakened their hold on representation is not new (Harvey, 2020). Some studies argue that the acknowledgement of feminism that began in the 1990s is associated with texts directed at female audiences (Tasker & Negra, 2005). Lemish and Lahav (2004) located this trend in Israeli media in the 1990s, finding more progressive representation of men in advertisements directed at female audiences than those directed at general audiences. The evolution of a gender gap in Israeli voting, like the one found in other countries (Gedalya-Lavy, 2016), might have accelerated this development—as Israeli women politicians responded by striving for dialogue with a feminine audience through women's magazines. I suggest that the positive coverage might have encouraged women politicians to appear within this sphere.

However, my findings indicate a complicated and contradictory terrain of negotiation. On the one hand, I find a gender-blind coverage of women politicians and, occasionally, feminist coverage in terms of rhetoric. The feminist voices that emerge in the coverage of women politicians resonate with both liberal feminism and radical feminism, reflecting the multiplicity of feminist voices in the Israeli scene (Fogiel-Bijaoui, 2016). On the other hand, feminism is instrumentalized for political gain. It often serves in the representation as a marketing tool (such in the case of Livni and Shaked). Moreover, in terms of visual images, the coverage of women politicians is often feminine and sometimes sexual. This discrepancy echoes Susan Douglas's concept of "enlightened sexism" (2010). Douglas identified two contradictory trends that emerged in Western popular media in the 1990s. In the first, high-powered women became highly visible and feminist discourse penetrated popular culture; conversely, the media continued to represent women through sexiest images. Based on Douglas' argument, I suggest that the marking and performing of visual representation of femininity regarding Israeli women politicians blurs and hides the feminist development. In other words, the feminine or sexual visual representation serves to soften the potential threat of the politicians' messages relating to existing gender roles.

The need to soften feminist coverage can also be explained in the context of stubborn conservative trends in Israeli society. Journalists and the women politicians themselves perceive that they need to maneuver between contradictory cultural expectations reflecting the double standards women in power are held to, as well as the often-conflicting expectations put on them. It is assumed these women will practice both "professionalism" (e.g., determination and ambition) and "femininity" (e.g., softness and sexuality). This reminds us that politics is still a realm of male hegemony, perceived as a gender-incongruent profession for women, that violates feminine gender roles (Raicheva-Strover & Ibroscheva, 2014). In the Israeli context, despite some progress in both the descriptive representation of women politicians and the feminist public discourse, the social reality is still a patriarchal one (Fogiel-Bijaoui, 2016). More specifically, the findings indicate how both women politicians and media professionals evaluate Israeli society's conservative norms and expectations around the performance of gender and feminine appearance.

The cover page of women's magazine is the result of premediated and calculated deliberations of journalists and professionals. The high-profile women politicians who appear as "cover girls" often take part in the decision-making in this production process. This study's findings indicate that the women politicians manage their representation, reacting to their perception of public needs and how their image is seen in the context of gender politics. They need to perform a divided strategy: both establishing what is considered a professional face and preserving what is considered feminine appearance. This strategy seems to demand self-awareness and self-monitoring, requiring their efforts and resources (Halevi, 2012). This conclusion warrants further research, ideally based on in-depth interviews, to gain understanding about the tactics and strategies of women politicians with respect to gender when they deal with the media, as well as about the perceptions and practices of editorial staff when they cover women politicians.

While popular women's magazines are identified with the private sphere, these magazines in Israel cover women politicians as serious political actors and as part of the political game. The serious political coverage proves the relevance of this seemingly trivial form of journalism and its impact on the democratic process in the public sphere, suggesting they can be evaluated for their political and civic potential (Lachover, 2019; Saarenmaa & Ruoho, 2014; Ytre-Arne, 2013). In this sense, women's magazines challenge the patriarchal logic that segregates the private and public spheres (Pateman, 1989). Within the current era of individualization of politics, commercial women's magazines, which typically empower the individual woman (Gill, 2007), seem to be an ideal media space for women politicians who seek to reach a women's audience.

Acknowledgments I thank Sofia Haytin for her help in documenting and analyzing the study's corpus. I also wish to thank the anonymous reviewers for their attentive reading and insightful comments.

REFERENCES

Bystrom. (2021). Gender and political communication. In Ross, K. (Ed.), *The international encyclopedia of gender, media, and communication* (pp. 559–564). Hoboken, NJ: Wiley Blackwell.

Campus, D. (2013). *Women Political Leaders and the Media*. Palgrave.

Douglas, J. S. (2010). *The Rise of Enlightened Sexism: How Pop Culture Took Us from Girl Power to Girls Gone Wild*. St. Martin's Griffin.

Duffy, B. E. (2013). *Remake, Remodel: Women's Magazines in the Digital Age*. University of Illinois Press.

Ette, M. (2021). Journalism and Gendered Mediation. In K. Ross (Ed.), *The International Encyclopedia of Gender, Media, and Communication* (pp. 771–775). Wiley Blackwell.

Favaro, L., & Gill, R. (2018). Feminism Rebranded: Women's Magazines Online and "the Return of the F-Word." *Digitos, 4*, 37–65. Retrieved from https://openaccess. city.ac.uk/id/eprint/23943

Fogiel-Bijaoui, S. (2016). Navigating Gender Inequality in Israel: The Challenges of Feminism. In E. Ben Rafael et al. (Eds.), *Handbook of Israel: The Major Debates* (pp. 423–436). De Gruyter Oldenbourg.

Gallagher, M. (2005). *Who Makes the News? Global Media Monitoring Project.* WACC.

Gedalya, E., Herzog, H., & Shamir, M. (2011). Tzip(p)ing Through the Elections: Gender in the 2009 Elections. In A. Arian & M. Shamir (Eds.), *The Elections in Israel—2009* (pp. 165–193). Transaction Publishers.

Gedalya-Lavy, E. (2016). *The Puzzle of Gender and Politics: Voting and Media Framing in Israel (1969-2013).* Ph.D. dissertation. Tel Aviv University.

Gill, R. (2007). *Gender and the Media.* Polity Press.

Goodyear-Grant, E. (2013). *Gendered News: Media Coverage and Electoral Politics in Canada.* UBS Press.

Gough-Yates, A. (2003). *Understanding Women's Magazines: Publishing, Markets and Readerships.* Routledge.

Greenwald, G., & Lehman-Wilzig, S. (2019). Is She Still 'the Legendary Jewish Mother'? A Comparative Look at Golda Meir's and Tzipi Livni Election Campaign Coverage in the Israeli Press. *Israel Affairs, 25*(1), 42–64.

Halevi, S. (2012). Damned If You Do, Damned If You Don't? The Debate on a 'Feminine' Leadership Style in the Israeli Press. *Feminist Media Studies, 12*(2), 195–213. https://doi.org/10.1080/14680777.2011.597100

Harp, D., & Bachmann, I. (2018). Gender and the Mediated Political Sphere from a Feminist Theory Lens. In D. Harp, J. Loke, & I. Bachmann (Eds.), *Feminist Approaches to Media Theory* (pp. 183–193). Palgrave Macmillan.

Harvey, A. (2020). *Feminist Media Studies.* Polity.

Hayes, D., & Lawless, J. (2013, April 11–14). A Non-Gendered Lens: The Absence of Gender Stereotyping in Contemporary Congressional Elections. In *Paper Presented at the Annual Meeting of the Midwest Political Science Association, Chicago, IL.*

Herzog, H. (2000). Women's Magazines: A Mirroring or a Challenging Space? *Kesher, 28*, 45–52.

Hovav, O. (2021, August 18). Without Chrome and with Competition by Social Media: What Is Women's Magazines Direction? *Haaretz.* Retrieved from https://www. haaretz.co.il/gallery/media/.premium-MAGAZINE-1.10121638

Inter-Parliamentary Union. (2020). Retrieved from https://www.ipu.org/our-impact/ gender-equality

Itzkovitch-Malka, R. (2021). Gender in Israel. In R. Y. Hazan, A. Dowty, M. Hofnung, & G. Rahat (Eds.), *The Oxford Handbook of Israeli Politics and Society* (pp. 211–225). Oxford University Press.

Jalalazi, F. (2013). *Shattered, Cracked, or Firmly Intact? Women and the Executive Glass Ceiling Worldwide.* Oxford University Press.

Jamieson, K. H. (1995). *Beyond the Double Bind: Women and Leadership.* Oxford University Press.

Johnson, S., & Prijatel, P. (2013). *The Magazine from Cover to Cover* (3rd ed.). Oxford University Press.

Keller, J., & Ryan, M. E. (2018). Introduction. Mapping Emergent Feminisms. In J. Keller & T. Maureen (Eds.), *Emergent Feminisms: Complicating a Postfeminist Media Culture* (pp. 1–22). Routledge.

Kitch, C. (2006). Useful Memory' in Time Inc. Magazines. *Journalism Studies, 7*(1), 94–110. https://doi.org/10.1080/14616700500450384

Lachover, E. (2014). Women in Politics as Depicted in Israeli Popular Women's Magazines. In M. Strover & E. Ibroscheva (Eds.), *Women in Politics and Media: Perspectives from Nations in Transition* (pp. 15–30). Bloomsbury.

Lachover, E. (2017). Signs of Change in Women's Representation in Israeli Politics and Media: Prominent and Less-Prominent Politicians. *Journalism, 18*(4), 446–463. https://doi.org/10.1177/1464884915610991

Lachover, E. (2019). The Political and Civic Potential of Popular Women's Magazines: The Israeli Case. *International Journal of Communication, 13*, 3403–3421. Retrieved from https://api.semanticscholar.org/CorpusID:201360379

Lee, J. (2021). Gender, Politics, and the News Media in Japan. In K. Ross (Ed.), *The International Encyclopedia of Gender, Media, and Communication* (pp. 573–577). Wiley Blackwell.

Lemish, D. (2004). Exclusion and Marginality: Portrayals of Women in Israeli Media. In K. Ross & C. M. Byerly (Eds.), *Women and Media: International Perspectives* (pp. 39–59). Blackwell Publishing.

Lemish, D., & Lahav, I. (2004). Much Ado About Nothing? Masculinities in Israeli Advertising. *Feminist Media Studies, 4*(2), 147–163.

Mann, R., & Lev-On, A. (2015). *Annual Report: The Israeli Media in 2014: Agendas, Uses, and Trends.* Ariel Institute for the Study of New Media, Politics, and Society [Hebrew].

Marciano, A., & Yadlin, A. (Online first 2021). Media Coverage of Covid-19 State Surveillance in Israel: The Securitization and Militarization of a Civil-Medical Crisis. Media Culture and Society.

McRobbie, A. (2000). *Feminism and Youth Culture: From "Jackie" to "Just Seventeen"* (2nd ed.). Routledge.

Meeks, L. (2012). Is She Man Enough? Women Candidates, Executive Political Offices, and News Coverage. *Journal of Communication, 62*, 175–193. https://doi.org/10.1111/j.1460-2466.2011.01621.x

Norris, P., & Inglerhart, R. (2008). *Cracking the Marble Ceiling: Cultural Barriers Facing Men Leaders.* Harvard University Press Report.

Pateman, C. (1989). Feminist Critique of the Public/Private Dichotomy. In C. Pateman (Ed.), *The Disorder Women: Democracy, Feminism and Political Theory* (pp. 118–140). Polity Press.

Paxton, P., Hughes, M. M., & Barnes, T. D. (2021). *Women, Politics and Power. A Global Perspective.* Rowman & Littlefield.

Rahat, G. (2019). *The Decline of the Group and the Rise of the Star(s): From Party Politics to Personal Politics.* The Israel Democracy Institute.

Raicheva-Strover, M., & Ibroscheva, E. (2014). Introduction. In Raicheva-Strover & Ibroscheva (Eds.), *Women in politics and media. Perspectives from nations in transition* (pp. 1–12). New York and London: Bloomsbury.

Ribke, N. (2015). *A Genre Approach to Celebrity Politics: Global Patterns of Passage from Media to Politics.* Palgrave Macmillan.

Rodrigues Cardoso, C., & Cardoso, D. (2021). Women's Lifestyle Magazines. In K. Ross (Ed.), *The International Encyclopedia of Gender, Media, and Communication* (pp. 1611–1618). Wiley Blackwell.

Ross, K. (2014). A Nice Bit of Skirt and the Talking Head: Sex, Politics, and News. In C. Carter, L. Steiner, & L. McLaughlin (Eds.), *The Routledge Companion to Media and Gender*. Routledge.

Saarenmaa, L., & Ruoho, I. (2014). Politics Politicians and the Welfare State: Women's Magazines in the Nordic Style. *European Journal of Communication, 29*(3), 289–303. https://doi.org/10.1177/0267323114523887

Tasker, Y., & Negra, D. (2005). Postfeminism and Contemporary Media Studies. *Cinema Journal, 44*(2), 107–110.

Tuchman, G. (1978). *Making News: A Study in the Construction of Reality*. Free Press.

Tzameret-Kertcher, H., Chazan, N. H., & Herzog, H. (2020). *Gender Index: Gender Inequality in Israel*. The Center for the Advancement of Women in the Public Sphere and The Van Leer Jerusalem Institute.

UNDP (United Nations Development Program). (2015). *Human Development Report*. Retrieved from http://bit.ly/1OpvncX

Van Dijk, T. A. (1988). *News as Discourse*. Lawrence Erlbaum Assoc.

Van Krieken, R. (2019). *Celebrity Society: The Struggle for Attention* (2nd ed.). Routledge.

Van Zoonen, L. (2006). The Personal, the Political and The popular: A Woman's Guide to Celebrity Politics. *Celebrity Studies, 9*(3), 287–301. https://doi.org/10.1177/1367549406066074

Winship, J. (1987). *Inside Women's Magazines*. Pandora.

Young, B. (2011). *Power Dressing: First Ladies, Women Politicians and Fashion*. Merrell Publishers.

Ytre-Arne, B. (2013). Changing Magazine Journalism: Key Trends in Norwegian Women's Magazines. *Nordicom Review, 34*, 75–88. Retrieved from https://www.nordicom.gu.se/sites/default/files/kapitel-pdf/06_ytre-arne_0.pdf

Seizing the Opportunity: Political Participation of Libyan Women and Their Partaking in Communication Platforms

Haala Hweio

INTRODUCTION

Libya is not an exception to the patriarchal nature of Middle Eastern and North African societies where women suffer from limitations on their rights and duties as well as their ability to launch initiatives and contribute to nation building. For a long time, Libyan women did not have a sustained experience in active political and civic participation. Muammar Gaddafi's totalitarian regime, which prohibited the party system and criminalized all oppositional ideologies, had not given Libyans in general any space to express themselves politically throughout the 42 years of his rule. Women suffered from social restrictions in addition to the political ones imposed by the regime. The conservative nature of Libyan society applied more limitations on women's participation in the public sphere. Those limitations, along with the political constraints, made women less likely than men to find windows for public engagement, politically and socially.

The Libyan 2011 revolution opened new doors for women to undertake new roles in public space. Politics and civil society were new domains for women in Libya but that did not stop them from taking advantage of the new political opportunities opened by the revolution. They led initiatives in civil society work and women empowerment projects.

H. Hweio (✉)
Naperville, IL, USA

L. H. Skalli, N. Eltantawy (eds.), *The Palgrave Handbook of Gender, Media and Communication in the Middle East and North Africa,*
https://doi.org/10.1007/978-3-031-11980-4_15

Yet, those achievements are far from being considered sustainable gains for women. Different factors are pulling women back to their old place in society. Those factors include the dominant culture which needs more than sudden political and social transformations to change. Another factor that contributes to the decline in women's participation is the rise of Islamic fundamentalism Islamism, which takes a reactionary approach to women's public engagement.

This chapter provides a historical overview and discussion of the ability of Libyan women to create and seize engagement opportunities in the areas of politics and media.[1] It starts by analyzing the political and social environments during the monarchical era and then moves to analyzing women's opportunities in participating in politics and media under Gaddafi's regime. It highlights women's presence at every sign of political openness. The third section discusses new prospects for women's participation as part of the rapid political and social changes following the revolution of February 2011. The last section draws on personal interviews with a group of Libyan activists to discuss women's activism in the aftermath of the revolution and during the state-building process.

Putting Gender Activism in Libya in Perspective[2]

This chapter focuses on the changes in women's engagement in politics and media over time starting from the formation of the Libyan modern state and ending with the social and political changes caused by the social uprising in 2011 and beyond. The sudden revolutionary changes altered the nature and direction of gender activism within Libyan society. Examples from various countries around the world demonstrate that women have made strong contributions in politics and communication during times of political instability, such as revolutions, civil wars, and social uprisings. Yet, women were excluded from the political arena in the aftermath of political upheavals and had to continue to fight to remain engaged in the political decision-making processes and stay active in the public arena.

One interesting case is Vietnamese women's role in the liberation movement against French colonization. The patriarchal family structure in Vietnam is similar to the Libyan family structure. Women in Vietnam were part of the labor force mainly working as peasants on family land or as maids (Tetreault, 1995). However, the years of war against the French (1946–1954) witnessed women's engagement in activities like mobilization and information gathering in support of the revolt. Furthermore, in the early 1950s, women were on the frontlines of the war, serving as members of small groups of commandos when

---

[1] Some sections on women in media in this chapter were published in the author's article "The Libyan Revolution and Women's Participation in Politics & Media," *African Conflict & Peace Building Review*, Vol. 8, No. 2, (Fall 2018), pp. 63–92.

[2] A version of this section was published in the author's article "The Libyan Revolution and Women's Participation in Politics & Media," *African Conflict & Peace Building Review*, Vol. 8, No.2, (Fall 2018), pp. 63–92.

"about 840,000 female guerrillas operated in the north and some 140,000 in the south" (Tetreault, 1995: 115).

The Vietnamese liberation movement against the French is comparable to the Libyan revolutionary fight against Gaddafi's regime in more than one aspect, including the mobilization of women during the liberation process and the unprecedented level of women's engagement in the revolution. However, the outcome of the Vietnamese revolution, just like in Libya, brought little recognition to women, as they were pushed back again in terms of their political and civic engagement. As Mary Tetreault (1995: 130) noted, "the paucity of women in important positions in government and industry in Vietnam today demonstrates the failure of the regime to consolidate the cultural as opposed to the class and political gains made by the revolution."

In her book *Why Women Protest*, Lisa Baldez (2002) studies women's protest movements in Chile under two different governments: the socialist government of Salvador Allende and the military government of Augusto Pinochet. She explains why women mobilize and why gender was the baseline for the protest movements studied in her book, despite the differences between them in terms of motivations and ideologies. Baldez argues that women are mobilized when three factors are present: tipping, timing, and framing. She explains tipping as the point when different women's organizations are unified to form a movement, and timing and framing are necessary conditions for it to happen. For women's mobilization to succeed, Baldez puts forth two conditions: partisan realignment, which is described as "the formation of new coalitions among political parties" and certain cultural norms about gender differences that are held by the society (5). Baldez presents an argument on why women organize themselves by forming gender-based organizations, claiming that despite the different ideologies and political stances women might have, they all share similar grief, and a lack of political representation in the decision-making process. She asserts that "Appeals to gender identity bridge women's different and sometimes contradictory interests: exclusion from political power. No matter what specific agenda women's organizations wish to pursue, they cannot pursue it efficiently without political access" (11).

Although Baldez's framework provides a valid explanation as to why women mobilize under the gender umbrella and their mechanism to do so (tipping, timing, framing), she applies her method exclusively to societies with stable political institutions and active party systems. She asserts that partisan realignment or "the fundamental changes in the issues that political parties represent" is an essential condition for women's mobilization: "Women's movements emerge in response to a realignment, understood here as the formation of new coalitions among political parties" (Baldez, 2002: 7). It is important to point out that Baldez's theory does not really apply well to the case of Libya, where women formed gender-based organizations in the context of collapsed state institutions. The mobilization occurred within a newly formed political party system in a country with no previous experience with one. Moreover, it was led by women who had lived under a dictatorial regime for more than four decades.

A closer example to Libya is that of Lebanon, another Arab country with a similar social and framing structure. The brutal Lebanese civil war, which lasted for more than fifteen years, took thousands of lives, destroyed the infrastructure of the country, and damaged its industrial sector and its main income source: tourism. The role of women in the Lebanese war was largely to provide meals, medical assistance, and emotional support to the fighters. Yet, their role was crucial because "[a]ctive involvement must not be understood solely as bearing arms, even though women were engaged in combat on all sides in the conflict but should also include the great number of women who were engaged in supportive activities, essential for the male combatants' efficiency" (Karame', 1999: 196).

The war gave Lebanese women an opportunity to move out of their traditional roles and forced society to change some stereotypical views regarding their accepted economic and social roles (Shehadeh, 1999). However, despite women's achievements in various domains, women in Lebanon in the years after the war struggled for better political status. Decision-making positions were still dominated by men, and women's political presence was almost non-existent. In the first postwar parliamentary elections held in 1992, only 3 of the 128 members of Parliament were women, all of whom won their seats "for and through traditional parameters," as they were either sisters or widows of prominent male political figures and "None was known for any political or feminist activism" (Shehadeh, 1999: 327). Two of the three women were reelected in 1996 (Shehadeh, 1999: 328).

These are a few examples that show that the social framing of gender roles would most likely remain the same even after dramatic political and social changes. The previous cases of women's engagement in the political and social aspects of public life during critical times show similar outcomes with some variations. The gains women manage to obtain through their active participation in times of war or political instability might not be permanent. Women, in most cases, are pushed back to their original position in society when the unusual political, economic, and social circumstances are over. This chapter focuses on Libyan women to provide insights on their gender activism and their future engagement prospects in public life and the limitations of their role in the state-building process.

WOMEN'S PUBLIC ENGAGEMENT OPPORTUNITIES DURING THE MONARCHY

The social structure of Libyan society during the first half of the twentieth century until independence in December 1951 was like most of the Arab world. The patriarchal nature of the society gave men the lion's share in participating in public life with all its political, social, economic, and cultural aspects (Metz, 2003, p. 112). This masculine nature led the community to deal with women often as second-class citizens with respect to their rights and duties and in terms of the ability to propose initiatives and to contribute to public life. Conservative attitudes regarding women dominated society until the early 1960s (Metz, 2003, p. 112).

Multiple factors contributed to the lack of political and social opportunities for women during this period. These factors include the profound social traditions, poor economic conditions, and low literacy rates. The profound social traditions linked the family honor, particularly that of the men, to the conduct of the females in the family. Based on this, women were treated as vulnerable creatures that required constant care and protection. Women's public behavior was strictly controlled to the extent that "the slightest implication of un-avenged impropriety, especially if made public, could irreparably destroy a family's honor" (Metz, 2003, p. 112). This constant pressure by society made it more convenient for families to keep their wives and daughters at home and away from the public eye to avoid any sullied reputation. It also contributed to the well-accepted tradition that allowed families to marry off their daughters at a relatively young age, where they were expected to (mainly at their husband's home) take care of the family (Metz, 2003, p. 112).

Monarchical system attempted to improve women's social and legal rights through laws and regulations (Harris, 1986, p. 33). Those rights included a "woman's right to choose her husband, the right for divorce, the right of political participation through voting. These regulations also gave women the right to own properties, and the right to establish forums and associations" (Obeidi, 2013, p. 5). Another law, passed to protect women from getting married at a young age, stated that no girl should be married against her will (Harris, 1986, p. 34).

However, social change is a long-term process and the rights women gained through those progressive regulations took a long time to be implemented. Only a small number of women took advantage of those rights, a reality that was reflected in the limited participation of women in public life compared to men.

Further, poor economic conditions limited women's participation in public life. By the time of its independence in December 1951, Libya was one of the poorest countries in the world. The per capita income was $30 in 1951. In 1960, just one year after oil was discovered in Libya and before the rapid development in the industry, the per capita income was $100 (El Fathaly & Palmer, 1980). During this time frame, more than 70% of the labor force worked in the agricultural sector (El Fathaly & Palmer, 1980). Women's role was mostly limited to their work in the fields with other family members. It is worth noting that most agricultural areas in Cyrenaica were destroyed during WWII (Vandewalle, 2006, p. 51), which means that for women in the eastern part of the country, even that option of work was limited. In addition, their lack of skills and qualifications, limited other job options for women to the ones with low skill requirements (Obeidi, 2013). The hard economic conditions in the 1930s and 1940s led women to search for more financial resources by establishing small businesses at home to make clothes, shoes, horse saddles, and crochet products (Alusta, 2006). Women were absent even from jobs traditionally practiced by women like nursing, administrative positions, and teaching (Vandewalle, 2006, p. 52).

Low literacy rates was also a factor in limiting women's public engagement opportunities. During the 1950s, Libya adopted a six-year social and economic development plan to improve the country's economic performance, which was hindered by long-held social beliefs. One of the areas of improvements in the plan was the status of women and their participation in the labor force (Vandewalle, 2006, p. 52). The 10% literacy rate by the time of independence (Vandewalle, 2006, p. 51) was a direct result of the poor economic levels in the newly independent state. Up until the end of the first half of the twentieth century, the education system in Libya was extremely underdeveloped.

Despite all the discouraging circumstances regarding women's education, the first half of the twentieth century saw a few women who rose above those circumstances to create new opportunities for themselves within the Libyan society. The names of Hameeda Tarakhan and Hameeda Elenayzi stand out as examples of trailblazers who led the way for women to changing society's perception of the role of women. Hameeda Tarakhan was a cofounder of the first nursing school, female teacher institute, and the girl scout organization in Libya (Majdey, 2014). She also established the first women's association in 1954, through which she and her colleagues provided services to help women find jobs, learn crafts, or get financial assistance.

Even though the active participation of pioneer women was limited to the elite whose families were able to educate them and challenge the conservative norms of the society (Obeidi, 2013), those women took the lead in the process of women's education in Libya by teaching and administrating the first Libyan schools for girls in Benghazi, Tripoli, and Derna. This was supported by the new literacy law of 1952 that made school education mandatory for both sexes (Obeidi, 2013). Furthermore, Libyan women were granted the right to vote in 1964 even though their actual political participation was limited and optional (Obeidi, 2013).

Women's political participation under the monarchy shows that the focus of pioneer women was not in getting elected to Parliament or being chosen for a political position. Rather, the main goal was building "a strong social base for women's participation through spreading awareness of the importance of women's role in public life. They encouraged public engagement for women by establishing several women's associations and forums that flourished during the 1950s and 1960s" (Hweio, 2018, p. 68).

The civic efforts of Libyan women started with the establishment of the Women's Renaissance Society in Benghazi in 1954 followed by the formation of another women's organization in 1957 in Tripoli. Those organizations led the women's movement in Libya, which demanded—through petitions and demonstrations—equal political and civil rights for women in Libya (Bugaighis, 2012). They were women's way to create new communication methods with the society.

The efforts of those women contributed to awakening women's realization of their role in the social and political arenas and their capabilities of making changes in society.

They encouraged public engagement by the establishment of several women's associations and forums that flourished during the 1950s and 1960s. They also found a voice for women in the media by establishing magazines and radio shows targeting women. One advocate for women's rights and cultural awareness through media channels was Khadija Al Jahmi, who finished her primary school education in the Italian school in Benghazi with the support of her father and against all cultural traditions. She then traveled to Egypt to continue her higher education and came back with a teaching certificate and eagerness to improve women's conditions in Libya. In 1956 she was offered a position on Libyan radio, which made her the first female voice on Libyan radio (Alusta, 2006). Her career in the media lasted for decades, during which she produced and hosted many radio shows targeting women and family issues. Some of her notable shows include "Lights on the Society," "Woman's Corner," "Child's Corner," and "People's Lives." She was also the first female news presenter (Alusta, 2006).

In 1964, Khadija established the first women's magazine, which she used to reach out to women and encourage them to practice their newly gained rights and participate in the development process of their country. She showed great devotion to her cause, taking the magazine's issues in her car to distribute them (Alusta, 2006). She also founded the first youth magazine, *Alamal* [*Hope*], in 1975. Khadija Al Jahmi's efforts, along with those of her devoted female colleagues, contributed profoundly to awakening women's realization of their role in social and political arenas and their capabilities of making changes in society. This would, however, change when Gaddafi led a military coup against the monarchy in September 1969 and started a dictatorial regime that lasted for forty-two years.

WOMEN'S PUBLIC ENGAGEMENT OPPORTUNITIES DURING GADDAFI'S REGIME

Women's activism under Gaddafi was a segment of the political system created and directed by Gaddafi. Under dictatorships, the ceiling for political opportunities is normally low and communication platforms are limited since he had had complete control over all venues of public life. The limitation in political opportunities also resulted from the high risks that arise from challenging the regime.

This section analyzes the risks associated with engagement under Gaddafi's dictatorship. It sheds light on the general environment of political freedom and political opportunities under the Gaddafi regime, including the political opportunity choices that were available for women. It also discusses the environment within which women gauged their way to use the limited communication platforms available to them. In the early stages of Gaddafi's regime, the political culture in Libya, developed during the monarchy era, was still not affected by Gaddafi's new ideology. The new social and political dogma presented by Gaddafi soon faced opposition from wide sections of the population, especially intellectuals and university students. This resistance produced further state intervention (Simons, 1993).

In 1976 when the regime interfered in the elections of Benghazi university student association, clashes erupted on the campus of Benghazi University and ultimately led to the new phenomenon of public executions, where three university students were executed in Benghazi on April 7, 1977 (Makhlouf, 1993). Public executions took place in the following years in different parts of the country and became the new method of dealing with domestic opposition.

The ruthlessness of the regime made it difficult for citizens to express their opinions. The situation was even harder on women, who would face two challenges: the regime's brutality and society's restrictions. However, some cases of women publicly opposed to Gaddafi were recorded during the first and second decades of Gaddafi's regime.

Female students were engaged in the students' movement of the 1970s and 1980s. They were present during the bloody events of 1976. Women's engagement did not take the form of armed resistance or violent opposition but in the form of verbal mobilization, providing logistic support to male associates, and printing and distributing flyers against the regime (Al-Ta'aeb, 2015). However, the way the regime reacted to those actions was not different than its reaction toward any other opposition.

A group of female students was active in mobilizing the students on the campus of Tripoli University in 1976 as a response to the regime's executions of the university students in Benghazi. Seventeen female students went from classroom to classroom calling for suspension of classes and urging students to go out on demonstrations. They were arrested and tortured for a few days before they were released with travel restrictions and a suspension from university (Al-Ta'aeb, 2015).

Fatima Al-Ta'aeb was one of them. Her story with the regime did not stop there. Even after what she went through with her friends, they did not stop searching for venues to express their resistance. Fatima, along with her younger sister Zakiea and three of her college friends who shared the previous prison experience with her, tried to contact the opposition abroad and offered their help: she reported, "They did not reply to our request. We then formed a cell and sent our names to them" (Al-Ta'aeb, 2015).

After a failed attempt to assassinate Gaddafi in 1984, the cell's information was leaked. All cell members were arrested. Fatima, a mother of a two-year-old daughter, was transferred from her city Benghazi to Tripoli with her sister and another member of the cell, with their heads covered in black plastic bags and their hands cuffed:

> They put us in isolated cells for three days, they would call us late at night for investigation, they would hit us and call us names and make us sign on papers

without reading them. We would spend the whole day with our heads covered and our hands cuffed. This torture lasted for three months then we were transferred to a women's criminal jail in which a new section was built just for us; the political prisoners. (Al-Ta'aeb, 2015)

Fatima took full responsibility and claimed that her younger sister knew nothing about the cell: "There was an aged guard who used to bring food to our cell. Every time he entered the room, I see tears in his eyes. One day when he was delivering the food, he whispered to me that my sister was released" (Al-Ta'aeb, 2015).

Fatima and her female friends spent four years in the political prison. There were ten people in a small room with no visits allowed. Their release came as part of a blanket amnesty in 1988. Their husbands, who never gave up on them, came to Tripoli to take them home to Benghazi. Fatima's daughter, who was about six years old by then, did not recognize her (Al-Ta'aeb, 2015).

Women, as a component of Libyan society, did not stop searching for opportunities to project their voice. The brutal reaction toward opposition including female political activities which took place in the first and second decades of the Gaddafi regime tuned down in the third decade when the regime started using different strategies to deal with women's activism.

After the invasion of Iraq in 2003, Gaddafi's fear of facing Saddam Hussein's fate made him anxious to repair his relations with the West. He terminated his program of Weapons of Mass Destruction and opened the country for foreign inspectors (Murphy, 2004).

Normalizing relations with the West required Gaddafi to apply limited reforms to gain the trust of the world powers. These reforms included improvement of human rights conditions and liberties and changing the regime's strategies toward opposition were led by Saif Al-Islam Gaddafi, Gaddafi's second son, who was seen as his father's most likely successor (BBC News, 2012). The reforms included changing the regime's strategies towards the opposition. Deals were made with long-term opposition groups like the Muslim Brotherhood movement in order to include them in the political system (Altaweel, 2015).

Individuals and associations took advantage of the new political openness to lobby for more human rights reformation. Women were part of the process. Azza Maghur, a lawyer and human rights activist, worked for years to improve legal rights for women in Libya. She had multiple encounters with the regime during the last decade of the Gaddafi rule when she took advantage of the new political openness. She called for improvement in women's rights.

Azza states that her activities were constrained by the regime. She recalls one of her latest clashes with the regime just a few months before the revolution: "In November 2010, I spoke with the chairman of the Bar Association in Libya about the issue of not having an active civil society in Libya. I told him that since a normal civil society is not allowed, there is a need to visualize a different type of it" (Azza Maghur, personal interview, May 11, 2016). Azza and a group of lawyers decided to hold a public seminar to discuss the issue. "We planned for the seminar in my office. At that day I felt scared; when you live under a dictatorship for a long time you would feel scared when you cross the line. I felt the danger that evening; I felt we were crossing the line" (Azza Maghur, personal interview, May 11, 2016).

The seminar was held in the Bar Association in November 2010. Azza presented a paper that criticized the conditions of civil society in Libya and compared it to civil society activities the Libyans created under the Italian colonization. "I concluded with the prediction that the civil society in Libya will evolve virtually through social media and one day it will come out and change reality. I remember that the whole room had a burst of outrage; members of the revolutionary committee movement attacked us verbally and demanded that I apologize for what I had said in my presentation. I went home that night with an alarming feeling all over me" (Azza Maghur, personal interview, May 11, 2016).

Azza published her paper online and after a few days she received a phone call from the main office of the revolutionary committee. She called a friend and gave her the number of Human Rights Watch. "I told her if anything happened to me, call them. I went there without even telling my husband. A member of my staff went with me. I told him if I did not come out in two hours to go tell my husband to take my daughters and flee the country" (Azza Maghur, personal interview, May 11, 2016).

Azza, who acted based on her knowledge of the brutal history of the regime, knew that she did nothing wrong when she used a peaceful way to oppose the system: "I was doing my job as a lawyer; I had no anticipation of authority" (Azza Maghur, personal interview, May 11, 2016). There were seven men from different security institutions waiting for her in a dark meeting room:

> Their words were full of indirect threat. I asked them if any of them read my article? And I found out that only one did read it. I asked that guy if there was any instigation in my paper and he said that I used a scientific approach and that he did not see any incitation in it. Then I argued with them, saying that they lost communication with the youth who started a new type of civil society in the shadow. I told them "you don't want anyone to tell you what's right and what's wrong." I felt that I managed to convince them. (Azza Maghur, personal interview, May 11, 2016)

After she left, Azza knew that other participants in the seminar were also questioned: "A few days later, I met a friend who was close to the leadership of the revolutionary committee movement. He told me that our seminar was a big issue and Gaddafi was going for more brutal ways to punish us and even execute our chairman but other voices in his close circle convinced him to listen to us" (Azza Maghur, personal interview, May 11, 2016).

Azza's experience with the regime in its final years proves the slight changes in the regime's approach toward opposition voices. The margins of political opportunity somewhat expanded, but Gaddafi's dictatorship remained brutal.

Under authoritarian regimes, communication platforms become a mobilizing tool to deliver the regime's propaganda. The nature of mass media under

Gaddafi's regime indicates that this important source of public communication was paralyzed for a long time. The policies undertaken by the regime-imposed restrictions on the freedom of the media and allowed only one voice to be heard. All of which played a significant role in stopping people from using the media to shape their opinions. Even more, government control over mass media created a negative relationship and lack of trust with the public. The media was used as another oppressive tool to stop people from challenging the regime.

Within this context, women who worked in media outlets during the Gaddafi regime faced two types of restrictions: political restrictions, in the form of regime control over the media, and social restrictions from the conservative Libyan society, which considered women working in the media improper. Some female journalists had to switch careers from TV to print media, which "was more socially acceptable for women. Working as a TV presenter was an expression of emancipation not tolerated in the conservative Libyan society" (Issawi, 2014).

Women's Public Engagement Opportunities During the Revolution

A basic assumption in social movements literature explains that opportunities become possible when changes in political and social settings take place and lead to the vulnerability of the established order (Wickham, 2002). Social movements scholars specify five conditions under which political and social opportunities can be prolonged (Wickham, 2002, p. 2):

1. The extension of participation to new actors.
2. Changes in political alignments.
3. Emerging divisions among elites.
4. The appearance of influential allies.
5. A decline in the state's capacity or will to repress dissent.

Based on these conditions, the possibility for political and social opening is subject to the type of political and social environments and the degree of political flexibility the government obtains. Therefore, increasing opportunities for public engagement under dictatorship regimes is much harder than developing those opportunities within a democratic environment. Wickham (2002) stated, "In authoritarian settings, in which the risks of participating in an opposition movement are high and the prospects of effecting change are, at best, uncertain, even the most aggrieved citizens may retreat into self-preserving silence. Hence the burden is on movement organizers to create the motivations and venues for political protest and, in so doing, enable citizens to overcome the powerful psychological and structural barriers to participation erected by the authoritarian state" (p. 204).

Thus, the likelihoods to develop new opportunities become limited under nondemocratic regimes and more likely to happen as part of a major political and social event like an uprising or a revolution. Such huge events would disturb the previous political and social balance to create the perfect environment for the five conditions mentioned above to thrive.

The usage of political opportunities and constraints in studying Libyan women's participation in the revolution represent the basic idea of creating and seizing the opportunity. Taking into consideration the limitations of women's pre-revolution public participation, one would expect that women would lean on the society's profound vision of women as recipients of care and citizens with no leadership abilities. Women had to decide whether to be free riders, a position that comes with no shame in this case, or decide to take initiatives and participate profoundly in the revolution despite the risk that comes with that participation.

Holding back and being free riders was expected, welcomed, and even accepted by the Libyan conservative patriarchal society. However, women decided not to be free riders; the involvement of women in the Libyan revolution against Gaddafi's regime was splendid.

Even though the revolution against Gaddafi's tyranny was an impulsive popular action, two factors contributed to inflaming the spontaneous event: the other Arab uprisings which took place in neighboring countries, especially in Tunisia and Egypt, and the increased tension in Benghazi which started to become part of the city's daily life until it was surmounted with the arrest of Fathi Terbil, the lawyer in the infamous case of Abu Salim prison, on February 15, 2011.[3]

At that night, the mothers, wives, and daughters of Abu Salim's victims protested in front of the internal security building in Benghazi demanding Terbil's release (Obeidi, 2013). "The ladies chanted that night, 'Wake up, Benghazi, this is the day you've been waiting for'; there and then, the revolution started (Nadine Nasrat, personal interview, November 13, 2015).

The women's protest lasted for a few hours, and the lawyer was released in the early morning of February 16 (AlArabiya, 2011); however, Benghazi did not rest. The next day, a small number of protestors, mostly lawyers and human rights activists, started a sit-in in front of the court building in Benghazi, holding signs demanding better human rights and urgent reforms. Iman Bugaighis, along with her sister Salwa, were among the first handful of people who protested at the court that day. She recalls what happened:

---

[3] The Abu Salim case refers to the infamous event of June 29, 1996, in which the regime responded to the strikes of political prisoners in Abu Salim Prison demanding better conditions by killing 1270 political prisoners in about three hours. The regime hid the crime for years and families of the victims were not informed of the killing of their loved ones until 2003, when rumors started to spread about the massacre and Saif Al-Islam Gaddafi took charge of the issue through his human rights organization and tried to resolve the situation before it received international attention.

I told my sister, "If you go out to protest, I will come with you." She called me and said, "They are going to the court." I was preparing to grade exam papers for my class in the college of dentistry; I put the papers aside and came back to them six months later! I picked up my daughter from school and dropped her off at my mother's place. My sister did the same with her kids; she only went with her husband and her oldest son. We left home around noon and did not know if we [would] come back. (Iman Bugaighis, personal interview, November 4, 2015).

The young protestors led the crowds, carrying the demands for Gaddafi to step down. The regime forces met the unarmed protestors with live bullets and anti-aircraft missiles. At that time, there was no turning back: "It was too late, the blood was already shed" (Nadine Nasrat, personal interview, November 13, 2015).

When considering the brutal history of how Gaddafi dealt with opposition, it is worth noting that women came out of their comfort zone during the most threatening and dangerous days of his rule. The decision made by Libyan women to participate in the revolution was reflected in the level of participation and the number of turnouts in the protests and social programs to help the wounded and search for the missing during the war. Women were the backbone of the revolutionary movement by providing logistic services to the front line from nursing to cooking thousands of meals a day for the revolutionists at the battlefront (Bugaighis, 2012, p. 3).

Tripoli, the capital city, suffered from a siege that lasted for six months. During this time, the people had to respond to the regime's brutality by using different forms of resistance. Even there, women were involved in the revolution as they "hid fighters and cooked them meals. They sewed flags, collected money, contacted journalists. They ran guns and, in a few cases, used them" (Barnard, 2011). Moreover, women smuggled weapons to the revolutionaries, tended wounded rebels, and some of them worked as guides for NATO to find airstrike targets in Tripoli (Barnard, 2011).

In the case of the Libyan revolution, women earned their opportunity from day one when the mothers of Abu Salim's victims protested in front of the security building commanding the release of their attorney. Those women were the only segment in the Libyan society that was permitted to protest. The permit given to those families was meant to absorb the popular outrage that was fueled by the crime committed by the government by killing more than 1200 prisoners in Abu Salim prison in three hours. Years of silent protests in Benghazi made those women the perfect starters of the uprising. Fathi Terbil, the attorney for the victims' families, explained the circumstances under which those women played a major role in initiating the uprising:

In the last four years of Gaddafi's regime, the mothers, sisters, and wives of the Abu Salim Massacre used to protest every Saturday to demand justice for their beloved ones. They took advantage of the regime's signs of openness, which were the result of national and international pressure. Therefore, women played a huge role in preparing for the revolution and participating in it. The bravery of those wives, daughters, mothers, and sisters was unimaginable. They created the rebellion culture through their weekly protests. (Obeidi, 2013, p. 9)

Women's choice to seize opportunity did not come without a risk. Najla Elmangoush was willing to take that risk when she agreed to go on the third day of the revolution to a radio station located in Abu-Dezzerah, a small town located in the Benghazi suburbs. She went with two other female activists. The three women were accompanied by a group of young revolutionary men to check whether they could use the radio station to broadcast the revolution's updates. Najla describes that moment:

> When we started the broadcasting, we all sat [in] a circle and handed the micro-phone to each other to say one thing: "Libya is free." It was a wonderful feeling and a touching moment I will cherish forever; we were all crying.... I did not think at that time of the risky situation we were in. I did not want to think that our broadcasting was live and Gaddafi's air forces could have easily located our position and strike us. I was like a child exploring a new toy. When I recall that day, I always ask myself, "What was I thinking when I did that?." (Najla Elmangoush, personal interview, December 5, 2015)

Najla read the first declaration of the uprising and requested people to remain calm and to submit any arms in their possession to the collection points in the city. She and her companions stayed in the radio station until a late hour that night (Najla Elmangoush, personal interview, December 5, 2015).

When looking at women's actions in the beginning of the revolution and how they chose to rise for the occasion, a question must be asked: why didn't women choose to be free riders? Why did they choose to risk their lives and reputations by being in the heart of the event?

One activist answers those questions when stating "I did not join the revolu-tion to pursue a personal dream, I did so because I always believed that we deserved a better life. Part of me wanted to rebel against the social and political restrictions we suffered from. That's why I was working for more than twelve hours a day during the revolution without feeling tired; the revolution was our hope" (Najla Elmangoush, personal interview, December 5, 2015).

Hana El-Gallal, the international law professor who joined the revolution on February 17, 2011, and was present during the first official meeting of the Transnational Council, offered another illustration of women's motivations for joining the revolution:

> There are hidden memories we all have; those memories affect our decisions in life. I was a child during the 1980s and I lived through Gaddafi's public execu-tions of university students. I always wondered why the older people at that time did not support the youth and stop Gaddafi from doing what he did to them. I always thought things could've been different had they stood up to his actions. When the uprising started in 2011, I was … the same age my parents were in the 1980s; I felt responsible not to let the youth down. I did not want to repeat the mistake the generation before us did back in the 1980s. Therefore, when the youth went out on the streets, I went with them. (Hana El-Gallal, personal inter-view, November 15, 2015)

Women in Communication Platforms During the Revolution

The February 2011 uprising came as a shock to conservative society in Libya and to women themselves. The revolution showed how ready Libyan women were for change.

The unexpected public role of Libyan women in the beginning of the revolution brought them into the spotlight. This new reality required exceptional will to break long-lasting cultural traditions that limited women's role in society. To challenge societal norms and traditions, women had to first face the authority of the patriarchal figures within their own family. Seeking the approval of a male figure was important for two main reasons: first, to provide support and to help her with her new roles and, second, to protect her from the society's possible negative reaction. Shahrazad Kablan, the first female anchor to appear on TV during the revolution, sums up this social need for approval:

> If women in our society did not have a husband, a father, or a brother to support them and stand behind their brave decisions to get involved in public space, women would not be able to do what they have done in the revolution. The easiest thing people would say is that he is not a "man" because he allowed his female relative to have an active public role. A man must have special qualities to be in that position, he must be very strong to face society's backlash on him. (Shahrazad Kablan, personal interview, March 6, 2016)

Kablan is an example of a pioneer, being the first female to break a long stigma in Libyan society regarding women's work in the media. Kablan, who worked as a teacher and educator in the United States for years, was the first female anchor on the first nongovernmental TV station, Libya Alahrar TV, which was launched in Doha, Qatar, on March 30, 2011, in support of the Libyan revolution.

WOMEN'S PUBLIC ENGAGEMENT OPPORTUNITIES AFTER THE REVOLUTION

When the chair of the National Transitional Council delivered the liberation speech on October 24, 2011, he officially signaled the start of the state-building process.

Women started the state-building phase willing to maintain their newly gained political and social status. However, women's presence in the public sphere witnessed a backlash. Women, who scored new records of participation and created new opportunities in the first two years after the revolution, started to lose their position as a full partner in the state-building process. Three main reasons for the decrease in women's engagement opportunities are worth mentioning: the assassination of Salwa Bugaighis on June 25, 2014, the rise of Islamist groups, and the lack of security due to the proliferation of arms.

Those new factors show that obstacles to women's participation go beyond the traditional perception of women. The lack of security and the absence of the rule of law along with the extreme levels of violence among the unchecked militias, the rise of extremist Islamist groups, and the increased number of war crimes are all indicators of the challenges women encounter in new Libya.

The call for a limited role for women in politics came from different fronts, from Islamist groups and armed militias to elected members of the General National Congress (GNC). Examples of violations against female politicians and activists ranged from verbal abuse to assassination. Mohamed Kilani, an Islamist member in the GNC, demanded the female members of the GNC to be seated in a different room from men because "GNC members are distracted by their colleagues who wore make up, dressed indecently and mingled with men" (LWPP, 2014a). A member of GNC physically attacked a female member because she disagreed with him, only to become the head of Dawn of Libya Operation, the biggest militia group in Tripoli (LWPP, 2014a).

Female members of the Council of Representatives (CoR) received their share of threats and attacks as well. Houses of some female members and candidates were robbed and burned down, while several female representatives received threats to burn their houses down (LWPP, 2014a).

However, the attacks against women were escalated to a new level with the murder of Salwa Bugaighis, a lawyer and human rights activist and Vice Chair of the National Dialogue Preparatory Commission. Salwa, who was one of the first Libyans to participate in the uprising against Gaddafi, had to flee the country, just like other activists, after receiving death threats. She came back to Benghazi to vote in the parliamentary elections held in June 2014. She posted her photos at the voting center on social media and spent the day encouraging people of Benghazi to go out and vote (LWPP, 2014b). That same day, she was brutally killed and her husband was kidnapped her husband (The Guardian, 2014). An investigation was opened on the murder, but the murderers were never arrested.

Salwa's murder was a "decisive event" (Azza Maghur, personal interview, May 11, 2016) and a turning point for women's activism in Libya, as most female activists fled the country after receiving death threats, the thing that made "the whole women's movement reverse to an idle status. After Salwa's assassination, women came under huge familial and societal pressure to stop or reduce their activities for their own safety" (Nadine Nasrat, personal interview, November 13, 2015).

After the assassination of Salwa Bugaighis, more women were murdered in different Libyan cities. Fariha Al-Berkawi, a former GNC member, was killed in her home city, Derna. Also, Salwa Henied, a member of the national security under the Gaddafi regime, was killed by uncharted killers. Other female activists and journalists were assassinated, and the killers were never arrested.

Since then, most female activists fled the country due to increased violence against women and after receiving threats (LWPP, 2014b). However, Libyan women did not stop their efforts to secure a sustainable and meaningful place for them in the Libyan political and civic arenas. Women's rights organizations continued their work to support women's rights through holding meetings and workshops abroad.

Efforts toward creating a new discourse started to take place amid these critical times in Libya. A new wave of women's activism has started to take place. Projects led by youth rely on social media platforms to get their voices heard. Their tools changed from direct activism on the ground to using social media as their means of action. Women are trying to create their opportunities even if they do that from behind the keyboards and by using nicknames.

Conclusion

Gender activism and engagement opportunities depend, for the most part, on the type of regime and the window for political participation available for the citizens. Libyan women, however, did not only seize the opportunities, but they also created their own. Even when political participation was at its lowest levels during Gaddafi's rule, individual cases tell the story of women who tried to make their voice heard under the most oppressive circumstances.

Those stories, however, remained limited to a small number of women who seized or created their prospects until the revolution in 2011. Women then acted collectively; they were present in every aspect of the revolutionary act. Their participation is not connected to individuals, though some individuals took the initiative; it was the uprising of a whole segment of the society. Women in the revolution were aware of their role, their duty, and their potentials. Therefore, their strong presence during the revolution and the opportunities they obtained were targeted and attacked. Attempts to exclude women from the political scene and the state-building process show a backlash in the progress made to secure a sustainable presentation of women in the political arena.

Today, women are no longer acting collectively to seize political opportunities. Instead, female activists and politicians are acting either as independent agents or through their own limited-resourced organizations in exile to improve women's chances to take part in the state-building process. Specifically, some activists focus their efforts on conflict resolution strategies as their means of action.

References

AlArabiya. (2011, February 27). *Fathi Terbil: A Young Lawyer Who Started a Revolution*. Retrieved February 12, 2016, from AlArabiya.net: http://www.alarabiya.net/articles/2011/02/27/139488.html

Al-Ta'aeb, F. (2015, February 12). *Behind the Walls*. YouTube.

Altaweel, K. (2015, June 13). *Saif El-Islam Gaddafi the Failed Reformer Who Counted on the Muslim Brotherhood*. Retrieved May 15, 2016, from Al Hayata http://www.alhayat.com/Articles/9501460/%2الإصلاحي-الفاشل D%2D%2سيف-الإسلام-القناةي D%2D%2D% 2D%2D%2D%2الإخوان D%2حين-راهن-على

Alusta, A. M. (2006). *I am Khadija Aljahmi (Ana Khadija)*. General Council of Culture.

Baldez, L. (2002). *Why Women Protest: Women's Movements in Chile*. Cambridge University Press.

Barnard, A. (2011, September 12). *Libya's War-Tested Women Hope to Keep New Power.* Retrieved October 24, 2011, from The New York Times http://www.nytimes.com/2011/09/13/world/africa/13women.html?nl=todaysheadlines&emc=tha22

BBC News. (2012, October 9). *Libya's Saif al-Islam Gaddafi Profiled.* Retrieved May 18, 2016, from BBC News http://www.bbc.com/news/world-africa-14617511

Bugaighis, W. (2012). Prospects for Women in New Libya. In *The International Conference on Women's Participation in Politics.*

El Fathaly, O. E., & Palmer, M. (1980). *Political Development and Social Change in Libya.* Lexington Books.

Harris, L. C. (1986). *Libya: Qadhafi's Revolution and the Modern State.* Westview Press.

Hweio, H. (2018, Fall). The Libyan Revolution and Women's Participation in Politics and Media. *African Conflict and Peacebuilding Review, 8*(2), 63–92.

Issawi, F. E. (2014). Women and Media: Libyan Female Journalists from Gaddafi Media to Post-Revolution: Case Study. *Cyber Orient, 8,* 1. Retrieved from http://www.cyberorient.net/article.do?articleId=8865

Karame', K. H. (1999). Maman Aida, A Lebanese Godmother of the Combatants: Fighting without Arms. In L. R. Shehadeh (Ed.), *Women and War in Lebanon.* University Press of Florida.

Libyan Women's Platform for Peace (LWPP). (2014a, October 15). *Human Rights and Women in Libya: LWPP's UPR Submitted to the UN OHCHR.* Retrieved January 25, 2015, from Libyan Women's Platform for Peace: http://www.libyanwomensplatformforpeace.wordpress.com/2014/10/

Libyan Women's Platform for Peace (LWPP). (2014b, December 11). *The Story of Salwa.* Retrieved January 15, 2015, from Libyan Women's Platform for Peace: libyanwomensplatformforpeace.com/2014/12//قصة-سلوى/

Majdey, M. (2014, October 15). *Cairo Dar.* Retrieved August 20, 2015, from www.cairodar.com: www.cairodar.com/358935

Makhlouf, M. (1993, January 6). *The Phenomenon of Public Executions in Libya: Punisment Philosophy and Popular Courts: Al-Hayat Newspaper,* 10922.

Metz, H. C. (2003). Libya: A Country Study. In S. Bianci (Ed.), *Libya: Current Issues and Historical Background.* Nova Science Publishers.

Murphy, S. (2004, January). U.S./UK Negotiations with Libya Regarding Nonproliferation. *The American Journal of International Law, 98*(1), 195–197.

Obeidi, A. (2013). The Impact of the Revolution and the Transitional Period on Women's Empowering Policies in Libya: Reality and Challenges. In *Women and the Arab Spring.* Mesbar.

Shehadeh, L. R. (1999). A War of Survival. In L. R. Shehadeh (Ed.), *Women and War in Lebanon.* University Press of Florida.

Simons, G. (1993). *Libya: The Struggle for Survival.* St. Martin's Press.

Tetreault, M. A. (1995). Women and Revolution in Vietnam. In M. A. Tetreault (Ed.), *Women in Revolution in Africa, Asia, and the New World.* University of South Carolina Press.

The Guardian. (2014, June 25). *Salwa Bugaighis, Libyan Human Rights Activist, Shot Dead in Benghazi.* Retrieved January 22, 2015, from The Guardian http://www.theguardian.com/world/2014/jun/26/salwa-bugaighis-libyan-shot-dead-benghazi

Vandewalle, D. (2006). *A History of Modern Libya.* Cambridge University Press.

Wickham, C. R. (2002). *Mobilizing Islam: Religion, Activism, and Political Change in Egypt.* Colombia University Press.

CHAPTER 16

Facebook's Role in Empowering Egyptian Women During COVID-19: Case of the 2020 Parliamentary Elections

Amany Ahmed Khodair and Reman Abdel All

INTRODUCTION

In Egypt, the influence of new media, primarily Facebook, has noticeably risen to impact political development. In the last few years, Facebook overrode traditional media, especially television, as the primary source of information. Therefore, it can play an essential role in shaping ideas and values and be a powerful tool to mobilise actions such as visiting election polls.

This study's main objective is to understand the political impact of Facebook on Egyptian women by examining their reliance on Facebook to make political decisions. Besides, Facebook's role in mobilising women voters in the 2020 elections will also be examined. This study aims to answer three chief questions: To what extent did Facebook contribute to empowering women in the 2020 elections? Has it replaced traditional media in promoting political participation? Was the COVID-19 pandemic one of the factors that led or paved the way to heavier reliance on social networks, including Facebook?

A. A. Khodair (✉)
Suez Canal University, Ismaïlia, Egypt

The British University in Egypt, El Sherouk City, Egypt
e-mail: Amany.Khodair@bue.edu.eg

R. A. All
Suez Canal University, Ismaïlia, Egypt

© The Author(s), under exclusive license to Springer Nature Switzerland AG 2023
L. H. Skalli, N. Eltantawy (eds.), *The Palgrave Handbook of Gender, Media and Communication in the Middle East and North Africa*,
https://doi.org/10.1007/978-3-031-11980-4_16

This study argues that women in Egypt rely on Facebook as a primary source of information and are thus motivated to act in line with the mainstream public opinions at any given point in time. This fact was heavily utilised by women candidates running in the 2020 parliamentary elections.

To test this argument and for research purposes, this study limits the scope of research to the Suez Canal region. The rest of the study is organised as follows: The first section presents the conceptual and theoretical framework. This is followed by a brief examination of the data collection and methodology used. We report the main empirical results before drawing conclusions and making prudent policy recommendations for public policy decision-makers in Egypt. These suggestions put forward the importance of considering Facebook as an agenda-setting tool and highlight its role in public policy implementation.

Conceptual and Theoretical Framework

Social Media and Political Participation

Political participation refers to "voluntary behaviour" learned/acquired by interacting with societal groups such as family, school, and others. The individual's exercise of political participation as an acquired process is based on the availability, capacity and motivation, the opportunities provided by society, political and ideological traditions, and the conditions that determine the nature of the political climate prevailing in a particular society (Milbrath, 1981). The general public undertakes such activities to influence public policy, either directly or by affecting the selection of persons who make the policies (Uhlaner, 2015). Some traditional activities of political participation can also be effectively undertaken via social media platforms such as Facebook.

The emergence of social networks for participation has created an active role for Internet audiences in the political process through discussions, participation, and voting. Further, social media sites have had a qualitative impact on political activists due to the perception that they are more interactive, connected, and involved than traditional media (Marichal, 2013).

According to Andersen and Medaglia (2009), social media, in general, and Facebook, in particular, can have a role in assisting political campaigns, supporting candidates or their cause, contacting officials through official pages, voicing criticism or protesting, and discussing societal issues with fellow citizens. Facebook can enhance political participation as it informs the public on political matters and choices in a faster and more precise manner than ever before. This is increasing political participation in response to recruitment or mobilisation through the use of social media platforms.

McClurg (2003) believes that social network interactions have a strong influence on an individual's tendency towards political participation, as it provides them an opportunity to gather the information that promotes their political actions. Social networks also help facilitate all political involvement and participation. It was also found that Facebook users who join groups on the Facebook platform seek political involvement and obtain information for the purposes of discussing more political issues compared to other issues (Conroy et al., 2012). Social networking sites provide an excellent opportunity to reach individuals who are less interested in politics. Further, those politicians who respond or interact with their comments are commended and are more appealing to voters (Enli & Skogerbø, 2013).

Facebook in Egypt

Facebook has gained significant importance in Egypt during the last decade, especially in terms of its impact on political life. This was primarily because Facebook had a pivotal role in the January 25 revolution. The role played by social media networks in the revolution had multiple elements that indeed reshaped the political sphere. Facebook, in particular, gained popularity during the January 25 revolution due to its ability to influence political mobilisation. Facebook was used to mobilise the masses towards significant revolutionary demands such as freedom, equality, democracy, and social justice.

Many Egyptians used such platforms to interact spontaneously, although these interactions soon developed into waves of political mobilisation for democratic change (Zahran, 2012). Facebook was employed by supporters to advance political demands through demonstration or civil disobedience. Facebook contributed to transferring virtual anger into real anger by facilitating responses to calls for protests and assembly (Al-Gabory, 2015). Facebook also impacted the organisation and coordination of political action. Most activists used this tool to mobilise protesters and organise them by facilitating communication between them related to the dates and sites of their gathering. Activists used social media to transmit information, photos, and video clips through Twitter, Facebook, and YouTube (Al-Salehy, 2017). Therefore, these sites, especially Facebook, were considered strategic organisation tools for political mobilisation.

Another strength of Facebook is that it enabled activists to challenge state monopoly over information. In addition to the politicisation of Egyptian youth, Facebook helped convert large silent youth groups into political activists using social media to express opinions, spread ideas, and engage in discussions without fear (Kamel, 2014). Given the impact of Facebook on mobilising the masses, state agencies decided to interrupt Internet services in Egypt on January 28, 2011 (Elsebahy, 2013).

Many sources, including the British newspaper *The Guardian*, acknowledged the role of Facebook in the revolution by referring to the Egyptian revolution as a "social media revolution" (Shearlaw, 2016). The number of Facebook users increased dramatically in the early years of the uprisings, and has continued to increase since. A report by the Egyptian "Techno Wireless", a company specialising in electronic marketing and mobile networks, confirmed that the Internet users in Egypt increased from 21.2 million before the revolution to 23.1 million users in 2012 alone (Reuters, 2011). Egyptians ignored traditional media and started following events and news about the revolution via social media platforms.

Since 2011, it has become clear that the impact of Facebook on the political and social transformations in Egypt has gone well beyond its simple role as a tool for communication (Kamel, 2014). Increasing dependence on Facebook in Egypt is reflected in the increasing number of users that reached approximately 42,400,000 by 2020, which account for 40.1% of the population (Napoleoncat Stats, 2020). According to the same study, nearly 32% of these users fall in the age range between 25 and 34 years old (Statista, 2021). However, it is worth mentioning that females do not constitute the majority of Facebook users, particularly in Egypt, since 64% of the users are males (Napoleoncat Stats, 2020).

Studies have shown that political participation is linked to personal exposure to more information through social media networks, which results in increased interest in politics and participation (Velasquez & LaRose, 2015). Researchers have also demonstrated how Facebook has become a tool that reflects the nature of the relationship between the state and society and between the elite and the masses (Hawadsy, 2018). This is seen in the changing attitude of government officials towards social media platforms: today, most governmental institutions in Egypt, as well as the presidency and miliary, have their official pages on Facebook. According to some, this tool (Facebook) has even replaced some of the traditional, yet weak, functions of political party functions such as mobilisation of voters (Rady, 2003).

Women Empowerment and Political Representation

This section draws on insights about women's political empowerment (WPE) and the internet-based political empowerment to argue that Egyptian women, owing to COVID-19, turned to Facebook during the 2020 elections to acquire information/awareness, increase participation, and influence voting for election.

Pirannejad and Janssen (2019) categorised their Internet-based political empowerment into two general concepts utilised in this research: political awareness and participation. Their research demonstrates that Facebook provides all citizens with a large volume of political information in a rapid fashion and at no cost. Digital tools bring people together on one platform (which may be impossible by direct communication), and give them better access to monitor public figures, engage in online discussions/debates, and exchange views. This, they argue, affects political awareness, knowledge, and potentially higher levels of participation. Social media can also influence the voting process during elections.

Women's empowerment is defined as the process that enhances women's ability to make strategic decisions. It also refers to women's ownership of resources that can be used to meet their goals and achieve successes. Accordingly, researchers highlight the importance of three key interconnected elements needed to empower women—resources, management, and achievements—each of which has a different meaning (Huis et al., 2017). Resources refers to materials, social and human expectations, and allocations, while management refers to a woman's ability to define her strategic goals and act based on those goals. This results in a wide range of outcomes that vary from achieving a decent standard of life to achieving proper women political representation (Rahman, 2013).

According to Buznytska (2019), WPE is a process by which women can accomplish equal representation, attain political authority, and ensure equal political power to all members of society. Egyptian women broke the ceiling in 2017 by having the first ever female governor—a position that was strictly reserved for men. Currently, 19% of women in Egypt hold senior management positions which is in line with the goals set by the National Strategy for the Empowerment of Egyptian Women 2030 Vision and Pillars (2017). Women also constitute 27% (162 seats) of the Egyptian cabinet.

The Egyptian parliament is a bicameral legislature composed of an upper (the Senate) and a lower house (the representatives' house).[1] The 2014 constitution and the current electoral law (#46/2014) provided affirmative action for protecting the representation rights of six segments of Egyptian society: workers, farmers, youth, Christians, disabled persons, and Egyptians abroad, including women (Khodair and Abdall, 2016). The 2020 elections for the House of Representatives ensured 25% seats for women, a 30% increase compared to the previous house (2015) when women secured an unprecedented 89 seats (13%) (*National Election Authority Official Website*, 2021). The current 2020 House of Representatives elected includes 148 women, whereby 142 were elected through the list, 6 were elected in the single-member constituency system, and 14 appointed by the president.

---

[1] The 2020 Article 5 of Law No. 140 (*National Election Authority Official Website*, 2021) amended some provisions of the Law on Exercising Political Rights promulgated by Law No. 45 of 2014. The Egyptian House of Representatives is now composed of 596 members, including 568 elected members and 28 appointed members by the president (5% of elected members). The elected members are divided into 284 elected with "winner-takes-all lists" and 284 elected by the single-member system (*State Information Service Official Website*, 2020).

Percentage of Women in the Egyptian House of Representatives

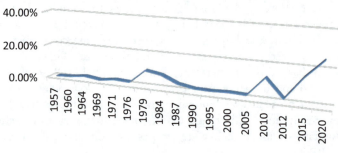

prepared by the authors

Adly et al. (2017)

In 2019 the establishment of the Egyptian Senate was also among the constitutional amendments indicating specific tasks for the council. These include discussing proposals to amend one or more articles of the constitution, drafting general plans for social and economic development, approving peace and alliance treaties, and treaties related to sovereignty rights (the Tahrir Institute for Middle EAST Policy 2019).

According to Law No. 141 of 2020, the Senate consists of 300 seats, 100 elected members by the single-member system, and 100 elected using the "winner-takes-all lists" system. Further, 100 seats are appointed by the President of the Republic, provided that no less than 10% of the total number of seats are allocated to women. The Republic is divided into 27 districts devoted to the single system election and 4 districts to the list system election. Two constituencies of the four list districts are allocated 15 seats each, and the other two are allocated 35 seats each. Each electoral list must include several candidates equal to the number to be elected in the district and several reservists. Each 15 seat list must comprise at least three women. In comparison, each 35 seat list must include at least seven women.

In the current 2020 Egyptian Senate, no women were elected via the single-member system, 10 were elected through the "winner-takes-all lists" system, and the president appointed 20, bringing the total number of female members to 30 (10% according to the electoral law). Here, it is important to point out that the president appointed 20 women. However, the law stipulated 10% was to overcome the fact that women were not elected by the single-member system, which is the hardest for women candidates as there is no affirmative action in this type of voting.

It is worth mentioning that the importance of the 2020 parliamentary elections is derived from the fact that it is the first after a new electoral law was approved in the wake of constitutional amendments in 2019 (National Election Authority Official Website, 2021). Additionally, the 2020 election was notable for women because Phoebe Fawzy, who is interviewed later in this research, is a Coptic woman who has become the Egyptian Senate's first female undersecretary (Hosny, 2020).

QUANTITATIVE ANALYSIS

This study analyses women's use of Facebook during the 2020 elections. It aims to empirically assess the role of Facebook in empowering Egyptian women during COVID-19. Approximately 330 Egyptian women from the Suez Canal governorates (Ismailia, Port Said, and Suez) were surveyed (total number surveyed was 385) and 3 parliamentarians were interviewed: Ms Phoebe Fawzy who is a journalist and a political activist serving as the second deputy speaker of the Egyptian Senate, Ms Amal Rizkallah, member of the Egyptian House of Representatives from Ismailia, and Ms Amal Asfour, Academic Dean of the AASTMT Portsaid Campus.

Additionally, three interviews were conducted with candidates who ran for elections but failed to secure a seat in the House of Representatives or the senate, including Ms Manal Madbouly, a retired television anchor from Ismailia governorate. Also interviewed was Ms Gehan Farouk, a member of the National Council of Women, as well as Ms Magda Mahmoud, an independent senate candidate from Suez governorate. These interviews contributed to assessing the role of Facebook in empowering women during the 2020 elections.

The survey draws on a random sample of Egyptian women eligible to vote. It comprises only female voters from various sectors of society in the Suez Canal governorates, including homemakers, employees, academics, and students from Canal universities. Additionally, semi-structured interviews were conducted with women activists, previous election nominees, and current members of the parliament as previously mentioned.

The surveyed sample returned 330 questionnaires. This represents an 85.9% response rate. The quality and validity of response data were established by conducting a reliability test using Cronbach's alpha (Sekaran, 2003). The SPSS (22) reliability analysis was performed separately for the indicators of each scale (Table 16.1).

Generally, reliability coefficients (Cronbach's alpha) of 0.6 or higher are considered adequate (Sekaran, 2003). As illustrated in Table 16.1, the overall

Table 16.1 Reliability analysis of the surveyed sample

Variable	Number of items	Reliability (Cronbach's Alpha)
Assessing to what extent Facebook contributed to empowering women during elections	8	0.753
Assessing the role of Facebook versus traditional media in promoting political participation	10	0.757
Assessing the effect of COVID-19 on Facebook usage	5	0.747

reliability coefficients for Cronbach's alpha ranged between 0.747 and 0.757, so all variables included in the study are reliable.

Data Analysis Methods

Basic descriptive statistics were analysed to ensure that the distortion of the questionnaire response outputs was negligible. The descriptive analysis results (see Appendix) illustrate that the standard deviation is not significant, revealing that there is only a weak distortion of the collected data for all variables. These results imply the homogeneity of the surveyed sample.

Although 79.3% of the respondents initially believed that Facebook contributes to spreading rumours and stirring up disputes, 73.5% believed that it is an effective tool for spreading ideas and exchanging opinions, especially regarding women candidates. There was general agreement that Facebook contributes to empowering women during elections, as 67.2% of the sample strongly agreed that Facebook is the best and fastest way to get information about candidates, especially women. The fact that was ascertained by Fawzy who believes that social media, and particularly Facebook, has become a pivotal source of communication between the candidate and the voters. Acting as an alternative media outlet, it provides a space for getting in touch with people's demands, problems, and suggestions. Besides, it presents a mechanism for responding and interacting with constant changes on the ground (P. Fawzy, Interview, April 25, 2021).

However, although Facebook offers an open space for exchanging ideas and views, it also allows for the spread of rumours and inaccurate information. This fact could contribute to several social, political, and economic problems. According to Fawzy, Facebook must be used with caution: it requires the user to be critical in filtering information and choosing what to believe and what to disregard, which is a skill highly lacking in our society (P. Fawzy, Interview, April 25, 2021).

Moreover, 66.2% of questionnaire respondents maintained that it increases their ability to analyse political events and engage in free discussions. Women find Facebook an arena to freely express themselves without censorship or obstacles. In addition, 65.2% and 62.7%, respectively, think that women are affected by ideas presented on Facebook more than the ideas of family members. The tool is considered important for identifying women candidates, examining programmes, and conducting comparisons. Conversely, 52.1% of the respondents relied on Facebook to determine their votes when it came to choosing women candidates.

With respect to assessing the role of Facebook versus traditional media in promoting political participation, a total of 76.6% of the respondents obtained local community news through Facebook. Additionally, 74.9% and 64.8% perceived Facebook as a powerful electronic tool that is more critical than traditional media (such as radio and TV).

However, all interviewed candidates, whether they won or lost the elections, believed that Facebook is essential but needs to be complemented with traditional media and direct contact with members of society and potential voters. Amal Asfour, a member of representatives from Port Said who used Facebook to announce her electoral programme, stated that she did utilise Facebook in reaching out to voters. However, she believes that Facebook empowered her to reach only a certain sector of the community; whereas, other segments of the society needed other means of communication (A. Asfour, Interview, April 1, 2021). Fawzy asserted that with the spread of COVID-19 and the consequent ban on gatherings, Facebook became the most important platform for discussing social events. This is in addition to many online applications that compensated for face-to-face meetings like zoom (P. Fawzy, Interview, April 25, 2021).

The results also show that 63.5% did not rely on Facebook, whereas, 58.3% partially depended on Facebook in determining their votes. It is worth mentioning that 56.8% of respondents have a personal page and another public page (this is common in Egypt even if not electoral candidates). They use these to communicate with the local community and participate in community discussions, especially voting in elections.

The elections took place during the peak of COVID-19 spread. This has made it difficult or nearly impossible for candidates to conduct face-to-face meetings or conferences with voters. Therefore, social media, particularly Facebook, offered valuable space for candidates to not only present their views and electoral programmes but to also receive feedback and recommendations that can be included in their programmes (P. Fawzy, Interview, April 25, 2021).

There was a general agreement that the COVID-19 pandemic has influenced Facebook usage. Overall, 65.5% of the respondents avoided relying on Facebook before the pandemic to make political decisions, especially voting in elections. They believed that the diversity of opinions negatively affects their ability to make an objective decision. However, 64.7% of respondents claimed that despite not having full confidence in what is being discussed on Facebook concerning the elections, they had no other alternatives but to turn to it due to the pandemic. Moreover, 64.5% of respondents felt that with the conditions resulting from the COVID-19 pandemic, Facebook was the best way to identify candidates from their homes during the lockdown. Out of the total survey takers, 51.6% of respondents were not Facebook users before the COVID-19 pandemic but were compelled to turn to it during elections to help identify candidates (G. Farouk, member of the Egyptian National Council for Women Suez governorate branch, Interview, March 21, 2021).

(a) *A one-sample t-test was performed to evaluate the role of Facebook in empowering women during elections (Douglas Lind 2010). The results are listed below:*

Table 16.2 shows a one-sample t-test evaluating the role of Facebook in empowering women during elections.

Table 16.2 One-sample t-test for the role of Facebook in empowering women during elections

			Test value = 3			
	T	df	Sig. (2-tailed)	Mean difference	95% confidence interval of the difference	
					Lower	Upper
Role of Facebook	24.117	329	0.000	0.70779	0.6501	0.7655

Table 16.3 One-sample t-test for the role of Facebook versus traditional media in promoting political participation

			Test value = 3			
	T	df	Sig. (2-tailed)	Mean difference	95% confidence interval of the difference	
					Lower	Upper
Facebook versus traditional media	21.619	329	0.000	0.65584	0.5962	0.7155

As the sig = (0.0) is less than α = 0.05, we can conclude that there is a significant difference between the mean of agreement, the value three (the median), and the mean difference = 0.70779. This indicates that the studied sample agrees with Facebook having a role in empowering women during elections.

(b) *A one-sample t-test was performed to evaluate the role of Facebook versus traditional media in promoting political participation (Lind 2010). The results are listed below:*

Table 16.3 shows a one-sample t-test used to evaluate the role of Facebook versus traditional media in promoting political participation.

As the sig = (0.0) is less than α = 0.05, we can conclude that there is a significant difference between the mean of agreement, the value three (the median), and the mean difference = 0.65584. This indicates that the studied sample agrees that Facebook has become more important than traditional media (radio and TV).

(a) *A one-sample t-test was performed to evaluate the effect of COVID-19 on Facebook usage (Lind, 2010). The results are listed below:*

Table 16.4 shows a one-sample t-test used to evaluate the effect of COVID-19 on Facebook usage.

Table 16.4 One-sample t-test for the effect of COVID-19 on Facebook usage

			Test value = 3			
	t	*df*	*Sig. (2-tailed)*	*Mean difference*	*95% confidence interval of the difference*	
					Lower	*Upper*
Effect of COVID-19	14.605	329	0.000	0.46797	0.4049	0.5310

As the sig = (0.0) is less than $\alpha = 0.05$, we can conclude that there is a significant difference between the mean of agreement, the value three (the median), and the mean difference = 0.46797. This indicates that the studied sample agrees that COVID-19 has increased reliance on Facebook for seeking information on elections.

Discussion and Conclusion

Women have realised the important role that Facebook can play in empowering them as an accessible communication tool. It can support them in reaching out to voters, and enabling them to influence, recruit, and mobilise voters. Analysis of the results shows that the COVID-19 pandemic expanded this role. However, they also realised that they cannot rely on Facebook alone. Other means of communication are needed (M. Mahmoud, Interview, March 31, 2021). Findings show that 58.3% of respondents and all interviewed candidates agreed that nothing can replace direct communications such as public rallies and door-to-door campaigning.

It is also evident through the interviews that winning the elections affects the candidate's opinion on the importance and role played by Facebook in empowering them. Amal Rizkallah, a candidate who won the 2020 elections, asserted the importance of Facebook in empowering her by voicing her views and informing the public of her activities and parliamentary achievements (Interview, March 23, 2021). This view was not shared by the candidates who failed to win a seat in the 2020 elections. Manal Madbouly, a television anchor who decided to run for parliament in the 2020 elections, confirms that she lost interest in Facebook after losing the elections. Madbouly maintains that although Facebook is an easy instrument to reach a wide range of people, this advantage is undermined by the fact that it attracts a specific category of users— not all segments of society use Facebook. Further, she argues that it can sometimes confuse users' thoughts due to the conflicting and contradictory ideas being shared (Interview, April 5, 2021).

Thus, Facebook alone cannot achieve the empowerment of women. Other sources for political communication/publicity are required—a fact confirmed by the three parliamentarians interviewed by the authors in this research

(Phoebe Fawzy, Amal Rizkallah, and Amal Asfour). Contrastingly, interviewed candidates who failed to secure a seat in the 2020 elections believed that Facebook is an important communication tool that may empower women since it is less costly than holding local campaign conferences or using traditional media coverage.

In conclusion, the analysis has shown that for Egyptian women, Facebook acts as both a valuable source of information and a tool for mobilising public opinion. Understanding this fact and considering the COVID-19 pandemic context, women candidates for 2020 parliamentary elections heavily utilised Facebook in their campaigns. Nevertheless, the effectiveness of this strategy was limited as a result of two main drawbacks. First, the reach of Facebook is limited to particular societal strata, failing to influence votes in other sectors of the community, particularly in rural areas. Second, its credibility is highly questioned, especially in the absence of mechanisms to verify the authenticity of posted content, be it information or news.

These limitations and obstacles could be avoided in the future for the sake of empowering women in Egypt. We recommend that politically active women use other means of communication besides Facebook to mobilise voters. The Egyptian National Council for Women can also play a vital role in this regard by offering training and guidance to women activists on the optimal use of social media in supporting their efforts to run for elections. In addition to this, revisions of the legal framework that governs the use and information publishing process of social media should be conducted on regular basis.

APPENDIX

No	Statement	Mean	Std. deviation	CV	Agreement rate %	Rank
1. Assessing to what extent Facebook contributed to empowering women during elections						
1	Facebook made me interested in following the political programmes of the women candidates	2.984	1.251	41.9%	59.7%	7
2	I am a Facebook user because it is an effective tool for spreading ideas and exchanging opinions, especially with regard to women candidates	3.677	1.069	29.1%	73.5%	2
3	I relied completely on Facebook in determining my electoral vote when it came to choosing women candidates	2.605	1.185	45.5%	52.1%	8

(*continued*)

(continued)

No	Statement	Mean	Std. deviation	CV	Agreement rate %	Rank
4	I believe women are affected by the ideas that they receive via Facebook more than they are affected by the ideas of their surrounding family members	3.260	1.151	35.3%	65.2%	5
5	Facebook increases my ability to analyse political events and engage in free discussions	3.312	1.044	31.5%	66.2%	4
6	Facebook contributes to spreading rumours and stirring up disputes	3.964	1.130	28.5%	79.3%	1
7	Facebook is the best and fastest way to get information about candidates, especially women	3.362	1.146	34.1%	67.2%	3
8	I believe Facebook is very important in identifying women candidates' programmes and conducting comparisons	3.134	1.149	36.7%	62.7%	6
2. Assessing the role of Facebook versus traditional media in promoting political participation						
1	I have always participated in the elections since January 25, 2011	3.071	1.238	40.3%	61.4%	5
2	I do not consistently participate in elections	2.792	1.241	44.4%	55.8%	9
3	I have a personal Facebook account that helps me know about my local community news	3.830	1.002	26.2%	76.6%	1
4	With Facebook, I no longer have a need for radio and television, "traditional media"	3.241	1.300	40.1%	64.8%	3
5	Facebook as an electronic communication tool has become more important than traditional media (such as radio and television)	3.745	1.066	28.5%	74.9%	2
6	I consider myself very active on Facebook as I have a personal page and another public page through which I communicate with the local community and participate in community discussions, especially voting in elections.	2.841	1.232	43.4%	56.8%	8
7	I fully trust what is discussed on Facebook pages in relation to the elections	2.625	1.253	47.7%	52.5%	10
8	I did not depend on Facebook in determining my electoral vote	3.173	1.193	37.6%	63.5%	4
9	I currently acquire all my information about the local community from Facebook	2.929	1.220	41.7%	58.6%	6
10	I partially relied on Facebook in determining my electoral vote as I believe that nothing can replace direct communication with candidates via public rallies	2.915	1.158	39.7%	58.3%	7

(*continued*)

(continued)

No	Statement	Mean	Std. deviation	CV	Agreement rate %	Rank
3. Assessing the effect of COVID-19 on Facebook usage						
1	I do not have full confidence in what is being discussed on Facebook in relation to the elections, but there were no other alternatives due to conditions of the COVID-19 pandemic	3.236	1.116	34.5%	64.7%	2
2	With the conditions resulting from the COVID-19 pandemic, Facebook was the best way to identify candidates from our homes during the lockdown	3.225	1.096	34.0%	64.5%	3
3	Even before the COVID-19 pandemic, I have always relied on Facebook to make decisions related to politics, especially voting in elections, as the diversity of opinions helps me decide and thus choose my representative	2.553	1.095	42.9%	51.1%	5
4	Before COVID-19, I avoided relying on Facebook to make political decisions, especially voting in elections, as I assumed that the diversity of opinions negatively affects my ability to make an objective decision	3.274	1.189	36.3%	65.5%	1
5	I was not a user of Facebook, but I was compelled to turn to it during the election period to identify the candidates due to COVID-19 conditions	2.581	1.217	47.1%	51.6%	4

References

Adly, H., M. Ezzat, A. Fawzy, R. Bahy & M. Nazir (2017). The Political Participation of Woman/Al-Mosharak Al-Siyasiya Li Al-Mara'a. Friedrich Ebert Stiftung. Retrieved from http://library.fes.de/pdffiles/bueros/aegypten/15390.pdf

Al-Gabory, K. (2015). The Role of Social Media in the Egyptian 25th of January/Door Wasael Al-Tawasol Al-Igtmaei fi 25 Ynayer. *Political Science Journal*. Tekrit University. Retrieved from https://portal.arid.my/ar-LY/Publications/Details/1281

Al-Salehy, S. (2017). *The Role of Social Media in International Politics/Door Wasael Al-Tawasol Al-Igtmaei fi Al-Siyassa Al-Dawleya*. Published PhD Thesis. Arab Democratic Center. Retrieved from https://democraticac.de/?p=50855

Andersen, N., & Medaglia, R. (2009). The Use of Facebook in National Election Campaigns: Politics as Usual? In A. Macintosh & E. Tambouris (Eds.), *Electronic Participation* (pp. 101–111). Springer.

Buznytska, H. (2019). *Does Women's Political Empowerment Improve Gender Balance in Peacekeeping? A Large N Study of Troop Contributing Countries*. Master's thesis, Goteborgs Universitet, Department of Political Science.

Conroy, M., Feezell, J. T., & Guerrero, M. (2012). Facebook and Political Engagement: A Study of Online Political Group Membership and Offline Political Engagement. *Computers in Human Behavior, 28*(5), 1535. https://doi.org/10.1016/j. chb.2012.03.012

Elsebahy, N. (2013). *The Impact of Social Media Outlets on the Presidential Elections: A Case Study.* The Department of Journalism and Mass Communication in Partial Fulfillment of the Requirements for the Degree of Master of Arts.

Enli, G. S., & Skogerbø, E. (2013). Personalized Campaigns in Party-Centred Politics. *Information, Communication & Society, 16*(5), 757. https://doi.org/10.108 0/1369118X.2013.782330

Hawadsy, S. (2018). The Debate on the Role of Social Media/*Gadaleyat Door Mawake' Al-Tawasol Al-Igtmaei. Geel Journal for Political Studies and International Relations.* Retrieved from https://jilrc.com/archives/8602.

Hosny, R. (2020, December). First Coptic Female Deputy to Egypt's Senate Speaker: Sailing Uncharted Waters. *Mawteny.* Retrieved from https://en.wataninet.com/ politics/parliament/first-coptic-female-deputy-to-egypts-senate-speaker-sailing-uncharted-waters/34364/

Huis, M. A., Hansen, N., Otten, S., & Lensink, R. (2017). A Three-Dimensional Model of Women's Empowerment: Implications in the Field of Microfinance and Future Directions. *Frontiers in Psychology, 8.* https://doi.org/10.3389/ fpsyg.2017.01678

Kamel, S. H. (2014). The Value of Social Media in Egypt's Uprising and Beyond. *The Electronic Journal of Information Systems in Developing Countries, 60*(1), 1. https:// doi.org/10.1002/j.1681-4835.2014.tb00426.x

Khodair, A., & Abdall, R. (2016). Egypt's 2015 Parliamentary Elections: Assessing the New Electoral System. *International Affairs and Global Strategy, 44*(1), 2224–8951.

Lind, D. (2010). *Basic Statistics for Business and Economics* (7th ed.). McGraw Hill Higher Education.

Marichal, J. (2013). Political Facebook Groups: Micro-Activism and the Digital Front Stage. *First Monday, 18*(12). https://doi.org/10.5210/fm.v18i12.4653

Mcclurg, S. D. (2003). Social Networks and Political Participation: The Role of Social Interaction in Explaining Political Participation. *Political Research Quarterly, 56*(4), 449–464. https://doi.org/10.1177/106591290305600407

Milbrath, L. W. (1981). Political Participation. In *The Handbook of Political Behavior.* Springer. https://doi.org/10.1007/978-1-4684-3878-9_4

Napoleoncat Stats Website. (2020). Retrieved from https://napoleoncat.com/stats/ facebook-users-inegypt/2020/01#:~:text=There%20were%2042%20400%20 000,group%20(14%20000%20000)

National Election Authority-Official Site. (2021). Retrieved from https://www.elections.eg/images/pdfs/laws/PoliRightsAmendments2020-140.pdf

National Strategy for the Empowerment of Egyptian Women 2030 Vision and Pillars. (2017).

Pirannejad, A., & Janssen, M. (2019). Internet and Political Empowerment: Towards a Taxonomy for Online Political Empowerment. *Information Development, 35*(1), 80. https://doi.org/10.1177/0266666917730118

Rady, Z. (2003). The Use of Social Media in the Arab World/*Istkhdam Mawake' Al-Tawasol Al-Igtmaei fi Al-Alam Al-Arabi. Journal of Education, 26*(1).

Rahman, M. A. (2013). *Women's Empowerment: Concept and Beyond.* Springer.

Reuters, S. (2011, March 2017). *A Big Increase in Internet Users in Egypt After the January Revolution (Arabic Version)*. Retrieved from https://www.reuters.com/article/oegin-egypt-internet-mn6-idARACAE72G1PN20110317

Sekaran, U. (2003). *Research Methods for Business* (4th ed.). Wiley.

Shearlaw, M. (2016, January 26). Egypt Five Years On: Was It Ever a "Social Media Revolution"? *The Guardian*. Retrieved from https://www.theguardian.com/world/2016/jan/25/egypt-5-years-on-was-it-ever-a-social-media-revolution

State Information Service Website. (2020). Retrieved from https://www.sis.gov.eg/Story/212570

Statista Website. (2021). Retrieved from https://www.statista.com/statistics/1028451/facebook-user-share-in-egypt-by-age/

Uhlaner, C. J. (2015). Politics and Participation. In *International Encyclopedia of the Social & Behavioral Sciences*. Elsevier. https://doi.org/10.1016/B978-0-08-097086-8.93086-1

Velasquez, A., & LaRose, R. (2015). Youth Collective Activism Through Social Media: The Role of Collective Efficacy. *New Media & Society, 17*(6), 899. https://doi.org/10.1177/1461444813518391

Zahran, G. (2012). Regional Trends and Their Relationship to the Center/Al-Itgahat Al Manatikeyya Wa e'lakatha bi Al-Markaz. In *The Egyptian Revolution: Drivers, Trends, and Challenges*. Arab Center for Research and Policy Studies.

PART IV

Introduction to Gender-Based Violence

Gender-based violence (GBV) is a multidimensional phenomenon that is per-petrated by various actors including intimate partners, family, community members, as well as state actors and representatives. GBV occurs in various forms (physical, sexual, emotional, psychological, and economic) and takes place in different spaces including home, school, workplace, and numerous other public spaces. As in many parts of the world, entrenched patriarchal gen-der norms and repressive conservative ideologies have not only made GBV ubiquitous in MENA, but have also turned it into a taboo subject confined to a spiral of silence that condemns the survivors to an isolated experience of trauma.

The frequency and severity of the violence that individuals endure across the MENA region remains largely underreported given the legal, social, and per-sonal burden that the survivors face (Zahia, 2013). National surveys on GBV are rather scarce and, when available in a few countries, tend to be dated and/ or incomplete given the quasi-absence of systematic recording and reporting mechanisms (Skalli, 2020). Despite this, or probably because of it, human rights activists and women's movements across the region have made GBV one of their rallying causes regardless of the unpopularity of the topic among national governments and policy makers. Their activism, which spans several decades, has resulted in the formation of national, regional, and transnational alliances around GBV and put steady pressure on governments to commit to policy, legal, and social reforms necessary for ending violence against women. National activists have also mobilized numerous communication tools to raise public awareness through articles in popular press, radio programming, street marches, sit-ins, as well as letters and petitions to law makers. Years of agitation have produced a few successes including anchoring GBV within broader strug-gles for gender equality and greater commitments by governments in MENA to sign international conventions such as the CEDAW. Most recently, the region has seen modest legal gains that criminalize sexual harassment and rape.

However, academic research on gender-based violence has not followed the same developments on the ground. By and large, it has remained limited in disciplinary scope and thematic focus which has given the existing body of work the following distinctive characteristics. First, there is a tendency to reduce gender to only women and approach GBV with the assumption that only women are victims of violence even if gender-based violence includes all persons regardless of gender, sexual orientation, or gender identity. The result of this reduction is a serious gap in our knowledge about the various forms of violence endured by persons and social groups presumed to be among the perpetrators of violence rather than its victims. Second, research has predominantly focused on only two types of violence at the expense of practically all other forms: the violence of representation and sexual harassment in public spaces. The violence of representation includes the reproduction and circulation of stereotypical gender images and roles in cultural/media products, national educational materials, promotional campaigns, and newer digital spaces and platforms (ALSAQER, 2019). Given the resilience and pervasiveness of gender-based stereotypes, scholarship in this area has been insightful and continues to be instrumental in targeting public awareness.

With respect to sexual harassment in public spaces, the vexing phenomenon has garnered greater scholarly attention over the last few decades, and increasingly so since the 2011 democratic uprisings. One can argue that 2011 has seen a turning point in both research and mobilization around sexual harassment. This is the case partly because greater access to and advances in digital technologies have allowed citizens to witness, record, and diffuse numerous forms of violence perpetrated against women, including state-sponsored violence against women activists. This is seen in the last days of the Mubarak regime during which gang rape and sexual assault turned Egyptian streets into the infamous "circles of hell" under the indifferent watch of security forces (Nezra, 2014).

Finally, research on GBV in MENA has been mostly produced by health/clinical studies (Mojahed et al., 2020; Lilleston et al., 2018) and sociology and women's studies (Kizilhan et al., 2020, while communication and media scholars have only recently started broadening research beyond the violence of representation. Using a variety of quantitative and qualitative methodologies, researchers are increasingly examining the broader role, uses, and potential of newer technologies in reinforcing or fighting GBV. Recent publications have, for instance, explored the uses of new technologies for healing and recovering from GBV trauma in conflict-affected areas including Iraq and Syria (Alsaquer, 2019; Hosseini, 2019). Others are examining ways survivors of violence mobilize social media to interrupt their social isolation, resist victimhood, and create safe spaces for dialogue (Eltantawy, 2018). Others still are trying to assess the effectiveness of social media and digital tools in creating an intergenerational solidarity among activists to push for legal reforms in their countries (Skalli, 2014).

Despite these laudable efforts, serious gaps remain in our research about communication and GBV in MENA. The chapters in this part seek to address some of these gaps by broadening the areas of inquiry to include struggles with

GBV in intimate settings as well as the workplace. The contributors in this part contextualize the discussion beyond the few countries that are typically over-represented in research (Egypt, Lebanon, and Jordan).

Leila Tayeb's chapter takes us to post-Gaddafi Libya to discuss "digital intimacy" in the context of war, political transition, and national reconstruction. Tayeb's research spans the ten-year period following the 2011 uprisings to examine the impact of conflict on social interactions and human relationships in their mediated forms. By examining practices of in-app chatting, texting, phone calls, and social media video creation, Tayeb delivers powerful insights into novel forms of "interpersonal violence and patriarchal policing" conveyed in and through new sites. She contends that militarized societies, such as Libya, lead to greater presence and investment online, which, in turn, create greater vulnerability to online violence and attacks. Online spaces, she demonstrates, create more "complex intertwining between the range of forms of violence" that target and traumatize women.

Tamara Kharroub's chapter situates the discussion on digital technologies and GBV in the context of Palestine. Kharroub focuses on the tragic case of 21-year-old Israa Ghrayeb, the late social media personality, whose tragic killing by her family demonstrates the complex role social media plays in simultaneously empowering and endangering the lives of young women in deeply conservative communities. What ended Israa Ghrayeb's short life, according to Kharroub, was more than the brutal physical violence perpetrated by her family, as captured by cellphone camera and shared online. It was also the violence of indifference from the police and hospital staff who failed to protect the young woman when she called for help. It was the violence of indifference from the government that failed to acknowledge and investigate this case of GBV and criminalize its perpetrators. The outrage at all these forms of violence created intense debates online and mobilized online/offline activists to demand justice and legal reform.

It is the same violence of indifference that Sarah Benamara's chapter on Algeria seeks to capture in discussing the relationship between national media and the legal system on domestic violence and femicide. Benamara focuses on Algeria's 2015 domestic violence law to examine the disparities between media narratives surrounding this law and the actual experiences of Algerian domestic violence survivors. She contends that traditional media and television in particular are still playing a great role in traditional societies despite the increasing penetration of digital technologies. Her analysis cautions against the nefarious powers of mediated misinformation, disinformation, and distortions even in societies that criminalize GBV.

The last two chapters in this part discuss sexual harassment in different contexts to highlight interesting trends in both Egypt and Kuwait. Nahed Eltantawy's "Egyptian Women's Cyberactivism: The Ongoing Battle Against Sexual Harassment and Violence" turns our attention to Egyptian women's mobilization of digital tools to break away from the taboo that has long silenced women survivors of GBV. Eltantawy analyzes two recent GBV cases in Egypt to demonstrate how female-led activism has empowered survivors to come forward with their personal stories to build legal cases against the perpetrators.

In the case of Kuwait, Fatima Alsalem discusses sexual harassment in the workplace to draw attention to the implication of GBV on women's personal and professional lives. Drawing on a survey of 24 Kuwaiti female journalists and in-depth interviews with 8 female journalists, Alsalem provides interesting insights on how sexual harassment feeds into larger societal and institutional barriers that curtail Kuwaiti women's professional development in the media industry. Findings from the survey and interviews not only confirm that GBV is multidimensional but that women are likely to experience the compounded effects of its multiple dimensions.

Ultimately, the chapters in this part provide insights on the levels and forms of GBV in the personal and professional lives of women. The consensus from these chapters is that digital tools and spaces can and do play a complex role in how GBV is experienced, discussed, and responded to in the MENA region.

References

Alsaqer, L. (2019). Towards a "Transformative" Image of Arab Women in Anti-Violence Adverts: Semiotics Analysis of Arab Social Media Adverts. *Media Watch, 10*(3), 586–596. Eltantawy, N. (2018). I am Untouchable! Egyptian Women's War Against Sexual Harassment. In S. Khamis & A. Mili (Eds). *Arab Women's Activism and Socio-Political Transformation: Unfinished Gendered Revolutions* (pp. 131–148). Palgrave Macmillan.

Hosseini, B. (2019). Women's Survival Through Social Media: A Narrative Analysis. *Asian Journal of Women's Studies, 25*(2), 180–197.

Kizilhan, J., Steger, F., & Noll-Hussong, M. (2020). Shame, Dissociative Seizures and Their Correlation Among Traumatised Female Yazidi with Experience of Sexual Violence. *The British Journal of Psychiatry, 216*(3), 138–143.

Lilleston, P., Winograd, L., Ahmed, S., Salamé, D., Al Alam, D., Stoebenau, K., et al. (2018). Evaluation of a Mobile Approach to Gender-Based Violence Service Delivery Among Syrian Refugees in Lebanon. *Health Policy and Planning, 33*(7), 767–776.

Nazra. (2014). "Qanun Nashaz" – A Campaign on the Legal Issues Associated with Violence Against Women in Both Public and Private Sphere. http://nazra.org/en/node/388

Salhi, Z. S. (2013). Gender and Violence in the Middle East and North Africa: Negotiating with Patriarchal States and Islamism. In Z. S. Salhi (Author), *Gender and Violence in Islamic Societies: Patriarchy, Islamism and Politics in the Middle East and North Africa* (pp. 12–42). I.B. Tauris.

Skalli, H. L. (2014). Young Women and Social Media Against Sexual Harassment in North Africa. *Journal of North African Studies, 19*(2), 244–258.

Skalli, L. H. (2021) Violence Against Women in North Africa. In: Yacob-Haliso O., Falola T. (Eds.), *The Palgrave Handbook of African Women's Studies*. Palgrave Macmillan.

CHAPTER 17

Digital Intimacy and Violence in Contemporary Libya

Leila Tayeb

Toward the height of Libyan militia leader Khalifa Haftar's 2019–2020 attempt to seize control of Tripoli militarily, I sat in an apartment in that city as part of a small group of women in our twenties and thirties. The second eldest among us[1] wanted to get married and had recently downloaded Tinder for the third or fourth time. Swiping through profiles, she narrated aloud details that might make us laugh or commiserate in bemoaning the state of available men. One profile stuck out differently: a tall, blond, muscular man in green military fatigues against what did not appear to be a local backdrop. Together we mused over this profile's potential significance. Were we encountering intimate evidence of the recently reported influx of Russian snipers? Had this "Russian" forgotten to turn off his geolocating apps?

During the past decade in Libya, the quotidian dangers of war have ebbed and flowed, and many have spent long hours at home. Family members, friends, intimate partners, work colleagues, classmates, and acquaintances have all used phone calls, texting, and an ever-shifting gamut of apps to keep in contact, whether with those outside of Libya, in another city or neighborhood, or even between households in the same building. Pre- and non-marital intimate

---

[1] Interlocutors' names, where used, and some other identifying information have been changed to protect anonymity.

L. Tayeb (✉)
Northwestern University in Qatar, Education City, Doha, Qatar
e-mail: leila-tayeb@northwestern.edu

L. H. Skalli, N. Eltantawy (eds.), *The Palgrave Handbook of Gender, Media and Communication in the Middle East and North Africa,*
https://doi.org/10.1007/978-3-031-11980-4_17

relationships,[2] in particular, have come to be increasingly heavily reliant on digital communication as mixed-gender spaces for socializing have repeatedly been the targets of militia violence in the years since 2011.[3] Women's mobility especially has seen dramatic curtailing in the two metropolises of Tripoli and Benghazi, where urban conflict has at different times been overwhelming in both places. Militia groups have consistently targeted women activists across the country in the years since 2011, producing a chilling string of kidnappings and assassinations.[4] Further, women simply moving about independently, en route to work and other daily destinations, have also been targets of carjacking, kidnapping, and murder. These two trends have lent credence to patriarchal logics that argue for the confinement of women to the home in the name of their protection. Women grappling with these forces in their families find themselves needing exceptional reasons to justify leaving the house.

It is within this broader context that a scene like the one I describe above unfolds. The "Russian sniper" appearing on Tinder illustrates the extent to which the conditions and logics of war extend themselves into the—ostensibly

[2] My research for this chapter has primarily reflected the conditions and constraints of heterosexual intimacies in this period in Libya. The wide range of practices that exceed these normativities are certainly extant and subject to a different set of constraints and violences, upon which ethnographic research is sorely needed.

[3] Cafés, in particular, that are open to mixed-gender youth have faced militia attacks in both Tripoli and Benghazi in the years since 2011. Most often the militias taking action describe the closures or disruptions of business as being a result of something other than the gender-mixing taking place. For example, Tripoli's Kitty Cat Café, which operated for a brief period circa 2017, was ostensibly in violation of public health codes, while the nearby Coffee & Book slowly declined after its bookshelves were removed.

[4] An incomplete list of only the most well-publicized incidents, in chronological order: TV journalist Naseeb Kernafa was tortured and killed, along with her driver, in the southern city of Sebha on 29 May 2014. Salwa Boughaigis, human rights lawyer and activist, was assassinated in her Benghazi home on 25 June 2014, hours after using her Facebook page to publish photos of herself voting. Three weeks later, former MP Fariha al-Barkawi was shot and killed beside a gas station in Derna. In February of the following year, human rights activist Intissar al-Hassairi was murdered along with her aunt in Tripoli, their bodies discarded in the trunk of their car. More recently, MP Seham Sergiwa was abducted by gunman in July 2019, and remains missing at the time of this writing. Political activist Hanan al-Barassi was assassinated in Benghazi in November 2020. See: https://raseef22.net/article/1075282-militias-end-womens-aspirations-of-participating-in-libyas-democratic-process; https://www.theguardian.com/world/2014/jun/26/salwa-bugaighis-libyan-shot-dead-benghazi; https://news.blogs.nytimes.com/2014/06/26/slain-libyan-rights-activist-documented-her-last-hours-online/; https://www.reuters.com/article/us-libya-security-idUSKBN0FM1N620140717;https://www.ibtimes.co.uk/libya-female-activist-intissar-al-hasaari-shot-dead-tripoli-1489296; https://www.theguardian.com/world/2019/jul/31/abducted-libyan-mp-seham-sergiwa-torture-fears; https://www.theguardian.com/world/2020/nov/10/gunmen-shoot-dead-female-libyan-dissident-in-busy-benghazi-street; https://unsmil.unmissions.org/women-peace-and-security-libyan-context; https://www.libyanjustice.org/news/joint-statement-libya-must-end-systematic-impunity-and-investigate-the-killing-of-lawyer-and-political-activist-hanan-al-barassi

protected—domestic sphere both symbolically and materially. This example is one among many. Whether the particularities involve geolocated mercenaries, the gendered policing of siblings, the politics of respectability and reputation, or new partisan limits on family approval for marriage, gendered hierarchies of power and privilege are intimately entangled with and affected by shifts in the post-2011 Libyan civil war. Primary among these hierarchies are those that stem from and shape practices of partnering. This chapter explores how the modes, conditions, and politics of forming and maintaining intimate relationships in and outside of Libya have changed concurrently with the past decade's war and its attendant processes of increased militarization and widespread traumatization. While young people have widely invested in the cruelly optimistic attachment (Berlant, 2011) of looking in particular to the social norm of marriage as a way of imagining security, the continuation of life, and a future beyond the ongoing conflict, whether in or outside of Libya, they have also negotiated the encroachment of the war into the intimate spheres of their lives, including the avenues by which they seek a potential partner, the grounds on which they obtain broader familial agreement, and the gendered traumas that shape their relationships. These processes have sustained each other and structure a particular set of impasses that underscore the crisis of Libyan patriarchy, while at the same time enabling its continued reproduction.

Militarization and Digital Intimacy

In examining the relationship of digital intimacy and violence in the Libyan context, I draw together recent research in the emerging field of digital intimacy studies with feminist theory on militarization and war in order to root my ethnographic observations. These observations in turn stem from research over the course of ten years, primarily in Tripoli and Benghazi, in which I have used ethnographic methods to attend to the imbrication of performance and performativity in daily life. The qualitative data presented in this chapter combines informal interviews undertaken during 2020 and 2021 with relevant stories and experiences from earlier fieldwork. I use the phrase "digital intimacies," following Elisabetta Costa and Laura Menin, to describe "the spheres of personal relationships, affects and sexuality mediated by new digital communication channels," and to focus especially on "love and romance, as well as on premarital and sexual relationships" (2016: 138–139). It is within these spheres, as Costa and Menin argue, "that the transformations brought about by the Internet and mobile phones become particularly intense" (139). Their work, and the ethnographic research that makes up a 2016 special issue of the *Middle East Journal of Culture and Communication* that they coedited, illustrate the analytical importance of the spatial for understanding how digital intimacies are enabled, shaped, and constrained. As they write, digital media are not simply tools for communication, but "a configuration of *places* where young people spend a significant amount of their time" (141). When, as in Libya in recent years, other kinds of places are less or inaccessible as a result of war, digital places come to factor even more heavily for individual and communal meaning making and for undertaking practices of affiliation and self-fashioning. They also come to be more impactful sites for interpersonal violence and patriarchal policing.

The modes of privacy and publicity that characterize digital sites and practices allow for experimentation and novelty in self-fashioning and relationship construction, while also often producing cleavages between various performed selves. As Costa and Menin write, "By multiplying private and secret channels of communication, [...] digital technologies have facilitated the formation of relationships that have no legitimacy in the offline world, or are restricted by predominant gendered norms, social constraints and religious beliefs. In these emerging private online spaces, people can stretch the boundaries of their social worlds and creatively re-imagine emotional and sexual possibilities" (140). This reimagining might entail engaging in pre- or extra-marital relationships that are otherwise proscribed or simply unsettling prior normative conventions around how the lead-up to marriage should play out. At the same time, however, "the new opportunities for public visibility, display, fame and popularity opened by social media platforms such as Facebook, Instagram, or Twitter have brought about new risks of moral threat and public reproach. [...] In digitally mediated 'public' spaces, people present and tactically perform moral gendered selves that often stand in contrast with their practices in 'secret' online spaces" (140–141). It is precisely at the intersection of these modes of privacy and publicity that risk and the likelihood of harm are brought into sharp relief. I think of one interlocutor who, after a conflict with a man she was "talking to" via private social media channels, viewed her love interest's public social media story in which he ranted about a nameless woman he implied knowing intimately, using violent slurs to target her sexual propriety. My interlocutor was left to worry about the potential harm done to her reputation via this public rant, while at the same wondering if she was indeed the person the video was ostensibly describing or if, rather, this person she had believed herself to be in exclusive conversation with was instead pursuing (and demeaning) multiple women simultaneously. In the awareness of this field of risk, the pressure increases to perform exceedingly moral gendered selves in public-facing social media (Jyrkiäinen, 2016).

Thinking along a spectrum from the targeted killings I described earlier to these comparatively mild reputational attacks, I use the category of violence in this writing to refer to a range of injurious structures, events, and processes, some of which are a direct outcome of the post-2011 war, while others are rooted in the longer durée. I am especially concerned with the process of militarization, which I understand to mean "the degree to which a society's institutions, policies, behaviors, thought, and values are devoted to military power and shaped by war" (Kohn cited in González & Gusterson, 2019: 6), and how militarization affects intimate forms of violence, such as spousal abuse and other domestic violence. While militarization in Libya is by no means new to the post-2011 political context, the degree to which local and national military conflict came to define the parameters of civilian life during and subsequent to the revolution made this period distinct. What had been the circumscribed sphere of national military institutions shifted to a much more diffuse constellation of armed revolutionaries and, subsequently, local militias, after civilians took up weapons in the fight to overthrow Muammar Gaddafi.[5] Where few family homes contained guns in the years prior to 2011, many did after, as a result of the popular participation in the uprising and war. While campaigns were held to gather up these arms in the first few years after the revolution, political instability made some people reluctant to hand over their weapons. As such, arms proliferation became one important aspect of a broader process of the militarization of civilian daily life. An ease of access to weapons in turn increases the lethality of domestic violence, already a subject for which official statistics do not exist and access to refuge for victims is scarce (Khalifa, 2020).

The increasing militarization of society and the increased concentration of public life in online spaces together create greater and more complex intertwining between the range of forms of violence at issue here. Social media usage is high in Libya in comparison to global trends (Kemp, 2021). In a country with official population estimates of approximately 7 million, Libya had over 6.5 million Facebook users, more than 5.5 million Facebook Messenger users, and nearly 2 million Instagram users in 2021, according to NapoleonCat. In this context of widespread use, women especially have been subjected to targeted attacks in social media settings. These online attacks are often traumatizing for the women they target, both because of the damage they can inflict on an individual's reputation for personal and professional contexts and because of the threats of offline violence that they often include. As one Libyan political scientist attests, "the pattern in Libya is that online violence goes beyond verbal and written violence to incitement and threats to life, and its impact extends beyond the person to all their family members. In addition, the verbal culture of society makes an oral accusation proof from the first word, it makes what is said in online violence an accusation that affects the reputation of the person without evidence" (Elfarsi quoted in Jurasz et al., 2021: 14–15). Thus, the harm inflicted through online attacks functions in nonlinear relation to offline effects, wherein targeted individuals—and their families—have been assassinated, forced to flee the country, withdrawn their public participation, and suffered long-term damage to their mental health. Some recent research documents this spectrum of online-offline violence against women who are active in the public sphere (Jurasz et al., 2021), and indeed much greater attention is warranted to understand how the nexus of online and offline gendered violence has adversely affected Libyan women's ability to participate in democratic institutions and public life. In addition, as this chapter shows, even when women engage in other, less publicly visible, kinds of quotidian

---

[5] For more on the shift from revolutionary to militia formations, see Tayeb (2020) and Wehrey (2018: 85–103).

communication, including entering platonic and romantic relationships online, they continue to grapple with many of the same vulnerabilities.

It should be no surprise, then, that as an ethnographer I encounter evidence of widespread trauma among my interlocutors, while I myself have also had traumatic experiences in the course of doing fieldwork.[6] I maintain my use of the notion of trauma because I am interested in the temporality it produces, even while I take heed of the wariness with which some scholars of crisis regard the term. Lauren Berlant writes that "[c]risis is not exceptional to history or consciousness but a process embedded in the ordinary that unfolds in stories about navigating what's overwhelming" (2011: 10). For Berlant, a notion like "crisis ordinariness" is thus more accurate than trauma, which carries a "fundamentally ahistoricizing logic" and "conventionally focuses on exceptional shock and data loss in the memory and experience of catastrophe" (2011: 10). In contrast to the conventional trauma theory to which Berlant is responding, I draw here on theories of complex trauma that attend to the ways that traumatic experiences accumulate and produce altered modalities for engaging with the present (Schwartz, 2021). I contend that in contemporary Libya the crisis ordinariness which undoubtedly structures daily life shapes and is shaped by the individuated and collective traumatic disorders that in turn spare almost no one. Traumatic experience is indeed itself quite ordinary: the category, as I use it, encompasses the wide range of moments and ways that bodies and their nervous systems are sent into high alert, only to be suspended there when neither fight nor flight nor freeze alleviate the stimulus that produced a stress response. Traumatic disorders are the ways that bodies adapt to the accumulation of a series of these experiences over time, through heightened or dulled sensitivity, and come to confuse present conditions with past ones in ways that fundamentally alter individuated capacities for relating and intimacy.

The sections that follow weave a narrative discussion of digital intimacies in the context of ongoing conflict with ethnographic vignette. They trace the encroachment of war into the intimate spheres of young Libyans' lives, including the avenues by which they seek a potential partner, the grounds on which they obtain broader familial agreement, and the gendered traumas that shape their relationships. The conclusion explores how this period has seen both a shoring up of conventional normativities and prospects for the production of new moralities.

---

[6] On ethnography and trauma, see the Trauma and Resilience blog series edited by Beatriz Reyes-Foster and Rebecca Lester at anthro{dendum}: https://anthrodendum.org/author/ trauma-and-resilience/. For a discussion of efforts in the cultural sphere to combat the social effects of trauma in the Libyan context, see Gana (2020).

FINDING A PARTNER

Young people in Libya, as elsewhere, increasingly seek out potential intimate partners via digital platforms. A convergence of factors, some in line with global trends and others more particular to the contingencies of post-2011 Libya, have animated this broad shift toward communication via app and this shift has in turn imposed new prospects and constraints. Avenues for seeking potential partners, across a spectrum of more and less conservative social norms, are also a site in which young people grapple with the effects of ongoing war in the most intimate spheres of their lives. Even what might be thought of as the most conventional of methods for meeting potential marital partners, that of family referral, has both come to incorporate digital communication and to illustrate the contours of war in the intimate. In this format, a parent, elder sibling, or other relative introduces a potential match, along with that person's broader family reputation, itself shaped by and performed via social media. The prospective couple might meet in person with family chaperones and, subsequently, may have opportunities to meet repeatedly in person, under the conditions of particular hours of the day and particular venues. However, the pair may just as likely be limited to—or even prefer—communication via phone, text, and app. This may be because one party is residing outside of Libya, quite often as a result of the war. It may be because of a perceived lack (by one or both members of the couple or by other family members) of respectable gender-mixed locations to meet in person. It may be because a more traditional initial or subsequent meeting at home is less feasible if extended family members are abroad, again due to the war. It may often also be because restricting communication to the digital realm enables one or both parties "to control and shape what they present to others" and keep hidden aspects of their behavior that would be deemed morally unacceptable, thus playing a "cynical embellishment game" to grapple with family or societal pressures (Jyrkiäinen, 2016: 186, 195). The cynicism of this game is often paramount and sometimes (dis)places patriarchal power onto the women agents of heteronormative marital structures. One interlocutor, who was pursuing this traditional form of partnering while leaning into the compartmentalization afforded by restricting this relationship to the digital in its courtship stage, described to me his expectations of his mother and sisters' relationship to his future spouse in stark terms: "They will choose her and then they will hate her." Here the distance produced by both war-impelled displacement and digital media enables both the projection of moral responsibility in gendered terms away from the couple form and the maintenance of a public-facing self-image that is unaffected by private behavior. The digital in instances like this one offers greater privacy for the couple both with each other and from each other.

When dealing with fewer family constraints, a potential couple might initially meet at a shared workplace. As a result of the relative scarcity of gender-mixed café options, workplaces made up of mostly young people tend in Libya to function as important social spaces. This is of course not exceptional, and at the same time Libyan youth in the post-2011 environment confront particularly diffuse policing of these kinds of work-social spaces, wherein actors beyond company management—parents, neighbors, or militia members—may intervene in what they see as problematic conduct. Let me offer an example: during late 2014, I spent a few weeks regularly attending work hours at a local radio station in Tripoli. This radio station occupied a converted villa and was made up of rooms dedicated for office space, a recording studio, a small kitchen, and a reception area with couches where a living room might otherwise have been. Station employees came in and out throughout the day as they tended to projects or went live on the air, while guests also appeared at various times. Working and socializing in the station often extended into the evening hours. One such evening caused a conflict. Friends of friends of young station employees came to use the small open reception area as a dance floor to practice a routine for their upcoming wedding. A small group of station regulars gathered around to watch the practice, but it was interrupted after only a few minutes when the one older member of the station, who was around the age of the young employees' parents, deemed the activity inappropriate. While there were no formal workplace policies that this dance rehearsal violated, the elder present was either himself offended by the mixed gender spectacle or feared consequences resulting from someone else—neighbor, parent, militia—being offended. The way the policing unfolded made the latter distinction immaterial. In such a context, where even mixed gender company between fiancés is often suspect (though in this instance it was unclear how much the mixed gender aspect weighed against the dancing aspect), young people exploring a partnered relationship generally prefer to move their primary contact online. In the digital realm, they are afforded much greater privacy.

A third way that Libyan youth seek out potential partners is that which has become primary in much of the world: with the initial meeting online. It is worth taking a minute to lay out the different forms that such first contacts take, as they comprise both global and more local or regional practices. Dating apps, proximity-based and others, are one such form. Tinder is the one my interlocutors have most often recounted using. While this app is in some parts of the world primarily known for enabling "hook-ups," in Libya it does not necessarily suggest an avenue for forming no-strings-attached sexual relationships. At the same time, however, as the broader context of dating practices suggests, reputation is both paramount and precarious for unmarried women, and, even more than on other online platforms, female Tinder users most often guard their identities through pseudonyms and photos not of themselves. Such a user might, for example, use a profile under a name like Desert Rose and post profile pictures that show landscapes scenes, flowers, cakes, or religious quotes, images of famous or unknown people (these may sometimes be intimate, of a couple kissing, for example), and/or of famous or stock photo "doppelgangers." Men much more often post their real first names and photos of themselves, though they may also have privacy concerns (sometimes for other reasons, however, e.g. if married). This imbalance in personal information disclosed leads to a different set of swiping practices than in places where names and photos are more often expected to reflect reality. Men using the platform describe swiping right (indicating openness to a match and the possibility of conversing) on all profiles marked as women, regardless of name, photos, or textual description. Indeed, one interlocutor spoke of the app temporarily disabling his access to more profiles as a result of swiping right too quickly and seemingly indiscriminately. In this way, Tinder ends up functioning somewhat more similarly to apps such as Bumble, which were designed to empower women to have greater selection and make the first contact in heterosexual online dating.

Other widely used social media platforms are also avenues for dating among young (and not-so-young) Libyans. An interested party will often send a friend or follow request to initiate contact on Facebook or Instagram. Women sometimes navigate the volume of these requests by posting a statement in their profile bio, which is visible to non-friends in some instances, declaring that they do not accept friend requests from men they don't know. Such a practice operates at once as a way of ostensibly decreasing the frequency and number of such requests, and as a field for patriarchal respectability politics, wherein women signal chastity to their immediate and broader social networks. When a request is accepted, direct messages move from the request folder to the main folder and both parties can see read messages; from there the pair may begin a conversation and potentially move to phone calls and beyond. One pair, Iman and Zuheir, met initially in person in a work context and subsequently became friends on social media. It was the latter setting that enabled a deepening of their relationship; eventually, in the context of the "boredom" of the pandemic, they began to chat daily. Communicating via message and phone call, they built trust and closeness. Over time they began to meet in person, going out for lunch or on walks in the city. Even then, online communication remained primary: as the place they spent the most time together, the place they worked out disagreements, expressed growing affections, and navigated their disparate pasts and potential shared futures.

As Facebook, Instagram, and even Tinder if connected to these platforms give users information about online friends in common, a further removed avenue for making new contacts online is that of apps like Telegram, which were designed for internet-based calling and have been modified by users to facilitate introductions. Telegram offers a "find nearby" function, which, if activated, makes a user's name and profile picture visible to others within a specified proximity. This capability allows users to form local private chat groups[7] or to talk to new people one-on-one without exchanging phone numbers. One interlocutor showed me the unanswered "hello" messages from men not in her contacts list that crowded her inbox. In densely populated areas,

---

[7] This is one way that Telegram, along with similar apps such as Signal, has been used by extremist groups, activist movements, and other collectives who aim to avoid monitoring. See, for example, Feldstein and Gordon (2021).

users might find success with this function from home or work, though this carries the risk of being physically located. For greater volumes of new contacts, some people opt to use the "find nearby" feature in a café or restaurant, especially if it is mixed gender. This strategy seems to be practiced throughout the broader Arab region, and especially in places with greater degrees of gender segregation in daily life. Ethnographers have noted the use of Bluetooth for similar discreet introductions in UAE cafes (Laure Assaf 2021, personal communication), and in family restaurants in Yemen (Nevola, 2016: 158).

These forms of proximity-based introductions, in online settings not specifically geared toward dating, are perhaps only a slight modification of an in-person practice that predates and continues alongside them: the phone number throw. In this practice, men "give" their phone number to women in brief interactions in public settings. As a woman gets in or out of a parked car, or walks along a street, for example, a man may throw a crumpled paper to (at) her on which his phone number is written. Or he may yell the number to (at) her, beginning his utterance with the name of the mobile carrier of the numerical prefix associated with it. I have also seen an iteration of this in which he writes a phone number in the dust on her parked car's window. This practice is widespread enough in Libya that no further explanation or contextualization is needed in the interaction, as he assumes that she knows what the content of this string of numbers is and why he is directing this information at her. The word "interaction" here is used loosely, as the woman involved may not be consenting to participation, one way in which such practices normalize broader forms of gendered violence and harassment. These practices are also closely linked with one final mode of introduction, in which a man dials random local phone numbers in order to strike up a conversation with any voices that he perceives to be "female" and perhaps "young." In this practice, which likewise blurs the line between consensual introduction and frightening harassment, the man on the line often begins talking without identifying himself, implying that he and the person who has answered the call already know each other. This can be both confusing to the receiver and a cause of "problems" within her home, as a male relative overhearing the call may take this tone of familiarity as evidence of her scandalous conduct.

OBTAINING FAMILIAL AGREEMENT

Salma has lived in Tripoli since a few years after the start of the uprising. She, her parents, a few of her adult siblings and their families, and some of her aunts and uncles all moved from Benghazi to Tripoli when conditions in Benghazi became untenable. As the war there made its way into their suburban neighborhood and as extended family members involved in the conflict became widely known, the family grew increasingly afraid of the prospect of becoming collateral damage and fled to the relative safety of Libya's western capital. There they would not entirely avoid the possibility of being targeted for their family name, but they could more easily blend into the relatively cosmopolitan urban environment and live quiet civilian lives.

Among the many ways the move from Libya's biggest eastern to biggest western city has transformed Salma's life, both in the present and in how she is able to imagine and plan toward the future, is in the realm of dating and marriage. Describing her family as "conservative," Salma, one of four sisters and now in her early thirties, has long known that she would be expected to marry in a way that followed familial norms and expectations. In her case, this would likely mean meeting her future partner through prescribed familial channels, and even more importantly, that the man would need to come from a "good family." For Salma's parents, a good family entails not only people they consider broadly to be peers in terms of social class, status, and whiteness (Tayeb, 2021) but, more specifically, those families with whom they share historical and regional affiliations. For Salma, this will most likely mean that the family should be from urban Benghazi, or even more preferably, from urban Benghazi with nineteenth-century origins in the western city of Misrata.

If these dynamics are not enough to manage, work within, or struggle to expand in normal times, they have become even more burdensome as a result of the ongoing conflict. This is in part a result of the increased difficulties that come with trying to begin, build, maintain, and progress a relationship toward marriage that displacement engenders. It is also a result of the partisanship produced in and through the war. Several years after the family move, Salma finds herself expected to produce a suitable husband whose family background both aligns with the criteria described above and is aligned politically with her family's position. To simplify, this means his family should be *from* the east, but (publicly) opposed to the dominant political actors of these years *in* the east.

Salma's story illustrates a fraught but not uncommon way that the post-2011 conflict has encroached on the domestic lives of young Libyans and shaped new modes of patriarchal structure and constraint. The particularities of a story like this are characteristic of the ongoing negotiations that have come to make up civilian daily life in the circumstances of the war, negotiations which are at once pragmatic, contingent, and producing potentially lasting effects to social order. One essential question that structures both the feasibility of a possible relationship and the likelihood of obtaining broader familial agreement for marriage is: where does the potential spouse live? This question is certainly not exclusively produced by conditions of conflict, but the fact of and the shape of the war give it new facets. Where a potential spouse lives might be important because of distance from extended family, or because of frontlines of the war and the relative safety of a particular place, as well as the traversability of particular roads, or because of opportunities for a life outside of Libya and (at least physically) away from the war. All of these factors, alongside the changed partisan dynamics at play in Salma's situation, make for a changed and changing calculus as to which families might be "good families" and which youth are more and less marriageable.

Navigating Gendered Traumas

In the summer of 2016, I was on the freeway in Tripoli driving home one evening when I encountered unexpected and sudden traffic. After a few minutes of confusion, it became apparent that the entire freeway had been blocked and cars were funneling onto a single-lane exit. This was a summer during which civil unrest took the form of protest over frequently absent electrical power. The weather was hot, cash shortages left most people waiting in long lines outside their banks in often futile attempts to withdraw the small dinar amounts they were allotted, and inflation, as well as the prices of basic goods, were skyrocketing. Forced to a dramatic reduction in speed on the highway, I remember seeing people on the road, and fire, and then more fire, but rerouting to the residential roads that run closer to the coast didn't seem to be any large difficulty and I continued driving calmly. I followed the cars in front of me to take the next major thoroughfare, but we found it also blocked, this time with smaller bits of fire, burning tires, and rocks. My calm was shaken after I turned at the next intersection from which it was possible to continue westward and, after a few minutes of sitting in stopped traffic, cars began spinning to drive the other way. It now seemed that I did not know a reliable route home. Each time I got caught in a place with lots of traffic and blocked exits, I would see men in the cars beside me noticing that I was there driving alone.

Beginning to fear, I spun my car around quickly and flew as best as I could down an underpass to avoid what seemed to be another group of cars getting ready to create a blockade. Apparently out of options, I drove down toward a beach road I knew to be unreliable, but then second guessed my own idea to head this way. When I realized I had lost phone service in the area, I turned back, at once trying to think what to do and trying to call male cousins and a trusted male friend. I thought I should perhaps go back toward downtown to seek shelter with this friend, but I was already pretty far from there and I was unsure which roads would be open. Plus, his phone was either out of service or busy—when the power went out that summer (and other times of year), the already shaky phone reception got especially bad.

I finally got ahold of one of my cousins as I got back onto a main road going toward downtown; he said he was also headed home and would come find me. I pulled to the side of the road in a place where things seemed calm and did my best to describe where I was. I had stopped across the street from a kebab place that was still open and I thought maybe I would go ask them to let me wait in there, but that would also be a strange thing to do. It didn't seem to have any women inside and the door was wide enough to render the whole restaurant visible from the busy street. Before I could decide, a group of cars skidded up the road ahead of me coming from the direction where I had just been and blocked the road in front of me. Two men in a car looked at me and then tried to block me from moving as I narrowly avoided them and wheeled quickly around the corner onto a side street. Finding myself at a dead end after a few fast turns, I went back and found the same blue car. At this point fully panicking, I drove as quickly as I could toward the third and last road option and pulled up to a tiny corner vegetable shop with a light on, having decided by now that I had better choose a stranger to trust and get off the street. The blue car skidded up alongside my window as I tried to get out of the car. I was sure they were going to throw me in their trunk. I realized I had better calm down and I rolled down my window, most definitely failing to appear unfazed as I asked what they needed. The man in the passenger seat threw a ball of rolled up paper at me: his phone number.

I can't remember when they drove away or if they simply moved far enough so that I could open my door or how I got out, but I remember slipping trying to grab both handles of my open purse and lock the car door. I rushed into the vegetable shop and asked if the man working could please describe the location to my cousin. He didn't look me in my face, perhaps scandalized that I was there alone at night or merely wary that I was bringing him trouble. His assistant seemed less annoyed. Both thankfully tolerated my presence anyway and the owner spoke to my cousin a few times as he tried to find the place, but eventually insisted I go wait in the car because he wanted to close his shop and still had far to go home. I explained why I had come there and why I was scared. They said nothing.

I recount this tense experience because of the ways it is evocative of the interweaving of gendered social norms and traumatic experience, and because I read in this scene both a kind of crisis ordinariness and the exceptionality more conventionally associated with trauma. This night was both particularly frightening and impactful (for me) and profoundly ordinary in the social scripts through which it played out. While I would assert myself as a victim of gendered harassment in this story, both in its playing out and in its aftermath I was subjected to patriarchal policing by both strangers and family in deeply banal ways. I also include this vignette here because its telling exposes me and not my interlocutors, and at the end of the day I am more willing to risk subjecting myself than them to the reputational damage that being a woman undertaking quotidian activities in Libya can currently engender.

Perhaps a sense of wartime lawlessness is apparent, but what about this vignette speaks to digital intimacy? More broadly, in what ways does a public encounter such as this one extend into intimate and domestic spheres? I describe above my fear of being kidnapped. The crumpled and thrown phone number that assuaged that alarm produced in me in that moment a physical shock. This shock was at once violent and the cessation of another violence. Read in retrospect, that crumpled paper and the gesture through which it landed on me weave together the promise of the joy of potential intimacy with the risk of lasting harm that attends this promise. Presumably, the man who threw this phone number may have believed I would call him (though in this instance, the violence of the encounter makes that possibility particularly untenable in my view). Almost certainly, he acted to assert his gendered power as a way to participate in homosocial bonding (Pereira, 2020), perhaps even taking pleasure in my evident fear.

Violent intimacy animates even this relatively public encounter; it structures the many other gendered traumas that push their way into my interlocutors' lives. Militia members are embedded in families: their gendered traumas (e.g. pressures to conform to violent masculinities) encroach in direct and indirect ways into their relationships with partners, siblings, parents, and children, enabling secondary and even cyclical primary traumatization. These families and those with no militia involvement bear traumas of displacement and loss as a result of ground conflicts and aerial bombardments.[8] Earlier examples in this chapter evidence the trauma that results from less obviously war-produced gendered violence that is nonetheless shaped by the contingencies of the current conflict: the way that domestic violence is linked to (often justified in relation to) public perceptions and family reputation, the way that acts of violence against women in public spaces are used to justify women's confinement, the ways that victims of these horrific attacks are blamed in their aftermath.

Desiring Stability/Producing New Moralities

Faced with more than a decade of post-revolution conflict, the young people that came of age during and in the aftermath of the 2011 Libyan uprising have yearned for stable futures while fearing these will remain out of reach. In this regard, young Libyans are like other millennials around the world who, facing climate disasters, pandemics, and the ruthlessness of late capitalism, grapple with the intertwining of optimism and dread. Attempting to find agency in mostly intolerable conditions, many of my interlocutors look toward normative genres for life, family, and work, even while they may also transgress these via their online relationships. In this concluding section, I consider this pairing: the potentialities of digital media and the intimacies that they enable for producing new moral norms, alongside the pulls of older and more well-established normativities as modes for imagining realistic futures.

Indeed, both digital media and the social upheaval that attends revolution and war are particularly fertile sites for the production of new moral grammars and norms. As Costa and Menin put it, "[o]n digital media, people do not simply privately transgress the existing social norms but also create new normativities and new moral norms" (2016: 141). This is not necessarily a process full of intentionality. One of the ways that it happens is via the collaborative construction of idioms of practice (Gershon, 2010): the "conventional ways of interacting created among loosely bounded groups of people" using particular media and then narrating and negotiating their experiences (Gagné, 2016: 170–171). From these idioms of practice, people form, share, and endorse others' judgements about acceptable behavior, resulting in new (near or ostensible) consensus around, for example, the appropriate media in which to

---

[8] The Libyan conflict has the terrible distinction of being a frontier in the use of AI-directed aerial drones, adding new dimensions to the tragedies inflicted via bombing campaigns. See Cramer (2021).

communicate a breakup message (Gershon, 2010) or what kinds of personal information should be divulged on Instagram versus Facebook. A similar process takes place in the aftermath of a revolution, as those who saw themselves as participants in particular work to take stock of what is newly possible in changed political conditions. An especially salient characteristic of Libya's 2011 revolution was participants' near-exclusive focus on what they collectively opposed, with almost no public discourse around what they might demand in its place (Tayeb, 2017). In the years that followed, people observed and narrated new quotidian realities as they emerged, idioms of practice that often differed within Libya from locale to locale and that sometimes shifted rapidly, even while agents of the changes were not always evident.

Yet, while the production of new norms has been both feasible in post-2011 Libya and unfolding, for better or worse, the interlocutors whose lives and stories inform this chapter have spoken with me much more about pathways for the future that are by and large conventional, even if they express other "if only" yearnings in terms less concrete. One might understand this in terms of resignation, a prevalent enough affect for Libyan youth who are relentlessly asked to be an audience for political elites' cynicism and international analysts' descriptions of Libya as intractably both socially conservative and politically doomed. But I don't think resignation explains the prevalence of young peoples' attachments to the conventional, images of marriage and children, bourgeois consumption, or even studies and a career abroad. These attachments are clearly sustaining in some way, making it improbable to think outside them, or, more terrifying to lose them than to hold tight in dissatisfaction. Berlant reminds us that "one of optimism's ordinary pleasures is to induce conventionality, that place where appetites find a shape in the predictable comforts of the good-life genres that a person or a world has seen fit to formulate" (Berlant, 2011: 2). They go on to demonstrate, famously, the cruel optimism of attaching to the good-life genres that, in practice, become an obstacle to one's flourishing. This structure persists as much in post-revolution Libya as elsewhere. What the continuation of war offers is a deferral: as long as conflict shapes all aspects of living on, including emotional intimacies, digital and otherwise, hope for a post-conflict good life cannot be foreclosed.

REFERENCES

Berlant, L. (2011). *Cruel Optimism*. Duke University Press.

Costa, E., & Menin, L. (2016). Digital Intimacies: Exploring Digital Media and Intimate Lives in the Middle East and North Africa. *Middle East Journal of Culture and Communication*, *9*(2), 137–145. https://doi.org/10.1163/18739865-00902002

Cramer, M.. (2021, June 3). A.I. Drone May Have Acted on Its Own in Attacking Fighters, U.N. Says. *New York Times*. Accessed June 29, 2021, from https://www.nytimes.com/2021/06/03/world/africa/libya-drone.html

Feldstein, S., & Gordon, S. (2021, March 13). Are Telegram and Signal Havens for Right-Wing Extremists? *Foreign Policy* Accessed June 15, 2021, from https://foreignpolicy.com/2021/03/13/telegram-signal-apps-right-wing-extremism-islamic-state-terrorism-violence-europol-encrypted/

Gagné, M. (2016). Nadir's Intimate Biography: Fantasy, Gay Hook-Up Apps, and Intimate Productions in Beirut. *Middle East Journal of Culture and Communication, 9*(2), 165–181. https://doi.org/10.1163/18739865-00902004

Gana, H. (2020). Building Bayt Ali Gana. *Lamma: A Journal of Libyan Studies, 1.* Accessed from https://escholarship.org/uc/item/2zd7w09d.

Gershon, I. (2010). *The Break-Up 2.0: Disconnecting Over New Media.* Cornell University Press.

González, R., & Gusterson, H. (2019). Introduction. In R. González, H. Gusterson, & G. Houtman (Eds.), *Militarization: A Reader.* Duke University Press.

Jurasz, O., Elmessiry, M., Mohamed, M., Molyneux, T. Ożyńska, D., Rechdane, M., & Kazan, S. (2021). *"We Will Not Be Silenced": Online Violence Against Women in Libya.* Lawyers for Justice in Libya (LFJL). Accessed June 11, 2021, from bit.ly/3l3PKWO

Jyrkiäinen, S. (2016). Online Presentation of Gendered Selves Among Young Women in Egypt. *Middle East Journal of Culture and Communication, 9*(2), 182–198. https://doi.org/10.1163/18739865-00902005

Kemp, S. (2021). *Digital 2021: Libya. DataReportal.* Accessed June 11, 2021, from https://datareportal.com/reports/digital-2021-libya

Khalifa, A. (2020, May 14). Libya's Forgotten Half: Between Conflict and Pandemic, Women Pay the Higher Price. *Open Democracy.* Accessed June 11, 2021, from https://www.opendemocracy.net/en/north-africa-west-asia/libyas-forgotten-half-between-conflict-and-pandemic-women-pay-the-higher-price/

Nevola, L. (2016). Love, Mobile Phones and the Codification of Intimacy in Contemporary Yemen. *Middle East Journal of Culture and Communication, 9*(2), 147–164. https://doi.org/10.1163/18739865-00902003

Pereira, C. (2020). The Construction of Virility and Performance of Masculinity in the Language Practices of Young Men in Tripoli. *Lamma: A Journal of Libyan Studies, 1.* Accessed from https://escholarship.org/uc/item/2zd7w09d

Schwartz, A. (2021). *The Complex PTSD Treatment Manual: An Integrative, Mind-Body Approach to Trauma Recovery.* PESI Publishing.

Tayeb, L. (2017). *Shahi al-Huriya*: Militant Optimism and Freedom Tea. *Communication and the Public, 2*(2), 164–176.

Tayeb, L. (2020). Militia Soundscapes in Post-Qaddafi Libya. *Arab Studies Journal, 28*(1), 64–83.

Tayeb, L. (2021). What Is Whiteness in North Africa? *Laterality, 10*(1). https://doi.org/10.25158/L10.1.20

Wehrey, F. (2018). *The Burning Shores: Inside the Battle for the New Libya.* Farrar, Straus, and Giroux.

CHAPTER 18

Palestinian Women's Digital Activism Against Gender-Based Violence: Navigating Transnational and Social Media Spaces

Tamara Kharroub

Israa Ghrayeb is a 21-year-old Palestinian woman from a small town in the West Bank. She was a successful makeup artist and an independent woman, who supported her family financially and had more than 12,000 Instagram followers—a significant number for her small community. In August 2019, Ghrayeb was beaten to death by her male relatives after posting an Instagram story at a coffee shop with a man who had proposed to her. Ghrayeb's is one of millions of stories of women in the Arab region and across the world who experience violence and abuse. But in this particular case, social media became a central component of the narrative as the details of Ghrayeb's killing were broadcast online and social media posts went viral generating news headlines and widespread regional and international outrage. Ghrayeb's social media and mobile phone use, through recording and sharing conversations with her friends and posting pictures and videos to her followers, along with the social media campaigns after her death, would become a focal point of the case. Israa Ghrayeb relied on social media to market her makeup work and connect with her clients. But a social media post was the catalyst that led to her killing, yet

T. Kharroub (✉)
Arab Center Washington DC, Washington, DC, USA
e-mail: tkharroub@arabcenterdc.org

© The Author(s), under exclusive license to Springer Nature
Switzerland AG 2023
L. H. Skalli, N. Eltantawy (eds.), *The Palgrave Handbook of Gender, Media and Communication in the Middle East and North Africa*,
https://doi.org/10.1007/978-3-031-11980-4_18

317

she utilized technology and social media to document her abuse and share her narrative with friends and the world. The story of her death began with a social media post and evolved online with a growing assembly of social media spectators, investigators, and supporters.

According to her friends, Ghrayeb's female cousin complained about her Instagram post with her soon to be fiancé to Israa's brothers, claiming it brought shame to the family (in some conservative communities, it is considered inappropriate for an unmarried couple to be seen alone together in public). Some report that Israa's friends shared an audio recording of this conversation on social media platforms. Another phone conversation between Ghrayeb and her cousin surfaced online, in which Ghrayeb admonished her cousin and explained that her family consented to the relationship and was aware of the outing. Following this incident, Ghrayeb was admitted to Al-Hussein hospital on August 10 with a fractured spine and bruises on her body and face. According to friends and media reports, she was assaulted at home and fell from the second floor of their house while attempting to escape her family's abuse. While at the hospital, she posted pictures to her Instagram story; a smiling Ghrayeb with visible injuries (Bateman, 2019) and a picture of text informing her clients that she is having surgery and canceling appointments scheduled for August and September. In another photo of the hospital room, she wrote, "I am strong and I have the will to live, if I didn't have this willpower, I would have died yesterday." She added, "May God be the judge of those who oppressed me and hurt me" (Alfares, 2019). Shortly after, a video believed to be recorded by a nurse was shared on social media appearing to show a hospital corridor with a voice of a woman screaming and pleading to the sound of thuds. Friends and activists alleged that the video was of Israa screaming while being assaulted a second time by her two brothers, brother-in-law, and father. Witness accounts report that her family explained to hospital staff they were performing an exorcism on Israa whom they believed was possessed by a demon, but the family backtracked and disputed the authenticity of the video after Israa's death. Ghrayeb was discharged from the hospital days later and no investigation was conducted despite what health officials later admitted were signs of abuse (Bateman, 2019). She died on August 22 at home from a head injury, as she went into a coma before her heart stopped (Ghoneim, 2019). In an attempt to counter the social media storm, her brother-in-law, Mohammed Safi, a sheikh and one of the family members accused online by Israa's friends and social media activists of assaulting Ghrayeb, offered a video interview to a local reporter which was also widely shared on social media. In the interview, he claimed there was no abuse and that Israa was possessed and suffered mental health issues (Bateman, 2019). Her family released a statement after her death on social media saying she jumped off the second-story balcony, breaking her spine and suffering cuts to her face, which eventually caused her death. The statement also said that she had been possessed by demons, which is why she was screaming when she was admitted to the hospital and was receiving help from local clerics (Shaalan & Agencies,

2019). But Ghrayeb's friends and online activists disputed the family's narrative and pointed out gaps where the story did not add up.

Ghrayeb's death sparked public outrage in Palestine and beyond, as the narrative was evolving and unraveling online before everyone's eyes (and ears) and accessible to anyone with an Internet connection, a Facebook account, and Arabic language proficiency. The gruesome details of the story, Ghrayeb's voice, words, pictures, and her harrowing screams, and the absurdity and audacity of her family's claims, along with the inability or unwillingness of hospital staff and police to protect her, the lack of serious investigation, and the government's inaction, all shocked and angered social media users across the Arab cybersphere as they watched and listened to this young woman's pleas. The Palestinian women's movement #Tal3at was born as Palestinian activists launched social media campaigns and called for protests in different cities and outside the office of Palestinian Prime Minister Mohammad Shtayyeh in Ramallah (Bateman, 2019). The hashtag #WeAreAllIsraaGhrayeb was trending on Twitter, while other social media campaigns like "No honor in honor crimes" and "JusticeforIsraa" went viral in the Arabic-language online world for months. Even Arab pop stars, celebrities, and popular media personalities from across the region like Nancy Ajram, Elissa, Nishan, Shams, Amr Adeeb, and Ola Fares posted about Ghrayeb's death and called for action and accountability (e.g., Ghoneim, 2019).

The wide-scale outrage and online storm and the public pressure both in Palestine and in the Arabic-language virtual domain forced the Palestinian Prime Minster to respond by announcing further investigation and highlighting the need to strengthen legal protections for women. Further forensic tests were ordered, and on September 12, the Palestinian Authority attorney general Akram al-Khatib held a news conference announcing that the pathology reports showed that Ghrayeb died from severe respiratory failure due to a collapsed lung, which was caused by multiple serious injuries from domestic violence. He confirmed that the videos of her screams at the hospital were authentic and said that the investigation concluded that Ghrayeb had been repeatedly subjected to psychological and physical violence. He further announced that prosecutors charged three individuals for assault that led to unintentional killing under article 330 of the penal code, a charge that can carry a sentence of at least five years in prison (Begum, 2019). Additionally, the Palestinian Authority's Ministry of Women's Affairs announced that it will introduce a new family protection law that would amend the penal code regarding legal protections for victims of domestic violence, the minimum age for marriage, harsher penalties for perpetrators, and police training for dealing with domestic violence cases (Abumaria, 2019).

While activists awaited the implementation of these promises and the trial and sentencing of the perpetrators (who were released on bail), they believed that the case of Israa Ghrayeb will be known as a turning point for ending the culture of impunity for the crimes of femicide and gender-based violence in Palestine. The circumstances surrounding Israa's case, especially the sophisticated use of social media and its transnational pan-Arab reach, played an important role in bringing justice, through exposing the crimes, giving the victim agency and ownership of her narrative, reaching a wider public, generating mass public outcry and solidarity, pushing for accountability, and exerting pressure on the government to take action. In this chapter, the #Tal3at movement and the killing of Israa Ghrayeb are used as an instrumental case study to better understand the role that social media plays in Palestinian women's activism against gender-based violence particularly in shifting the space for action and creating a platform for informal justice, while at the same time exploring the challenges of mirroring offline structural inequalities and posing the risk of transnational decontextualization. This case study utilizes data collected from social media accounts and posts related to the case of Israa Ghrayeb and the #Tal3at movement and draws from theories of space activism and the Palestinian sociopolitical environment in order to make conclusions about the emerging Palestinian women's movements and their use of social media technologies to combat violence.

GENDER-BASED VIOLENCE IN PALESTINE

Although women in the MENA region have long mobilized for their rights and freedoms and taken part in political protests and national movements, Arab Women today continue to rank worst in the world, scoring 40% in the Gender Gap Index which measures gender-based gaps in access to health, education, economy, and politics (World Economic Forum, 2018). Additionally, the experiences and grievances of Arab women are often trivialized and relegated to peripheral secondary issues on the social and political agendas. While women protested alongside men during the waves of uprisings that swept the region since 2011, today 10 years after the Arab Spring, Arab women remain marginalized in all aspects of society, patriarchal norms remain prevalent, and reporting of sexual harassment and gender-based violence is on the rise, with some countries worse for women than before the Arab Spring (Boros, 2013). One of the alarming issues facing Arab and Palestinian women today, especially during and following the coronavirus pandemic lockdowns, is gender-based violence. Sometimes referred to and measured as violence against women and girls (VAWG), intimate partner violence (IPV), or domestic violence (DV), the broader term of gender-based violence (GBV) is conceptualized using the CEDAW definition as "any act of gender-based violence that results in, or is likely to result in, physical, sexual or psychological harm or suffering to women, including threats of such acts, coercion or arbitrary deprivation of liberty, whether occurring in public or in private life" (OHCHR, 1993). Gender-based violence is a global silent pandemic, with 30% of women worldwide experiencing violence in their lifetime and 35% who may get sexually assaulted during their lifetime (WHO, 2013). The lockdown measures and stay-at-home orders instituted as a result of the global coronavirus pandemic starting in early 2020 caused a spike in reporting of cases of violence against women, which UN

Women termed the "shadow pandemic" (2020a). With women trapped at homes with their abusers, reports and surveys from around the world showed that cases of domestic violence and calls to hotlines dramatically increased during 2020, ranging from 20% to 33% increase in Argentina, the Catalan region of Spain, Cyprus, France, and Singapore, to 50% in Brazil, and as high as 300% in the Hubei province in China, as reported by UN Women (2020a). Additionally, due to closures intended to curb the spread of covid-19, psychosocial support and healthcare services as well as legal means available to victims of domestic violence were disrupted, and sometimes the continual presence of abusers at home made it difficult for women to safely access help or call support centers resulting in a decline in calls in some cases. Even before the coronavirus pandemic, violence against women and girls was largely underreported where less than 40% report the crime or seek help, of whom most seek help from family members and friends and only 10% go to the police (UNDESA, 2015, 2020).

Violence against women is a worldwide silent pandemic, but underreporting is particularly problematic in the Arab world due to a variety of reasons including attitudes that domestic violence is a private matter and taboo and keeping it private is associated with preserving the family honor, in addition to some invalid claims of Islamic religious justification (Douki et al., 2003). As such, the overwhelming majority of women who experience violence in the region do not seek formal help from public service providers such as police, health workers, or legal entities. According to a study commissioned by USAID, only 5.4% of Tunisian women who experience domestic violence report it to government institutions or civil society groups, 3.8% to the police, and 2.3% seek help from healthcare providers, while 3% in Morocco and 1.4% in the West Bank and Gaza file formal complaints (Banyan Global, 2016). But even with the gross underreporting, the numbers are still alarming. In the Middle East and North Africa (MENA) region, 37% of women experience physical and/or sexual violence by a partner or non-partner (WHO, 2013). Recent reports show that these numbers have increased during 2020 as a result of the covid-19 quarantine and lockdown measures, in addition to the added trauma of impeding women's access to help, safe spaces and shelter, and healthcare and psychosocial support services due to the movement restrictions. Following the imposition of curfews to curb covid-19, the number of domestic violence cases rose fivefold in Tunisia (UN Women, 2020b) and increased by 100% in Lebanon (AbiRafeh, 2020). The state of gender-based violence in Palestine is no different, where 29% of women were subjected to violence by their husbands in 2019, 24% in the West Bank, and 38% in the Gaza Strip (Palestinian Central Bureau of Statistics, 2019). The numbers increased after the lockdown in 2020, for example, five Palestinian women were killed as a result of domestic violence between early March and mid-April 2020 and calls to women's support organizations rose by 30% (Najjar, 2020). Of the Palestinian women who experience domestic violence, 61% do seek help or talk to family members, while 3% consult a lawyer, 1% seek psychological, social, or legal services, and only 1% file a complaint with the police (Palestinian Central Bureau of Statistics,

2019). The fear of shame and retaliation as well as the belief that speaking out will not bring about change to their violent situation has forced Palestinian women to silently accept violence at home. However, in the last few years, technology has created a radical shift in attitudes, new means for speaking out, and additional avenues for accountability.

Navigating Space, Effecting Change: Palestinian Women's Online Activism Against GBV

The role of social media in activist movements, including its benefit as well as its limitations, has now been well documented and analyzed. The 2011 protests of the Arab Spring represent a prominent example of utilizing social media tools for activism and achieving political and social change. The role of the Internet was hailed as an imperative part of the movement as it was used to share information, mobilize activists, document abuses, and facilitate protest organizing, among others. It has been shown that online activism has the capability to empower marginalized groups, including women, to overcome restrictions or limitations. Arab women have employed the Internet and social networking sites to bypass state and patriarchal hegemony and control, amplify their voices, tell their stories, connect with the wider public, create solidarity domestically and transnationally, and enforce their grievances on the national and transnational agendas. Arab women's online activism succeeded in achieving real change on the ground, through accelerated sharing of information, mobilization, connectivity, and wide-scale publicity. Palestinian women, in particular, have been able to utilize the cybersphere to overcome the various geographic, political, and patriarchal obstacles that have restrained women's participation and activism.

One area in which Palestinian women's online activism has been prominent in the last two years is the fight against gender-based violence (GBV). The story of Israa Ghrayeb's murder and the role social media played in enabling the victim and her supporters to tell her story and rapidly transmitting this information to a wide audience acted not only as a platform for accountability but also as a wake-up call and a catalyst for birthing a renewed movement in Palestine. Several online groups and campaigns were established or gained prominence and followers. For example, #Bekafe "Enough against domestic violence" was founded in November 2019 triggered by Israa's killing, with its first campaign calling for stand-in outside the Bethlehem Court, during the first scheduled hearing for the trial of Israa's killers, to demand a fair and transparent trial. Another campaign, "Yes for family protection laws," was founded in August 2020 and works to raise awareness and advocate for legal change in Palestine. One of the prominent and most interesting movements for the purposes of this discussion is *Tal'at* or #Tal3at (Tal3at, n.d.). Also triggered by the killing of Israa Ghrayeb, Tal3at is a Palestinian feminist movement the name of which translates in Arabic to "women stepping out." Tal3at was launched when activists called for protests against gender-based violence in Palestine to take place on September 26, 2019, along with the campaigns "No honor in honor crimes," #WeAreAllIsraaGhrayeb, and #JusticeforIsraa, which were already trending online. During the lockdown, in April 2020, Tal3at called on Palestinians via Twitter to bang pots and pans from their windows and balconies in protest against GBV and to express solidarity with women living with violence under lockdown (#Tal3at, 2020). The #Tal3at movement is unique in the way its founders and activists chose to interact with the context in which it exists and negotiate space for gender activism within Palestinian society. As I propose elsewhere (Kharroub, 2021), examining the intersection of media, transnationalism, and women's movements from the spatial feminist approach is needed in order to better understand how Arab and Palestinian women's movements navigate online spaces and gendered environments to carry out their women's rights activism and achieve change.

Alternative Space for Action

Patriarchal norms have always demarcated public and private spaces in terms of gendered classifications. Women are traditionally confined to the private space, whereas the public space is historically considered a male arena marked by its restrictions on women's place in society, be it in the social, political, or economic arenas. The public space is a gendered space where women's visibility, access, and opportunities are constrained by patriarchal social norms that define what is deemed appropriate behavior for women in the public realm and in turn define women's space for action. Drawing from conceptualizations by Kelly (2003) and Lundgren (1998), space for action is the space in which women operate with agency and freedom, a "life-space" (Lundgren, 1998) representing the options available for women to exist, occupy space, and carry out their lives. As such, women's space for action is limited by the above-mentioned gendered restrictions and structural inequalities, where boundaries are set for women (and men) in public space in all areas of life. For that reason, we see great reluctance by Arab and Palestinian women to report gender-based violence, where bringing the private to the public is viewed as a violation of these gendered boundaries and is therefore considered shameful. But the Internet equips women with tools that transcend this distinction between public and private. The Internet and social media afford women's activism freedom of expression, agency over their spaces, and to some extent the protection of private space in the public arena. For example, Saudi women use fake names and conceal their pictures online as a tactic to allow them to operate and mobilize in the public space without risking their lives (Guta & Karolak, 2015). As such, women use the ability afforded by the Internet to challenge the private-public construction of space and negotiate their identities and presence in a way that enables them to operate safely in the public sphere. To overcome the historical construct of public space of excluding women and privileging men, women use the Internet from their private space to operate in a public space, hence expanding their space for action. For example, in 2011, Manal Al Sharif filmed herself driving in Saudi Arabia and called on Saudi women to challenge the driving ban. The YouTube video went viral and mobilized thousands of Saudi women to drive (The Guardian, 2013), which ultimately contributed international exposure and the pressure that resulted in lifting the ban. In Egypt, the YouTube video of 26-year-old Asmaa Mahfouz calling on Egyptians to join the protests went viral on social media and became a symbol of sparking the Egyptian revolution (Democracy Now, 2011). In both cases, social media served to amplify the voice and action of an individual occurring in a private space and broadcast them to a larger public, generating mass public reactions that ultimately led to change. In many respects, the diffusion of mobile phones and mobile Internet access have particularly given women the freedom and control over their private spaces away from the patriarchal control of their families (Sreberny, 2018), and unlocked the possibilities for these individual yet monumental acts.

In the same way, Israa Ghrayeb took control of her space for action and defied patriarchal norms through the use of her mobile phone, Internet connection, and social networking sites. Ghrayeb recorded private conversations which she shared with her friends, who then broadcast them widely to a large online audience in the public sphere, thereby allowing her to tell her individual story of domestic violence and abuse to the world. Similarly, the Palestinian #Tal3at movement embodies that interplay between private and public space. The word *Tal'at* or *Tal3at* in Arabic translates to "women stepping out" or "women going out on the streets." As such, the #Tal3at movement was designed to operate beyond the online sphere to mobilize and organize on the streets. Tal3at represents a call for action, calling on Palestinian women to step out on the streets and take agency over the public space; through its name, it loudly and explicitly and therefore unapologetically challenges the traditional constructions of the gendered business of the public sphere. Here, Tal3at activists were able to take advantage of the private characteristics of the digital space to launch a mass movement in the public space. Their first activity on September 6, 2019, was organized online and garnered thousands of protestors (men and women) on the streets of 12 cities in Palestine and beyond, coming together against gender-based violence in Palestine (Marshood & Alsanah, 2020). While the public space continues to confine and silence Palestinian women, the Internet has afforded them an alternative space for action and activism against gender-based violence.

A Transnational Geolinguistic Space

In addition to providing women safe access to the public space and expanding their space for action, Internet and communication technologies (ICTs) have also enabled Palestinian women to operate in a transnational space for action, connecting with hundreds of thousands of activists across the region. The media industry in the Arab world is unique as a transnational market in a large geolinguistic region that includes more than 427 million people across 22 countries in the Middle East and North Africa (The World Bank, 2019), who predominantly speak Arabic. Geolinguistic regions are defined as "imagined communities of speakers of the same language and participants in similar cultures which form the geolinguistic regions exploited by the media entrepreneurs" (Sinclair et al., 1996, p. 25). The countries with Arabic as their official or main language form the Arab geolinguistic region and have had the advantage of sharing and circulating information and media content since the eighteenth century. This transnational media sphere contributes to creating a sense of unity despite the distance, geography, and borders. This unifying characteristic of the Arabic geolinguistic region has been clearly reflected in the media environment since the days of the print industry with the traditional saying "Egypt writes, Lebanon prints, and Iraq reads," and into the time of the "Voice of the Arabs" popular pan-Arab radio service in the 1950s and 1960s, which Egyptian president and proponent of the pan-Arabist ideology Gamal Abdel Nasser used to promote his movement's messages across the Arab world (Chiba, 2012). The advancement of satellite technologies in the 1990s and the Internet in the 2000s has greatly contributed to the strengthening of a transnational pan-Arab media environment that not only transcends geographic borders and distance but also overcomes government control of information and communication tools, thus revolutionizing the Arab information sphere. Today, with 90% of young Arabs using at least one social media platform every day (ASDA'A BCW, 2019) and mobile social media penetration more than doubling to 44% in five years (GSMA Intelligence, 2019), the Internet and communication technologies provide new avenues for expression, diversity of information, and spaces for transnational connectivity and mobilization. These platforms have not only played a vital role in facilitating activism movements most prominently during the protests of the "Arab Spring" but also created a new transnational Arabic-language space for women's rights activism.

Against this backdrop, the story of Israa Ghrayeb transpired before a large transnational Arabic-speaking audience online. This large geolinguistic online community became important actors in the case, as Arab social media users took the role of investigative reporters analyzing and scrutinizing every video, text post, image, recording, statement, and interview. Activists and celebrities across the region rapidly spread Ghrayeb's story, presented arguments, expressed anger at government inaction, named and shamed those responsible, and mounted the public pressure on the Palestinian Authority, especially with prominent pan-Arab figures weighing in. Here, the Arab digital sphere became a platform for informal justice (e.g., Fileborn, 2016), as an alternative space parallel to the failed formal justice system. The transnational online community represented an alternative space for action for Palestinian activists and helped hold the perpetrator and the government accountable. This transnational pan-Arab cyberspace generated a new space for instant solidarity among feminist movements across the region. Through eliminating borders and occupying virtual space, Arab feminists generate an "energy effect" (Sreberny, 2015) to inspire activism, amass solidarity, and bring women's issues into public contestation and thereby elevating them from the social to the political agendas (see Mouffe, 2005) and increasing the likelihood of effecting policy changes.

MIRRORING STRUCTURAL INEQUALITIES AND PATRIARCHY

While the Internet and social networking sites may have revolutionized Arab women's struggle for equality and expanded women's space for action and agency, they are also subject to the existing structural inequalities in the offline realm. Multiple levels of structural inequalities are mirrored and incorporated in the virtual digital environment, from the digital divide and patriarchal norms to authoritarian powers and colonial and globalization hegemonic dynamics. First, historically, women's rights activists hail from the educated upper and middle-class, a phenomenon that carries over into the virtual sphere which tends to be exclusive for women with connectivity, literacy, and technical skills. In that respect, the digital divide and the gender digital divide remain an obstacle in the region. The Internet penetration rate in the Arab world is around 50%, with lower rates among women at 44.2% compared to 58.5% for men (International Telecommunications Union, 2019). This reality, coupled with literacy rates, leaves already marginalized women and rural populations excluded from the benefits and opportunities offered by ICTs. Another manifestation of gender-based violence in the digital sphere is cyberviolence. Rapid advances in technology and the rise in the use of virtual spaces during the covid-19 pandemic have presented an increase in cyberviolence against women around the world. Violence against Palestinian women has also branched out into the social media arena in recent years, with new forms of cyberviolence and harassment. Studies show that online gender-based violence against Palestinian women mirrors the violence they experience offline (Odeh, 2018). This virtual violence can take the shape of surveillance and monitoring, stalking and tracking technologies, censorship, discrimination, exclusion, denying access, sexual harassment, exposure to sexual content and images, bullying, hacking, extortion, and blackmail. According to Palestinian Police Spokesperson Loay Zureikat, cybercrimes in Palestine are on the rise and most of the cases involve blackmail and extortion against women and girls related to illegally obtaining private photographs (Odeh, 2018). The research also showed that one in four women closed their social media accounts as a result of violence and harassment. These trends are alarming as Internet penetration rates increase, more women will be facing online violence and withdrawing from virtual spaces, creating a ripple effect of exclusion from opportunities and spaces for action.

Another domain where structural inequalities are replicated in the virtual sphere is digital repression. Authoritarian and repressive powers may also have the upper hand in the digital sphere, as control of the cybersphere is subject to traditional power structures and availability of financial resources. The last years have witnessed a rise in digital repression in the Middle East and North Africa (PEN America, 2013), where totalitarian regimes use hacking techniques, censorship, surveillance, and government-affiliated social media influencers to intimidate critics and control the narrative. For example, the government of Saudi Arabia employed targeted and highly organized Twitter campaigns against female journalists who were critical of the kingdom (Jones, 2020). The study by Jones (2020) shows a coordinated campaign by thousands of Twitter accounts from Saudi Arabia using hacked private photographs of the women and orchestrating sexual harassment and smear attacks online. Another study demonstrates how gulf monarchies like Saudi Arabia are using Twitter bots (i.e., automated accounts) for the mass production of tweets and coopting social media influencers in order to spread propaganda (Leber & Abrahams, 2019). Transnational firms like the Israeli NSO group are involved in selling spyware technologies to authoritarian governments around the world (Ensor, 2018). Meanwhile, the United Arab Emirates has developed spyware to track and surveil activities (Schectman & Bing, 2019), while the Egyptian regimes jailed TikTok female influencers for "indecent" videos (BBC News, 2020). Women activists who challenged the driving ban in Saudi Arabia were targeted in smear campaigns (BBC News, 2018) and arrested and tortured (Burleigh, 2020). Palestinian women endure a double repression in this case, from the Palestinian Authority on one hand and from the Israeli occupation on the other. For example, Palestinian female journalists and activists have been arrested by both the Palestinian police and the Israeli occupation forces for social media posts critical of the Palestinian and Israeli authorities (MADA, 2016). It has become clear that the liberating promises of ICTs come with a warning, as repressive regimes with a wealth of financial and technical resources are capable of taking control over virtual social media spaces using tactics like propaganda, surveillance, censorship, hacking, harassment, intimidation, smear campaigns, Internet and social media blackouts, and offline arrests and tortures. New spaces for action can become new spaces for oppression and patriarchy.

The Palestinian Women's Movement and Digital Activism in Context

Since its inception, the Palestinian women's movement has had to confront the realities of colonialization and military occupation, and as a result has drawn its legitimacy as a movement from carefully balancing between feminism and nationalism. To understand Palestinian women's social media activism, one must understand this tension between the women's rights agenda and the national liberation agenda and the context within which this mobilization exists today. Palestinian women's activism cannot be detached from the political context in which it operates. Since the 1920s, the Palestinian women's movement has been intertwined with the larger geopolitical conditions and the Palestinian national struggle for independence. For example, when the first Palestinian women's union was created in 1921 in Jerusalem, it became instrumental in mobilizing against the British Mandate and the creation of a Jewish state in Palestine (Jad, 1995; Kuttab, 1993). Up until 1947, Palestinian women continued to be at the forefront of the national movement, through participation in protests, congresses, fundraising, aid work, and meetings with and letters to the government, while at the same time emphasizing their feminist agenda (Fleischmann, 2003). The 1948 and 1967 wars, which resulted in the dispossession of Palestinians and fragmentation of Palestinian society, forced the Palestinian women's movement to turn into charitable relief and aid work and address the needs of a displaced population (Kuttab, 2009). At the same time, the wide-ranging destruction of Palestinian political, economic, and cultural infrastructure after 1948 and 1967 was coupled with a democratizing effect (Taraki, 1991), as the old traditional social and class structures no longer existed and the lack of autonomy and governance in a society under occupation created a need for grass-roots and civil society organizations to be established and respond to the newly created Palestinian realities. This new political reality allowed various segments of Palestinian society to integrate into Palestinian institutional life and enabled the mobilization of youth, students, workers, and women. The new Palestinian women's movement asserted the importance of women's rights in conjunction with the political and national agenda and played a central and sustaining role in the 1987 *Intifada* (Kuttab, 1993, 2003). However, the suppression of the *Intifada* and the ensuing creation of the symbolic Palestinian National Authority in the post-Oslo period in the 1900s led to the monopolization of power through authoritarian mechanisms, which in turn resulted in the institutionalization of women's activism into specialized work (Kuttab, 2009) and the "NGO-ization" of women's movements (Jad, 2003). This professionalization of women activism served to delink the women's movement from the national struggle for liberation and at the same time separated the women's rights agenda from the political process, thus limiting its scope and impact (Kuttab, 2009). Moreover, the geographic fragmentation of the Palestinian population into Bantustans under Israeli occupation within the West Bank, East Jerusalem, and Gaza, as well as the separation from Palestinian citizens of Israel, Palestinians in refugee camps across the region, and Palestinians in the diaspora, each community with its own set of localized issues and priorities as well as different political and legal contexts, presented additional structural challenges to women's right organizing.

This left Palestinian women facing not only patriarchal norms and structures, the authoritarian rule of the Palestinian Authority, and the violence and oppression of the Israeli occupation but also geographic fragmentation and structural challenges that complicated activism and mobilization. What the history of the Palestinian women's movement demonstrates is that Palestinian women activists have always had to grapple with the tension between feminism and nationalism. From the 1920s and through the first *Intifada* in the 1980s, Palestinian women participation in the national struggle provided legitimacy for their activism and role in society (Fleischmann, 2003). While women's rights and gender equality constituted an important part of their mission, Palestinian women activists understood that their reality of living under a settler colonial occupation prioritized basic human and political rights and building a nation-state (Kuttab, 2009). The Palestinian women's movement today continues to deal with the additional burden and complexity of simultaneously balancing the women's rights agenda and the national political agenda so as to prevent the trivialization of the fight for gender equality. It is in this context that, the #Tal3at movement's slogan can be understood. Tal3at's Facebook page is called "Free women = free homeland," which is also the motto of the movement on Twitter and the chants heard at protests asserting that "there is no free homeland without free women." Founders and members of Tal3at insist on centering women's rights within the struggle for national liberation, explaining that their movement is based on the foundations of emancipatory politics, where violence is understood in its multilayered gendered, economic, social, and political forms and where patriarchal violence is perceived in connection with colonial violence (Marshood & Alsanah, 2020). In fact, the reality of the occupation for Palestinians seeps into the dynamics of gender-based violence as well, whether in preventing Palestinian police and social service access and jurisdiction over Area C of the West Bank, by being perpetrators of physical, sexual, and psychological violence against Palestinian women, or by perpetuating patriarchal systems in dealing with gender-based violence cases among Palestinian communities in Israel (e.g., Najjar, 2020). As such the reality of the occupation cannot be detached from gender-based violence in Palestine. In this respect, Tal3at challenges and counters the prevalent professionalization of women's activism and sidelining of women's rights agendas by the Palestinian Authority. This overarching revolutionary political feminism may have contributed to the large-scale mobilization the movement achieved in various—geographically and politically—disconnected Palestinian communities, among both women and men. In fact, the movement utilized social media tools to transcend this geographic fragmentation and geopolitical divides, uniting Palestinians in what members call a "de-fragmented feminist solidarity" in one virtual space under the banner of collective liberation. Tal3at's first activity included coordinated protests in 12 cities in the West Bank, Jerusalem, Gaza, Israel, and the Palestinian diaspora like in Germany. What the Tal3at example shows is that Palestinian women's movements have been able to situate their struggle within the large political struggle without deprioritizing or depoliticizing women's rights.

Turning to the larger global context, the transnational nature of social media connectivity presents an added risk of decontextualization of the Palestinian women's agenda. As seen here, Palestinian women's activism is a rumination of Palestinian lived experiences and is therefore focused on the Palestinian reality and motivated by responding to the challenges facing Palestinian men and women. However, transnational exposure may elevate transnational and international agendas at the expense of national interests (e.g., Nisbet & Myers, 2010). Additionally, when local messages are transformed globally through online platforms, they are prone to manipulation and bias where a process of digital reflexivity alters the original activists' message to fit an international or transnational audience, which in turn might function as "contained empowerment" for women (Newsom & Lengel, 2012). For example, the NGO-ization and external funding and training of Palestinian women's activism gradually forces an adoption of international definitions and agendas that might produce reformative rather than transformative change; only addressing individual grievances at the expense of collective structural transformation (Kuttab, 2010). The visibility of individual cases, like that of Israa Ghrayeb, allows transnational and international pressure that can lead to accountability in the case, but rarely does it alter the underlying patriarchal structures that caused the injustice in the first place. An additional component of Palestinian women's activism against GBV is the risk of being exploited by orientalist views and anti-Palestinian entities and western media to appropriate a narrative removed from the context of the Israeli occupation and further dehumanize Palestinians and propagate the misconception of Palestinian violence. This is likely another reason why movements like Tal3at insist on situating the fight against gender-based violence within the larger struggle for Palestinian freedom and rights.

In conclusion, transnational social media platforms have the potential to empower women and create alternative spaces for action, solidarity, and informal justice, in parallel to the gendered public space and patriarchal systems. The cybersphere affords Palestinian women's activism against GBV a new avenue to overcome the structural obstacles they face including institutionalization, NGO-ization, authoritarianism, geographic fragmentation, patriarchal structures, and military occupation. As seen in the case of Israa Ghrayeb, ICTs play an important role in turning the once private issue of GBV into a public and political concern, through publicizing an individual story, mobilizing thousands of activists, garnering mass transnational support, and holding those responsible to account, thus enabling social and legal change. However, while cyberspace has allowed women to overcome gendered restrictions and challenge patriarchal norms, the digital sphere is not immune to the existing structural inequalities and authoritarian and patriarchal control. The analysis of Ghrayeb's case and the #Tal3at movement shows that "online activism spaces are simultaneously empowering and restrained by hegemony," yet they are capable of providing the motivation and tools to achieve change (Newsom & Lengel, 2012). As such, Palestinian women's movements fighting GBV carefully navigate the transnational online sphere in order to have agency over their spaces for action, all while situating their women's rights activism within the larger national political movement.

REFERENCES

#Tal3at: Free women = Free homeland -#حر وطن = حرة نساء :طالبات [@tal3at_sept26]. (2020, April 18). مساء السابعة الساعة الاثنين يوم. [Tweet]. Twitter. Accessed from https://twitter.com/tal3at_sept26/status/1251519340958138369

AbiRafeh, Li. (2020, May 4). For Arab Women and Girls, the Crisis Is Just Beginning. *Al Jazeera*. Accessed April 29, 2021, from https://www.aljazeera.com/opinions/2020/5/4/for-arab-women-and-girls-the-crisis-is-just-beginning

Abumaria, D. (2019, October 1). PA Finally Working on Family Protection Law. *The Jerusalem Post*. Accessed April 29, 2021, from https://www.jpost.com/Middle-East/PA-finally-working-on-Family-Protection-Law-603345?fbclid=IwAR2Gyh_xlu-W5-_8B8o7ajRSRa_gRJ_8PAp6q3LC5htB3FqGncDxr07ACzs

Alfares, O. [@OlaAlfares]. (2019, August 29). لم أستطع النوم هذه الليلة..صوت صراخها في المستشفى في الفيديو المتداول لا يفارقني. [Tweet]. Twitter. Accessed from https://twitter.com/OlaAlfares/status/1167265187705032707

ASDA'A BCW. (2019. *A Call for Reform: A White Paper on the Findings of the 11th Annual ASDA'A BCW Arab Youth Survey 2019*. Accessed from https://www.arabyouthsurvey.com/pdf/downloadwhitepaper/download-whitepaper.pdf

Banyan Global. (2016). *Gender-Based Violence in the MENA Region: Context Analysis*. USAID. Accessed from https://banyanglobal.com/wp-content/uploads/2018/02/MENA-Context-Analysis.pdf

Bateman, T. (2019, September 16). Israa Ghrayeb: Palestinian Woman's Death Prompts Soul-Searching. *BBC News*. Accessed April 29, 2021, from https://www.bbc.com/news/world-middle-east-49688920

BBC News. (2018). Saudi Arabia Women's Driving Activists 'Targeted in Smear Campaign'. *BBC News*. Accessed April 29, 2021, from https://www.bbc.com/news/world-middle-east-44187840?ocid=socialflow_twitter

BBC News. (2020). Egypt TikTok: Female Influencers Jailed Over 'Indecent' Videos. *BBC News*. Accessed April 29, 2021, from https://www.bbc.com/news/world-middle-east-53557576

Begum, R. (2019, September 18). When It Mattered, Palestinian Law Failed Israa Ghrayeb. It's High Time that Changed. *Al Araby*. Accessed April 29, 2021, from https://english.alaraby.co.uk/english/comment/2019/9/18/the-lethal-cost-of-being-a-woman-in-palestine

Boros, C. (2013. *Poll-Egypt Is Worst Arab State for Women, Comoros Best*. Thomson Reuters Foundation. Accessed April 29, 2021, from https://news.trust.org/item/20131108170910-qacvu/?source=spotlight-writaw

Burleigh, N. (2020, December 1). Trump and the West's Enabling of Saudi Arabia Enables the Torture of Loujain al-Hathloul. *NBC News*. Accessed April 29, 2021, from https://www.nbcnews.com/think/opinion/trump-west-s-enabling-saudi-arabia-enables-torture-loujain-al-ncna1249563

Chiba, Y. (2012). The Geographical Transformation of Arab Media: The Decline of Offshore Media and the Rise of the Media City. *Asian and African Area Studies*, *12*(1), 79–103.

Democracy Now! (2011, February 8). *Asmaa Mahfouz & the YouTube Video that Helped Spark the Egyptian Uprising*. Democracy Now!. Accessed April 29, 2021, from https://www.democracynow.org/2011/2/8/asmaa_mahfouz_the_youtube_video_that

Douki, S., Nacef, F., Belhadj, A., Bouasker, A., & Ghachem, R. (2003). Violence Against Women in Arab and Islamic Countries. *Archives of Women's Mental Health*, *6*(3), 165–171. https://doi.org/10.1007/s00737-003-0170-x

Ensor, J. (2018December 3). Israeli Software Company 'Shared Hacked Messages' from Khashoggi with Saudi, Lawsuit Claims. *The Telegraph*. Accessed April 29, 2021, from https://www.telegraph.co.uk/news/2018/12/03/israeli-software-company-shared-hacked-messages-khashoggi-saudi/

Fileborn, B. (2016). Justice 2.0: Street Harassment Victims' Use of Social Media and Online Activism as Sites of Informal Justice. *British Journal of Criminology, 57*(6), 1482–1501.

Fleischmann, E. (2003). *The Nation and Its New Women: The Palestinian Women's Movement 1920-1948.* University of California Press, USA.

Ghoneim, N. (2019, August 31). Palestinian Woman Murdered in Honor Killing After Posting Instagram Video with Fiancé. *Egyptian Streets.* Accessed April 29, 2021, from https://egyptianstreets.com/2019/08/31/palestinian-woman-murdered-in-honor-killing-after-posting-instagram-video-with-fiance/

GSMA Intelligence. (2019. *The Mobile Economy Middle East & North Africa 2019.* Accessed from https://data.gsmaintelligence.com/api-web/v2/research-file-download?id=47743179&file=2866-261119-ME-MENA.pdf

Guta, H., & Karolak, M. (2015). Veiling and Blogging: Social Media as Sites of Identity Negotiation and Expression Among Saudi Women. *Journal of International Women's Studies, 16*(2), 115–127.

International Telecommunications Union. (2019). *Measuring Digital Development: Facts and Figures 2019.* Accessed April 29, 2021, from https://www.itu.int/en/ITU-D/Statistics/Documents/facts/FactsFigures2019.pdf

Jad, I. (1995). Claiming Feminism, Claiming Nationalism: Women's Activism in the Occupied Territories. In A. Basu (Ed.), *The Challenges of Local Feminisms: Women's Movements in Global Perspective.* Westview Press.

Jad, I. (2003). The NGOization of Arab Women's Movement. *Al Raida, 20*(100).

Jones, M. O. (2020, June 9). *Twitter Thread.* 6:00 p.m. Accessed from https://twitter.com/marcowenjones/status/1270475823947173888

Kelly, L. (2003). The Wrong Debate: Reflections on Why Force Is Not the Key Issue with Respect to Trafficking in Women for Sexual Exploitation. *Feminist Review, 73*(1), 139–144.

Kharroub, T. (2021). Arab Women's Activism in a Transnational Media Landscape: Negotiating Gendered Spaces. *Feminist Media Studies, 21,* 692. https://doi.org/10.1080/14680777.2021.1919732

Kuttab, E. (1993). Palestinian Women in the Intifada: Liberation Within Liberation. *Arab Studies Quarterly, 15*(2).

Kuttab, E. (2003). *Palestinian Intifada in the Context of Globalization: A Gender Review* (Vol. 70). Nour Publishing House for Arab Women.

Kuttab, E. (2009). The Palestinian Women's Movement: From Resistance and Liberation to Accommodation and Globalization. In *Vents d'Est, vents d'Ouest: Mouvements de femmes et féminismes anticoloniaux* [online]. Graduate Institute Publications. https://doi.org/10.4000/books.iheid.6310. Accessed from http://books.openedition.org/iheid/6310

Kuttab, E. (2010). Empowerment as Resistance: Conceptualizing Palestinian Women's Empowerment. *Development (Society for International Development), 53*(2), 247–253.

Leber, A., & Abrahams, A. (2019). A Storm of Tweets: Social Media Manipulation During the Gulf Crisis. *Review of Middle East Studies (Tucson, Ariz.), 53*(2), 241–411.

Lundgren, E. (1998). The Hand that Strikes and Comforts: Gender Construction and the Tension Between Body and Soul. In R. E. Dobash & R. P. Dobash (Eds.), *Rethinking Violence Against Women* (pp. 169–198). Sage.

MADA- The Palestinian Center for Development and Media Freedoms. (2016). *Social Media… A New Venue to Censor and Prosecute Journalists.* Accessed April 29, 2021, from https://www.madacenter.org/en/article/248/

Marshood, H. & Alsanah, R. (2020, February 25). Tal'at: A Feminist Movement that Is Redefining Liberation and REIMAGINING PALEStine. *Mondoweiss.* Accessed April 29, 2021, from https://mondoweiss.net/2020/02/talat-a-feminist-movement-that-is-redefining-liberation-and-reimagining-palestine/

Mouffe, C. (2005). *On the Political.* Routledge.

Najjar, F. (2020, April 2). Domestic Abuse Against Palestinian Women Soars. *Al Jazeera.* Accessed April 29, 2021, from https://www.aljazeera.com/news/2020/4/20/domestic-abuse-against-palestinian-women-soars

Newsom, V. A., & Lengel, L. (2012). Arab Women, Social Media, and the Arab Spring: Applying the Framework of Digital Reflexivity to Analyze Gender and Online Activism. *Journal of International Women's Studies, 13*(5), 31–45. Accessed from http://vc.bridgew.edu/jiws/vol13/iss5/5

Nisbet, E. C., & Myers, T. (2010). Challenging the State: Transnational TV and Political Identity in the Middle East. *Political Communication, 27*(4), 347–366. https://doi.org/10.1080/10584609.2010.516801

Odeh, S. (2018November). *A Violent Network: Gender-Based Violence Against Palestinian Women in Virtual Space.* Kvinna till Kvinna in Cooperation with 7amleh-The Arab Center for the Advancement of Social Media.

OHCHR. (1993. *Declaration on the Elimination of Violence Against Women.* Accessed from https://www.ohchr.org/en/professionalinterest/pages/violenceagainstwomen.aspx

Palestinian Central Bureau of Statistics. (2019). *Preliminary Results of the Violence Survey in the Palestinian Society.* Ramallah – Palestine. Accessed from http://www.pcbs.gov.ps/Downloads/book2480.pdf

PEN America. (2013, December 3). The Rise of Digital Repression: Interactive Infographic. *Global Investigative Journalist Network.* Accessed April 29, 2021, from https://gijn.org/2013/12/03/the-rise-of-digital-repression-interactive-infographic/

Schectman, J. & Bing, C. (2019). American Hackers Helped UAE Spy on Al Jazeera Chairman, BBC Host. *Reuters.* Accessed April 29, 2021, from https://www.reuters.com/investigates/special-report/usa-raven-media/

Shaalan, H., & Agencies. (2019, September 12). Three Family Members Charged in Killing of Palestinian Woman. *Ynet News.* Accessed April 29, 2021, from https://www.ynetnews.com/articles/0,7340,L-5587436,00.html

Sinclair, J., Jacka, E., & Cunningham, S. (1996). *New Patterns in Global Television: Peripheral Vision.* Oxford University Press.

Sreberny, A. (2015). Women's Digital Activism in a Changing Middle East. *International Journal Middle East Studies, 47*(02), 357–361.

Sreberny, A. (2018). Women's Digital Activism: Making Change in the Middle East. In M. Zayani (Ed.), *Digital Middle East: State and Society in the Information Age.* Oxford University Press. https://doi.org/10.1093/oso/9780190859329.003.0005

Tal3at - حرة نساء حر وطن. (n.d.). *In Facebook [Facebook page].* Accessed April 29, 2021, from https://m.facebook.com/%D9%88%D8%B7%D9%86-%D8%AD%D8%B1-%D9%86%D8%B3%D8%A7%D8%A1-%D8%AD%D8%B1%D8%A9-2703156423090972/

Taraki, L. (1991). The Development of Political Consciousness Among Palestinians in the Occupied Territories, 1967-1987. In J. Nassar & R. Heackock (Eds.), *Intifada: Palestine at the Crossroads.* Praeger Publishers.

The Guardian. (2013). *Dozens of Saudi Arabian Women Drive Cars on Day of Protest Against Ban.* Accessed April 29, 2021, from https://www.theguardian.com/world/2013/oct/26/saudi-arabia-woman-driving-car-ban

The World Bank. (2019). *Population, Total – Arab World (Dataset). DataBank.* Accessed April 29, 2021, from https://data.worldbank.org/indicator/SP.POP.TOTL?locations=1A

UN Women. (2020a). *COVID-19 and Ending Violence Against Women and Girls. Issue Brief.* Accessed from https://www.unwomen.org/-/media/headquarters/attachments/sections/library/publications/2020/issue-brief-covid-19-and-ending-violence-against-women-and-girls-en.pdf?la=en&vs=5006

UN Women. (2020b). *Gender-Responsive Measures to Combat COVID-19 Urgently Needed to Preserve and Advance Tunisia's Progress on Women's Rights, Warns UN Women. Press Release.* Accessed from https://arabstates.unwomen.org/en/news/stories/2020/06/press-release-tunisia-urgent-need-for-gender-responsive-measures-to-combat-covid-19

United Nations Department of Economic and Social Affairs - UNDESA. (2015). *The World's Women 2015: Trends and Statistics.* Accessed from https://unstats.un.org/unsd/gender/downloads/worldswomen2015_report.pdf

United Nations Department of Economic and Social Affairs - UNDESA. (2020). *The World's Women 2020: Trends and Statistics.* Accessed from https://worlds-women-2020-data-undesa.hub.arcgis.com/app/50dd1b2d6167437693178836261522e6

World Economic Forum. (2018). *The Global Gender Gap Report 2018.* Accessed April 29, 2021, from http://www3.weforum.org/docs/WEF_GGGR_2018.pdf

World Health Organization. (2013). *Global and Regional Estimates of Violence Against Women: Prevalence and Health Effects of Intimate Partner Violence and Non-Partner Sexual Violence. Situation Report.* Accessed April 29, 2021, from https://www.who.int/publications/i/item/9789241564625

Uncovering Narratives: The Effects of Algerian Media and Legal System on Survivors of Domestic Violence

Sarah Benamara

INTRODUCTION

In October 2020, in the midst of the Covid-19 pandemic, the death of 19-year-old Chaima sparked outrage across Algeria and led women to defy the mandated quarantine to protest her brutal murder. To many, this case highlighted the lack of protection that women receive from law enforcement against abusers and harassers. Chaima knew her murderer and had reported him to the police four years earlier for attempted rape, but no action had been taken. As a protester from Algiers states, "Women file a complaint and wait three or four years for it to be resolved and for a judgment to be rendered. These are unacceptable conditions. Algeria is for Algerian men *and* women" (BBC, 2020). Protesters turned online too, creating a movement with the hashtags #WeLostOneOfUs and #JesuisChaima (I am Chaima) (The Africa Report, 2021) to voice their opinions on Algeria's restrictive family law.

The outrage was exacerbated in the following year when a chain of femicide cases took place including the murder of Warda Hafadh and TV journalist Tinehinane Laceb by their respective husbands. These cases, which gained wide media coverage (Hammadi, 2021), sparked anti-violence campaigns and the birth of the *Femicides Algerie*, a running database of women who were

S. Benamara (✉)
Boston, MA, USA
e-mail: benamasa@bc.edu

L. H. Skalli, N. Eltantawy (eds.), *The Palgrave Handbook of Gender, Media and Communication in the Middle East and North Africa*, https://doi.org/10.1007/978-3-031-11980-4_19

335

murdered by domestic abusers. Even after the 2015 criminalization of domestic violence, many highlighted the massive shortcomings of the law. Ultimately, those outraged by the murders called for harsher sentencing for abusers and a complete abrogation of the current family law, to be replaced with a more encompassing definition of domestic abuse and protection of women against all forms of violence.

The Algerian Penal Code was modified in 2015 to grant additional protection from domestic abuse. Articles 263–276 of the penal code provide a definition of torture, list the type of people capable of domestic abuse by the different articles, and outline the related financial and imprisonment punishments. Article 263 states, "Torture is understood to mean any act by which pain or grave suffering, whether physical or mental, are intentionally inflicted on a person regardless of the motive." The remaining articles are very thorough in listing different types of physical harm such as mutilation, amputation, deprivation of the use of a limb, permanent illness, castration, and blindness. They further assign different sentences according to the duration of the harm inflicted on the survivors. If the harm inflicted is remediable within 15 days, the abuser's sentence will not exceed 10 years. If the inflicted harm lasts longer than 15 days, then the sentence can be up to 20 years, or in the case of murder, a life sentence in prison. While mental pain is referenced in Article 263, it is neither defined nor mentioned again in the remaining articles. Lastly, the section mentions the type of people who can be held liable for domestic abuse. The articles reference domestic violence perpetrators as ascendents, descendants, a spouse, a successor, or a guardian(s) (Algerian Penal Code, 2015). This classification neglects to account for abuse done by siblings or non-biologically related people living in the same household. These aforementioned gaps and the arbitrary classification of sentencing based on the healing of physical wounds, while helpful in establishing the general notion that domestic abuse should be punishable, leaves too much ambiguity and ultimately too much vulnerability for survivors of abuse.

The gaps in the legislation translate to larger concerns in the process of implementing the laws. The process of proving domestic violence is arbitrary and often leaves women more vulnerable, as it requires long wait times and multiple doctor visits before a case can be brought forward. Unfortunately, in the public media discussion of whether these laws are beneficial for society, many people seem unaware of the arduous process of filing a domestic violence case, and the likelihood of winning one.

The media have undeniably impacted some of the change occurring in the MENA region and elsewhere. However, they do not always positively contribute to solving the issues at hand. In Algeria's case, while there recently has been a lot of activism on social media against domestic violence, traditional media have promoted dialogue likely to support domestic violence or denounce the need for domestic violence laws. After the 2015 domestic violence law was implemented, the two largest national channels, Ennahar TV and Echourouk, conducted street interviews on the reactions to the law. "A real Algerian woman, if her husband doesn't beat her sometimes, she'll feel ... he's not manly," exclaimed an Algerian woman to a television reporter on the national network Ennahar TV (2015). This woman, along with other female and male interviewees, asserted that being beaten "normally" is acceptable, and even sometimes necessary in marriage. Those opposed to the law expressed their support for the survivors and voiced their frustration with the legal system. One woman stated that "we hear of these rights but do not see them" (Ennahar, 2016). In terms of representation of opinion, both channels used a 50/50 approach, where 50% of the opinions were for the new reforms, and 50% were against it. This approach does not enable the viewers to understand the popular opinion among those interviewed. Traditional media enabled abuse sympathizers to voice their opinions and spread misinformation about the new law, such as claiming that there will be a spike in domestic violence cases and that women will "abuse the system" to steal their husband's money, the most important perspective, that of the domestic violence survivor, has largely been left out of the discourse. Considering that more than 92% of Algerians consume traditional and social media, it is worth looking at these platforms to see how they affect, if at all, the actions of domestic violence survivors (BBC Media Action Data Portal, 2018). The split public opinion on domestic violence, the ambiguous laws and arduous process of filing for domestic abuse, and the lack of legal precedence can all contribute to a survivor's perception of security and acceptance in society.

This chapter aims to explore the understudied phenomenon of media discourse on women in Algerian society and its effects on the likelihood of women engaging with the more reformed legal system. To gather first-hand data on the topic, the author interviewed domestic violence survivors from different socio-economic and geographic backgrounds in Algiers, Oran, and Ain Sefra. The interviews serve to understand the resources available to survivors, their experiences within the legal system, and their understanding of how media affected their decision to leave or remain in their abusive relationships. This chapter also examines different reports on media and domestic violence in Algeria produced through independent research (including National Council on Human Rights).

Perceptions of Domestic Violence in Algerian Media

When the domestic violence law emerged in March 2015, over 30 articles were published in popular newspapers in the cities of Oran and Algiers. Vibrant discourse emerged that mainly supported or criticized the new law, and many denounced the Islamist party for criticizing the law and claiming that it would "break up the family unit" (Middle East Eye, 2015). On March 3, *Le Quotidien d'Oran* wrote, "There are no foreign pressures that have brought about this law, which was imposed through the religious and cultural beliefs of the society." It further elaborated by stating, "To not take the necessary measures to stop domestic violence against women is contrary to the principles of Sharia

Law, which protects women and their dignity" (2015). A month later, on April 7, *El Moudjahid* supported the claims of the Minister Mounia Meslem, who stated that this was a great first step in changing the mentalities toward this taboo. While people sung the praises of the new law, many expressed in print media its shortcomings, with some going so far as to call this new provision in the Family Code a "double edged law" (Benhamed, 2015). On March 4, *El Watan*, which was highly critical of the clauses in place, stated, "Nevertheless, this law is not enough to protect women against assault and battery, forced marriages, rape, and the many intimidations they suffer from their families" (2015). *Liberté*, on February 5, asserted that "this bill, which the government keeps on presenting as a protection for women, is, in fact, only a decoy to those who are very fragile and prone to the pressures they will inevitably suffer from family and society" (Hamma, 2015).

The Islamist party came under fire by all these newspapers for being explicitly opposed to the implementation of this law. Some reiterated the Prime Minister's belief that this law stems from Sharia law, as the protection of women is an important pillar. They then went on to mock and criticize the Islamist party, which claimed that this law would "disrupt family order." *El Watan* even titled one of their articles on the new law, "When the Conservative-Islamists are Against Women" (Tlemcani, 2015). These newspapers approached the issue from different angles to highlight journalists' reactions to the law and discuss concerns about its implementation in society. Newspaper articles on domestic violence also provided great opportunities for journalists to elaborate on the rights this law brought to women, and in many cases even outlined the prison sentences that abusers could face for different violations. Overall, newspapers overwhelmingly sided with domestic abuse survivors and urged the betterment of women's rights in the country.

Today, the average citizen consumes visual media instead of print. About 99% of Algerian households have at least one television set. With increasing access to social media, they are relying more on satellite and online platforms to quickly access news. In all my discussions surrounding domestic violence, people alluded only to television and social media for examples of debates or discussions on domestic violence. While mainstream papers are known to appeal to the more liberal educated crowd in Algeria, television is not. It is consumed by all citizens, and therefore aims to be "representative." Ennahar TV, founded in 2012, promoted itself as a news outlet that would represent the average citizen and promote freedom of speech. It did this by attempting to display the diversity of opinions people hold, mainly through street interviews. It is difficult to assess this diversity of opinions on a complex issue such as domestic violence, especially in the absence of recent national surveys. Although television is popular among Algerians, it is misleading to rely on the opinions they present as a gauge of where public opinion stands on domestic violence. Many of the responses sought from citizens interviewed for television are either *strongly* for or *strongly* against domestic violence as well as the 2015 law.

On one of the segments on Ennahar TV, the host interviewed people in a popular shopping mall about the new domestic violence law. The voices selected for television were polarized. Those against the new law had passionate reactions stating that men have become more disadvantaged than women, especially because women will use this tool frivolously against their husbands. Another man asserted that "it is true that we are against domestic violence towards women, but for someone to be sent to jail for 20 years if he makes a *mistake*—that is a prejudice against men" (Ennahar TV, 2015). The segment, true to its mission to be "representative" of diverse perspectives, did feature opinions that were strongly for the law, showing men and women of varying ages praising the law for empowering women and stopping the abuse many endure.

The same polarized opinions were reproduced by the other leading national network, Echourouk TV (2016). However, media's most harmful contribution to domestic violence in the nation has been depriving domestic violence survivors from having a voice on a national platform. The absence of their voices and perspectives perpetuates misunderstanding and stereotypes about what a domestically abused woman looks like.

DOMESTIC VIOLENCE IN MENA

Domestic abuse, as defined by the United Nations, is "a pattern of behavior in any relationship that is used to gain or maintain power and control over an intimate partner." They further define the types of abuse that exist such as physical, sexual, emotional, economic, and psychological. Examples of methods used to inflict abuse are "any behaviors that frighten, intimidate, terrorize, manipulate, hurt, humiliate, blame, injure, or wound someone." Domestic abuse can happen to anyone regardless of gender, race, age, sexual orientation, religion, socio-economic background, or education level (United Nations, n.d.).

On a global scale, approximately 27% have reported experiencing intimate partner violence, according to a World Health Organization report (2021). Based on figures from the Arab Barometer, one of the most reliable public opinion research entities in the MENA region, domestic violence percentages fall within this same range. Based on the last cycle of research which was administered from 2018 to 2019, domestic violence is reported to be relatively high in Yemen (26%), Morocco (25%), Egypt (23%), Sudan (22%), and Algeria (21%), while self-reported rates are lower in Libya (7%) and Jordan, Lebanon, and Tunisia (6% each) (Arab Barometer, 2020). However, statistics are likely much higher both globally and in the MENA region. The incidence is often underreported for a variety of reasons, including social pressures, fear of reprisal, shame, and absence of support network for the survivors. While the real numbers remain difficult to capture, the MENA region continues to lack the infrastructure to support domestic violence survivors.

At the legal level, more than half of MENA countries have yet to pass legislature that protects women from domestic violence (Congressional Research

Service, 2020). The countries that did adopt legislature for this issue did so only within the past six years, raising questions about whether there has been sufficient time to enact any change. Structurally, there are numerous unresolved issues, including lack of shelters for victims, legal knowledge on a survivor's rights (if their country has passed legislation protecting women), and lack of validation from officials such as police (Arab Barometer, 2020). Given these obstacles, it is much more difficult for a woman to leave an abusive relationship in the MENA region than in other parts of the world. Therefore, women are more likely to turn to relatives (with a high likelihood that they will turn to a female relative) before institutions. It is difficult to say whether this is a result of a cultural preference to resolve familial problems without institutional interference, whether survivors do not trust the system, or whether they are just unaware of the resources and options that exist. Regardless, this shows that more effort is required to develop adequate resources and encourage survivors to seek out and utilize these resources (Arab Barometer, 2020).

As in other parts of MENA, social media has become a platform that Algerian activists are using to raise awareness about gender-based issues. Much of the discourse and subsequently public attention has been women's experiences with sexual assault and harassment in the public sphere. After the #Metoo movement rose to prominence in the United States, similar efforts emerged across the Middle East. The #Notyourhabibti (Palestine), #AnaKaman (Egypt), #EnaZeda (Tunisia), #Masaktach (I will not be silent—Morocco), and #LanAsket (I will not be silent—Kuwait) movements are some of the few campaigns that swept their respective countries and allowed women an opportunity to share their experiences and voice their concerns (Middle East Eye, 2020). A few institutions in the region also took part in launching their own campaigns to encourage women to participate in public discourse. The UN Regional Gender Group in the Arab States started the #Ismaani (Hear Me) campaign to "galvanize women and men from the region to shine a spotlight on cases of sexual harassment and abuse" (UN Women, 2019). The American University of Beirut launched #Mesh_Besita (It's not ok) to spark debate on the lack of sexual harassment protections in the MENA region (AUB, 2021). All these movements have been praised as an effective method to raise awareness of the pervasive and prevalent sexual harassment in MENA.

Unfortunately, media coverage and academic research surrounding domestic violence remain significantly scarce. Public discourse surrounding domestic violence usually takes place after a domestic violence murder takes place. After a short lapse of time, however, attention to the subject matter dies out. Given the limited scholarship on domestic violence in Algeria, this chapter aims to fill this void by gathering first-hand accounts from domestic violence survivors in Algeria to better understand the complexities of the phenomenon.

BACKGROUND ON INTERVIEWEES

The people who arguably hold the most knowledge on the social and legal realities of domestic violence are the survivors themselves, and specifically, those who had the opportunity to pursue a legal way out of their situation. The interviewees in this chapter have been contacted through women's shelters in Algiers or through my own personal and social network. The personal in-depth interviews were conducted between December 2017 and February 2018.

Each interviewee was subsequently assigned an identifying marker for the purposes of confidentiality.

In the interviews, the women were asked to describe their abusive relationships, the steps they took to leave these relationships, the actors that played a role in assisting them, their divorce and/or legal experiences, their knowledge on how domestic violence is discussed in the media, and whether they were cognizant of or acted according to media discussions of domestic violence.

The women interviewed came from a range of ages, where the youngest woman was in her late 20s, while the oldest woman was in her early 50s. All the women had children with their abusive ex-husbands. Most of the women interviewed resided in women's shelters at the time they were spoken to. One woman was at *SOS Femmes en détresse* (SOS Women in Distress), which is a UNHCR-supported shelter in Algiers, which aims to help women who are fleeing horrendous domestic environments. They are a transitional shelter that houses women and provides financial and psychological support, while trying to reintegrate them into society by helping them find permanent housing and a job. Four women were at *Dar el Hassana*, a government-run shelter that provides refuge for homeless women. This shelter, unlike SOS, houses a variety of women, including orphans, those with mental illnesses, and domestic violence survivors. It is the largest shelter in Algeria and houses on average of 50 women at any time. Women are allowed to enter and exit as they please, and many make use of the psychiatric services there. This highly secure shelter maintains a great reputation even within the international community, as many nations donate annually to it through their embassies.

The last two women interviewed came from higher socio-economic backgrounds (within the middle class) whose stories were referred to me through relatives. While women in the shelter come from lower socio-economic statuses, those who did not need the shelters provide a perspective on the barriers women of a higher social status still face.

Despite the increasing numbers of domestic violence survivors in the nation, jumping from approximately 1000 reported in 2012 (CIDEFF, 2012 report) to approximately 4000 in 2017 (Human Rights Watch, 2017), the frequency of women at shelters and in court has remained the same since the end of the Civil War (Dar el Hassana and SOS Women in Distress, 2017). Due to the scarcity of shelters and the confidentiality of court cases, it is difficult to find female domestic violence survivors and therefore gather a more representative view of the experiences they face. Nonetheless, this chapter highlights the opinions of the few women who were able to come forth with their stories and underscores the commonalities among the women's experiences and recommendations. The stories outlined in this chapter can be viewed as relative successes, where success is defined as their removal from these abusive environments. Each woman's story varies, yet these women from different parts of Algeria and of different backgrounds hold similar opinions and *recommendations* for helping other domestic violence survivors.

REALITY OF DOMESTIC VIOLENCE IN ALGERIA

The media, mainly television, has continued to circulate information about domestic violence and its survivors that are riddled with misconceptions. Many Algerians interviewed on Television segments have stated that this law is "discriminatory towards men" and will entice women to "search for minor reasons to take their husbands to court" (Ennahar TV, 2015). What is not acknowledged in the media, however, is the long, tedious, and often dangerous process that domestic violence survivors need to endure in order to bring their cases to court. The women who shared their stories in these interviews had a more holistic view about the reality of domestic violence in Algeria, and their experiences led them to disagree with mainstream sentiments. Many of them explained that the legal "protection" granted to them does not extend beyond the walls of the courts. The reality for domestic violence survivors is made of a series of barriers when they seek legal protection. As one interviewee stated, "you hear of all these custody and divorce rights, but when you enter the terrain then it's a whole other reality" (2A, 2017).

The pre-trial process alone can be enough to discourage women from filing for divorce. Women, who were in abusive relationships anywhere from 5 to 20 years, had to successfully navigate the pre-trial process, oftentimes with little financial and emotional support. Seeking a legal way out of their relationships was also dangerous, as their husbands sought to physically confine them or control their lives. Once they did find an opportunity to leave, the women found themselves with little professional assistance and no accommodations that would allow them to be removed from their abusive partners before and during the trial. In addition, the institutions they sought for help were mired in corruption. Those stemming from a higher socio-economic background were usually able to overcome these challenges, while others obtained divorce with great difficulty or fled to women's shelters.

The first step in filing for divorce based on domestic violence is obtaining a 14-day certificate from a court doctor. This report is a crucial piece of evidence in court since it details the injuries they endured for the past 14 days of the report. But as one woman pointed out "14 days does not encompass all that I have experienced in my relationship" (2B, 2017). As these certificates only document one incident out of the many that they experienced, it misses out on the full extent of physical and *mental* abuse the survivors face. This certificate is then taken to the police, where it will ideally be processed, then produce a court date. In smaller towns, however, finding a court doctor is not guaranteed. One woman from Biskra, who escaped her house one night after getting severely beaten by her drunken husband, was unable to find a court doctor for a few days.

She instead filled out a descriptive abuse report at the hospital, which was refused at the local police station because it did not come from the doctor. When she finally received the 14-day certificate and filed it at the police station, she encountered a friend of her husband who tried to shame her for following through with the process. She recalls, "He tried to discourage me by saying 'No this is your husband, you shouldn't put him in prison. This time he'll straighten out.' So, I returned to him" (2B, 2017). Upon hearing that she filed a complaint against him, her husband told her that if she did not retract that claim, he would have his friends testify against her in court. Specifically, the friend's testimony would accuse her of prostitution and adultery, which would separate her from her three children. She explained, "I was afraid. I was afraid about my reputation, my parents, and my children—if he makes a claim like this in court, I would lose my children. So I stopped the investigation. I cried as I signed the documents to stop the investigation. If the officials were doing their jobs properly, they would have known that I was reluctantly dropping the charges" (2B, 2017).

Another woman from Algiers faced a similar situation. She sought divorce after 19 years of marriage due to her husband's abuse and infidelity. A mother to four children, she was physically and mentally abused by her husband, and later by her oldest son. The first time she sought help, her husband convinced her children to talk her out of it. "He closed all my doors," she said, in response to her life before her divorce (2C, 2017).

Survivors of emotional abuse find seeking a divorce to be immensely more difficult, as emotional abuse is not always recognized as abuse in court. When a professor at a University in Mascara brought her case forward for emotional abuse, she found it difficult to prove. Her husband was unemployed but controlled all her finances: "He was living on my money" (2D, 2017). The longer she stayed with him the more she realized that his controlling tendencies and mental abuse made her feel insecure and submissive. She explained that her high level of education did not make her immune to abuse. Yet, it was the reason she stayed in the marriage because others did not believe she was being emotionally abused. "With him I was degraded, because he made me think I was less than him, even though I was more educated than him. What I endured was discreet violence. Like how a drop of water on rock does nothing at first, but eventually erodes and breaks it" (2D, 2017). She eventually brought a divorce case forward on the basis of infidelity and neglect because she knew she had no evidence for abuse that was not physical. Her divorce was granted, but she lost her house in the process.

The false notion often circulated by the media that women will find it easier to file for divorce and therefore abuse this new Algerian law is very misguided. As one interviewee remarked, "you can't do it unless you are absolutely certain you want to leave and have someplace to go. That's why so many people stay silent because they have no place to go" (2A, 2017). Domestic abuse survivors navigate a flawed system to get the rights they deserve and are promised under the Algerian law. By requiring time-consuming processes before the trial, survivors are left to return and defend themselves against their abusers, leaving them in exceptionally unsafe environments.

Once women successfully overcome the pre-trial barriers, they face the trial process, where their full rights are not necessarily guaranteed. As lawyers are not required for trial, women often forgo or are unaware of the additional reparations they can legally obtain. Under law, if a man is to blame for divorce (for infidelity, abuse, or any other unacceptable conduct) then he is required to provide financial assistance and reasonable housing accommodations to his wife after the divorce. All the divorced women interviewed stated that their ex-husbands defaulted on their payments after the divorce. While defaulting on payments can result in more fees and possible jail time, they still got away with it by rigging the system. They typically pay one month then use their proof of payment in court to argue that they were consistently making their payments. The courts accept this and the women eventually give up on getting their payments.

While trial can lead to losses for the women, it is important to highlight the advantages that it can give them as well. With a 14-day certificate and witnesses, women are almost always granted divorce by the judges. Judges are widely known for siding with survivors and use trial as an opportunity to denounce the behavior of the abusive partners. In the case of the woman from Ain Sefra, recounting her abuse in court gained her the sympathy of the judge, and ultimately allowed her the custody of her daughter. She sought a divorce after her husband took her daughter away from her for weeks. The woman initially sought the help of the police but was turned away because they would not consider this an abduction case. This drove her to court for a divorce, with the goal of getting primary custody of her daughter. In court, she divorced him on the basis of infidelity, as well as physical and emotional abuse. The judge eventually granted her this, and publicly offered his support. He told her "Put yourself first and think about your own future. If you think this man will get better we can close the case, but if you don't think he will change then I will grant you this divorce" (2A, 2017). To this the woman responded, "I have lived through the period of terrorist [Algerian Civil War] for ten years, and these past five years brought me back to those days. I do not feel safe in my own home" (2A, 2017). The woman was granted a divorce and custody of her daughter. The husband, unsatisfied with this decision, took the case to the district court where the judge decided to uphold the verdict from the lower court.

When another woman from Ghilisane took her husband to court for domestic violence, the husband profusely tried to deny the claim. The judge, however, told him that there was undeniable proof of the abuse because of the certificate, police statement, and the witnesses who came forward. He immediately granted the woman a divorce. While the system has its flaws, these authority figures that are upholding the new laws are important for maintaining the legitimacy of the process. Many of the judges expressed sympathy, and the women recall that the trial made them feel validated in their experiences and decision to leave.

Throughout these interviews, many of the women emphasized that their families and neighbors had the most impactful effect on their situations. Upon finding out about the abuse, family members urged the women to leave, and took steps to ensure they could. The woman from Biskra recalled her neighbors' efforts to help her after she spotted her with swollen eyes and bruises on her body. She took her to the hospital and paid for her medication. Later, the woman's uncle drove her and her children to Algiers. The woman decided to leave her husband when her efforts to get a divorce failed. Her family was unable to financially support her, so her uncle later brought her to a domestic abuse shelter, where she would be assisted with housing and employment (2B, 2017).

In the interview, the woman from Ain Sefra outwardly stated, "It is because of the help of my parents that I am standing here" (2A, 2017). After her parents discovered the abuse, her father urged her to divorce her husband, and convinced her to move to her parent's house with her daughter. Her mother and father supported her financially and provided childcare when she decided to work. Other women highlighted the support they received from their neighbors inside and outside of court.

The woman from Ghilisane detailed her last night being abused by her husband before she sought help, and mentioned that without her neighbors, the police would never have been called. They heard the abuse, contacted the police, and later physically prevented her husband from getting close to her while the police were on their way. One of her neighbors, a doctor, was able to treat her injuries immediately and even issued her a 14-day certificate that night. Many of them later testified against him in court (2E, 2017). The woman from Algiers, who faced abuse from her oldest son after her husband left, was saved by her passing neighbor. She described her neighbor as a highly respected "man of religion," who entered her home and physically restrained the son. The woman also spoke about an anonymous neighbor who would leave groceries on her doorstep as a gesture of support (2C, 2017). For many of the women, the decision and ability to divorce or leave their husbands came only after the support of neighbors and family. They navigated the legal process, corruption, and lack of resources and accommodations with the support of social networks.

These stories of survival offer more insight into some of the paths taken by women who endured domestic abuse. Differences in socio-economic status, resource availability, and emotional support all contributed to the different paths and outcomes that the women had. There are some common threads, however. All the women interviewed recounted an abusive incident that made them realize that they had to leave the relationship they were in. They all mention neighbors or family members who supported them and assisted them in seeking legal protection or leaving. For those who successfully went through trial, they all mention the ways in which their ex-husbands were able to default on their payments without consequences. These common experiences highlight flaws in the system and give accurate insights on domestic survivors' reality, which is ignored by the mainstream media. Leaving these stories out of the media also helps to perpetuate misconceptions on what a survivor should look like.

Given the disparity between the reality of domestic violence and media discourses on the topic, the reactions of many women were unsurprising. All but one of the survivors had seen segments on television that discussed domestic violence. The indifference toward the media discourse manifested itself in different ways. The woman from Biskra, who had seen media segments, said that the discourse did not concern her when she was in an abusive relationship. She did not have the privilege to care, and was focused instead on finding ways to safely leave her husband and take her children with her. She instead opted to shift the conversation to discuss legal measures and resources that could be put in place that would support and benefit all survivors who left abusive relationships (2B, 2017). The woman from Ghilisane, who had also seen some television segments on domestic violence, did not care for what people had to say. After quoting some of the opinions toward survivors, I asked her if the negative or positive opinions that she had heard on television mattered to her, especially when she was still in the abusive relationship. She dismissed the question, and instead rhetorically asked, "But why would anyone ever hit someone?" (2E, 2017).

The woman from Algiers first expressed hope about the new law but said that her experiences soon altered her attitude. She stated, "When I first heard of the changes that took place in the Family Code, that's when I thought that the Algerian woman could start to breathe." Shortly after the emergence of the law, however, she was proved wrong and relied solely on her own experiences in an abusive relationship and during the court process to inform her opinions on domestic violence (2C, 2017). Her own experiences trumped those in the media and led her to become dismissive of the media discourse. Similarly, the woman from Mascara, who was the only one who did not see the segments, said that she did not care for the portrayal of domestic violence survivors in the media because she does not believe anything that the media puts out (2D, 2017).

The only direct effect the media had was on the woman from Ain Sefra. She explained how an advertisement for a women's organization that aired during a popular television news segment gave her hope. This organization, based out of Tlemcen, Algeria, was composed of women who were fighting for custody of their children. The women in the televised segment came from diverse backgrounds; a few of the members also included female lawyers, who offered their assistance for free on these cases. After seeing this organization, the woman reached out for help. She said that while she did not get a reply from the organization, she also did not adamantly pursue that option because she was able to hire an attorney and rely mostly on herself. When asked about the debates on the media segments, the woman from Ain Sefra expressed the same indifference as the aforementioned women. "You see people on TV talking. Even before the law came out, people talked about this on television, but I'm telling you that in practice it is not the same as it is portrayed. It's all talk in the media, but in reality, their [legal protection] is nothing" (2A, 2017).

Yet, the women's indifference to media discourse on domestic violence is very informative and indicative of a much larger issue. It reveals that the women have lost trust in the media and cannot rely on it as they seek protection in their lives. According to these women, neither condemning nor supportive statements toward survivors lead to any change in the outcome of the survivor's life.

Ultimately, the research gathered here shows that the aforementioned media articles and TV segments that voiced opposition to the domestic violence law and sought to slander the intentions of domestic violence survivors had little effect on the interviewed survivors. Many of the women expressed that in the midst of their violent relationships, the media and society's perceptions of domestic violence mattered little to them. They were preoccupied with the immediate and urgent need to remove themselves and their children from the abusive living situation. What they have previously seen on television or print was unimportant and did not affect their decisions to come forward with their abuse in court. Instead, their decisions were influenced by the state of their own well-being, their financial status, knowledge about existing resources, and the presence of loved ones who reached out to help them.

If the media had any effect on the survivors, it was surprisingly a positive one. Some of the women mention leveraging the media to find resources and communities that later helped them escape their abusive relationships. The media, specifically television and social media, enabled some of the women to find shelters, allowed them to contact people who provide resources for domestic violence survivors, and enabled them to find support groups. More recently, the media launched awareness campaigns and gave women and allies a new platform to do their own reporting, lobbying, and denouncing of violence against women. These efforts have grown substantially in the last few years. Platforms such as *Femicides Algerie* and the willingness of reporters to draw attention to the violence that women endure shows an active shift in support for survivors and a growing vocal intolerance for abuse. The case of Algeria shows us that the media can be a powerful tool to be utilized by domestic violence survivors.

References

UN Women | Arab States. (2019). *A Hashtag for Women from the Arab States.* Accessed from https://arabstates.unwomen.org/en/news/stories/2019/2/a-hashtag-for-women-from-the-arab-states

Alayli, A. (2020, June 1). *Domestic Violence and Arab Women's False Choice During COVID-19.* Arab Barometer. Accessed from https://www.arabbarometer.org/2020/06/domestic-violence-and-arab-womens-false-choice-during-covid-19-pandemic/

Middle East Eye. (2015, March 6). *Algeria Passes Law Banning Domestic Violence Against Women*. News. Accessed from http://www.middleeasteye.net/news/algeria-passes-law-banning-domestic-violence-against-women-596359589

Algerian Penal Code. Secrétariat Général du Gouvernement. (2015). Accessed from https://resourceequity.org/record/2720-algeria-penal-code/

Allouche, Y. (2020, July 13). *'Silent Pandemic': How Women in the Middle East and North Africa Are Threatened Online*. Middle East Eye. Accessed from https://www.middleeasteye.net/news/women-middle-east-north-africa-threats-harassment-abuse-sexism-online

American University of Beirut. (2021). *Sexual Harassment Campaign: B3DA #mesh_basita for Law No. 205*. Accessed from https://www.aub.edu.lb/cibl/news/Pages/SexualHarassmentCampaignB3daMeshBasitaforLawNo205.aspx

Benhamed, W. (2015, April 7). Un Prix national de lutte contre la violence à l'égard des femmes: Il sera institutionnalisé le 25 novembre de chaque annee. *El Moudjahid*.

BBC News. (2020, October 8). *Chaïma: Algeria Women Protest Over Teen's Rape and Murder*. n.d. Accessed from https://www.bbc.com/news/world-africa-54465180

Echourouk TV. (2016, March). الأحمر.

Ennahar TV. (2015, March 10). صرّح جبا: آراء الشارع الجزائري حول حماية المرأة من العنف. Accessed from https://www.youtube.com/watch?v=kQR6MFGuNE0&app=desktop

Ennahar TV. (2016, November 26). صرّح جبا: العنف ضد المرأة ف الجزائر.. إلى أين ؟ Accessed from https://www.youtube.com/watch?v=7cUYsbALSxo

F.B. (2015, March 4). *Violence à l'égard des femmes: Que cesse l'impunité!*. El Watan.

Ghanem, D. (2021, March 19). *Covid-19 Has EXACERBATED Algeria's Femicide Problem*. The Africa Report.com. Accessed from https://www.theafricareport.com/73396/covid-19-has-exacerbated-algerias-femicide-problem/

Hamma, N. (2015, February 5). *La Clause qui fausse tout. Liberté*.

Hammadi, S. (2021). La haine de la femme, *Libertie-Algerie*, https://www.liberte-algerie.com/actualite/la-haine-de-la-femme-353457

Le Quotidien d'Oran. (2015, March 3). *Projet de loi sur la protection de la femme contre la violence: Louh nie toute pression étrangère*.

The Algerian Media Landscape. (2018). Summary of key results from a nationwide survey, *BBC Media Action Data Portal*, https://dataportal.bbcmediaaction.org/site/assets/uploads/2020/03/Algeria-Survey-key-results-FINAL.pdf

Tlemcani, S. (2015, March 30). *Lorsque les islamo-conservateurs s'allient contre la femme*. El Watan.

United Nations. (n.d.). *What Is Domestic Abuse?* United Nations. Accessed from https://www.un.org/en/coronavirus/what-is-domestic-abuse

United States, Congress, Congressional Research Service, et al. (2020, November 27). *Women in the Middle East and North Africa: Issues for Congress, Congressional Research Service*. Accessed from https://crsreports.congress.gov/

"Your Destiny is to Stay with Him". (2017). State Response to Domestic Violence in Algeria, *Human Rights Watch*, https://www.hrw.org/report/2017/04/23/your-destiny-stay-him/state-response-domestic-violence-algeria

World Health Organization. (2021, March 9). *Violence Against Women*. World Health Organization. Accessed from https://www.who.int/news-room/fact-sheets/detail/violence-against-women

INTERVIEWS

2A. (2017, December 29). *Woman from Ain Sefra in Ain Sefra, Algeria.*
2B. (2017, December 21). *Woman from Biskra in Algiers, Algeria.*
2C. (2017, December 24). *Woman from Algiers, in Algiers, Algeria.*
2D. (2018, February 14). *Woman from Mascara, in Mascara, Algeria.*
2E. (2017, December 24). *Woman from Ghilisane, in Algiers, Algeria.*

CHAPTER 20

Egyptian Women's Cyberactivism: The Ongoing Battle Against Sexual Harassment and Violence

Nahed Eltantawy

For decades, Egypt has remained one of the main MENA countries where gender-based violence and sexual harassment have plagued the country as a central social and legal problem (Sadek, 2016). A 2015 study conducted by the United Nations Population Fund, the National Council for Women, and the Central Agency for Public Mobilization and Statistics revealed that, on an annual basis, approximately 7.8 million Egyptian women are victims[1] of all forms of violence by a male partner, relative, or strangers in public places (UNFPA website). A UN study in 2013 found out that over 99.3 percent of all Egyptian females surveyed admitted to experiencing some form of sexual harassment in their lifetime (El-Deeb, 2013). Yet, Egyptian women's active participation in the Arab uprisings of 2011 has encouraged many women, who

---

[1] Throughout the chapter, the term victim will be used to refer to women in both case studies instead of survivors. According to RAINN (Rape, Abuse & Incest National Network), the term victim is used within the criminal justice system to describe someone who has experienced a crime. The word "serves also as a status that provides certain rights under the law," and does not in any way imply weakness, assume guilt or assign blame" (RAINN, 2015). The case studies analyzed in this chapter both involve victims of sexual assault in criminal justice cases, which is why the term "victim" was applied throughout.

N. Eltantawy (✉)
Nido R. Qubein School of Communication, High Point University,
High Point, NC, USA
e-mail: neltanta@highpoint.edu

L. H. Skalli, N. Eltantawy (eds.), *The Palgrave Handbook of Gender,
Media and Communication in the Middle East and North Africa*,
https://doi.org/10.1007/978-3-031-11980-4_20

once accepted such humiliating and painful experiences with shame and self-blame, to increasingly find their voice and stand up to their harassers and abusers (Eltantawy, 2017; Ibrahim, 2019). Today, a growing number of female activists continue to combat violence and sexual harassment via social media activism as well as other forms of activism.

This chapter applies a thematic analysis of posts on the Instagram account of the Egyptian feminist activist group, Assault Police, between July 1 and November 9, 2021. Assault Police was created in July 2020 to expose the multiple sexual harassment and sexual assault crimes of 21-year-old Egyptian, Ahmed Bassam Zaki. Assault Police has since posted on several sexual assault and violence incidents against women, leading to widespread national and international media attention, and encouraging many victims of Zaki and other male perpetrators to share their stories. The chapter will analyze these social media discourses relating to Assault Police, utilizing collective action and empowerment theories, in order to develop a deeper understanding of Egyptian women's cyber activism as well as the challenges that women continue to face in their ongoing battle against gender-based violence and sexual harassment.

GENDER-BASED VIOLENCE AND CYBERACTIVISM IN MENA

Hashtag activism in the MENA region is not a new phenomenon. Since the 2010/11 Arab Uprisings, protestors in Tunisia, Egypt, Yemen, Syria, and elsewhere in the Middle East and North Africa region heavily relied on hashtags to spread updates and capture regime abuses on Facebook and Twitter (#Arabspring, Eltantawy & Wiest (2011). For the women in the region, cyberactivism has since been a major tool of empowerment and advocacy (Basch-Harod, 2019; Hurley, 2021; Tazi & Oumlil, 2020). As Annabelle Sreberny suggested in 2015, for MENA women, "it is reasonable to suggest that access to the Internet, the development of social media platforms in English and Arabic, and the growing popular awareness of change have produced a more conducive environment for women's political activities and thus for a general enlargement of what counts as the 'sphere of the political'" (p. 357). Skalli (2014) describes these social media activists as "a young generation of young brave, articulate and assertive women prepared to fight for their dignity against all odds," using all forms of media and all communication platforms accessible (p. 256). Muslim women worldwide have utilized social media to participate in the Twitter #MosqueMeToo movement, where they shared their personal experiences with sexual violence in a religious setting (Guha et al., 2019). Women have been utilizing social media to fight for more rights, such as Saudi Arabian women's struggles over the years to obtain the right to drive and to eliminate the male-guardianship system (Altoaimy, 2018; Doaiji, 2017) and Egyptian women's battle against sexual harassment (Allam, 2018; Cochrane et al., 2019; Eltantawy, 2018).

Theoretical Framework: Collective Action and Empowerment

The themes identified in this thematic analysis largely focus on collective action and empowerment, two concepts that have been visible and significant in MENA over the last two decades. The Arab uprisings introduced to the region collective action by various groups and organizations via social media and digital technologies (Eltantawy & Wiest, 2011; Moussa, 2017; Steinert-Threlkeld, 2017). It is also during this period that women and other minorities experienced empowerment as they contributed to the protests and voiced demands, side by side with men (Alvi, 2015; Fecteau, 2017).

According to Cloud (2021), collective action theory refers to "any form of organized social or political act carried about by a group of people in order to address their needs" (Cloud, 2021, para. 2). Examples of collective action include protests, voting, or any other examples where a group works to address some form of struggle. "Virtually any form of organized group effort to address some form of inequality may be considered collective action. Many of the examples are struggles for equal rights, such as women's suffrage or the struggle for gay and lesbian rights" (Cloud, 2021, para. 2). Not all collective action results in positive change, according to Seo (2019). "While some collective actions have resulted in influencing public opinion or policies, there are many other examples of collective actions failing to bring about change" (Seo, 2019, p. 2753).

Empowerment theory refers to the process by which marginalized individuals can gain control over their lives and valued resources (Perkins & Zimmerman, 1995). Empowerment literature reveals that empowerment can be viewed as both a process and an outcome (Cattaneo & Goodman, 2015). The empowerment process incorporates any actions, activities, or steps taken by an individual, whereas the outcome refers to the level of empowerment an individual achieves (Jupp et al., 2010; Nachshen, 2005). This leads to empowerment and action-taking. Empowerment literature shows that there are different forms of empowerment that include: the *power to*, as in the power to take action, the *power with*, which is collective empowerment to become part of a community, as well as the *power from within*, as in self-empowerment and the power to gain control (Batliwala, 1994; Calvès, 2009; Kabeer, 1994; Rowlands, 1995; Zimmerman, 2000).

In the case of Egypt, digital technologies and social media have contributed to collective action and empowerment, both in positive and negative ways. On the positive side, digital technologies have enabled minorities and activists to rely on social media to create collective virtual spaces to plan protests, dispute concerns, or even simply vent regime frustrations (Eltantawy & Wiest, 2011; Fischer, 2013; Hafez, 2016). In terms of empowerment, social media has demonstrated how virtual campaigns can lead to youth and women's empowerment, as it offers these groups a voice and gives them a space to make demands that is often lacking in the public sphere (Miladi, 2016; Shata & Seelig, 2021).

On the other hand, following the Arab uprisings and the positive focus on social media's impact, a resurgence in cyber authoritarianism gradually swept the Middle East and Egypt. This included tighter online security, massive arrests of activists and prominent revolutionaries and social media personalities, and the introduction of new cyberlaws that aimed to control and monitor cyberspace (Deibert, 2015; Kassem, 2020; Salib, 2016). In terms of empowerment, just as social media can empower youth and women, it can also be a detriment and put them in the public eye and bring too much attention to them, which, in turn, can put their lives in danger. Scholars argue that social media platforms "are complex and contradictory spaces for feminisms" that allow women to form new and creative methods of activism. Yet, these same platforms are where women face bullying, harassment, and even violent threats, when they often attempt to raise awareness on certain issues (Locke et al., 2018). Digital technologies and social media, therefore, are complex, and it is for this reason that collective action and empowerment are a significant focus of this chapter. While recognizing the great impact of social media for grouping and bringing minorities together and enabling them to formulate and organize and empower, it is also important to realize that social media and digital technologies have their drawbacks and their risks, and are likely, in some cases, to bring negative attention to activists, and even cause threats.

Egypt, Sexual Harassment, and Gender-Based Violence

Sexual harassment in its various forms has plagued Egyptian society for decades (Sadek, 2016). Several reports released within the last 15 years confirm that Egypt is one of the worst countries in MENA when it comes to sexual harassment (Sadler, 2019). The Egyptian Center for Women's Right's released a 2008 report stating that 83 percent of Egyptian women and 98 percent of foreign women in Egypt confirm experiencing sexual harassment in Egypt (Hassan & Shoukry, 2008). A 2013 UN-funded study confirmed that 99.3 percent of women and girls in Egypt experienced sexual harassment. Paul Amar (2011) explains how Egyptian authorities used sexual harassment as a tool against women. For years, Egyptian security forces utilized *baltagiya* (thugs) to cause chaos during male-dominated protests in Egypt to confirm the Orientalist stereotype of the savage Arab male. Yet, when educated, professional women began to participate in such protests, security forces had to change their tactics. This is when they began to resort to sexual harassment as a tool to police and terrorize female protestors.

> The state responded by shifting its aims from using demonized masculinity in order to delegitimize political opposition to using state-imposed sexual aggression in order to undermine class respectability. Women who protested were sexualized and had their respectability wiped out: not just by innuendo and accusation, but literally, by sexually assaulting them, in public and by arresting them as

prostitutes, registering them in court records and press accounts as sex criminals and then raping and sexually torturing them in jail. (Amar, 2011, p. 309)

Gender-based violence continues to be a prevalent problem in Egypt that impacts girls and women across the country. This involves various forms of violence, including physical, psychological, and sexual violence (Magdy & Zaki, 2021). A United Nations Fund for Population Activities (UNFPA) 2015 survey revealed that over 7.8 million Egyptian women experience some form of violence annually from a spouse, fiancé, family, or strangers in public places (unfpa.org). Over the past 10 years or so, multiple incidents of sexual violence against women have forced the media and the government to pay more attention to gender-based violence in Egypt and to the existing laws for those who assault women (Sadek, 2016). The women of Egypt have been fighting this violence for years. In fact, according to Skalli (2014), their battle started in the 1990s with the establishment of women's rights groups, such as the Egyptian Center for Human Rights.

EGYPT AND CYBERACTIVISM

Egyptian women have been active on social media for years. Cyberactivism has been a main outlet for women who often find their urgent problems and demands excluded from the public sphere. These young cyberactivists, "not only disrupt this patriarchal logic, but also puncture the silence that normalizes sexual harassment in the quotidian of their lives" (Skalli, 2014, p. 248). Egyptian women had been utilizing social media to fight sexual harassment years before the MeToo movement took off in the United States and the rest of the world (Ibrahim, 2019). One of activists' oldest and most prominent forms of resistance to sexual harassment is HarassMap, a website created by a group of volunteers in 2010 that with a crowdsourcing map identifies geographic areas where incidents of harassment take place. "The impact of the organization has resulted in international recognition, awards and support" (Cochrane et al., 2019, p. 402). Following the Egyptian Revolution of 2011, where female activists were as prominent and as active online and offline as their male counterparts, the organizational power of women's movements in Egypt grants them significant cultural attention (Zakarria, 2019). Several anti-harassment movements were formed post-2011 that utilized online and offline spaces, with the goal of spreading awareness on the sexual harassment pandemic and documenting violations. Among the most prominent initiatives were OpAntiSH, Tahrir Bodyguard, I Saw Harassment, and Imprint Movement (Zakarria, 2019). Through these collective efforts, activists are gradually able to change society's perception of sexual harassment from a taboo topic that is off limits, to one that is openly discussed, and one where female victims are no longer ashamed or afraid to share their experiences or fight their assailants (Eltantawy, 2018; Skalli, 2014; Zakarria, 2019).

METHODOLOGY AND THEORETICAL FRAMEWORK

This chapter applies a thematic analysis to examine Instagram posts by the activist group, Assault Police (@assaultpolice) with the goal of determining the dominant themes in these posts. Assault Police posts have impacted many Egyptian women and have led to multiple arrests and charges for men accused of sexual assault. The analysis specifically focuses on posts relating to two case studies, the case of Ahmed Bassam Zaki and the Fairmont Hotel rape. In April 2021, Zaki confessed to the assault and blackmailing of six women, including minors, and was sentenced to over eight years in prison for several crimes, including the blackmail and sexual assault of three minors ("Egypt: court hands man 8-year jail term in #MeToo case," 2021). Victim accounts that helped bring the case to court were collected in July 2020 by @AssaultPolice via their Instagram account ("Egypt: court hands man 8-year jail term in #MeToo case," 2021).

The Fairmont Hotel rape was a crime that took place in 2014, when a then-18-year-old female claimed that she was drugged and gang-raped by a group of affluent men in the luxury Fairmont Nile Hotel. The victim said the men wrote their initials on her body, filmed the rape, and then circulated the video among their close friends. According to @assaultpolice, there were other victims of similar assaults by the same offenders. The case resurfaced in July 2020 when @assaultpolice called on all women who were victims of these perpetrators to share their stories ("Setback to Egypt's #MeToo movement as rape witnesses reportedly charged," 2020).

@Assaultpolice is an Instagram activism account that was launched in July 2020 by a 23-year-old philosophy student, Nadeen Ashraf. Ashraf was responsible for the initial activism and attention the account brought to the major assault cases of Zaki and the Fairmont Hotel rape. Yet, according to Ashraf, since these major cases, the group has expanded and is now run by herself, along with several volunteers who collectively work to raise awareness on sexual assault, search for new cases, translate posts, create graphics, and connect with families, schools, and organizations interested in raising awareness and helping curb sexual assault and sexual harassment in Egypt (@Assaultpolice post August 2020). Today the Instagram account has over 346,000 followers.

Data Collection

The chapter analyzes @Assaultpolice Instagram posts from July 1, 2020, to November 9, 2021, which is the period that both incidents were national stories in Egypt. This is also the entire period that @assaultpolice has been actively posting on Instagram. Since then, the group has not posted any additional posts. Only posts relating to these two specific cases, the Zaki and Fairmont Hotel cases, were analyzed for this chapter. All posts on the site were examined, but only posts related to these two specific cases were analyzed. A total of 25 posts on Zaki and 17 posts for the Fairmont Hotel case were analyzed.

Analysis of Case Studies

In analyzing these case studies, a thematic discourse analysis was applied. Caulfield (2022) defines thematic analysis as a qualitative method of analyzing data that allows researchers to identify common themes, topics, or patterns that reappear in the data. Thematic analysis, which was originally developed in psychology research (Braun & Clarke, 2006), allows for the deductive or inductive development of themes. In this chapter, themes were inductively created based on a close analysis of the data sample. In analyzing the Ahmed Bassam Zaki case study, four themes were identified: raising awareness, exposure and evidence, support and empowerment, and call to action. In the Fairmont Hotel rape case, three themes were identified: raising awareness, support and empowerment, and call to action.

Ahmed Bassam Zaki Themes: In analyzing posts on Zaki's case, four dominant themes were identified: raising awareness, evidence, encouragement and empowerment, and call to action. Some posts fell under more than one of these themes, as they offered encouragement and a call to action, or they offered evidence but also words of encouragement, etc.

Raising Awareness: These were informative posts to raise awareness and explain the details of each incident. Other awareness posts explained issues relating to the case or warned followers or victims from taking specific actions that could impact the legal case against Zaki.

The very first post for the group on July 1, 2020, is a graphic headlined, "Who is Ahmed Bassam Zaki? A Sexual Predator." The graphic offers a bio on Zaki and the assault crimes he committed against various victims and how he has been allowed to do so without any punishment for several years.

In another post, @assaultpolice explain how posting personal information on Zaki's family or physically harming Zaki can hinder the legal case that would bring justice to all his victims (Fig. 20.1). The group explains in simple and gentle language to its followers that the best way to seek justice is through evidence collection and the courts, and not through physical attacks on Zaki or personal attacks on his family via social media.

An example of a post that combines call to action and empowerment is a July 4th, 2020, post, where the group announced that Zaki has been arrested (Fig. 20.2). On the one hand, the graphic includes a colorful drawing of diverse colored arms holding onto each other, with the words "stronger together" written above. This is a simple yet empowering message, as it demonstrates how this collective of activists and victims were able to get Zaki arrested in record time. The post also warns that this may not be enough to keep Zaki behind bars. The group makes it clear that more concrete evidence is needed to make sure "this monster" is not released (@assault police, July 4, 2020).

Exposure and Evidence: The posts under this theme helped expose criminal action and/or wrongdoing at the hands of those in power who are supposed to seek justice. These posts, on the one hand, helped the investigation by offering concrete evidence against Zaki, such as audio or written accounts from

Ahmed Bassam Zaki is under arrest.
They WILL let him go free if women don't start coming forward.
Everything I've been working on for ASSAULT POLICE was to reach this
point... But for this monster to he prosecuted and go to prison, we HAVE
to all take action together.

IF YOU HAVE BEEN SEXUALLY HARASSED OR ASSAULTED BY AHMED BASSAM ZAKI. NOW IS THE TIME TO COME FORWARD.

WE HAVE TO STOP HIM FROM DOING THIS TO OTHER GIRLS IN THE
FUTURE.

1. You will remain anonymous to the public.

2. You do NOT have to provide concrete
evidence: This is the investigative police's job.
If you are telling the truth, they WILL prove it.
Don't be scared if you deleted your chats.

3. WE HAVE SECURED ONE OF THE BEST
LAWYERS IN THE COUNTRY. YOU ARE IN
GOOD HANDS!

email **reportabz@gmail.com** & we will jump start the
process with our lawyer immediately.

DO NOT EMAIL IF YOU ARE NOT WILLING TO COME FORWARD TESTIFY WITH OUR LAWYER

Fig. 20.1 @Assaultpolice, July 3, 2020

Zaki's countless victims. On the other hand, it exposed and embarrassed those
who failed to bring justice and forced society or social media followers to no
longer be silent and to start talking openly about assault. It gives the victims
the green light to talk in a safe space and be heard, knowing that they are
not alone.

One telling example includes an anonymous victim of Zaki who sent @
assaultpolice an audio recording of Zaki blackmailing her to perform sexual
acts or he would send her family nude photos of her. In the post, @assaultpolice
state that these photos could be photoshopped.

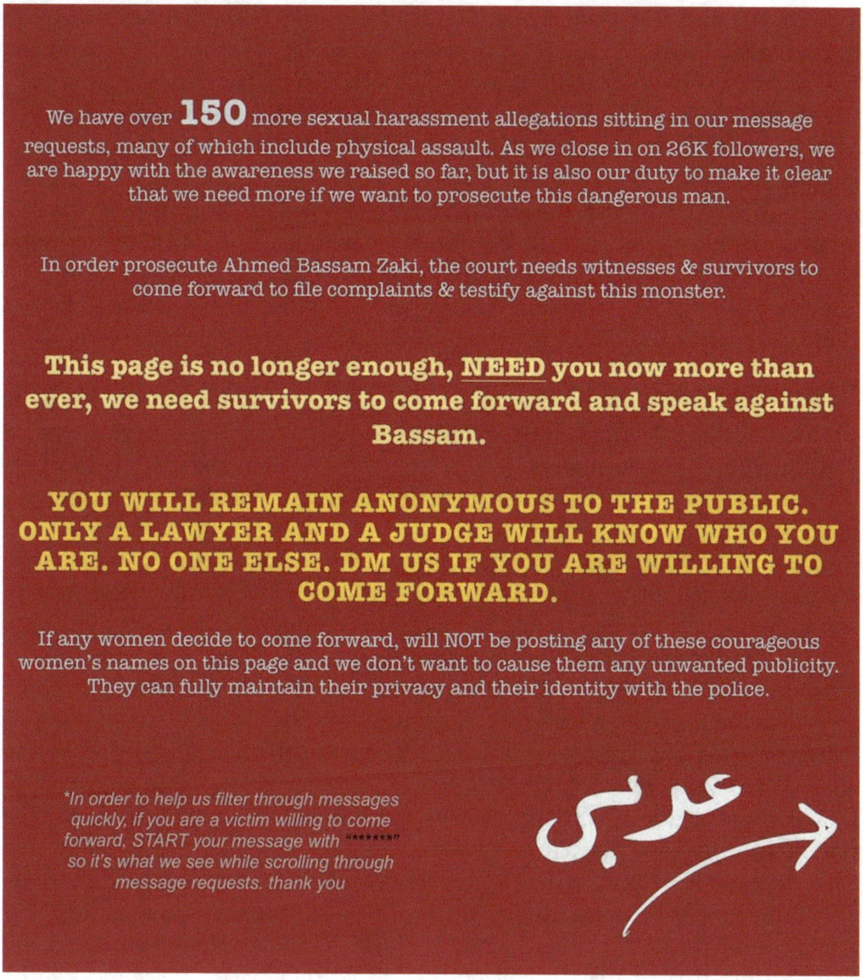

We have over **150** more sexual harassment allegations sitting in our message requests, many of which include physical assault. As we close in on 26K followers, we are happy with the awareness we raised so far, but it is also our duty to make it clear that we need more if we want to prosecute this dangerous man.

In order prosecute Ahmed Bassam Zaki, the court needs witnesses & survivors to come forward to file complaints & testify against this monster.

This page is no longer enough, <u>NEED</u> you now more than ever, we need survivors to come forward and speak against Bassam.

YOU WILL REMAIN ANONYMOUS TO THE PUBLIC. ONLY A LAWYER AND A JUDGE WILL KNOW WHO YOU ARE. NO ONE ELSE. DM US IF YOU ARE WILLING TO COME FORWARD.

If any women decide to come forward, will NOT be posting any of these courageous women's names on this page and we don't want to cause them any unwanted publicity. They can fully maintain their privacy and their identity with the police.

*In order to help us filter through messages quickly, if you are a victim willing to come forward, START your message with "******" so it's what we see while scrolling through message requests. thank you

عربي

Fig. 20.2 @Assault Police July 4, 2020

An example of a post that exposed wrongdoing by those in power was a July 9, 2021, post titled, "How educational institutions enabled sexual harassment in the case of Ahmed Bassam Zaki." The post includes quotes from some of his victims or friends of victims who complained to administrators at affluent educational institutions that Zaki attended. The post reads, "The educational institutions he attended played a huge role in silencing young girls and even concerned boys who were worried about their female classmates. Young students united to compile evidence and report Ahmed's behavior to the adults they felt would protect them, only to be ignored and dismissed" (@assaultpolice, July 9, 2021).

Support and Empowerment: These were mostly posts that offer words of encouragement to the brave women who are speaking up on such a difficult and sensitive issue in a conservative society where such taboo topics are usually not discussed in public. It is also telling victims that they are not alone and that they have an army of supportive activists, fellow victims, and others who are supporting them.

In a July 1, 2020 post, the group added a detailed message by one of Zaki's victims, recounting her assault by him. With the post, the group typed words of encouragement to their audience, saying: "The chilling story of one of Ahmed Bassam Zaki's victims. It's very painful to read, but it needs to be out there. To everyone submitting their stories, you are incredibly brave. We WILL get justice for you."

This post combines the themes of evidence and empowerment. It clearly details one victim's assault by Zaki and explains how this story must be heard and we can no longer be silent. It also empowers women and commends them for speaking up, promising them that they will be rewarded with justice for such bravery.

A July 5th, 2020, post, included quotes from a few of Zaki's victims who testified in front of a judge. The women explained how they went in very scared but were surprised to find the judge very supportive and encouraging.

One woman was quoted in the post as saying, "Grateful that I was able to make my case with this person. I want to assure all girls that decide to come forward, that they are making the right decision and that there is nothing to worry about. I can't believe this is happening. For the first time I don't t feel alone" (@assaultpolice, July 5, 2020).

The post includes a second woman's account following her testimony. The post is a positive one that aims to comfort hesitant or scared victims and to tell them they are not alone. It is also encouraging as it demonstrates how supportive authorities have been, thus giving women faith and hope that they will attain justice through the legal system. Finally, it allows Zaki's victims to feel that they are part of a larger collective and that they have a voice and can be heard. The victims said, "for the first time I don't feel alone." This is empowering and comforting for her and others, who can take this message to mean they have a collective of activists and supporters who are listening and standing up with them against their perpetrator.

One of the most significant posts that fall under the empowerment theme was on July 8, 2020, when the group posted an adjustment to sexual assault laws in Egypt, offering more protection for the identity of victims in sexual assault cases. The post is titled, "We have officially amended the law ☺" and the group wrote, "THIS IS HOW POWERFUL YOUR VOICES ARE. KEEP SHARING. KEEP TALKING ABOUT THIS. CHANGE IS COMING!" (@assaultpolice, July 8, 2020).

In another post on July 11, 2020, the group posted a graphic with international news headlines on the case of Zaki's arrest, thanks to Egyptian women and the #MeToo movement. @Assaultpolice wrote, "We did this & we are not slowing down!" (@assaultpolice, July 11, 2020).

In the above examples, women are empowered and made to feel proud of their collective action. The group demonstrates to their followers that together, we can, and we do bring about change.

Call to Action: These were posts that invited women to come forward and speak up or called on authorities to take the appropriate action against the assaulters.

One example is a July 1, 2020, post, which offers a third victim's account of her sexual assault and attack at the hands of Zaki. @Assaultpolice explain how the victim was forced to move away from her family and friends to get as far away as possible from Zaki. They thank her for her bravery for coming forward, then call on others to do the same: "You are not alone, come forward, together we can expose this person & bring him to justice" (@Assaultpolice, July 1, 2020).

In another graphic, on July 2nd, 2020, @assaultpolice announce that they have collected accounts and evidence from over 150 victims of Zaki. But they call on all of his victims to come forward (Fig. 20.3). They explain that the only way to bring justice is through the collective evidence and accounts of all his victims combined.

Fairmont Hotel Rape themes: In this case study, @assaultpolice revived interest in the 2014 rape because they believed that the assault video was still circulating. They invited followers to come forward with any information or evidence. They also confirmed that there were six sexual assault victims in total who experienced gang rapes by these affluent perpetrators. It is important to note here that @assaultpolice faced death threats during their campaign against the perpetrators, which forced the account administrators to deactivate the account from late July to mid-August of 2020 (Allinson, 2020). This impacted the number of posts released by @assaultpolice on the Fairmont Hotel rape case. So, overall, there were fewer posts to analyze, compared to the Zaki case. The main dominant themes identified in the Fairmont case are: raising awareness, supports and empowerment, and call to action. The evidence theme was not identified here, and this could be because @assaultpolice was asking victims to email evidence to the group's designated email account or to email them directly to the specific authorities investigating the Fairmont case.

Raising Awareness: The posts under this theme aim to alert followers of urgent updates and explain details relevant to the Fairmont Hotel rape case. In one post, dated August 14, 2020, @assaultpolice alert followers that a recording is being circulated on Instagram of the Fairmont victim and her lawyer. These Instagram accounts threatened to reveal the victim's identity and spread negative rumors about her. The post from @assaultpolice warned followers of this, calling on them to protect the victim's identity. "If you hear her name, do not spread it. Protect her" (@assaultpolice, August 14, 2020). Another post on August 24th, 2020, informs followers that the Egyptian prosecutor issued an arrest warrant for the perpetrators of the Fairmont Hotel rape.

Fig. 20.3 @assaultpolice, July 2, 2020

In another update post, dated March 15, 2021, @assaultpolice informs followers that authorities released one of the Fairmont Rape perpetrators who were arrested six months earlier. "There are no words to be said," the post reads (@assaultpolice, March 15, 2021). A following @assaultpolice post from March 19, 2021, offers followers an update on all six perpetrators in the Fairmont Hotel rape case (Fig. 20.4). They inform followers that one of the accused was released, three were in prison, and two had escaped out of the country.

Then, on May 11, 2021, @assaultpolice announced that the public prosecutor ordered the release of all alleged rapists in the Fairmont case due to lack of evidence. The group simply added the hashtag #JusticefortheFairmont survivor to show how unfair and unjust this decision was.

The final post from @assaultpolice on the Fairmont case, which also happens to be the group's last post to this date, came on November 9, 2021, almost nine months after the Fairmont case investigations started. The post announced that three of the perpetrators received sentences, ranging from 15 years to life

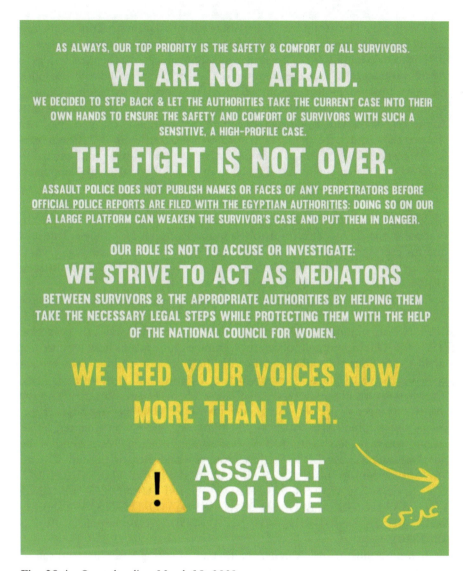

Fig. 20.4 @assaultpolice, March 19, 2021

for taking part in another gang rape in the North Coast (@assaultpolice November 9, 2021).

Support and Empowerment: Posts that fit under this theme focused on spreading/sharing positive updates and words of encouragement. These posts demonstrate to victims who came forward and to @assaultfollowers that justice will be served. An August 16th, 2020, post shows a video graphic demonstrating @assaultpolice's support to victims of the Fairmont Hotel perpetrators. The graphic explains how these victims were being threatened with exposing their identities. The group used the hashtag #Iamthefairmontvictim to encourage all followers to show support for the victims by claiming that they too were victims to help empower these women and show unity with them, as well as to create confusion and keep the identities of the actual victims hidden. The video graphic displayed multiple examples from the social media community of women who were already joining this social media campaign to protect victims. At the end of the video, @assaultpolice writes, "the night you raped her, you violated thousands of women. She is not alone. #Arrestthemnow" (@assaultpolice August 16, 2020). This post empowers victims and displays to them and to those who threaten them that they have an army of social media supporters who are standing up to protect them. The post also has a call to action at the end, addressing authorities and asking them to arrest these perpetrators now.

A September 24th, 2020, post, for example, includes a graphic with photos of three of the six perpetrators involved in the Fairmont Hotel rape. This post informs everyone that these men have been arrested, and the message accompanying the post reads, "THIS IS A BIG VICTORY, JUSTICE IS BEING SERVED" (@assaultpolice, September 24th, 2020).

Call to Action: Similar to posts on the Zaki case, posts under this theme encouraged followers to act. An example would be a post from August 13, 2020, which combines the themes, raising awareness and call to action (Fig. 20.5). Here, @assaultpolice post a graphic that explains how they are not afraid to continue this fight or justice for the Fairmont victims. They explain how they strive to act as mediators between victims and authorities to make sure victims take all the necessary legal steps. Then, they end the post with the words, "we need your voices now more than ever." The message that accompanies the graphic starts with, "If you think one share won't matter, let us remind you that this account had 0 followers a month ago." At the end of the post, @assaultpolice calls on various groups, whose help is needed. "Be an active participant in this historical movement: SUPPORT THE FAIRMONT GIRLS. GEN-Z TWITTER, WE NEED YOU. INFLUENCERS, WE NEED YOU. TV HOSTS, WE NEED YOU. MEDIA OUTLETS, WE NEED YOU. PUBLIC FIGURES, WE NEED YOU" (@assaultpolice, August 13, 2020).

In another post that falls under the themes of raising awareness and call to action, @assaultpolice, on March 19, 2021, offer a detailed timeline with all updates on the Fairmont Hotel rape case (Fig. 20.6). At the end of the post, in red, the post calls on followers to report any updates to a government-designated email.

Conclusion: It is fair to claim that in the two case studies addressed here, collective action by followers of @assaultpolice contributed to the impact the group had on the two sexual assault cases addressed in this chapter. In the case of Bassam Ahmed Zaki, collective action prompted victims to come forward and speak up about their assault incidents; it prompted them to contact authorities and hand in all audio/video or social media evidence that would help put Zaki behind bars. In the Fairmont Hotel rape case, collective action helped

TIMELINE OF FAIRMONT GANG RAPE CRIME

2014

— 25/04: Fairmont Crime committed & filmed.

— 2014-2020: Video circulates widely.

2020

— 25/07: Incident breaks to public via social media.

— 29/07: Assault Police Account deactivated due to threats.

— 29/07: GangRapistsOfCairo Account begins reporting on case.

— 30/07: Evidence submitted to NCW & PPO.

— 05/08: NCW announces receiving an official report.

— 13/08: Someone voice records private conversations between survivor and her lawyer.

— 15/08: Threats to expose Fairmont survivor's identity.

Fig. 20.5 @assaultpolice, August 13, 2020

protected the anonymity of the assault victim when @assaultpolice launched the #Iamthefairmontvictim campaign. It is also what prompted victims to come forward and submit evidence via email to @assaultpolice or to authorities, again, helping the victims attain justice.

Cattaneo and Goodman (2015) discuss the centrality of empowerment to the field of domestic violence, describing the Empowerment Process Model, a model that identifies characteristics of empowerment and the empowerment-building process for persons who lack power. The authors discuss how this model assists the powerless to set personal goals to increase their personal power, take specific action, and make progress toward reaching these goals. In defining empowerment as it relates to domestic violence victims, Kasturirangan (2008) explains that victims of domestic abuse often begin the process of empowerment with a sense of powerlessness, "characterized by internalized devaluation and limited access to resources" (p. 1467). Victims at this point engage in self-blame and overall sense of defeat or helpless acceptance of their current situation (Kasturirangan, 2008; Watts & Abdul-Adil, 1997).

TIMELINE OF FAIRMONT GANG RAPE CRIME

— 24/08: PPO issues arrest warrant for all accused rapists.

— 29/08: Witnesses detained.

— 30/08: Accused rapist Omar Hafez arrested.

— 01/09: Smear campaign begins against witnesses & survivor.

— 24/09: Three accused rapists arrested in Beirut.

2021

— 06/01: Witnesses released.

— 24/02: PPO issues urgent call for Fairmont video.

— 15/03: Accused rapist Khaled Mahmoud is released on bail (50k).

— **#JusticeForTheFairmontSurvivor**

Fig. 20.6 @assaultpolice, March 19, 2021

Kasturirangan (2008) argues that empowerment programs that aim to help victims should focus on developing "critical awareness," which is an understanding of a person's current circumstances and barriers, which can then help victims create and achieve goals to overcome these barriers (Kasturirangan, 2008; Kieffer, 1984; Watts et al., 1999; Zimmerman, 2000). The Instagram posts analyzed in this chapter demonstrate how @assaultpolice assisted victims who felt voiceless and powerless, set justice as a goal, and worked to help these victims attain this goal. In other words, @assaultpolice applied the Empowerment Process Model discussed by Cattaneo and Goodman (2015) and helped victims both understand their status quo and the barriers that needed to be broken to achieve justice. They explained that the only way to achieve justice was by telling their stories and by talking to authorities so that the perpetrators can be tried and punished.

Additionally, this study arguably reveals the empowerment process potential of @assaultpolice's Instagram account to target violence against women. With regards to the empowerment process, the study demonstrates how @assaultpolice utilized social media to inform, explain, and spread awareness on the two sexual assault cases by continuously providing facts, updates to create awareness among their followers on the two cases and on what needs to be done to help the victims attain justice. The chapter also shows how @assaultpolice offered self-encouragement and confidence to both the victims as well as users reading about the two assault cases. @assaultpolice enabled the victims to believe in their abilities and to take control. As one of Zaki's victims confirmed, it was the first time she felt heard. Thus, one can argue that this leads to an empowerment outcome. The @assaultpolice posts also encouraged non-victims to take a stance to support the victims of these assault cases. This was clear in the Fairmont Hotel rape case when the #Iamthefairmontvictim campaign was launched to protect the identity of the real victim. Additionally, witnessing victims speak up about their experiences empowered other assault victims by giving them a space to voice opinion and share their personal stories. During the time @assaultpolice covered the two assault cases, there was a gradual trickle of sexual assault stories from several followers of the group. In fact, a few of the stories shared were from men who had experienced sexual harassment or assault and were speaking about it for the first time (@asaultpolice, July 18, 2020). Afshar (1998) argues that if empowerment is to be meaningful, it must enable those "who are most affected by violence to find ways of articulating the pain and accommodate the slow process of healing" (p. 3). The posts analyzed in this study demonstrate how empowerment via @assaultpolice offered users the facts and resources to build awareness and the tools and means to assist victims of abuse to recover and survive such pain.

The examples analyzed in this chapter demonstrate Egyptian women's unrelenting resistance to sexual assault via cyberactivism. The posts by @assaultpolice that focus on the two cases of Ahmed Bassam Zaki and the Fairmont Hotel rape demonstrate how women empower each other to break the traditional barriers of shame that have long been tied to cases of sexual harassment and assault, to take collective action, to tell their stories and be heard, and to fight for justice.

Yet, this chapter also demonstrates that while Egyptian women have accomplished a lot, thanks to their years of hard work, determination, and thanks to digital technologies and social media, society and gender bias still hinder their progress in many ways. We witnessed this in the Fairmont Hotel rape case with how the victim's anonymity was threatened and @assaultpolice had to appeal to its mass supporters to make sure the victim remained anonymous. This once again demonstrates the paradoxes of digital technologies that can all at once contribute to and hinder empowerment and collective action.

REFERENCES

"Egypt: court hands man 8 year jail term in #MeToo case" (2021, April 11). *Deutsche Welle*. Accessed from https://www.dw.com/en/egypt-court-hands-man-8-year-jail-term-in-metoo-case/a-57163302

"Gender-based violence". (2015). *UNFPA.org*. Accessed from https://egypt.unfpa. org/en/node/22540#:~:text=Gender%2DBased%20Violence%20in%20 Egypt&text=Other%20data%20available%20for%20domestic,since%20the%20 age%20of%2015

Afshar, H. (1998). Introduction: Women and Empowerment – Some Illustrative Studies. In H. Afshar (Ed.), *Women and Empowerment: Illustrations from the Third World* (pp. 1–10). St. Martin's Press.

Allam, N. (2018). Activism Amid Disappointment: Women's Groups and the Politics of Hope in Egypt. *Middle East Law and Governance, 10*(3), 291–316.

Allinson, T. (2020, September 17). *Setback to Egypt's #MeToo Movement as Rape Witnesses Reportedly Charged*. Deutsche Welle. Accessed from https://www.dw. com/en/setback-to-egypts-metoo-movement-as-rape-witnesses-reportedly-charged/a-54958956

Altoaimy, L. (2018). Driving Change on Twitter: A Corpus-Assisted Discourse Analysis of the Twitter Debates on the Saudi Ban on Women Driving. *Social Sciences, 7*(5), 81.

Alvi, H. (2015). Women's Rights Movements in the 'Arab Spring': Major Victories or Failures for Human Rights? *Journal of International Women's Studies, 16*(3), 294–318.

Amar, P. (2011). Turning the Gendered Politics of the Security State Inside Out? Charging the Police with Sexual Harassment in Egypt. *International Feminist Journal of Politics, 13*(3), 299–328.

Ashraf, N. (2020, August 20). *@Assaultpolice Instagram post*. Accessed from https://www.instagram.com/p/CEH5ipwlcpw/?utm_source=ig_embed&ig_rid=88858e9f-b997-457f-9448-000ba71846ee

Basch-Harod, H. (2019). #MeToo and the history of "Hashtag Feminism" in the MENA region. IEMed: Mediterranean yearbook, (2019), 306–310. Retrieved from: https://www.iemed.org/publication/metoo-and-thehistory-of-hashtag-feminism-in-the-mena-region/

Batliwala, S. (1994). *Women's Empowerment in South Asia: Concepts and Practices*. Asian South Pacific Bureau of Adult Education.

Braun, V., & Clarke, V. (2006). Using Thematic Analysis in Psychology. *Qualitative Research in Psychology, 3*(2), 77–101.

Calvès, A. E. (2009). Empowerment: The History of a Key Concept in Contemporary Development Discourse. *Revue Tiers Monde, 4*, 735–749.

Cattaneo, L. B., & Goodman, L. A. (2015). What Is Empowerment Anyway? A Model for Domestic Violence Practice, Research, and Evaluation. *Psychology of Violence, 5*(1), 84.

Caulfield, J. (2022). How to Do Thematic Analysis: A Step-by-Step Guide & Examples. *Scribbr*. Accessed from https://www.scribbr.com/methodology/thematic-analysis/

Cloud, D. (2021). *Collective Action: Definition, Theory, Logic & Problems*. Study.com. Accessed from https://study.com/academy/lesson/collective-action-definition-theory-logic-problems.html

Cochrane, L., Zeid, Y., & Sharif, R. (2019, May 24). Mapping Anti-Sexual Harassment and Changing Social Norms in Egypt. *ACME: An International Journal for Critical*

Geographies, 18(2). Accessed February 7, 2022, from https://www.acme-journal. org/index.php/acme/article/view/1745

Deibert, R. (2015). Authoritarianism Goes Global: Cyberspace Under Siege. *Journal of Democracy, 26*(3), 64–78.

Doaiji, N. (2017). Saudi Women's Online Activism: One Year of the "I Am My Own Guardian" Campaign. *The Arab Gulf States Institute in Washington Issue Paper #11.* Accessed from https://agsiw.org/saudi-womens-online-activism-one-year-guardian-campaign/

El-Deeb, B. (2013). *Study on Ways and Methods to Eliminate Sexual Harassment in Egypt.* UN Women. Accessed from https://web.law.columbia.edu/sites/default/files/microsites/gender-sexuality/un_womensexual-harassment-study-egypt-final-en.pdf

Eltantawy, N. (Ed.). (2017). *Women and Media in the Middle East: From Veiling to Blogging.* Taylor & Francis.

Eltantawy, N. (2018). I Am Untouchable! Egyptian Women's War Against Sexual Harassment. In S. Khamis & A. Mili (Eds.), *Arab Women's Activism and Socio-Political Transformation: Unfinished Gendered Revolutions* (pp. 131–148). Palgrave Macmillan.

Eltantawy, N., & Wiest, J. B. (2011). Social Media in the Egyptian Revolution: Reconsidering Resource Mobilization Theory. *International Journal of Communication, 5,* 1207–1224.

Fecteau, A. (2017). The Arab Spring and Women's Rights Activism on Facebook. In L. Touaf, S. Boukhil, & C. Nasri (Eds.), *North African Women After the Arab Spring* (pp. 77–96). Palgrave Macmillan.

Fischer, F. (2013). *Cascades of Collective Action? Analyzing the Impact of Protest History and Social Media on Regime Change in the Context of the 2011 Uprisings in Egypt and Syria.* Open Access Repository. Accessed from https://www.ssoar.info/ssoar/bit-stream/handle/document/44144/ssoar-2013-fischer-Cascades_of_collective_action_Analyzing.pdf?sequence=1&isAllowed=y&lnkname=ss oar-2013-fischer-Cascades_of_collective_action_Analyzing.pdf

Guha, P., Stabile, C. A., & Gajjala, R. (2019). Introduction: Sexual Violence, Social Movements, and Social Media. *Ada – A Journal of Gender New Media & Technology, 15.* Accessed from https://adanewmedia.org/2019/02/issue15-gajjala-guha-stabile/

Hafez, S. (2016). *Virtual Space and Collective Action in Egypt. Post-Revolutionary Communities on Facebook.* Middle East Information & Research Project. Accessed from https://merip.org/2017/05/virtual-space-and-collective-action-in-egypt/

Hassan, R. M. & A. Shoukry (2008). *"Clouds in Egypt's Sky," Sexual Harassment: From Verbal Harassment to Rape.* Egyptian Center for Women's Rights. Accessed from https://www.academia.edu/42743647/Clouds_in_Egypts_sky

Hurley, Z. (2021). # reimagining Arab Women's Social Media Empowerment and the Post digital Condition. *Social Media + Society, 7*(2), 1–14.

Ibrahim, A. (2019). Cyberactivism and Empowerment: Egyptian Women's Advocacy to Combat Sexual Harassment. *The Journal of Social Media in Society, 8*(2), 167–186.

Jupp, D., Ali, S. I., & Barahona, C. (2010). Measuring Empowerment? Ask Them. *Sida Studies in Evaluation, 1,* 7–99. Accessed from https://www.oecd.org/derec/swe-den/46146440.pdf

Kabeer, N. (1994). *Reversed Realities: Gender Hierarchies in Development Thought.* Verso.

Kassem, N. (2020). Social Media in Egypt: The Debate Continues. In N. Miladi & N. Mellor (Eds.), *Routledge Handbook on Arab Media* (pp. 74–87). Routledge.

Kasturirangan, A. (2008). Empowerment and Programs Designed to Address Domestic Violence. *Violence Against Women, 14*(12), 1465–1475.

Kieffer, C. H. (1984). Citizen Empowerment: A Developmental Perspective. *Prevention in Human Services, 3*, 9–36.

Locke, A., Lawthom, R., & Lyons, A. (2018). Social Media Platforms as Complex and Contradictory Spaces for Feminisms: Visibility, Opportunity, Power, Resistance and Activism. *Feminism & Psychology, 28*(1), 3–10.

Magdy, D., & Zaki, H. A. (2021). After COVID-19: Mitigating Domestic Gender-Based Violence in Egypt in Times of Emergency. In *Social Protection in Egypt: Mitigating the Socio-Economic Effects of the COVID-19 Pandemic on Vulnerable Employment.*

Miladi, N. (2016). Social Media and Social Change. *Digest of Middle East Studies, 25*(1), 36–51.

Moussa, M. B. (2017). From Arab Street to Social Movements: Re-theorizing Collective Action and the Role of Social Media in the Arab Spring. *Westminster Papers in Communication and Culture, 9*(2), 45–68.

Nachshen, J. S. (2005). Empowerment and Families: Building Bridges Between Parents and Professionals, Theory and Research. *Journal on Developmental Disabilities, 11*(1), 67–76.

Perkins, D., & Zimmerman, M. (1995). Empowerment Theory, Research and Application. *American Journal of Community Psychology, 23*(5), 569–579.

RAINN. (2015). *Victim or Survivor: Terminology from Investigation Through Prosecution.* SAKI-Sexual Assault Kit Initiative. Sakitta.org. Accessed April 1, 2022, from https://sakitta.org/toolkit/docs/Victim-or-Survivor-Terminology-from-Investigation-Through-Prosecution.pdf

Rowlands, J. (1995). Empowerment Examined. *Development in Practice, 5*(2), 101–107.

Sadek, G. (2016). (rep.). Egypt: Sexual Violence Against Women. In *The Law Library of Congress* (pp. 1–24).

Sadler, N. (2019). Myths, Masterplots and Sexual Harassment in Egypt. *The Journal of North African Studies, 24*(2), 247–270.

Saliba, I. (2016). *Killing Them Softly. Assessing Pre-emptive Repressing in Russia and Egypt.* WZB Berlin Social Science Center Conference. Accessed from https://www.research-gate.net/publication/315799708_Killing_them_softly_Assessing_Preemptive_Repression_in_Russia_and_Egypt

Seo, H. (2019). Collective Action in Digital Age: A Multilevel Model. In *Proceedings of the 52nd Hawaii International Conference on System Sciences.* Accessed from https://scholarspace.manoa.hawaii.edu/bitstream/10125/59712/0272.pdf

Shata, A., & Seelig, M. I. (2021). The Dragonfly Effect: Analysis of the Social Media Women's Empowerment Campaign. *Journal of Creative Communications, 16*(3), 331–346.

Skalli, L. H. (2014). Young Women and Social Media Against Sexual Harassment in North Africa. *The Journal of North African Studies, 19*(2), 244–258.

Steinert-Threlkeld, Z. C. (2017). Spontaneous Collective Action: Peripheral Mobilization During the Arab Spring. *American Political Science Review, 111*(2), 379–403.

Tazi, M., & Oumlil, K. (2020). The Rise of Fourth-Wave Feminism in the Arab Region? Cyberfeminism and Women's Activism at the Crossroads of the Arab Spring. *CyberOrient, 14*(1), 44–71.

UNFPA Egypt. (2015). The Egypt Economic Cost of Gender-Based Violence Survey (ECGBVC) 2015. Accessed January 27, 2022, from https://egypt.unfpa.org/sites/default/files/pubpdf/Costs%20of%20the%20impact%20of%20Gender%20Based%20Violence%20%28GBV%29%20WEB.pdf

Watts, R. J., & Abdul-Adil, J. K. (1997). Promoting Critical Consciousness in Young African American Men. *Journal of Prevention and Intervention in the Community, 16*(1/2), 63–86.

Watts, R. J., Griffith, D. M., & Abdul-Adil, J. (1999). Sociopolitical Development as an Antidote for Oppression: Theory and Action. *American Journal of Community Psychology, 27*, 255–271.

Zakarria, J. (2019). Public Feminism, Female Shame, and Sexual Violence in Modern Egypt. *Journal of International Women's Studies, 20*(7), 113–128.

Zimmerman, M. A. (2000). Empowerment Theory: Psychological, Organizational, and Community Levels of Analysis. In J. Rappaport & E. Seidman (Eds.), *Handbook of Community Psychology* (pp. 43–63). Plenum.

CHAPTER 21

"Don't Touch Me": Sexual Harassments, Digital Threats, and Social Resistance Toward Kuwaiti Female Journalists

Fatima Alsalem

Introduction

Kuwaiti journalist Hidaya Sultan Alsalem's brutal public murder in 2001 has been the subject of much discussion. Hidaya was aware of being targeted; she had received many threats after she published an article in which she had insulted the killer's tribe. After 10 years in prison, the killer was released in 2019 when a *diya* (blood money) of 33 million dollars was collected, constituting the largest known amount of blood money paid in Kuwait. The killer's release from prison sparked a debate on violence against female journalists in Kuwait. Discussions, both online and offline, centered on the challenges female journalists face, including the threats and harassment they encounter while doing their job. Some defended the killer, focusing on his bravery in protecting his tribe's dignity. Some others argued that Hidaya had crossed a social line and that she should not have been a journalist at all. Yet others felt journalism is not safe for women who should ideally stay home. A few people went so far as to say that Hidaya deserved to be killed for her opinions. Public attention to this incident has reignited the debate on women in the media, especially in conservative societies. This study explores the cultural and social obstacles faced by female journalists in Kuwait and how public perceptions and expectations impact their careers and lives. Interrelated factors that discourage women from

F. Alsalem (✉)
Kuwait City, Kuwait

L. H. Skalli, N. Eltantawy (eds.), *The Palgrave Handbook of Gender, Media and Communication in the Middle East and North Africa,*
https://doi.org/10.1007/978-3-031-11980-4_21

working in journalism are examined, such as social acceptance, gender discrimination, digital threats, sexual harassment, and cultural influences.

The study uses a mixed-methods approach, including a survey of female journalists working in Kuwait and in-depth interviews with eight female journalists, to examine their attitudes toward their careers, workplace practices, media culture, violence, harassment, and marginalization. To provide a comprehensive picture of the status of female journalists in Kuwait, the study analyzes female journalists' perceptions of their own roles, the social and cultural perceptions of their jobs, and the violence, threats, sexual harassment, and challenges they face. It also describes the types of violence that female journalists encounter and discusses how these incidents affect the public perceptions and social acceptability of women working in the field. In identifying the main challenges and difficulties female journalists face in Kuwait, the study hopes to find ways to, and inform research on, how they can be better treated, positioned, and perceived. The study employed a cross-sectional survey with both structured and close-ended questions to fully understand the main challenges faced by female journalists in Kuwait, by way of harassment, threats, and cultural resistance. The survey asked general questions regarding the type of journalistic work they do, why they chose to work in journalism, how they thought society perceived them, their main challenges, sexual harassment at work, assaults, and digital threats they received as journalists.

BACKGROUND

Kuwait has a population of approximately 4.2 million (The World Bank, 2021). As of 2020, the number of Kuwaitis who work for the government is about 323,358, 59.1% of them women; of the 73,303 who work in the private sector, 50.4% are women (Central Statistical Bureau [CSB] Kuwait, 2020). According to census data, the country enjoys a 100% literacy rate among nationals (CSB Kuwait, 2020). This high literacy rate is mainly due to the free school education offered by government, with primary and intermediate education being compulsory. There are also various educational centers in the country for literacy and religious training, including literacy training for the elderly. Although women increasingly form a greater share of the workforce, their occupation choices are limited. According to a government report, women constitute 84.5% of the total workforce of the Ministry of Education and 70% of the total number of workers in the Ministry of Health, compared with only 33.1% in the Ministry of Information (CSB Kuwait, 2020). The same report shows that in the private sector, Kuwaiti women constitute only 0.4% of the information and communication sector and 1.6% in the arts, entertainment, and recreation sectors. However, the number of Kuwaiti female journalists or media persons is unknown because of lack of specific data; statistics show that women constitute less than 1% of the information and communication sector (CBS Kuwait, 2020).

While Kuwaiti women are seen as the most liberal in the Gulf region (Alsalem, 2021), many of them feel marginalized, especially in the news media

The freedom that Kuwaiti women enjoy enables them to be more outspoken and independent when compared to their Khaleeji counterparts (Mamoun, 2018). Mamoun (2018) argues that Kuwaiti women have unprecedented courage due to the social, political, and economic atmosphere that is different in Kuwait when compared to other countries in the region. Nevertheless, social upbringing in the Arab world mostly prepares women for their roles as mothers and housewives (Aldweelah, 2009). Scholars have argued that women have been socialized into a passive role (Alajimi, 2000). Thus, women's disengagement from working in the media or as journalists does not stem from restrictions or laws against them, but rather from a set of norms that women themselves hold about working in the media or as journalists.

The male dominance of the profession of journalism and the status of women in keeping with their cultural and social backgrounds in many countries seem to have strengthened the general perception that journalism is not suitable for women. Chen et al. (2020) suggest that women have been marginalized in the workplace and society for many years, and the issue is not different in journalism. In their research on female journalists in Nigeria, Jibril and Abubakar (2017) argue that any attempt by women to practice journalism is stereotypically seen as unusual and unfit. Studies have argued that there is a noticeable bias, worldwide, against women in journalism and what they are capable of, and they are also often seen as out of the newsroom league (Frank, 2013; Jibril & Abubaker, 2017; Sakha & Shah, 2019). Sakha and Shah (2019) argue that women are not welcome in journalism and are not accepted socially not because of any lack of professional skills but simply for being women. This worldwide idea and stereotype of women being unfit and not good enough for journalism also applies to Kuwait.

The second factor that prevents women from practicing journalism is social and cultural pressures. Although Kuwaiti women are seen as advocates of their sex and more culturally open than their counterparts in other Gulf and Arab countries (Alsalem, 2021), they still face many cultural barriers and unseen "social rules." Although the culture supports working women, it discourages women from practicing certain jobs that require working in the field or need women to expose their identities and pictures in public. For example, Kaya (2018) argues that the deeply gendered structural inequalities play a significant role in preventing women to work in politics and to run for the parliament. Moreover, women running for the parliament are exposed to sexist prejudices, criticism, and public defamation (Kaya, 2018). That is because women are expected to protect their reputation and those who do not do so are considered "too free" and liberal in the Kuwaiti context.

Third, the guardianship nature of the relationship between most women and their spouses, brothers, or fathers prevents their engagement in journalism. In a male-dominated culture, as in Kuwait, men often determine women's career choices, which, in turn, might affect women's motivation to be actively involved in the news media industry. Aldweelah (2009) argues that cultural traditions play a great role in the choice of career in Kuwait, where certain jobs (such as journalism) are seen as masculine, and women entering these industries is considered as "going against" tradition. Despite that females constitute 73.5% of the total number of students at Kuwait University and outnumber males in all majors (the only state university in Kuwait), their career paths are mostly limited to Ministry of Health and Ministry of Education (Kuwait University, 2017). Salami (1999) argues that women do not make it to top positions at work or to influential jobs such as journalism, not because of their intellectual incapability but because of the cultural restraints that have kept them outside the newsroom.

Violence Against and Sexual Harassment of Women

Although Hidaya was the only female journalist killed in Kuwait, the number of journalists subjected to sexual harassment, assault, threat, or attacks remains unknown. Although sexual harassment and violence against female journalists are well documented around the globe, such issues are rarely discussed in Kuwait. It is not acceptable to speak about sexual harassment or assault in public, and women who face these issues usually remain silent and fear speaking up. Sakha and Shah (2019) argue that female journalists experience pushing, touching, and punching when they go to cover stories in public but do not report or share these incidents even with their female colleagues because of fear of gossip. Moreover, as harassment is the norm in many cultures, numerous female journalists decide to stay silent because otherwise they would be seen as "making a big deal out of nothing" (Sakha & Shah, 2019).

Additionally, women are often seen as sex objects and are expected to act and dress to attract viewers and to tolerate harassment (Sakha & Shah, 2019). In Kuwait, a few incidents have occurred with callers sexually harassing women presenters on TV who would then laugh or pretend to not understand the harasser (Sputniknews, 2018). In an interview, Kuwaiti media host Maha Mohammed admitted that she has lost her media dream because of the harassment she was subjected to when she was working as a broadcaster (Elfenn, 2021).

In 2018, a famous Kuwaiti journalist, Haleema Boland, publicly accused a male journalist for sexually harassing her on Twitter via private chat. In return, the journalist replied that she was the one who talked to him first (Sputniknews, 2018). Many people took the accusations as a joke, while others defended the male journalist. Sexual harassment against women is rooted in the culture in some parts of the world, including Kuwait, and women who are outspoken and decide to be vocal about it are looked down upon (Melki & Mallat, 2016; Sakha & Shah, 2019).

In 2021, Kuwaiti blogger Asia Alshammari ignited a social controversy after she recorded a video while being harassed, and said "the problem exists in Kuwait and women don't report it because they fear being prevented from going out by their parents"; "I will not be silent from now on," she continued. Asia's claims provoked widespread reaction in Kuwait because sexual harassment is a very sensitive topic and has rarely been discussed (Alkhaldy, 2021).

Following in the footsteps of the worldwide #Metoo campaign, Kuwaiti women's rights activists and feminists have launched a campaign against sexual harassment after Asia's video went viral—"I will not be silent"—(len askot) to raise awareness of the existence of sexual harassment in Kuwait, empower women to speak for themselves, and start reporting harassments and assaults. The (len askot) "I will not be silent" campaign is the first time Kuwaiti women speak out publicly to confront harassment defying the conservative traditions and the culture of "shame" in Kuwait. Through the "I will not be silenced" account on Instagram, dozens of testimonies began to be published about being stalked, harassed, or assaulted (Aljazeera, 2021).

As a result of the campaign, a young Kuwaiti female journalist working for the Alqabas online newspaper went undercover and filmed a shocking video of herself being sexually harassed and assaulted in public (Albawaba, 2021). The video was published on the newspaper's website and social media accounts, evoking mixed reactions on Twitter. Some people expressed their outrage and shock, while others justified the harassment as a typical outcome for a woman not wearing a hijab and *being out alone*. Aladala TV broadcast a special episode on sexual harassment in Kuwait, which caused a lot of controversy after the female presenter ended a phone call with a Kuwaiti social activist who blamed the harassment on women's attractive appearance and clothes (Alkhaldy, 2021).

Simorangkir (2020) posited that women endure unwanted sexual attention and offensive conduct as the price of getting accepted into the workforce. According to IWMF's global study on female journalists, 14.3% of female journalists have experienced intimidation, threats, and abuse at the workplace (Simorangkir, 2020). The same report found that many women are reluctant to report these harassments for fear of losing work opportunities and other negative consequences. In their study of Lebanese female journalists, Melki and Mallat (2016) found that 65% of female journalists in Lebanon faced sexual harassment at least once, and 88% believed that sexual harassment is a serious problem for female journalists. A baseline study by Somali female journalists (SWJ, 2017) found that sexual harassment is a sensitive topic and not openly discussed in many African countries. The report found that only 13% of the surveyed journalists felt comfortable sharing their experiences of sexual harassment, while 20% said that if exposed to harassment, they would be afraid to report it (SWJ, 2017). In terms of online sexual harassment, a study of female journalists in Nepal found 67% saying they had experienced some sort of abuse online (Koirala, 2020).

According to the Attitudinal Survey on Violence Against Women's report in Kuwait, 42.6% of the sample considered violence against women as a topic of concern (Alsalem, 2018). The same report found that physical abuse was the most common type of violence against women (30.7%), followed by psychological abuse (25.3%) and verbal abuse (24.9%). Yet, only 27.4% would report to the police in case they were a victim of violence (Alsalem, 2018). According to research, sexual harassment can be categorized into four types (Koirala, 2020; Simorangkir, 2020). The first is the verbal form of harassment, which includes unwelcome sexual advances, propositions or pressure for sexual activity, offensive flirtation, and inappropriate jokes. The second is nonverbal, including sexually suggestive gestures, pictures, or texts. The third comprise physical forms, including any form of unwanted physical contact or touch. The last is harassment by authority, which involves any demand by supervisors or managers for sexual favors in lieu of certain job benefits, promotions, or salary increases, even when deserved by the female employee.

Female journalists' safety and challenges are neglected in Kuwait, and the topic is not discussed due to its sensitive nature. Even though sexual harassment, threats, intimidation, and social resistance are not exclusively targeted at female journalists, female employees are significantly more prone to harassment than male employees (Koirala, 2020; Simorangkir, 2020). Moreover, research has shown that female journalists are more exposed to such challenges compared to women in other occupations for three reasons: (1) lack of social support, (2) the mixed-gender nature of journalism that exposes women to sources and male colleagues, making people assume that they are more accepting of such acts and "culturally open," and (3) male domination of the field, leading to women working in junior positions and dependent on male bosses for promotions and career development (Simorangkir, 2020).

The contribution of this study lies in the fact that it highlights female journalists in Kuwait are not only a small minority but also face intimidation, social resistance, threats, and sexual harassment. The issue of sexual harassment has recently attracted increased attention due to amplified social media awareness campaigns about violence against women and the importance of reporting sexual assaults. Although there is no empirical data on sexual harassment and threats to Kuwaiti female journalists, evidence from social media accounts, personal blogs, and online forums suggests that sexual harassment is a significant issue. The apparently low number of women who choose to work in journalism in Kuwait and the daily lived experiences of harassment as expressed on social media points to a need for more in-depth and culturally sensitive research on the topic. Although the scope of this study is limited to one country, our study of the Kuwaiti experience could prove relevant for countries with similar sociocultural contexts.

The study examined how sexual harassment and threats might influence female journalists. Specifically, it focused on how sexual harassment, digital threats, and assault might influence women's choice of journalism as a profession and how it affected the social perception and acceptance of their career choices. Based on the above, the following questions were put to the purposively selected women journalists:

RQ1. What type of sexual harassment, threat, and intimidation do female journalists face in Kuwait?

RQ2. How have sexual harassment and abuse personally affected you?

RQ3. What type of protection and prevention against sexual harassment and abuse do you take?

RQ4. What type of social pressures do female journalists face?

METHODOLOGY

The study employed a mixed-methods approach that included surveying and interviewing in-depth 24 and eight female journalists, respectively, who are working at 13 local newspapers, three TV stations, and four radio stations. For the quantitative method, the study employed a purposive sampling method and the author contacted journalists and sent them an electronic copy of the survey using Google Docs. The female journalists were contacted based on personal connections with the author or by targeting them via social media.

The surveys were distributed between April 1 and May 1, 2021. The cross-sectional survey was developed with both structured and close-ended questions to fully understand the main challenges faced by female journalists in Kuwait, by way of harassment, threats, and cultural resistance. To provide an empirical basis for ensuring the reliability of the instrument, a pilot study was conducted with five female journalists to test the suitability and appropriateness of the instrument. Participants were assured of confidentiality and anonymity, and participation was voluntary. The questionnaires were administered in Arabic. After data collection, the author used SPSS for data entry and analysis.

For qualitative data, in-depth interviews with eight female journalists were conducted in Arabic between March 22 and May 15, 2021, using a purposive sample. The interviewed journalists represented online, television, radio, and print in Kuwait. Sampling was performed using a non-random snowball technique. All interviews were conducted face-to-face with the author. The researcher did not record the interviews but depended on taking notes from the interviews to ensure privacy and allow respondents to speak with full honesty without fear of being recorded. To protect confidentiality and avoid any retribution, the names of all respondents and the organizations they work for have been withheld. After participants gave their consent, interviews were conducted for approximately 40–60 minutes. The interviews were then analyzed to explore the theme of sexual harassment and examine certain responses to it, particularly prevention and protection.

The survey questionnaire measured the prevalence of verbal, nonverbal, physical, and threatening sexual harassment incidents, their perpetrators, and the outcome. In addition, the questionnaire measured female journalists' working conditions and cultural barriers. Qualitative interviews sought in-depth information about the circumstances, reactions, and outcomes of sexual harassment. The journalists were asked general questions regarding the type of journalistic work they do, why they chose to work in journalism, how they thought society perceived them, their main challenges, sexual harassment at work, assaults, and digital threats they received as journalists. The findings below capture the main strands of the interview responses to these questions.

RESULTS

To analyze the qualitative data, the study employed Chen et al. (2020) long interview technique, which allows researchers to code the interviews into themes and broad categories. The author read the notes and transcriptions from the interviews several times before the initial analysis. Based on the analysis, the author produced the most prominent themes by grouping interrelated ideas into themes.

Four main themes emerged from our data: journalism as a side job, which discusses that working in journalism does not provide job security or social status; intimidation, violence, and harassment, which discusses the type of abuse female journalists face, the sexual harassment and other abuse, and their perpetrators; reporting and protection, which discusses the best strategies for dealing with harassment and protection of women in the field; and, finally, social resistance, which focuses on the cultural barriers faced by female journalists.

Journalism as a Part-Time Job

The vast majority of the surveyed participants, or 66.7%, were TV journalists; 20.7% were radio journalists, and only 12.5% were newspaper journalists. In terms of job description, 37.5% (N = 9) were photojournalists, 20.8% (N = 5) were news producers, 20.8% (N = 5) were journalists, 12.5% (N = 3) were news editors, and 8.3% were presenters. In terms of type of recruitment, 62.5% (N = 15) were employed full-time, 33.3% (N = 8) were part-time, and 4.2% were freelancers (Table 21.1). This indicates that the majority of female journalists surveyed were full-time workers, with 37.5% engaged in a part-time or side job. Consistently, qualitative interviews suggested that the majority of female journalists worked on TV, and more than half of them were employed part-time in journalism as they all had day jobs at government institutions. Interviewees felt that journalism did not provide job security, and they would rather work in government to assure consistent income. In addition, female journalists said that journalism was not "a real" job. One senior investigative journalist said:

Table 21.1 Distribution of positions of female journalists in the news industry

Occupation	%	N
Journalist	20.8	5
Photojournalist	37.5	9
Presenter	8.3	2
News Producer	20.8	5
News Editor	12.5	3

I work in a government job that provides me with job security and a high salary, so I consider my journalism job as a job I do in my free time. Journalism does not give me prestige or social status, but it is a nice part-time job to do while getting an extra amount of cash. To be honest, I consider journalism a passion more than a real job. (Personal communication, March 25, 2021)

This dilemma raises a question about journalism as a profession among women in Kuwait. Alsalem (2020) argues that Kuwaitis account for only 55% of the total population of journalists in the country due to their societal perceptions and media organizations' policies. Some studies (Abdullah, 2006; Alrajhi, 2017) have found that journalism does not attract many qualified Kuwaitis because of lack of job security and longer working hours than other jobs. A Kuwait newspaper journalist in her late 50s described her job in journalism for the past 30 years as a personal preference:

I do not work in journalism for financial benefits because other jobs provide more, and I do not work for social status as female journalists in Kuwait are not respected well. I work because I love my job despite my family's rejection. (May 14, 2021)

Intimidation, Threats, Violence, and Harassments

The second theme answered RQ1, which asked about the types of sexual harassment, digital threats, intimidation, and abuse female journalists face. As seen from Table 21.2, the most frequently reported act of intimidation, threats, and abuse that female journalists face was "abuse of power or authority" (75%). Moreover, more than half of the respondents (54.2%) reported being "publicly humiliated or threatened with humiliation" and "forced to make concessions to gain job promotions." In addition, 41.7% of respondents reported being

Table 21.2 Types of threats or intimidation experienced by respondents related to their jobs

Threats	N	%
Abuse of authority	18	75
Publicly humiliated or threatened with humiliation	13	54.2
Forced to make concessions to gain job promotions	13	54.2
Insulted and criticized publicly	10	41.7
Threatened with verbal abuse	7	29.2
Threatened with destroying reputation	5	20.8
Threatened with violence	5	20.8
Name calling and verbal abuse	3	12.5
Threats of hurting family members or friends	2	8.3
Threatened with job loss in case of pregnancy	2	8.3

"insulted and criticized publicly." In addition, when respondents were asked an open-ended question regarding the main challenges they faced in their job, several points were repeatedly emphasized. The oft-reported challenge was that they were forced to make concessions, such as accepting harassments, accepting dinner invitations, or wearing revealing clothes, to gain promotions and approval of their supervisors. In fact, one political news journalist revealed that she was forced to accept unwanted sexual text messages because she did not want to lose her job.

When asked, "have you ever experienced any physical violence in relation to your work?," all respondents (100%) said "no." However, 45.8% of female journalists reported experiencing "verbal threats," while 37.5% reported facing "verbal violence." A senior political journalist said that she was the only woman working with 20 male journalists, and that she experienced all types of verbal violence and intimidation:

> I was called Bu Mohammed (the father of Mohammed) instead of Um Mohammed (the mother of Mohammed) by my co-workers as an act of demeaning and was told that I was in a job not suitable for women. One co-worker once told me that he did not respect me anymore because I said I smoke hookah (shisha). (May 7, 2021)

Second, in terms of sexual harassments, female journalists were asked, "Have you ever experienced any sexual harassment in relation to your work," to which more than one-third (37.5%) of the respondents said "yes." The most frequently reported act of sexual harassment was "unwanted comments on dress or appearance" (45.8%). Moreover, 29.2% of the respondents reported being frequently asked out for dinner against their will, and a small number (4.2%) reported acts such as "unwanted physical contact and touching," "suggestive remarks," and "verbal threats."

In-depth interviews revealed that female journalists face many sexual harassments in the office and in the field. Journalists report that they receive gifts and free trips at the price of cooperating with the abuser. Most interviewed journalists revealed that they get unwanted dinner invitations all the time. One journalist admitted to being invited to join an official trip to Iraq with a politician and was told that they would have fun together. Ironically, the most successful strategy journalists adopt to prevent unwanted sexual harassment is to act as if they do not understand or completely ignore. An investigative journalist mentioned that:

> I received a very weird text message from a famous ex-parliament member inviting me to join him on a trip oversees. I was shocked but ignored the message and acted as if I did not understand it. (March 25, 2021)

Interestingly, the majority of respondents did not consider inappropriate comments or sexual jokes as a form of sexual harassment, and said that the only form of sexual harassment they would report is when it involves touching or physical contact. Regarding the place of sexual harassment, half of the respondents reported incidents of sexual harassment (50%) in the office. The next most frequently reported locations were social media (20.8%) and the street while reporting (12.5%). Close to a third of the perpetrators were managers (29.2%), while 25% were colleagues. Of the female journalists, 20.8% claimed they did not know the perpetrators, and 16.7% said the acts of sexual harassment were committed by their sources and interviewees. Moreover, 4.2% of acts of sexual harassment were committed by the police. One example came from the same senior political journalist mentioned above:

> I was sexually harassed by one of my sources who used to text me with inappropriate texts and sexual pictures, and kept inviting me to his hotel room and when I stopped responding, he threatened to fire me from my job. (May 7, 2021)

Another example came from a young journalist who contacted a senior government official for access to an international forum held in the country, who said: "I contacted a senior government official and politely asked to get a press access to the forum and I was surprised when he said, 'what will I get in return?'" (May 15, 2021).

Third, regarding digital threats, 45.8% of respondents said they had experienced digital harassment, while more than one-third (37.5%) of respondents reported being impersonated online, and 33.3% said they had experienced online bullying and digital abuse. Moreover, 20.8% of respondents had experienced hacking of their social media personal accounts. A young broadcast journalist said:

> My co-worker sexually harassed me verbally for more than a year and tried to touch me in the staircase before I ran away with panic and screamed "do not touch me". The harasser later started to threaten me on social media and started posting stories about me to destroy my reputation. I was so terrified that my father would read the tweets or someone would tell him. (May 12, 2021)

Consequences of Sexual Abuse and Harassment

To answer RQ2, regarding the consequences and effects of sexual harassment and abuse on female journalists, the survey asked, "How did your experience of being sexually harassed affect you?." Table 21.3 shows that about one-third of respondents (33.3%) said they felt unsafe at work. In addition, 29.2% of respondents said the harassment had made them feel depressed and lose interest in work. The broadcast journalist quoted above, who had experienced digital threats, said:

> I started missing work and took a very long sick leave after my experience with both physical sexual harassment and digital threats because I felt ashamed,

Table 21.3 Effects of sexual harassment and abuse

Effects	N	%
Depression and loss of interest	7	29.2
Psychological effects	2	8.3
Unsafe at work	8	33.3
Change of workplace (department change)	6	25.0
Leave work	1	4.2

humiliated, and lost interest in work. I ended up going to therapy and suffered from extreme depression and anxiety. (May 12, 2021)

Moreover, 25% of respondents said they had to change their work or departments as a result of harassment, 8.3% cited psychological effects, and 4.2% had to leave their jobs.

In terms of sexual harassment and abuse reporting, the majority of respondents who experienced sexual harassment said they had not reported it (66.7%). Of those who did, 25% said they went to the police. Far fewer reported to their managers (4.2%) or another authority (4.2%). When asked, "why did you decide against reporting the sexual harassment?" for a qualitative response question, many women said they feared being blamed for it or for their reputation. Female journalists believe it is against tradition and social norms to speak about harassment, let alone report it to the authorities. Journalists said reporting sexual harassment is not a good idea because it is neither socially accepted nor appropriate for their status or reputation. Women believe reporting harassment would backfire, and the authorities would always blame the victim. A broadcast journalist said: "I will never report sexual harassment because people would blame me or think I want attention" (May 5, 2021).

Prevention and Protection

To answer RQ3 about the type of prevention and protection that female journalists have against sexual harassment and abuse, the survey asked, "does your organization take any measures to protect your personal security?," to which half of the respondents replied in the negative. About 37.5% said that their organizations offered a complaint unit, while only 4.2% said their organizations provided training and awareness courses, and another 4.2% said they provided emotional support. Respondents were asked an open-ended question about ideal measures to protect personal security, and several recommendations were emphasized. The most-suggested preventive measures are:

- Provision of security guards when they are out in the field
- Self-defense training courses
- Legal support
- Hotline to report harassments and assaults

The in-depth interviews revealed that most female journalists believe they are not protected against harassment and abuse from their organizations and, thus, they needed to protect themselves. One journalist said: "I usually wear neutral colors when at work or in the field so that I don't attract unwanted attention. In fact, I started wearing all white to 'meld' with all the men wearing dishdashas" (a long white robe traditionally worn by the men) (March 25, 2021).

Social Resistance

RQ4 sought information about the social pressure and resistance that female journalists face. The survey asked respondents about their social perception and acceptance of their jobs as female journalists. Half of the respondents were satisfied (29.2%) and very satisfied (20.8%) about the social perception of their job, 4.2% were not satisfied at all, and 8.3% were not satisfied. Moreover, 37.5% were neither satisfied nor dissatisfied with the social perception of their job as journalists. Moreover, when asked about family members' approval of their job as journalists, only 8.3% of the respondents said they were not satisfied, 41.7% said they were satisfied, and 25% said they were very satisfied with their job. However, a newspaper journalist in her late 50s described her family's resistance as follows:

> My father had no problem with me working in a newspaper but my mother did. My mother's side of the family is very religious; they used to cut out my news stories and show it to her to prove that my job was against traditions and religion. Later, in the late 1970s, after a few years of my journalism job, I was married and stopped by my husband's family from working in a newspaper. (May 14, 2021)

When asked about their job satisfaction, 50% of female journalists said they were satisfied with their job, and 20.8% were very satisfied. In contrast, 12.5% of the respondents said that they were not satisfied or not satisfied at all. A young journalist said: "I love journalism and I'm very satisfied with my job. Although I face harassment and unwanted attention sometimes, I can deal with it and to be honest, it does not stop me from doing my job" (May 15, 2021).

The survey also asked female journalists about their perception of their jobs and the main challenges. As shown in Table 21.4, 37.5% of surveyed journalists said that women were stereotyped at work and that is how they were treated. Equally, 37.5% of respondents agreed that there is sexism at work. Moreover, 34.8% of female journalists said they had been replaced at work that was initially assigned to them because of someone else's looks or relationships. Similarly, 30.4% of female journalists said that they had been replaced at work because of someone else's appearance, and 33.3% of the surveyed female journalists felt excluded at work by their male colleagues, all of which means that although women have broken the glass ceiling of the journalism profession in Kuwait and are generally satisfied with their job, they still feel excluded,

Table 21.4 The main challenges that female journalists face at work

Statements	% of those who agree and strongly agree
Being a woman is one of the struggles I face at work.	25
Being a woman negatively impacts my work and promotion.	25
There is a stereotype of women at work and I'm treated accordingly.	37.5
My male colleagues exclude me sometimes.	33.3
I'm not appreciated the way I deserve because of my gender.	25
There is sexism toward women at work.	37.5
A woman was preferred over me because of her appearance.	30.4
I was assigned a job and my name was changed to a replacement because of this person's relationships or appearance.	34.8

marginalized, and judged by their looks. A young broadcast journalist said: "I admit that my looks have helped a lot with my job and I cannot deny that, but I also work hard every day to prove that I should be treated and judged for my skills, not my looks" (May 12, 2021).

Another investigative journalist who has covered many international events, often at the invitation of the government, said: "I know that journalism can be challenging, but to be honest I never felt excluded or marginalized. I think my family name and social status play a big role in my success" (March 25, 2021).

An open-ended question in the survey asked female journalists to state the main challenges they faced at work, and the most common answer was "being women," as they are judged every day because of their gender. Moreover, they said they are not being appreciated at work, and their male counterparts receive more benefits and promotions. This shows that women face sexism at work and feel that they have to work harder than men to be noticed and recognized.

Discussion and Conclusions

This study has drawn on rich data from in-depth interviews and surveys of female journalists in Kuwait to examine their experiences with sexual harassment, abuse, and digital threats. The findings strongly suggest that sexual harassment of female journalists is frequent in Kuwait. The study found that more than one-third of female journalists faced sexual harassment related to their work. Although most acts of sexual harassment were unwanted comments and verbal harassment, 4.2% reported physical contact and touching. This means that female journalists not only face verbal harassment but also physical harassment that might turn into violence and abuse. Surprisingly, women do not consider verbal harassment a big deal and seem prepared to accept it and move on. The interviews revealed that the majority of female journalists do not get offended by verbal sexual harassment and ignore it as a part of their job. This might be explained by the general culture of "shame" where women feel obligated to stay silent because it's shameful to tell others that they were harassed because she would be considered as attention seeker. Moreover, women have been socialized for many years to be victim blamed. In addition, the male-dominant authoritative culture give men the right to verbally express and harass women while it is expected of women to remain silent.

The study also revealed that female journalists are frequently asked out and invited to dinner by their managers or sources, which suggests they face a lot of pressure and need to sacrifice just to keep their jobs. More than half (54.2%) of the surveyed journalists reported being forced to make concessions to gain job promotions. This could involve accepting invitations or gifts from the very perpetrators. When asked about the types of threats and intimidation female journalists face at work, the majority (75%) said that they face abuse of authority; this could relate to sexism, where the men feel they are entitled to more because of their gender. Many female journalists claimed to have been abused and sexually harassed by politicians taking advantage of their position, who do not fear reporting or police interference due to the power they enjoy. A newspaper journalist claimed that a politician had threatened to fire her from her job if she did not accept his invitation to visit him in his hotel room. In addition, politicians take advantage of female journalists' need for information and insider insights, using that need for their own advantage.

Half of the sexual harassment incidents have taken place in office, 20.8% through social media, and 12.5% in the field while reporting. This shows that, unlike what most people think, reporting and field work of journalism is not the biggest problem faced by female journalists but misogyny at work. Most acts of sexual harassment happen at the office—29.2% of the perpetrators were managers, while 25% were colleagues. This shows that the office work culture of journalism is adverse to women, not the profession itself.

Sexual harassment not only endangers female journalists physically but can also affect them psychologically and affect their careers. Kuwaiti female journalists are disturbed by the sexual harassment at work, and many of them have decided to shift to another profession or undermine their career to protect their safety and dignity. In fact, 25% of the respondents admitted to changing jobs or departments as a result of sexual harassment, while 4.2% had quit.

Those who decide to keep their jobs suffer from psychological outcomes because they are forced to accept sexual harassment or pretend or ignore. In-depth interviews have shown that many female journalists ignore harassment, mainly because they believe that they have to let go and cooperate with their perpetrators simply to keep working. Additionally, reporting sexual harassment incidents is not socially accepted or expected. Women in conservative societies like Kuwait believe that reporting such incidents may harm their reputation, and that victims of sexual harassment are always blamed. More than two-thirds of the respondents who experienced sexual harassment did not report it. Likewise, when asked about reporting sexual harassment, the interviews revealed that most female journalists who had experienced harassment did not and would not report it because they believe it is against the norm and fear that people would perceive them as seeking attention. Female journalists are trapped in a system that denies them from speaking out about sexual harassment and abuse because the culture tends to blame the victim.

However, as the #MeToo movement has successfully influenced people around the world to publicly talk about sexual harassment, it has equally influenced Kuwaitis to start addressing the issue in public. For decades, women have kept silent or silenced in a male-controlled culture supported by traditional values. Nevertheless, more women are now aware, and the #len_askot (I will not be silent) movement is normalizing reporting sexual harassment and empowering women to speak up.

In terms of digital threats, the study found that 45.8% had experienced digital harassment and 33.3% said they had been bullied online and experienced digital abuse while others had experienced hacking and identity theft. Moreover, social media has become a nightmare to some journalists as their perpetrators use these platforms to threaten, intimidate, and hurt their reputation.

Despite social resistance to and cultural pressure on women's career choices, the study found that journalism has gained social acceptance in Kuwait. The majority of female journalists are satisfied with their jobs, as are their families. The survey showed that most journalists believe their families are satisfied with their jobs and they do not have to worry about family approval. The majority were also satisfied with the social perception and approval of their job as journalists. This shows that women in Kuwait do not face social resistance as before and in the last two decades, society has become more liberal and accepting of women working in the field or appearing on TV. However, female journalists believe they are treated based on social stereotypes of women at work, there is sexism against women in the news room, and nearly one-third say that their male colleagues exclude them from discussions and meetings. Revealingly, 25% of female journalists consider "being a woman" as their main struggle at work and negatively impacting their career. This suggests women feel marginalized in the journalism domain regardless of their satisfaction and positive public perception of their job. Moreover, female journalists feel they are underappreciated because of their gender, and 30.4% said that physical appearance plays a significant role in job assignments and promotions.

Thus, Kuwaiti female journalists may not suffer from social pressure and cultural resistance per se but derived from the newsroom culture and their male colleagues' exclusion and stereotyping. In conclusion, female journalists believe that their gender negatively impacts their job and that they have to work harder to be recognized or appreciated by their male bosses and managers, which makes them inferior and submissive.

REFERENCES

Abdullah, A. (2006). *Technology and Internet-Related Information Behaviors of Print Journalists in Kuwait.* Unpublished Dissertation Submitted to University of Pittsburgh, Pennsylvania.

Alajimi, M. (2000). *Kuwaiti Women and Political Participation: A Scientific Analysis.* Dar Aljadeed.

Albawaba. (2021). *Bibi Al Khothari Kuwaiti Female Journalist Documents Being Harassed Live.* Albawaba Online. Retrieved from https://www.albawaba.com/ar/ 1410434-اختيار-المحرر/الإعلامية-الكويتية-بيبي-الخضري-توثق-لحظة-التحرش-بها-في-شارع-عام

Aldweelah, A. (2009). *The Degree of Political Awareness Among Kuwaiti Working Women in Higher Education and Its Effect on Students.* Kuwait Center for Research and Studies, Almansouriyah, Kuwait.

Aljazeera. (2021). (Len askon) Kuwaitis Launch an Online Campaign Against Sexual Harassment. *Aljazeera Online.* Retrieved from https://www.aljazeera.net/news/ women/2021/2/9/حملة-عبر-العيب-ثقافة-يتحدين-كويتيات

AlKhaldy, K. (2021). I Won't Be Quiet: Kuwaitis Against Harassment. *Alaraby Aljadeed Online.* Retrieved from www.alaraby.co.uk

Alrajhi, M. (2017). Journalists Job Satisfaction in Kuwait. *Jordan Journal of Social Sciences, 10*(2), 165–181.

Alsalem, F. (2018). Attitudinal Survey on Violence Against Women. *Abolish153.* Retrieved from www.abolish153.com

Alsalem, F. (2020). Journalism in Kuwait: Print Journalists' Practices, Professional Values and Perceived Roles. *Media Watch, 11*(4), 736–748.

Alsalem, F. (2021). The Power of Social Media Influencers: A Study of Public Perception of Credibility. *Journal of Gulf Studies and the Arabian Peninsula, 181*(62).

Central Statistical Bureau (CSB), Kuwait. (2020). *The Labor Market Information System Report.* Retrieved from https://lmis.csb.gov.kw/En/IntegratedData_View.aspx

Chen, G., Pain, P., Chen, V. Y., Mekelburg, M., Springer, N., & Troger, F. (2020). 'You Really Have to Have a Thick Skin': A Cross-Cultural Perspective on How Online Harassment Influences Female Journalists. *Journalism, 21*(7), 877–895.

Elfenn. (2021). Maha Mohammed: I Was Subjected to Harassment and Abduction. *Elfenn Online Newspaper.* Retrieved from https://www.elfann.com/news/ show/1238798/مها-محمد-تعرّضت-للتحرش-والاختطاف-وأتحمّصت-جنينها-عبر

Frank, S. (2013). *Women and Journalism.* Tauris & Co.

Jibril, A., & Abubaker, A. M. (2017). Public Perception of Female Journalists in North-East Nigeria. *Journal of Communication and Media Research, 9*(2), 108–119.

Kaya, K. (2018). Attitudes of ELL students rowards the course of English literature. Doctoral dissertation, Selcuk University, Konya, Turkey.

Koirala, S. (2020). Female Journalists' Experience of Online Harassment: A Case Study of Nepal. *Media and Communication, 8*(1), 47–56.

Kuwait University (2017). *Students Statistics 2016/2017. Office of the Vice President for Planning.* Kuwait University. Retrieved from http://www.planning.kuniv.edu.kw/ Statistics_Ar_1.aspx

Mamoun, M. (2018). Kuwaiti Fashionistas Are the Highest Paid. *Alqabas Newspaper.* Retrieved from https://alqabas.com

Melki, J., & Mallat, S. (2016). Block Her Entry, Keep Her Down and Push Her Out. *Journalism Studies, 17*(1), 57–79.

Sakha, T., & Shah, N. (2019). Challenges Faced by Women in Journalism: An Analytical Case Study of Situation in Pakistan. *Pakistan Journal of Women Studies, 26*(2), 149–172.

Salami, I. (1999). Women in Benin historical drama: Emotan of Benin (Ernest Edyang) and Imaguero (Evinma Ogieria XII). *Journal of Theatre and Communication Studies, 4*(1), 34–56.

Simorangkir, D. (2020). Work-related sexual harassment and coping techniques: the case of Indonesian female journalists. *Media Asia, 47*(1-2), 23–33.

Sputniknews. (2018). *Haleema Boland Accuses a Male Journalist of Sexually Harassing Her on Twitter (in Arabic)*. Retrieved from https://arabic.sputniknews.com/mosaic/201812021037142745-حليمة-بولند-تحرش-إعلامي/

SWJ. (2017). Baseline Study on the Working Conditions of Somali Women Journalists. *Somali Women Journalists Organization*. Retrieved from https://swj.so/

The World Bank (2021). *Population of Kuwait*. Retrieved from https://data.worldbank.org/indicator/SP.POP.TOTL?locations=KW

CHAPTER 22

Gender in Yemeni Media: Hostility and Marginalization in a Fractured Media

Amel Al Ariqi

The term "gender" in Yemeni society is itself much misunderstood. Bilkis Zabara, head of the Centre for International Development and Gender at Sana'a University, explained: "They've written articles stating how the word gender itself is haram ('sin' or 'prohibited' according to Islam, Ed.), and that we, under the influence of the West, are trying to spread bad habits and customs in our society" (As cited in Cordes, 2013).

The prominent woman Yemeni journalist, Raufa Hassan, founder of the Media Faculty and the Empirical Research and Women's Studies Centre at Sana'a University, was attacked and denounced by religious and political figures when she introduced the English word gender to the public during a conference discussing women's rights. In 2000, she had to leave the country for five years after the government shut down her centre, under the pretext that "gender" did not exist in Arabic, and presumably spread "moral corruption and homosexuality, an evil conspiracy to undermine the family" (Al Sharjabi, 2013, p. 19). When she returned to Yemen in 2004 to resume her media teaching and writing, the interpretation of the word gender had also been clarified and translated into Arabic as "social role." The centre re-opened in 2005, this time called the Gender-Development Research and Study Centre (Belqees TV, April 2017).

Yet, the anti-feminist backlash from some influential ultraconservative Islamist members of parliament and conservative clerics compelled most feminists to adopt a more pragmatic approach in their media messages and use less

A. Al Ariqi (✉)
Reading, UK

© The Author(s), under exclusive license to Springer Nature Switzerland AG 2023
L. H. Skalli, N. Eltantawy (eds.), *The Palgrave Handbook of Gender, Media and Communication in the Middle East and North Africa*,
https://doi.org/10.1007/978-3-031-11980-4_22

provocative labels and terms, such as advocacy in women's empowerment or women's rights (Nasser, 2018).

Although Raufa died in 2011 at the age of 53, her legacy continues to inspire women and men in Yemen, especially those who work in the media sector. It also highlights the challenges of developing gender-sensitive media in a conservative patriarchal society controlled by strict social and tribal masculine norms where men and women are not equal.

Method

This chapter takes an overview of how gender issues have been addressed in the changing Yemeni media landscape over the last two decades. It relies on qualitative data collected from the few available research papers and reports published between 2005 and 2020 focusing on Yemeni women media professionals. Given the lack of contemporary academic studies on gender and media in Yemen, most of the quotes and cases in this chapter come from published reports, articles, and videos on social media platforms of Yemeni journalists and writers who focused on gender issues in Yemen. Data were collected between February 2021 and April 2021, with the goal of identifying the impact of the current media status on the representation of women in the media workforce, the presentation of women in the media, and the main gender-related messages delivered by Yemeni media.

A Fractured Media Landscape

Never Free, Never Independent

Yemen has witnessed many changes and crises in its recent modern history, which have led to years of political and economic instability. In turn, this has affected the status of the media, which has never been independent or non-partisan.

After the unification in 1990, Yemen's Ministry of Information monitored the country's media through the control of printing presses, the granting of newspaper licences, and ownership of the country's television and radio stations. Under the Press and Publications Law (1990), newspapers and magazines had to be government-licensed. This was the foundation for a more repressive media environment by prohibiting content perceived critical of religion or encouraging sectarianism and inciting violence. Criticism of the ruling authorities was a red line and only tolerated if it was deemed constructive. Foreign satellite television channels and internet began to enter Yemeni homes in the 1990s, but an underdeveloped network and difficulties connecting the country's rural population have hindered their penetration.

Following the 1994 civil war between southern separatists and the Sana'a-based government, the authorities started to increasingly intervene in media production and the freedom of expression that had characterized the country's early years of unification (Battaglia, n.d.).

In 2010, the media was opened up to private investment. This was given a further boost by the 2011 uprising, popularly known as the Arab Spring, which signalled initial optimism for greater media freedom. However, the media market did not develop as expected after the uprising. Instead it became absolutely dominated by political parties. This was most obvious in the print media, followed by broadcast TV and websites (Battaglia, n.d.).

By 2014, there were nine government-controlled media, 50 independent and 30 party-affiliated newspapers. There were approximately 90 magazines, 50 of which were private or party affiliated. A number of Yemeni-orientated satellite channels opened abroad in addition to several private radio stations and online news publications within the country (Battaglia, n.d.).

War Changed the Media

The most significant event that affected the media landscape is the war, which erupted on March 25, 2015. Indeed, six years of regional proxy civil war have fragmented the media landscape and undermined freedom of speech in Yemen. The 2021 World Press Freedom Index ranked Yemen 169 out of 180 countries, describing press freedom as an "appalling situation" as the division into areas controlled by the conflict's rival parties exacerbated media polarization. Yemeni journalists have been subjected to abduction, torture, murder, and imprisonment. Death sentences have been handed down in politicized trials that lack the most basic legal procedures. Many journalists gave up journalism to avoid reprisals although this has not stopped them from being persecuted for what they had written in the past. Other media professionals have been internally displaced or fled the country (Reports without Borders RSF, 2021).

While the current conflict has destroyed the Yemeni print press, as most publishers suspended their print editions and the English-language press has completely disappeared, broadcasting and online media survived. A number of Yemeni-orientated satellite channels opened abroad, in addition to several private radio stations and online news outlets, with limited access to what is happening in the field (Battaglia, n.d.).

There were 21 radio stations, eight of which are affiliated with the Sana'a government, and 24 private (FM) radio stations, 20 of which are in Sana'a, in addition to 27 television channels, seven of which are governmental. The number of media websites has reached 252 (Saleh, 2018).

Professional journalism in Yemen has reached a low point, as regional and political polarization has forced journalists still working to sacrifice impartiality for propaganda. A recent survey, conducted by the Studies and Economic Media Centre in Yemen, found Yemeni TV news and political analysis programmes were presented in a partisan manner. Most programmes and news on Yemeni channels cover only military achievements, while neglecting to discuss peace or peace initiatives. The study found the monitored programmes were dominated by inflammatory language and an exciting tone to impart an emotional quality to the subject matter appealing to the public's feelings towards the other party (SEMC, 2017a, p. 24).

Underrepresentation and Suppression

Yemeni Women Journalists in the Workplace

According to the 2021 Global Gender Gap Report by the World Economic Forum, Yemen ranks 152 out of 153 countries with the biggest gender gap in the world. Because of gender inequality in the economy, only 6 per cent of Yemini women participate in the labour force, in contrast to 70.8 percent of men. The media sector is no exception (World Economic Forum, 2021, p. 14).

There is no recent comprehensive information covering all governorates of Yemen to show the real figures of representation of Yemeni women working in the media, whether staff or freelance. However, what available data there is confirms Yemeni women are still underrepresented in leadership positions. Prior to the current conflict, women working in the Yemeni media faced rejection and disapproval for their choice of profession (Kafi, 2005). This negative attitude came from their own family members and the wider society. Some families show a conditional acceptance of the media profession if it adheres to the ethics and values of society (Al Kafi, 2005). The study also found the majority of women media workers contributed to family expenses from their income, whether they are married or unmarried. Some female media workers provide for the whole family after the death of a father or husband. This indicated the profession was not considered a luxury or an attempt to prove oneself, but rather a way to overcome the economic difficulties faced by Yemeni families.

Among challenges Yemeni women media professionals face are the restrictive social norms and traditions, lack of training, inequality of opportunities and promotion, low wages, and harassment from society or colleagues in addition to a lack of the technical tools and equipment required for better production. They also feel marginalized and received less encouragement or appreciation from management compared to male colleagues (Kafi, 2005).

This situation has become even more dire. A recent study, by Mohamed Farhan, (2017b) underlined that despite the increasing number of Yemeni media outlets since 2011, especially broadcast, the number of women in the media is still very low even compared to the small number of female graduates from the media colleges in Yemen. There are about 140 female graduates annually from various departments of journalism, radio, and television. Only half of these women go on to work in the media sector while the others move on to different fields or remain unemployed.

Farhan's research (2017b) found the majority of Yemeni women media professionals are employed in TV, radio, and online outlets. Only 170 women journalists are members of the Yemeni Journalists Syndicate, which represents a mere 11 percent of the total membership of 1500. Yemeni media institutions are not discrimination-free. For example, in the South, the recruitment of women, mostly by the government, is often a matter of "tokenism" to silence critics, or fill a gap when no suitable man is available for the job.

The study listed various causes and forms of discrimination against women. This includes their exclusion from male-only Qat-chewing sessions held outside work hours where decisions are made. Chewing Qat in segregated gender groups is a Yemeni social habit that occurs daily. Conservative community attitudes towards women's media work prevents them from working at night or travelling on professional assignments without a family companion. The social expectation of patriarchal gender norms and distribution of roles weigh heavily on them too. Unfortunately, media outlets are not taking these as a reason to provide more regulations—such as maternity leave or access to facilities such as separate toilets, eating, and praying areas for women journalists. Instead, they are using prevailing gender norms as justification to employ men instead of women.

A 2018 survey of several governorates found the number of women working in government media, state news agencies, and broadcast radio and TV to be a mere 13 per cent of the media labour force. Only 160 women, 3 per cent of media workers, had positions of managers or head of departments. The representation of women in private radio was greater than men at 30 percent (compared to 21 per cent for males), while the lowest representation of women was in private websites at a rate of 7 per cent compared to 17 per cent for men (Saleh, 2018).

Women Journalists in a Broken Media

Problems faced by women media workers in Yemen were exacerbated by the war, as social oppression and economic obstacles are worsening their opportunities. While Yemeni men are typically engaged in two struggles: ending political and economic injustice, Yemeni women face several struggles to end their own political, economic, and social injustice. War has exacerbated concerns over their own safety and security.

The grip of the Houthis in the Yemeni capital Sana'a and fragile security in other governorates in Yemen have posed a major threat to women's presence in media roles. Many women journalists have been out of work due to fear of threats and abuse against them while in the field. Before the war, traditional cultures provided some protection for women in public spaces but the war has eroded that protection for female journalists (Farhan, 2017a, b).

The war has caused hundreds of women journalists to lose their jobs as many newspapers and news websites have closed. Others left Yemen in search of work opportunities elsewhere. Many also relocated to other governorates in Yemen, including Taiz, Aden, and Marib, for fear of harm they may suffer because of their continued work (Farhan, 2017a, b).

One of the journalists interviewed for this chapter, W. Albadwi W states: "It took me two years to realize the war would last and there was no point in remaining paralysed by fear. I decided to resume my journalistic activities. However, I found it almost impossible to work in the current media environment, where most Yemeni media outlets have turned into trumpets belonging to parties in the conflict, or what I call 'military media,' which mean messages are mobilization and incitement against 'the others.' Other media are not committed to professionalism, and really do not care about credibility and impartiality, and their audience follow them as a source of information" (personal communication, April 4, 2021).

Wedad, a Yemeni woman journalist since 2007, faced numerous challenges from family, society, and within the media sector before she established the Cultural Media Centre in 2011, a non-governmental civil and cultural media institution. Through the centre, Wedad launched a one-year project "Safe Sister" to build a community of Yemeni women journalists and activists working to promote women's rights. As she explains: "It was shocking to realize most pioneering professional Yemeni women journalists had left the country during the war, and others lost their jobs and source of income due to their refusal to work with parties that did not respect their professionalism."

Gender-Based Violence in the Profession

The nature of attacks on women journalists can differ according to where they are working and the location of the media outlets for which they work. For example, cases of abuse show female journalists in the north are more vulnerable to attempted murder and physical abuse. Those in the south, such as Aden and Hadramout, are subjected to arbitrary dismissal, salary cuts, and bias, especially if they work for media outlets affiliated with the north. Male journalists are subjected to physical attacks, kidnap, torture, and murder both in the south and north (Albadwi, W, personal communication, April 4, 2021).

Besides the Yemeni Journalist Syndicate, there are several non-government organizations, like the Yemen Media Observatory (Marsadak, n.d.), which track and document violations and crimes against human right activists and journalists. Examples of attacks on Yemeni female journalists between 2014 and 2020 recorded by Marsadak include the case of Nadia Al-Saqqaf, who was the first woman appointed as Information Minister in Yemen. A few months after her appointment, she had to flee the country when the Houthis took control of the Ministry of Information. They confiscated her home and property and issued a death sentence against her in November 2020.

In 2015 Nahla al-Qdsi, a reporter and editor, was beaten by Houthi gunmen in the capital Sana'a while filming a demonstration. In 2013, Nahla had been threatened over her coverage of labour strikes in the Hodiedah governorate. In 2016, journalist Boushra Al-Nashair was shot by Houthis who at first refused to allow her to be taken to hospital. Her leg was later amputated after developing gangrene due to delayed treatment. The same year, Nadra Abdel Qadous Mohamed, editor of the 14th of October newspaper in Aden, was subjected to a negative campaign through social media and some news websites following her call to re-open the newspaper after it was shut in 2015. Hadbaa Al-Yazidi, a reporter in Hadramout governorate in south-eastern Yemen, said the Hadrami community did not accept her and she was harassed by male colleagues because she worked for a northern channel.

In 2020, correspondent Abeer Abdullah and her team were attacked by Islamic militia in Taiz, in south-west Yemen, who attempted to arrest them and confiscate their camera. The same year, at least 25 female journalists were dismissed from the Aden-based Saba news agency, south Yemen, without any explanation given.

Further, most women journalists throughout Yemen are subjected to defamation campaigns on social media and websites. Often these target the victim's gender, morality, national loyalty, and extend the attacks to their family. Such smears are especially damaging in a country where the code of honour is crucial in preserving women's dignity (Rassam, 2021, p. 10). These cases and many others illustrate the type and scope of violence targeting women journalists in Yemen. Other constraints are interfering with the exercise of their profession.

In 2003, the Yemeni government imposed the wearing of the headscarf (hijab) for women broadcasters on television after criticism of what was called failure to adhere to Islamic etiquette in an Islamic country. This move aimed to prevent the Islamist opposition party, Islah, and some religious groups from using it as an issue in the election campaign at that time (Munser, 2003). Since then, he majority of Yemeni women who appear on TV, as presenters, guests, or actors, wear the hijab. A handful of Yemeni women have decided not to wear it on TV, challenging the view of wider society (both men and women praise the women who wear it and criticize those who do not). Most of the Yemeni women presenters who do not wear a scarf, who usually present serious political programmes, are outside Yemen. They are still subjected to online smear campaigns because of their decision. It should be noted that female foreign correspondents in Yemen are expected to wear both the hijab and modest clothing.

Standing Against the Storm

Despite the social, political, and institutional discrimination against Yemeni women media workers, many continue to fight back in a daily struggle to break the stereotypical narrative about them. Many have been recognized for their courage and bravery. For example, Hadeel Yamani, who received a 2017 Courage in Journalism Award from the International Women Media's Foundation (IWMF), was the first female Yemeni war correspondent. Yemeni writer and journalist, Bushra Al-Maqtari, was recognized by the German Palm Award for Freedom of Speech and Press, and the Françoise Giroud Award for Defense of Freedom and Liberties and Wedad Al Badwi, who received the prize for her work at the Iraqi Women Journalists Forum, among many others.

Media Insensitivity to Gender Issues

Media Consumption and Trust

The 2017 survey by SEMC found that despite audiences remaining high, the majority of the Yemeni public no longer trusts traditional local media. The lack of public confidence in the traditional media pushed more people to find information from alternative new sources, including social media (SEMC, 2017b, p. 4).

According to Internet World States, there were 3.2 million social media users in Yemen in January 2021. The number increased by 700,000 (+28 per cent) between 2020 and 2021. This was equivalent to 10.6 per cent of the total population. The top three most frequently visited web pages are Facebook, YouTube, and Twitter. Several reports from Arabbarometer revealed Yemen is still experiencing a gap between men and women in internet usage and access (Raz, 2020).

As users of social media, Yemeni women are not visible in terms of their profile pictures, and some choose also not to use their real names. This can be explained by the majority of Yemeni women wearing the niqab (veil) in public, or when there are male non-relatives present. Some publish their photos wearing the hijab and a few will use their photos without one, but most of the last group are living abroad.

Yemeni women's space on social media is sometimes invaded by men using fake profiles, leading women to be more cautious about the images they post and closed groups they form. There have been cases of profile-hacking or posting photos from stolen mobile phones of Yemeni girls, which have put their lives at risk.

Media, Activism, and Gender Issues

Unlike many of the 2011 uprisings in Arab countries, the role of social media was not central in Yemen, where there was little Facebook and Twitter usage, according to The Arab Social Media Report (Salem et al., 2011).

However, the media landscape witnessed the emergence of several outlets not owned by the regime. This created a unique momentum and gave more space to discuss gender issues, like early marriage for girls, street harassment, and the political participation of women.

These issues were raised on rare occasions like International Women's Day, or when UN agencies were launching or funding media campaigns to support women's rights and gender equality. During the two years of political transfer from Salah to Hadi, many campaigns used the internet and social media platforms, mainly Facebook, like Safe Street, which aimed to confront sexual harassment against women and girls in the streets of Yemen.

Social media has helped expose gender-based violence, like sexual harassment, domestic violence, and male violence against women in a way not possible before. One of the reasons for this is the ability to report incidents anonymously, without fearing the consequences, which could otherwise be devastating to the victim and her family. For example, families of women victims of harassment often ignore it, as they believe the negative implications for the woman's career and family reputation outweigh any pursuit of justice (Al-Saqaf, 2015). Sharing a video clip online was another demonstration of how powerful the internet can be in triggering public discussion around sensitive issues, such as shocking images of victims of domestic violence going viral. Many of these cases were not necessarily first published on social media by journalists, but became journalistic material after being picked up by local media websites.

It is debatable whether coverage of some stories of violence actually causes more harm to the victims. Many cases of early marriage, or violence against children, feature photos and videos published on social media or in the press, without the consent of the victims or their families. According to many activists for children and women's rights, this can lead to their being stigmatized or their suffering from long-term psychological damage. In the absence of a journalism code of conduct or agreed ethics, this debate is still unresolved in Yemen.

Social media also allowed the proliferation of hate speech and misogyny against Yemeni women in general and Yemeni women activists in particular. This is obvious in some individual profiles and platforms of extremist ultraconservative Islamists.

It is critical to note that while social media provided platforms for Yemeni journalists and others who consider themselves citizen journalists, it also had an impact on perceptions of the professionalism, credibility, and objectivity of journalism.

What to Cover, How to Cover, When to Cover

Lack of female representation in the workplace, or on social media, is not the only indicator of the gender-insensitive media landscape in Yemen. The poor, or sometimes absent, coverage of gender issues is also a strong indicator of the institutional prejudices against women and other gender groups.

For example, among the biggest taboos in Yemeni society and its media are sexual freedom, gender identity, and homosexuality, due to extremely conservative norms influenced by a strict interpretation of Shari'a law. The Yemeni Penal Code imposes penalties ranging from 100 lashes to death by stoning for non-marital sex, while homosexuality is punishable by death.

The authorities block access to websites that express support for LGBT rights. This policy of censorship extends to publications and broadcasting in Yemen. The magazine Al Thaqafiya was shut down in 2012 by the government for publishing a review of the Egyptian film Heena Maysara (translates to "Till things get better"). The reviewer, Yemeni filmmaker Hamid Aqbi, expressed some support for LGBTQ rights while discussing the film (Al-Saqaf, 2015).

Even if social media has helped highlight sensitive issues that were off-limits in Yemen, discussion of LGBTQ community rights is not welcome. Hind Aleryani, who describes herself as an activist and a journalist, was attacked online by both her followers in Yemen and her critics, when she wrote in her blog about the LGBTQ community calling for more rights in Yemen and the Arab World (Al-Bowaba, 2020).

The 2010 UN assessment on Violence against women in Yemen noted traditional Yemeni media outlets rarely addressed issues related to gender equity and gender-based violence. The assessment found this was because the media often considered the issues as sensitive. It also noted traditional media outlets are not conveying consistent messages to curb violence against women.

Many broadcasters used the term the safe age for marriage instead of child bride or child marriage to avoid backlash from a society with one of the highest rates of child marriage in the world. There is no clear law regulating the minimum age for marriage in Yemen and many girls are forced to marry under 18.

Media coverage of gender equality and women's political participation is negligible. Some media outlets only cover occasional events highlighting women's issues, such as International Women's Day, or events sporadically implemented by women's organizations. Apart from that, programmes on issues from a gender perspective are not an integral part of media coverage.

Even with occasional attention to women's issues, some Arabic and Yemeni media platforms—while striving to promote awareness of women's rights and gender equality—continue to discriminate against women by using stereotypes and traditionally harmful expressions (Al-Jaadbi, 2020).

Arabic editors, both men and women, still use such terms and phrases as "the fair sex," to refer to women, and "she has the courage of men," or "a woman with the strength of a thousand men" (when describing a woman being brave). They also use such phrases as "he was like a woman" (referring to a cowardly man), and the use of the term "spinster" for an unmarried woman (Al-Jaadbi, 2020).

Headlines in cases of domestic violence and adultery, for example, "implicitly reduce the blame on the perpetrator to place a portion of it on the victim" (Al-Jaadbi, 2020).

These examples, among others, show how male and female journalists received no training about gender-sensitive reporting. It is not enough to encourage women into journalism; it is critical to provide them with training because female journalists are educated and influenced by the same patriarchal ideas.

CONCLUSION

Yemeni women suffer from multiple layers of invisibility which obscure their complex identities and lived realities. They suffer from media misrepresentation, marginalization in the socioeconomic sphere, and stereotypical portrayal of women and men that sustains socially endorsed gender biases.

The deeply entrenched gender inequality rooted in a patriarchal society have created a media landscape not only insensitive to gender issues but, in many situations, supportive of the hostility towards women. The ongoing conflict in the country has exacerbated the marginalization of women's issues in the media by creating "military" media outlets, or polarizing political ones.

Moreover, given the political fragmentations in the country, there are no institutions to create and implement laws to protect women and journalists of either gender. In the absence of a functioning government and an effective parliament, the role of civil society is critical for the functioning of independent media. For this to happen, civil society organizations will need the financial and technical support from the private sector and independent international organizations.

Solving the media deficiencies in covering gender issues can be achieved not only through an increase in women's representation in the media sector but also appropriate professional training that transforms the media landscape into a more gender-sensitive environment.

REFERENCES

Al Sharjabi, A. M. (2013). *Yemeni Women's Rights Are a Struggle Between "Gender", Gulden and "Gendarmerie"*. Assafir Al-Arabi. Accessed from https://assafirarabi.com/ar/2752/2013/05/29/

Al-Bowaba. (2020, January). *Prominent Yemeni Activist Under Fire for Defending LGBT+ Rights in the Middle East*. Accessed from https://www.albawaba.com/node/prominent-yemeni-activist-under-fire-defending-lgbt-rights-middle-east

Al-Jaadbi, J. (2020, March), *Women in Journalism: Discriminatory Terminology and Stereotypes*. Accessed from https://manasati30.com/society/11374/

Al-Saqaf, W. (2015). *Sexual Rights and the Internet Report Yemen*. Accessed from https://www.giswatch.org/en/country-report/sexual-rights/yemen

Al-Zarqa, A., & Beleeqa TV. (2017, April 27). *Raufah Hassan; Years of Creativity and Modernization* [Video]. YouTube. Accessed from https://www.youtube.com/watch?v=CL_TQbdpoRU&t=2193s

Amnesty International. (2019, December 16). *Yemen: One of the Worst Places in the World to be a Woman*. Accessed from https://www.amnesty.org/en/latest/campaigns/2019/12/yemen-one-of-the-worst-places-in-the-world-to-be-a-woman/

Battaglia, L. S. (n.d.). *Yemen Media Landscape*. Accessed from *https://medialandscapes.org/country/yemen*

Cordes, S. (2013, August). *One Year After the Women Took to the Streets of Yemen*. KVINFO. Accessed from https://kvinfo.dk/one-year-after-the-women-took-to-the-streets-of-yemen/?lang=en

Farhan, M. (2017a). *An Evaluative Study Yemen TV Performance*. Studies and Economic Media Center SEMC. Accessed from http://economicmedia.net/en/?p=1315#more

Farhan, M. (2017b). *Current Status of Yemeni Women Journalists Challenges in Peace and War*. Studies & Economic Media Center (SEMC). Accessed from http://economicmedia.net/en/?p=1506

Kafi, M. A. (2005). *The Conditions of Female Media Workers and Obstacles to Professional Practice in Society and Yemeni MEDIA institutions.* Accessed from http://www.abhatoo.net.ma/page-principale

Munser, H. (2003, Feburary). *Yemeni Women Broadcasters Are Compelled to Wearing Headscarf, Shutting Nightclubs.* Accessed from https://elaph.com/Web/Archive/1045545743970952500.html

Nasser, A. (2018). *Making the Most of the Space Available.* Goethe-Institute/Perspectives. Accessed from https://www.goethe.de/prj/ruy/en/fra/21549306.html

Rassam, H. (2021). *Media Coverage of Women's Issues in Yemen - An Analytical Study. Women"s Voice Platform.* Mashaker Media. Accessed from https://drive.google.com/file/d/1Itk2_vk5NFS-dyCgSfCzUgWFPuS3MbPy/view

Raz, D. (2020, September). *The Arab World's Digital Divide.* Accessed from https://www.arabbarometer.org/2020/09/the-mena-digital-divide/

Reporters Without Borders (RSF). (2021). *World Press Freedom Index-2021.* Appalling Situation. Accessed from https://rsf.org/en/yemen

Saleh, H. (2018). *Including Women's Issues in Yemeni Media.* Gender-Development Research and Studies Centre. Accessed from https://gdrsc.net/en/2020/10/1958/.

Salem, F., et al. (2011, May) *Civil Movement: The Impact of Facebook and Twitter.* Dubai School Government. Accessed from https://journalistsresource.org/wpcontent/uploads/2011/08/DSG_Arab_Social_Media_Report_No_2.pdf

Studies & Economic Media Center (SEMC). (2017a). *Evaluation Study of the Media Coverage of the War in Yemen.* Accessed from http://economicmedia.net/EN/wp-content/uploads/2017/09/War-Media-Study-Yemen-.pdf

Studies & Economic Media Center (SEMC). (2017b). *Yemen Media Landscape.* Accessed from http://economicmedia.net/en/?p=2101

The UN. (2010). *The 2010 UN Assessment on Violence Against Women.* Accessed from https://www.un.org/womenwatch/ianwge/taskforces/vaw/Country_Assessment_on_Violence_against_Women_August_2_2010.pdf

World Economic Forum. (2021, March). *Global Gender Gap-Insight Report 2021-P14.* Accessed from https://www3.weforum.org/docs/WEF_GGGR_2021.pdf

Yemen Media Observatory in Yemen–(Marsadak). (n.d.). Accessed from https://www.marsadak.org/main

Yemen: Law No. 25. (1990). *On the Press and Publications.* Accessed from https://aceproject.org/ero-en/regions/mideast/YE/yemen-law-no-25-on-press-and-publications-1990/view

PART V

Introduction: Gender and Expressive Cultures

The linkages between gender and cultural expressions are communicated through a variety of spaces, forms, and platforms. Whether one analyzes popular, visual, and street art, music or theater, performances, literary works, or mediated content, these linkages are invariably structured by dimensions of power and control, gender dynamics and hierarchies, as well as processes of contestation and subversion. Although the cultures of the Middle East and North Africa are rich, dynamic, and diverse, the gender dimension of expressive cultures has remained largely understudied.

Scholars of MENA cultures and artistic expressions have been mostly engaged, over the last few decades, in redirecting research away from the long tradition of the reductionist and paternalistic gaze of Orientalist cultural anthropology. Contemporary research has therefore redefined the theoretical, epistemological, and methodological frameworks that recognize cultural expressions as complex sites of meaning-making and power struggles, identity formation, and political contestation (Armbrst, 1996; El Hamamsy & Soliman, 2014; Sabry, 2010, 2012; Swendberg, 2012; Valassapoulos, 2013). Through rigorous analysis of the region's film industries and television productions, visual arts, popular music, performances, and other cultural expressions, scholars have built a robust foundation for comprehending significant trends in MENA cultures. One important trend is the critical role that expressive cultures have played at each major moment of MENA's recent histories ranging from colonial occupations and struggles for independence to political and social movements for civil liberties and political freedoms. In all these instances, expressive cultures have been both constitutive and reflective of the demands and dreams of the region's citizens. Given this trend, expressive cultures have been intensely political as well as politicized, closely monitored and controlled by MENA's political and religious centers of power.

This is an important point to underscore because expressive cultures have not suddenly emerged during or after the 2011 democratic uprisings, as many observers or scholars of MENA might suggest. Rather, the region has been home to vibrant cultural movements and underground music scenes whose artists have been engaged in indigenizing global music forms (heavy metal, rock, hip hop, or rap) (Levine, 2008) and experimenting with other artistic forms that resonate with their complex realities. Despite censorship and threats of persecution by the region's security apparatuses, MENA artists turned to cultural expressions to articulate their generational consciousness and reflect on the tensions and contradictions within the political and social fabrics of their societies leading up to the 2011 uprisings (Skalli, 2011, 2013). The prolific literature that has emerged after the 2011 uprisings [see, e.g., Shilton (2021), Kraidy (2017), Gröndahl (2013)] is therefore less a discovery of expressive cultures themselves than an affirmation of the ingenuity of MENA artists in adopting and adapting various media and forms of expressions to their contextual needs.

Despite this, scholarship on gender and expressive cultures in MENA remains, with rare exceptions, very limited. The groundbreaking work of Lila Abu-Lughod and Deborah Kapchan has charted a path for a feminist anthropology of MENA cultures that examines the multiple ways in which gender articulates with cultural forms, the politics of everyday lives, knowledge production, as well as regimes of power and discipline in MENA. Their insights have directed our attention to the extent to which expressive cultures (Bedouin poetry, popular music, and performances) are productive sites of negotiation over gender roles and relations and contestation over political and religious authority, sexual identities, morality, and heteronormativity.

The chapters in this part build on and extend this line of research by focusing on a wide range of cultural expressions and using a variety of analytical tools and methodologies. They situate us in Tunisia, Morocco, Algeria, Iraq, Palestine, and Egypt to provide conceptual insights and empirical analyses of the gendered dimensions of expressive cultures. Despite contextual differences and the chapters' focus on different cultural expressions, there are fascinating overlaps and complementarities worth signaling at the outset. These include the researchers' conscious efforts to (a) heed the intersection of gender with age, class, and race within their specific localities, (b) attend to shifting local and global forces which shape and inform expressive cultures in MENA, and (c) transcend the tendency of romanticizing "resistance" in their reading of gendered cultural expressions.

Brinda Mehta does this by turning our attention to the writings of the award-winning Iraqi poet, Dunya Mikhail, to examine the poetics of pain, loss, and remembrance. Poetry in this context is approached as a medium for retrieving, recording, and memorializing women's embodied experiences of conflict, in the phenomenological meaning of embodiment. As Brinda puts it, Mikhail's "*In Her Feminine Sign* pulsates with the rhythmic sensations of life, death, and resistance to infuse the sterility of conventional war chronicles with the breath, sound, and feelings of those most impacted by war in the form of lived narratives, human emotions, and corporeal archives." By analyzing Mikhail's collection of poetry and other writings, Brinda delivers an effective analysis of gender dimensions often marginalized in the scholarship on conflict and memory in

MENA. Engagement with Mikhail poetry enables her to problematize acts of witnessing, remembrance, and memory-making and tease out ways in which these processes are inherently gendered.

Polly Withers situates us in another context of conflict to deliver a convincing analysis of how subcultural music in contemporary Palestine engages with and negotiates gender roles and gendered practices in complex and unanticipated ways. Specifically, Polly problematizes such concepts as "agency," "empowerment," and "gender dissent" in post-Oslo Palestine. She does so by questioning the tendency of reducing cultural production in MENA to uncontextualized "revolutionary" metanarratives one is likely to find in much of Western media and liberal approaches to expressive cultures. Through keen observations and nuanced readings of youth subcultural practices, she contends that narratives of "spectacular acts of gender dissent" are not only simplistic but also misleading. They typically mask how the empowerment of masculinities and femininities is a complex process mediated by class, race, and geopolitical forces. Acknowledging these mediating forces is necessary to comprehend how young adults' cultural engagement with music and performances simultaneously "ruptures and reproduces" dominant structures of gendered power.

Cristina Moreno provides a similar nuanced reading of empowerment through expressive cultures in her chapter on female rappers in the Moroccan urban cultural scene (1990s–2000s). Moreno refutes the tendency to frame female Hip Hop artists as the "voice of women" in MENA or the "voices of the revolution" during the Arab uprisings. This reductionist framing, she contends, prevents the appreciation of the artistic contributions of women rappers and their deft negotiations of national contexts and international forces to position themselves as artists. Through this analysis of the music aesthetics and politics of Moroccan female rappers, she demonstrates how these artists "have learned to navigate politics, moral codes and a growing social media penetration in order to create and build their own artistic careers." Moreno's contribution invites further research in the gendered world of artistic production and performance while she rightfully cautions against the temptation to exaggerate or essentialize gender justice.

It is precisely because of the paucity of research on women artists in MENA that Lilia Labidi devotes her chapter to three women artists from North Africa: the Tunisian Safia Farhat, the Moroccan Chaibia, and the Algerian Baya. Labidi, a scholar and artist herself, asks questions about the role of women artists in their societies, as well as the nature and meaning of their artistic contributions. She goes to great lengths to show why and how the work of female artists has been marginalized if not unrecognized by art historians within and outside the region. Yet, the life trajectories and artistic productions of the three artists, as Labidi demonstrates, are fascinating and anchored in the realities of their societies and the cultural tradition of Islamic miniatures while fully engaged with broader global artistic trends and influences.

Zoe Hurley's chapter on Middle Eastern women's comic performances on Instagram provides a rare glimpse into the politics of laughter by examining the intersection of gender, humor, and social media affordances in MENA. Zoe focuses on three comic social media influencers to discuss how their humorous Instagram performances open spaces for empowerment while articulating constraints on women's freedoms and daily practices. Her research highlights the political significance of women's laughter as it articulates traditional Middle Eastern "modes of social critique ("hazl" (farce), "tahakkum" (taunt), and "sukhri'iya" (poking fun, including forms of sarcasm and irony)" in new spaces created by newer digital technologies. To do this, she proposes a "novel feminist postdigital framework" that highlights how young women participate in the destabilizing power of humor by capitalizing on opportunities created by new digital spaces and mobilizing these to bargain with patriarchy.

Alma Khasawnih's chapter takes us to the post-revolution graffiti art in Egypt to examine the meaning of these cultural spaces and modes of expression. Khasawnih argues that although graffiti is an ephemeral art form, its social and political implications in the repressive context of Egypt transcend ephemera and contextual constraints. Graffiti created by women and women-centered groups are acts of defiance and challenges to the hegemonic narratives of the uprisings. They are also sites for redefining and imagining womanhood beyond the confines of patriarchal structures. In fact, bargaining with patriarchy and rethinking structures of power are the running threads in this part's chapters.

REFERENCES

Abu-Lughod, L. (1986). *Veiled Sentiments: Honor and Poetry in a Bedouin Society.* University of California Press. El Hamamsy, W., & Soliman, M. (2014). *Popular Culture in the Middle East and North Africa.* Routledge.

Grondahl, M. (2013). *Revolution Graffiti: Street Art of the New Egypt.* Cairo University Press.

Kachpen, D. (1996). *Gender on the Market: Moroccan Women and the Revoicing of Tradition.* University of Pennsylvania Press.

Kraidy, M. (2017). *The Naked Blogger of Cairo.* Harvard University Press.

Levine, M. (2008). *Heavy Metal Islam: Rock, Resistance, and the Struggle for the Soul of Islam.* Broadway Books.

Skalli, L. H. (2013). Introduction. *Middle East Journal of Culture and Communication,* 6(1), 5–14. doi: https://doi.org/10.1163/18739865-00503001

Skalli, H. S. (2011). Youth, Media and the Art of Protest in North Africa. *Jadaliyya.* https://www.jadaliyya.com/Details/24130

Swedenburg, T. (2012). Egypt's Music of Protest: From Sayyid Darwish to DJ Haha. *Middle East Report,* 42(265).

Tarik, S. (2010). *Cultural Encounters in the Arab World: On Media, The Modern and the Everyday.* I.B. Tauris.

Tarik, T. (Ed.) (2012). *Arab Cultural Studies: Mapping the Field.* I.B. Tauris.

Valassopoulos, A. (Ed.) (2013). *Arab Cultural Studies: History, Politics, and the Popular.* Routledge.

CHAPTER 23

Redefining the Archive: Birdsong, Tied Circles, and Woman-Space in Dunya Mikhail's *In Her Feminine Sign*

Brinda J. Mehta

Our claytablets are cracked
Scattered, like us, are the Sumerian letters
"Freedom" is inscribed this way
Ama-ar-gi
—Dunya Mikhail

Feminist poetry occupies an important position within the spectrum of Iraqi literature from antiquity to the present day. Enheduanna, the high priestess of the goddess Inanna, is the first recorded poet in history. She is the foremother of female literary creation in ancient Mesopotamia. Enheduanna establishes a strong woman-centered genealogy of feminist poetry through the ages in what is now contemporary Iraq. Centuries later, a Sufi mystic named Rabia of Basra (714–801 CE) became Islam's first Sufi woman saint. Rabia initiated a revolutionary gendered understanding of women's shifting roles in society through the prism of transcendent poetry, religion, asceticism, and the idea of divine love. She argued that women had equal access to spiritual transcendence as men through critical thinking, the reevaluation of women's roles in religion, and the development of women's creative potential through Sufi mysticism (Monte, 2017). In a more contemporary context, trailblazing feminist poets

B. J. Mehta (✉)
Mills College, Northeastern University, Oakland, CA, USA
e-mail: b.mehta@northeastern.edu

L. H. Skalli, N. Eltantawy (eds.), *The Palgrave Handbook of Gender, Media and Communication in the Middle East and North Africa*,
https://doi.org/10.1007/978-3-031-11980-4_23

407

such as Daisy Amir, Lamia Abbas Amara, Nazik al-Malaika, Dunya Mikhail, and Najiba Ahmad revolutionized the structure and content of Iraqi poetry. They introduced free verse formations; articulated their feminist concerns about love, gender roles, and patriarchal politics; included the voices of Kurdish women authors; critiqued social taboos and conventions that delimited a woman's right to (self-)expression; expressed their exilic consciousness; and boldly documented their feminist responses to war and conflict in searing verse (Al-Hassan, 2020). Award-winning poet Dunya Mikhail occupies a place of prominence within this pantheon of creative artists through her strong sense of ancestral consciousness and her poetic reflections on the ravages of war.

Multiple wars have scarred the recent political and social landscapes of Iraq to create a country under siege by internal and external forces—Saddam Hussein's Ba'athist dictatorship (1979–2003), a US-led invasion and occupation in 2003, and the ensuing post-occupation sectarian violence exacerbated by *Daesh* or the Islamic State. Within this climate of anxiety, insecurity, and sociopolitical destabilization, Dunya Mikhail's poetry grafts landscapes of pain and resistance to bear witness to the horrors and traumas of Iraq's succession of wars while highlighting the poet's resistance to this violation. These writings represent a deeply insightful medium to evoke the most horrific realities of war, displacement, and loss. I argue it is this precise need to overcome suffering and loss through poetry that motivates Mikhail to construct an important woman-centered archive of marginalized histories and stories within these negating circumstances. These poems nevertheless include "a circular embrace of humanity" as a form of humanitarian consciousness (Bernea, 2020).

The sidelined perspectives of women are symbolized by the poeticized "feminine sign," a uniquely feminized alphabet that punctuates Mikhail's recent collection of poetry titled *In Her Feminine Sign* in the original English version (2019). In this essay I demonstrate how the feminine cipher reveals Iraq's wounded geographies of death, absence, violence, and desolation. These experiences are preserved within the feminine sign's womb-like folds as a symbol of the many losses suffered by women in particular when they are confronted by war and violence. At the same time, war as an historical event or a fact of history is not the focus of this poetry: "Writing was a way to turn a catastrophic event into an aesthetic one," asserts Mikhail (Pearce, 2021). Instead, the human experiences engendered by war take center stage to highlight the traumas, violence, and hardships suffered by casualties and survivors alike in these poetic writings. *In Her Feminine Sign* responds to current events in Iraq: "Yet while poetry has profoundly influenced Arab politics it has also been transformed and reshaped by it," argues Waed Athamneh in *Modern Arabic Poetry: Revolution and Conflict* (2017, 8). Mikhail subverts the "poetry for poetry's sake" dictum in this aesthetic reshaping by positioning her poetry as a medium of feminist and social justice consciousness; this poetry demonstrates its ongoing engagement *in* and *with* a war-torn world.

An Iraqi-Christian from Baghdad, Dunya Mikhail is an award-winning author whose prestigious accolades include a John Simon Guggenheim

Fellowship, the Kresge Fellowship, the Arab American Book Award, and the United Nations Human Rights Award. Her literary repertory comprises seven books of poetry translated into multiple languages (*In Her Feminine Sign, The Iraqi Nights, The War Works Hard*), a poetic memoir (*Diary of a Wave Outside the Sea*), a harrowing non-fiction account of the Yazidi tragedy of 2014 in *The Beekeeper: Rescuing the Stolen Women of Iraq* [2018], and her first novel written in Arabic titled *The Bird Tattoo* in translation (2021). Mikhail started writing war poetry during her most formative years in Iraq where she also worked as a journalist for *The Baghdad Observer*. Mikhail embraces a polyglot sensibility in her work to translate and accommodate Iraq's rich cultural and religious heritage in verse. Fluent in Aramaic, Arabic, and English, her writings reflect a deep sense of ancestral historicity on the one hand. On the other hand, her creative imaginary is animated by a "bare to the bones" imagery and lyricism as a form of political critique.

Mikhail adopts a multitudinous fluidity in her poetry enabling her to traverse time and space in her imagination as she connects the past with the present, the exilic *here* with the rooted *there*, and the human and non-human in seamless continuity. Seemingly disparate associations find new meaning in fluid juxtapositions that mirror the poet's exilic consciousness situated in the *betwixt* and the *between*. Identifying with the venerable Enheduanna, Mikhail associates the ancestral poet's ethic of "flame keeping" with the contemporary writer's responsibility to craft poetic flames in verse as a form of protest against oppression and war. At the same time, these flames also represent poetry's aesthetic and moral potential to transform, transcend, and uphold the "common truth" (Jarrar, 2015, 15) in the fires of inspiration. Mikhail's writings emerge from within the agonizing depths of war and political injustice to highlight the "common truth" about the human cost of this devastation in the form of deep wounds. These wounds are both sensed and expressed in visceral language. The anti-war sentiment of Mikhail's poetry and her refusal to become a praise singer of Saddam Hussein's regime ultimately resulted in the censorship of her writing in Iraq and her eventual exile to Michigan in 1996. She currently teaches Arabic at Oakland University.

In Her Feminine Sign is inspired by the poet's visit to the temple of Lalish in Iraq's Kurdish Sinjar province. Mikhail visited the shrine to pay her respects to the bravehearted Yazidi women whose testimonies are chronicled in her non-fictional testimonial text, *The Beekeeper: Rescuing the Stolen Women of Iraq* (2018). The primary focus of her visit, however, was to thank the man who saved the women from further perdition at the hands of *Daesh*.[1] The intrepid beekeeper Abdullah provided Mikhail with a first-hand narration of the women's ordeals that are at the core of *The Beekeeper*. In turn, Mikhail honors the

---

[1] *Daesh* is a Sunni jihadist terrorist organization that has espoused a violent ideology of hate. Claiming to be an Islamic Caliphate endowed with the power to exercise unilateral religious control over Muslims, *Daesh* has engaged in unspeakable acts of militarized terror leveled against Christians, Yazidis, and moderate Muslims in Iraq and Syria.

women in her poetry by demonstrating how the horror of human abjection can also inspire deeply meaningful writing. *In Her Feminine Sign* emerges from these depths of sorrow, pain, and horror while simultaneously denouncing the heinous violence committed against the women; these poems also commemorate the dead. The temple of Lalish is a very sacred place for the Yazidis, a symbol of their religious identity and ancient cultural and spiritual traditions. Within the temple walls "the columns are draped with prayer cloths, and pilgrims may make their wishes by first untying a knot, thus releasing the previous pilgrim's wish to be granted, then tying and retying the knot three times while reflecting on their own wish. On the third turn, they tie it tight, having made their wish" (Levi, 2019). Together with Abdullah, Mikhail participates in this sacrosanct ritual whose significance lies in the repeated tying and untying of a circular knot. This ritualistic action liberates the wishes of the pilgrims who visit the holy shrine. While performing the ritual, Mikhail reflects on the hidden meanings concealed and then released from within the knot's folds. This moment of meditative reflection is a creative act and a source of poetic inspiration.

The circular movements of this time-honored ritual invite parallels with the circularity of "feminine words" in Arabic represented by "a circle with two dots over it." It also provides the basic structure and motivation for this poetic collection ("The Stranger In Her Feminine Sign," 11). The circle generates multiple meanings through its concentricity. It refers to both gendered language ("everything has gender/in Arabic," 11) and cultural sanctity while offering a protective cocoon to enfold the forgotten stories of the women. Just as successive waves of pilgrims liberate the wishes of those who come before them in this "town of tied wishes," so also the women await with bated breath for the arrival of the poet-stranger who will visit the sanctuary one day in order to collect their stories "and adorn them to her circle." They hope to welcome this special guest who "will arrive/today in her feminine sign" (11) and free them from the burden of "old wishes/to make space for the new" ("The Stranger," 12). The violations experienced by these women at the hands of *Daesh* cannot be articulated in ordinary words. They can only be imagined in poetry's supra-sensory language beyond the materiality of mundane vocabulary: "In poetry, the sensory details are the necessary means by which the supra-sensory realm is evoked" (Sun, 1995, 113).

This supra-sensorial "third space" archives the women's pain in the tied circle. It is the poet's responsibility to unveil these emotions in figurative verse through the sensory ritual of touching, feeling, experiencing, and finally expressing this pain in poetic expression. For this reason, Mikhail expects her readers to "feel" her poems rather than merely read or analyze them. She wants the reader to experience a sense of linguistic impotence in their inability to find the right words of sympathy and consolation for the women's distress, just as the women are unable to express themselves using mere words. Poetry becomes a medium to express the unsaid through a sensory experience connecting language and body in "tied" or intimate circularity. The pain and violence hidden within the tied circle also refers to the way the *Daesh* perpetrators would "tie" the hands of the women before leading them to a hapless fate of death or rape (Griffith, 2019, 6). Accordingly, the women seek the poet's help to find a new language to both articulate and then exorcise their knotted pain. Their need for self-expression is located in "the tied circle" of wishes ("The Stranger," 11) that must be untied to liberate these repressed emotions and experiences.

The title of the collection references a key moment in the poet's own consciousness referenced by the use of the preposition "in." The preposition "*in* her feminine sign" reveals how the poems are influenced by the poet's reawakened feminist sensibilities located within the "tied circle." This positionality enables her to both see and empathize with the suffering of the Yazidi women as she attempts to recover from her own state of shock when she hears about their repeated violations by *Daesh*. This convulsive moment morphs into the inspiring force of creation. The poet joins these women "in" bonds of feminist solidarity and deep compassion. It is her ethical responsibility as a poet to find the appropriate words to name this un-nameable violence by using "a special sentence,/the gift she'll bring to town." This is a daunting task when she comes face to face with the human devastation in the Yazidi lands of Sinjar. She must tread cautiously by choosing the appropriate "verb/or a noun" because her words can be a gift or a curse by having the power to either heal or re-traumatize. "With one touch" her words could transform "into a flower that blooms/for only an instant/before it withers and dies" ("The Stranger," 12). She must offer the promise of hope (symbolized by the blooming flower) in her reflective verse while guarding against the loss of hope through untied, inappropriate, or dead poetry.

Moreover, the poet herself needs to heal after transcribing the women's horrific ordeals in *The Beekeeper*, which explains her initial hesitation to undertake the project of the "tied circle" and her "lateness" for "those who wait" ("The Stranger," 12). While giving voice to the women, she must also find release from the trauma of memory in the unraveling knots of poetry. The process of untying these poetic knots leads to an epiphanic revelation in verse. This moment of revelation is symbolized by the illuminating waxing and waning of the moon, the poet's lunar muse: "How the moon/hides in her red circle" ("The Stranger," 11) states the narrator as she negotiates the knotted spaces of exile between Iraq and the US, the in-betweenness of "Baghdad in Detroit" (15). *In Her Feminine Sign* attempts to provide a sense of poetic closure to the horrors of the past through the tied circle symbol while suggesting that this horror could be unleashed or untied at any moment through male dreams of power and conquest. This violence nullifies the women's wishes for peace through the gendering of language in Arabic: "Dream is male/Wish is female" ("The Stranger," 11).

In Her Feminine Sign is crafted in two distinctive languages, Arabic and English. The poems are written "from right to left and from left to right" ("Author's Note," 7) to highlight the poet's linguistic and exilic ambidexterity needed to straddle the interstitiality of exile. Mikhail insists the English version is an autonomous text and not a translation from the Arabic. She states: "The reason I didn't think of it as "translation" is that I allowed myself to be free in the "rewriting" of the poem as if trying to give it two lives that relate to each other but are not exactly a copy of each other" (Saeed, 2019). Writing the volume twice represents the poet's "new original" (Saeed, 2019), wherein she goes back and forth between the two versions to mirror her exilic trajectories between the US and Iraq and the tenuousness of exile in general. At home in her native Arabic, this language enables the poet "to hear the music the words make or not make together." She must, at the same time, find a sense of homing in the English language whose cadence is unable to "translate" the musical rhythms of Arabic. Yet, English represents a medium of negotiation through a mirroring effect: "English doesn't play music for me but it helps me see my text better because it makes me more sensitive towards the Arabic," she states (Saeed, 2019). The two languages nevertheless intersect at a liminal point in the poet's consciousness to represent both loss and recovery, hope and anguish, the timeless and the ephemeral.

The volume is divided into three (dis)continuous parts—"Tied Circle," followed by "Tablets," and concluding with "T/here"; the three sections are nevertheless tied together by the highly fluid and lyrical idiom of the feminine circle. This language is expressed in the Arabic *taa'marboota*, the feminized signifier for nouns. The three sections mirror the cyclical patterns of the moon in the form of poetic plenitude. This system of writing is expressed in the Arabic style known as *al-sahl al-mumtane*, "language that delivers information and emotion with great fluidity but without excess, a kind of lucid restraint that contains multitudes" (Khalaf Tuffaha, 2019). This form encapsulates the intensity of thought and feeling in liminal verse that is nevertheless replete with signs and signifiers likened to the pregnant fullness of the moon. In other words, these poems are animated by ethereal moonscapes configured like the "tied circle," a symbol of transcendence and creative inspiration. The second section "Tablets" refers to the ancient Sumerian system of writing on clay tablets, the first recorded form of inscription dating back to 3100 BC. This script is a highly figurative, "imaged" language initially expressed in the form of pictographs and later developed into cuneiform to include sounds and meaning (Gelb, 2019). This metaphoric language is poetic in nature using pictogram-inspired images to convey thoughts and feelings in the absence of words. These images accompany each poem to provide visual language when words fail.

Like the ancient tablets, the poems in this section are compressed in haiku-like form with a difference. Termed "Iraqi haiku" by the poet, the poetic Iraqi tablets bend the 5-7-5 structure of the traditional three-lined Japanese haiku by "untying" its syllabic restrictions to capture the depth of feelings and emotions that cannot be expressed in words. The haikus are accompanied by the poet's own drawings that recreate the prehistoric Sumerian tablets. The poems do not have descriptive titles. Instead, they are structured in numerical order like the ancient clay tablets. The reconfigured Iraqi haiku with its accompanying images is a language of the senses; its expressiveness goes beyond the literalness of words to enter the infinity of the full moon's zero circle: "When the moon is full/it looks like a zero" ("11," 37). This anti-structure gives Mikhail the freedom to discover the Iraqi haiku's hidden expressions that remain concealed "behind" conventional structure.

The third section "T/here" reflects the poet's exilic consciousness suspended between the *here* and *there* and her search for belonging beyond exile. Does such a third space exist, and if so, what are the poet's rights of access to this transcendent space filled with "so much war and so much love" ("What We Carry To Mars," 57)? Is exile a tenuous middle passage or a point of no return for the estranged poet who experiences a sense of nowhere-ness amid the fractures of exile? Does poetry provide a sanctuary space within the fullness of the "tied circle," a protective womb of comfort for both the poet and the ravaged mothers and sisters of her homeland, or does it dissipate into an abysmal vortex of lost hope and irrevocable personal pain expressed in sorrowful tones?: "It's true that pain/is like air, available/everywhere,/but we each feel/our pain hurts the most" ("15", 49). Undulating poetic rhythms express the unpredictable personal trajectories of pain to maintain the tension between the possible anticipation of freedom and the impossible disavowal of pain's "atmospheric" vibrations. These sensory pulsations must be preserved in an audible recording of airborne birdsong, "like the air," as the expressive language of the elusive goddess.

War Is the True Survivor Among Us
—Mikhail

In Her Feminine Sign pulsates with the rhythmic sensations of life, death, and resistance to infuse the sterility of conventional war chronicles with the breath, sound, and feelings of those most impacted by war in the form of lived narratives, human emotions, and corporeal archives. Mikhail creates what Anna Harris terms a "sensory archive," comprising "a body of sensory knowledge that is continually played and experimented with in different ways, shared between others to become something different yet again" (2016). This knowledge is a source of experimentation, transformation, movement, regeneration, and creativity preserved in a non-institutionalized open-ended archival space. *The Feminine Sign* recreates this space in nature. As a form of "life cycle" (Brothman, 2001, 52), this mobile archive is a resource "for the potential discovery or recovery of memories that have been lost" (Hedstrom, 2010, 136) through a gendered re-engagement with the past and a corresponding reevaluation of the present through the feminine sign's prismatic lens.

The conventional archive as a national resource plays an important role in the construction of a nation's identity, history, and memory. At the same time, whose memories are deemed worthy of recording and for what purpose? Can the archive be manipulated by those in power to record a particular version of history by privileging some memories over others? What is deliberately remembered and what is conveniently forgotten to create a "feverish" state of "forgetfulness, amnesia, the annihilation of memory" (Derrida, 2011, 11)? Is the archive capable of recording a memory of loss for dispossessed groups when the right to document is denied or monitored by state policing and colonial theft as in the case of Iraq? Within such ambiguity, why is an alternative feminine archive needed to record the truncated experiences of women who are dually marginalized by "a neo-feudal corporatism—an emerging global system ruled by a superpower/corporate military complex" of national and international aggressors (Jacqueline Ismael & Shereen Ismael, 2007, 258)?[2] My essay addresses the last question.

Mikhail's poetry creates an archive of simultaneous loss and recuperation through the gendering of women's memories that are rescued from the confines of state amnesia and the devastation of war. State-sanctioned memories "wield power over the shape and direction of historical scholarship, collective memory, and national identity" through partial recording and mnemonic exclusions (Schwarz & Cook, 2002, 2). In a contrapuntal twist, Mikhail's writings urge the reader to look for women's obscured stories in non-conventional places such as in a grandmother's hair braids, for example: "her braid/each hair a history" ("My Grandmother's Grave," 24). The intricate braids document the grandmother's intimate life story in a highly textured archival weaving intertwined with the complex history of Iraqi women. These poems revise the traditional "idea" of the archive in which the nation's history is memorialized in government institutions, state buildings, official documents, and public monuments. Instead, Mikhail's poems construct living archives of memorialized senses and feelings expressed in soundscapes, nature, and ruins. This connection between poetry, recording, and feeling is best revealed in Arabic through the close association between *sh'ir* (poetry) and feeling (*shi'ur*) as described by Mikhail in her interview with Sobia Khan (2015, 12).

The search for the feminine sign in these poems is an act of retrieval—a search for lost archival knowledge that has been wrenched from the hands of the maternal guardians of this ancient wisdom by male gods and godheads: "Ama-ar-gi is what we weep," states the distraught poet (59). These figures include the ancient goddesses Inanna and Nisaba, Enheduanna,[3] and the contemporary poet herself. Nisaba is the Sumerian goddess of writing, learning, and agriculture, while the Babylonian Inanna is "the goddess of love and war, and she's both masculine and feminine. She was in both upper world and underworld. She's pretty much like Iraq with all of its contradictions," asserts Mikhail in her interview with Khan (11, 2015). This pantheon of Iraqi god-

---

[2] At the same time, the preservation of the archive acquires special salience in times of war when an invaded nation's records are destroyed, plundered, or stolen.

[3] "The first known poet in history, Enheduanna was an Iraqi woman. She wrote about Inanna on tablets in the cuneiform language. The interesting thing about her is that she had a position or title. It was "The Keeper of the Flame," states Mikhail in a New Directions interview (April 2010). Enheduanna lived in the twenty-third century BCE in ancient Mesopotamia. For more details on the priestess-poet, consult Betty de Shong's *Princess, Priestess, Poet: The Sumerian Temple Hymns of Enheduanna.* University of Texas Press. 2009.

desses and poetesses guards a repository of wisdom that extends across the cosmic geography of Ama-ar-gi, a Sumerian word that signifies "returning to the mother" ("Ama-ar-gi," 58). The cartography of Ama-ar-gi stretches from the ancient Sumer and Babylonia of mythological times to contemporary war-torn Iraq and the exilic spaces of Detroit, Michigan. It is animated by the voice of the mother as the ultimate *Ursprache*, an interiorized language that provides "the key to unlocking what lies behind the gaps and silences that surround women's creative contributions to history" (cooke, 2001, xxxvi). As the primal breath, this language corresponds with the original trace of Derrida's "sound-image" (1976, 63), a psychic imprint of voice and presence expressing itself in a sororal echo across ancient lands.

Mikhail's poetry has many lives and incarnations within this transnational sonorous space; it is (re)located within a wondrous circle of women's inter-twining memories, myths, histories, and stories. The feminine sign rescues Iraq's stolen maternal heritage from the ravages of war, militarization, and male-centered histories by resurrecting the maternal ethos of the divine god-dess in a circular invocation of life, breath, and protective care: "She's still look-ing/down at her baby/after 4800 years" ("Song Inside A Fossil," 13). These mythologized timelines cover a lifespan of 4800 years; they are nevertheless marked by the shadows of the many women who still remain invisible and voiceless in history, these "faces of the absentees" (13). Only a poetic invoca-tion uttered "in her feminine sign" will provide the right words to name this un-nameable absence in a sensory incantation. This "sound-image" contains the one hundred names of the goddess Nisaba: "How shall I call you/when you have one hundred names?" cries the poet ("Nisaba," 17). The poet is chal-lenged to find the precise name or the specific sound bite that will invoke the goddess's benevolent presence in her poetic supplications amid so much loss and destruction.

> **Deep wounds don't speak, they can only be felt**
> —Mikhail – *The Beekeeper*

In Her Feminine Sign is an invitation to enter an archive "with a difference" in which sights, sounds, and ciphers compel the reader to listen to the forgot-ten maternal voices of the past and present; these ethereal voices emerge from "inside her mother's belly" ("15," 38). In this form of circular movement, the contemporary poet goes back in time to merge with the ancestral high priestess-poet-princess Enheduanna and the goddess-scribe Nisaba in a timeless rhyth-mical encirclement, this "life cycle" evoked by Brothman (2001, 52). The poet creates a sensory archive through the womb-like figure of the tied circle as a site of creativity, metamorphosis, and limitless possibility: "This tied circle transforms into the moon, a stone that binds friendship, birdsong over ruins ... and a hymn to Nisaba ..." (New Directions, 2019). The transformative dimen-sions of this regenerating sign facilitate ancestral connections and mythical interventions in poetry. For example, the identification with Enheduanna is a point of access to the mystical realm of the eminent Inanna, the penultimate bearer of the feminine sign.

Inanna's voice of plenitude is the poet's muse urging her to break the silence around the story of women's ancestry, creativity, knowledge, and suffering in a highly symbolic language, "one that deviates from the familiar simply because it is both different and feminine" (Fatna El Bouih, 2008, i). The feminine sign has the power to unveil the eclipsed "circle with two dots" as a feminized affirmation of presence represented by these ancient muse-turned-scribe role models. The symbol of the "tied circle" or *taamarbuta* in Arabic references a more inclusive perspective completed by "a verb/or a noun phrase ... /a word complete on its own" in order to reveal the names and faces of those who remain hidden behind words and history ("The Stranger in Her Feminine Sign," 11).

The *taamarbuta* reflects the search for inclusivity as the poet meditates on the political, social, and religious fractures that compromise human dignity and the right to exist peacefully in Iraq. Her writings follow the trajectory of the 2003 US-led invasion, occupation, and its aftermath in both poetry and non-fictional prose to demonstrate how war-related violence has fractured her beloved country into sectarian Sunni, Shia, Christian, and Kurdish enclaves that deny the peaceful existence of Iraqis. These fractures are referred to as "circles with cracks" in the poem "What We Carry to Mars" (55). These circles of hope are nevertheless compromised by deeply entrenched cracks that highlight Iraq's ongoing struggles with the multiple scars of war and violence.

The search for this feminized tongue remains beyond the limitations of the patriarchal language of war in which "history is male" (11). It can only be expressed in the song-like rhythms of poetry "throbbing with songs/that cause sadness and elation/and something so obscure/no one has a name for it" (11), a lyricism echoed amid the sounds of nature. These poetic soundscapes represent the ethereal language of the feminine sign in the form of a coded language, "something so obscure" and nameless ("The Stranger," 12). It is primarily deciphered through birdsong, sighs, and cries. This as-yet-to-be-named language is comparable to Algerian author Assia Djebar's evocation of the "fourth language" emerging from the depths of bodily pain and loss as a way to both mourn and protest the ignominy of war and violence. This is a highly communicative spirit language composed of "scab words" that reveal the muffled sounds and wounded words of devastated bodies: "The fourth language, for all females ... remains that of the body ... the body which, in trances, dances or vociferations, in fits of hope and despair, rebels ..." (*Fantasia*, 1987, 180). This voice of rebellion nevertheless emerges progressively in fits and starts from within the ceremonial feminine circle as a point of articulation. It follows the cadence of the poet's liberating verse to reveal the hidden face of "a goddess who found/her lost universe in the last minute" ("Eva Whose Shadow Is A Swan," 22). The feminine sign performs a timely search and rescue mission to restore the goddess's lost universe as a way to restore peace and cosmic equilibrium.

STRUCTURING THE FEMININE SIGN

The pre-symbolic articulation of the feminine sign enables the poet to give life and texture to the un-nameable language of death, for example, a language that can only be sensed and heard in birdsong, the quiet rippling of water, or the gentle rustling of autumn leaves: "All of us are autumn leaves/ready to fall at any time," muses the poet ("5," 36). In other words, the imminence of death can only be intuited through the body while the reality of death amid war's wanton destruction can only be announced by the presence of wild flowers on unmarked mass graves: "Those colorful flowers/over the mass graves/ are the dead's last words" ("17," 38). The beautiful flowers are nevertheless tainted by bloodied horror represented by the concealed mass graves. Their dual symbolism reveals nature's manifest glory in Iraq while simultaneously marking the country's concealed sites of violence. The poet's organic understanding of death is part of her planetary consciousness that gives voice and presence to the dead who lie "under stars/that don't know their names" ("16", 49). Her sensory language animates the "flowery" expressions of pain used by the dead as a form of symbolic *deadspeak*. *Deadspeak* is a manifestation of the "fourth language" capable of reverberating among the stars while enunciating the "deadly" words of the departed.

The celestial stars have the "illuminating" potential to transform anonymity into commemoration in cyclical patterns of regeneration that keep the dead alive in memory. The spirits of the dead manifest regularly in symbolic form when "they appear every time/in the greenness of the grass," to circumvent the finality of physical death: "We are not upset when/the grass dies," reassures the poet—"We know/it will come back," she affirms with confidence ("23," 45). The poems in this section are reminiscent of existential mediations on the impact of war and exile, the meaning of life and the senselessness of death, the nostalgia for home, the in-betweenness of exile, the loss of the ancient mother tongue, and the wonders of nature. These reflections continue to haunt the poet as she ponders the never-ending cycles of violence and destruction that punctuate the human condition in Iraq. This violence has led to dramatic inversions represented by the waning moon ("N," 65), "cities moving backward" ("Rotation," 75), wrinkled maps ("N," 67), "mass graves" ("17," 38), blood swollen rivers ("My Grandmother's Grave," 25), and "the killed ones" ("11," 33).

> **Change each form of your thoughts into**
> **a bird.**
> **Let them fly**
> **To other parts of the world**
> **—Rumi ("In the Silence")**

Birds are an integral part of Mikhail's poetry. As a symbol of the human soul, they represent goodness, joy, innocence, beauty, wisdom, and intelligence. In Sufi thought, "the image of flying birds has long been a universal symbol of the human soul rising towards a higher reality" (Johan, 2019, 696). Their magical wings have the transcendent power to lift the soul to heaven, thereby making them divine intermediaries between heaven and earth. Their flight to the supra-terrestrial realm of *life beyond earthly life* is experienced through the soundwaves of eternal song that animate the feminine sign, "but the bird who survived sings" ("Song Inside A Fossil" 14). These "circling" songs of liberation and survival commemorate the resilient spirit of Iraq that must nevertheless be lifted from the depths of despair and silence to regain its historicity compromised by loss: "The survivor has the memory/of thirst and of two silent birds" ("Song Inside A Fossil," 13). The memory of Iraq's past glory represented by its venerable mother cultures, these "two silent birds," has been both tarnished by the manmade thirst for war and silenced by political oppression. It remains frozen in a state of limbo, "their circular embrace is/a song inside a fossil," waiting for the liberating power of the poet's song-like words that will release it from "life in a cage" ("Song Inside A Fossil," 14). This poetic release will give new meaning to both life and the afterlife through the resuscitating power of archival memory-words that go beyond the limiting confines of death: "Though birds don't know/what poison means" ("Song Inside A Fossil," 13). If poison represents the death of memory, poetry in turn personifies the creative return to life represented in bird imagery.

The birds represent the many lost souls of Iraq who are looking for a home after their forced displacement resulting from war, violence, exile, and death: "Some of our tribal members/died in war, some/died regular deaths./None of them died from joy" ("23," 39). The migrating patterns of the birds provide ambulatory mappings to mark the passage from despair to joy and vice versa. The poet wonders: "I don't know why the birds/sing/during their crossings/over our ruins" ("My Poem Will Not Save You," 27). For the birds, these ruins do not represent the end of life but a spiritual renaissance instead. Ruined cities will be reconstructed in memory to rise like the phoenix amid "the shells/when they fall/onto a sleeping town" (27). At the same time, the aerial configurations created by the circular bird flight patterns outline a borderless cartography invalidating artificial borders and boundaries between the *here* and *there*: "If birds' memories are circles, a line/must bisect them, tracing their migration/to places that are neither homelands nor exiles" ("Songs Inside A Fossil," 13). The birds excavate the ancestral mappings of Ama-ar-gi described as "returning to the mother" ("Ama-argi," 58) through their de-territorialized memorial journeys in which borders are replaced by song, "only songs for places" ("Salwa," 19), and forgetfulness finds cathartic release in "a circle with everyone inside" ("Nisaba," 17). The mobile archive reveals its importance in its capacity to function as "an agent of political continuity and social solidarity, helping … societies to hang together over time by serving as important self-affirming symbols of community, identity and memory" (Brothman, 2010, 158–160). The circular contours of the memorialized archive are an embracing space of inclusivity, peace, and communion when artificial boundaries that are dissolved in liquid songs of solidarity and communities regain their lost identities in memory.

The poet must follow the example of the singing birds by poetically creating an undifferentiated territoriality between home and exile to minimize the trauma of otherness. This limitless space is the home of Ama-ar-gi's transcendent feminine sign; this signifier embraces differences and exilic sensibilities across vertical and horizontal timelines and de-territorialized geographical expanses in a reconfigured mapping of home and belonging. This otherworldly map is as vast and inclusive as the nature-as-archive trope itself: "But what if the world, for birds,/is all exile, till they leave it behind" ("Song Inside A Fossil," 13), wonders the poet. The birds, as divine guardians of this sacrosanct space, provide the necessary routes of access through their circular movement and ethereal song in a memorialized journey of the senses. This journey represents a form of nesting for both the migrating birds and the war weary souls who are looking for "a way of coming back to life" ("Song Inside A Fossil," 14) within the embracing space of Ama-ar-gi: "Paradise is Ama-ar-gi,/no victors at all" ("Ama-ar-gi," 58). The paradisiac return to a healed homeland nevertheless remains a work in progress, "all truths come late" ("16," 34), until that liminal moment in time when Iraq is able to banish all the conquering local and foreign aggressors who have battered "us/without discrimination" ("18," 44). Until this transcendent moment of final release, the poet and her people can only find temporary sanctuary in the "idea" of the goddess's promised return expressed in the conditional tense: "Ama-ar-gi might be a moon/that follows us home, a shadow/that stumbles on its true self" ("Ama-ar-gi," 58), a symbol of hope and future relief: "Her shadow/is still here/feeding the birds" ("24," 35).

BAGHDAD: BONE CITY

In this sensory journey, delimiting maps are replaced by songs of access, "she has no map,/only songs for places" ("Salwa," 19). These songs of welcome are inscribed in the very historicity of Baghdad, an ancient city of peace long known for its rites of hospitality: "That city whose doors stayed open/for passerbys, tourists, and invaders" ("22," 50). As a poet from Baghdad, Mikhail herself subscribes to this poetics of welcome in her writings: "In poetry I am the native citizen who welcomes others, the way I was welcomed by others who came before me," she admits (Pearce, 2021. Baghdad opens its welcoming gates to guests who avail of its generosity; these very rituals of greeting are compromised by hostile invaders and their barbaric invasions, "then the barbarians arrived" ("My Grandmother's Grave," 25). These aggressions alter the peaceful cityscapes of Baghdad represented in its natural and cultural heritage by creating bloodied sites of perdition instead. These locations are marked by "corpse-lilies" (24), rivers of death ("My Grandmother's Grave," 24), ruins, "the bone-city I am choked by" ("4," 31), and expansive landscapes of devastation: "We strolled roadsides/piled with rocks blasted/from bridges and buildings/now bent and cratered" ("Eva," 21). Baghdad's ancient architectural marvels are disfigured by bombs and constant shelling to create a city in alienation of its own identity through the colonizing imprint of the outsider. The sacking of this ancient city by multiple invaders through time immemorial [4]— Abbasid, Mongol, Tartar, Turk, Persian, British, and the recent US invasion and occupation—has endowed it with an existential schizophrenia in which war and peace play a tug-of-war game of control: *"I am from Baghdad*, I replied,/*a city we call the "home of peace,"/though war has lived in it/for two hundred years*" ("Eva," 21). Baghdad's duality as a city of "peace and blood" (Marozzi, 2014) nevertheless maintains its equilibrium under the watchful eye of its protecting spirit Inanna. The goddess is ready to engage in battle with the foreign "barbarian" in order to protect her sanctuary-city from destruction. Her actions bear witness to her love for her city, which is why she is represented as the goddess of both love and war.

The poet wonders how to find the right words to commemorate her devastated city when confronted by its destruction by outsiders and internal forces. Her search for the lost maternal archive is punctuated by the search for Ama-ar-gi's lost alphabet as she ruminates on how to recreate language from loss and the displacement of exile. "My hand brushes the map/as if rubbing an old scar," she cries as she uses scabs and the congealed blood of "corpse-lilies" to describe this wounding ("My Grandmother's Grave," 25). How does the poet excavate the "debris words" that remain scattered among ruined cities and artificial maps? Baghdad is reduced to a broken ghost town battered by "the wind and rain" ("18," 44) and the spectral shadow-presence of the dead in the form of "specks of sand" ("20," 34). The only visible vestiges of life are found in skeletal remains, bone fragments, and decomposed bodies, "now smashed like berries" ("12," 33). The poet must find alternative sources to document the city's scarred history beyond authorized textbooks and government sources that do not reveal the faces of "naked emperors" responsible for this destruction, those who "passed by the Tigris/and more ships …" ("My Grandmother's Grave," 25). In other words, Baghdad must be imaged appropriately through what I term the poet's *corpse-quill* as a deeply sensorial form of writing with the senses. The ancient Sumerian clay tablets that structure Part Two of this poetic collection represent the essential *corpse-quills* that preserve the city's dust-filled traces of memory. The poet looks for vital "debris words" ("Song Inside A Fossil," 13) as clues amid the dusty remains to perform an act of poetic renewal. The city represents an important archive of memory located in bones, corporeal signifiers, dusty ruins, and orality. It reflects anteriority through its monumental past as well as futurity through a process of reconstruction or ultimate homing, like "a soul/searching for home" ("11," 33). The city provides testimonial documentation of life amid the ruins, "from under the shrapnel" ("My Poem Will Not Save You," 26), to reveal a palimpsest-like composition of

---

[4] Consult Justin Marozzi's *Baghdad City of Peace, City of Blood: A History in Thirteen Centuries* (2014), for more details.

deeply sedimented histories and personal stories. These narratives are waiting to be unearthed by the poet's quivering *corpse-quill* as she sifts through the ruins with her testifying debris words. The erasure of these stories will foreshadow the city's death-in-memory in the absence of a sustaining narrative. This danger leads to the poet's warning: "Their stories didn't kill me/but I would die if I didn't/tell them to you" ("21," 45).The poet documents Baghdad's cyclical historicity of combined suffering and resilience in an open-ended refrain "whose song/has no beginning/or end" ("7," 32) to reveal the city's powers of regeneration. The city's resilience is captured in "restless motion, multiple chronologies and levels of meaning" (Sheringham & Wentworth, 2016, 519).

Baghdad's polyphonic sounds are expressed as a lament in times of distress, a hymn of elation in joyful times ("The Stranger," 12), migrating bird song, and Salwa's anxious humming (19). These "arche-sounds" represent the primal mother language needed to record memory in a commemorative space as a site of identity and belonging (Rao, 2008, 179). The lilting rhythms are a form of archival weaving similar to the physical braiding of stories that construct a literary mosaic of interconnected experiences and emotions. When the poet goes in search of inspiration to write "an epic about suffering," she discovers the stray tendril of a woman's hair "among the ruins/of her mud house." The epiphanic moment of discovering a lost chapter in Iraq's war story symbolized by the lone tendril helps her to find "my epic there" ("1," 41). The tendril enables the poet to document a more humanized representation of the war by highlighting its human cost. The lonely tendril provides testimony of the woman's solitary suffering, while her braided hair reveals an entire spectrum of complex feelings knitted together in an epic knotting of pain.

The individual tendril, "each hair a history," links the woman to an entire community of sufferers through shared bonds of empathy expressed in clay inscriptions. The tablets are compared to "the dates ripening before their sorrows" ("My Grandmother's Grave," 24). The epic narrative resounds with personal and communal expressions of "ripe" pain that are united in a reverberating chorus of collective mourning. These ethereal voices extend upwards to join the sweet symphony of the migrating birds in a thunderous echo. This primal vibration resonates with the haunting voice of the mother, "Ama-ar-gi-/that's how we return to the mother,/strangers from strangers" (59), who welcomes her suffering children into a paradisiac space where there are "no losses no demons" (58). The flight to Ama-ar-gi is facilitated by the uplifting notes of the singing birds that guarantee safe passage into this transcendent space for these "strangers from strangers" (59).

This melodic rite of passage is transcribed in text by the poet as she experiences a similar moment of transcendence when she dreams of reconnecting with her outer worldly lunar muse, the mother goddess: "Ama-ar-gi might be a moon/that follows us home" (58). The mother-moon connection provides the poet with a homing space in writing through the preeminence of the mother's Voice—"the song, the first music of the voice of love, which every woman keeps alive … The deepest, the oldest, the loveliest Visitation. Within each woman the first, nameless love is singing" (Cixous, 1986, 93). This primary Visitation expresses itself in the lyricism of the poet's embodied voice-in-text. This ultra-sensory language is the meditative voice of poetic reflection wherein, "song by song/I scatter my birds/away from the fog of smoke" ("Baghdad in Detroit," 15).

Poetry's luminous Voice unveils manmade illusions and smoke screens destined to obscure the truth amid the hazy fog of smoke, "all truths come late" ("16," 34). Poetry reveals its function of truth telling as exemplified by Mikhail's refusal to become a political praise singer, a truth that is expressed through her credo: "I was born./I write poetry./I will die" ("23," 35). She reveals the true agenda of an engaged poet through her creative mission that remains straightforward and unadorned by obfuscation. The poet's protest song must be daring in its capacity to stand up for the truth by asking difficult questions even at the risk of being considered seditious. She exposes an age-old war truth amid her questioning: "When a challenge happens,/killing offers the easiest solution" ("Black and White," 61). At the same time, this poetry must reveal its relevance by reflecting the dark and joyous times in which it is created. While Mikhail has no pretention of starting a revolution with her poetry, she nevertheless insists on poetry's art of asking the right questions without compromise or deflection. She simultaneously refuses to provide ideological responses as a form of demagoguery: "I am sorry/my poem will not/block the shells/ when they fall/onto a sleeping town" ("My Poem Will Not Save You," 27). Mikhail does not weaponize her poetry even as she describes the devastation of war that "will not raise the dead" (27). A poet is not a miracle worker, "many mistakes in life/will not be corrected by my poem" (28), she states with humility. Yet, poetry provides the x-ray vision needed to image a more humanitarian "touch," one in which "their songs/give us that touch" ("My Poem Will Not Save You," 28).

On the flip side, the poet's spiritual twinning with the mother goddess Inanna receives an inverted twist in an ill-fated pairing between the home city Baghdad and the city of exile Detroit. The forced umbilical connection between the two transatlantic cities is conditioned by war and the poet's exilic displacement to the US resulting from the US-led war and Saddam Hussein's militarized dictatorship. Baghdad and Detroit share a tenuous borderline positionality through a mismatched spatial twinning that reveals the disparate connections between the two cities. The poem "The War in Colors" demonstrates how America's multiple wars against Iraq and other global south countries degenerate into an obsessive video game with brightly highlighted foreign targets. This remote control reality becomes a colorful spectacle to be observed from afar: "Iraq in purple/Syria in yellow/Kuwait in blue/Afghanistan in red/Vietnam in green" (63). These wars represent colorful war candy to be consumed at leisure by voracious appetites that are nevertheless protected by virtual borders between the *here* and *there* in the form of digital maps: the "digital map on the wall/displays American wars/in colors" ("The War in Colors," 63).

Accordingly, July 4th firework displays in Detroit are a sign of US patriotism on independence day. These spectacular sights and sounds meant to entertain and awe the US masses are nevertheless synchronized with the deafening explosion of live bombs in Baghdad through the US military's "shock and awe" campaign of death: "On the Fourth of July/here in Detroit/I hear the echo of Baghdad explosions./They say it is the sound of fireworks" ("Baghdad in Detroit," 15). For the exiled poet, the two cities mirror their seemingly incongruent yet interconnected realities in spectral echoes that delimit the porous boundaries between entertainment and destruction. She carries the soundscapes of war with her during the process of migration as she crosses the Tigris to the Detroit River like an escaping butterfly (15) only to confront the ghosts of war in her newly adopted home. Haunted by the trauma of war, she experiences a ghosting effect in exile through trauma's circular ambulation across time and space. The poet's inherited war traumas seek resolution in the supposedly peaceful space of exile where "no bombs today to scare her away./They say this is the Detroit River" (15). Yet, peace can only be *imagined* in Detroit when anti-Arab racism, "this, then is how the map grew borders," threatens the poet with another forced departure to a foreign elsewhere: "We will leave at the end of the raid./They say this is the tunnel to Canada," she warns the reader ("Baghdad In Detroit," 15). The trauma of a third possible displacement haunts the poet as she reflects on the permanence of her exilic condition expressed in a renewed identification with the Sumerian ancestors and the search for the feminine archive, "scattered, like us, the Sumerian letters" ("Ama-ar-gi," 58).

In conclusion, *In Her Feminine Sign* represents Dunya Mikhail's cosmic search for the immortal mother goddess amid the devastated landscapes of war in Iraq and the exilic spaces of the US. This search redefines the place and meaning of the archive through the poetic search for what is lost, forgotten, and un-representable. The obscured twin dots of the feminine sign recover the poet's lost sense of plenitude as she contemplates her separation from the ancestral world of the goddess Inanna, her homeland Iraq, and her exilic status in the US. Her existential musings on life and death are expressed in the sensory language of debris words, songs of migration, ruins, and natural sounds that are integrated in the feminine archive's embodied "fourth language." The recovery of the lost maternal world of "Ama-ar-gi" marks the first step toward healing after years of war and suffering. Poetry represents Mikhail's effort to reverse the deeply entrenched psychological, spiritual, and physical imbalances conditioned by war and authoritarianism in Iraq by stopping the abysmal regression of "the cities moving backwards" and the silencing of "our untold stories" ("Rotation," 75). These inversions compromise the soul of her country and delay the return of the goddess even as "the flamingoes/have migrated back to Iraq," a sign of renewed hope and possibility ("Flamingo," 74).

REFERENCES

Al-Hassan, H. (2020). *Women, Writing and the Iraqi Ba'thist State*. Edinburgh University Press.

Athamneh, W. (2017). *Modern Arabic Poetry: Revolution and Conflict*. University of Notre Dame Press.

Bernea, I. (2020, November 12). A Descendant of Enheduanna, the Sumerian Poet. *Atelier LiterNet*. Retrieved from https://atelier.liternet.ro/articol/22967/Ilinca-Bernea-Dunya-Mikhail/A-descendant-of-Enheduanna-the-Sumerian-poet.html#.X7U7sxzT6T4.twitter

Brothman, B. (2001). The Past that Archives Keep: Memory, History, and the Preservation of Archival Records. *Archivaria, 51*, 48–80.

Brothman, B. (2010). Perfect Present, Perfect Gift: Finding a Place for Archival Consciousness in Social Theory. *Archival Science, 10*, 141–189.

Cixous, H. (1986). *The Newly Born Woman*. Translated from the French by Betsy Wing with an Introduction by Sandra M. Gilbert. University of Minnesota Press.

cooke, m. (2001). *Women Claim Islam: Creating Islamic Feminism Through Literature*. Routledge Press.

Derrida, J. (1976). *Of Grammatology*. Johns Hopkins Press.

Derrida, J. (2011). *Archive Fever*. Chicago: University of Chicago Press.

Djebar, A. 1987. *Fantasia: An Algerian Cavalcade*. Translated from the French by Dorothy S. Blair. Quartet Books.

El Bouih, F. 2008. *Talk of Darkness*. Translated from the Arabic by Mustapha Kamal and Susan Slyomovics. The University of Texas Press.

Gelb, I. J. (2019, March 20). *Sumerian Language*. Encyclopedia Britannica. Retrieved from https://www.britannica.com/topic/Sumerian-language

Griffith, K. (2019, November 14). Dunya Mikhail's The Beekeeper and in Her Feminine Sign. *War, Literature & the Arts: An International Journal of the Humanities, 31*. Retrieved from https://www.wlajournal.com/wlaarchive/31/GRIFFITH.PDF

Harris, A. (2016, October 13). The Sensory Archive. *The Senses and Society, 11*(3), 345–350. Retrieved from https://www.tandfonline.com/doi/full/10.1080/17458927.2016.1212473?scroll=top&needAccess=true

Hedstrom, M. (2010). Archives and Collective Memory: More than a Metaphor, Less than an Analogy. In T. Eastwood & H. MacNeil (Eds.), *Currents of Archival Thinking*. Santa Barbara, CA.

Ismael, J. S., & Ismael, S. T. (2007). Iraqi Women Under Occupation: From Tribalism to Neo-Feudalism. *International Journal of Contemporary Iraqi Studies, 1*(1), 247–268.

Jarrar, R. (2015, August 15). The PEN Ten with Dunya Mikhail. *PEN America*. Retrieved from https://pen.org/the-pen-ten-with-dunya-mikhail/

Johan, I. M. (2019). Bird Symbolism in Persian Mystical Poetry. *International Review of Humanities Studies, 4*, 695–716.

Khan, S. (2015). My Poetry Has Two Lives, Like Any Exile: A Conversation With Dunya Mikhail. *World Literature Today, 89*(5), 10–13.

Levi, C. (2019, August 20). Taking a Walking Tour of Lalish's Main Temple. *Kurdistan, 24*.

Marozzi, J. (2014). *Baghdad: City of Peace, City of Blood: A History in Thirteen Centuries*. Da Capo Press.

Mikhail, D. (2019). *Her Feminine Sign. Bilingual Arabic-English.* New Directions Publishing.

Monte, J. (2017). *The Legendary Life and Poetry of Islam's First Woman Sufi Saint Rabia al-Adawiyya.* Self Published.

New Directions. (2019). *In Her Feminine Sign.* New Directions. Retrieved from https://www.ndbooks.com/book/in-her-feminine-sign/

Pearce, L.. (2021, May 2). Aesthetic Enthusiasm: An Interview with Dunya Mikhail. *Michigan Quarterly Review.* Retrieved from https://sites.lsa.umich.edu/mqr/2021/05/aesthetic-enthusiasm-an-interview-with-dunya-mikhail/

Rao, V. (2008). *City as Archive: Contemporary Urban Transformations and the Possibility of Politics.* International Association of Educating Cities. Arts Gràfiques Bobalà, SL. Retrieved from https://www.edcities.org/en/wp-content/uploads/sites/2/2015/04/Vyjayanthi-V-Rao-EN.pdf

Saeed, H. (2019, July 8). Dunya Mikhail: 'Writing It Twice Is My New Original. *Arab Quarterly.* Retrieved from https://arablit.org/2019/07/08/dunya-mikhail-writing-it-twice-is-my-new-original/

Schwarz, J., & Cook, T. (2002). Archives, Records and Power: The Making of Modern Memory. *Archival Science, 2,* 1–19.

Sheringham, M., & Wentworth, R. (2016). City as Archive: A Dialogue Between Theory and Practice. *Cultural Geographies, 23*(3), 517–523.

Sun, C.-C. (1995). *Pearl from the Dragon's Mouth: Evocation of Scene and Feeling in Chinese Poetry.* University of Michigan Press.

Tuffaha, K. L. (2019, Autumn). *In Her Feminine Sign* by Dunya Mikhail. Book Review. *World Literature Today.* Retrieved from https://www.worldliteraturetoday.org/2019/autumn/her-feminine-sign-dunya-mikhail

Feminism Ruptured, or Feminism Repaired? Music, Feminisms, and Gender Politics in Palestinian Subcultures

Polly Withers

INTRODUCTION

On stage, the DJ is pumping a heady mix of Berlin-Detroit-style techno through the bar. We're in the garden, and the sun is just about setting. The characteristically monotonous, 4/4 beat creates an aggressive, almost militaristic, rhythmic structure to the music. In the emerging darkness, the drum machines and pad synthesisers seem to glow eerily in time with the quick-tempo pace. Neon yellows and soft blues flash as electricity pulses through the equipment. There are few melodies, no lyrics. Instead, the repetitive, mechanic sounds push a charged, edgy energy across the party. On the dance floor, we move almost robotically to keep up with the beat.

The DJ is petite. From the audience space, her small frame seems dwarfed by the mixing desk and headset slung around her neck. Her brunette hair hangs lightly around her shoulders. She wears a loose-fitting, dark-coloured vest, ripped off at the sleeves. Low-slung, baggy jeans and sports trainers complete the androgynous look. Around her slender wrists are an assortment of fabric bands from previous festival attendance—those ubiquitously youthful markers of having been somewhere 'cool' in the recent past. They move melodically as she works the decks. To the left of the mixers, the DJ's friend, similarly

P. Withers (✉)
LSE Middle East Centre, LSE, London, UK
e-mail: P.Withers@lse.ac.uk

L. H. Skalli, N. Eltantawy (eds.), *The Palgrave Handbook of Gender, Media and Communication in the Middle East and North Africa*, https://doi.org/10.1007/978-3-031-11980-4_24

dressed in low-slung slacks and with short-cropped hair, stands to offer occasional assistance. She giggles and photographs the young woman on her iPhone while she performs.

These ambiguous sartorial practices ripple across the audience, too. Partygoers mix and mash-up normative gendered iconography on and through their bodies. Several men wear their long hair tied up in dreadlocked buns, while women might cut theirs off entirely. Tattoos and facial piercings are abundant, and androgynous clothing is standard. Some partygoers have even gone full 'rave' and are wearing luminous vests or leather bondage outfits. Differently to the municipal space of the street, then—where (in Ramallah at least) modesty norms more clearly delimit male-female intimacies—those in this party dance or socialise with one another across the gender binary. Alcohol, too—the consumption of which is socially prohibited in wider publics—flows in abundance between friends, and from the bar to the crowd, in this enclaved space.

Through pleasure, play, and symbolic (re)imagination, then, these sartorial performances and social practices upend local gender norms while reiterating global notions of queer hipster 'cool'. As these young men and women corporeally self-fashion 'new' DIY masculinities and femininities through transnational markers, they unsettle one gender order while activating another. Their bodies are thus formed and transformed by gathering in bars to listen to techno music—which, as this chapter argues, crafts new alliances that also fortify and manufacture novel iterations of difference.

Setting the Scene

I attended this techno-electronic dance music (EDM) party with some Palestinian friends in the Summer of 2018. The gig took place at *Bar Radio*, formally known as *Beit Aneeseh*, in the West Bank's de facto capital, Ramallah. At the time, I lived in Sheikh Jarrah, in Jerusalem, where I was staying for a year to extend my previous research on popular culture in Palestine. Like many others in this party, I had thus travelled across Israel's illegal apartheid wall to attend. Networking young Palestinians with access above and below colonial borders, parties such as this one index Palestine's mushrooming 'alternative' (*badila*) music scene. Unlike its European counterparts, this subculture defies rigid categorisation. Scenesters mix trap, hip-hop, EDM, trance, and techno with Arabic melodies, instrumentation, and poetic repertoires to create hybrid (cf. Kraidy, 2005) sounds. Musicians, DJs, producers, promoters, and fans' interpersonal synergies, rather than sonic preferences, are its bedrock. Through music, then, this growing subculture connects predominantly middle-class youth in the related, but distinct, urban areas of Ramallah, Bethlehem, Jerusalem, Haifa, Nazareth, and Yaffa. It also extends ties to some in the diaspora: Amman-based Palestinians with West Bank IDs, for instance, occasionally also attend or play West Bank shows.[1]

I have argued elsewhere that, in Ramallah, EDM and techno parties occur with increasing frequency. Participatory music rituals have always formed and reformed social and political identities in the community in Palestine—especially before the Palestinian Liberation Organization (PLO) institutionalised art and culture to their national resistance aims (see McDonald, 2006). *Subcultural* music, however, and its associated 'underground' gigs expanded rapidly after the 1993 Oslo Accords and the West Bank's successive neoliberalisations (see Khalidi & Samour, 2011; Turner, 2015; Haddad, 2016; Dana, 2019). Likewise, middle-class Palestinians in Haifa have cultivated such a successful nightlife scene that the city's downtown area now forms an urban enclave where Israeli-Jews, rather than Palestinian-Arabs, are the guests. The growth of this subculture across historic Palestine thus extends new belongings and novel identities to those with the social, discursive, and imaginative capitals required for access. Constituting a neoliberal politics of self and consumption, parties transgress gender norms while further reinforcing post-Oslo class cleavages (Withers, 2021).

This chapter opens with a related, but distinct, reflection. As this scene grows, it attracts widespread journalistic and academic interest. Over the past five years or so, musicians, DJs, and hipster youth have become increasingly visible in transnational media ecosystems. Indie and mainstream presses alike habitually encode alternative music and underground parties with 'revolutionary' messages. Moreover, spectacularising *gendered* dissent, women and girls hold particular value in these media circuits. Female DJs, such as those in the event I attended above, are routinely splashed across regional and European/US news items as progressive agents of social change—often to vaguely articulated status quos. The Israeli-Jewish centre-left broadsheet *Haaretz*, for instance, recently published a piece with the headline: "Meet the Female Arab DJs Setting the West Bank Free" (20/06/2017). To be clear, this Israeli-Jewish author is *not* suggesting that Palestinian (here homogenised as Arab) women have "set the West Bank free" from Israeli settler-colonisation. Instead, the article focuses on female DJs unconventional self-making practices. Mobilising the tradition/modernity binary, the author suggests that individuals with ostensibly 'Western' cultural tastes 'empower' themselves through globalised music, fashion, and consumption. The orientalist notion that Palestinian spaces are synonymous with cultural 'backwardness' and undifferentiated gender oppression thus underpins such stories.

As highlighted above, young adults certainly *do* interrupt *some* gender norms through their aesthetic and corporeal performances in parties. In so doing, however, they at the same time initiate *novel* controls. The problem with dominant media (and some academic) accounts, then, is that fronting romantic resistance tropes restricts our understanding of the *complex* ways that music

---

[1] For a detailed overview of Israel's complex system of identification cards, see Tawil-Souri (2011).

communicates gender in Palestine—and beyond. Most critically, such simplistic frames dilute questions about what women—and which women—are being 'empowered' to do through subcultural participation. Furthermore, by centring liberal definitions of agency as individual rupture, customary representations ignore how intersecting (classed, sexuality-based, geopolitical, racialised, etc.) forces enable and constrain these 'liberated' femininities and masculinities. This chapter therefore proposes a different interpretation of this subcultural network and its gender politics. Moving beyond the resistance/domination binary (cf. El-Zein, 2017; Moreno-Almeida, 2017; Withers, 2021), the piece examines the *contradictory* ways in which alternative music mediates, enacts, and/or challenges gender roles and gendered practices in occupied Palestine.

Music is often ignored in feminist communication studies. Instead, scholars routinely chart how social media enables and disables different feminisms. The myriad ways that popular cultural forms, like techno, are also engaged in the formation of feminism are thus overlooked. This chapter therefore addresses this gap. It argues that alternative music constitutes a significant, yet ambiguous field of popular feminist struggle. Here, the chapter's thinking leans heavily on Stuart Hall's (1998) definition of popular culture as a terrain of contest. For Hall, the vernacular is: "one of the sites where [the] struggle for and against a culture of the powerful is engaged... it is the arena of consent and resistance. It is partly where hegemony arises, and where it is secured" (1998, 453). The popular, in other words, mediates and constitutes conflicts between competing gender, race, class, sexuality, and geopolitical interests. As such, this chapter questions how young people's subcultural participation, as well as the modes and discursive framings of their interventions, might transgress *and* repress different gendered formations through music, dress, and dance.

Moreover, this contribution is especially concerned with asking if, and theorising why, young adults do or do not narrate their embodied actions as specifically *feminist* practices. Given that mainstream media represents women and girls' subcultural agencies as gender dissent, the chapter questions if women *actually* mobilise such frames to conceptualise their music. In addition, the chapter is specifically interested in asking if *some* feminist discourses emerge with greater force than others through people's creative actions and narratives. As media theorist Sarah Banet-Weiser (2018) argues, media and popular culture are fields where *multiple* feminisms circulate and compete for recognition. Do certain feminist subjects, or specific feminist politics, therefore traffic with more weight than others in Palestinian popular music? And if so, how are such dominant feminisms entangled with other pre-existing configurations in contemporary Palestine? Put differently, if the popular is a site where struggles over gender, sexuality, geopolitics, and class surface, (how) do such conflicts shape the feminist visions that achieve greatest visibility via subcultural communications?

Here, it is important to stress that there is nothing inherently emancipatory about women's musical agencies. It is well established in Middle East gender studies that women might uphold restrictive gender norms as much as, and sometimes even more than, their male counterparts (Kandiyoti, 1988; Abu-Lughod, 1998; Mahmood, 2005). Indeed, as Nicola Pratt (2020: 7) shows in her work on women's activism in Jordan, Lebanon, and Egypt, feminist politics can fracture *and* repair hegemonic power at different scalar levels instantaneously. Echoing Hall's reflections on popular culture, Pratt's research further underscores the need to approach women's artistic modalities through intersectional lenses. For this research, this means thinking about how middle-class women might, for instance, challenge patriarchal restrictions on women's mobility by going to clubs and raves, and yet, in so doing further reinforce capitalist structures that equate gendered emancipation with individual consumerism.

Indeed, and as is additionally reflected in the feminist media literature, the 'cost' of gendered cultural resistance is not spread equally between people in a shared social backdrop. Those with the capacity to dissent from gender norms often benefit from extra material, economic, or social capitals and/or enjoy added supports (from family, peers, religious elders, etc.) in the community (Stokes, 2007): privileges that are both gendered and classed. Gendered or feminist praxis could, in other words, reinscribe while it challenges power across different, but connected, platforms.

As such, this chapter brings these media and Middle East gender debates into dialogue to chart the type and scale of agency an action involves, before it is simply celebrated as dissent (cf. Banaji, 2017: 194–197). It draws on over one hundred interviews with musicians, DJs, and fans and more than 200 participant observations at parties, raves, and concerts, gathered during more than two years of ethnographic fieldwork (2012, 2014, 2015, 2017–2018) in Palestine (Ramallah, Haifa, Jerusalem), and its diaspora (Amman and London), to advance the argument. It also employs ongoing analysis of artists' audiovisual productions (songs, music videos, lyrics) to support the discussion.

Overall, the chapter makes two core contributions to communications scholarship on the gender/culture nexus in Middle East and North Africa (MENA) media. First, it suggests that, and shows how, young adults challenge certain gender stereotypes through their songs and subcultural practices. Scenesters particularly disrupt heteropatriarchal expectations about identity and desire through their lyrics and digital productions. In this first sense, then, music communicates critical gender politics while crafting distinctive feminist subjects in Palestine.

Second, however, it would be a mistake to assume that popular music therefore enacts utopian sites of wholesale gender 'emancipation'. While transgressing some gender norms, performances—and in particular musicians' framings of their performances—instantiate novel restrictions. As the chapter will show, young people's discursive practices habitually centre transnationally mobile (neo)liberal (cf. Ong, 2007) scripts of gendered freedom, sutured to ideas about individual agency, choice, and autonomy. Currently, the ways in which MENA media (re)shapes gendered subjectivities and feminist politics along (neo)liberal lines is undertheorised in the Palestine-focused literature. Speaking to this gap, the chapter instead shows how music *also* mediates capitalist transformations of youthful femininities and feminisms in Palestinian urban spaces. The chapter concludes that as young women and men challenge local gender codes, they simultaneously constitute de-fanged postfeminist (Gill, 2007; Dosekun, 2020) sensibilities rooted in highly individuated notions of gendered 'empowerment'. Thus, neither fully resistant nor entirely comprised, scenesters' embodied gendered practices instead highlight the ambiguous and contradictory ways in which music communicates gender in Palestine's fractured post-Oslo landscape.

HISTORICISING THE PRODUCTION OF GENDER IN PALESTINE

First, however, to understand the gender dynamics of alternative music in Palestine, it is important to grasp how gender itself is produced and maintained in the Palestinian case. In Israeli-dominated Palestine, as in any colonised context, it is not possible to theorise gendered subjectivities without unpacking how gender, race, class, and sexuality intersect under colonial rule. As established in the global south gender literature, colonial elites require ideological supports to legitimise their monopoly over land and resources. This largely took (and takes) place via the invention of race. By manufacturing the "rule of colonial difference" (Chatterjee, 1993: 10), colonial discourse enforced the coloniser's superiority and annihilated indigenous' claims to lands, knowledges, and livelihoods. Crucially, these racialised hierarchies rely on gender and sexuality to operate (Abu-Lughod, 1998; Najmabadi, 1991; Pratt, 2020: 8–9). To legitimise colonial violence, racist colonial patriarchies crafted the downtrodden 'Oriental' woman. Pointing to women's veiling, arranged marriages, gender segregation, and polygamy, Europeans used orientalist binaries to present 'non-Western' women as sexually 'oppressed' members of inherently 'barbaric' societies (Ahmed, 1992; Yuval-Davis, 1997; Yegenoglu, 1998). Such constructs became (and continue to be) core justifications for colonial enterprise. Then and now, the 'girl effect', or the idea that global south women need 'rescuing' from 'miserable' global south lives, continues to animate such gendered geopolitical arenas as the US-led war 'on terror', the aid industrial complex, and global fashion and beauty advertising (Spivak, 1985; Abu-Lughod, 2002; Sensoy & Marshall, 2010; Nguyen, 2011; Switzer, 2013; Calkin, 2015; Skalli, 2015).

Because, then, racialised colonial power is gendered, women's bodies, behaviours, and sexualities became (and continue to be) critical arenas through which patriarchal nationalists perform anti-colonial resistance (Hammami, 1990; Pratt, 2020: 9). In their struggle for independence, 'modernising' elites fashioned a 'new' woman to counter her 'Oriental' counterpart. Suturing women's 'liberation' to anti-colonial state-building, this 'reformed' feminine subject was to be educated and publicly visible, as well as a dutiful heterosexual housewife and 'modern' mother (Abu-Lughod, 1998; Najmabadi, 1998; Kandiyoti, 1991). Enabling and constraining women's agencies, this 'modern yet modest' (Najmabadi, 1991: 49) figure became the symbol and object of self-rule premised on a national modernity both like and unlike Europe's (Pratt, 2020: 10). Such gendered frames transformed women's bodies into icons of 'uncontaminated' cultural and national 'purity' (Chatterjee, 1989). Here, then, female 'respectability', articulated through 'modest' dress and decorum, becomes hyper-mediated vehicles through which patriarchal elites cultivate distinctions from colonial rule.

As Pratt argues (2020: 16), it is therefore crucial to note that social or legislative restrictions over women's corporeal actions are *performative*, rather than *reflective*, of national or cultural differences. Disciplinary norms about female virtue enact disidentification(s) from socially constructed and fluid 'others'. Under classic colonialism, for instance, modesty largely meant mandating sartorial and sexual difference from imagined European women. Today, however, and given the ongoing legacies of colonial rule across the globe, patriarchal forces largely (but not only) script gendered respectability across 'non-Western', 'non-American', or 'non-Israeli' scaffolds. There are two things that are significant to pull out here. First, it is not helpful to frame gender hierarchies in MENA or elsewhere as fixed evidence of cultural or religious 'backwardness' (Pratt, 2020: 12). As above, such norms take partial shape through gendered colonial encounters. And that second, while shifting through time and space, gendered virtue generally mandates a woman's sexual purity and implied obedience to men. 'Immodest' behaviour might therefore include activities that involve mixing with unrelated men or that obviously challenge male authority (Pratt, 2020: 10). Such discursive constructs are thus mapped to very *real* materialities of power that—as the chapter will highlight—help and hinder differently situated *actual* women in diverse ways.

In Palestine, Israeli settler-colonialism is obviously active and ongoing. The Israeli regime dominates almost all aspects of daily life for Palestinians across the occupied Palestinian territory (oPt) and in Israel-proper. Gender and sexuality are thus additionally weaponised regulated fictions in the colony. Across time, the shifting contours of female modesty (or perceived lack thereof) have mediated variously charged debates about cultural authenticity and national resistance versus imperial/colonial/Western pollutions.

As demonstrated above, while echoing pre-Oslo participatory cultural trends, subcultural music is rooted in Palestine's post-Oslo neoliberal political economy. The 1993 Oslo Accords and their aftermath ushered in widespread changes in everyday social, political, cultural, economic, and technological life in Palestine. In the years following the (failed) 'peace' process, cultural, consumer, and communicative technologies from previously distant places flooded into Palestinian society in the oPt and Israel (McDonald, 2006; Taraki, 2008). Global media and communications, subcultural music, digital culture, 'underground' aesthetics, 'hip' fashions, and consumer practices like bar-hopping and rave-going became increasingly available for scenesters-in-waiting with the necessary capitals for entrance. One of the enduring impacts of the post-Oslo period has thus been an expanded transcultural (cf. Kraidy, 2005) art and middle-class leisure scene, located within a neoliberal consumer order, in Palestinian urban centres across Israel and the oPt.

Given these rapid-fire shifts, many of the globalised cultural and digital forms that emerged following the Accords became suspect in some societal sectors. In particular, the presence of seemingly 'outside' (and more specifically 'American') popular modalities reactivated binarising debates over nationalism/neoliberalisation (often referred to as globalisation) and tradition/modernity (Maria & Shihade, 2012: 2)—tensions that, as outlined above, predominantly manifest through anxieties over the 'virtuous' versus 'non-virtuous' female body. This has two important implications for the arguments in the subsequent sections of this chapter. First, and as elsewhere, alternative music in Palestine is a contested cultural repertoire. The fact that music performances and parties largely comprise mixed gender crowds, involve alcohol, rotate around consumerism, and showcase unconventional dress and dance practices opens the scene to 'immodesty' charges. Women's bodies, queer sexualities, and non-binary sartorial choices are central in such disputes. Second, such contentious framings raise many interesting questions about the ways that young people *actually* navigate these fluctuating demands of patriarchal national modernity, as well as neoliberal capitalism, in their quotidian contexts.

Indeed, there is a long history of feminist organising in Palestine. Since (at least) British colonial rule, largely middle-/upper-class urban women mobilised against European colonialism and its gendered manifestations in society (Fleischmann, 2003). Forming the Palestinian women's movement, subsequent women across the social spectrum have, in various ways throughout Palestine's shifting histories, struggled against interconnected colonial and anti-colonial uses of women's bodies, voices, and views as political communiques (see, e.g. Peteet, 1991; Kuttub, 1993). This chapter, then, wants to question how such pre-existing feminisms, and pre-existing gender codes, interact with other feminist formations, and other gendered frames, through post-Oslo media cultures. In other words, if Oslo networked Palestinian society to transnational popular culture while cultivating neoliberal capitalism, how do such shifts impact the gender politics and feminist frameworks that alternative music mediates?

Performing Gender Transgressions in Underground Publics

In interviews with young women, several explained that music was important because it allowed them to express dissatisfaction with the gender norms that comprise female respectability. Fatima,[2] for instance, is a Muslim-identifying hip-hopper from Akka, a Palestinian-majority city in the north of modern-day Israel. When we first met, she was twenty-six and living at home with her par-

---

[2] All names have been changed, and full ethical permission to reproduce quotes was established before each interview.

ents, who are supportive of her musical goals. Fatima makes music as a semi-professional musician. She often plays local shows in Akka and Haifa (Palestinian-majority areas of current-day Israel) as well as further afield in Jerusalem, Ramallah, Jericho, and Bethlehem (in the West Bank). In our discussion, Fatima told me about the gendered stereotypes on which she uses her subcultural participation to push back. She first outlined such norms on transnational levels, telling me that:

> Hip-hop is strong music, its seen as strength, [but when others in] the community see women, it's like women should be like a lady [puts on an exaggeratedly high voice and laughs] – so that's why [stereotypical] ideas about women and hip-hop don't go together. I mean, you don't see a lot of female rappers in the world, not just here... [but] hip-hop is music where you talk about what you feel, what you want to change, and stuff like that... it's about communicating, exchanging thoughts and feelings... [And] as women we always have something to say. Whether in France, Europe, here, in the Arab world, women always have something to say. (Akka, 07/07/2018)

In this first half of her statement, Fatima universalises hip-hop as a conduit for fostering transnational feminist solidarities based on shared critiques of normative femininity. She argues that generic gender norms shape mainstream attitudes towards women in hip-hop scenes across Europe and the Arab world. For Fatima, such assumptions prohibit women from becoming public rap figures relative to men. As such, she frames music as cultivating cross-border networks for articulating feminist critiques of the belief that rap connotes a wholly masculine field of performance. Developing an explicitly feminine, if not feminist, hip-hop persona is thus important to Fatima because it allows her to construct alternative self-representations that challenge the gendered dynamics of hip-hop culture itself (cf. Morgan, 1999).

While highlighting transnational links, Fatima was additionally keen to drill down into some of the debates that shape ideas about rap media in her local context. Reiterating the above comments that 'American' or 'Western' symbols activate competing visions of social order, she continued (both naively and proudly) that:

> But here, for the Arab woman, there is another dimension. I'm a girl [and] our community, the older Arab community, will look at me in a different way – like it's forbidden, you know, for an Arab Muslim girl to do hip-hop, [Because] there is this idea that women's voices should be silent ['awra]... the voice of the woman can't be loud, it's forbidden... I mean even the way [people in the community: al-naas] look at the guys, it's as though they're doing something strange [because people think that] hip-hop came from America, not from here... so imagine how they look at me, as a girl and as a Muslim! (Akka, 07/07/2018)

While Fatima's simplistic language is unhelpfully totalising, her words nonetheless contextualise the much messier ways that gender and youth culture animate anxieties about post-Oslo flux. There are several elements to unpack here. First, as the rapper describes community perceptions of hip-hop culture, she alludes to the ways that inside-outside boundaries materialise via youthful bodies. As she puts it: "even the way [people] look at the guys (*shabab*, i.e. young men), it's as though they're doing something strange [because people think that] hip-hop came from America." Here, then, she suggests that adult culture frames hip-hop as strange or foreign (*gharib*) in order to exert generational restrictions over youthful behaviour. Her words thus show how parent culture produces youth 'indecency' to facilitate adult authority, and, moreover, that such controls take shape via pre-established repertoires for performing anti-colonial difference (with 'American' culture understood as the imperial power from which distance is sought).

Second, Fatima's statement opens windows for theorising the centrality of gender in this process. As she describes it, women and girls' bodies more specifically mark and mediate the borders between 'improper' disorder and 'proper' order. Her focus on *'awra* is in this sense interesting. In their research, Frances Hasso and Zakia Salime (2016: 16) highlight that, as a concept, *'awra* originates from an Islamic hadith expressing equivalence between women's voices and sexualised body parts (*sawt al-maraa 'awra*/literally: the woman's voice is defective). In its classic construction, they continue, *'awra* demands that women remain silent and covered in the company of unrelated men to avoid *fitna* (sexual disorder). In Fatima's view, patriarchal elders appropriate such religious texts to prohibit or at least negatively shape everyday attitudes towards female rappers in the community. For Fatima, then, hip-hop is an important resource because it enables her to produce value outside of such adult codes. As she proudly states: "imagine how they look at me, as a girl and as a Muslim!". Hip-hop is thus useful because it allows (some) young women to reckon, in the way Winegar (2006) meant, with the unequal expectations that underpin gendered respectability.

Furthermore, Fatima's musically mediated feminist politics resonate with other contemporary feminisms in the region. Both during and after the 2010–2013 uprisings, many young women protested against social practices based on concepts like *'awra*, as well as wider personal status laws premised on female modesty (see Hasso & Salime, 2016: 15–17; Pratt, 2020). If, then, patriarchal anti-colonial nationalisms foster regulatory gender idioms, feminist hip-hop media intermingles with broader political movements for interrupting and re-negotiating such symbols on local and regional scales.

Other young women echoed Fatima's view that music produces subjectivities outside of modesty dictates. Razan, for instance, emphasised the idea that the performing body can be a political medium for self-fashioning gender dissent. Razan is a punk-folk-rock singer and guitarist from Haifa. When we met, she was in her early twenties and living between her hometown and a city in Europe, where she was undertaking an artistic residency. Focusing on her embodied practices in her live shows, she said that:

I play guitar and I sing and I like to jump and I like to shout and I like to – you know? And all of a sudden there was this festival that we did in Bethlehem, and there was a reporter [who saw the show] and they [asked me] how is this possible? He was completely a moron, I got really pissed off, he kept saying women don't usually do that, how come you do that? What are you trying to do [she laughs]? I was like oh my god [pulls a sarcastic face]! I really can't remember what I answered but you know it was just like [makes a growling face] – I tried to scare him away, and said I do music and this is what I felt in the moment, and it feels good and that's it. (Haifa, 01/06/2018)

For Razan, live music performances are spaces where she can create and experiment with unruly gendered identities and modes of embodiment. Like Fatima, she frames subcultural participation as devices for challenging female respectability premised on women's self-contained bodily praxis. Instead, she cultivates a disorderly 'punk' sensibility that takes up and demands space via her body-in-motion. Critically, then, it is Razan's corporeal presence that mediates such disruption. As she puts it: "I like to sing and I like to jump and I like to shout... [because] it feels good and that's it."

Women like Razan and Fatima thus illustrate two things. First, that performances create feminist repertoires of intervention into everyday gendered social norms. And second, that young adults remix the cultural and consumer forms that became available after Oslo to pursue their own, local identity projects. As Constantine Nakassis (2013) argues in her ethnographic work on style and youth in India, this is not simply about desiring 'globality', as some earlier studies of globalisation-as-imperialism pushed. While globalised youth cultures are certainly not post-hegemonic (see Kraidy, 2005), neither do they produce the same impacts in the different, but connected, localities through which they circulate. Neoliberal globalisation always enters complicated living social, symbolic, and political worlds. As such, it would be a mistake to frame these young adults as (only) negotiating hegemonic globalised culture through music and style. Young women also use such repertoires to signify difference from 'here' (cf. Nakassis, 2013), with 'here' being the neighbourhood, hometown, or nation and its gendered socialites. Music is, then, a vehicle for asserting authority through values that parent culture undermines. By inscribing markers from putative 'outsides' (punk attitudes, 'American' hip-hop) with local and regional meanings, young people inflect female 'immodesty' with positive worth. As a primary point of departure, we can therefore theorise subcultural performances as cultivating *embodied* agencies (see Banaji, 2017) that disavow the patriarchal adult order of things, for those with access.

Music videos are especially salient sites for performing such distinctions from, and transgressions on, quotidian gendered containments. In the past five years or so, a small but clear corpus of Palestinian artists have produced audiovisual materials that directly engage regulatory ideas about gender. Within this work, the heterosexual wedding has proved a powerful trope for negotiating disciplinary expectations about sexuality and life-cycle 'achievements' for those with access. One particularly potent example is Jerusalem-based electro-pop artist Bashar Murad's 2018 *al-kul am bitjawaz* ("Everyone's Getting Married").[3] Bashar, who is the son a founding member of the influential Palestinian band *Sabreen*, publicly identifies as gay. Most of his songs and videos express critiques of gender norms: *al-kul am bitjawaz* is no exception. Overall, the lyrics tell the story of a young adult over-burdened with intertwined parental-societal pressures to get married as they approach thirty years of age. The chorus, for instance, repeats: *al-kul 'am bitjawaz hawale, uw ana mish arif rasi min ajrae* ("everyone around me is getting married, and I don't know my head from my toes"—i.e. I don't know what I'm doing in life). Through humour, then, the words express youthful disdain with adult certainties centred on heterosexual rituals.

The video is particularly stylised to produce this satirical critique. The digital text's central scenes revolve around Bashar. At first, we see him working as a waiter in a wedding party, where an older-looking lady propositions him to marry what we can assume is her younger female relative. Shaking his head ruefully, he replies: *"a-shoglay mish ana ma bidee, a-shoglay ino beitee ala adee"* ("it's not that I don't want to, it's that my house only fits me"—i.e. I don't have any space, emotional or otherwise, to fit another person into my life). The scene then shifts from the party to a garden wedding ceremony. Symbols of heterosexual nuptials adorn the frame—red roses and colourful confetti mark this convention. Now, the viewer sees Bashar in multiple roles: he plays the priest, the groom, and—as is revealed midway through the fictional ceremony—the bride. As each character, his dress is overblown and exaggerated. The priest appears in highly religious markers of orthodox Christianity, the groom has a thick moustache and tacky suit, and the bride wears a long, hyperfeminine white gown and lace veil.

Given the hyperbolic nature of these visual cues, we can assume that Bashar intends for this video to elicit humour from the viewer. The fact that the musician performs all three characters in the wedding, differentiated only sartorially, can in this sense be read as Butlerian (1990) intention to highlight how masculinities, femininities, and their associated identities (groom, priest, bride) are made real not through interiority, but performative processes constituted through theatre and dress. Moreover, because such gender-bending unravels within the context of a heterosexual marriage, we can further suppose that the young singer aims to assert that conformist sexuality is a similarly regulated fiction. In other words, it is lifetime monogamy, premised on heteropatriarchal ritual, that becomes abnormal in the song's imaginary—rather than queer desire or gender fluidity. For those with the required reading glasses, then,

---

[3] Women also critique gender normativity and patriarchal power in their music and media productions. In the post-MeToo movement, for instance, Palestinian artists like Maysa Daw and Safaa Hathot use their songs and videos to express and cultivate different feminist critiques of misogynistic masculinity. For further discussion of women's music and the diverse feminisms (anti-colonial, popular, postfeminist, etc.) that emerge through their songs and music videos, please see Withers (2022).

al-kul am bitjawaz challenges the disciplinary mechanisms that sustain heterosexual normativity.

There are two chief points to pull out here. First, and in line with Fatima and Razan's comments discussed above, this song and video use creativity and play to interrupt heteropatriarchal expectations about identity and desire. Through humour, it imagines a locality where Arab youth set the rules (cf. Elsayed & Zidani, 2020). Rendered hence, it showcases the critical ways in which music communicates gender in Palestine. We can thus frame the document as mediating queer feminist disruptions of heteropatriarchal power. Second, however, while the video *can* be read thus, it remains likely that *only* audiences who already assent to this view of heteronormativity will do so. In other words, there is an ideological framing of normative heterosexuality and marriage as inhibitors of personal liberty underpinning this piece. As such, this digital text certainly 'does' critical identity work in its *local* context. And yet, at the same time it converges with *transnationally familiar* pathways to gender-queer liberation. By expressing dissatisfaction with heterosexual parent culture, the song mediates youthful aspirations to live a wilful life unburdened by others' projections. Performing 'freedom' through individual personhood, this equates queer emancipation with choice-making, autonomy, and 'empowerment' (rather than, say, structural transformation of systemic hierarchies). As the track deconstructs regulatory desire through humour, it therefore activates novel borders around the extent to which the observer supports liberal individuality.

Indeed, humour is a tricky medium for performing social critique. Although laughter draws inclusions around those who share the joke, it excludes those who do not assent to the notion that marriage, for instance, curtails individual freedoms (cf. Zidani, 2020). For many women and girls around the globe, heterosexual courtship and domesticity remain aspirational goals of real or imagined economic security. Reading matrimony as parody is thus more readily available to audiences with the material, 'progressive', and educational capitals required to 'get the joke'. There is, then, a certain level of class power on display in this piece, of which the use of dress as gender-bending comedy is especially revealing. As described above, the performances in the video satirise bridal femininity by unambiguously placing Bashar, a person gendered male, into this feminised role. There are, as this chapter has argued, clear political dissents contained in such acts that should not be ignored. At the same time, however, because such disruptions mobilise hyper-mediated ideas about 'liberated' queer masculinity, they render less spectacular notions of queer desire invisible. Most immediately, pushing 'female' dress as drag parody consigns the long robes worn by Arab men to the category of 'skirt', thus feminising and subjugating those types of clothing that might also be affordable for older queer men who never 'came out'. Satire, in other words, cements difference as it rallies around identity.

My point here is not to denounce these social practices and those who facilitate them. Undoubtedly, songs like *al-kul am bitjawaz,* and musicians like

Razan or Fatima, create new gender and sexuality norms and mores through their music. Instead, it is important to use this productive tension to think, in the final section of this chapter, about the hegemonies that manifest through subcultural transgressions. Who has the capacity to take on and disobey gendered normativity in Palestine, and how do they discursively frame their actions? And are there any limits to the queer and/or feminist politics that music mediates?

Neoliberal Entrepreneurialism, Individual Gendered Success, and Transnational Feminist Capitals

Over the more than two years I spent conducting the research on which this chapter is based, almost all the musicians I met stated that their parents and/or other elites in the community supported their creative endeavours, albeit to varying degrees. Nonetheless, despite enjoying such extra social supports, with striking frequency, these young adults equated their musical success with personal hard work. This tendency especially punctuated my discussions with young women whose familial class privileges were enhanced after Oslo. In interviews, we often talked about the gendered asymmetries that shape this subculture. As is the case in countless music networks around the world, men dominate (and gatekeep) publicly visible roles, such as singing or playing instruments on stage, relative to women in the Palestinian underground. While there are plenty of female DJs, musicians, singers, and musicians in this scene, women more typically occupy positions as bedroom artists, fans, or audience members than they do public performers—especially in such stereotypically hyper-masculine subfields as rap and hip-hop.

The fact that several women with public roles accounted for their musical achievements via individuating narratives is therefore interesting. In our discussion, for example, Palestinian-Jordanian-Canadian event-planner and artist-promoter Lubna told me that alternative music in Palestine, as elsewhere, is a "man's world." When we met, Lubna was in her early thirties. She is largely based in Amman, but often hosts alternative parties across the West Bank. She said:

> I'm just lucky that my parents understand my work... I'm glad my parents are accepting ... [but] I have a strong personality... the point is that I'm a driven person, I love what I'm doing, and I'm working my butt off to get there. That could be anyone. It could be a man, a woman, transgender, whatever, it could be whatever you want, it doesn't matter... I know a lot of strong women in the industry, but I don't think it's about gender, I think it's about standing your ground no matter what your age, sex, gender, sexuality – it's important to just be yourself as a human. Run after what you want (Amman, 02/03/2014).

In this statement, Lubna argues that her ability to earn a living from the culture industries is down to her own hard work as a "driven person" with a "strong personality." Deploying entrepreneurial metanarratives, she insists that structural blockages to power "[do not] matter." Instead, she employs the neoliberal mantras of resilience, personal gumption, and individual discipline to explain her accomplishments. Her account thus shows how post-Oslo capitalist transformations are shaping and reshaping gendered subjectivities in the region.

Given her turning away from systemic accounts of social inequality, I was interested to hear what she thought about the gendered hierarchies that structure her subcultural milieu. She said:

> There are many more male artists [in the scene] than female artists, which is sad because a lot of these [male] artists are looking for female vocals and they can't find them. Be it religion, be it family, be it social, I'm not quite sure. I think everyone has their own mix of how they grew up and what they stand for, that they need to either fight or be against. I just feel – I know that there's a big need for female vocals, I get that all the time, requests for female vocalists... many bands are forming looking for [female singers] and there's not many. (Amman, 02/03/2014)

The depoliticised position Lubna here adopts is both naïve and highly informative. Stating that "religion...family [or] social" themes prevent *some* women from subcultural participation, she enacts her own discursive distance from these *always already other* groups. Lubna, in other words, presents herself as what media scholar Simidele Dosekun (2020: 17) describes as "empowered *already*." Dosekun's work focuses, among other things, on style and spectacular femininity in middle-/upper-class communities in contemporary Nigeria. Part of this work theorises how postfeminism—that is, the notion that today's women have 'been liberated' and therefore no longer require feminist politics (see Gill, 2007)—emerges in contexts where the putative 'pastness' of feminism is historically harder to assert (2020: 13). Dosekun argues that one way in which postfeminism takes root in such backdrops is through local class hierarchies. The elite women in her study, she suggests, deploy the 'plight' of their 'downtrodden' rural and/or working-class counterparts to signify their own gendered 'empowerment'. Hence, Dosekun's class privileged subjects can *bypass* feminism precisely because other local 'poor women' continue to need 'empowering' (2020: 16).

There are clear parallels between Dosekun's participants and Lubna's words. By using "religion, family, or social" factors to explain gendered inequalities in the music scene, the young creative claims her own postfeminist 'liberation'. As in Dosekun's analysis, while *she* can achieve individual success because she is "a driven person [which has] nothing to do with gender," other 'poor women' continue to be entirely 'stuck' in unchanging 'local traditions'. It is this assumed distance, then, from these *other others* that allow actors like Lubna to disavow feminism while situating herself as a "strong woman" who is no longer 'burdened' by gendered asymmetries. Her words thus insatiate a highly individuating class project, fashioned on achieving hierarchal difference from her peers, rooted in transnationally mobile (cf. Ong, 2007) postfeminist frames.

This postfeminist attitude structured many of my conversations with middle-class young women. Manal, for instance, makes music as an EDM and techno DJ in and around Haifa and Ramallah. At the time of our interview, Manal was in her late twenties. She is originally from Nazareth, but was then living in Haifa, where she was studying for a degree at the university. I asked Manal how she perceived her work as a DJ, and wondered if she would ever use the label "feminist" or "feminism" to narrate her practice. To which she emphatically replied:

> I'm *so* far from politics! I have nothing to do with politics! Even to say that I'm a feminist – I mean, I'm pretty sure I come out as a feminist, and a strong woman, and I'm definitely with that 100 per cent, but I don't stand in the way and say I'm a feminist... if feminism is to have the same rights as a man, absolutely; but... the women that are so much into feminism, I just feel like, with all due respect... all that matters is the final result. You know, if you go see a painting in a museum, you're gonna ask who painted it [and] it doesn't matter if it was a man or a woman... I don't look at my music and think: "oh because of politics I'm doing this", or "because of feminism I'm doing this", no! ... We have to all be one and one, together. So that's why I'm far from that. I don't like to get into it, cos I don't see any point of it. (Haifa, 31/01/2018)

Manal powerfully repudiates feminism: she "doesn't see any point of it." Like Lubna, she argues that her musical achievements have absolutely nothing to do with pre-existing histories of feminist mobilisations in Palestine. And again, like Lubna, she deploys neoliberal entrepreneurial scaffolds to position herself as a "strong woman." By depoliticising systemic oppressions, she shows how post-Oslo class power enables transgressions on gendered social norms in the community.

Finally, then, this point is not to belittle Manal or others' individual accounts of their social practices. Instead, such narratives are significant because they allow us to theorise how post-Oslo media culture *also* networks *some* class privileged young women to transnationally migratory (cf. Ong, 2007) feminist rationalities. As these young women engage in local and regional efforts to undo the patriarchal codes that forge female respectability, they at the same time shape and participate in truncated feminist politics focused on individual, rather than structural, 'empowerment'. This highlights how young adults are connected through "scattered hegemonies" (Grewal & Kaplan, 1994), or pockets of power, above and below local, national, and regional borders through subcultural media (see also Dosekun, 2020). Thus, it is not simply the case that homogenous imperial 'Western' feminisms annihilate unitary 'authentic regional' gender relations. Instead, paying attention to intersections between class and gender in popular cultures in Palestine allows us to trace how women in the global south form and are formed by transnational media worlds. Neither resistant nor compliant, musical feminisms in Palestinian subcultures thus simultaneously contest and co-operate with different power relations as they travel through local and transnationally mediated networks.

CONCLUSIONS

This chapter explored intersections between feminist politics and subcultural music. Using the empirical case study of Palestine, it suggested that there is not a singular 'type' of feminism that underpins Palestinian underground music. Instead, local, regional, and transnationally mobile feminist formations vie and compete for domination. What this shows us, then, is that subculturally identifying young adults embark on *contradictory* feminist work, in the way Hall (1994) theorised. First, young women's practices and embodied agencies *do* cultivate distinct feminist subjectivities rooted on, and in gendered critiques of, among other things, heteronormative and heteropatriarchal status quos. Music performances especially—and intentionally—uproot historic ideas about female modesty. In this sense, young women continue Palestine's long histories of feminist organising and mobilising against patriarchy under British and Zionist (settler-)colonialisms, through music.

Second, however, while youth *practices* depart from gendered hegemonies, their *narratives* are much more ambiguous. In our discussions, and differently to the mainstream media accounts with which I opened this chapter, young women *also*, at times at least, shied away from—or even disavowed—naming their cultural actions as specifically *feminist* interventions. Adopting postfeminist frames, they foster individuating feminisms. Such discourses thus demonstrate how neoliberal transformations in Israeli-dominated Palestine are reshaping youthful, middle-class gender and feminist politics. Neither utopian nor dystopian, this piece therefore concluded that popular music constitutes a dialectic struggle between the 'undoing' and the 'redoing' of feminism in Palestine and beyond.

The chapter therefore makes two contributions to feminist media studies in general and feminist Middle East media studies more specifically. First, and in terms of Middle East–focused feminist media studies, there has to date been no systematic examination of how late-capitalist shifts are reshaping feminisms in Palestine or MENA. By thinking about the complex ways in which neoliberal transformations interact with pre-existing gender dynamics, the chapter thus points to new lines of enquiry for future research. Second, and more broadly, the chapter further demonstrated the importance of music and popular culture for feminist politics. Thus, whereas feminist communications scholarship routinely overlooks how music shapes feminisms around the globe, this chapter highlighted the centrality of popular music for feminist struggle. Moving forwards, the research presented here thus aims to generate further lines of feminist enquiry focused on the relationship between contemporary feminist formations, gendered subjectivities, and popular music in Palestine, the Middle East, and beyond.

REFERENCES

Abu-Lughod, L. (1998). *Remaking Women: Feminism and Modernity in the Middle East*. Princeton University Press.

Abu-Lughod, L. (2002). Do Muslim Women Really Need Saving? Anthropological Reflection on Cultural Relativism and Its Others. *American Anthropologist, 104*(3), 783–790.

Ahmed, L. (1992). *Women and Gender in Islam: Historical Roots of a Modern Debate*. Yale University Press.

Banaji, S. (2017). *Children and Media in India*. Routledge.

Banet-Weiser, S. (2018). *Empowered: Popular Feminism and Popular Misogyny*. Duke University Press.

Butler, J. (1990). *Gender Trouble*. Routledge.

Calkin, S. (2015). Post-Feminist Spectatorship and the Girl Effect: 'Go Ahead, Really Imagine Her'. *Third World Quarterly, 26*(4), 654–669.

Chatterjee, P. (1989). Colonialism, Nationalism, and Colonised Women. *American Ethnologist, 4*, 622–633.

Chatterjee, P. (1993). *The Nation and Its Fragments*. Princeton University Press.

Dana, T. (2019). Crony Capitalism in the Palestinian Authority: A Deal Among Friends. *Third World Quarterly, 41*(2), 247–263.

Dosekun, S. (2020). *Spectacular Femininity*. University of Illinois Press.

Elsayed, Y., & Zidani, S. (2020). Reimagining the Arab Spring: From Imagination to Creativity. In H. Jenkins, G. Peter-Lazaro, & S. Shreshtova (Eds.), *Popular Culture and the Civic Imagination: Case Studies of Creative Social Change* (pp. 162–172). New York University Press.

El-Zein, R. (2017). "Resisting Resistance": On Political Feelings in Arabic Rap Concerts. In T. Sabry & L. Ftouni (Eds.), *Arab Subcultures* (pp. 152–176). I.B. Tauris.

Fleischmann, E. (2003). *The Nation and Its "New" Women: The Palestinian Women's Movement, 1920-1948*. University of California Press.

Gill, R. (2007). Postfeminist Media Culture: Elements of a Sensibility. *European Journal of Cultural Studies, 10*(2), 147–166.

Grewal, I., & Kaplan, C. (1994). *Scattered Hegemonies*. University of Minnesota Press.

Haddad, T. (2016). *Palestine Ltd.: Neoliberalism and Nationalism in the Occupied Territory*. IB Tauris.

Hall, S. (1998 [1994]). Notes on Deconstructing "the Popular". In J. Storey (Ed.), *Cultural Theory and Popular Culture: A Reader* (pp. 455-466). Routledge.

Hammami, R. (1990). *Women, the Hijab and the Intifada. Middle East Report*. Accessed October 20, 2021, from https://merip.org/1990/05/women-the-hijab-and-the-intifada/

Hasso, F., & Salime, Z. (2016). *Freedom Without Permission: Bodies and Space in the Arab Revolutions*. Duke University Press.

Kandiyoti, D. (1988). Bargaining with Patriarchy. *Gender & Society, 2*(3), 274–290.

Kandiyoti, D. (1991). Identity and Its Discontents: Women and the Nation. *Millennium, 20*, 429–443.

Khalidi, R., & Samour, S. (2011). Neoliberalism as Liberation: The Statehood Program and the Remaking of the Palestinian National Movement. *Journal of Palestine Studies, 40*(2), 6–25.

Kraidy, M. (2005). *Hybridity*. Temple University Press.

Kuttub, E. (1993). Palestinian Women in the Intifada: Fighting on Two Fronts. *Arab Studies Quarterly, 15*(2), 1–69.

Mahmood, S. (2005). *Politics of Piety*. Princeton University Press.

Maria, S., & Shihade, M. (2012). Hip Hop from '48 Palestinians. Youth, Music, and the Present Absent. *Social Text, 30*(3), 1–26.

McDonald, D. (2006). Performing Palestine. *Jerusalem Quarterly, 25*, 5–18.

Moreno-Almeida, C. (2017). *Rap Beyond Resistance*. Palgrave Macmillan.

Morgan, J. (1999). *When Chickenheads Come Home to Roost: A Hip-Hop Feminist Breaks It Down*. Simon and Shuster.

Najmabadi, A. (1991). Hazards of Modernity and Morality; Women, State and Ideology. In D. Kandiyoti (Ed.), *Women, Islam and the State* (pp. 48–76). Palgrave Macmillan.

Najmabadi, A. (1998). Crafting an Educated Housewife in Iran. In L. Abu-Lughod (Ed.), *Remaking Women: Feminism and Modernity in the Middle East* (pp. 91–125). Princeton University Press.

Nakassis, C. (2013). Youth Masculinity, 'Style' and the Peer Group in Tamil Nadu, India. *Contributions to Indian Sociology, 47*(2), 245–269.

Nguyen, M. (2011). The Biopower of Beauty: Humanitarian Imperialisms and Global Feminisms in the Age of Terror. *Signs, 362*, 359–383.

Ong, A. (2007). Neoliberalism as a Mobile Technology. *Boundary Crossing, 32*(1), 3–8.

Peteet, J. (1991). *Gender in Crisis: Women and the Palestinian Resistance Movement*. Colombia University Press.

Pratt, N. (2020). *Embodying Geopolitics: Generations of Women's Activism in Egypt, Jordan, and Lebanon*. University of California Press.

Sensoy, O., & Marshall, E. (2010). Missionary Girl Power: Saving the 'Third World' One Girl at a Time. *Gender and Education, 22*(3), 295–311.

Skalli, L. (2015). The Girl Factor and the (In)Security of Coloniality: A View from the Middle East. *Alternative: Global, Local, Political, 40*(2), 174–187.

Spivak, G. (1985). Can the Subaltern Speak? In C. Nelson & L. Grossberg (Eds.), *Marxism and the Interpretation of Culture* (pp. 271–313). Macmillan.

Stokes, C. (2007). Representin' in Cyberspace: Sexual Scripts, Self-definition, and Hip-Hop Culture in Black Adolescent girls' Home Pages. *Culture, Health & Sexuality, 9*(2), 169–184.

Switzer, H. (2013). (Post)feminist Development Fables: The Girl Effect and the Production of Sexual Subjects. *Feminist Theory, 14*(3), 345–360.

Taraki, L. (2008). Enclave Micropolis: The Paradoxical Case of Ramallah/Al-Bireh. *Journal of Palestine Studies, 37*(4), 6–20.

Tawil-Souri, H. (2011). Colored Identity: The Politics and Materiality of ID Cards in Palestine/Israel. *Social Text, 29*(2), 67–97.

Turner, M. (2015). Peacebuilding as Counterinsurgency in the Occupied Palestinian Territory. *Review of International Studies, 41*(1), 73–98.

Winegar, J. (2006). *Creative Reckonings: The Politics of Art and Culture in Contemporary Egypt*. Stanford University Press.

Withers, P. (2021). Ramallah ravers and Haifa hipsters: Gender, Class, and Nation in Palestinian Popular Culture. *British Journal of Middle Eastern Studies, 48*(1), 94–113.

Withers, P. (2022). Digital Feminisms in Palestinian Hip Hop. *Journal of Global Hip Hop Studies, 2.2*, pp. 159–177.

Yegenoglu, M. (1998). *Colonial Fantasies: Towards a Feminist Reading of Orientalism*. Cambridge University Press.

Yuval-Davis, N. (1997). *Gender and Nation*. SAGE Publications.

Zidani, S. (2020). Not Arabi or Ajnabi: Arab Youth and Reorienting Humor. *International Journal of Communication, 14*(20), 3202–3219.

CHAPTER 25

Moroccan Hip Hop Queens: A (Her)Story of Rap Music in Morocco

Cristina Moreno Almeida

Hip Hop culture is well-established in Morocco with a vast number of practitioners and fans within and beyond Moroccan borders. Since the mid-1990s, the Moroccan rap scene has thrived, conquering the stage at national and international music festivals; rap songs are regularly played on the radio; and rappers are regular guests on television programmes. Particularly from the 2010s, rap music and Hip Hop culture have benefited from a growing number of social media users as a consequence of the development of ICTs and better quality internet connectivity. Platforms such as YouTube and Instagram have provided a space for both practitioners and fans to release and listen to rap music regardless of traditional media and cultural industry gatekeeping.[1] In building such a flourishing scene, female rap artists or *femcees* have played an important role in disrupting an otherwise male-dominated scene.[2] The presence of women rappers has, however, remained uneven and at times scarce. A low participation of

---

[1] I have discussed the main tenets of Moroccan rap history and politics in *Rap Beyond Resistance: Staging Power in Contemporary Morocco* (2017).

[2] The use of female and male in this chapter is intended to highlight issues concerning these categories but is not intended to negate non-binary and queer identities.

C. Moreno Almeida (✉)
School of Language, Linguistics and Film, Queen Mary University of London, London, UK
e-mail: c.morenoalmeida@qmul.ac.uk

© The Author(s), under exclusive license to Springer Nature Switzerland AG 2023
L. H. Skalli, N. Eltantawy (eds.), *The Palgrave Handbook of Gender, Media and Communication in the Middle East and North Africa*, https://doi.org/10.1007/978-3-031-11980-4_25

femcees is not unique to Morocco, but a common feature worldwide. In the country with the largest rap industry in the world, the United States, female performers have encountered a similar pitted scenario. The Grammy Awards withdrawal of "Best Female Rap Artist" category in 2004 illustrates the struggle of femcees in the United States. The decision was backed up merely two years after the category was created because the Awards claimed to have gathered only thirteen candidates for this entry instead of the required minimum of twenty-five (Concepcion, 2007, pp. 24–25). In spite of the industry's disbelief in female rap, throughout the years women's voices have steadily made headway not only into the US music industry but also in Morocco. Especially since 2017, new rap music by Moroccan female artists has increasingly bloomed, setting high expectations for the future of Hip Hop in North Africa.

There is a long tradition of Moroccan women performers whether singers, dancers, singer-dancers, composers, lyricists and instrumentalists. Across the country, women perform in urban centres or rural areas, as part of traditional Amazigh *ahidus* and *ahwash* performances or Andalusian ensembles, as well as the transgressive *shikhat*. Within the field of contemporary music, many women have made a name for themselves. Some classic Moroccan artists include the late Haja El Hamdaouia known for singing Moroccan Chaabi and Aita, Hayat El Idrissi who specialised in interpretations of Oum Kalthoum songs, Latifa Raafat known for singing exclusively in Moroccan Darija and Naima Samih whose career took off after participating in the 1970s talent music show Mawahib. Particularly prominent internationally are Samira Said and Najat Aatabou. Samira Said is a venerated superstar with a particular following in Egypt. Najat Aatabou gained popularity with her hit "Hadi Kedba Bayna" (This Lie is Obvious, 1992) later sampled in the song "Galvanize" (2004) by the Chemical Brothers. Since the 2000s, a number of female artists have explored music genres such as pop and rap, but also rock, indie and electronic music. Besides the rappers discussed in this chapters, some of prominent artists include Oum (fusion-soul), Khansa Batma (fusion-rock), Hindi Zahra (jazz-soul), Dounia Batma (Arabic pop) or younger singer-composers such as Nada (indie-electronic). Together with these and many other women performers, female rappers have played an important role in perpetuating the vibrancy of Morocco's music scene.

The road towards a rich female rap scene, however, has suffered from times with no notable femcee in the limelight. This momentary silence has led some anglophone media to report North African and Middle Eastern female rappers as exceptional and unique within their countries. These reports often blend rappers like Malikah living in Lebanon but born in France to an Algerian family with artists living outside the region such as Shadia Mansour of Palestinian origin but based in the UK all as the voices of Arabic Hip Hop (see, e.g. "7 Female Rappers Shaping Hip-Hop in the Middle East" 2018, "The Six: Female rappers from the Middle East who are changing the game" 2018 and Hamad 2020). Year after year, these articles produce similar lists iterating the names of the same rappers. As a result, reports on female rap performers from Middle

East and North Africa (MENA) are mostly fragmented and unnuanced. While such a mediatic picture suggests a monotonous and unexciting domain for artists, the Moroccan case evidences a long and interesting herstory of women rappers.

Against a backdrop of existing mediatic accounts of female rap in MENA, this chapter chronicles the stories of some of Morocco's most popular femcees as well as of crucial events throughout the past twenty years. In this chapter I look back into the history of Moroccan femceeing to pay homage to those women whose music has shaped Moroccan rap. I analyse key elements in women's cultural production such as lyrics, music videos, performance, language as well as their presence on social media presenting the Moroccan female rap scene holistically. In order to fill in the void in knowledge that particularly affects the beginnings of the female rap scene, I carried out interviews with some of the women I had encountered during my years researching and working on the Moroccan rap scene (2011–2015). Cultural analysis and interviews carried out for the purposes of this work focusing on women complement my previous work on the Moroccan rap scene. The chapter, following for the most part a chronological order, opens by narrating the different experiences that led the first women to enter the Hip Hop scene in the late 1990s and beginning of the 2000s. The following section considers the moment when female rappers gained notoriety within national and international media. At this point, the chapter looks into the significance of local Hip Hop networks of solidarity to then moves onto 2017 as a significant year for Moroccan female rap. In closing, the last section discusses some of the particularities inherent to Moroccan femceeing, suggesting an increase in female collaborations to continue building the road ahead.

IN THE BEGINNING

When Widad Mjama aka Queen T (Thug) was first invited to be one of the leading singers of the rap group Thug Gang, there were not any other female rappers that she knew of in Morocco. At the end of the 1990s, the Kingdom was transitioning to what was marketed as a new era with King Mohammed VI leading the way towards development, modernity and democracy. Daughter of an Arabic teacher and with a mother in the military, Widad, as she is still referred to within the Hip Hop community, grew up in the neighbourhood of Mers Sultan in downtown Casablanca. In those days, there were no studios available such as Boultek or L'uzine which opened over a decade later where Thug Gang and other music bands could rehearse. Widad, however, lived in one of the hot spots of the city's Hip Hop scene. At the time, the Mohammed V Square hosted families strolling and feeding flocks of pigeons, as well as rappers and break-dancers who occupied this space to practice their craft. From the streets of Maarif to Yasmina and Nevada, at the Ligue Arab Park, crowds of young people wearing baggy pants and oversized t-shirts proliferated, attracted to Hip Hop's youthful creativity. For many in Morocco including Widad,

Tupac was a key figure of inspiration refuting assumptions that rap was mainly introduced in Morocco through France. Together, young people would listen to cassettes of their favourite US rappers and translate from English to Moroccan Darija lyrics of songs they did not fully understand.

Thug Gang was initially formed by Houcine aka Shot, Walid Ben Selim and Toufik Hazeb aka Don Bigg. When the latter left the group, Houcine and Walid heard Widad rapping one of Tupac's song during a basketball practice. It was then when her artistic career began. In 2001, Thug Gang which by then had added other MCs such as Mehdi Koman who won the third edition of L'Boulevard (short for *Festival du Boulevard des Jeunes Musiciens*).[3] At what soon became one of the most prestigious music festivals in the country, Widad met other femcees for the first time:

> At that time, there was another female rapper, Nawal, part of the group Silent Weapons and Asmae, I don't remember in which group she was … There was a brief moment where I was the only one, but then it started to pick up even if it was always smaller than male rappers. (Unpublished interview with author, December 2, 2020)

In the next five years, the Moroccan rap scene quickly flourished. Rap and breakdancing battles were taking place in different youth centres all around the country. Moroccan rappers featured on national television and new music festivals began programming rap music. The birth of Hit Radio in 2006 was also pivotal in supporting local rap music as it would soon reach large audiences all around the country. By the time rap became omnipresent in the Moroccan music scene, Widad and Walid left to continue their studies in France. Widad returned to Morocco in 2011 with the aim of applying everything she had learned in France and, as she says, give back to her country. However, things had changed for her. In 2013, Widad went back to France, where together with Walid she formed the extremely successful electro-Hip-Hop band N3erdistan.

In those years, rapper Tendresse emerged as the new star femcee. Hanane Lafif, aka Tendresse, was born in Casablanca and like Widad frequented popular places among rappers like Yasmina or the club La Cage. By 2010, Tendresse had become a well-established rapper invited to numerous music festivals all around Morocco and playing internationally at concerts in Brussels and Madrid in 2011. After this success, Tendresse paused her career for a few years due to family issues although she never stopped writing and recording music. Tendresse has consistently published new music videos on her YouTube channel.[4] She released in 2020 the EP *Lagertah* and the album *The One* with

---

[3] Watch here Widad Queen T live with Thug Gang at la F.O.L. in Casablanca in 2002. https://www.youtube.com/watch?v=LzTvDvE3pw4 (Accessed May 11, 2021).

[4] See Tendresse YouTube channel at: https://www.youtube.com/channel/UCKJr1q-r5M1R373SVtokqpw (accessed May 11, 2021).

material she had been working on during her brief hiatus from the public eye. Her work is praised by male and female rappers due to her impeccable flow, blunt lyrics and a strong stage presence. Tendresse's prolific career has kept her relevant for twenty years, becoming a reference point especially for new female rappers.

A childhood of solitude and abuse drew Tendresse towards Hip Hop. She is the youngest of eleven brothers and sisters. She was unaware until later in her life that she had been adopted. When growing up all her sisters were married so she shared her childhood and teen years with seven brothers who closely oversaw and controlled every aspect of her life. Her brothers constantly beat her and forbade her to invite friends over, to paint her nails or to listen to music. Contrary to Widad who remembers a house full of music, in Tendresse's conservative household playing music was considered *haram* (forbidden). For this reason, Tendresse first found a safe space in composing poetry and later in rap lyrics. Writing allowed her to express everything she was going through. As she says,

> It was difficult for me to talk, to express myself, to say what I had in my mind. The medium for me was my paper. I would never fail my paper because it was my friend. I wrote first poems in French and I wrote poems in [Classic] Arabic. That helped me to ease a bit, to free what I wanted to tell, because I couldn't speak to anyone at home quite simply, of what I had lived during my childhood and adolescence. My childhood wasn't easy, but I could get out of there, forge a personality, and because I only grew up with boys at home, I was sort of like a boy … Otherwise I would lock up myself in the toilet during my childhood to be able to write poems or rap because it was almost forbidden … being an artist or whatever was almost forbidden. I had to follow their orders. It was a difficult childhood, it was only the light of my mother, may she rest in peace, otherwise everything else was dark. (Unpublished interview with author, December 11, 2020)

At twelve years of age, Tendresse was raped by a twenty-eight-year-old man while on holidays with part of her family. After being assaulted, still with her face covered with bruises and in tears, she went back home and wrote down what she had experienced. She feared to be further beaten by her family so did not confide in anyone. However, one of her brothers found the text and responded employing what Loubna Hanna Skalli (2014, p. 253) calls the patriarchal blame/shame logic: "My brother told me: 'Today you're a whore like the rest of them'" (unpublished interview with author, December 11, 2020). Penalised for being the victim, Tendresse started writing profusely to avoid, as she told me, becoming insane. The turn from writing poetry to rap lyrics happened after listening to French rapper Manau and his song "La Tribu de Dana" (1998). Although she had never stepped into a recording studio, soon after in 2002, she started frequenting home studios where she began producing her first songs. To evade her family's constant monitoring, Tendresse simulated going to the hammam but would instead stop at the studio: "That was my small secret, but my paradise at the same time" (unpublished interview with author, December 11, 2020). The studio as much as the hammam turned out to be a space where she felt secure from her brothers, providing Tendresse with a sense of belonging and self-worth.

Tendresse's artistic and her Arabic given name Hanane mean tenderness. Even if her name might suggest a fragile nature, Tendresse is outspoken and confident, displaying a lack of fear to speak out her mind. She occupies the focal point of the camera in her music videos. She swears in her songs showing the middle finger even when that contravenes conservative and mostly accepted public language conventions for a young woman: "Fine wald lka7la wald lfa7la, b9a gha wld l9a7ba wld l9a7ba" (Where is the son of the black? The son of the strong woman? The only one left is the son of a bitch, son of a bitch). In these lyrics from her song "B.W.B" (*Brani Wst Bladi*, Foreigner in My Country, 2020), Tendresse speaks about abuse, poverty and homelessness: topics with which she can relate due to her own life experience. In this song's music video, a rapid delivery of lyrics happens while images alternatively show the rapper dressed in torn clothes and real-life images of young poor Moroccans roaming the city at night. The last shot of "B.W.B." addresses those who think their actions do not have consequences by writing: "Le [*sic*] roue tourne on ne récolte que ce qu'on sème faites attention au karma liouma 3andak ghda 3andi" (The wheel turns, we only reap what we sow, watch out for karma, today you have, but tomorrow I will).[5] The hardships of everyday life in Morocco and lost futures are a recurrent theme in Tendresse music. After twenty years as a rapper, Tendresse continues working in her craft out of love for rap and Hip Hop, leaving behind an invaluable footprint for new generations of rappers.

FEMCEES ON THE MEDIA

Near the end of the 2000s, four young femcees entered the music scene with their single "Maghribiya" (Moroccan Woman, 2008). Originally from different cities, the members of Tigresse Flow meet in Casablanca as undergraduate students. Their song, a chant demanding the empowerment of Moroccan women, worked well within national mainstream media. As the first all-female rap group to gain popularity, the members of Tigresse Flow, Miss Wiba (Wahiba Achik), Mc Flow (Hind), Fatinez (Fatima-Zahra) and Soultana (Youssra Oakuf), soon found themselves performing on television, radio stations and at music festivals. Together they have won multiple prizes: the first prize at Ouf du Bled Festival in Casablanca in 2006, Le Tremplin du Boulevard in 2007 and Génération Mawazine—part of the state-sponsored music festival Mawazine— in 2008. Crucial in the group's success was a well-balanced performance palatable to broader audiences exhibiting urban youthfulness and feminist lyrics free from vulgar expressions. By mid-2000s, feminists' groups in Morocco had succeeded in their demands for a new Family Code (2004). This reform was in

---

[5] All translations into English are by the author of this chapter.

tune with Eurocentric perspectives on progress, development and modernity positioning the new King as the champion of women's right (Kozma, 2003, p. 127; Massad, 2015). An all-female rap group aligned well with the image of change Morocco had been promoting; however, the public success of Tigresse Flow did not materialise into economic support. After winning Génération Mawazine which entails funding to produce an album, the festival did not follow through with the promise of a record deal. As Soultana ("Moroccan Rap is the Voice of the People", 2014) claims, the festival's organisation believed it was not worthwhile investing in female artists because women would soon abandon their music careers. Although winning this contest does not guarantee a successful career, such a claim suggests that while putting female rappers on stage was good for the festival's image, these femcees and their career prospects were not taken seriously or considered profitable.

Two years after reaching stardom, the members of Tigress Flow split up. In 2012, Miss Wiba paused her career for personal reasons, while Hind and Fatima-Zahra decided to leave rap altogether. As a solo artist, Soultana released the song "Sawt Nssa" (The Voice of Women, 2010), continuing with the group's feminist gaze. In this song, Soultana addresses prostitution, a leitmotiv that would be also part of other femcees' work. Soultana has continued to perform at national and international festivals but she has also focused on her studies in the United States. International anglophone media often reports on Soultana as the "only female rapper in Morocco" ("Moroccan Rap is the Voice of the People", 2014) or "Morocco's First Female Rapper" ("7 of the Best Arab and North African Female Rappers", 2020; "Rapper Soultana Is The Voice of Moroccan Women", 2019; Natour, 2019). Even if newer rappers have gathered millions of views and followers on social media as this chapter later discusses, up until as recently as 2020 media outlets still name Soultana as the single female Moroccan rapper "Shaking Up the Arab World" (Natour, 2019). Hailing Soultana as the only female rapper in Morocco reflects poorly on journalistic practices, but it also presents a distorted view of femceeing in the MENA region. Even if the number of female rappers is low in larger rap industries in Europe and the United States, rarely do anglophone reports single out *one* rapper from each European country or the United States. Contrary to the MENA region, such reports do not fall into methodological nationalism (see, e.g. Roberson 2020), or when they focus in one country they show a variety of top artists (see, e.g. Patterson, 2012).

Further, when speaking about women and rap in MENA, the story is often less concerned with the rapper's artistry and popularity within local audiences. One article reads "Morocco's Soultana raps for social change" (Rohan, 2014), while another claims "Female Rappers Push Limits in Conservative Morocco" (Pfeiffer, 2009). Stories frequently present women using rap as a useful "tool." This is the case with how Afghan female rappers are portrayed, writing headlines such as "Afghan Rapper Voices Women's Rights" (Assadi, 2013) or "Afghan Teen Uses Rap to Escape Forced Marriage" (Bloom, 2015). There is no doubt that rap may have a positive influence on these artists and their audiences. These headlines, however, focus on the need for female liberation in one region as if women's rap beyond the Global North only mattered in its capacity to explicitly and directly drive social change. Such reporting dispossesses women in MENA from being valued for their artistry. Utterly neglected are conversations that speak on female aesthetics or artistic innovation like delivery skills, flow, groove, visual artwork and so forth in the case of rap. As the case of Tigresse Flow suggests, instead of being artists who speak on social issues, the value of these femcees depends on how they respond to anxieties of liberating Muslim women. For female rappers in MENA, liberation is only possible through the markers of modernity that have been agreed by Global North.

In indulging stories of exceptionality, these reports overlook the stories of Miss Wiba, also member of Tigresse Flow, and of similar all-female rap groups that emerged around the same time. Inspired by the socially engaged themes of US rap, Miss Wiba started recording songs as early as 2003 under the alias of Dirty Flow. Throughout the years she has continued to write new songs, recording them in the studio as well as attending every event organised by the local Hip Hop community. As she told me in our last conversation (unpublished interview with author, March 15, 2021), in spite of pausing her career after Tigresse Flow parted ways, she sees her future career together with Soultana coming back as a group. All-female rap crews also flourished in other parts of the country. Particularly Salé, a neighbouring city to the capital Rabat, has been an important place for Hip Hop culture. Bnat HH or S-Girlzz whose members later joined other groups such as Bnat L'Blad created in 2008 with Sista Fonkee, Nigrita, Vicky and DJ Rach and Bnat Bladi formed by rappers Naghma and Fleury together with the singer Enigma have all emerged from this city. Bnat L'Blad also participated in Génération Mawazine in 2012 as well as the Festival Voix de Femme in Tetouan that same year. Even if of brief success and even if of little interest to traditional media, these groups have guaranteed the continuity of local female rap.

Hip Hop Networks and Solidarity

By the 2010s, Moroccan rappers had built strong ties not only among themselves but also with local music producers, home recording studios, video directors, lighting technicians, graphic artists, photographers and many others involved in music production. Establishing strong networks has resulted in a well-developed and lively rap scene. These interconnected groups have mostly emerged around urban centres as shown throughout this chapter in Casablanca and Salé, but also Marrakech, Meknes, Tangiers, Agadir and Rabat, including smaller nodes in towns such as Oujda and Asfi. Within networks where men outnumber women, femcees assert that for the most part they have felt welcome and respected. Widad, who was encouraged to join Thug Gang by two male rappers, asserts: "What I do remember really well is that the guys were really kind. There was a lot of respect. At that time, it was about performance: you rap well, or you don't" (unpublished interview with author, December 2,

2020). Tendresse and Miss Wiba reported similar experiences, as the latter claims: "We felt welcome by the Moroccan rap scene and audience. They encouraged us to continue our rap careers" (unpublished interview with author, March 15, 2021). In Casablanca, these two female rappers benefited from the supporting atmosphere of rapper Chaht Man's studio. Chaht Man, who is one of the founding members of the popular group Casa Crew, has enabled throughout the years a space at his studio where new rappers record their first songs. It is at this studio where Tigresse Flow produced their maxi album *Gangsta Rap* and where Tendresse still records her music.

One female artist who has taken advantage of Hip Hop networks between Marrakech, Asfi and Casablanca is the singer Manal. Manal Benchlikha entered the rap scene as the only female voice for the song "Mantsayadch" (I Won't Be Fooled, 2014). This song was part of a campaign launched by Hit Radio to promote voting among young people. For this project, Manal performed together with four well-known male rappers, Dizzy DROS, Muslim and the duo Shayfeen as well as the singer Ahmed Soultan. At the time, Manal's manager was DJ Van who had been a member of the rap group Fnaire and therefore part of the Marrakech rap scene. Later, Cilvaringz, a Dutch Moroccan rapper member of the Wu-Tang Clan based in Marrakech, became her manager. Manal debuted as a rapper in 2018 with two songs: "Taj" featured by Shayfeen and "Slay" with rapper ElGrande Toto. Both music videos have both enjoyed great success on YouTube, gathering collectively over 80 million views. In spite of this success, the rap community perceived Manal as a commercial product who had gained notoriety thanks to her collaborations with already known rappers and the networks they had already curated. The fact is that both of these rap songs were written by the male performers, hindering her efforts to become a credible rapper. It was clear among rap connoisseurs that both songs were catered to broader audiences. Manal's performance in these songs differs from the work of other female rappers whose lyrics sound more intimate and personal. After her success with the greater audience, Manal has turned to pop music with songs like "Niya" (Naive, 2020), confirming the perception of the rap community. After releasing this song, Manal asserted on her Instagram account that rap had only been part of her artistic exploratory path and that she was moving on to other music genres for her upcoming album.

Establishing your credibility within the rap family requires authentic, personal and credible performance and lyrics. Khtek, a female rapper originally from Khemisset, a small city next to Rabat, has collaborated early in her career with established male rappers. Nonetheless, Houda Abouz aka Khtek entered the rap scene's radar after her freestyle "Unpredictable" (2019) became viral on Instagram. Soon after, she was called to rap side by side with ElGrande Toto, Don Bigg and Draganov in the song "Hors Serie" (Special Edition, 2020) as part of an ad campaign for McDonald's. Unlike Manal's demure style, Khtek exhibits unique lyrics, skills and performance. As Tendresse, Khtek does not shy away from employing a language that, although perceived as vulgar by conservative sectors of society especially when spoken in public, remains faithful to everyday youthful interactions:

Hna kayn ghi rap qui domine,	Here only rap dominates
I seem sweet I can be mean	I seem sweet I can be mean
Ghelta b7alla 3fatti fel khra,	I'm a mistake like stepping on poo
f had l'game ana lekhra	In this game, I'm the last one
Ma kanrappich l wlad Descartes	I don't rap for the people of Descartes
hadchi l zwaml w l7erraga	This is for *zwaml*[6] and *harraga*[7]

Interlocking English with Darija, these lines from her single "KickOff" (2020) suggest a break with French as Morocco's colonial language and widely used by upper classes. Here, Khtek plays with double meanings to claim that her music is not for French people or the people of Descartes, nor the Moroccan bourgeoisie, that is, those who attend the French international school in Rabat called Lycée Descartes. Her songs are for those who fall within the cracks of Moroccan society such as undocumented migrants and LGBTQAI+ community which she is known to support. Khtek's voice is deep and husky and enjoys creatively experimenting with different forms of make-up and costumes, ultimately surprising the audience in each music video she produces.

Not every female rapper has felt supported by their peers. Born Sanae Rayhani, rapper Krtas Nssa has been vocal regarding the fact that while notable members of the rap community and Moroccan cultural industry claimed to support her career publicly, privately they have ignored her calls. The artist grew up in another important epicentre of Moroccan Hip Hop, the city of Meknes. Listening to local rappers who had been successful in the music scene like Mehdi K-libre and H-Kayne, Krtas Nssa started writing first and then rapping in her early teens. In 2014 when she was still a teenager, she participated in the talent show *Big Up* broadcasted on the Moroccan national channel Medi1 TV. As part of the show, rapper Muslim acted as one of the judges. Although she managed to make it far as the only rapper left among the other contestants, once the show ended, neither the show's management nor Muslim answered her calls. In those years, the rap scene was void of any popular female voices, but her perseverance would lead Krtas Nssa to be one of the leading femcees of a new generation of women rappers. By releasing three music videos in 2017 she reclaimed a new era for the herstory of Moroccan rap revamping a scene that seemed to be perishing. These songs, "Rainbow," "Madame," and "Zid L'alcool," belonged to her first EP called *KN* (2018a, b, c). Through this body of work, Krtas Nssa proved that she had the necessary rap skills and punchlines to be taken seriously as one of the new names of the rap scene. In her lyrics, Krtas Nssa reflects on social issues using the art of ego-tripping to

---

[6] The word *zwaml* (the plural of *zamil*) is a derogative word that means effeminate.

[7] *Harraga* is a word used for those undocumented migrants who cross the Mediterranean Sea.

perform a pulse with her opponents. These might be other rappers or the country as is the case with the song "Madame." Here, she speaks on the double life some women are forced to lead, arguing women are compelled to leave the country in order to act freely:

Ghanquittek ghadi ndi m3aya soura	I'm leaving the country and leave behind a picture
Sorry	Sorry
Madame bagha ghir dkoura	The woman only wants strong males
Dayra 7ijab 3ryana f'doura	She has a veil on, but she's naked in the backstreet
Ghadi tl9aha f'stori medkoura	You'll see it in her Instagram story

In the chorus of the song, she blames the country for not letting women lead their lives in a different way:

Bladi ghadya bya b'lour	My country is taking me backwards
Khayfa Lante7 yzetmoli f'lard	I'm afraid to fall and be stepped on
Chayfaha f'mnami labsa lbyad	I'm seeing her in my sleep wearing white
Khayfa la tdini w matraja3ch	I'm afraid that it takes me and won't come back

Krtas Nssa's songs are carefully curated with rhymes that work well in creatively narrating the difficulties of being a young woman. Her feminist views also guide the artwork for her EP *Otite* (2019). The cover of this EP shows the female reproductive organs in red with two boxing gloves substituting the ovaries. Through this artwork she confirms her commitment to continue fighting in spite of the hurdles women find along the road. In a later song, Krtas Nssa continues exploring women's role in society through the topic of prostitution. The song and music video "Bent Lil" (lit. woman of the night, 2020), partly sung in French, serves the rapper to denounce society's hypocrisy in neglecting the role of men: "He tells her woman of the night, and I tell him son of a bitch." In the description of the YouTube video, she writes in Arabic:

أتمنى أن نتوقف عن التركيز على المرأة في مسألة العفة ونعتبرها مصدر الشر فالمرأة الفاسدة لم توجد إلا لأن الرجل صفق لها وشجعها! ولو أن كل امرأة فاسدة
متبرجة وجدت احتقارا من الرجال لما انهال علينا سيل العاهرات الذي نراه في هذا الزمان.

I hope we stop focusing on women regarding the issue of chastity and consider them the source of evil. An immoral woman cannot exist without a man encouraging her! And if every corrupt, exposed woman had found men's contempt, we would not have been hit by the torrent of prostitutes we see in this time.

Prostitution has been a relevant topic in Moroccan culture, especially after Nabil Ayouch's movie "Much Loved" (2015). Telling the lives of four female sex workers, the movie was banned in Moroccan cinemas but widely watched as unauthorised copies roamed the internet. Both the song and the movie showcase the patriarchal blame/shame logic that continues to limit women's lives, including those who dare to challenge conservative social boundaries as the following section discusses.

LOVE AND FAME IN THE AGE OF SOCIAL MEDIA

By 2017, rappers and audience had grown accustomed to interacting on social media, especially on image-sharing sites such as YouTube and Instagram. These platforms also increased new and upcoming femcees' visibility not only within the rap community, but also with other users interested in closely following their daily Instagram Stories updates. The opportunity to share music online and to gain followers through active social media use meant that while women artists secured agency, local cultural and media gatekeepers lost their power. In this regard, Krtas Nssa, Khtek and singer Manal have accumulated in 2021 a high number of followers on Instagram: 144 k, 279 k and 2.4 million, respectively. This acquired visibility may act as a double-edged sword when it comes to MENA women's self-(re)presentation practices. A perceived hypervisibility and agency threatens what Omnia El Shakry (2013) calls "patriarchal bargain," that is, granting women in MENA presence in public spaces as long as they stay politically silent and adhere "to bourgeois norms of respectability" (El Shakry, 2013, p. 84). Rapper Ily, a social media star with over 1.3 million followers on Instagram to this day, has put this bargain into question by publicly exposing matters traditionally kept within the private sphere such family affairs and being in non-marital romantic relationship. Her story deserves a closer look.

Rapper Ilham El Arbaoui aka Ily released her first hit song "Khelouni"[8] (Leave Me Alone) in 2018 gathering over 20 million views on YouTube up until 2021. The music video shows a confident and daring rapper exhibiting a behaviour aimed at disrupting conservative social norms. Shot at night, the video shows Ily with two other friends smoking and drinking at a table beside a swimming pool. Structured as a diss song,[9] Ily's lyrics are far from explicitly discussing feminist struggles. Ily's controversial relationship with other female rappers and regular posts where she appears close to male performers have enticed the curiosity of social media users. Over the recent years, her Instagram followers have been invited to watch aspects of her most intimate life such as her difficult relationship with who she alleges to be her father, the famous chaabi singer Abdelaziz Stati, and with her former boyfriend, the popular rapper 7liwa (pronounced hliwa).

Public displays of affection on social media or romantic love themes are not common in Moroccan rap. Some romantic love rap songs have appeared over the past years. On February 14, 2019, Tendresse released the love song "Nta"

---

[8] See video at https://www.youtube.com/watch?v=Gd_70kdfZXw (accessed May 11, 2021).

[9] A diss song is a type of rap song intended to disrespect or defy a particular rapper or rappers in general.

(You) where she sings to a past romantic relationship. Conversations about the reasons behind the absence of these themes in Moroccan rap prompted after Dizzy DROS released "Nota" (2020). This song speaks openly about the difficulty of publicly admitting having romantic love feelings and calls the audience in the lyrics to "just say that you are in love." The fact is that public displays of romantic affection are punished by law in Morocco. Throughout the MENA region, audio-visual production companies edit foreign movies and TV shows to delete any scene or storylines considered inappropriate such as kisses between lovers or homosexuality. Especially when it comes to non-marital relationships, many public figures including male rappers shy away from disclosing them on their social media profiles. The fact that Ily shared her love story with the well-known rapper 7liwa crossed the lines of public propriety. While it attracted the curiosity of social media users, it also had a negative effect on her credibility as a rapper.

Rappers in Morocco have mostly directed their expressions of love towards their parents as this kind of love is socially praised and extremely well received by audiences. One such song is Muslim's "Mama" (2018) which has over 129 million views on YouTube.[10] Following the success of these themes, in 2020 Ily released the song and music video "Baba" (Dad) where the rapper remembers her childhood with her father Abdelaziz Stati. In the lyrics Ily sings "Even if I grew up alone, your picture is always in my heart" (Wakha kbert ghi bouhdi ma3ya wehda ou nta sorteq kayna dima fqelbi ldakhel). Contrary to Muslim, Ily's song was released after several public statements where her relationship with Stati emerged as complicated. Stati had publicly rejected being Ily's father in 2018 (Tantani, 2018). Ily, on her side, had reaffirmed her own identity as an artist rapping in the song "Khelouni": "Smiti Ilham machi Bent Stati" (I am Ilham not the daughter of Stati). For this reason, posting old pictures with Stati and recreating memories with her father during her childhood in "Baba" meant a change in Ily's public attitude towards Stati. This song served as well to redirect a damaged image after the events that occurred at the rapper's first performance on a big stage.

In 2018, Ily was invited to perform in L'Boulevard. Nearly two decades after Widad won the first prize for best rap group, the festival gathers an audience of around 30,000 people each day. Invited by the collective Block 10, Ily went on stage that year to perform one song as a new upcoming rapper. The audience, however, did not receive her well, booing and throwing bottles of water at her. In the midst of insults calling her *kahba* (whore) among other slurs, the rapper braved to finish her performance, but left the stage visibly upset. Having attended concerts in Morocco over a decade, I have witnessed audience being vocal in showing their discontent if their favourite rappers are not on stage. This response towards a then new and young female rapper, however, proved to be particularly tough and cruel. Ily's romantic relationship and

---

[10] See video at https://www.youtube.com/watch?v=RNRkJ0DksjU (accessed May 11, 2021).

her issues with her father proved to be detrimental on stage as the audience there was not interested in her music.

Meanwhile, Ily's nemesis, rapper Psychoqueen (Kawtar) also claims to have been physically assaulted. The rapper released her first clip "Mama" at the end of 2017 as part of the new wave of female emcees. In spite of the title, the song is mostly a diss track alluding at her Instagram clashes with other rappers. In 2018, a few days after she had released the song "Chui pas la" (I'm not here), Psychoqueen was attacked during an Instagram Live. In January 2020, she appeared once again on her Instagram Stories covered with blood and asking for help after being attacked in the street. The fact that both events were shared on her social media has raised suspicions claiming the artist staged these attacks to gain fame and notoriety. Staged or not, everyday harassment towards women has been and still is reported at length. For this reason, while social media conveys opportunities for female empowerment in the region (see Hurley, 2021), breaking the patriarchal bargain online may result on discrediting young female rappers' artistry and putting their lives in danger.

Setbacks from perceived online overexposure have led some new female rappers to conceal their identities. In 2021, increasingly popular femcees such as Chimera la Bruna, Minerva, Alpha the Rapper and Madrina have decided to start their artistic careers without showing their face in their music videos or on their Instagram accounts. Their disguise allows them to explore their artistry keeping the audience's attention in their rap skills and music avoiding the nuisances and dangers for women of being exposed to large online audiences. While Alpha the Rapper employs artwork and avatars in her song covers, other femcees have mostly chosen to appear wearing ski masks or cagoules. Chimera La Bruna devotes her song "Ski Mask" (2020) to consciously embody her hidden artistic persona. That said, covering her face does not mean following Islamic modest fashion. The artwork of her song "Freesoul" (2021) shows an avatar of a woman wearing a black ski mask with a naked torso and holding a mic. Her lips are red as her eyes which emit red thunder. Alpha the Rapper's avatar for her song "Fatality" (2020) shows a masked woman sporting a tight suit resembling a female superhero while she carries a sword and holds a fireball. Their creative performance might not fit with Eurocentric notions of female empowerment and women's agency (see Hurley, 2021); after all, they are covering their faces instead of showing them. As part of their exploration into the rap scene, however, this strategy shields young women from unwanted attention and harassment in their daily lives, granting them an initial safe space to start their careers.

Moroccan Femceeing

Contrary to the preferred ways media usually speaks on Moroccan female rap, femcees' stories evidence that women have been part of the rap scene since its very beginning. Moroccan women have set a path for other new performers to follow and to continue building a strong female rap scene. As this chapter shows, not every femcee has chosen the same route or devoted lyrics to the same topics. Throughout the past twenty years, rappers have addressed inequality as women, but also have devoted great part of their lyrics to engage with young people and poverty discussing difficulties unprivileged youth face in a country they believe has little to offer them. Their artistry, performance and presence vary according to their own choices, networks and life experiences. During the past twenty years, women rappers in Morocco have been compelled to negotiate, engaged and developed their aesthetics and politics in finding their place within a male-dominated culture. From the use of language, stage performance and presence on public spaces including social media to how their stories have been mediatised, one thing becomes clear: femceeing in Morocco is not an easy job. On the one hand, there is a certain expectation for rap artists and women in general to engage with explicit political messages that exclusively speak about "women's issues" (see Ait Mous et al., 2019). On the other hand, a knowledgeable rap audience demands skill sets established by male rappers. Femcees' qualities and credibility are therefore often validated according to their male counterparts. To this, Widad complained that "the measuring cup is always a male rapper, this female is *as* good as such guy" (unpublished interview with author, December 2, 2020).

Different stories in this chapter confirm that female rappers are interested in speaking about issues that particularly affect women. The problem, as Lila Abu-Lughod (1990) argued thirty years ago, is that looking obsessively for forms of resistance and resisters obscures important processes, conversations and negotiations within women's creative cultures in the MENA. In this case, femcees also discuss other problems at large that affect Moroccan youth. Furthermore, while in rap the search for resistance has mostly translated into a focus on lyrics that speak about women's issues, radical performances and boundary pushing occur in many other spaces such as artwork, the use of material culture such as ski masks, the way in which make-up is applied, beat-making, the use of social media or developing rap skills such as delivery or flow. In spite of such expectations, Widad admits that she always felt she could write about the themes she was interested about: "If I felt the need of talking about feminism, then I wrote about it, but not necessarily, aren't we all feminist now anyway?" An obsessive search for explicitly feminist rappers and feminist lyrics may deter us from understanding implicit ways these women are pushing boundaries within their own communities.

An added complication is that femcees find themselves in a world where hetero-masculinity sets the rules. Female performers have mostly capitalised on combative moves combined with vigorous voices in order to adapt to these hetero-masculine expectations of what rap *is*. Rappers from Tendresse to Khtek, Manal and Chimera la Bruna often show the middle finger as an act of defiance to what is appropriate to their gender. Rappers have also employed vulgarity to their advantage to increase in toughness and gain credibility or as Manal who by blurring these images safely capitalises in vulgarity without shocking the broader audience. Soultana and Krtas Nssa have chosen to write songs rendering visible Moroccan women's issues. Ily, however, has rebelled against certain constraints by crossing the lines of propriety. In different ways, they have all appealed to young women's agency. They have tackled issues on prostitution as well as opening debates regarding what it means to be a young unmarried woman in this time and age, and the effects of social media on Moroccan women. Femceeing through lyrics, performance and lifestyle defies the patriarchal bargain as it invites women to be publicly loud, visible and present in whatever form they chose to do it.

One key point in order to move the Moroccan female rap scene forward is to create stronger networks of collaborations between femcees and other female artists and technicians. Up until now female artists have mainly featured in men's songs. With the exception of the work of all-female groups, most rappers have been surrounded mainly by male artists, crews, music producers and even technicians. Further, especially within the second wave of female rap, male managers have intervened in the careers of artists like Ily, Psychoqueen and Manal. While male presence might be helpful in navigating the rap scene, it can also curtail these artists' agency. Noting this issue, Tendresse is willing to create an 'All Stars' song, gathering the network of femcees she has built over the years. Such an event must also pay attention in order to include women directing music videos, producing beats and getting involved in the technical side of creating music. The future of Moroccan femceeing is bright as the number of rappers is increasingly growing. Therefore, campaigning towards a strong female-led scene is key in helping new and upcoming artists to jump the hurdles of patriarchy and to develop their own set of artistic rules.

REFERENCES

7 Female Rappers Shaping Hip-Hop in the Middle East. (2018, May 1). *Scene Arabia*. https://scenearabia.com/Noise/Female-Rappers-Arab-Women-Hip-Hop-Middle-East.

7 of the Best Arab and North African Female Rappers. (2020, March 11). *Egyptian Streets*.

Abu-Lughod, L. (1990). The Romance of Resistance: Tracing Transformations of Power Through Bedouin Women. *American Ethnologist, 17*(1), 41–55. https://doi.org/10.1525/ae.1990.17.1.02a00030

Ait Mous, F., Bendana, K., & Vince, N. (2019). Women in Northern African History. In *Oxford Research Encyclopedia of African History*. Oxford University Press. doi:https://doi.org/10.1093/acrefore/9780190277734.013.685.

Assadi, R. (2013, October 28). *Afghan Rapper Voices Women's Rights in Kabul*. BBC.

Bloom, D. (2015, October 13). *Afghan Teen Uses Rap to Escape Forced Marriage*. CNN.

Ciucci, A. (2012). The Study of Women and Music in Morocco. *International Journal of Middle East Studies, 44*(4), 787–789. https://doi.org/10.1017/S0020743812000906

Concepcion, M. (2007, June). A Bad Rap? Facing Declining Sales and Limited Opportunities, The Female Hip-Hop Industry Ponders Its Future. *Billboard, 24–27*.

El Shakry, O. (2013). Rethinking Entrenched Binaries in Middle East Gender and Sexuality Studies. *International Feminist Journal of Politics, 15*(1), 82–87. https://doi.org/10.1080/14616742.2012.742760

Hamad, M. (2020, July 21). 13 Arab rappers to listen to instead of Drake. *Gulf News.*

Hurley, Z. (2021). #reimagining Arab Women's Social Media Empowerment and the Postdigital Condition. *Social Media + Society, 7*(2), 205630512110101. https://doi.org/10.1177/20563051211010169

Kozma, L. (2003). Moroccan Women's Narrative of Liberation: A Passive Revolution? In J. Mcdougall (Ed.), *Nation, Society and Culture in North Africa* (pp. 112–130). Frank Cass Publishers.

Massad, J. (2015). *Islam in Liberalism.* The University of Chicago Press.

Moreno-Almeida, C. (2017). *Rap Beyond Resistance: Staging Power in Contemporary Morocco.* Palgrave Macmillan.

Moroccan Rap is the Voice of the People. (2014, May 2). *KVINFO.* https://kvinfo.dk/moroccan-rap-is-the-voice-of-the-people/?lang=en.

Najat Aatabou. (1992). *Hadi Kedba Bayna.*

Natour, R. (2019, May 23). *This Female Moroccan Rapper Is Shaking Up the Arab World.* Haaretz. https://www.haaretz.com/life/.premium-this-female-moroccan-rapper-is-shaking-up-the-arab-world-1.7279479

Patterson, J. "JP." (2012, October 9). Top 7 British Female Rappers Making Noise. *Billboard.* https://www.billboard.com/articles/columns/the-juice/480284/top-7-british-female-rappers-making-noise

Pfeiffer, T. (2009, May 20). *Female Rappers Push Limits in Conservative Morocco.* Reuters.

Rapper Soultana Is The Voice of Moroccan Women. (2019, May 28). *Morocco Travel.* https://moroccotravelblog.com/scalia_news/rapper-soultana-is-the-voice-of-moroccan-women/

Roberson, S. (2020, January 9). 13 Female Rappers to Watch Out For In 2020. *Revolt.*

Rohan, J. (2014, February 18). Morocco's Soultana Raps for Social Change. *Morocco World News.*

Skalli, L. H. (2014). Young women and social media against sexual harassment in North Africa. *Journal of North African Studies, 19*(2), 244–258. https://doi.org/10.1080/13629387.2013.858034

Soultana. (2010). *Sawt Nssa.*

Tantani, A. (2018, September 17). *Abdelaziz Stati: "Ily n'est pas ma fille, elle ne m'intéresse pas".* Le 360.

The Six: Female Rappers from the Middle East Who Are Changing the Game. (2018, November 18). *Arab News.* https://www.arabnews.com/node/1406756/art-culture

Discography

Ahmed Soultan, Dizzy DROS, DJ Van, Manal BK, Muslim & Shayfeen. (2014). *Mantsayadch.*

Alpha the Rapper. (2020). *Fatality.*

Chimera La Bruna. (2020). *Ski Mask.*

Chimera La Bruna. (2021). *Freesoul.*

Dizzy DROS. (2020). *Nota.*

ElGrande Toto feat. Khtek, Draganov, Don Bigg. (2020). *Hors Serie.*

Ily. (2018). *Khelouni.*

Ily. (2020). *Baba.*

Khtek. (2019). *Unpredictable.*

Khtek. (2020). KickOff.

Krtas Nssa. (2018a). Rainbow, EP *KN*.

Krtas Nssa. (2018b). *Madame*, EP *KN*.

Krtas Nssa. (2018c). *Zid L'alcool*, EP *KN*.

Krtas Nssa. (2019). EP *Otite*.

Manal. (2020). Niya.

Manal Feat. ElGrande Toto. (2018). *Slay*.

Manal Feat. Shayfeen. (2018). *Taj*.

Manau. (1998). *La Tribu de Dana*. *Panique Celtique*. Polydor.

Muslim. (2018). *Mama*.

Najat Aatabou. (1992). *Hadi Kedba Bayna*.

Psychoqueen. (2017). *Mama*.

Psychoqueen. (2018). *Chui pas la*.

Soultana. (2010). *Sawt Nssa*.

Tendresse. (2019). Nta.

Tendresse. (2020a). *B.W.B.* EP *Lagertah*.

Tendresse. (2020b). EP *Lagertah*.

Tendresse. (2020c). *The One*.

Tigresse Flow. (2008). *Maghribiya*.

Tigresse Flow. (n.d.) *Gangsta Rap*.

CHAPTER 26

Women Artists and Contemporary Art in the Maghreb: Insights from the Works of Aicha Filali, Sana Tamzini, and Khadija Tnana

Lilia Labidi

To the memory of my colleagues
Noureddine Sraieb,
Moncer Rouissi.
Barbro Klein.

SETTING THE SCENE

The Tunisian artists, Aicha Filali and Sana Tamzini, and the Moroccan artist Khadija Tnana are central figures in contemporary and conceptual art in the Maghreb. Their installations have contributed to producing a new artistic discourse and have attracted the attention of galleries in their own countries as well as abroad.

This discussion is based on biographical elements and exchanges about their works taken from personal interviews and electronic conversations with the

This chapter draws on material developed during my research project, "Women artists in today's Arab world: creativity and social justice," at the Swedish Collegium for Advanced Study (SCAS), Uppsala, Sweden, 2016–2017.

L. Labidi (✉)
University of Tunis, Tunis, Tunisia

Woodrow Wilson Center, Washington, DC, USA

© The Author(s), under exclusive license to Springer Nature Switzerland AG 2023
L. H. Skalli, N. Eltantawy (eds.), *The Palgrave Handbook of Gender, Media and Communication in the Middle East and North Africa*,
https://doi.org/10.1007/978-3-031-11980-4_26

artists. Aicha Filali and Sana Tamzini made catalogues of their personal exhibits available for this research and shared photos of their work, as did Khadija Tnana. The chapter draws on their writings, reviews in the press, and videos on the internet, to explore their roles in the public spaces of their respective countries. This chapter analyzes their work and their responses during the recent critical period in the history of the Maghreb before and after the uprisings that started in Tunisia in December 2010 (Labidi, 2017), and discusses how their work is related to their personal histories.[1] The section below explores the context within which their work was produced and explains how and why I became interested in the work of Arab women artists.

ART AS A RESPONSE TO CENSORSHIP AND REPRESSION

My interest in artistic production in the Arab world, particularly in that of women artists in the Maghreb, grows out of my experience as a Tunisian anthropologist and psychoanalyst who was struck by the lack of attention paid to the role of women in the struggle against colonialism. Between 1980 and 2000, I collected the life histories of Tunisian women political activists.[2] I saw the important role played by images in their oral poetry and discourse as they denounced colonial oppression.[3] Noureddine Sraieb calls these oral poets "secular preachers," referring to their role in raising awareness in the Maghreb populations of the importance of the struggle against colonialism.[4]

---

[1] Where a reference is not given for a quoted statement, the statement comes from personal communication between the artist and the author. I would like to thank Aicha Filali, Sana Tamzini, and Khadija Tnana for their cooperation throughout this research project.

[2] That project led to several publications, among them: *Génération des années 30: la mémoire vivante des sujets de l'histoire*. Tunis: CERES, Tunis University, 1985. (L. Labidi with A. Zghal); *Joudhour al-harakat al-nisa'iyya: riwayaat li-shakhsiyyaat tarikhiyya* [Origins of feminist movements in Tunisia: personal history narratives]. Tunis: Imprimerie Tunis Carthage, 1987, republished in 1990 and then in 2009 with one additional personal narrative that had previously been censored, as well as presenting all the personal narratives in Modern Standard Arabic as well as in Tunisian Arabic; and *Qamus as-siyar li-lmunadhilaat at-tunisiyaat, 1881–1956* [Biographical Dictionary of Tunisian Women Militants]. Tunis: Imprimerie Tunis Carthage, 2009b.

[3] Chedlia Bouzgarou, a political prisoner held by the French colonial authorities in Tunisia, would recite her poems during marriage ceremonies to encourage women to become politically active. See Lilia Labidi. *Joudhour al-harakat al-nisa'iyya: riwayaat li-shakhsiyyaat tarikhiyya* [Origins of feminist movements in Tunisia: personal history narratives]. Tunis: Imprimerie Tunis Carthage, 2009a. (3rd edition). p. 145–146.

[4] Noureddine Sraieb takes the term "secular preachers" ("prédicateurs profanes") from the Moroccan anthropologist Hassan Jouad, whom he refers to in *Revue du monde musulman de la Méditerranée*. N 51. 1989. p. 9–10. Research in the social sciences and the humanities only recently began to pay attention to women's oral poetry in Tunisia, following January 2011 when a festival of "al-Jazel" poetry, with women poets who respond to one another, was organized in a number of cities in 2011. In 2018, Raya Choubani collected, in the company of Megda Mrabet— both of whom were university faculty members—several poems of Mongia Labidi titled *Ekbess (Be strong)*, *Tounes Mchat (Tunis is finished)*, *Bint Tounes el Horra (Daughter of Free Tunisia)*, and *Entakhabnek (We elected you)*, which had a political character related to the democratic transition in Tunisia. On 20 July 2021 Maha Chabbi posted on her Facebook page a video where Mongia Labidi recites her poem *Miskina Tounes Miskina (Poor Tunis, Poor)* which was seen by 2213 viewers and gathered 208 comments.

In this chapter, I show how the work of Maghrebi women visual artists gives expression to protest during and after the uprisings and plays a role like that of oral poets. I discuss how these artists reinvent the grammar of their artistic language in a manner similar to the women artists in the Arab world who, in the 1940s, innovated in abstract art and helped lay the foundations for an aesthetic of feminist art. Like them, these artists participated in the construction of values and a reformulation of ethics (Labidi, 2014). I have also produced several art works as a response to the censorship and repression under the Ben Ali regime characterized by government eavesdropping on telephone conversations, close surveillance, cancelation of academic conferences, censorship, and restricted meetings and demonstrations. Starting in the 1990s, and seeking to circumvent and denounce this censorship and repression, I began to use forms of artistic expression such as photo-collage, happenings, and installations. I will point to two examples of these works that were shown in public.

"Mqartssa" ("Wrapped Up")

The work "*Mqartssa*" (Fig. 26.1) is a happening I presented at a conference "Image, images et société" that I organized at the Ibn Khaldoun Cultural Center in Tunis in 2000. This happening was developed in the context of the

Fig. 26.1 *Mqartssa* (Wrapped)

project "Construction of public morality in the Arab world and Africa" that I carried out in Tunisia, Senegal, Egypt, and South Africa from 1997 to 2001. The aim of "*Mqartssa*" was to indicate that words were forbidden and even silence disallowed by the authorities. I expressed this by presenting approximately a dozen women—my students all participating voluntarily—enveloped in newspaper standing during the conference's first session.

When a conference participant approached one of these "mummies," the young woman inside the paper envelope played a recording machine where a woman's voice spoke of her suffering in speeches that were developed during several working sessions that I had with my students. To see these women lined up like mummies, each enveloped in newspapers affixed with scotch tape and without any part of their bodies or faces showing, and then to hear voices in lamentations and denunciations, was a shock to a number of the conference participants.

Interestingly, a woman journalist who attended this conference wrote an article (I. H., 2000) about this which was censored. Some weeks later, after the foreign media accused the ruling regime of censorship, this article and a photo of the happening were published by the newspaper, the same newspaper that had been used to wrap the women's bodies.

"ElMahress" *(The Pestle)*

This work (Fig. 26.2) is an installation where items in the form of body parts of women and young girls are strewn over the ground on a kilim rug and amassed in the form of a hill. The body parts are indicated by socks and tights, of different sizes and colors, stuffed with newspaper, displaying the lower parts of bodies. These body parts indicate the murders and wounds from domestic, social, and political violence. The installation was organized with my students, during the conference "Culture et société" (June 2001), to denounce violence against women.

The installation was strategically placed in the main room on the first floor of Tunis' Ibn Khaldoun Cultural Center, where participants could not miss it.[5] A few conference participants, of both sexes, indicated how shocked and troubled they felt at the sight of the mass of body parts. Although this exhibit was meant to last for only one day, the Artists Union, which had its headquarters in this Cultural Center, requested this exhibit for two additional weeks.

[5] Soumeya Beltifa (interviewer). "Lilia Laâbidi, psychanalyste et anthropologue. 'Il est important d'investir dans la formation et la promotion des jeunes, futurs chercheurs de demain.'" (*Le Temps*, 18 June 2001).

Fig. 26.2 *ElMahress* (The Pestle)

EXISTING SOURCES FOR WRITING THE HISTORY OF WOMEN ARTISTS IN THE MAGHREB: THE CASE OF TUNISIA

As I began to examine the role of Maghrebi women artists, I was struck by the lack of sources on women's art in the region. Taking Tunisia as an example, this section briefly reviews the role that women artists occupy in the discourse of art critics and other cultural agents.[6] First, the catalogue of an exhibition organized in 1984 and an article from 2016 dealing with the subject of abstract art shed some light on the participation of women in local artistic activity. Ali Louati, author (1984) and director of the National Center of Living Art in Tunis, shows no surprise at the absence of women in the exhibition, despite the fact that Safia Farhat (1924–2004) had already shown in 1976 a series of her abstract drawings in her exhibition, "*Souffle divin*" ("Divine breath") (Filali, 2005). Experts also agree that that her tapestries have abstract patterns.[7]

---

[6] Fatima Mazmouz makes the same observation concerning research on art in Morocco. Roger Calme. L'interview/Plasticienne Fatima Mazmouz. Le Temps de se rétablir. https://zoes.fr/2021/12/09/linterview-plasticienne-fatima-fatima-mazmouz-le-temps-de-se-retablir/

[7] Alia Nakhli. "L'écrit dans les arts visuels en Tunisie (1960–2015)." *Perspective. Actualité en histoire de l'art.* (no date indicated). https://www.researchgate.net/publication/323518325_L%27Ecrit_dans_les_arts_visuels_en_Tunisie_1960-2015

This exclusion of women artists may be explained in part by the conflicts between members of the *Ecole de Tunis* (a group of artists formed in the 1940s who dominated the Tunisian art scene of which Safia Farhat was a member) and the artists who emerged during the 1960s and 1970s and promoted abstract art. But we also must consider the status of women in society. The lack of, or at best scant, attention accorded to women artists and their contributions to abstract art reminds me of the words of Madiha Umar (1908–2005), an Iraqi artist and author of Syrian origin who introduced calligraphic art into Iraq. When asked by a doctoral student why her role as a precursor of the *Hurufiyya* (calligraphic) art movement was not recognized, she responded: "It is because I am a woman" (Oweis, 2008, 257). This limited attention given to women's artistic work may be a particular instance of myopia towards women's contributions, seen also in many other parts of the world.[8]

In his book on contemporary art, Ali Louati (2017) devotes three chapters to Tunisian women artists from the 1990s. He discusses Fatma Charfi M'Seddi's 1999 memoir of the Gulf War,[9] Feryel Lakhdar's opulent women figures of the Tunis bourgeoisie in 2012, and Aicha Filali's exhibit *Ana/Chroniques* in 2015. While women artists started receiving some attention in the 1990s, the absence until quite recently of museums of modern art[10] and biographies of women artists or other writings that treat their works pushed some of those artists to commit their own resources and networks to present their works.

In Saudi Arabia, for example, Safeya Binzagr transformed her house into a museum and produced writings on her own work. As an author and artist, Safeya's paintings deal with the country's heritage and explore themes such as marriage, traditional dress, old architecture, religion, and desert life. Prevailing segregation in Saudi Arabia prevented her from attending the opening of her first exhibit in the 1970s in her country (Binzagr, 1979). In 2000 she transformed her home into a library open to researchers and a museum where she exhibits her work she refused to sell since 1973. In Tunisia, the artist Aicha Filali opened a private museum in 2016 on Safia Farhat's family land and named the museum in Farhat's honor, with an exhibit devoted to Farhat inaugurating

---

[8] Edward J. McCaughan. "Navigating the Labyrinth of Silence: Feminist Artists in Mexico". Social Justice. Vol. 34, No. 1 (107), Art, Identity and Social Justice (2007), pp. 44–62. p. 51. This same myopia is seen in Tunisia: in the seven issues of the bilingual Tunisian feminist magazine *Nissa* that appeared in 1985 and 1986, only one article published in the French language section is devoted to a woman artist, here to Shehrazade Rhaïem on the occasion of an exhibition of her works at the Ettaswir gallery. The article has a brief introduction by Anne Marie Khatib, a photo of the work "Complicité," and a text by Shehrazade Rhaïem, "Portraits de femmes: Pourquoi Virginia Woolf?" *Nissa* 2, 1985. p. 5.

[9] Fatma Charfi M'Seddi (1955–2018), a Tunisian-Swiss artist, worked in a variety of domains, such as photography, video, installations, happenings, and so on.

[10] Museums in the Maghreb devoted to modern art began to appear in the 2000s, with the National Museum of Modern and Contemporary Art of Algiers (MAMA) inaugurated in 2007 and the Museum of Modern and Contemporary Art of Rabat in 2014. There were no associations of women artists in Tunisia. Safia Farhat was member of the executive committee of the UNFT (Union Nationale de la Femme Tunisienne) in 1956, 1958, and 1960.

the museum. Since then she organizes annually an exhibit bringing together various Tunisian artists.

Silvia Naef (2017) imputes the scarcity of art publications in the region to the fact that relevant bibliographies are produced especially in languages foreign to the region, and also to the scant interest the states have in preserving archives. Nadira Laggoune-Aklouche (2011) discusses the hostile criticism directed at women organizing exhibits of women's artistic works and at women researchers who reflect on these productions. They are criticized for giving visibility to second-class artists or contributing to the ghettoization of women artists.

Encountering Women Artists and Contemporary Art in the Maghreb

This section focuses on the work of three Maghrebi women artists—Tunisian artists Aicha Filali and Sana Tamzini and Moroccan artist Khadija Tnana—whom we can see as forces for change (Salwa Mikdadi Nashashibi, Laura Nader, Etel Adnen (1994)).

Aicha Filali

Aicha Filali was born in 1956 in a milieu of anti-colonial militants who came to occupy ministerial positions in the newly independent Tunisia. Filali discovered the world of art through her aunt Safia Farhat (1924–2004)—an artist and first woman director of the Tunisian School of Fine Arts in 1966. As explained in her interview, she became familiar with the art of miniature while living with her parents in Algeria where she became acquainted with the work of Mohammed Racim (1896–1975), the founder of the Algerian miniature school.

Since 1984, Filali has been exhibiting her work in collective and individual exhibitions.[11] Her rich and varied work includes modern clothing made with traditional textiles, jewelry, quilts with digital montage printed on textiles, sculptures of people in their daily lives inspired by archeological discoveries from the Pharaonic period in Egypt, and sculptures of imperial army soldiers in China. She is the author of several catalogues, often in book form, devoted to her exhibits (Filali 1995, 2001), as well as other writings on art.[12]

---

[11] She defended a doctoral thesis in aesthetics and the sciences of art and taught, and for a time was director at the Tunis Higher Institute of Fine Arts. She is currently director of the Radès Center of Living Arts, founded by Safia Farhat and her husband Abdallah Farhat.

[12] Among the awards she has received are the UNESCO prize for artisanry in the Arab region in 1994 and the prize awarded by the Tunisian organization CREDIF (*Centre de recherches, d'études, de documentation, et d'information sur la femme*) in 2005, and she was decorated as Officer of the Order of the Tunisian Republic in 2020.

Among her work prior to the 2011 uprisings, there is a series of nine postage stamps produced between 1979 and 1985 for the Tunisian Post Office.[13] One of them, designed in 1981, is devoted to "Pilgrimage to Mecca" (Fig. 26.3). This was produced during a year marked by tensions between the government and the Islamic Tendency Movement (an Islamically oriented opposition political movement). It was also the year when Decree 108 was issued that forbid wearing the hijab for students and employees of public institutions. Therefore, this stamp occupies a special place in the relations between the government, which sought to control religious discourse, and the Islamic Tendency Movement.

This stamp portrays figures aligned in circles around the Kaaba which has a black covering, called *kiswa* (a garment), that is raised slightly on one side, like a blink of the eye, showing cement blocks. In the upper section a hand is placed on either side of the dome on top of the Kaaba, in a position of prayer and pointing towards the heavens. The figures arranged in circles are Arabic letters,

Fig. 26.3 Pilgrimage to Mecca

[13] The themes for this series are International Children's Year (1979), the 20th anniversary of the Association of Blood Donors (1981), the Pilgrimage to Mecca (1981), the Tunisian Red Crescent (1982), the Conference of Plenipotentiaries of the UIT (1982), Palestine (1983), Saluting the Flag (1983), the 4th School of Molecular Biology (1984), and the 3rd Week of Civil Protection (1985). Among a total of 124 artists who have contributed stamps to the Tunisian Post Office, 34 are women.

Fig. 26.4 Palestine

taking up the "*Talbiyah*" recited by the pilgrim to the Hajj or 'Umrah pilgrimages: "*Labbayk Allaahumma labbayk*" (Here I am, O Allah, here I am).

In 1983 Aicha Filali produced a stamp testifying to the importance of Palestine in the Tunisian imaginary (Fig. 26.4). On the right of this stamp features the Al-Aqsa Mosque in Jerusalem, and superimposed on this is the name Palestine in Arabic characters and in the same golden color as the dome of the mosque. On the stamp's left are symbols of an occupied country struggling for its freedom—a grill of barbed wire from which a pigeon in the colors of the Palestinian flag has just escaped. Behind the barbed wire we see broken red ropes that may be signs of torture or traces of gunshots by the Israeli army upon the Palestinian population.

In 2005 one of Aicha Filali's works addressed masculine sexuality. "*Le canapé polygame*" (The polygamous sofa) (Fig. 26.5) shows women's brassieres of different styles, sizes, and materials. They are stuffed with latex covering a couch and spread to convey fantasy, as Anouar Jerad wrote in the introduction to the exhibit's catalogue.[14] The artist Nadia Jelassi, a curator and Filali's colleague at the Tunis Higher Institute of Fine Arts, provides an interpretation of

---

[14] A collection of furniture reinterpreted in response to an invitation from a furniture maker who was celebrating the centenary of its Italian furniture brand, about which Anouar Jerad wrote in the "Introduction" in *Univers féminin: meubles et objets présentés dans le cadre de Z.I. EXPO 2005*. Organized by Emporio and Gallery Ammar Farhat, February–March 2005.

Fig. 26.5 *Le canapé polygame*

Le Canapé polygame by referring to literary works from the Arab world and from the West, using the concepts of "the empire of signs" and "the empire of the senses," arguing that it would be a mistake to see in this work the practice of Islamic polygamies. For her, Aicha Filali's creative act conjugates images of a particular East and West, with "*Le Canapé polygame* linking *A Thousand and One Nights* with the intrigues of Messalina [a wife of the Roman emperor Claudius known for her active sexuality] and the tales of Shehrazade with the adventures of Casanova" (Jelassi, 2009, 82).

While Aicha Filali produced installations before 2011, her projects after January 2011 and since the end of censorship are deeply critical and socio-politically oriented. Her bittersweet view of Tunisian society makes her an artist whose conceptual art documents the socio-political context. Without ever abandoning her humor and her acerbic tone and without having to circumvent censorship as in the past, she criticizes what she sees as anachronistic development in her society since the fall of Ben Ali regime and rise of Islamists on the political scene. In 2012 she participated in the exhibition "Dégagements" at *l'Institut du Monde Arabe* (IMA) in Paris where the symbolic and abstract dominated. Her sculptures "Bourgeons Di(n)vers" ("Diverse Tree Buds," with a play on the word *din* (religion)), and "Bourgeons en palabres" (Tree Buds in debate) show the tree under which the community discusses subjects that concern its members. The green buds on the various branches signify fruits, most of which haven't yet emerged while others emerged as pencils. These refer to

Fig. 26.6 *Tounes tintakhab*

freedom of the press while a high-heeled shoe alludes to women's rights. Both confront a crescent on top that suggests the power of religious institutions.

The exhibit *"Ana/Chroniques"* held in 2015 at the Abdelaziz Gorgi gallery in Sidi Bou Said[15] provided Aicha Filali with the opportunity to experiment with digital collage, using old miniatures found online, the artist's photos taken in the Tunis medina, and Arabic calligraphy, all brought together for a particular theme. Among these works is *"Tounes tintakhab"* ("Tunisia votes") (Fig. 26.6) which measures 75 by 50.5 centimeters. It conveys the concerns of voters of all political orientations regarding the results of Tunisia's 2014 plural-ist and independent legislative and presidential elections. The title in Arabic calligraphy is at the top of this digital collage. To the right and on the bottom of this work, there are inked fingers of the voters, as occurs in current voting practice. In the upper left corner, the artist places in Arabic characters informa-tion about the elections from the Independent Higher Instance for the Elections (ISIE). Next to this information are the two palaces at play in these elections: the presidential palace in Carthage and the governmental palace in Kasbah place. The center features election urns, some with rabbits on top, sur-rounded by figures taken from ancient Persian and Indian miniatures, with a photographer in a suit holding a camera in the upper right of the work.

---

[15] Sidi Bou Said is a town near Tunis known for its role in the art world, *Ana/Chroniques.* Tunis, Sud Éditions, 2015.

Fig. 26.7   Cover of the exhibition catalogue '*Man Antom*'

The question "Who will win the elections?" is represented by the rabbits on the election urns, similar to rabbits emerging from the hats of magicians, referencing the no less than 70 candidates in the first round of the presidential election.[16]

In the introduction to the catalogue of the exhibit "*Ana/Chroniques*," Aicha Filali indicates that she chose to mix periods and styles, invoking the past to address the present, using hybrid modes of expression that are known in the history of art to show the complexity of the Tunisian context. The revolution that was led by youth resulted, ironically, in the election as president of the 88-year-old Béji Caid Essebsi who had occupied a number of governmental positions under Habib Bourguiba, from July 1965 to September 1969. Essebsi based his campaign on defending Bourguiba's legacy and women's rights.

Aicha Filali's exhibition "*Man Antom*" (Who are you?), which shows several of her works in various styles, was presented in 2016. The exhibition catalogue's cover (Fig. 26.7) shows several graffiti including "*Tahya Tounes horra dimocratia*" (Long live free democratic Tunisia) and "*La Illaha ila allah. Mohamed Rasoul Allah*" (There is no god but Allah, Mohamed is the messenger of God). On the lower left, there is a crescent with a star which is a symbol

---

[16] Judge Kalthoum Kannou was the only woman among the 70 candidates.

Fig. 26.8 *Harim ettemsé7*

found on the Tunisian flag. Each of these phrases or symbols represents a particular social group.

This exhibit is one of her productions after January 2011 that openly criticize political Islam. One of her works in this exhibit is the installation "*Harim ettemsé7*" (The Crocodile's Harem) (Figs. 26.8). This is a sculpture in textiles and other materials that refers to the Turkish television film *Harim al Soltan*, telecast daily on the private channel *Nessma*.[17] This installation shows a crocodile covered with gray pearls and a turban on its head, wearing green Nike sneakers on its feet, with a full black beard with its ends dyed with henna. The crocodile, wearing some Islamist symbols, is stretched out with its head on a prayer rug in the direction of Mecca. Behind the large crocodile, which is like the sultan, four smaller crocodiles are grouped in pairs with different colors, rings on their fingers and slippers on their feet. This work refers to polygamy that had been outlawed in Tunisia since the promulgation of the Personal Status Code in 1956. Aicha Filali conveys a fear related to the sexual fantasies of Tunisian men, which *Le Canapé polygame* had treated with humor in 2005. This work suggests women's fear of the return of polygamy in Tunisia after the

[17] This series was very successful among women, both old and young, attracting about 150 million Arab viewers. Harim al Soltan, directed by Meral Okay, deals with the tenth sultan of the Ottoman dynasty (1520–1566) and the intrigues among the favorites of his harem. See Thomas Seibert. Istanbul. "Les spectatrices arabes accros aux séries turques" (24 May 2013).

https://www.courrierinternational.com/article/2013/05/24/les-spectatrices-arabes-accros-aux-series-turques controversial term "complementarity" instead of "equality" between men and women was suggested by Islamist women parliamentarians during the drafting of the post-revolution Constitution. Feminists ultimately succeeded in rejecting the term; the crocodiles allude to the expression "crocodile tears," to signify the hypocrisy of the Nahdha Party members.

Sana Tamzini

Sana Tamzini was born in 1975 in the Tunisian city of Kairouan. After her studies at the Higher Institute of Fine Arts in Tunis, she undertook further training in museum studies in Austria and the Faculty of Environmental Design at the University of Montreal. As a faculty member of *l'Ecole supérieure des sciences et technologies du design*, she has had several residencies, and, since the end of the 1990s, she has exhibited in several foreign capitals. She is known for, among other things, her use of lighting in her installations.[18]

Following January 2011, Tamzini took on the direction of several Tunisian institutions including the National Center of Living Art in Tunis (2011–2013) and Fine Arts Sector at the Ministry of Culture and Heritage Protection (2015–2016). Under her leadership, the National Center of Living Art found new dynamism and artistic collaborations. She set up several exhibitions for women and projects and activities for young Tunisian artists who had refused to participate in state-run exhibitions prior to 2011. She also promotes artistic freedom and greater mobility of cultural agents through her presidency of the Federation of Cultural Associations (FACT) of the Fanak Fund.

Her political orientation regarding the artistic practice of women artists and of young artists from Tunisia's interior and her installations where light plays a fundamental role make her one of the most innovative artists of her generation. When she produced "*Free*" (Freedom) (Fig. 26.9) in the framework of citizens' art taking place in the Tunis medina in January 2011, she shed light on what she had experienced as a teacher and welcomed the "new Tunisians" that she had been awaiting since the self-immolation of Mohamed Bouazizi on 17 December 2010 in Sidi Bouzid. Speaking with the Kasbah demonstrators, Tamzini and her students discussed how the inhabitants and neighbors of Kasbah Place experienced these demonstrations and sit-ins and what would happen if they barricaded the streets of the neighborhood. She worked with the slammer Anis Zgarni, the artist Rachida Amara, other artists, as well as her students on the theme of Neighborhood Committees that emerged during the demonstrations (December 2010 and January 2011).

Employing a white material used in building construction to reduce sound, although it burns the skin when touched, Tamzini worked on a happening where the members of the group were enveloped in this material and attached to one another to block a street in the medina near government buildings,

---

[18] Several of her installations were presented in the catalogue *Proximity*, produced in partnership with the municipality of Tunis, 2008.

Fig. 26.9 *Horr*

obstructing access. The choreography of their movements expressed the aim of freeing oneself, freeing the group, and being born as a new Tunisian. Sana Tamzini said, "I dreamt of freedom. For me, everyone should speak ... "*Free*" (Freedom), was created to express that we had just emerged from a repressive, heavily policed society ... It must not be forgotten that before January 2011 we always had people attending our courses who later would report what was said to the head of the Institute." But when I suggested to her that in January 2011 the residents of various neighborhoods had organized spontaneously into committees in order to protect themselves from robberies and attacks, she answered, "I ended up by assimilating the Neighborhood Committees to the plainclothes police who attended my courses" (Labidi, 2016).

Khadija Tnana

Born in 1945 in Tetouan (Morocco) into a bourgeois family, Khadija Tnana was a law professor and cultural figure before becoming an artist, painter, and a playwright in the 1990s. After legal studies in Morocco she went to Paris to prepare her doctorate. Living on rue Bonaparte between 1969 and 1975 she found many art galleries, and, she says, "I absorbed the colors of the paintings that were exhibited but I didn't have the courage to interrupt my legal studies and begin studying art." While in Paris she joined the Moroccan Socialist Union of Popular Forces Party (USFP).

Returning to Morocco in 1983, she decided to live in the city of Fès where, in addition to teaching at the Law Faculty, she became a successful USFP candidate in the municipal elections and for nine years was the mayor's advisor in charge of cultural affairs. Realizing that there were several associations working for women's rights but none that focused on women's creative work, she decided to focus her own activities on women's creativity, organizing a number of cultural events in that area. Disillusioned with political activism, she left Morocco at the end of the 1980s for Barcelona where she registered for a year of training in the arts, involving drawing for several hours a day with a model.

In her work she uses materials taken from her immediate surroundings, like ground coffee beans, red and brown soil found in northern of Morocco, manuscript pages that she paints upon, wood, canvas, and acrylic painting, among other materials. She has spoken of her refusal to name her works as a way to avoid influencing the gaze of those looking at them. Her résumé lists only dates, the titles of group exhibitions, the names of the cities where the exhibition was held, and the places where she had residencies in Morocco and Europe.

In 1993 she joined a group of Mediterranean artists called "Ras El Hanout" (a Maghreb spice mixture, here symbolizing a variety of artistic styles). After ten years of collaboration and organization of exhibits in Morocco and several European countries, the artists decided to end this experience because of a lack of funds. In recent years, she returned to live in Tetouan, her region of origin. Wanting to make a permanent contribution to her country, Tnana told me she had considered, back in 2009, to set up a foundation, but never did because of hurdles in the Moroccan administration.

Tnana is the author of three dramatic works that extend the themes of her visual art. With regard to her play "Tata Mbarka," a name given to black slave women in Morocco, she says, "I took inspiration from my family's history. My grandfather, an important judge in Tetouan, had a black woman slave. When I was a child, I didn't understand why this woman was always in the kitchen. I wrote the play in homage to her."[19] One of her drawings—a scratched pencil drawing that shows a woman in the center with a man emerging from the hair on her head symbolizes, for her, her feminist orientation and her approach of reinterpreting myths (Fig. 26.10).

In 2010 she was contacted by Mostapha Romli, director and founder of the artistic foundation Ifitry, who provided her with a space and material to carry out her work. This foundation allows her to have exchanges with artists from different countries (Japan, North and South America, Europe) who were in residence at Ifitry. Tnana participated in several biennials in Morocco and Dakar and an exhibition at the Pisa Museum in Italy, Berlin, and other places. In return, she gave to Romli all of her work, saying, "He'll know best what to do with it."

[19] "*Tata Mbarka*" was directed by Naima Zitane (Zitane directed the play '*Diali*' ("Mine" [women use the term "mine" to avoid using the word "vagina"])). This play has been performed in several cities in Morocco, France, Italy, Belgium, and Tunisia. She also wrote *Louiza*, her second play, directed by Hamza Boulaiz (a young artist who founded the first theatrical caravan in Morocco), which treats the issue of incest. Her third play, *Le mur* (The Wall), treats questions related to women and politics.

Fig. 26.10 *Reinterpreting the myth*

Her art works address two main themes: namely, social and political injustice and the woman's body and sexuality. The first theme includes works which treat the "*Harragas*" (clandestine migrants) who often die at sea in their attempt to cross the Mediterranean. She sees this as the body "facing a wave that is a monster." She also depicts prostitution, where women are obliged to sell their bodies to survive and support their families. She painted the Palestinian Intifada with children throwing stones at the Israeli soldiers, and she exhibited it as part of a collective exhibition in Egypt. Regarding the second theme, that of the body and sexuality of women, she says, "I have treated sexuality in my work to show the violence of men who are attracted only by the sexual organs in a woman's body, but it is for specialists to determine how to treat these problems."

In a series inspired by the Indian Kama Sutra, written between the sixth and seventh centuries, Tnana produced several versions of installations with the generic title "Kamasutra." One version is composed of 30 wooden boxes that are used in schools, each containing an erotic drawing. She ends her description of this work, which was exhibited in Italy, by saying that "the bearded ones arrived and since then my works are repressed." Another version, which she referred to as "*Kamasutra maghrébine*," is composed of several hands of Fatma on very thin paper affixed to a cardboard. It shows erotic figures in different sexual positions on each of the 246 items that form a large *khomssa* (hand of

Fig. 26.11   *Kamasutra Maghrébine*

Fatma) (Fig. 26.11). This untitled work, which measures 3.80 by 2.60 meters, was exhibited in Italy following January 2011.[20] The installation, exhibited at the Modern Art Center in Tetouan in March 2018, was judged too daring and was withdrawn from the exhibit on the opening day.[21] In protest, the artist created a happening, installing herself in the area where her work was to be exhibited, with her mouth gagged and her hands and feet tied, to indicate to visitors that she had been censored.[22]

[20] She dedicated this work to Cheikh Nefzaoui, a Tunisian religious figure and author of "The Perfumed Garden," an erotic manual written in the fifteenth century and designed to transmit sexual education to youth.

[21] Ghita Zine. "Interview 'Kamasutra', une installation interdite par le Centre d'art moderne" (6 March 2018).https://www.yabiladi.com/articles/details/62479/tetouan-kamasutra-installation-interdite-centre.html

[22] Qods Chabaa. Video. "Scandale. Une oeuvre 'osée' de Khadija Tnana a été censurée." (3 March/2018)   https://m.le360.ma/culture/video-scandale-une-oeuvre-osee-de-khadija-tnana-a-ete-censuree-158415 le

Fig. 26.12 *Trafficking of women*

In line with her views favoring freedom of expression, Khadija Tnana signed her name on the manifesto, "We women and men, Moroccan citizens, declare that we are outlaws, in solidarity with Hajar Raissouni, journalist accused of fornication and abortion."[23] She has also produced an installation seven meters long dealing with the trafficking of women (Fig. 26.12) and composed of many small feet grouped into two large feet, one pointing north and one south, "to denounce trafficking of women from northern countries like Bosnia, Romania, and others from African countries in the south, taken by a mafia that promises them work, clothes, etc., but finally lands them in prostitution, as a new form of slavery." On the feet Khadija Tnana has drawn and painted women's bodies torn to bits. When she hears comments that her subjects are sinister, she responds that her work is dark because she is depicting political subjects, and that the women she portrays, while still sensual, have demands that should be satisfied. This installation was exhibited at the Dakar Biennial and at the

[23] Group manifesto, "Nous, citoyennes et citoyens marocains, déclarons que nous sommes hors la loi "(Le Monde, 9 September 2019) https://www.lemonde.fr/idees/article/2019/09/23/nous-citoyennes-et-citoyens-marocains-declarons-que-nous-sommes-hors-la-loi_6012648_3232.html

Fig. 26.13   *Too bad for Mr. Benkirane*

exhibit, "Femmes, artistes marocaines de la modernité, 1960-2016" ("Women, Moroccan artists of modernity"), organized in Rabat in 2016.[24]

Tnana also produced an installation in response to Morocco's Prime Minister Abdelilah Benkirane, who compared women to a chandelier that lights up a home. She described this to me as, "Too bad for Mr. Benkirane" (Fig. 26.13). Here she installed 72 bowls of *lben* (sour milk) under a chandelier, with the number of bowls alluding to the number of *houris* promised to Muslim men when they reach paradise. Such bowls are normally used in the Friday couscous meal prepared for the men returning from the mosque and who find their women dressed in their finest clothes. The message here according to Tnana is: "It is not for him to tell us what needs to be done. Each woman is free to decide. I painted these blue bowls with women in a variety of poses. Sometimes one woman per bowl, sometimes several women in erotic, provocative poses."

Another installation (Fig. 26.14) shows a room with a school bag hanging on the right and a school costume on the left, a tape recorder that gives out sounds coming from a schoolyard, and a wall in the center displaying the number of the laws that allow a judge to authorize the marriage of a minor if he believes she is sufficiently mature for married life. This installation denounces

[24] The exhibit was organized by the Mohammed VI Museum of Modern and Contemporary Art (MMVI) in Rabat, from 23 November 2016 to 8 March 2017, with Rim Laâbi as curator.

Fig. 26.14 *No to the forced marriage of young girls to their rapists*

families' early withdrawal of their daughters from school, against the daughters' wishes, to force into marriage. Tnana participated in 2019 in the first biennial in Rabat devoted to contemporary art, titled *La source mystérieuse* (The mysterious source). Her work showed a woman lying down, giving birth, although the viewer sees only from behind the head. This is a nod to Gustave Courbet's 1866 painting, "The origin of the world," showing that life is created from inside the woman.

In conclusion, the works of the artists I discussed in this section are situated within the political contexts of the Maghreb and reflect their own particular experiences and reactions according to what Pierre Bourdieu might call their *habitus* (1979). Although belonging to similar social classes, each expresses in her own way and from her own psychological orientation what was otherwise inexpressible and sometimes horrific. The works of Aicha Filali, close to caricature and where irony plays an important role, have contributed to a critical discourse on specific socio-political situations. Sana Tamzini's works recall memories of historical moments that enable her to shed light on violence and address her own suffering (including surveillance) following January 2011. And the subversive artistic language of Khadija Tnana denounces critical historical and cultural phenomena including child marriage.

The Contributions of Women Artists to the History of Contemporary Art in the Maghreb

Among the changes that appeared in Tunisia and Morocco after January 2011 is a relative loosening of censorship that allowed the creative energies of women artists to be expressed.

The post-uprisings have seen the emergence of new associations devoted to art, art galleries run by women, private museums, residencies for artists, and women acting as curators for exhibits. Women artists have produced street art, video, photography, and cartooning and made significant contributions to a new art language and aesthetics. In Tunisia, a multidisciplinary and inclusive feminist festival, *Chouftouhonna* (You saw them), began in 2015 and, in 2016, an occasional publication called "*Etat d'urgence*" (State of emergency) appeared, focusing on cultural affairs and visual art.[25] In Morocco, in addition to exhibitions devoted to women artists, the first Rabat biennial on contemporary art was dedicated in 2019 to women artists.

This context enabled Aicha Filali to pursue her critique of society with humor and without the fear of censorship. Sana Tamzini was able to address in the happening "*Free*" (Being free) the theme of predators and violence, while Khadija Tnana found new momentum in her work at art residencies in Morocco and abroad (Clement 2018) where she continued to address the same themes related to the body, sexuality, exclusion, and violence. Installations and happenings enabled her to denounce institutional structures and cultures that constructed men as superior to women.

In Morocco, the suicide of Amina El Filali in March 2012 mobilized many artists, among them Khadija Tnana who produced an installation denouncing the forced marriage of young girls to their rapist. When members of the Justice and Development Party, the Islamist party that headed the government in Morocco, called for "clean art," Moroccan intellectuals and artists denounced this notion, while Khadija Tnana produced a series of paintings showing scenes of sexual violence and rape, inscribing on one of them, "*L'art propre, loi sale*" (Clean art, dirty law) (Fig. 26.15).

The installations, happenings, and other artistic forms used by the three artists discussed in this chapter have demonstrated how artists participate in the art of resistance. The aesthetic morality conveyed in the works of Aicha Filali, Sana Tamzini, and Khadija Tnana inspires a new ethics and model for social action (Maaouia, 2011; Meskini O. E. 2006). Although the three artists produced contemporary art well before the "Arab Spring," these popular uprisings resonated among each of them, as can be seen in their installations and happenings. Although they belong to different generations and engage with artistic processes that are rather different, they allow us to see similarities in their responses to the historical, cultural, and political contexts in the contemporary Maghreb.

While miniatures are like pages from the history of past societies, describing their customs and daily life, the installations of Aicha Filali, Sana Tamzini, and Khadija Tnana are works that testify to the tensions, power relations, and

---

[25] These Tunisian initiatives came from artists: "*Etat d'urgence*" appeared between 2016 and 2017; the *Chouftouhonna* festival, started in 2015 by the association *Chouf*, is run by a new generation of inclusive feminists, bringing together racial and sexual minorities and welcoming women artists from Tunisia and elsewhere (the festival was suspended during the Covid-19 pandemic).

Fig. 26.15 L'Art Propre, Loi Sale

relations between the sexes in Muslim societies in today's globalized world. Their choices for a new artistic grammar were not accidental. Given the critique expressed in the works of Aicha Filali, Sana Tamzini, and Khadija Tnana, one can suggest that they have constructed an aesthetics of resistance that expresses outrage and invites the viewer to think and say the unspeakable.

The works of Aicha Filali, Sana Tamzini and Khadija Tnana have contributed to historicize violence. No longer striving for beauty, each from her own particular subject position constructs a critique of the socio-political and cultural system, encouraging a rethinking of the contribution of women artists to the art history of the region. These women artists are the contemporary poets promoting a renewal of art practice in Tunisia and Morocco and putting forward new elements for an aesthetics of feminist art.

References

Beltifa, S. (2001). Lilia Laâbidi, psychanalyste et anthropologue. "Il est important d'investir dans la formation et la promotion des jeunes, futurs chercheurs de demain." Le Temps, June 18.

Binzagr, S. (1979). *Saudi Arabia: An Artist's View of the past*. Three Continents Publishers.

Bourdieu, P. (1979). *La distinction. Critique sociale du jugement*. Minuit.

El Khatib, A. M. (1985) Complicité. *Nissa 2*.

Filali, A. (1995). *Mémoire de terre*. MIM.

Filali, A. (2001). *Fragments Odorants*. MIM.

Filali, A. (2005). *Safia farhat, une biographie*. MIM.

Filali, A. (2015). *Ana/Chroniques*. Sud Éditions.

I. H. (2000). Des jeunes filles déguisées en momies. *La Presse de Tunisie*. March 16.

Jelassi, N. (2009). "Canapé polygame. Canapé, soutiens gorge, mousse." In *Etat de sièges. Lecture d'oeuvres*. Tunis : Unité de recherche: Pratiques artistiques modernes en Tunisie. Programme de recherche. Ministère de l'Enseignement Supérieur, Tunisie.

Labidi, L. (2009a). *Joudhour al-harakat al-nisa'iyya: riwayaat li-shakhsiyyaat tarikhiyya [Origins of Feminist Movements in Tunisia: Personal History Narratives]*. Imprimerie Tunis Carthage.

Labidi, L. (2009b). *Qamus as-siyar li-lmunadhilaat at-tunisiyaat, 1881–1956[Biographical Dictionary of Tunisian Women Militants]*. Imprimerie Tunis Carthage.

Labidi, L. (2014). Political, Aesthetic, and Ethical Positions of Tunisian Women Artists, 2011–2013. *Journal of North African Studies, 19*(2). Special Issue on Women, Gender, and the Arab Spring, pp 157–171.

Labidi, L. (2016). State, Institutional, and Symbolic Violence Against Women: The Struggle Since the "Arab Spring" and the Contribution of Arab Women Cartoonists. *Feminismo/s (Spain)*, 145–174.

Labidi, L. (2017). Women's Rights and Tunisian Women's Literature of Denunciation. In B. Badri & A. Tripp (Eds.), *Women's Movements in Africa* (pp. 61–96). Zed Press.

Labidi, L., & Zghal, A. (1985). *Génération des Années 30: La Mémoire Vivante des Sujets de L'histoire*. CERES, Tunis University.

Laggoune-Aklouche, N. (2011). Femmes, Artistes, en Algérie. *Africultures, 2011*(3), N 8, 20–27. https://www.cairn.info/revue-africultures-2011-3-page-20.htm.

Louati, A. (1984). *L'Abstraction dans la peinture tunisienne*. Ministère des Affaires Culturelles and le Centre d'Art Vivant de la ville de Tunis.

Louati, A. (2017). *Artistes de Tunisie et d'ailleurs. Ecrits sur l'art contemporain 1983–2016*. Contraste Editions.

Maaouia, M. (2011). L'histoire contemporaine de l'art à l'épreuve de l'usage idéologique. In R. Triki (Ed.), *Le contemporain des arts* (pp. 177–218). Editions Wassiti.

Meskini, O. E. (2006). Art et résistance chez Adorno. In R. Triki (Ed.), *Poïétique de l'existence. Stratégies contemporaines des arts* (pp. 17–26). Editions SUNOMED-Wassiti.

Mikdadi Nashashibi, S., Nader, L., & Adnen, E. (1994). Forces of Change. In S. Mikdadi Nashashibi, L. Nader, & E. Adnen (Eds.), *Forces of Change: Artists of the Arab World* (pp. 13–37). International Council for Women in the Arts, The National Museum of Women in the Arts.

Naef, S. (2017). Writing the History of Modern Art in the Arab World: Documents, Theories and Realities. In J. Allerstorfer & M. Leisch-Kiesl (Eds.), *"Global Art History". Transkulturelle Verortungen von Kunst und Kunstwissenschaft* (pp. 109–126). Transcript Verlag.

Oweis, F. S. (2008). *Madiha Umar. Encyclopedia of Arab American artists (Artists of the American Mosaic)* (pp. 255–258). Greenwood Press.

CHAPTER 27

Laughable Resistance? The Role of Humour in Middle Eastern Women's Social Media Empowerment

Zoe Hurley

Somalian-Canadian stand-up comedian, Hoodo Hersi, tells *hijab* jokes and makes digs at intersectional feminism (Hersi, 2020). During her set, she claims not to identify as a feminist due to the fatigue of already "climbing the mountains" of black and Muslim identity. Moreover, she tells audiences, "There's nothing interesting happening at the top of the female mountain … it is just a bunch of white women skiing!" (Hersi, 2020). This is a swipe at second-wave feminism's Caucasian privilege, Eurocentrism and apparent irrelevance to Muslim women's lives (Mohanty, 1988; El-Saadawi, 1983). Simultaneously, the humour is a refractive strategy that deflects from inherent tensions underpinning patriarchy as a systemic condition that constitutes women in terms of deficit. This study considers the extent to which refractive comedy, defined as indirect humour, is indicative of Middle Eastern women's comic self-effacing strategies as a form of empowerment in the Middle East and North African (MENA) region (Hurley, 2019a, b). Middle Eastern women's comedy represents a gap in social media literature but is an important concern that could help develop insights into how women in MENA challenge women's oppression. The central question of this study asks, to what extent are the humorous performances of Middle Eastern women influencers on social media a refractive strategy for empowerment?

Z. Hurley (✉)
Zayed University, Dubai, United Arab Emirates
e-mail: Zoe.hurley@zu.ac.ae

489

L. H. Skalli, N. Eltantawy (eds.), *The Palgrave Handbook of Gender, Media and Communication in the Middle East and North Africa*, https://doi.org/10.1007/978-3-031-11980-4_27

This question is addressed through a novel feminist postdigital framework. Feminist postdigitalism is defined as a critical theory and postcolonial approach for considering the intersecting offline/online practices of women's lives (Hurley, 2021a; Hurley & Al-Ali, 2021). This concern with women's technology-entangled experiences helps to explore a corpus of comic performances by Middle Eastern women influencers. Influencers are defined as microcelebrities who monetise content online (Senft, 2013; Marwick, 2015). I take the case of three women social media influencers to consider how humour intersects with the sociopolitical fabric of countries in MENA. Although influencers tend to use a range of applications to promote their personal brand, I focus on Instagram, the image- and video-sharing platform. Other applications in the Middle East are growing in popularity, but Instagram is selected since it has a predominantly female user-base that is under the age of 34 (Barnhart, 2021). I begin with a review of literature, discuss the conceptual framework and planes of enquiry and then offer presentation and discussion of the findings.

Literature Review

The literature review reorientates the current field of scholarship surrounding Middle Eastern women influencers from a feminist postdigital perspective. The feminist postdigital framework has a transnational concern with how globalisation and capitalism affect women across nations, races, classes, religions and sexualities in varying ways and as scattered hegemonies (Hurley, 2021a; Grewal & Kaplan, 2006). The rationale of the feminist postdigital framework is made explicit in following with the view that any theoretical agenda is underpinned by the conceptual beliefs and values of the researcher (Braun & Clarke, 2006). The academic articles, texts and websites reviewed are taken from Google Scholar and academic databases. Key search terms were divided between two thematic domains: first, comedy-related search terms including 'Middle Eastern women's comedy', 'Middle Eastern women comedians', 'comic Middle Eastern women influencers' and so on and second, empowerment terms including 'Middle Eastern women's empowerment/agency/resistance' and so on. Next, I discuss some key issues underpinning the MENA context and women's empowerment.

Empowerment

The strict control of information by government-owned press in MENA traditionally marginalised women's issues, including education and positions of authority, while social media has been credited with facilitating empowerment (Odine, 2013). Yet, 'empowerment' is a vague term that has been defined according to varying political orientations. For instance, commercialised discourses have implied that women on social media are already empowered and even 'have it all' (Duffy & Hund, 2015). This is due, in part, to social media's perceived affordances of visibility and networking. But women's increased invisibilities, via social media, may involve gendered self-promotion practices that routinely disempower. This is partly because social media occurs within broader global and neoliberal visual practices that market the lifestyles, customs and activities of women while obscuring the extent of digital labour and inequalities behind the scenes (Abidin, 2017).

Across MENA, as in Western contexts, what empowers some women may not benefit others since empowerment is not a one-size-fits-all category (Hurley, 2019b, 2021a). Middle Eastern women are not homogenous and MENA is a vast and diverse region. Moreover, 'patriarchy' refers to varying forms of gender domination that are specific to any given context, time, class, ethnicity and sexuality. Patriarchy is thus situated and dependent upon "the intimate inner workings of culturally and historically distinct arrangements between the genders" (Kandiyoti, 1988, p. 275). Forms of feminist political resistance, agential processes of empowerment and what makes people laugh could differ significantly. Consequently, the extent to which Middle Eastern women influencers' uses of comedy might bring about empowerment is also highly variable.

In this study, empowering women's comedy is defined as humorous performances that could expand women's agency within and/or beyond the domestic sphere while developing resistance to being overpowered. Simultaneously, feminist postdigital theorising recognises that agency cannot be considered as located exclusively within social actors, while patriarchy limits and moulds agency through several mechanisms (Mohanty, 1988). Feminist postdigitalism views agency as necessary for empowerment but goes beyond individualised notion of agencies that precede or are separate to technologies (Hurley, 2021a). This is important since it acknowledges that agencies (and empowerment) are not simply a decision on behalf of social actors, irrespective of structural inequalities bolstering patriarchy in its various (dis)guises. To illustrate further, I discuss varying facets of MENA's comedic media history which has always been politically charged around issues of agency.

Comedy

The term 'comedy' comes from ancient Greek and is defined as a genre of fiction and theatre that intends to be humorous and induce laughter. A comic performance followed the conventional structure of *parados* (chorus of performers), *agon* (witty debate between the principal actors) and *parabasis* (chorus speaking directly to the audience) (Cartwright, 2013).

Another central premise of comedy is to pit two groups, ages, genders or societies against one another. Northrop Frye (1957) depicted these as opposing sides as a 'society of youth' and 'society of the old'. Essentially this involves the struggle of the powerless youth against the societal conventions. The youth, being devoid of agential power, resort to irony, satire and humour to provoke laughter and destabilise the authority of the old.

There is a long-established literature surrounding comedy as a subversive medium characterised by transgression, social ambivalence and the traditions of carnival (Bakhtin, 1984). However, for Mikhail Bakhtin (1984, pp. 11–12) the laughter of the carnival is not necessarily exclusively binary or divisive. Conversely, it could also be all inclusive, pervasive and simultaneously allusive: "laughter is ambivalent: it is gay, triumphant, and at the same time mocking, deriding. It asserts and denies, it buries and revives. Such is the laughter of carnival." From a Bakhtinian perspective, humour is thus not only a mode of attack but also a ritual of release, catharsis, celebration, probing and pushing of established boundaries. These are not necessarily overturned or dismantled but they are explored and considered afresh. Katherine Rowe (1995, p. 3), writing about female comedy and 'unruly women' in Western contexts, therefore suggests "laughter is a powerful means of self-definition and a weapon for feminist appropriation."

In the MENA context, Middle Eastern women might arguably occupy quite different subject positions to Western women, who are also not uniform and differ in terms of ethnicities, class, sexuality and so on. Indeed, postcolonial feminist scholars writing about "unruly Muslim women" in Western contexts suggest the veil or *hijab* and Muslim woman herself is an affront to Western liberalism and confounds the basic beliefs of Western liberal feminism (Sheth, 2006).

Considering the lacuna surrounding women's comedy in the MENA context, it is important to explore Middle Eastern women's laughter-invoking practices. In terms of MENA's history of comedy, Middle Eastern humour continues to be under-researched and untheorised (Cheurfa, 2019). MENA's social actors have their own languages, dialects, vernaculars and unique national practices, while humour is an essential aspect of everyday lives and evident in political cartoons, memes, gifs and social interactions. The existence of humour in Middle Eastern culture, especially in literature, can be traced to the pre-Islamic period and is considered to have played a major role in poetry, Arabic civilisation and tribal rivalries. Contemporary Middle Eastern humour is considered inherently political and involving "*hazl*" (farce), "*tahakkum*" (taunt) and "*sukhri'iya*" (poking fun, including forms of sarcasm and irony) (Cheurfa, 2019, p. 185). Humour and political satire have always been a prominent element in most Middle Eastern films and television series but are changing dramatically as a result of the enormous shifts that have taken place at the economic, social, educational and industrial levels.

Moreover, MENA is a diverse region and there are considerable geopolitical differences between countries. While Islam is the dominant religion and Arabic is the main language, there are significant minority groups, other religions and linguistic diversities (Abed & Davoodi, 2003). Not surprisingly Middle Eastern women's modes of humour vary enormously. The linguistic barriers between MENA nations sometimes make it difficult for Arabic-speaking audiences across the region to comprehend one another's television shows and films. For example, Moroccan or Saudi Arabian films and TV shows are normally produced in Moroccan and Saudi dialects of Arabic, respectively, making it hard for the other Arabic-speaking audiences to understand and appreciate the jokes in these materials (Alharthi, 2014). However, despite factors inhibiting television and cinematic comedies, there have been recent productions in MENA countries such as Kuwait, Saudi Arabia, the United Arab Emirates, Qatar, Bahrain, Tunisia, Iraq, Jordan and Yemen. In Saudi Arabia, for example, *Tash Ma Tash* (No Big Deal) is a hugely popular television comedy series that ran for 18 seasons during the holy month of Ramadan (AlSaeid, 2015).

Nevertheless, comedy is often situationally specific and does not easily translate across cultural and linguistic borders. Furthermore, Middle Eastern humour, like humour elsewhere, can be highly gendered and often centres around the censoring of women's independence, autonomy and power (Fisher, 2012). For example, mother-in-law jokes, wife skits and comedy concerning the sexual purity and/or nubile attractiveness of young women often have a distinctly misogynist tone (Fisher, 2012). But misogyny is clearly not limited to MENA and some of the significant architects of institutionalised Middle Eastern patriarchy were Ottoman, British and French colonial rulers. The trade-off for Middle Eastern rulers, losing control over the public sphere, was often compensated for via the submission of women. Simultaneously, comedy can be viewed as a coping mechanism to compensate for a sense of powerlessness (Willems, 2011). However, despite the guise of benign amusement, the effect of jokes can go beyond ridiculing gender inequality and instead promote physical violence against women. Nayef and El-Nashar (2014, p. 131) state that this is a deeply serious matter and that, "in a patriarchal social system like that of Egypt, which already disparages women as the 'marked' and the 'different', such jokes should not be dismissed lightly as 'just jokes.'"

These concerns begin to indicate the extent to which different forms of patriarchy present women with distinct 'rules' and call for varying situated strategies to maximise security and optimise life options and degrees of empowerment with varying potential for active or passive resistance in the face of oppression. Deniz Kandiyoti (1988, p. 275) refers to this as the "patriarchal bargain." When considering Middle Eastern women influencers' uses of humour, the notion of the patriarchal bargain could indicate how women might strategise within a set of concrete constraints, including different modes of humour and comic performance. Patriarchy is intersectional. By this I mean that it impacts upon social actors in varying class, racial, secular/non-secular and gendered terms. In the MENA context, the patriarchal bargain can also involve modes of refractive humour which deflect from the seriousness of Middle Eastern women's jibes at power and localised patriarchy.

Modes of humour and women's opportunities to be performatively humorous are increasing significantly in MENA due, in part, to the emergence of social media (YouTube, Twitter, Facebook, Instagram, Snapchat, TikTok, WhatsApp, etc.). Humour on social media platforms, including Instagram and TikTok, is being progressively utilised by young Middle Eastern women performers for social and political purposes while evading censorship. Middle

Eastern women influencers, as the technological agents of humour, are more able to transgress cultural taboos and challenge patriarchy, while laughter is invested with a de-stabling power that could unsettle patriarchal authority. At the same time, the apparent frivolity of social media humour enables Middle Eastern women influencers to veil criticisms as mere 'amusements' rather than as an outright attack and grab for power.

Simultaneously, the humorous female body can be linked to what Bakhtin (1984) has called the "lower body stratum," grotesque and carnivalesque body of excess, transgression and laughter (Keck & Poole, 2011). Rowe (1995, p. 19) argues that unruly comic women are generally "too fat, too funny, too noisy, too old, too rebellious" which unsettles social hierarchies. Muslim women comedians in Western contexts, for example, Hersi (2020), frequently base comic skits around Muslim women being too covered, veiled and *hijabed* while not conforming to the European hegemonic feminine visual availability. In the MENA context, women's comedy has a far-reaching transnational history that continues to play an arguable yet generally unrecognised role in Middle Eastern women's bargains with local patriarchies (Kandiyoti, 1988). Next, I outline the study's conceptual framework and methods for exploring Middle Eastern women's refractive veils of comedy on social media.

Conceptual Framework

Feminist Postdigitalism

To consider Middle Eastern women influencers' humorous performances, enquiry develops through a novel feminist postdigital framework. Feminist postdigital theory conceives of social media's offline/online intersections in relation to MENA's social, political, economic and gendered circuits (Hurley, 2021a; Hurley & Al-Ali, 2021). Importantly, feminist postdigital research has a transnational agenda that is concerned not only with the exchange of people, languages, commodities and meanings across borders, but is also a de-Westernising perspective with a critical research agenda to reveal social actors on the margins of power (Grewal & Kaplan, 2006; Mahler, 2018; Hurley & Al-Ali, 2021). This is crucial because, while Middle Eastern women influencers are increasingly visible, refractive comic performances could occur below the radar of controversy and not necessarily be understood from Western perspectives. The feminist postdigital framework helps to address the central research question of the study which asks, to what extent are the humorous performances of Middle Eastern women influencers on social media a refractive strategy for empowerment? The planes of enquiry are discussed next.

Planes of Enquiry

Theorising was first informed by secondary texts, including academic scholarship, news articles, Middle Eastern women and Muslimah's comic YouTube videos and Middle Eastern women influencers' Instagram posts. Second, 12 months of focused digital analysis was carried out. This included iterations with a team of three bilingual Arab-English-speaking research assistants. Their ability to speak English, standard modern Arabic and other Arabic dialects was crucial since Middle Eastern women influencers' code-switching, between English and a number of Arabic variations, can be central to the comedy.

The study also drew on my previous research, focus groups and interviews with Middle Eastern women's social media influencers (Hurley, 2019a, b, 2021a). In this study, the influencers selected are featured due to their popularity, substantial number of followers and availability within the public domain. The focus on these influencers also enables zooming in on a cross-section of Middle Eastern women's comic social media performances. Instagram account links, posts and videos were stored as a corpus on Google Drive. Table 27.1 presents the influencers' biodata and broad summary of the corpus.

The feminist postdigital framework enabled data to be explored at three different levels, which include the following:

1. Listing of the observable *structures* and elements of the Middle Eastern women's comic Instagram posts collated within the corpus
2. Description of the dialogic *modes of humorous address*
3. Classification of the *style* of comic performances and *technological affordances* of Instagram employed for humorous effect

All the above were considered in combination to address the research question of the study asking to what extent the humorous performances of Middle Eastern women influencers on social media are refractive strategies for empowerment. To address the question, interpretive analysis of the observable elements, considering multiple and tacit meanings of the posts, some possibly occurring below the radar, could be developed. The resulting analytic categories focused on structure, mode, style, interpretative and coalescing aspects of comedy. These nodes of the feminist postdigital framework are summarised as follows:

Table 27.1 Influencer corpus

Influencer	Name	Location	No. followers	Number of posts
@darin00013	Darin Al Bayed	Saudi Arabia—Lebanese origin	4.2 m	492
@rawsanhallak	Rawsan Hallak	Jordan	613 k	657
@amyroko	Amy Roko (pseudonym)	Saudi Arabia	1.5 m	189

- *Dramatic structure* of the social media comic performances, including digital equivalents of *parados* (performers), *agon* (witty dialogues and debates) and *parabasis* (audience engagement strategies).
- *Modes of humorous address* by influencers as well as dialogic interactions, responses and parasocial engagements with followers. The modes of humour here include varying types of comedy in *hazl*, (farce), *tahakkum* (taunt) and *sukhri'iya* (poking fun, including forms of sarcasm and irony).
- *Styles of humour* and mediation of technological affordances including audiovisuality, synthetic embodiment via audio-dubbing, graphics, text, spoken language, emojis, hashtags, modality and any features communicating meaning.
- Interpretive aspects of the influencers' comic Instagram posts, in terms of localised social meanings at overt and tacit levels. This helps to reveal the refractive aspects and interpretive meanings that might have dialogic significance below the radar.
- Culmination of the above is considered in relation to the broader MENA and transnational contexts of the women influencers' comic Instagram posts. As well as identifying correlations and differences between the corpora of posts, the framework also helps to address the research question.

The Instagram corpus was categorised and analysed according to the overlapping feminist postdigital analytic categories. Subsequently, this enables exploration of the meanings of the comic social media practices embedded, embodied and combined within the collapsed MENA/social media context. In terms of ethics, all the Instagram accounts are freely available within the public domain. Ethical considerations were informed by a cautious approach to the MENA region's strict social media censorship and internet laws (Hurley, 2021a). As a feminist postdigital scholar, I am self-reflexive that analysis always involves researcher subjectivity. I have attempted to address this through firstly acknowledging it; secondly, adhering to the feminist postdigital framework; and thirdly, through drawing on a broad spectrum of Middle Eastern women's Instagram posts to convey the multiplicity of social meanings.

Self-reflexivity is an important value of the feminist postdigital study, since it is acknowledged that the researcher always speaks from a particular gender, class, racial, cultural and ethnic background (Denzin & Lincoln, 2005). In terms of my own background, while originally from the United Kingdom, having partly grown up there, I am a transnational woman academic and have spent my adult life in Muslim countries in Asia and the Middle East. I am aware that the digital medium allows researchers to sometimes remain a completely inconspicuous observer and that this raises questions about the researcher's role in digitised spaces. In the presentation of the findings, I therefore identify researcher interpretation through writing in the first person. In the next section, I present some key findings emerging from the planes of feminist postdigital framework. I begin with @darin00013.

Findings

In many of @darin00013's video stories on Instagram, dramatic structure involves voice-overs from other source material. In Example 1, @darin00013 takes on the persona of an Egyptian man through audio-dubbing while she speaks to her forlorn-looking friend who has under-performed in a school exam.

Example 1: @Darin00013 (English Translation):
"How much did you get then?"
  "No need to know…"
  "Tell me!"
  "I got 15 out of 50…"
  "You got 15!? 15 marks/points?"
  "Yes."
  "And you're upset? Who's the idiot that told you that you failed? I got half a point!"
  "Really?"
  "I swear!"
Caption: *"When you have a failing supporter" "Mention the one who's like this"*
@darin00013 (2021)

The dramatic structure of this scene is the digital equivalent of *agon*, defined as a witty dialogue between principal actors. Through lip-syncing to a male voice, @darin00013 embodies the persona of what might be called a 'beta male' while celebrating her friend's apparent success in failing an academic test. There are different variations of the beta male, but in this case, they are defined as the academic, financial and career 'losers' in comedies (Greven, 2013). @darin00013, via the male audio-dubbing, explains to her friend that you have not *"failed"* if you only score *"15 out of 50"* in a school test, since she only ever managed to achieve *"half a point"* in any exam!

In terms of local interpretive aspects of this scene, struggles surrounding masculinity are a popular theme of comedy that has a longstanding history in Egyptian cinema (Hamam, 2012). While Egyptian comedies have been criticised as formulaic, fragmentary and unconvincing, film theorist Iman Hamam (2012, p. 186) says that they constitute what may be called a *"sha'abi"* genre. *Shaabi* means 'of the people'. It originated in Cairo in the 1970s as a new form of urban music expressing the difficulties and frustrations of modern Egyptian life. *Shaabi* lyrics can be intensely political yet filled with humour and *double entendre*. Egyptian comedies draw on these elements, aligning narratives with music and modern settings occupied by the everyday city dweller (Hamam, 2012). Class and gender are tightly interwoven within Egyptian films to manifest a series of political anxieties about Egypt's class divide, corruption and generations of youth confronting unemployment, while conveyed through humour.

@darin00013's mode of humour is a variant of the 'beta male' narrative, defined as 'celebrating' low expectations (Greven, 2013). It draws on the formats of Egyptian comedy's structures for confronting class struggle. The audio-visual overlay provides a simple template for replicating a comic trope of disaffected youth. In terms of modes of humour, Example 1 includes features of *hazl* (farce) and *sukhri'iya* (poking fun, including forms of sarcasm and irony). This is not a mode of attack but a style of humour to compensate for a sense of powerlessness (Willems, 2011). Simultaneously, @darin00013's *hazl* and *sukhri'iya* manifest with particular similarities to carnival culture and grotesque realism. This includes @darin00013's overdetermined facial gestures and animated body language, in an extremely exaggerated form of disguise, scatology, fragmentation and distortion (Bakhtin, 1984).

In my opinion, the skit's ambiguity and dialogism (multiplicity of voice and perspective) are intensified through the backdrop of the female bedroom and dressing table that displays medals, certificates and symbols of academic achievement. However, these indexes of intellectual status are undermined by the action in the foreground and *hazl* of @darin00013 telling the younger girl (forlornly posed in a purple onesie) that scoring even half a point in an academic test is an achievement.

Dialogic interpretation considers the multiplicity and intertextuality of voices, perspectives and texts within any given genre or speech act (Bakhtin, 1984). Dialogism here reveals @darin00013's own fluid performative gender positionality as a social media influencer of Lebanese origin based in Saudi Arabia. Both Lebanon and Saudi Arabia, to differing extents and for varying reasons, face uncertain economic futures due to the global downturn of oil and gas economies. Thus @darin00013, speaking to Saudi, Egyptian, Lebanese and transnational audiences, taps into the underpinning anxieties surrounding economic instability in MENA. She can do so through recycling Egyptian comic tropes of disaffectedness via her embodied stance as a modern young woman living in Saudi Arabia. While there is no music in this particular skit, there often are diegetic and non-diegetic soundtracks in a number of @darin00013's posts on Instagram that convey a sense of Egyptian *shaabi* (Hamam, 2012).

However, @darin00013 is clearly situated in the feminine domestic sphere of the home and girl's bedroom. The rise of women and girls' performances on social media has been championed as contributing to the transformation of a female 'bedroom culture' (McRobbie & Garber, 1976; Kennedy, 2020). But performances by women influencers and social media's entry into the traditional domestic sphere of Middle Eastern women change the conceptualisation of the bedroom as a private or space safe from surveillance (Hurley, 2021b; Hurley & Al-Ali, 2021). Next, in Example 2, the findings illustrate some of the pertinent inequalities enmeshing women in MENA's domestic sphere.

Example 2
@rawsanhallak

@rawsanhallak is the Instagram handle for Rawsan Hallak, the stand-up comedian, civil engineer and social media influencer from Jordan. Her Instagram stories and videos regularly focus on Middle Eastern women's lives. For instance, her post captioned *"Jealousy: a new episode of Tarma's daily life. #Tarma's dailylife #love #jealousy #Jordan #Amman"* begins with @rawsanhallak inserted within a Looney Tunes cartoon background and soundtrack. Three varying portraits of @rawsanhallak are inserted within the background, each with a differing expression, one smiling, another angry and one laughing. These icons illustrate the comic and cartoonish fictionality of the Instagram performance and that @rawsanhallak is playing a range of characters. An English translation of the Arabic-transcribed Instagram video is presented next.

Example 2
Transcription of @rawsanhallak's comic video story

Scene 1 (wife sitting and eating seeds while watching TV and commenting on a show)

> **Wife** (commenting on an actress on TV): *Stay like that, just stay like that. Romance? What romance? At the end he's just going to cheat on you dear.*
> (Husband walks in the house and wife gets up to greet him and they both start singing a recent Arabic song and are happy.)
> **Husband** (while singing the song sings a specific lyric): *"The neighbour's daughter has caught my attention."*
> **Wife** (face changes and is now angry): *"STOP right there! Who is this neighbour's daughter? Huh? And she caught your eyes as well? Listen, my favourite song is I will pull your eyes out.*
> **Husband:** *Calm down, clam down; how did your mood change so fast? We were just singing and all happy.*
> **Wife:** *You mean you were the one happy and singing and in a great mood.*
> **Husband:** *So, you'd prefer I come angry and unhappy? Will that make you happy? And aren't you going to let me come inside the house? And no welcome home my love?*
> **Wife:** *Welcome? Wow now you talk in English. Listen, who is this neighbour's daughter that you're singing for?*
> **Husband:** *UFFFF, this is just a song!*
> **Wife** (shouting): *And my mind is going crazy!!*
> (husband walks away)

Scene 2 (wife enters the kitchen and starts preparing food and then husband enters the kitchen)

> **Husband:** *Darling, do you want anything? I'm going out with my friends.*
> **Wife:** *No, I want your wellbeing, enjoy.*
> **Husband:** *And I won't be late like yesterday, inshallah.*
> **Wife** (face changes from being calm to annoyed): *WAIT! I changed my mind* (goes closer to her husband). *I've noticed you put three and a half extra sprays from your perfume today. And you've also blow-dried your beard.*

Husband (laughing): *You reminded me of the sentence, "a lion's bite instead of an evil eye."*
Wife: *And now you're changing the subject.*
Husband: *Ugh, not every time you have to make me stand this way, enough with the jealously! I'm going to go crazy because of you, UFFT!*
Wife: *Okay Hamoodah, I swear, I swear I will make you go crazy this time.*

Scene 3: (husband sitting outside, dejected on the pavement; a random girl passes by and assumes he's a homeless person and gives him money. He takes it. His wife sees this and runs towards him)

> **Wife:** *Who is this that you just smiled at? Isn't it enough that you already left the house, and now you're sitting here and flirting with women while you're out of the house?*
> Husband gets up mumbles a few lyrics from an Arabic song and starts running away and wife starts singing the same song along the lines of: *"you leave me, I hate my life, I get lost, and he won't find me."*

The dramatic structure of Example 2 is a digital version of *parados* (performance). It is crafted in televisual sitcom style, shaped by non-diegetic music of the comic soundtrack and the heightened diegetic noise of @rawsanhallak eating popcorn. This layering of sound indexes the rhythm and suspense of the skit as her husband arrives home. Significantly, the skit is devoid of the calibrated amateurism, often associated with social media (Abidin, 2017). Calibrated amateurism involves influencers' attempts to display their authenticity and parasocial engagement with followers by showing supposedly unscripted events. This can include breaking the fourth wall of fiction, via diegetic sound and natural lighting, while revealing the selfie stick, camera or method of recording the narrative. Alternatively, @rawsanhallak's Instagram videos are highly choreographed through the stylistic affordances of television sitcom and cartoons. In relation to mode, it is a form of *sukhri'iya* (poking fun, including forms of sarcasm and irony) and a heightened sense of comic fictionality, conveyed through the actors' facial expressions and body language which are exaggerated and contrived.

Interpretive meanings of the scene, in relation to MENA's social meanings at overt and tacit levels, indicate that the comedy is derived from the perverse gender logics and politics of inequalities. In the skit, the husband is at the mercy of his irrational wife's jealousy, fuelled by popular culture, music and soap opera. Initially the wife seems to have the upper hand, exposing her husband for dousing himself in perfume and *"blow-drying"* his beard. But, at a tacit level, I suggest that the scene reveals the woman's insecurities about male fidelity, challenges of monogamy and deeper-rooted concerns about marriage. Furthermore, while illustrating the tenacity of the popcorn-eating @rawsanhallak, ultimately the authorial mode curates sympathy for the male protagonist and implies that men are the ones 'suffering' most in patriarchal marriage due to controlling wives. Simultaneously, other women are positioned as potential competitors for a husband's attention, including neighbours and even female strangers passing by.

In @rawsanhallak's skit, the style and modes of comedy do not culminate to subvert patriarchal power but instead reinforce the hegemony of men's sexual agency, reminding women of the patriarchal bargain. This is contradictory to the idea of women's empowerment via humour. I suggest that the scene might be interpreted as a warning to women to laugh off men's infidelities rather than confronting and consequently losing their husbands, as @rawsanhallak does by the end of the skit. This is cautious comic *sukhri'iya* about aging wives unable to compete on the platforms of female attractiveness. As the scene progresses, @rawsanhallak's appearance deteriorates from her pretty flowered veil and red lipstick into a raggedy headwrap and contorted face. The skit ends with her husband turning his back on her, kicking off his slippers, fleeing from the feminine domestic realm and returning barefoot—to the *shaabi*—or male-dominated street. This denouement illustrates that humour is not automatically empowering but could also be corrective, censoring and hegemonic. Nevertheless, the same skit is open to varying audiences' interpretations and next I consider the role of audience reaction as *parabasis* (chorus of interactions).

Example 3
@amyroko and friend's Instagram video story

@amyroko is a Saudi Arabian influencer who wears the traditional Gulf-Arab (*Khaleeji*) black *niqab* (facial covering) and *abaya* (coat). The dramatic structure of the Instagram scene studied involves the *parados* of her and her friend—Hadeel Marei—who is a famous influencer in her own right. @amyroko and Marei dance from the bedroom to the kitchen and fridge, as they eat cereal straight out of the packet. Joyous, upbeat Arabic music plays, with lively singing and ululation, which is the term for the wavering, high-pitched vocal sound resembling a howl with a trilling quality. In Arabic it is called *zaghārīt* and is performed to honour someone or something. In this Instagram video, the ululation honours @amyroko and her friend's dance to the kitchen to eat more food. The text caption on the video says, "*Me and my friend at 5am going to the kitchen after we've had three dinners.*" The song playing is translated as "*Come over for dinner.*" The two phrases playing from the song translate *to* "*Welcome to dinner/dinner's ready/dinner's served*" and "*Welcome Arabs.*" The caption translates to: "*For God's sake how many times do you eat/have dinner in a day?*"

@amyroko has made a name for herself on Instagram, subverting the *mise en scene* of *shaabi*, driving across the Saudi Arabia, while rapping, dancing and all the while wearing a *niqab* (facial covering). She is also an outspoken advocate for young Saudi women's empowerment (Tay, 2020). Marei is a regular performer in her posts and the two are clearly partners in comedy. The structure of the skit is led by *parados* (performers). In terms of mode, it is a form of *sukhri'iya* that is self-effacing and pokes fun at the women's compulsive visits to the kitchen. It is also high *hazl* (farce) concerning the number of people turning to food for comfort during Covid-19 lockdowns.

At tacit levels, the scene also conveys the mundanity of the feminine domestic sphere. This shatters the illusion of digital feminine mystique of earlier Instagram microcelebrity trends, suggesting that women "have it all" while confined by stereotypical gender roles in the home (Duffy & Hund, 2015; Hurley, 2019a; Abidin, 2020). @amyroko reveals young Saudi Arabian women confined and bored in the female domestic sphere during Covid-19. But Melanie Kennedy (2020) writing about the rise of the 'e-girl aesthetic' suggests that "boredom is a feeling experienced by the privileged" (p. 1074). However, it is not clear how Kennedy defines privilege or if boredom is necessarily exclusive to the rich (as anyone earning a minimum wage for repetitive labour might verify). Conversely, the theme of women's domestic boredom runs through the Middle Eastern influencers' stories while laughter is presented as an antidote.

Regarding issues of interpretation in the MENA context, some of the followers commenting on the skit are deeply critical of @amyroko's dancing while wearing a *niqab*. The criticism expressed against @amyroko comes from an Islamic perspective and situated expectations of how *niqabbed* women should behave. As indicated, the lively wedding music, ululation (*zaghārīt*) and beating of the drums to celebrate the girls' dance to the fridge is a highly irreverent mode of *hazl* (farce). But some of the followers' comments are a digitally reversed form of *parabasis*, whereby @amyroko's Instagram followers play the role of the critical chorus. The research assistants working with me explained that some Muslim women wearing a *niqab* could become subject to collective expectations of *niqabbed* women in the MENA context to adhere to certain modes of behaviour. The affordances of *niqab*, to veil and conceal, are not necessarily open licence for the farcical *hazl*, cheekily performed by @amyroko and her friend. The comments of @amyroko's followers evolve as an inversion of *parabasis* since the audience of followers speak directly to the performers via their written comments. Consequently, while comedy is often considered a version of carnival, subverting traditional authority, audiences on social media might also offer a chorus of correction to reinforce patriarchy. Nevertheless, some comments on the video skit are less critical, revealing the dialogism of humour and a variation of responses. Next, I offer some further discussion of the findings.

DISCUSSION

Comedy is an allusive genre that transforms, reconfigures and adjusts according to design, media and context. On Instagram, comedy can draw on the technological affordances of audio-visual dubbing, music, text, hashtags and calibrations of televisual crafting and choreography. Each of the Middle Eastern women influencers discussed draws on these affordances. But while they have varying comic styles, all engage in degrees of patriarchal bargaining to greater and lesser extents. I provide a broad summary of each of the influencers' pertinent comic negotiations.

The hugely popular @darin00013, with 4.2 m followers, uses the structures of *agon*, defined as witty dialogue. She enunciates some of the challenges that face MENA youth, concerning education and lack of employment. As illustrated, @darin00013 uses social media as a platform to speak to her followers from the confines of her bedroom. Due to audio-visual dubbing, she transgresses gender and generation to articulate Middle Eastern youths' disaffections. Through tacit associations with *shaabi* Egyptian cinema, her comic social media videos articulate through *hazl* and *sukhri'iya*s and speak in the mode of the street. In terms of addressing the research question of the chapter and whether @darin00013 offers an example of a humorous refractive strategy for empowerment, the example presented certainly indicates the agency of young Middle Eastern women in MENA, via social media, to become stakeholders in the discussion surrounding youth in the region. This enables @darin00013 and her followers to comment on political issues without leaving their bedrooms and thus covertly highlighting the female realm as a potential staging post for refractive dissent.

We also find @rawsanhallak confined with the female domestic sphere, watching soap operas, preparing food for her husband while seemingly agitated by jealousy and insecurity. Although Rawsan Hallak is an engineer by trade, there is no reference to her professional capabilities as she embodies the character of a traditional yet deluded housewife. In this instance, rather than comedy enabling a transgression and liberating role, as some of the literature suggests, we find @rawsanhallak resorting to the patriarchal bargain. This reminds her women followers that they should not question their husbands to prevent them from running away, back to the male-dominated *shaabi* (street). This could be interpreted as a deeply reactionary message that is disturbing rather than funny. But Hallak is playing the character "*Tarma*"—the housewife. Rather than performing under the façade of authenticity, more typical of earlier Middle Eastern women influencers, she is overtly constructing a persona (Hurley, 2019a). In representing marriage as comic performance, @rawsanhallak might also be considered a self-elected sage, resorting to the only tools available within Jordan's patriarchy. These social media tools include carefully crafted cartoonish *mise en scene*, sitcom-style performance and grotesque realism to sweeten the bitter taste of her message.

Yet, despite her craftsmanship, @rawsanhallak's rejection of women's ability in marriage to authentically relay their feelings, discontent and anxieties about patriarchy's shortcomings could demean their agency and empowerment. Ultimately, this performative compromise tethers women to the male hegemony of patriarchy. Next, I discuss summative points concerning @amyroko.

@amyroko, although hugely popular and admired by some, both for and despite her gender transgressions as a *niqabbed* woman, is on the receiving end of follower-led *parabasis* and negative audience engagement. Although she does not show her face, her social media antics render her visible and thereby controversial in the MENA context. Yet, @amyroko also works with other leading influencers in the region and is part of an engagement pod of Middle Eastern women who perform on one another's social media accounts. This indicates not only the growing community of practice of Middle Eastern women influencers but also the women's homosocial spaces in the Middle East context that might sometimes be sanctuaries of laughter to challenge patriarchal compromise. For instance, as mentioned @amyroko's sidekick is the notable Middle Eastern influencer—Hadeel Marei. Marei is the Egyptian content creator, producer and performer gaining visibility on social media in MENA, with 729k followers on Instagram and 1.7 million on TikTok. Unlike @rawsanhallak's cautious bargaining with patriarchy, @amyroko and Marei in their social media skits rally against the constraints of Middle Eastern patriarchy while pushing against the limitations of comedy deemed appropriate for women. In an interview with *Vogue Arabia*'s Michaela Somerville (2021), Marei states:

> There is a certain mold that holds women—our jokes are expected to be about our age, looks, shape, or being ultra-fem. I'm steering away from that reductive concept, and defying the cultural norms that tell me to be more docile and calm … I'm inspired by trauma.

This statement provides rationale for why Marei and @amyroko are using their platforms on social media to perform sardonic skits, transcending the boundaries of *hazl* (farce), *tahakkum* (taunt) and *sukhri'iya* (poking fun), to deride "molds" encapsulating Middle Eastern women. This discussion indicates that collectively, women's comedy in the Middle East is executed via varying and sometimes intersecting modes of *hazl*, *tahakkum* and *sukhri'iya*, as coping mechanisms to confront the patriarchal bargain. As Bakhtin (1984) suggests, laughter is catharsis for momentary release from constraints. But in the MENA context on social media, beneath the refractions of amusement are bitter issues of gender inequality which some Middle Eastern women influencers are challenging. In the concluding section, I discuss implications, limitations and recommendations for future research.

CONCLUSION

Overall, just as women's empowerment is not a one-size-fits-all category, this study illustrates that neither is Middle Eastern women's humour. Middle Eastern women influencers deploy varying modes of comedy to critique, probe and bargain with patriarchy. The central question of the chapter asks, to what extent are the humorous performances of Middle Eastern women influencers on social media a refractive strategy for empowerment? In answer to this question, I have illustrated how humour and comic performances can be varying forms of double-speak to offer refractive social critique. Middle Eastern women's humour can also be loud, proud, too much and dubbed and/or occur below the radar. MENA is a complex context which routinely censors women's modes of behaviour in the public and domestic sphere. Middle Eastern women, like other social actors on the margins of power, continue to navigate patriarchal bargains. But the popularity of Middle Eastern women's humour on social media indicates an irreverent agency that could be invaluable for advocating women's equality. Simultaneously, while a range social taboos have traditionally banished Middle Eastern women from the public gaze, the engagement pods of women influencers, such as @amyroko and friends, are increasingly visible and demonstrate the promise of women social media influencers working collectively.

The limitations of the study are that it skims the surface of a small corpus of influencers' Instagram accounts and could do more to consider the interactions of social media audiences. Future research could extend the feminist postdigital framework to consider refractive issues of precariat migrant women, from Asia, Africa and Eastern Europe, working in MENA, often without citizenship status. Their uses of social media, on apps like TikTok and WhatsApp, are loaded with humorous retort but represent a gap in knowledge. Nevertheless, the findings of the study are generalisable to other contexts whereby women's humour operates across a spectrum of discursive modes. This study develops feminist postdigital reorientations for thinking about women's refractive and overt humour on social media. Finally, the enquiry offers fine-grained theorising of some Middle Eastern influencers' *hazl*, *tahakkum* and *sukhri'iya* for laughter in the face of continuing systemic oppression of women.

References

Abed, G., & Davoodi, H. (2003). *Challenges of Growth and Globalization in the Middle East and North Africa*. Retrieved 26 June 2021, from https://www.imf.org/external/pubs/ft/med/2003/eng/abed.htm

Abidin, C. (2017). #familygoals: Family Influencers, Calibrated Amateurism, and Justifying Young Digital Labor. *Social Media + Society*, April–June, 1–15. doi: https://doi.org/10.1177/2056305117707191.

Abidin, C. (2020). Mapping Internet Celebrity on TikTok: Exploring Attention Economies and Visibility Labours. *Cultural Science Journal, 12*(1), 77–103. https://doi.org/10.5334/csci.140

Alharthi, A. (2014). Humour and Culture. *International Journal of Humanities and Cultural Studies, 1*(3), 1–13.

AlSaeid, N. (2015). *Screens of Influence: Arab Satellite Television and Social Development*. Askance Publishing.

Bakhtin, M. (1984). *Rabelais and His World*. Indiana University Press.

Barnhart, B. (2021). *The Most Important Instagram Statistics You Need to Know for 2021*. Retrieved 7 September 2021, from https://sproutsocial.com/insights/instagram-stats/

Braun, V., & Clarke, V. (2006). Using Thematic Analysis in Psychology. *Qualitative Research in Psychology,* 3(2), 77–101. https://doi.org/10.1191/1478088706qp063oa

Cartwright, M. (2013). *Ancient Greek Comedy.* Retrieved 2 May 2021, from https://www.worldhistory.org/Greek_Comedy/

Cheurfa, H. (2019). Comedic Resilience: Arab Women's Diaries of National Struggles and Dissident Humour. *Comedy Studies,* 10(2), 183–198. https://doi.org/10.1080/2040610x.2019.1623501

Denzin, N., & Lincoln, Y. (2005). *The Landscape of Qualitative Research.* Sage.

Duffy, B., & Hund, E. (2015). "Having it All" on Social Media: Entrepreneurial Femininity and Self-Branding Among Fashion Bloggers. *Social Media + Society,* 1(2), 205630511560433. https://doi.org/10.1177/2056305115604337

El-Saadawi, N. (1983). *Memoirs from the women's prison.* Zed Books.

Fisher, M. (2012). *The Real Roots of Sexism in the Middle East (It's Not Islam, Race, or 'Hate').* Retrieved 3 May 2021, from https://www.theatlantic.com/international/archive/2012/04/the-real-roots-of-sexism-in-the-middle-east-its-not-islam-race-or-hate/256362/

Frye, N. (1957). *Anatomy of Criticism.* Princeton University Press.

Greven, D. (2013). "I Love You, Brom Bones": Beta Male Comedies and American Culture. *Quarterly Review of Film and Video,* 30(5), 405–420. https://doi.org/10.1080/10509208.2011.575669

Grewal, I., & Kaplan, C. (2006). *Scattered Hegemonies.* University of Minnesota Press.

Hamam, I. (2012). Disarticulating Arab Popular Culture: The Case of Egyptian Comedies. In T. Sabry (Ed.), *Arab Cultural Studies: Mapping the Field* (pp. 186–213). Bloomsbury.

Hersi, H. (2020). *Hoodo Hersi - The Reason She's Not a Feminist.* Retrieved 2 May 2021, from https://www.youtube.com/watch?v=LLhy2FKv6jg

Hurley, Z. (2019a). Imagined Affordances of Instagram and the Fantastical Authenticity of Gulf-Arab Social Media Influencers. *Social Media + Society,* 5(1).

Hurley, Z. (2019b). Why I No Longer Believe Social Media Is Cool …. *Social Media + Society,* 5(3), 205630511984949. https://doi.org/10.1177/2056305119849495

Hurley, Z. (2021a). #reimagining Arab Women's Social Media Empowerment and the Postdigital Condition. *Social Media + Society,* 7(2), 205630512110101. https://doi.org/10.1177/20563051211010169

Hurley, Z. (2021b). Dialogic Theorising of Emirati Women's Technology Enhanced Learning in the United Arab Emirates. *Studies in Technology Enhanced Learning,* 1(2). https://doi.org/10.21428/8c225f6e.b70d4b5a

Hurley, Z., & Al-Ali, K. (2021). Feminist Postdigital Inquiry in the Ruins of Pandemic Universities. *Postdigital Science and Education.* https://doi.org/10.1007/s42438-021-00254-4

Kandiyoti, D. (1988). Bargaining with patriarchy. *Gender and Society,* 2(3), 274–290. https://doi.org/10.1177/089124388002003004

Keck, A., & Poole, R. (2011). *EBSCOhost | 70199996 | Gender and Humour: Reinventing the Genres of Laughter.* Retrieved 3 May 2021, from https://web.a.ebscohost.com/abstract?direct=true&profile=ehost&scope=site&authtype=crawler&jrnl=16131878&AN=70199996&h=J0Cz6E%2fqiIgJEw%2boMx%2bltb4btAcHm1o4FkOUP6CdsAfjFNx1bm9OMFZoy%2by2eE1BzVnP4v7WRIgbGM%2fR2xiFSg%3d%3d&crl=c&resultNs=AdminWebAuth&resultLocal=ErrCrlNotAuth&crlhashurl=login.

aspx%3fdirect%3dtrue%26profile%3dehost%26scope%3dsite%26authtype%3dcrawle r%26jrnl%3d16131878%26AN%3d70199996

Kennedy, M. (2020). 'If the Rise of the TikTok Dance and e-Girl Aesthetic Has Taught Us Anything, IT's that Teenage Girls Rule the Internet Right Now': TikTok Celebrity, Girls and the Coronavirus Crisis. *European Journal of Cultural Studies, 23*(6), 1069–1076. https://doi.org/10.1177/1367549420945341

Mahler, A. (2018). *From the Tricontinental to the Global South: Race, Radicalism, and Transnational Solidarity*. Duke University Press.

Marwick, A. (2015). Instafame: Luxury Selfies in the Attention Economy. *Public Culture, 27*(1 75), 137–160. https://doi.org/10.1215/08992363-2798379

McRobbie, A., & Garber, J. (1976). Girls and subcultures. In S. Hall & T. Jefferson (Eds.), *Resistance Through Rituals: Youth Subcultures in Post-war Britain* (pp. 209–223). Hutchinson. Reprinted in A. McRobbie (Ed.) *Feminism and Youth Culture from Jackie to Just Seventeen* (pp. 12–25). Macmillan, 1991.

Mohanty, C. (1988). Under Western Eyes: Feminist Scholarship and Colonial Discourses. *Feminist Review, 30*, 61. https://doi.org/10.2307/1395054

Nayef, H., & El-Nashar, M. (2014). Promoting Masculine Hegemony Through Humour: A Linguistic Analysis of Gender Stereotyping in Egyptian Sexist Internet Jokes. *International Journal of Linguistics and Communication, 2*(4). https://doi.org/10.15640/ijlc.v2n4a5

Odine, M. (2013). Role of Social Media in the Empowerment of Arab Women. *Global Media Journal*, Spring.

Rowe, K. (1995). *The Unruly Woman: Gender and the Genres of Laughter*. University of Texas Press.

Senft, S. (2013). Microcelebrity and the Branded Self. In J. Hartley, J. Burgess, & A. Bruns (Eds.), *A Companion to New Media Dynamics* (pp. 346–354). Wiley.

Sheth, F. (2006). Unruly Muslim Women and Threats to Liberal Culture. *Peace Review, 18*(4), 455–463. https://doi.org/10.1080/10402650601030328

Somerville, M. (2021). *Why Egyptian Creator Hadeel Marei Is Poised to Be the Next-Generation Queen of Comedy*. Retrieved September 6 2021, from https://en.vogue.me/beauty/egyptian-comedian-hadeel-marei/

Tay, A. (2020). *Meet the Women Under the Abayas: Amy Roko*. Retrieved September 8, 2021, from https://www.harpersbazaararabia.com/featured-news/under-the-abaya-amy-roko

Willems, W. (2011). Comic Strips and "The Crisis": Postcolonial Laughter and Coping with Everyday Life in Zimbabwe. *Popular Communication, 9*(2), 126–145. https://doi.org/10.1080/15405702.2011.562099

CHAPTER 28

Egyptian Women's Graffiti and the Construction of Future Imaginaries

alma aamiry-khasawnih

Since the start of the 25 January Revolution in January 2011, protestors have used walls of public and private buildings in urban and rural areas to engage in debates with each other and the state around revolutionary demands, document revolutionary happenings, and share their political and cultural views. While these ephemera documented revolutionary happenings, commemorated martyrs, and celebrated heroes, it also challenged hegemonic ideologies of Egyptian womanhood and articulated future imaginaries of what constitutes an Egyptian woman. Through close readings of select graffiti created by women and women-led groups and contextualizing it within nationalist constructions of Egyptian women's identity, I demonstrate that these ephemera challenge hegemonic characterizations of acceptable Egyptian womanhood and open up space for imagined alternative future definitions of what it means to be an Egyptian woman.

Through memoirs and academically published works, Egyptian women described their diverse roles in the revolution and their full participation,

a. aamiry-khasawnih (✉)
Department of Women's, Gender, and Sexuality Studies, The College of New Jersey, Ewing, NJ, USA
e-mail: khasawna@tcnj.edu

509

L. H. Skalli, N. Eltantawy (eds.), *The Palgrave Handbook of Gender, Media and Communication in the Middle East and North Africa*,
https://doi.org/10.1007/978-3-031-11980-4_28

inclusion, and camaraderie with fellow male protestors.[1] They described the freedom they felt during the first few weeks of the revolution, where they used their voices and bodies to fight alongside men, to lead protests, to stand face to face against state security agents, and to help bring down President Hosni Mubarak's regime in conditions largely free from sexual harassment and patriarchal protections. These narratives soon changed when male protestors and state security agents began targeting women protestors through various forms of sexual violence. Violence took the shape of mass rape and harassment of female protestors while participating in the demonstrations (Amar, 2011; Mikdashi, 2013; Hafez, 2014a, b; Abouelnaga, 2016), police and army personnel targeting female protestors by arresting them and subjecting them to rape while in detention through virginity tests (Amin, 2011; Mohsen, 2012; Seikaly, 2013; Hafez, 2014a, b), and excluding women from official political participation in shaping new national political agendas and the writing of the new constitution. In their 2013 "Position Paper on Sexual Violence Against Women and the Increasing Frequency of Gang Rape in Tahrir Square and its Environs," Nazra—a feminist studies organization in Cairo—argue that these gender-based violences were aimed at deterring women from participating in public political life and provoking patriarchal protections over women. Paul Amar (2011) demonstrates that acts of sexual violence by male protestors helped narratives that all male protests are violent and should be policed and criminalized by the state. Yet, this violence was not only perpetrated by protestors. Sherene Seikaly (2013) analyzes the arrests and virginity tests that Samira Ibrahim, along with 17 other women, was subjected to after being arrested on 9 March 2011 (the day after International Women's Day). Seikaly provides close readings of a military general's explanation of these violences as a way to distinguish respectable women from unrespectable women. The general said that the women arrested were "not like your daughter or mine … [w]e didn't want them to say we had sexually assaulted or raped them, so we wanted to prove that they weren't virgins in the first place" (Seikaly, 2013, lines 45–48). In other words, the military doctor Ahmed Abdel El-Mogy "punctured Samira's hymen to prove that it has (not) existed. For if it did not exist, and she was not a virgin, her rape would then be impossible. He raped her so that she could not claim that she was raped" (Seikaly, 2013, lines 49–51). By invoking familial relationships (daughters) and politics of respectability, the general makes it clear which women he perceives to belong to the nation and which ones do not. Women who belong to the nation are the ones who are at home, protected by their families, and not protesting against the state with male protestors. Samira Ibrahim, and many other women with her that day, understood that this violence that is cloaked under the guise of familial (national) honor is intended for her to regret demanding her existence in public space and life and her defiance to the nationalist patriarchal constructions of ideal Egyptian

---

[1] For more on women's inclusion and participation in the revolution during the first 18 days, see Naib (2011), Prince (2014), Soueif (2012), and Naber and Hameed (2016).

womanhood that demand that she stay home (Seikaly, 2013). Ibrahim, instead of shouldering the shame of the sexual violence she experienced as the state had planned she would, sued the military for rape. While she lost her case in a military tribunal that acquitted El-Mogy of rape in March 2012, she was victorious in December 2011 when civilian court judge ruled that "virginity tests" are illegal (Seikaly, 2013, lines 54–56). Ibrahim's resistance to state tactics of fear and violence by suing the military was commemorated in a number of stencil graffiti around Cairo and Egypt showing her portrait always with a colorful veil and a determined gaze either positioned above a military tank and an army of the medical doctor demonstrating her supremacy over them or with statements such as "You cannot break me" stencilled below.

The violence against women and the criminalization of men both aim at silencing popular dissent against the state by instilling fear in women protestors so that they no longer participate and their families who, in order to protect them, forbid them from taking to the streets. This violence aims also at perpetuating the idea that women need to bargain with the state to provide protection for their safety (Hafez, 2014a). For example, slogans such as "Egypt's daughters are a red line" are used in protests denouncing the violence against Egyptian women use similar familial discourses that position Egyptian women as daughters and Egyptian men as their protectors. This, Hafez contends, continues to uphold national "patriarchal obligations" to protect women who seek the state's protection from men.

While precarious conditions of state-sanctioned and activated violence against women increased, women and women-led groups participated in the rich and diverse ephemera of graffiti and murals that marked the 25 January Revolution. In their engagement, women asserted their active engagement in the revolution, feminist demands to be fully included in public life without harassment, and patriarchal politics of respectability.

This essay takes up the ways this graffiti has gendered the revolution by focusing on Egyptian women protestors' experiences in the revolution, noting that Egyptian women have different realities than those of Egyptian men, thus elucidating gendered differences experiences in public life and demanding systemic change that will ensure unobstructed participation by women. I take these important interventions a step further by suggesting that the graffiti I examine in this essay not only genders the revolution, it also creates visual articulations of alternative future imaginaries of what constitutes Egyptian womanhood and belonging. I take into account the different points of intersection between histories of the women's and nationalist anti-colonial movements, constructions of the ideal Egyptian national womanhood, the ongoing revolution and women's roles in it, gender-based violence, and visual culture production. I looked at hundreds of images of graffiti found in books such as *Walls of Freedom: Street Art of the Egyptian Revolution* by editors Basma Hamdy and Don Karl (2014) and Mia Gröndahl's (2012) photography book, *Revolution Graffiti: Street Art of the New Egypt*, on social media such as

Facebook and Twitter, and across various popular and scholarly publications. After considering images of graffiti created by women and women-led groups, closely reading them through histories of nationalist discourses on ideal Egyptian women's bodies, put together with events that took place at the time of making the graffiti during the 25 January Revolution, I argue that this graffiti is not only part of the revolution, it is also part of longer and complicated movements and histories of decolonization and Egyptian women's movements. Therefore, what I make visible here are the ways these ephemeral works, although constructed in the present, are in conversation with the past in order to fashion the future. By utilizing this form of ephemeral in public spaces as a form of protest, women and women-led groups' graffiti is "dream[ing] and enact[ing] new and better pleasures, other ways of being in the world, and ultimately new world" (Muñoz 1, 2009).

BACKGROUND

Constructions of Egyptian Womanhood: A History

As part of the project against colonialism, nationalists sought to demonstrate that modernity was a cornerstone of an independent state. Kumari Jayawardena (1986) and Partha Chatterjee (2010) argue that to engage in anti-colonial and nationalist movements, colonized states took up Western models of governmental institutions that were created to manage and benefit middle-class citizens in order to fashion their own modernity. In the Egyptian context, this process created a bind for elite nationalists who needed to find ways to be modern while at the same time authentic to the other local Muslim and Arab traditions. This tension made for an increasingly complicated relationship between women's bodies and Egypt's national honor. In her book, *Egypt as a Woman*, Beth Baron (2005) traces Egyptian women's participation in nationalist movements from the early nineteenth century until the 1952 Free Officers' Revolution, which marked Egypt's independence from British colonialism. She illustrates how Egyptian women discussed imperialism, liberation, piety and veiling, marriage, work, and schooling, among other concerns in closed meetings, until they took to the streets in 1919 in what was referred to as the "Ladies Demonstration." Baron argues that at this stage of the movement, elite urban Egyptian women focused on articulating the nation as family: as women, they were wives, mothers, and daughters of the nation and the men as husbands, fathers, and sons of the nation. They also constructed themselves as "mothers of the nation" (Baron, 111–112). Indeed, the symbolism of women as "mother of the nation" enabled Egyptians to create some sense of solidarity regardless of class, ethnicity, and religion. At the same time, it perpetuated familial patriarchal hierarchies of obedience and silence (Baron, 135). Margot Badran (1995) contends that the symbolism of "mothers of the nation" affirmed women's reproductive and domestic roles rather than political ones and extended family honor as embedded within women's bodies and purity to the nation (40). The making of Egyptian women into "mothers of the nation" had its historic roots in the works of Qasim Amin, a modernist who is credited for advocating for women's liberation in Egypt. Lila Abu-Lughod (1998) demonstrates that while Amin and other Egyptian nationalists and modernists spoke of women's rights, including education and work, they mostly promoted modern bourgeois family ideals (256). This continued symbolism of "mother as nation" modified gender roles; in particular for those of elite women, it did not fundamentally challenge them (Baron, 1601).

Cathlyn Mariscotti argues in her book, *Gender and Class in the Egyptian Women's Movement, 1925–1939* (2008), that much of the scholarship written on the Egyptian women's movement in anti-colonial and nationalist movements focuses on narratives that are positivist and neo-orientalist (1–2). She contends that these narratives focus on upper-class women as most needing liberation because they were secluded and veiled, while lower-class women (urban and rural) were not (3). This analysis, Mariscotti argues, results in the use of gender as a tool to analyze elite women's lives, while non-elite women's lives get analyzed through ethnicity and religion (9). In their quest for further access to public life, elite women argued for the removal of the face veil. In order to do this, they made the claim that this form of veiling was antimodern and also unnecessary to prove their Egyptian-ness and commitment to Islam. To support their position, they utilized rural women's unveiled access to public life as a point of reference and argued that these women were Egyptian and Muslim. Many rural Muslim women at the time wore a headscarf when they left their homes but not a face veil. Therefore, elite Egyptian women articulated rural women as "symbols of freedom," thus fashioning themselves as "simultaneous belonging to the Muslim nation (*umma*) and as citizens of a secular nation-state (*watan*)" (Badran 10). Interestingly, the removal of the face veil was not seen as a challenge to Egyptian identity, because rural women had been participating in various social rights unveiled. According to Badran, this highlights an Egyptian feminist discourse whereby peasant women were constructed as "symbols of freedom" for both nation and women (Badran 92), yet perhaps only superficially. In her book, *The Hidden Face of Eve* (2015), Nawal Sa'dāwī argues that working outside the home and removing the veil were struggles of elite and middle-class women, but not those of working-class urban and peasant women whose economic need to earn an income or help work the fields made it impossible for them not to work outside the home, mix with men, and be unveiled (354–355). Sa'dāwī demonstrates that the work of elite feminist Egyptian women did not take into account the needs of working-class women because they were so far removed from the working classes (357). This disconnect resulted not only in a feminist agenda that did not speak to working-class women, it also meant that even though these women participated side by side next to men in the 1919 revolution and were martyred in large numbers, their activism and martyrdom went mostly unrecognized (358).

This complex understanding of Egyptian women's participation and role in anti-colonial and nationalist movements was illustrated through visual representation of Egyptian womanhood. Dina Ramadan (2013) demonstrates that the School of Fine Art was a significant tool to demonstrate that the "presence and appreciation of 'the fine arts' is a marker of a 'civilized nation'" (89). The School was a site where Egyptian national identity was constructed by encouraging students to search for "national art" in rural Egypt and pharaonic art. This resulted in fashioning the rural Egyptian landscape and people as unchanged and pure (106–107). Representations of peasants appeared as "generic type, nameless and iconized" (Radwan, 2017, 14; Kane, 2010, 51–52, Badran, 1995, 68). In these representations the *fallaha* (female farmer) was veiled, a custom more modern and contemporary than ancient (Radwan, 2017, 14; Baron, 2005, 67–68). As described earlier, urban women looked at rural women as free from face covering yet able to go outside. Representations of rural women as veiled reflected an elite male imagination, perhaps even orientalist imagination of rural women. Similarly urban women were represented as the keepers of culture and symbols of the nation. In both cases, Egyptian women, rural and urban, were constructed through patriarchal male imagination as symbols for the nation, its honor and freedom.These histories of feminist movements in Egypt since the early 1900s ground the ways Egyptian women's participation and ways their bodies have been articulated in the 25 January Revolution graffiti. For example, a mural commemorating five Egyptians (one woman and four men) killed in the Revolution in Nasr City shows a woman dressed in the Egyptian flag releasing white pigeons each carrying the name of one female and four male martyrs. By dressing the woman in the Egyptian flag, she becomes a national unifying symbol of a caring mother.

Graffiti and the Revolution

Graffiti in Cairo, like most cities around the world, existed before the 25 January Revolution and its messages were diverse in content and goals. For example, freehand graffiti advertised services such as fencing a garden to circumcisions and announcements of love between two people or the opening of a new hair salon in the neighborhood. Political graffiti could also be seen. "Be with the Revolution"[2] is a stencil first created by Mohamed Gaber, a member of the 6 April Youth Movement that was established to support the 6 April 2008 sit-in by women and children in El Mahalla El-Kubra against low wages and high prices of food (Beinin, 2011). Gaber created this stencil because he felt the labor movement was revolutionary and he was urging Egyptians to be part of this nationwide change. The stencil is both a play on sayings he would see on cars and on the street such as "Be with God" and a desire to reimplant the ideology of the revolution into public consciousness (El-Geme'i, 2017, lines 10–11). This is only an example of graffiti and murals (directly political

---

[2] Hossam el-Hamalawy' Flicker account. Uploaded on 27 January 2012. https://www.flickr.com/photos/elhamalawy/6774570489/. Retrieved 16 February 2018

and otherwise) before the 25 January Revolution that in many ways ground the graffiti in the revolution.[3]

Graffiti and murals were part of the 25 January Revolution from the start. Images of "Down with Hosni Mubarak" and "Leave" sprayed on various surfaces across Cairo were circulating on the news and social media platforms as the protestors gathered and marched toward downtown. Numerous scholars, journalists, and bloggers wrote about the graffiti of the revolution from different perspectives (Batrawy, 2012; Boraïe, 2012; De Ruiter, 2015; and Morayef's *Suzee in the City* blog, n.d.). Perhaps the most detailed and extensive writings are those of scholar Mona Abaza who demonstrates the significance of these ephemera in documenting, chronicling, and engaging with the revolution.[4] Ahdaf Soueif writes in her introduction to *Walls of Freedom: Street Art of the Egyptian Revolution* (2013), "The streets of the revolution were our world; and the street art of the revolution expressed and celebrated our world. It blossomed on the walls, speaking for us and to us, a miraculous manifestation of the creative energy of the revolution had released across the country" (5). Soueif writes that graffiti and murals of the revolution expressed demonstrators' "feelings ... thoughts and impulses, articulated, transmuted, and given form" to the collective of Egyptians who took to the streets since 2011 (5).

WOMEN'S VISUAL CULTURE AND REVOLUTION: NOON EL-NESWA

Egyptian women and women-led groups engaged with and responded to gender-based violence and exclusion by marking the walls with their own messages documenting the violence, suggesting ways of resistance, and thus opening up space for alternative futures. Noon El-Neswa, a collective that includes women and men whose goal is to focus on Egyptian women's issues, began a graffiti campaign named *Graffiti Harimi* (Women's Graffiti) on 9 March 2012. The campaign's goals were for women to reclaim public space and to feel they belong in them (Fecteau, 2012).

This campaign started with stenciling iconic Egyptian women singers and actresses from the 1950s and 1960s such as singer Umm Kulthum, as well as contemporary iconic women such as leader Widad Al-Demerdash who led the women's labor protests in El-Mahalla El-Kubra on 6 April 2008. Noon el-Neswa members El-Mosher and Diaa Elsayed stenciled an image of actress

---

[3] To read more about graffiti and murals before the 25 January Revolution, I suggest the following readings: Hamdy, Basma and Don Karl (editors), 2014. *Walls of Freedom: Street Art of the Egyptian Revolution*. Berlin: From Here to Fame Publishing; Parker, Ann and Avon Neal, 1995. *Hajj Paintings: Folk Art of the Great Pilgrimage*. Washington: Smithsonian Institution Press; Ayman Hassan (2007). "Murals of Salwa." In Alaa Khalid, Mohab Nasr, and Salwa Rashad (editors), *Amkena: Concerned with the Poetic of Places*. No 8. June 2007, 121–128, p. 125; and Donovan, Leonie and Kim McCorquodale (editors), 2000. *Egyptian Art: Principles and Themes in Wall Scenes*. Ministry of Culture, Foreign Cultural Relations, Egypt.

[4] For more on Abaza's writings on the revolution, see Abaza (2012a, 2012b, and 2014).

Suad Hosni[5] with the caption *El-bint zai el-walad* (A girl is like a boy)[6] in various locations across downtown Cairo. The statement, *El-bint zai el-walad*, comes from the song "Girls" from the television series *Tales of Him and Her*, directed by Yehia El-Alami in 1985. The television series focuses on the relationship and issues between Egyptian men and women. The song focuses on the importance and various characteristics of girls, such as being gentle and kind and focused on serving their country, among other descriptions that make them specific just as boys are. In bringing to the forefront shared Egyptian experiences and repurposing an iconic and well-respected Egyptian woman actress' statement that girls are just like boys, Noon El-Neswa reminds Egyptians of an ideology expressed and admired a number of years before. This in turn suggests that the notion that women are the same as men is not a new or strange idea; rather it is one that has been in their consciousness for nearly 30 years. By connecting the past to the present, Noon El-Neswa highlights a time in the near past where unveiled women who sang, danced, and acted were respected and admired members of the Egyptian nation and were, in many ways, ideal Egyptian women.

By using representations of Suad Hosni—and other iconic female stars such as singer Umm Kulthum and actress Faten Hamamah—in their stencils, Noon El-Neswa evoke a rich history of Egyptian cultural production that highlights Egyptian women's role in resisting patriarchy and dominant gender roles. In their essay, "Golden age divas on the silver screen: Challenging or conforming to dominant gender norms?" Abdel-Fadil and Van Eynde (2016) argue that Suad Hosni's cinematic roles "convey complex messages of gender and class relations" (18) and are a "challenge to the rigid class and gender systems" (22). Zeinab Nour, in her essay "Reflections of Feminism in Contemporary Mural Painting between Occidental and Oriental Societies" (2017), contextualizes Suad Hosni's stencil with others of "powerful Egyptian women alongside text advocating for women's equality" (11) within histories of women's struggle in Egypt and a way for Egyptians to respond to and engage with women's concerns (10). Nour also argues that the Suad Hosni stencil aims at "reminding the whole society that a woman could be strong and great just like a man, raising the value of women in the eyes of society" in general not only at specific political happenings (11). Invoking historical and culturally significant and widely identifiable strong women icons brings debates that challenged patriarchy, gender, and class expectations to the present where they are utilized to demand similar actions, and in turn envision a future where patriarchy and rigid gender and class expectations are deconstructed to create a reality where girls are like boys.

---

[5] Suad Hosni's name is spelled in multiple ways in English: Suad, Souad, or Soad, and Hosni is sometimes spelled Hosny. I followed the most frequent spelling of the name.

[6] An image of this graffiti can be found online in various websites; here it is on the Nazra Twitter account (@NazraEgypt): https://twitter.com/nazraegypt/status/178075817786621953.

In their stencil *matsanifnish* (Do Not Classify Me),[7] painted in various parts of the city, including Mohamed Mahmoud Street in Downtown Cairo, Noon El-Neswa brought a feminist future to the forefront of the revolution by demanding that women not be classified, categorized, sorted, or ranked based on their external appearance, in particular representations of religiosity of veiling or unveiling. The stencil shows portrait silhouettes of three women showing only their heads: the one on the right has shoulder length hair, the middle one is wearing a veil that covers her hair and neck, and the one on the left is wearing a niqab covering her hair and face with her eyes showing. Underneath the silhouetted stencils was the caption, *matsanifnish. Tasnif* in Arabic has multiple meanings including classification and sorting and putting into a type. Put another way, there is an assumption that a veiled woman is decent, a woman (Muslim, Christian, or anything else) whose hair is loose is indecent, and a woman wearing a niqab is presumed to be too religious (Nour, 2017). In her essay, "Cinematic Representations of the Changing Gender Relations in Today's Cairo," Dalia Said Mostafa (2009) argues that women find it no longer possible to follow strict traditions. Therefore, unlike stereotypical perceptions that veiled women are "obedient, shy and helpless," veiled Egyptian women "lead demonstrations ... student protests inside universities, ... sleep overnight at their factories, along with men, when they are on strike" (6).

It is important to note that a number of Muslim women in Egypt wear a veil in part to satisfy this performative assumption of morality in order to avoid harassment. In her documentary film, *Mamnou'* (Forbidden), Amal Ramsis (2011) considers the term *forbidden* and explores the different ways it is used as a way to stop individuals and groups from doing something without clear reasons or formal documents that the thing is actually illegal or inappropriate. For example, filming on the streets of Cairo is often stopped by police, shop owners, and others because it is forbidden, but it is unclear who forbids it or why. Ramsis also interrogates the different ways forbidden is used to stop women from doing certain things, such as visit friends and extended family members alone or seek certain types of employment, just because it is obscurely objectionable. In their interviews Egyptian women from diverse backgrounds explain that they opt to wear the veil so that they challenge what is forbidden and ease their family members' feelings that they are safe from male advances and harassment, and therefore are more able to leave their homes. This reasoning to veil demonstrates how veiling is not always a symbol of religiosity; rather sometimes it is a tool to challenge gender norms and allow for certain access to public space and civic engagement.

The stencil also conjures and challenges colonial anthropological categorizations of types, whereby anthropologists aiding colonizers sorted Indigenous peoples into clearly marked categories that flattened Indigenous communities'

[7] An image of this graffiti can be found online in various websites; here is an example on Soraya Morayef's blog, Suzee in the City: https://suzeeinthecity.files.wordpress.com/2013/01/073-001.jpg.

histories and lives. Edward Said (1978) describes "types" as a "methodologi-cally formative ... analytic device" used by Orientalists to demonstrate what they analyzed as "ontological difference" between mentalities and that these "types" continue to endure because of "similar kinds of abstractions" (259–260). By spraying three women's busts side by side and adding a demand not to be categorized, the stencil requires readers to question contemporary and historic structures that fashion Egyptian women into three distinct types: unveiled, veiled, and wearing a niqab. The stencil, therefore, protests oriental-ist, colonialist, and contemporary codifications and demands from its readers to contemplate their processes of constructing Egyptian women through nar-ratives of religiosity. In doing so, the stencil critiques the idea that displays of piety can be used as an indicator to classify women's adherence to faith and morals and in turn women's respectability.

Through public visual ephemera, the works of Noon El-Neswa were able to engage and respond to happenings of the revolution, while simultaneously connecting the past to the present in ways that challenge hegemonic and nor-mative articulations of who is and what constitutes an Egyptian woman. In doing so it opened up space to experiment and rework various imaginaries of Egyptian women accessing public space safely and to belong within difference.

The Fight Against Violence to Imagine a Future Free of Violence

As the revolution and protestors' demands to end state tyranny continued, state violence against protestors escalated. With this intensification, women protestors experienced a unique form of gender-based violence in the form of mass harassment and rape while they participated in demonstrations. In 2013, Mira Shihadeh and El-Zeft's *Circle of Hell* (Fig. 28.1) depicted the mass rape and assault some women protestors experienced during protests. Shihadeh is a Palestinian artist and yoga instructor who lived in Cairo since 1999 and began engaging with graffiti in the Egyptian Revolution as a result of feeling frus-trated. El-Zeft is a pseudonym for a Cairene artist who joined the revolution after watching videos of the police torturing Egyptians (Cairo Scene, 2015, lines 5–6). *Circles of Hell* became the name for the large circles that were cre-ated by men around women in protests that facilitated the assault on women. There were three circles: the first closest to the woman, stripped her and attacked her, the second pretended to come closer to rescue the victim but once they got closer they also participated in the assault, and the third circle distracted others from what was happening (Patry, 2013; Lindsey, 2016). A joint report, "Egypt keeping women out," by the International Federation for Human Rights (FIDH), Nazra for Feminist Studies, New Women Foundation, and Uprising of Women in the Arab World in 2014 states: "Between 3 and 7 July 2013, more than 85 cases of sexual assault, including several cases of rape, were perpetrated by mobs in and around Tahrir Square" (3). The report

Fig. 28.1 Mira Shihadeh and El-Zeft, Circle of Hell, 2011, paint. Mansour Street, Cairo, Egypt. (Copyright by artists, photograph credit: alma aamiry-khasawnih, 2013)

includes statistics from the UN Women's survey of April 2013 that "99.3% of Egyptian women reported having been sexually harassed, with 91% saying they feel insecure in the street as a result" (4). Nazra's "Position Paper on Sexual Violence and Rape" (2013) states that cases of mass rape of women protestors have gone disregarded by official and unofficial political parties, thus creating "general state of denial and collusion" (6). "Circle of Hell," a collaboration between Shihadeh and El-Zeft, was painted on a buffer-concrete wall built in Mansour Street off Mohamed Mahmoud Street and a few meters east of Midan El-Tahrir in Downtown Cairo. This buffer-concrete wall is one of several such walls that were built by state agents to separate Midan El-Tahrir from other parts of the downtown area and squeeze protestors in a specific area, thus creating a war zone (Abaza, 2013). The concrete walls were built from one ton cubes and put one on top of the other, thus making it impossible for people to walk through the street. The mural's central figure of this work is a woman who is trapped in a sea of preying men. The features of her face are soft, the eyes big with long lashes, her cheeks a little pink, her lips are red. Her hair is short and curly. The woman is surrounded by the faces of a large number of men whose eyes hold devious and dangerous looks all focused on the middle of the mass, their mouths slightly open with sharp teeth showing, their tongues protruding out with what looks like remains of blood around the lips. The sea of men's prying eyes continues into the horizon where three Egyptian flags fly above what looks like a demonstration. In the mass of men's heads there is a single woman whose eyes are defenselessly looking above, her eyebrows slanted downward, her lips are red and her mouth closed, her face is framed with black short curls. The single female face within a crowd of men draws attention to the middle of the image, where the action is. Speech bubbles surround the encirclement. They read (from right to left): "She wants it this way," "I am tired, what am I supposed to do?!", "Don't worry, we are coming to help you," "Honestly, tasty girl," "Can't you see what she is wearing?", "But this is not my sister!", and "I am free, man!". *Free* here means that he is unrestrained to do as he pleases. And *tired* in an earlier bubble means horny, too sexually frustrated to control one's self. The speech bubbles speak to a number of concerns women face as they engage in public life and activism. For example, statements that argue that the woman brought this violence onto herself because of what she was wearing are examples of patriarchal victim blaming discourses that are found across the world (Hastings, 2002; Al Ali, 2014; Carr, 2018).[8] These speech bubble statements highlighted hegemonic and unattainable politics of respectability whereby women are losing regardless of what they do and wear or where they go. The speech bubbles that focused on women's clothing suggest that if the woman was wearing something different she would not be subjected to sexual violence. This sentiment made women wear more conservative clothing when they are in public in the hope that they would be seen as more respectable and pious, therefore deserving to be protected and spared from harassment. Yet, as described above, most Egyptian women's experiences demonstrate that they experience sexual harassment.

In addition to putting the burden of respectability onto women, the speech bubble, "But this is not my sister!", also brought to the forefront concerns about respectability by suggesting that a respectable woman would have patriarchal protection with her, someone who identifies her as his sister or family member, and therefore making the woman respectable and honorable. This patriarchal logic is the same one that justifies the assault on women protestors at the International Women's Day protest in 2012 where they were arrested and subjected to virginity tests (see above for details). It is also the same nationalist logic described earlier whereby Egyptian women were constructed as modern citizens through familial structures of mothers and daughters. These logics make it such that respectable Egyptian women can only be respectable if they fit an imagined (unattainable and unreal) image of a mother, daughter, and sister. But clearly, women who are harassed are someone's mother, daughter, and sister, yet the lack of male chaperone makes women's presence in public vulnerable to harassment because there is no patriarch to claim her as respectable. Harassment, including sexual harassment, played a central role in the ways the Egyptian state and histories of nationalist movements control

[8] The issue of rape victim blaming has been addressed in various feminist perspectives in journals around war violence, interpersonal relationship violence, slut shaming, and others. The suggested citations are only a small selection of scholarly works that address this issue from a transnational feminist perspective.

political participation of women by inciting fear into them and deterring them from participating in the revolution, which they did to some degree. Yet in response to the discourse of patriarchal protection and to challenge it, graffiti writers continued to engage in conversation not only by documenting happenings, but also by contributing to a movement demanding the end of gender-based violence at all levels of public and political lives.

This movement is one that rejects the reproduction of Arab patriarchy that Sherine Hafez (2012) argues is reproduced through "construction of femininity and masculinity through idioms of honor and shame" (40) and what Deepti Misri (2011) refers to as the "disciplining power of shame" that women are expected to feel when they are victims of sexual and gender-based violence (603). This shame is employed by the state to create obedient and docile subjects that results in both pacifying women and giving the patriarchal state power. Yet, the moment women refuse this shame the "administrative masculinity falls apart" (Misri 607). An example of this refusal is the graffiti created by Mira Shihadeh in June 2012 in Ismail Mohamed Street in Zamalek, Cairo, of a woman using a spray can to disperse a group of men (drawn as stick figures) with the text "No to harassment" under it and then reproduced a number of times in various locations in Downtown Cairo.

This frustration took Shihadeh to the walls again, where she painted another graffiti of a curvy woman, posing with her right arm positioned on her right hip in defiance, her left leg forward balancing her body. Her left arm is extended and holding a can of spray paint. She is wearing a vibrant red short dress with short sleeves that comes just above her knees, with a black long sleeve shirt and black tights under the dress, red and black shoes with straps and high heels, and red lipstick. In this edition, the figure is wearing a red and black veil with a flamingo-like flower on the side. Her eyes look straight at the viewer with a piercing gaze. In her left arm there is a red color can, which is spraying eight stick figures away with its powerful force. The text between the figure and the flying figures reads "No to harassment."[9] The woman's figure looks powerful and unwavering. Her stance and action state that she is here to stay. Her small spray can produce the pressure of a fire hydrant. This freehand graffiti tells us first and foremost that women are capable, powerful, and assertive as demonstrated by the composition of the graffiti and the powerful action the woman is taking to defend herself.

Another example that engages women as actively defending themselves are a series of stencils demonstrating different techniques of self-defense using local Egyptian vernacular and humor that began appearing on walls across Downtown Cairo. One stencil is a silhouette of a woman with long hair in trousers kicking a man in the groin as he doubles over. The stencil has the caption "To the one who calls you a pony, kick him. Stop harassment." The

[9] An image of this graffiti can be found online in various websites; here is an example on Soraya Morayef's blog, Suzee in the City: https://suzeeinthecity.files.wordpress.com/2013/01/sidi-henesh-047-001.jpg.

colloquial Egyptian text uses the word *farasah*, a female horse. Often these self-defense stencils are accompanied by another stencil of a silhouette of a tight tank top over larger breasts, a short skirt, with the belly button showing with the caption "whatever shows or does not show, my body is free and cannot be humiliated." These stencils are often sprayed as a series and first appeared on the lower part of Mohamed Mahmoud Street on the walls of the private technology and start-up hub the GrEEK Campus.[10] The location of these stencils is significant because not only did Mohamed Mahmoud Street witness intense violence against protestors from the SCAF, it also was site of some of the most brutal sexual harassment and rape incidents. Hend Kheera's "Touching is forbidden. Castration awaits you!"[11] is a stencil of a woman with long hair, wearing a shirt, trousers, and high heels. The figure is standing with the knee bent, a hand on the hip and another on her face making her hip protrude up and her upper part shift left, thus making her stance seem more provocative and defensive. These series of stencils challenge victim blaming narratives and patriarchal narratives that women are helpless and in need of male protection.

In her stencil, "Rebel Cat,"[12] created by Bahia Shehab in 2013, is another example of refusing obedience. In this project, Shehab's cat is an "attempt to feminize the act of rebellion" (Shehab 1, 2016).[13] The stencil is of a cat sitting up, with her face facing the viewer and her tail hanging and curled beside her. The cat has a halo behind her head reminiscent of religious paintings. The cats are stenciled in a series next to each other, accompanied with another stencil that reads: "Rebel oh cat." "Rebel" here is not a noun, but a directive verb inviting the cat to engage in rebellion. The use of the cat in the project connects the call for women to rebel to the Pharaonic past when cats were respected and admired creatures often treated highly by ancient Egyptians. The work is also a play on cat-calling. By calling women to rebel, Shehab disorients the cat-calling from its context of harassment and reorients it toward an act of calling women to resist and participate in rebellion, thus energizing women to defy cat-calling and the idea that women are responsible for this violence. Instead, Shehab encourages women to disobey systems of violence that perpetuate the cat-calling and sexual violence. Shehab's stencils, perhaps in some cases subliminally, make clear that violence against women is not an individual concern or is only relevant to women.

[10] The current technology grounds of the GrEEK Campus are rented from the American University in Cairo who obtained the property in the early 1960s. Greek refers to the Greek schools that were in this area in the early 1900s.

[11] An image of this graffiti can be found online in various websites; here is an example on Soraya Morayef's blog, Suzee in the City: https://suzeeinthecity.files.wordpress.com/2013/01/graffiti-zamalek-downtown-maadi-073-1.jpg.

[12] To see an example of this graffiti, visit Bahia Shehab's website: https://www.bahiashehab.com/graffiti/rebel-cat.

[13] Shehab, Bahia. 2016. "Translating Emotions: Graffiti as a Tool for Change." In *Translating Dissent: Voices from and with the Egyptian Revolution*, edited by Mona Baker, 163–177. New York; London: Routledge, Taylor & Francis Group

These graffiti examples depict women as standing up against harassment without feeling shame, being blamed for the violence, and needing to refer to familial honor discourses or state protection from sexual harassment. They portray women actively defying shame and deconstructing gendered expectations of docility and obedience. These works therefore open up a possibility to imagine a different future whereby women are not bound to shame-ridden femininity (Misri, 607) or bargaining with a patriarchal state for their protection (Hafez, 2012), but as active, independent, and empowered women in their own right.

Conclusion

Graffiti is so powerful. There can be so many interpretations. It's a great way to start a dialogue. -Merna Thomas, Noon El-Neswa co-founder (Fecteau, 2012, line 61)

The graffiti works discussed here describe the ways women and women-led groups took to the walls to engage with the 25 January Revolution not only as active participants in it, but also as a way of highlighting Egyptian women's unique experiences in the revolution, challenging patriarchal state-sanctioned violence against women, where women are active in defending themselves against this violence without patriarchal protection, and opening up space to imagine a future where women are not categorized based on preconceived notions of religiosity and respectability. Therefore, these ephemeral works are of the moment and are keeping pace with the developments of the revolution. These ephemera were created within hours of the violent incidents that instigated them. They are a gendered narrative and archive of the revolution. They are a testament to women's role in the revolution, as well as the systemic violence that women face and have been facing for many years. Through these ephemera writers and creators illustrate their resiliency against patriarchal hegemony and determination to keep the issue of violence against women in the public domain.

In addition to all the above and what I have argued here is that these ephemeral visual productions are doing more: they are creating openings where different and alternative futures for Egyptian women (and Egyptians generally) are dreamed, articulated, visualized, and imagined today in order to be seen and lived in the future. In connecting the past to the present, a future is made clearer. By reading for acts of active, disobedient, and shamelessness in the graffiti, we see a future free of patriarchal expectations of acceptable Egyptian womanhood as embodiments of national and familial honor and respectability. Only in reading the graffiti further, beyond what it is and what it tells us about the present, are we able to gain insight into the future.

REFERENCES

Abaza, M. (2012a, March 10). *An Emerging Memorial Space? In Praise of Mohammed Mahmud Street.* Jadaliyya. http://www.jadaliyya.com/pages/index/4625/an-emerging-memorial-space-in-praise-of-mohammed-m

Abaza, M. (2012b, June 12). *The Revolution's Barometer.* Jadaliyya. http://www.jadaliyya.com/Details/26220/The-Revolution%60s-Barometer

Abaza, M. (2013). Walls, Segregating Downtown Cairo and the Mohammed Mahmud Street Graffiti. *Theory, Culture and Society, 30*(1), 122–139.

Abaza, M. (2014). Gender Representation in Graffiti Post-25 January. In M. H. Dal (Ed.), *Cairo: Images of Transition. Perspectives on Visuality in Egypt 2011–2013* (pp. 248–255). Columbia University Press.

Abdel-Fadil, M., & Van Eynde, K. (2016). Golden Age Divas on the Silver Screen: Challenging or Conforming to Dominant Gender Norms? *Journal of African Cinemas, 8*(1), 11–27.

Abouelnaga, S. (2016). *Women in Revolutionary Egypt: Gender and the New Geographics of Identity.* American University in Cairo Press.

Abu-Lughod, L. (Ed.). (1998). *Remaking Women: Feminism and Modernity in the Middle East.* Princeton University Press.

Al Ali, N. (2014). Reflections on (counter)Revolutionary Processes in Egypt. *Feminist Review, 106,* 122–128.

Amar, P. (2011). Turning the Gendered Politics of the Security State Inside Out? Charging the Police with Sexual Harassment in Egypt. *International Feminist Journal of Politics, 13*(3), 299–328.

Amin, S. (2011, May 31). *Egyptian General Admits 'Virginity Checks' Conducted on Protesters.* CNN. http://www.cnn.com/2011/WORLD/meast/05/30/egypt.virginity.tests/

Badran, M. (1995). *Feminists, Islam, and Nation: Gender and the Making of Modern Egypt.* Princeton University Press.

Baron, B. (2005). *Egypt as a Woman: Nationalism, Gender, and Politics.* University of California Press.

Batrawy, A. (2012, January 28). *Egyptians Move to Reclaim Streets Through Graffiti.* The San Diego Union-Tribune. https://www.sandiegouniontribune.com/sdut-egyptians-move-to-reclaim-streets-through-graffiti-2012jan28-story.html.

Beinin, J. (2011). Workers and Egypt's January 25 Revolution. *International Labor and Working-Class History, 80,* 189–196.

Boraïe, S. (Ed.). (2012). *Wall Talk: Graffiti of the Egyptian Revolution.* Zeitouna Publishing.

Cairo Scene. (2015, March 20). *Egypt's Forgotten Graffiti and the Revolution that Came from Zeft.* Cairo Scene. https://cairoscene.com/ArtsAndCulture/El-Zeft-Revolution.

Carr, J. L. (2018). The SlutWalk Movement: A Study in Transnational Feminist Activism. *Journal of Feminist Scholarship, 4*(Spring), 24–38.

Chatterjee, P. (2010). *Empire and Nation: Selected Essays.* Columbia University Press.

De Ruiter, A. (2015). Imaging Egypt's Political Transition in (Post-)revolutionary Street Art: On the Interrelations Between Social Media and Graffiti as Media of Communication. *Media, Culture and Society, 37*(4), 581–601.

Donovan, L., & McCorquodale, K. (Eds.). (2000). *Egyptian Art: Principles and Themes in Wall Scenes.* Ministry of Culture, Foreign Cultural Relations.

El-Geme'i, R. (2017, January 22). *Masrawi in Dialogue with Graffiti Designer of "Be with the Revolution" on the Sixth Anniversary of "January"* [The Article Is in Arabic]. Masrawy. https://www.masrawy.com/news/news_various/details/2017/1/22/1017205/%D9%85%D8%B5%D8%B1%D8%A7%D9%88%D9%8A-%D9%8A%D8%AD%D8%A7%D9%88%D8%B1-%D9%85%D8%B5%D9%85%D9%85-%D8%AC%D8%B1%D8%A7%D9%81%D9%8A%D8%AA%D9%8A-%D9%83%D9%86-%D9%85%D8%B9-%D8%A7%D9%84%D8%AB%D9%88%D8%B1%D8%A9-%D9%81%D9%8A-%D8%A7%D9%84%D8%B0%D9%83%D8%B1%D9%89-%D8%A7%D9%84%D8%AE%D8%A7%D9%85%D8%B3%D8%A9-%D9%84%D9%80-%D9%8A%D9%86%D8%A7%D9%8A%D8%B1-

Fecteau, A. (2012, March 10). A Graffiti Campaign Brings Strong Female Voices to the Streets. *Egyptian Independent.* https://ww.egyptindependent.com/graffiti-campaign-brings-strong-female-voices-streets/

FIDH et al. (2014). *Egypt: Keeping Women Out: Sexual Violence Against Women in the Public Sphere.* FIDH. https://www.fidh.org/IMG/pdf/egypt_sexual_violence_uk-webfinal.pdf

Gröndahl, M. (2012). *Revolution Graffiti: Street Art of the New Egypt.* American University in Cairo Press.

Hafez, Sherine. (2012). "No longer a bargain: Women, masculinity, and the Egyptian uprising." *American Ethnologist. 39*(1), 37–42.

Hafez, S. (2014a). Bodies That Protest: The Girl in the Blue Bra, Sexuality, and State Violence in Revolutionary Egypt. *Signs, 40*(1), 20–28.

Hafez, S. (2014b). The Revolution Will Not Pass Through Women's Bodies: Egypt, Uprising and Gender Politics. *The Journal of North African Studies, 19*(2), 172–185.

Hamdy, B., & Karl, D. (Eds.). (2014). *Walls of Freedom: Street Art of the Egyptian Revolution.* From Here to Fame Publishing.

Hassan, A. (2007, June). Murals of Salwa. In A. Khalid et al (Eds.). *Amkena: Concerned with the Poetic of Places.* No 8 (p. 125).

Hastings, J. A. (2002). Silencing State-Sponsored Rape in and Beyond a Transnational Guatemalan Community. *Violence Against Women, 8*(10), 1153–1181.

Jayawardena, K. (1986). *Feminism and Nationalism in the Third World.* Zed Books.

Kane, P. (2010). Egyptian Art Institutions and Art Education from 1908 to 1951. *The Journal of Aesthetic Education, 44*(3), 43–68.

Lindsey. (2016, January 24). *Feminist Street Art Sparked by the Egyptian Revolution. Things Worth Describing: Exploring Beautify Through Observation.* http://thingsworthde-scribing.com/2016/01/24/feminist-street-art-sparked-by-the-egyptian-revolution

Mariscotti, C. (2008). *Gender and Class in the Egyptian Women's Movement, 1925–1939: Changing Perspectives. Middle East Studies beyond Dominant Paradigms.* Syracuse University Press.

Mikdashi, M. (2013, January 28). *The Gendered Body Pubic: Egypt, Sexual Violence and Revolution.* Jadaliyya. http://www.jadaliyya.com/pages/index/9826/the-gendered-body-public_egypt-sexual-violence-and.

Misri, D. (2011). "Are You a Man?": Performing Naked Protest in India. *Signs: Journal of Women in Culture and Society, 36*(3), 603–625.

Mohsen, H. (2012, March 16). *What Made Her Go There? Samira Ibrahim and Egypt's Virginity Test Trial.* Al-Jazeera. http://www.aljazeera.com/indepth/opinion/2012/03/2012316133129201850.html

Morayef, S. (n.d.) *Suzee in the City.* http://suzeeinthecity.wordpress.com

Mostafa, D. (2009). Cinematic Representations of the Changing Gender Relations in Today's Cairo. *Arab Studies Quarterly, 31*(3), 1–19.

Muñoz, J. (2009). *Cruising Utopia: The Then and There of Queer Futurity.* New York University Press.

Naber, N., & Hameed, D. (2016). Attacks on Feminists in Egypt: The Militarization of Public Space and Accountable Solidarity. *Feminist Studies, 42*(2), 520–527.

Naib, F. (2011, February 19). *Women of the Revolution.* Al Jazeera. http://www. aljazeera.com/indepth/features/2011/02/2011217134411934738.html.

Nazra for Feminist Studies. (2013, February 4). *Position Paper on Sexual Violence Against Women and the Increasing Frequency of Gang Rape in Tahrir Square and its Environs.* Nazra for Feminist Studies. http://nazra.org/en/2013/02/position-paper-sexual-violence-against-women-and-increasing-frequency-gang-rape-tahrir

Nour, Z. (2017). Reflections of Feminism in Contemporary Mural Painting Between Occidental and Oriental Societies. *The Academic Research Community Publication,* 1(1), The Academic Research Community Publication, 2017-09-18, 1(1).

Parker, A., & Neal, A. (1995). *Hajj Paintings: Folk Art of the Great Pilgrimage.* Smithsonian Institution Press.

Patry, M. (2013, May 15). *Egyptian Artists Declare War on Sexual Harassment.* Index on Censorship. http://www.indexoncensorship.org/2013/05/egyptian-artists-declare-war-on-sexual-harassment/

Prince, M. (2014). *Revolution Is My Name: An Egyptian Woman's Diary from Eighteen Days in Tahrir,* translated by Samia Mehrez. American University in Cairo Press.

Radwan, N. (2017). Between Diana and Isis: Egypt's 'Renaissance' and the Neo-Pharaonic Style (1920s–1930s). In M. Volait, & E. Perrin (Eds.). *Dialogues Artistiques avec les Passés de l'Égypte: Une Perspective Transnationale et Transmédiale* (pp. 1–18). InVisu (CNRS-INHA) ("Actes de colloques").

Ramadan, D. (2013). *The Aesthetics of the Modern: Art, Education, and Taste in Egypt 1903-1952.* [Doctoral dissertation, Columbia University].

Ramsis, A. (Dir.). (2011). *Forbidden.* Egypt/Spain: Morgana Producciones. Film.

Sa'dāwī, N. (2015). *The Hidden Face of Eve: Women in the Arab World.* 3rd ed. Translated by Sharīf Ḥatātah. Zed Books.

Said, E. (1978). *Orientalism* (25th Anniversary Ed.). Vintage Books.

Seikaly, S. (2013, January 8). *The Meaning of Revolution: On Samira Ibrahim.* Jadaliyya. http://www.jadaliyya.com/pages/index/9814/the-meaning-of-revolution_on-samira-ibrahim

Soueif, A. (2012). *Cairo: My City, Our Revolution.* Bloomsbury.

PART VI

Gender and Entrepreneurship

What do we know about women, gender, and entrepreneurship in MENA? What are the opportunities and constraints women encounter in pursuing their entrepreneurial ambitions? How do advances in communication technologies facilitate or complicate women's ventures? While these questions are beginning to receive greater scholarly and policy attention, existing scholarship does not allow us to answer all of them because disciplinary divisions are impacting the research focus and methods. For instance, most entrepreneurship researchers are less interested in gender issues or feminist epistemologies when they focus on the marketing and business aspects of entrepreneurship. On the other hand, those who focus on women entrepreneurs do not necessarily examine the linkages between *entrepreneuring*, gender, and information/communication technologies. The chapters in this part of the handbook seek to fill precisely these gaps by examining ways in which digital technologies are engendering the business *as well as* the social dimensions of entrepreneurship in the contexts of Bahrain, Lebanon, United Arab Emirates, Jordan, and so on.

Existing literature on women and entrepreneurship in MENA falls within one of the following broad areas: entrepreneurial ecosystem, distinguishing character(istics) of the entrepreneur, and broad institutional arrangements that shape and inform women entrepreneurship in comparison to their male counterparts. Almost all governments across MENA have adopted the World Bank's "smart economics" (2012) approach to advancing women's business investments and entrepreneurship as a strategy to modernizing the region's economies. Yet, the same institutions that (discursively) encourage women to be entrepreneurs also inhibit their ventures given the entrenched gender biases, restrictive gender roles and expectations, and pervasive patriarchal ideologies (Khan, 2019; Manzoor, 2019).

The second area of research focuses on the individual entrepreneur, her educational attainment and competencies, leadership traits, and socioeconomic status as predictors of success. While many studies underscore such broad characteristics as resilience, innovation, and perseverance, others point to the impact of Islamic principles and work ethics on the entrepreneur's choices and decisions. In this context, researchers reveal through in-depth interviews with women entrepreneurs how Islamic texts and teachings act as both a source of inspiration and resilience to overcome challenge. Muslim women, it is shown, seek to achieve excellence (*itqan*) in the running of their businesses through good and hard work (*amal salih*), honesty and truthfulness (*sidik and amanah*), fairness and justice (*haqq and adl*), and benevolence (*ihsaan*) (Tlaiss, 2015; Tlaiss & McAdam, 2020).

Finally, an emerging area of research seeks to assess the connections between women's entrepreneurship and forms of empowerment. While the jury is still out on this issue, existing insights indicate that empowerment opportunities are likely to increase with advances in and greater access to digital technologies (McAdam & Harrison, 2019). The assumption here is that technologies would not only expand women's opportunities for developing "digital entrepreneurship" but will also help them overcome the institutional barriers that hinder their entrepreneurial ambitions and ventures (McAdam et al., 2020).

The chapters in this part build on some of these insights but explore other unaddressed issues in the contexts of Bahrain, Lebanon, Jordan, Kuwait, and the United Arab Emirates. Lynn Mounzer provides an overview of the gender entrepreneurship landscape in MENA while assessing the opportunities and limitations of information communication technologies (ICTs) in this sector. Mounzer focuses on UAE and Lebanon to draw attention to significant contradictions taking place in these and other countries in MENA. The region is home to one of the highest gender entrepreneurship gaps in the world, yet, it is also the region where access to and adoption of digital technologies is increasing at a dizzying speed. Again, while digital technologies can be powerful tools to overcome cultural barriers in restrictive environments, the region still records one of the highest gender digital gaps in the world. Until we resolve these contradictions, the region will fail to capitalize on women's entrepreneurial capabilities and the promises of ICTs.

Willow Williamson's chapter gives Jordanian and Kuwaiti women entrepreneurs a voice to define their own understanding of digital entrepreneurship and empowerment within the context of their own realities. Drawing on feminist methodology in data collection and analysis, Williamson reflects on the institutional definitions of women's entrepreneurship and economic development to situate these within the broader neoliberal policies embraced by international and national actors. She then juxtaposes this analysis to women's own unique experiences with gender and digital entrepreneurship. Doing so allows Williamson to demonstrate how women problematize the gender dimension of entrepreneurship, technologies, and empowerment in ways that escape official discourses and expectations.

Loubna Skalli's chapter engages with the social dimension of women's entrepreneurship in MENA. Specifically, the chapter focuses on the entrepreneurial trajectory and accomplishments of the Bahraini native, Esra'a Al Shafei, to examine the under-researched world of women's social entrepreneurship and the mobilization of digital technologies to engineer social change in repressive regimes. Interviews with Al Shafei between 2008 and 2020 and analysis of her *Majal.com*, along with the numerous digital initiatives she launched since 2006, provide a basis for examining the emergence of new entrepreneurial possibilities and disruptive social innovation in the age of digital technologies. Al Shafei's work, according to Skalli, complicates our understanding of social entrepreneurship as it intersects with gender and digital technologies in authoritarian contexts.

Taken together, the chapters in this part point to the many gaps in our understanding of how gender, entrepreneurship, and ICTs intersect. They also invite us to broaden the subject of our inquiry to understand what forms of empowerment this intersection allows and what spaces of exclusion it creates.

REFERENCES

Bastian, B. L., Beverly D. M., & Reza Zali, M. (2019). Gender Inequality: Entrepreneurship Development in the MENA Region. *Sustainability*, 11(22), 6472.

Khan, M. A. I. A. A. (2019). Dynamics Encouraging Women Towards Embracing Entrepreneurship: Case Study of Mena Countries, *International Journal of Gender and Entrepreneurship, 11*(4), 379–389.

Manzoor, A. (2019). Womenpreneurs in MENA Region. In *Gender and Diversity: Concepts, Methodologies, Tools, and Applications* (pp. 1144–1158). IGI Global.

McAdam, M., Crowley, C., & Harrison, R. (2019). "To Boldly Go Where No [Man] Has Gone Before" - Institutional Voids and the Development of Women's Digital Entrepreneurship. *Technological Forecasting and Social Change, 146,* 912–922.

McAdam, M., Crowley, C., & Harrison, R. (2020). Digital Girl: Cyberfeminism and the Emancipatory Potential of Digital Entrepreneurship in Emerging Economies. *Small Business Economics, 55*(2), 349–362.

Tlaiss, H. A. (2015). How Islamic Business Ethics Impact Women Entrepreneurs: Insights from Four Arab Middle Eastern Countries. *Journal of Business Ethics, 129,* 859–877.

Tlaiss, H., & McAdam, M. (2020). Unexpected Lives: The Intersection of Islam and Arab Women's Entrepreneurship. *Journal of Business Ethics, 171*(2), 253–272.

World Bank. (2012). *World Development Report: Gender Equality and Development.* https://openknowledge.worldbank.org/handle/10986/4391

CHAPTER 29

ICT Impact on Female Entrepreneurs in Lebanon and UAE

Lynn Mounzer

ICTs and Entrepreneurship in the MENA Region

Information and communications technologies (ICTs) encompass the combination of different types of communications networks and technologies, including the internet, wireless networks, cell phones, and other communication media (OECD, 2017; Ratheeswari, 2018). Globally, ICTs have transformed societies in fundamental ways, from politics and financial systems to social connections giving marginalized sections of societies—especially women—opportunities to achieve greater equality. In 2018, the share of female-led technology startups in the Middle East and North Africa (MENA) was more than double the global rate—35 percent compared to 10 percent globally (Middle East Exchange, 2018). Through technology, women in MENA are able to disrupt the old ways of doing business, create access to markets, and start or grow a business through technology.

However, despite similarities within the region, countries are distinct because of differences in cultures, resources, and varying levels of access to technology. While some countries in the region are global ICT leaders, others lag significantly behind. For instance, Yemen has the second slowest broadband globally, while the UAE has the fastest mobile network in the world (Radcliffe, 2021).

L. Mounzer (✉)
Wilson Center, Washington, DC, USA

Hokouki, Washington, DC, USA

In recent years, the region has drastically increased its connection with the rest of the world through digitization, greater internet accessibility, and higher levels of social media usage. In early 2020, the number of internet users in the region was more than 180 million and internet penetration was 67.2 percent, higher than the world average of 56.8 percent (Internet World Stats, 2020). Bahrain, Kuwait, and Oman reached nationwide mobile broadband coverage (Arezki et al., 2018). The growth of ICTs, especially mobile phones, across the MENA region provided an easy and vital communication medium.

Until recently, the exponential growth of digital consumption in the MENA region did not translate into an increase in digital entrepreneurship. The decline in oil prices hurt economies across the region and governments responded by encouraging small and medium enterprises (SMEs) to contribute to overall economic diversification and development. Ironically, the decline in oil prices and the high percentage of youth unemployment have created a fertile ground for innovation. Two-thirds of the MENA population is under the age of 35 (Bjerde, 2020) and the rates of unemployment among youth is over 26 percent (World Bank, 2020). However, this is a tech-savvy generation that uses technologies to create opportunities for themselves. This young population is now visibly concentrated in tech startup sector (Alkasmi et al., 2018).

Digital business activities started in 2010 in the region and have placed MENA among the top three fastest-growing regions in e-commerce (Fabre et al., 2019). This growth is evident in the increasing number of tech companies that went from 20 in 2000 to several thousand in 2020. Tech companies are improving the region's entrepreneurial ecosystem and providing employment opportunities. In 2017, 16 MENA-based startups alone created a total of 7816 jobs (Boustani et al., 2017). Despite this, many countries struggle with various restrictions, including slow internet speed, poor connectivity, inadequate network access and readiness, and state-owned or state-controlled telecom that reduce competition (Boustani et al., 2017).

This chapter focuses on the state of women entrepreneurship and ICTs in two countries: Lebanon and the United Arab Emirates (UAE). These countries provide examples of the broad conditions affecting ICTs and women's entrepreneurship in the Middle East. According to the 2020 Network Readiness Index (NRI), the UAE ranked 30 globally and is number one regionally, while Lebanon ranked 90 globally and second to last in the Middle East, followed by Yemen. The World Economic Forum's NRI ranks 134 economies based on their performance across 60 variables, measuring the propensity for countries to exploit the opportunities offered by ICTs (Dutta & Lanvin, 2020). The distinct economic, social, and technological structures between Lebanon and UAE provide an excellent comparison for discussing different realities of women's entrepreneurship and ICT.

ICTs and Women Entrepreneurs in the MENA Region

The MENA region has one of the highest rates of internet penetration globally. However, the digital gender gap is the largest worldwide (Raz, 2020). Around 23 million women in MENA are unconnected (Rowntree, 2020) and the number of male internet users is still higher than that of females, 61 percent to 47 percent (ITU, 2020a, b). Women are 9 percent less likely than men to own a mobile phone compared to -1 percent for women in Europe (Clement, 2020). This inequality is costly to society and the economy. It limits women's access to essential services, employment, participation in the digital economy, and access to information safely. For instance, the economic gender gap in the region remains one of the largest in the world, where female labor force participation is only 20 percent (World Bank, 2021).

It is misleading to overgeneralize the condition of women entrepreneurs across the MENA region, especially since the countries have different economic structures, social norms, and institutional characteristics. Women around the region face different barriers and opportunities to economic participation despite such common barriers as cultural norms, lack of access to finance, and unsupportive environment. They also face gender-based obstacles like lack of access or control over capital and access to information, technology, and networking. A recent study based on interviews with women entrepreneurs in MENA concluded that 60 percent of women in Egypt, 50 percent in Palestine, 50 percent in Oman, and 42 percent in UAE mentioned lacking access to loans and finance (Mounzer, 2020).

Despite this, nearly 25 percent of new startups in MENA over the past three years were led by women compared to 17 percent in the US (Digital Boom, 2019). In 2018, women-led businesses in the region were worth US$385 billion (Kesisoglu, 2018). Women in the region managed to overcome societal pressure, the digital gap, and structural disadvantages and leverage the internet to start or grow their businesses. In 2020, one in three tech startups in the region was owned by women (Digital Boom, 2019). The internet is helping women overcome physical barriers, while digital platforms liberate them from cultural constraints and safety concerns since they limit mobility cost, childcare, and social censure (Kteily & Ommundsen, 2018).

Technology, however, will not eradicate constraining social norms or discrimination from which women typically suffer. Research shows that MENA women entrepreneurs face numerous challenges including basic ICT training, language barriers, and e-payment literacy. They also face the risks that come with being online. For example, as e-business owners, women have to disclose personal information, which is likely to impact their privacy and subject them to discriminatory practices, especially in conservative societies like MENA (Michota, 2013).

The COVID-19 pandemic has further complicated the status of women and women entrepreneurs since it magnified the digital gap caused by gender inequity. The online shift in the private and public sectors abandoned women consumers and entrepreneurs who have little to no access to technology. The pandemic has also reinforced restrictive social norms and traditional family roles. Women face unequal allocation of unpaid care and domestic responsibilities, caring for the sick, the children, and the elderly of the family. This leaves them with no time or energy for work on their businesses. Finally, women who lack digital literacy and proper internet infrastructure were completely left out (Campbell & Khamis, 2020).

WOMEN ENTREPRENEURS IN LEBANON AND THE UNITED ARAB EMIRATES

Case of Lebanon: Lebanese Economy and ICTs

In 2013, the Lebanese central bank, Banque du Liban (BdL), issued Circular 331 designed to foster a knowledge-based economy (KBE) and provide fresh funding for the startup ecosystem. This introduced new digital services and increased the number of innovative startups from around 55 to above 250 companies. In 2020, most ICT companies in Lebanon were SMEs in the digital economy, employing about 6 to 50 people. The ICT sector in Lebanon is highly export-oriented, mainly to the MENA region (70 percent) and specifically to the Gulf Cooperation Council (GCC) countries (55 percent) (IDAL, 2020). Before 2019, the Lebanese ICT sector witnessed considerable development due to the modernization of enterprises, expansion in broadband capacity, and increase in the number of the skilled tech-savvy labor force.

However, Lebanon's ICT sector still suffers from weak infrastructure and expensive mobile services. According to the Global Innovation Index (GII), out of 129 countries examined, Lebanon ranked 87 in 2020, dropping six places since 2017. The GII ranks the world's countries and economies across innovational measures, environments, and outputs (Cornell University, INSEAD, & WIPO, 2019). In 2020, the infrastructure—including ICT access and use, online government services, and e-participation—dropped 9 points, from 91 in 2019 to 100 in 2020 (Cornell University, INSEAD, & WIPO, 2019).

Internet penetration reached 94 percent in 2019 (IDAL, 2020) and the number of internet users increased from 61 percent in 2013 to 78 percent in 2019 (World Bank, 2019). Although the internet penetration is high, connectivity is uneven (World Bank j, 2020). Yet, the percentage of internet usage is similar among gender—88 percent each (Raz, 2020). The country has a high number of state-owned telecom incumbents. As a result of this monopoly, consumers pay high prices for unreliable, low-quality services (Boustani et al., 2017). The deterioration of Lebanese internet infrastructure is making the country unable to compete globally or even regionally. Lebanon has one of the lowest average internet speeds in the world, ranking 167 out of 192 countries—lower than Iraq, a war-torn country in the region (Fast Metrics, 2020).

According to the NRI 2020, Lebanon lacks online government service, ICT regulations, cybersecurity, and secured internet servers (Dutta & Lanvin, 2020).

Although the Lebanese government promised to improve the telecom infrastructure by adding new landlines and fiber optic networks, the pandemic and the compound economic and financial crises halted any development (De Rosbo, 2020). In October 2019, the country faced a financial crisis brought about by a sudden freeze in capital inflows, which severely impacted the banking sector and the exchange rate. In August 2020, the Port of Beirut was destroyed by a massive explosion, creating more economic and structural damage. Economic hyperinflation negatively impacted the capacity of the telecom sector to provide fast and reliable networks, postponing the progress towards expanding 5G wireless internet.

WOMEN IN BUSINESS IN LEBANON

Reforms to the education system in Lebanon failed to eliminate traditional gender stereotypes prevalent in school curricula. In 2020, Lebanon's education rank dropped ten grades, from 113 in 2019 to 123 in 2020 (Cornell University, INSEAD, & WIPO, 2019). This led the Lebanese market to be highly concentrated in skilled workers but lacking in technical specialists, especially among women. This lack of gender-sensitive career guidance does not present women with the right information and knowledge (Avis, 2017) and has created skill gaps among women transitioning from employment to entrepreneurship (Andraos et al., 2019).

Although Lebanon has one of the highest densities of established business owners, women consist of only 15 percent of business owners compared to 42 percent of men (Badre & Yaacoub, 2011). Recently, Lebanon's global rank drastically dropped in numerous categories, including the ease of starting business. The ease of doing business rank examines 12 areas in a country, including starting a business, registering property, getting credit, paying taxes, enforcing contracts and regulations on employing workers, and contracting with the government (World Bank, 2020). Out of 190 countries, Lebanon ranked 133 in 2018 and 143 in 2020. Lebanon is also among the 50 most corrupt countries in the world. Business owners encounter bribery, uncontrolled bureaucracy, random licensing, high taxes, slow internet speeds, poor electricity provision, and inadequate protection of intellectual property (International Trade Administration, 2020).

Lebanon has a free-market economy, a highly educated labor force, and limited restrictions on investors (International Trade Administration, 2020). Legally, women and men have the same rights to access markets, endure the same number of procedures, and pay the exact amount to register a business. Hence, Lebanese women do not face legal discrimination in setting up a business, acquiring a loan, or owning property (World Bank, 2020). Lebanese law does not discriminate based on gender in setting up a business, obtaining a loan, or owning property.

Lebanon lacks consistent and dependable policies, which negatively affects both economic growth and political stability. Women entrepreneurs face a hindering legal environment that does not enforce sexual harassment laws and social security (Andraos et al., 2019). In 2009, the Lebanese government made it easier to register a business but increased the cost of starting a business in 2011 (Dib & Ghaziri, 2018).

Lebanese women are not explicitly prevented from opening businesses legally, but structurally they have more considerable obstacles and less help. Limited access to physical and financial assets and lack of collateral directly affect women's decision to become entrepreneurs (World Bank g, 2020). Given the complexity and cost of business registration, Lebanese women entrepreneurs are likely to stay in the informal sector (Dib & Ghaziri, 2018), rely on their personal savings and investment from family and friends, and more likely to reinvest existing profit to finance their businesses (CAWTAR, 2008).

Lebanon is actively encouraging the growth of the entrepreneurship ecosystem. New initiatives and programs are launched to combat gender inequality and promote gender inclusivity in the entrepreneurial ecosystem through funding, training, and incubating (Boustani et al., 2017). In the last couple of years, the government sought to improve the situation of the Lebanese women entrepreneur by encouraging new local and international initiatives like the Women Entrepreneurs Finance Initiative project "e-Commerce and Women-Led SMEs in Lebanon." These initiatives aimed at helping women entrepreneurs access global and national markets through e-commerce platforms (World Bank b, 2019) and BLC Bank Women Empowerment Initiative connected women entrepreneurs and provided SME Toolkit (McCartney et al., 2016).

Lebanese women entrepreneurs also benefitted from new initiatives that were set to support women's economic empowerment and improve their access to finance. For instance, Lebanon Investment in Microfinance Program gave 6000 loans (42.9 percent) to women-owned businesses totaling $11 million (Dailey, 2015). According to UN ESCWA, the overall access to venture capital financing for Lebanese startups has increased over the past years, 0.4 points, from 2.7 in 2012 to 3.1 in 2016 (Boustani et al., 2017).

While the Lebanese law gives women entrepreneurs the same rights as men to register a business, open a bank account, and sign a contract, it does not prohibit gender-based discrimination by creditors (World Bank g, 2020), primarily evident among smaller enterprises. SMEs in Lebanon account for 97 percent of all enterprises and 30 percent are solely owned by women. These women-led SMEs receive only a tiny fraction of all bank loans, 3 percent (Andraos et al., 2019). Therefore, they rely on micro-loans which can be damaging. These loans are short-term with quick repayment and meant to increase poor women's economic participation through entrepreneurship. However, they do not motivate growth; instead, they lead women entrepreneurs towards informal industries that do not stand a chance of surviving any shock (Abdo & Kerbage, 2012).

Women in Lebanon are at a great disadvantage in access to capital. The Lebanese Labor Law mentions equal wage between gender (Avis, 2017), but the gender-based pay gap is 6 percent or higher depending on the sector (Badre & Yaacoub, 2011). Additionally, the personal status laws limit the distribution of inheritance (property and capital), making it difficult for women to obtain needed collateral for financing. The persistence of gender discrimination in the labor market and society poses continued obstacle for women to access finance.

On the other hand, the unstable market and political environment in Lebanon create a halting ecosystem for women. The low growth affects women specifically since the Lebanese society favors men for the few available jobs (World Bank g, 2020). According to the World Bank, women's economic participation in Iraq, Jordan, and Lebanon report, 40 percent of Lebanese entrepreneurs considered women less committed to their work because of their household and caregiving responsibilities (World Bank g, 2020). Society downplays women's abilities and discourages them from achieving their business and entrepreneurial ambitions. A 2012 study in Saida, the third-largest city in Lebanon, found that people reinforce traditional gender stereotypes, suggesting that women are better in communication and caregiving jobs (Andraos et al., 2019). These gender stereotypes limit women's entrepreneurial ventures, creating doubt in women's capacities and affecting women's confidence in themselves and in their businesses.

ICTs and Women Entrepreneurship in Lebanon

Firms with female-majority ownership in Lebanon are only 5.3 percent compared to 94.7 percent male-owned firms (Crotti et al., 2019). The World Economic Forum Gender Gap report 2020 ranked Lebanon among the highest gender gaps globally (145 out of 153 countries) and in MENA region (14 out of 19).

Recent reports underline that digital platforms are acting as salvation for Lebanon since they create more job opportunities and offer women flexibility and balance (World Bank g, 2020). For instance, the *Social Media, Employment and Entrepreneurship* report found that 90 percent of participants in Lebanon considered social media an essential tool for startups. This optimism encouraged Lebanese women to use social networks (Facebook and Instagram) to connect with other entrepreneurs, reach customers, sell their products, and minimize the time and cost risks (Mourtada & Salem, 2012). Lebanese women embraced the new technology, which offered them the opportunity to become entrepreneurs, access new markets, and reduce their business operating costs (CAWTAR, 2008). Women capitalized on their "traditional" skills to start e-commerce and retail businesses (Maier & Nair-Reichert, 2008). During the hyperinflation and high unemployment rate in 2020–2021 in Lebanon, women stepped up, got creative, and started home-based businesses to support their families. One of my interviewees is a business owner who left her banking job after a significant salary drop to start a low-end jewelry business. She supported her two kids and husband—who was laid off—during rough times.

Additionally, the ease of use of digital communications like WhatsApp made it easy for women to start or expand their businesses, especially in rural areas. A recent study found that Lebanese women's adoption of digital social networks (Facebook and WhatsApp) has given women the ability to start a business within the social constraints imposed on them. They concluded that through these micro-online enterprises, women were able to supplement the family income during the challenging economic situation that Lebanon keeps facing (Farquhar et al., 2021).

Overall, gender plays an important role in the credibility and validation of women's business entrepreneurship in Lebanon. The masculine society in Lebanon grants men access to technology-related training and doubts that women can be tech-savvy (Muturi, 2006). The conservative social norms think less of women's business and consider it an attempt rather than a legitimate business (Samara & Terzian, 2021). Consequently, women find it difficult to break the barriers of technology learning and adoption. Without the skills to use the technologies, women remain on the lowest levels of the economic ladder (Maier & Nair-Reichert, 2008).

In addition, women are twice more likely than men to experience cyberbullying, which restricts their use of the internet and social networks for business (Mourtada & Salem, 2012; Maier & Nair-Reichert, 2008). They also face other digital threats, like hacking and data privacy violations, especially since women in Lebanon have smaller businesses and cannot afford to use advanced digital security measures (Aidis et al., 2020).

Case of United Arab Emirates Economy and ICTs

The UAE is an example of rapid growth and development in the region, especially in infrastructure and shift to the knowledge economy (Das et al., 2015). It is not only one of the most important economic centers but also the wealthiest country in the MENA region on a per capita basis (DFAT, 2021). The UAE is also the global leader in ICT usage and skills which places it at 10th place out of 134 countries (GEM, 2018).

The UAE government is very active in adopting, investing in, and promoting emerging technologies. In 2006, UAE passed an act to ensure universal access to ICTs, improved its legal framework, and created a personal data handling and privacy assurance legal framework in 2007 (Al Mazrouei & Krotov, 2016). They also started new initiatives to unlock digital transformation, such as Abu Dhabi Economic Vision 2030. In 2020, the UAE ranked 34 among 131 economies in the GII and among the top 3 innovation economies in Northern Africa and Western Asia. The country's strength was mostly in ICT access and use, and general infrastructure, government's online service, and electricity output (Bayona et al., 2020). Currently, UAE has the largest technology business park in the Middle East, the Dubai Internet City (DIC).

Since 2015, the government has focused on improving its technology and innovation sector to diversify its income and economy and break its oil dependency. The initiatives were designed to unlock digital transformation and improve the tech entrepreneurship ecosystem (Rashed Alzahmi, 2020). Currently, UAE has the majority of the region startups and the highest number of startup headquarters (35 percent) (Wamda, 2020; Hallak, 2019). More than half of the established businesses in 2018 in the UAE are using new technologies with a market share of 26.8 percent (GEM, 2018). As of January 2020, the UAE had 99 percent internet penetration and 9.73 million internet users (31 percent female) out of 9.83 million total population. Plus, 92 percent of the population has a mobile phone—one of the highest rates of mobile phone adoption and usage in the world—and 66 percent have a computer (Kemp, 2020). The major gap the UAE faces is the lack of ICT governance and regulation, as well as production of digital content (Dutta & Lanvin, 2020).

ICTs and Women in Business in UAE

Literacy rates among women in UAE increased from 92 percent in 2015 to 95.8 percent in 2020 (Our World in Data, 2015). In 2018, around 70–80 percent of computer science and IT students in UAE were women, compared to 15–20 percent in the US (Alhashmi, 2018). Emirati women are motivated and confident about starting a business (Erogul & Goby, 2011) which is why numerous private and public sector initiatives were conceived—like the Khalifa Fund and Womena. These initiatives are encouraging women entrepreneurship by filling the skills and capital access gaps (Shams, 2020).

However, the high number of educated women is not reflected in the participation of Emirati women in the labor force which remains one of the lowest globally (Crotti et al., 2019). Just like Lebanon, UAE has a vast gap between the academic and the business world, in terms of skills. Traditional gender roles continue to push women either to find a stable governmental job or to start a family.

Since 2019, the UAE government has introduced reforms and implemented initiatives to drive equality in business and increase the number of women's economic participation. Some of the reforms include paid parental leave, imposing criminal penalties on sexual harassment in the workplace, removing job restrictions for women in specific sectors, mandating equal pay for work of equal value, and prohibiting gender-based discrimination in employment (Abousleiman, 2021). UAE is ranked one of the best countries in the region in the Global Gender Gap Index—which measures the extent of gender-based gaps in economic participation, educational attainment, health, and political empowerment (GEM, 2018).

Although UAE is ranked 16 globally in ease of doing business and number 1 in the MENA region, Emirati women face numerous difficulties in becoming entrepreneurs. Unlike their counterparts in Lebanon, it is laborious for Emirati women to register their businesses. They are required to complete more procedures and spend more time than their male counterparts to legally start and operate a company (World Bank b, 2020). Additionally, Emirati women have to pay higher cost for business registration than men entrepreneurs (IFC, 2007).

The UAE government recently committed to driving gender equality and helping female entrepreneurs succeed. In 2017, the government deposited USD 50 million into a fund for women entrepreneurs hoping to fill in the gap in access to fund (Sadaqat, 2021). Since the governmental decision, the number of women entrepreneurs in the UAE started growing whereby 33 percent of women-led companies in 2017 generated a revenue of more than $100,000 (UPS, 2019).

Yet, Emirati women founders make up only 2.8 percent of all business owners. They still suffer from lack of access to early-stage funding due to gender biases and lack of experience and collaterals. They also face discrimination in the financial sector. Financial institutes do not have confidence in women entrepreneurs' products and business ideas, which make them less likely to offer them loans. Additionally, women pay higher interest rates than men and are required to nominate a male member of the family as a guarantor (Tahir, 2017). Just like Lebanese women, they also rely on their savings, borrowing from their family and friends and reinvesting businesses' earnings in order to start a business (Erogul & Goby, 2011; Das et al., 2015). This makes it difficult for women entrepreneurs to maintain or grow their businesses.

Despite this, Emirati women continue to defy the cultural norms by starting their businesses. In 2015, almost half of the SMEs (48 percent) in UAE were owned by women (Das et al., 2015). Plus, there is a growing number of public and private initiatives in UAE that aim to connect Emirati women entrepreneurs to mentors and provide them with opportunities to reach global markets, like the Dubai Women Establishment and SheTrades (Condamine, 2020).

ICTs and Women Entrepreneurship in UAE

The diffusion and adoption of ICTs in the UAE is a game changer, especially for women. Although ICTs are changing the lives of Emirati women by giving them access to numerous educational resources and professional opportunities, it is not changing the gender-specific barriers to business creation and development that women entrepreneurs face. Institutions and organizations still act as barriers to women entrepreneurship.

The UAE government started several initiatives to improve the tech entrepreneurship ecosystem by increasing the number of entrepreneurs and driving innovation (Rashed Alzahmi, 2020). In 2014, Emirati women made up 35 percent of tech entrepreneurs, compared with a global average of 10 percent (Bin Byat & Sultan, 2014). Various dynamics explain this. First, since the cost of starting a business in UAE is high, more women are shifting to online businesses to cut costs (Raza & Tahir, 2020). For instance, e-commerce shops are less expensive to start than an actual physical store. Second, women running online businesses are less likely to be affected by the traditional economic structures that discriminate based on gender. Online businesses prevent conflict between women and their families, especially when compared to working outside of their homes (Boey et al., 2020).

On the other hand, the availability of training and easy access to information, traditionally limited to men, is reducing the knowledge gap between Emirati women and the market and is contributing to women's market intelligence (Ben Moussa & Seraphim, 2017). The internet gave women a platform to acquire and develop their skills and achieve self-satisfaction (Ben Moussa & Seraphim, 2017). Similar to Lebanese women, Emirati women entrepreneurs are using digital social networks to network and engage with like-minded people, which helps them gain support, grow their skills, and eventually, succeed as business owners.

Finally, the UAE government effectively introduced several initiatives and laws to empower women and protect women online. The UAE government policies play a crucial role in promoting women's entrepreneurship. Notably, the existing strict penalties for online criminals and high cybersecurity provide a safe space for women to start an online business (Oxford Business Group, 2017). Plus, the number of incubators and accelerators providing support and mentorship for women entrepreneurs in the UAE has increased drastically in the last years (Bin Byat & Sultan, 2014).

Nonetheless, numerous challenges continue to restrain women from achieving their full potential as business entrepreneurs. The tribal traditions and patriarchal family represent the strongest institutional order in UAE which posit gender inequality and limit women's economic participation. Society views women as caregivers and men as breadwinners whilst working women and business owners are looked at with disapproval since men should be the only provider (Al Mazrouei & Krotov, 2016). The Islamic culture is segregating between genders in all parts of life, limiting women's entrepreneurship and growth (Shakir et al., 2010).

These cultural norms are also reflected in ICTs. Despite the small gap in internet usage rates between gender, 86 percent men to 83 percent women (Khokhar, 2017), Emirati women do not have online freedom. Instead, they face strict social and family control over what, when, how, and how much. Besides, the family structure compels women to delegate tasks for men like setting up a business, online transactions, and e-government work. This weakens the state of women's online presence and lessens their digital knowledge (Ben Moussa & Seraphim, 2017).

DISCUSSION AND RECOMMENDATIONS

Growth in the MENA region necessitates advancing the role of women in both society and economy. With the traditional nature of the region and the lack of employment opportunities, entrepreneurship can increase women economic participation. ICTs can give women—especially entrepreneurs—many opportunities for economic advancement by allowing them to sell products in different markets; reducing transaction costs; improving communication, training, and information access; and eliminating the "middleman" (Dutta & Goswami, 2015; Maier & Nair-Reichert, 2008). ICTs also provide women entrepreneurs with flexibility in location and hours (Melhem et al., 2009).

Digital technologies also have the potential to boost business and economic growth. Entrepreneurs need to embrace digital solutions to compete and survive. Encouraging ICTs will offer women entrepreneurs the tools to start and grow businesses. So how can private and public institutes increase women's participation in the ICT sector in the MENA region?

Laws and Regulations

Government policies play an essential role in economic growth. To empower and motivate more women to become entrepreneurs and enter the ICT sector, the governments should enhance regulations by providing exclusive incentives or tax exemptions for women registering, running, or investing in the ICT sector which would encourage Lebanese and Emirati women to start a business in the industry. They should also examine whether exciting laws and regulations allow the creation of an enabling business environment for women entrepreneurs and allow equal access to the internet and information. Further, they should study and understand the obstacles women entrepreneurs face and create policies accordingly. These policies should be gender-sensitive to avoid gender biases. Finally, they should create an entrepreneurship ecosystem that is gender-responsive to include women in its policies, promote women entrepreneurship, and create a supportive culture for women in tech through proper financing and training.

There is an absence of women-focused studies to understand the complex sociocultural barriers that impact women's adoption of ICTs. New policies should regulate ICT usage and protect women online. The Lebanese government should follow the UAE steps and move its operation online, which facilitates business registration and other procedures for women, especially ones living in rural areas.

Access to Funding

According to the Global Findex Database 2017, the MENA region had a high gender gap in account ownership, with only 24 percent in Lebanon and 16 percent in UAE in 2017. This gender gap is slowing financial inclusion, which is an essential factor for women's economic participation. Financial institutions should improve access to funds by closing the financial gap through the use of technology. For instance, India was able to narrow the gap by creating a biometric identification system and a zero-balance account scheme where people can open a bank account with depositing money (Ansar et al., 2018).

Training and Education

Literacy and education are essential determinants of economic development and are vital for social and economic development. The gender gap in literacy rate in the MENA region is declining, where female adult literacy rate is 73 percent compared to 85 percent for males (World Bank c, 2020; World Bank d, 2020). The ratio of women to men enrolled at tertiary level schools in the region is 1.07, which suggests that women outnumber men in tertiary education (d, 2020).

However, there is still a huge gap between women's improved education and their economic participation. Female labor force participation in MENA is declining, around 21 percent in 2016 to 19 percent in 2019 (World Bank b, 2021). Only 43 percent of the gender gap in economic participation and opportunity in the Middle East and North Africa has been closed—the second-lowest region (World Economic Forum, 2019). Women also lack confidence in their capabilities, especially when entering a technology sector dominated by men (Iclaves, 2013). Training and education are essential to eliminate unconscious biases regarding gender and technology. Schools and universities play a significant role in changing this by integrating digital communication and technology into their curriculum.

Furthermore, women entrepreneurs struggle to integrate technology into their businesses due to the lack of information, inadequate infrastructure, and high costs. Institutes and organizations should provide spaces and training that benefit women entrepreneurs and help them raise money or outsource technology. The government should address the digital divide problems by providing the right tools and guidance to push women towards innovative and growing sectors such as technology as mobile apps.

Networking and Mentorship

The traditional culture in the MENA region limits women's mobility and networking efforts. Networks are essential for women entrepreneurship, where they offer them a platform to collaborate, gain information, and develop their skills, ideas, and businesses. Therefore, there should be more initiatives to gather and connect women in the region to help each other grow through different technological platforms, such as social media (LinkedIn) and mobile apps. Additionally, mentorship supports women's development, especially in the digital sector. Mentors guide women and increase their confidence in their products, services, and themselves. Therefore, institutes should provide mentoring programs focused on improving women's skills and abilities not acquired through formal education.

Sociocultural

To change the social perception of women as caregivers which limit women's economic participation in specific sectors, private and public institutions should create campaigns to increase awareness of the importance of ICTs and women's participation in that sector. Increasing the visibility of existing female digital champions will help combat gender stereotypes.

Moreover, ICTs allow women entrepreneurs to work from home. This may slow their growth given the responsibilities that society imposes on women, but at least it will give them a chance to start. They also provide flexibility in mobility, where women do not need to live in the city to get access to suppliers and customers. Women are using social media platforms to sell their products and services to customers all over the globe.

The media plays another vital role by creating campaigns targeted for men to create awareness on the importance of sharing childcare and household responsibilities. Alongside that, the government should include equated maternity pay and tax-free childcare, which will provide women entrepreneurs with more time.

REFERENCES

Abdo, N., & Kerbage, C. (2012). Women's Entrepreneurship Development Initiatives in Lebanon: Micro-Achievements and Macro-Gaps. *Gender and Development, 20*(1), 67–80.

Abousleiman, I. (2021, February 24). *Why Gender Equality Reforms in the Arab World Can Benefit Everyone*. Retrieved from The National: https://amp-thenationalnews-com.cdn.ampproject.org/c/s/amp.thenationalnews.com/business/comment/why-gender-equality-reforms-in-the-arab-world-can-benefit-everyone-1.1171618

Aidis, R., Griffin, L., & Mohiuddin, S. (2020). *Women-Owned Businesses In Cross-Border e-commerce: A Diagnostic Toolkit*. United States Agency for International Development (USAID).

Alhashmi, T. (2018, January 11). *Cracking the Glass Ceiling: Arab Women in Technology*. Retrieved from Arab Gulf State Institute in Washington: https://agsiw.org/arab-women-technology/.

Alkasmi, A. J., El Hamamsy, O., Khoury, L., & Syed, A.-R. (2018). Entrepreneurship in the Middle East and North Africa: How investors can support and enable growth. Digital Mckinsey.

Al Mazrouei, M., & Krotov, V. (2016). Gender-related barriers to e-commerce entrepreneurship: the case of the UAE. *Polish journal of management studies*, 7–17.

Andraos, N., Pendleton, J., Simmons, K., Smith, D., Smith-Lunsford, S., & Spangler, A. (2019). *USAID Lebanon Gender Assessment*. United States Agency for International Development.

Ansar, S., Demirgüç-Kunt, A., Hess, J., Klapper, L., & Singer, D. (2018). *The Global Findex Database 2017: Measuring Financial Inclusion and the Fin-tech Revolution*. The World Bank.

Arezki, R., Mottaghi, L., Barone, A., Yuting Fan, R., Abou Harb, A., Karasapan, O. M., et al. (2018). *A New Economy for the Middle East and North Africa*. World Bank Group.

Avis, W. R. (2017). *Gender Equality and Women's Empowerment in Lebanon*. K4D Helpdesk Report. 175. Institute of Development Studies.

Badre, L., & Yaacoub, N. (2011). *The Labour Market in Lebanon*. Statistics In Focus, Central Administration of Statistic.

Bayona, P., Dutta, S., Garanasvili, A., Lanvin, B., León, L. R., Reynoso, R. E., & Wunsch-Vincent, S. (2020). *The Global Innovation Index 2020: Who Will Finance Innovation?* Cornell University, INSEAD, and the World Intellectual Property Organization.

Ben Moussa, M., & Seraphim, J. (2017). Digital Gender Divides and e-empowerment in the UAE: A Critical Perspective. *International Journal of Education and Development Using Information and Communication Technology*, 145–161.

Bin Byat, A., & Sultan, O. (2014). The United Arab Emirates: Fostering a Unique Innovation Ecosystem for a Knowledge-Based Economy. In S. Dutta, B. Lanvin, & S. Wunsch-Vincent (Eds.), *The Global Innovation Index 2014 The Human Factor in Innovation* (pp. 101–111). Cornell University, INSEAD, and WIPO.

Bjerde, A. (2020, January 13). *Fulfilling the Aspirations of MENA's Youth*. Retrieved from World Bank: https://blogs.worldbank.org/arabvoices/fulfilling-aspirations-menas-youth

Boey, I., Chua Abdullah, S., Kim, M., & Thi Bich Thuy, N. (2020). Female Entrepreneurship in the ICT Sector: Success Factors and Challenges. *Asian Women, 36*(4), 43–72.

Boustani, E., Denner, L., Dimassi, H., Farrell, M., Feller, J., Idlebi, N., et al. (2017). *Enabling Digital Opportunities in the Middle East*. Internet Society.

Campbell, E., & Khamis, S. (2020, September 27). *Info-Deficiency in an Infodemic: The Gender Digital Gap, Arab Women and the COVID-19 Pandemic - Arab Media & Society*. Retrieved from Arab Media Society: https://www.arabmediasociety.com/info-deficiency-in-an-infodemic-the-gender-digital-gap-arab-women-and-the-covid-19-pandemic/

CAWTAR. (2008). *Women Entrepreneurs in the Middle East and North Africa: Characteristics, Contributions and Challenges*. Center of Arab Women for Training and Research.

Clement, J. (2020, January 28). *Internet Usage Rate Worldwide in 2019, by Gender and Region*. Retrieved from Statista: https://www.statista.com/statistics/491387/gender-distribution-of-internet-users-region/

Condamine, J.-F. (2020, May 26). *Middle East Women Entrepreneurs Will Get Their Dues*. Retrieved from Gulf News: https://gulfnews.com/business/analysis/middle-east-women-entrepreneurs-will-get-their-dues-1.71649015.

Cornell University, INSEAD, & WIPO. (2019). *Global Innovation Index 2019*. Cornell University, INSEAD, and WIPO.

Crotti, R., Geiger, T., Ratcheva, V., & Zahidi, S. (2019). *Global Gender Gap Report 2020*. World Economic Forum.

Dailey, J. (2015). *Strengthening Lebanon's Economy by Supporting Women Entrepreneurs*. United States Agency for International Development (USAID).

Das, S. S., Jabeen, F., & Katsioloudes, M. I. (2015). Is Family the Key? Exploring the Motivation and Success Factors of FEMALE EMIRATI ENTREPRENEURS. *International Journal of Entrepreneurship and Small Business*, 375–394.

De Rosbo, S. (2020). *Lebanon - Telecoms, Mobile and Broadband - Statistics and Analyses*. BuddeComm.

DFAT. (2021, January). *United Arab Emirates Country Brief*. Retrieved from Australian Government Department of Foreign Affairs and Trade: https://www.dfat.gov.au/geo/united-arab-emirates/united-arab-emirates-country-brief.

Dib, T., & Ghaziri, H. (2018). *The Future of Entrepreneurial Ecosystem in the Arab Region*. UN ESCWA.

Digital Boom. (2019, August 18). Middle Eastern Female Entrepreneurs Outpacing Other Nations. Retrieved from Digital Boom: https://adigitalboom.com/middle-eastern-female-entrepreneurs-outpacing-other-nations/.

Dutta, S., & Goswami, A. (2015). ICT in Women Entrepreneurial Firms - A Literature Review. *Journal of Business and Management*, 38–41.

Erogul, M. S., & Goby, V. P. (2011). Female entrepreneurship in the United Arab Emirates: Legislative encouragements and cultural constraints. *Women's Studies International Forum*, 329–334.

Dutta, S., & Lanvin, B. (2020). *The Network Readiness Index 2020*. Portulans Institute, WITSA.

Fabre, C., Malauzat, A.-L., Sarkis, C., Dhall, T., & Ghorra, J. (2019, February 19). *E-commerce in MENA: Opportunity Beyond the Hype*. Retrieved from Bain: https://www.bain.com/insights/ecommerce-in-MENA-opportunity-beyond-the-hype/

Farquhar, J., Kachour, M., & Lichy, J. (2021). Entrepreneurship via Social Networks – "Connected Woman" in Lebanon. *Qualitative Market Research, 24*(4), 426–448.

Fast Metrics. (2020). Average Internet Speeds By Country. Retrieved from Fast Metrics: https://www.fastmetrics.com/internet-connection-speed-by-country.php

GEM. (2018). UAE Annual Report. UAEU & Global Entrepreneurship Research Association.

Hallak, J. (2019). *Women in Tech: Social Innovation in MENA*. Engineering for Change.

Iclaves. (2013). *Women Active in the ICT Sector*. European Commission.

IDAL. (2020). *ICT Sector in Lebanon 2020 Factbook*. Investment Development Authority of Lebanon.

IFC. (2007). *Women Business Owners in the United Arab Emirates*. IFC, Center of Arab Women for Training and Research.

International Trade Administration. (2020, September 29). *Lebanon - Country Commercial Guide*. Retrieved from International Trade Administration: https://www.trade.gov/knowledge-product/lebanon-market-entry-strategy

Internet World Stats. (2020, March 31). *Internet Usage in the Middle East*. Retrieved from Internet World Stats: https://www.internetworldstats.com/stats5.htm

ITU. (2020a). *Measuring Digital Development: Facts and Figures 2020*. International Telecommunication Union.

ITU. (2020b). *Measuring Digital Development: Facts and Figures 2020*. International Telecommunication Union ITU.

Kemp, S. (2020, February 18). *Digital 2020: Lebanon*. Retrieved from DataReportal: https://datareportal.com/reports/digital-2020-lebanon

Kesisoglu, A. (2018, October 1). *Unlocking Digital Opportunities Across The MENA Region*. Retrieved from Entrepreneur: https://www.entrepreneur.com/article/320910.

Khokhar, T. (2017, March 8). *Chart: In These Countries, Internet Use Is Higher Among Women than Men*. Retrieved from The World Bank: https://blogs.worldbank.org/opendata/chart-these-countries-internet-use-higher-among-women-men.

Kteily, K., & Ommundsen, K. (2018, July 20). *How Women Entrepreneurs Are Advancing the Arab World's Startup Scene*. Retrieved from ITU: https://news.itu.int/female-entrepreneurs-arab-world/

Maier, S., & Nair-Reichert, U. (2008). Empowering Women Through ICT-Based Business Initiatives: An Overview of Best Practices in E-Commerce/E-Retailing Projects. *MIT Press, 4*(2), 43–60.

McCartney, A., Yamamoto, C., Korayem, M., Ioffe Kasher, O., Joseph, R., Essmat, S., & Tilyayev, U. Y. (2016). *BLC Bank - Lebanon: Leading in Banking on Women - A Study*. IFC.

Melhem, S., Morrell, C., & Tandon, N. (2009). *Information and Communication Technologies for Women's Socioeconomic Empowerment*. The World Bank.

Michota, A. (2013). Digital Security Concerns and Threats Facing Women Entrepreneurs. *Journal of Innovation and Entrepreneurship*, 2–7.

Middle East Exchange. (2018, October 16). *Women Are Driving Change in the Middle East Tech Industry*. Retrieved from Wamda: https://www.wamda.com/2018/10/women-driving-change-middle-east-tech-industry

Mounzer, L. (2020, March 11). *Brief: Female Entrepreneurship in the Middle East and North Africa Region*. Retrieved from GenDev Consulting: https://www.gendev.consulting/blog/brief-female-entrepreneurship-in-the-middle-east-and-north-africa-region-wgxjm-e8p28.

Mourtada, R., & Salem, F. (2012). *Social Media, Employment and Entrepreneurship New Frontiers for the Economic Empowerment of Arab Youth?* Dubai School of Government's Governance and Innovation Program.

Muturi, N. (2006). Gender Empowerment Through ICTs: Potential and Challenges for Women in the Caribbean. *Revista de Estudios para el Desarrollo Social de la Comunicación*, 133–148.

OECD. (2017). *Information and Communication Technology (ICT)*. OECD Publishing. Retrieved from OECD: https://www.oecd-ilibrary.org/science-and-technology/information-and-communication-technology-ict/indicator-group/english_04df17c2-en.

Our World in Data. (2015). *Adult Literacy Rate, Population 15+ Years, Female (%)*. Retrieved from Our World in Data: https://ourworldindata.org/grapher/adult-literacy-female?tab=table

Oxford Business Group. (2017). *The Report: Abu Dhabi 2017*. Oxford Business Group. Retrieved from Oxford Business Group: https://oxfordbusinessgroup.com/overview/smart-cookie-innovative-ict-solutions-are-set-cut-costs-and-transform-government-services.

Radcliffe, D. (2021, October 8). *Technology in the Middle East: 21 Key Stats on the Good, the Bad and the Ugly*. Retrieved from ZDNET: https://www.zdnet.com/article/understanding-middle-east-technology-21-key-stats/

Rashed Alzahmi, S. M. (2020, August 28). *The Role Emirati Women Can (And Should) Play in the UAE's Digital Transformation Strategy*. Retrieved from Entrepreneur: https://www.entrepreneur.com/article/355456

Ratheeswari, K. (2018). Information Communication Technology in Education. *Journal of Applied and Advanced Research, 3(S1):45*, 45–47.

Raza, A., & Tahir, R. (2020). Motivations of the Female Entrepreneurs to Starting Online Businesses in the United Arab Emirates. *International Journal of Innovation and Technology Management*.

Raz, D. (2020, September 25). The Arab World's Digital Divide. Retrieved from Arab Barometer: https://www.arabbarometer.org/2020/09/the-mena-digital-divide/

Rowntree, O. (2020). *The Mobile Gender Gap Report 2020*. GSM Association.

Sadaqat, R. (2021, January 28). *Entrepreneurship: Invest in What Women Bring to the Table*. Retrieved from Khaleej Times: https://www.khaleejtimes.com/business/local/entrepreneurship-invest-in-what-women-bring-to-the-table

Samara, G., & Terzian, J. (2021). Challenges and Opportunities for Digital Entrepreneurship in Developing Countries. In L. Göcke, M. Soltanifar, & M. Hughes (Eds.), *Digital Entrepreneurship* (pp. 283–302). Springer.

Shakir, M., Urquhart, C., & Vodanovich, S. (2010). Same But Different: Understanding Women's Experience of ICT in the UAE. *The Electronic Journal on Information Systems in Developing Countries*.

Shams. (2020, October 8). *Why Should Women Entrepreneurs Consider the UAE To Start a Business?* Retrieved from Shams: https://www.shams.ae/community/blog/81/why-should-women-entrepreneurs-consider-the-uae-to-start-a-business

Tahir, R. (2017). Finding the Path: Female Entrepreneurs in the United Arab Emirates. *2017 ELLTA Conference*. Bangkok.

UPS. (2019). SheTrades MENA report 2019. UPS.

Wamda. (2020). *The State of Pre-Seed Startups in MENA*. Wamda.

World Bank. (2019). *Individuals Using the Internet (% of Population) - Lebanon*. Retrieved from World Bank: https://data.worldbank.org/indicator/IT.NET.USER.ZS?locations=LB

World Bank. (2020). *Doing Business Doing Business 2020*. World Bank.

World Bank. (2021, January 29). *Labor Force Participation Rate, Female (% of Female Population Ages 15+) (Modeled ILO Estimate) - Middle East & North Africa*. Retrieved from World Bank: https://data.worldbank.org/indicator/SL.TLF.CACT.FE.ZS?locations=ZQ&name_desc=false

World Bank b. (2019, September 25). *Revolutionizing Women-Led Businesses in Lebanon Through E-Commerce*. Retrieved from World Bank: https://www.worldbank.org/en/news/feature/2019/09/25/revolutionizing-women-led-businesses-in-lebanon-through-e-commerce

World Bank b. (2020). *Economy Profile of United Arab Emirates - Doing Business 2020 Indicators*. World Bank Publications.

World Bank b. (2021, January 29). *Labor Force, Female (% of Total Labor Force) - Middle East & North Africa*. Retrieved from World Bank: https://data.worldbank.org/indicator/SL.TLF.TOTL.FE.ZS?locations=ZQ

World Bank c. (2020). Population, total - Middle East & North Africa. Retrieved from World Bank: https://data.worldbank.org/indicator/SP.POP.TOTL?locations=ZQ

World Bank d. (2020, September). School enrollment, tertiary (gross), gender parity index (GPI) - Middle East & North Africa. Retrieved from World Bank: https://data.worldbank.org/indicator/SE.ENR.TERT.FM.ZS?locations=ZQ

World Bank g. (2020). *Women's Economic Participation in Iraq, Jordan and Lebanon.* World Bank.

World Bank j. (2020). *Women's Economic Participation in Iraq, Jordan and Lebanon.* World Bank.

World Economic Forum. (2019). *Global Gender Report.* World Economic Forum.

CHAPTER 30

Gender and ICT Entrepreneurship in Jordan and Kuwait

Willow F. Williamson

Introduction

This chapter is about women entrepreneurs in Kuwait and Jordan and their perspectives on what ICT entrepreneurship represents and makes possible. The governments of Jordan and Kuwait both support building an entrepreneurship ecosystem through funding, incubators, and events in order to empower women and encourage youth to rely less on the government sector for jobs. In Jordan, the Ministry of Digital Economy and Entrepreneurship (previously the Ministry of ICT) has a strategy that includes supporting policies to facilitate entrepreneurship, funding a national incubation plan, and working regionally to increase access to markets (Ministry of Digital Economy and Entrepreneurship, 2021). Similarly, Kuwait has a national strategy for "New Kuwait 2035" that embraces the private sector to lead the economy through digitization and provides support for people to start new enterprises. This includes a $7 billion fund for new business enterprises (European Business Review, 2020; Ministry of Foreign Affairs, 2021; State of Kuwait, Ministry of Home Affairs, 2021). The goal of both governments is for their citizens to rely less on government sector jobs. For Jordan, development of the private sector is also key to its

---

This chapter is part of a larger project on entrepreneurship and gender in the GCC and Jordan in a forthcoming book.

W. F. Williamson (✉)
Washington, DC, USA

© The Author(s), under exclusive license to Springer Nature
Switzerland AG 2023
L. H. Skalli, N. Eltantawy (eds.), *The Palgrave Handbook of Gender,
Media and Communication in the Middle East and North Africa*,
https://doi.org/10.1007/978-3-031-11980-4_30

economic development goals as the unemployment rate is at 23%, and women's participation in the workforce is at 14.6% (International Labor Organization, 2021). In Kuwait, the focus is to move away from a reliance on oil, which is 42% of its GDP and 92% of its export revenue (Organization of the Petroleum Exporting Countries, 2021). In addition, one in three Kuwaitis works in the public sector and the government policy is to simultaneously have only Kuwaitis in this sector while also decreasing reliance on public sector jobs (Al Mulia, 2021).

Both governments are pushing ICT entrepreneurship as a way to empower women, youth, and society overall to achieve the goal of increased private sector development. The governments use the concept of entrepreneurship to indicate that they are empowering their populations to create change. However, the concept of change is contained within the boundaries of economic participation as neither government is encouraging political change. In addition, there are some structural factors inhibiting entrepreneurship. There are different models in Kuwait and Jordan to encourage entrepreneurship. Kuwait has a large government fund to invest in entrepreneurs for start-up costs, which some entrepreneurs and investors say provides a safety net for Kuwaiti nationals that is not conducive to promoting a mindset of risk-taking to grow a new business. On the other hand, Jordan relies more on foreign aid to support entrepreneurship, and many entrepreneurs feel that once they do create their businesses they are burdened with high taxes (Hayat, 2016). There are entrepreneurs who say they want to move to Dubai, which they say is more business friendly and secure (Muna, 2016). These examples illustrate that the state and individual communication about and perceptions of entrepreneurship do not always align.

This chapter asks how gender plays a role in ICT entrepreneurship. Specifically, it foregrounds the voices of women entrepreneurs in Kuwait and Jordan. It employs feminist methodology and draws from 29 in-depth interviews with women entrepreneurs and other stakeholders, participant observation of ArabNet in Kuwait in 2016, and visits to incubators in 2016. The study focuses on how ICT entrepreneurship is used as a way to indicate innovation, problem-solving, and change. While some women entrepreneurs said that technology entrepreneurship is a new space with a different mentality from other sectors, other interviewees said that the tech sector is male dominated. While both ICTs and entrepreneurship are concepts that are often assumed to have male characteristics, they can in fact be gendered in a spectrum that features female traits (Adachi & Hisada, 2017, 451). Panel discussants and interviewees frequently said that the concept of entrepreneurship is gendered male because of the risk-taking and innovation it represents. However, some of the women interviewees countered this narrative, stating that in fact entrepreneurship favors female characteristics such as multi-tasking, creativity, and flexibility. For female entrepreneurs, some even viewed ICT entrepreneurship as a gender-neutral space to expand opportunities for women, from launching "pink businesses" to more disruptive models. However, for other interviewees, ICT entrepreneurship reinforced gender norms. Overall, entrepreneurs feel that they are willing to take risks, are open to others, and take initiative to fix a problem or need in society, ranging from social issues to consumer needs.

This piece includes elements from the author's forthcoming book on women's empowerment, entrepreneurship, and US public diplomacy in the Cooperation Council for the Arab States of the Gulf (GCC) and Jordan. First, the chapter provides a contextual framework on the role of gender in ICTs and entrepreneurship to understand what these concepts represent and how state-level and international actors use them to uphold neoliberal economic policies. It then details the methodology and the theoretical framework. The findings focus on the concept of the entrepreneurial mindset and the components that people defined as key to entrepreneurship. The chapter asks how women embrace or push against state goals for entrepreneurship. It asks: How do women entrepreneurs in Kuwait and Jordan understand and put ICT entrepreneurship into practice?

ICT Entrepreneurship and Gender

Governments and international scholars place expectations on women's entrepreneurship to meet state-level goals and policies. However, these definitions may not align with how women understand their own lived experience of entrepreneurship. Critiques of women's empowerment through ICTs and entrepreneurship are concerned with what motivates or facilitates change (Haugh & Talwar, 2016, 647). Debates in the literature center around how social, economic, and political contexts versus enabling factors such as technology or entrepreneurship contribute to meeting development and/or community goals (Hanson, 2008, 7). For example, while existing social movements may create the possibility for change, some credit ICTs and/or entrepreneurship as the starting point for creating change (Schroeder, 2013, 12–14). Still others see social entrepreneurship itself as a form of participation in social change (Hervieux & Voltan, 2018, 290). However, in fact, ICT entrepreneurship may not contribute to change, but instead function to uphold dominant norms and practices (Roberts & Soederberg, 2012, 955–56; Martinez Dy et al., 2017, 295–96). On the one hand, some argue that women's empowerment discourse instrumentalizes women to serve neoliberal economic goals or other political projects (Gurumurthy & Singh, 2009, 4). But, others make the case that ICTs and entrepreneurship have created possibilities for women to bring about individual and societal changes to their benefit (Al-Dajani & Marlow, 2010, 472–73).

Some of the factors that scholars have examined as enablers for entrepreneurship to flourish are policy frameworks (Autio et al., 2014), national culture (Wennberg et al., 2013), social networks (Anderson & Jack, 2002, 194), and the mindset and characteristics of entrepreneurs (Nicolopoulou et al., 2016). The assumption is that supporting entrepreneurship will grow markets and foster competition. These studies also provide normative frameworks for building policy and networks that better support women entrepreneurs, including suggestions for increasing ICT access (Mathew, 2010, 167, 171, 179), and examining underlying educational, employment, and financial factors that act as barriers to women entering the ICT sector (Zineddine & Kindi, 2011). International, national, and private sector actors have showcased both ICTs and entrepreneurship as tools for women's empowerment, which is in turn presented as a solution to alleviating poverty and changing women's status in society (Maier & Nair-Reichert, 2007, 45). However, Al-Dajani and Marlow's study on women migrant entrepreneurs in Jordan provides an example of how women entrepreneurs negotiate rather than disrupt traditional family structures (Al-Dajani & Marlow, 2010).

When scholars and entrepreneurs define ICT entrepreneurship as going beyond meeting economic goals, it is imbued with the power to create change on both an individual and societal level, but this approach can overlook the structural factors that affect the agency of entrepreneurs (Martinez Dy et al., 2018, 7). Estrin stipulates that innovation requires "open-ended exploration" without an agenda from leaders (Estrin, 2008, 37). But, who has access to defining what innovation looks like and what sectors and approaches qualify as innovative? The structural factors that inhibit entrepreneurship, ranging from funding and a lack of bankruptcy laws to societal norms and pressures, also play a role in who can chose to take the risks inherent to starting a business (Maier & Nair-Reichert, 2007, 47).

Therefore, while some illustrate how entrepreneurship creates possibilities for change, there are also constraints in the discourse. A more critical approach analyzes the discourse of entrepreneurship as a process that takes place in a social context (Hjorth & Steyaert, 2004, 1–5). Analysis of women and gender has a long history in development theory and practice and illustrates larger movements in understandings of what it means to include gendered analysis of social, political, and economic contexts. Bruni and his colleagues coined the term "entrepreneur-mentality" in reference to Foucault's "governmentality" to bring attention to the ways in which the concept is created as a site for action (Bruni et al., 2005, 11). An "entrepreneur-mentality" is itself a constructed discourse that both limits and defines what an entrepreneur is and can do. Bruni et al.'s discourse analysis of entrepreneurship situates it in the context of practice and representation to show how it can then constrain agency. Entrepreneurship is often conceptualized as an individualized activity for economic gain, but it is a "socio-politically situated activity," where the relationship between empowerment and entrepreneurship is even linked to gender norms (Al-Dajani & Marlow, 2013, 503). Furthermore, the study of female entrepreneurship creates categories where women are the other and male entrepreneurship is the dominant and thus invisible form of practice (Bruni et al., 2005, 14). In other words, the characteristics of entrepreneurs lead to them extending their activities beyond economic goals and into the family and society in general. Much of the research on female entrepreneurship focuses on essentialized differences between men and women, with large-scale quantitative studies on business performance which assume that female entrepreneurs need to change to fit into mythical male norms of entrepreneurial behavior (Henry et al., 2015, 19). Others suggest that the term "entrepreneur" only allows a discussion about women as individuals, minimizing the importance of larger structures of power, which constrain women's choices (Cornwall & Anyidoho, 2010, 147).

These debates about what ICTs and entrepreneurship represent and make possible have parallels with questions about women's empowerment and what it means in different contexts. Both highlight that discourse can create boundaries around what is considered empowerment or entrepreneurship. These constraints in turn limit the ways in which people think about disrupting social, economic, and political norms. Acknowledging the dynamics of power relationships and motivations behind policy is central to feminist methodology, which fundamentally examines what happens when policy is implemented on the ground. This is addressed by examining empirical evidence of women who are entrepreneurs and/or in the tech fields in Jordan and Kuwait.

Methodology

This study applies a feminist interpretive approach to increase understanding about how women experience entrepreneurship and think about what they can accomplish in Jordan and Kuwait. A feminist approach analyzes power dynamics in how a concept is defined and used (Ackerly & True, 2010, 28). It can also guide the researcher to be attentive to the contestations in how concepts are understood within a broader context of state security and policy making (Tickner, 2006, 21). Feminist scholarship is also engaged with the idea that research can contribute to making changes that improve women's lives and/or the subjects of research (Tickner, 2006, 28). However, gendering the concept of entrepreneurship also means understanding that "individuals can be gendered, but so can institutions, organizations, and even states" (Sjoberg, 2013, 46–47). In other words, gender is not simply about examining women and men, but is also a way to organize power and to understand what is valued and by whom.

The 29 in-depth interviews and participant observation were examined to understand how both entrepreneurs and state-level actors assigned meaning to ICT entrepreneurship in terms of economic and political change and stability. The conference and incubators provided representational data for the ways in which government and non-governmental actors were talking about and supporting entrepreneurship. The ArabNet conference in Kuwait in 2016 was a regional event that brought together speakers for panels on topics ranging from creating regional structures that support tech entrepreneurship, to fostering talent and digital entrepreneurship in government. The incubators were Sirdab Lab in Kuwait and Oasis500 (government and US AID funded) and ZINC (funded by Zain telecom company) in Jordan. These locations were selected as sites of observation and as places to conduct interviews with aspiring entrepreneurs in order to see and discuss how entrepreneurship was understood and being put into practice. The choice to compare Jordan and Kuwait in this chapter was made as they share some key characteristics in terms of their governmental support for entrepreneurship. However, they have different challenges in terms of women's participation in the workforce and access to funding. They also provided a useful comparison to unpack perceptions of state support for women's empowerment through entrepreneurship.

The in-depth semi-structured interviews were all conducted in 2016 with subjects ranging in age from approximately 24 to 55. In 2016 in Jordan and Kuwait, purposive and snowball sampling was used to choose US diplomats, female participants in US-funded programs, and other stakeholders in the entrepreneurship ecosystem including local government officials, entrepreneurs, and incubator directors. In both Jordan and Kuwait, the interview subjects were English speaking and university educated and had traveled extensively. The interviews were conducted in offices, homes, incubators, and cafes and their duration ranged from 30 to 90 minutes. The interviewees were asked about their understanding of entrepreneurship and about the role of government in promoting entrepreneurship. Entrepreneurs were also asked about their choices and any obstacles or opportunities that they had encountered.

First, the data was organized in NVIVO (qualitative analysis software) to identify themes about the ways that the subjects understand entrepreneurship. NVIVO can find word and phrase patterns, and the researcher can then also use it as a tool for comparing different groups (Bazeley & Jackson, 2013). Then, recurring themes were identified through a close reading of the texts and notes from participant observation. This chapter focuses on one of the main themes that women entrepreneurs identified as central to creating change, which is the idea of mindset. The next section unpacks three aspects of mindset: confidence, open mind, and willingness to take risk.

Entrepreneurial Mindset

This section first examines some structural barriers that women talked about in terms of workplace discrimination and participation. It then explores how women entrepreneurs described their own relationship to entrepreneurship, and how they characterized their mindset. Interviewees were asked about what they thought makes entrepreneurs successful, or motivates people to start pursuing entrepreneurship to begin with. The findings are divided into sections around the themes that interviewees identified. Each section also includes the ways in which people discussed the relationship that each theme had with technology.

Structural Factors

In Jordan, women were facing structural barriers not only to entrepreneurship, but to finding work, and acceptance in the workplace, in general. Only 14.6%

of women in Jordan are part of the workforce (International Labor Organization, 2021), and according to Muna, a single woman in her late 30s who works in journalism, programs that focused on women's empowerment were not accomplishing enough. She spoke about what she thinks of women's empowerment:

> I am bored of it now to be honest. You hear about it a lot. Everybody writes about it. But, I don't know if enough is being done. In Jordan, a lot of the women are educated, a lot of them have university degrees, which is really good. But, many of them end up being teachers for instance, or not working at all. And even those who work, I don't think they are taken seriously by their bosses, or their male colleagues, which is really sad. In our magazine last year, we tried writing about women in top positions and it was really difficult for us to find ten women in top positions, which tells you a lot really. (Muna, 2016)

Muna's comment about being bored about women's empowerment underscores how, for her, the idea of empowering women through entrepreneurship was not leading to enough women being in higher positions. She also drew attention to the disparity between women and men in the workplace and the barriers that women face in practice (Adely, 2012, 138–41). While in Jordan, women spoke about structural barriers such as job availability and funding for starting their businesses, one Kuwaiti woman spoke more about social norms as a barrier to starting her business.

A single woman in her 20s, Yara came from a financially successful family. She had her own resources to start her business. She had completed her studies in the US at a prestigious university, but her father wanted her to come back to Kuwait to work there. In her first job in the banking sector, she was discouraged because she did not feel challenged. She launched her own start-up and felt more stimulated than she had in her finance job. Some of her family members thought she was not doing anything serious until an established woman in the business community wrote about her on social media. After that, her family and friends realized she was working hard to build something. One of the ways that women spoke about overcoming social barriers was through the use of technology. Yara was interested in using technology to build her business. The women in both Kuwait and Jordan were all developing businesses that were ICT based.

One interview subject, Nina, organized a series of roundtable discussions on women and entrepreneurship in Jordan in 2011 and 2012. She specified that in the tech sector, women felt that there was a different mentality from other sectors that was helping women to overcome barriers. Nina was an American who was engaged in building incubators in the region. She said that she felt technology was bringing people together who wanted to provide products and services that they felt were needed. She said,

> There's certainly inequalities and it's a male dominated sector, and I think it's a really interesting time where women are coming into their own and a lot of the

women that I spoke to in the tech sector, whether we were in Jordan, or KSA, or Qatar, or Egypt, said, I feel a sense of opportunity in this sector that I don't have in more traditional sectors. (Curley, 2015)

On the one hand, she said that there was a focus on finding solutions, but on the other she said that there was a persistent idea that technology provided a new space for women as it had a different mentality from other sectors.

Confidence

The idea of how to express confidence is often assumed to be gendered male in entrepreneurship. For example, at pitches, entrepreneurs are expected to present their ideas to attract investors. The understanding of confidence that the women shared was that they learned a way to speak about themselves, a way to present themselves, that made them feel more comfortable with public speaking and/or marketing themselves and their products or ideas. However, women discussed the ways in which their work in the tech sector helped them build confidence through more female-associated traits such as relationship building and being community focused. For some, it was through the struggles they had to overcome, such as being taken seriously or doing something new. For others, working in the tech sector was empowering because they felt that people in tech were focused on finding solutions for their communities. Shams, in Jordan, talked about how technology can facilitate empowerment through the development of tangible skills. She had gone to a summer camp during high school and studied computer programming. At the time, her parents did not know what she would do with this skill, and she was the only girl in the course. For her, the most important part of empowerment through technology was building confidence and soft skills:

It is me, as a woman, [that I] understand my capabilities and [am] able to put these capabilities into something productive and believe in myself. For technology, of course it helps. I think women's empowerment, after working with Injaz,[1] is making sure the girl standing in front of you understands that she has a path in life. One of the things I told the girls, 'if you want to get married, get married, have children, but even if you don't go to university, just work to meet people, to see yourself and try different ideas.'

So, [that] is women's empowerment for me: [knowing] that I can do it. Technology may play 30% [a part of the empowerment], maybe I can open a webpage, but if I don't trust myself to do it, even with all the technology, I can't do it. I can tell you now, for women in IT, or technology, it can empower them because they can work from home. Technology for me is a facilitator, not the core. Technology it is not about technology, it is about people, because you take

---

[1] Injaz is a non-profit that started in Jordan and is focused on empowering youth through entrepreneurship.

the problem and you search for a technical solution for it, right? So, it builds something in you. (Shams, 2016)

For Shams, while technology was part of empowerment, ultimately empowerment came from people feeling the confidence that they could accomplish something. Shams, and others, mentioned that ICT-based enterprises had the potential to be more inclusive of women because it allowed them to work from home. In other words, for some women, it was more accepted by their families if they were not having to interact in work spaces outside of the home. For others, it provided flexibility to work from home with children or care for other family members at home. Shams had worked in the technology sector for over 15 years and felt that working with technology had helped her build confidence because she had been able to support her family. In addition, she also talked about the confidence she gained from her participation in the US-funded TechWomen[2] program:

Lots of things you notice when you come back, each day I notice something changed for me. For example, [it was the] first time I lived alone without my parents. I am not married and am the eldest, [I did] not even [have] pajama parties. It built my confidence in myself that I can live outside my family and community. I can rely on myself. When I used to receive job offers in Dubai, I used to reject them. I was afraid to go there, to live out of the norms of my community and to meet foreign people. I worked for 12 years and didn't know what a panel is, what is moderating a panel. So, that was a new experience for me, moderating a panel, what a pitch is, an elevator pitch, VC, Oasis 500, or what an angel investor might be. Startup weekend started 2014/15 for the first time, but for me, in 2013 all these terminologies were new. (Shams, 2016)

Shams was exposed to aspects of working in the tech and entrepreneurship sector during her participation in TechWomen that were new for her. It inspired her to volunteer to teach technology in schools to girls. She also used her coding skills to help other women in her network to build their businesses. She emphasized how she gained confidence through the experience of living by herself in the US, which she said had made her realize that she could leave Jordan for work if she chooses to. For her, these opportunities were possible because of her engagement in the technology sector.

Open Mind

The idea of the open mind referred to being open to others, to ideas, and beyond the borders of one's country. This concept is gendered female in that it focuses on creativity and building relationships beyond personal goals. Shams

---

[2] TechWomen is a US-funded public diplomacy program that started in 2010. It brings emerging women in STEM from the Middle East, Africa, and Asia to the Silicon Valley for training and internships.

expressed that working in the tech sector had opened up her mind to different ideas, but that ultimately she was driven to find solutions for people and the technology was simply a route to help people. In general, she felt that technology helped to open her mind to new ideas:

> Technology is a really big part of life. Any science, the arts, it is necessary to open your mind to a lot of things, so it changes you. It makes your thinking wider and I think it develops you to be an entrepreneur. I know how to optimize things, because I work with systems. Technology it is not about technology, it is about people, because you take the problem and you search for technical solutions. (Shams, 2016)

In this way, technology was again seen as a route to opening and creating possibilities. It was put into a positive light as a solution to problems. Shams felt that working in her field, and with people in the sciences and arts in general, required having an open mind. For her, this meant challenging herself to connect her skills in technology to people. For Yara in Kuwait, entrepreneurship also encouraged people to be more productive:

> I think it is very important for a number of reasons. I think that when people are engaged in healthy passionate pursuits, things like entrepreneurship where they are really working on something they really believe in, it takes them away from less productive pursuits. I also think entrepreneurship gives you the chance to widen your perspective, become a more well-rounded person. It takes you away from just the chance of maybe falling into the wrong groups, and doing the wrong things, becoming extreme in any sort of way. Because there are more important things now. You become more financially stable, hopefully, if you are successful at your entrepreneurial ambition. When you are financially stable, you have less of that unrest that makes you prone to being angry and resentful. When you are doing something that is so engaging, that takes so much of your time, you have little time to get, if you will, corrupted. I think a lot of what is going on in the Middle East is there is some kind of brainwashing going on for people that feel left out, or people that feel resentful that they don't have enough. But, when you are engaged in business, and it's successful and you are doing something you love, you feel that positivity, you are not so easily dragged into that. (Yara, 2016)

In talking about her experience on the Goldman Sachs 10,000 Women—US Department of State Entrepreneurship Program,[3] she said that someone running the program told her group that one of the goals of the program was to encourage entrepreneurship as a route to becoming more worldly and less nationalistic:

[3] This exchange program started in 2015 as a collaboration between Goldman Sachs and the U.S. Department of State to bring women from the Middle East to the US, including a three-week course in entrepreneurship at Harvard and meetings at Goldman Sachs in New York.

He said, if you have more connections to the outside world, because you are doing trade and business, it becomes less tempting for you to go into this nationalistic seclusionary modes of thinking, such as thinking only about 'protect my tribe, protect my religion, protect my country' kind of thoughts. It made a lot of sense to me. I remember telling the girls, this is why I think they are supporting us and they are paying to do all this. It's because when we are engaged in something productive, we don't have time to be doing, not so productive things.

Yara had been in the US for university and felt that she was able to act as a cultural interpreter for other women on the program. She emphasized that entrepreneurs have to be hard working. She also felt that entrepreneurs are thinking about being connected to the world and not just focused on Kuwait. Jamila, a Kuwaiti married with children had started her own business in 2014 after being first in a government position and then in the private sector. She defined the mindset of an entrepreneur:

An entrepreneur is someone who sees an opportunity, a gap in the market or the society and takes the initiative to be part of something new, to be part of change, to be a productive person rather than a consumer.

Jamila thought that the mentality of entrepreneurs could bring needed changes to her society. But there was also recognition of the structural factors that governments could support to facilitate the growth of the entrepreneurship ecosystem, such as through regulatory and institutional changes. Many of the subjects stated that while in 2010 many people did not know what entrepreneurship or innovation was or did, now the region has moved beyond this nascent stage. At ArabNet in Kuwait in October 2016, several panelists discussed how ICT provided new business opportunities, but also possibilities to create regional shifts to think beyond national borders toward implementing regulation that would ease the movement of goods between the countries of the Gulf, the Levant, and beyond. While in 2012, many were thinking of the changes in terms of broader political and social changes, even regime changes, now the conversation had shifted to a focus on changing specific laws to change the infrastructure and support the ecosystem in this way.

Risk-Taking

Many interviewees expressed risk-taking as a male trait, but then discussed risks they had taken in starting their own businesses. One of the main components that entrepreneurs identified as essential to their success was taking the risk to shift their idea of networking. They differentiated between family networks and the networks of support that they developed through incubators and conferences. Some of the women established networks for mentorship and support through their participation in US public diplomacy programs and incubators. Women used these networks, such as WhatsApp groups, to ask questions of other participants, both from their own countries and from the region. They expressed that sometimes, because they were operating under different conditions, they were able to help each other come up with unique solutions that they would not have considered before. Instead of viewing risk as something they had to face alone, they asked for help in order to figure out solutions for the challenges they faced.

At ArabNet in Kuwait, one panelist talked about how entrepreneurs start with their personal family network and move out from that. The panelist said that extended family was both an asset and a problem because of the pressures from family to not fail. Many subjects talked about how the fear of failure was an obstacle to launching their businesses. For entrepreneurs who did not have an extended family network and financing, they had to prove their business ideas to potential investors. This is the same for any entrepreneur globally, as having access to seed funding is the first step toward launching a business. Interviewees spoke about the importance of networks because of the centrality of family networks for both their personal obligations and for connecting them to opportunities. Sometimes women mentioned how networks could constrain their activities because networks also provided a space where they could be monitored and/or judged or supported by family and community. They were then taking a risk to do something without their family's initial approval. For example, Yara spoke about how her family network was not supporting her until a woman leader in the business community mentioned Yara's work in a national forum. It was only when this prominent leader praised her work that Yara's larger family network took her entrepreneurship seriously. But, she had to be willing to take the risk to begin with.

Beyond the family support, broader networks rely on mutuality and exchange, and it is not common for people with vastly different backgrounds to be in the same networks. However, all of the women spoke about the importance of giving back to their communities. This manifested in encouraging other women to be entrepreneurs or to mentor women and youth to be active volunteers. Some of the women said that there had been some negative reception to their efforts. On a small scale, one woman attributed this to jealousy, but on a larger scale, she felt it was due to the state wanting to control the entrepreneurship and women's empowerment discourse. For some of the women, volunteering and mentorship were concepts that they said were already present in their communities. For women who had started participating in the technology and entrepreneurship workshop circuit, they also were acting as mentors for newer entrepreneurs. Women are often only able to use the social capital that they have from their existing networks because they are so often excluded from some of the opportunities that men have to network, including some formal institutions and employment spaces. Therefore, entrepreneurship provided a space for taking the risk to change in terms of the kinds of networks that entrepreneurs were participating in building.

Discussion and Conclusion

The governments of Kuwait and Jordan have economic goals that they have tied to fostering entrepreneurship and communicating about economic change. If entrepreneurship indeed communicates ideas about change, these changes are not universally defined or understood. Even within the idea of changing a mindset or expanding networks, in reality, the governments are asking people to redefine their position in society toward taking more responsibility for government economic goals. However, women and men entrepreneurs have also constructed an identity around what ICT entrepreneurship means in practice.

This chapter provided evidence for how a small sample of women entrepreneurs in Kuwait and Jordan understood three components of an entrepreneurial mindset and what it meant to them to be an entrepreneur. It examined how confidence, open mind, and risk-taking have both gendered female and male traits. While some initially described confidence and risk-taking as male traits, the data showed that these elements can also contain gendered female traits. The data also provided evidence for the ways that women ICT entrepreneurs linked their understanding of what technology made possible to develop these three elements of an entrepreneurial mindset. Some of the examples included (1) building confidence through learning to use technology to help people/communities, (2) participating in entrepreneurship to help women to open their minds to new ideas and to think beyond nationalism, and (3) taking risks through building networks beyond the family through technology tools.

The theme that repeated was that through their mindset, entrepreneurs took initiative to fix or address a problem or need in society, whether social or market based. In addition to the financial, material reality of the risks inherent to starting a business (and sometimes to leaving well-paid government or private sector work to do so), women said that the idea of being open-minded was central to not only being an entrepreneur, but also to bringing entrepreneurial ideas to their jobs. They also identified being positive, connected to other women internationally, and contributing to change as part of this mindset. Ultimately, the project of empowering women, and society overall, through entrepreneurship is an ongoing process that is affected by power structures, and an empowered ICT woman entrepreneur is multidimensional and does not produce one result. Future research can consider economic class, citizenship status, and different kinds of entrepreneurs to analyze not only how people understand what entrepreneurship means, but also to address how these other contextual factors affect outcomes.

References

Ackerly, B., & True, J. (2010). *Doing Feminist Research in Political and Social Science.* Palgrave Macmillan.

Adachi, T., & Hisada, T. (2017). Gender Differences in Entrepreneurship and Intrapreneurship: An Empirical Analysis. *Small Business Economics, 48*(3), 447–486.

Adely, F. (2012). *Gendered Paradoxes: Educating Jordanian Women in Nation, Faith, and Progress*. University of Chicago Press.

Al Mulia, Y. (2021). *More than 6,000 Kuwait Citizens Left Private Sector in the Past Six Months*, July 18, 2021. https://gulfnews.com/world/gulf/kuwait/more-than-6000-kuwait-citizens-left-private-sector-in-the-past-six-months-1.80739149.

Al-Dajani, H., & Marlow, S. (2010). Impact of Women's Home-Based Enterprise on Family Dynamics: Evidence from Jordan. *International Small Business Journal, 28*(5), 470–486. https://doi.org/10.1177/0266242610370392

Al-Dajani, H., & Marlow, S. (2013). Empowerment and Entrepreneurship: A Theoretical Framework. *International Journal of Entrepreneurial Behavior & Research, 19*(5), 503–524.

Anderson, A. R., & Jack, S. L. (2002). The Articulation of Social Capital in Entrepreneurial Networks: A Glue or a Lubricant? *Entrepreneurship and Regional Development: An International Journal, 14*(3), 193–210.

Autio, E., Kenney, M., Mustar, P., Siegel, D., & Wright, M. (2014). Entrepreneurial Innovation: The Importance of Context. *Research Policy, 43*(7), 1097–1108. https://doi.org/10.1016/j.respol.2014.01.015

Bazeley, P., & Jackson, K. (2013). *Qualitative Data Analysis with NVivo* (2nd ed.). Sage. https://www.amazon.com/Qualitative-Analysis-NVivo-Patricia-Bazeley/dp/1446256561/ref=sr_1_1?ie=UTF8&qid=1492323734&sr=8-1&keywords=Qualitative+Data+Analysis+with+NVivo

Bruni, A., Gherardi, S., & Poggio, B. (2005). *Gender and Entrepreneurship: An Ethnographical Approach* (1st ed.). Routledge.

Cornwall, A., & Anyidoho, N. A. (2010). Introduction: Women's Empowerment: Contentions and Contestations. *Development, 53*(2), 144–149. https://doi.org/10.1057/dev.2010.34

Curley, N. (2015). *Interview Interview by Willow Williamson*.

Estrin, J. (2008). *Closing the Innovation Gap: Reigniting the Spark of Creativity in a Global Economy* (1st ed.). McGraw-Hill.

European Business Review. (2020). Kuwait Keen on Digital Transformation to Build a Society Based on Smart E-Services. *The European Business Review* (blog). January 20, 2020. https://www.europeanbusinessreview.com/kuwait-keen-on-digital-transformation-to-build-a-society-based-on-smart-e-services/.

Gurumurthy, A., & Singh, P. J. (2009). ICTD-Is It a New Species of Development? *IT for Change Perspective Paper Presented at the IT for Change*, Bangalore.

Hanson, E. (2008). *The Information Revolution and World Politics*. Rowman & Littlefield Publishers.

Haugh, H. M., & Talwar, A. (2016). Linking Social Entrepreneurship and Social Change: The Mediating Role of Empowerment. *Journal of Business Ethics, 133*(4), 643–658.

Hayat. (2016). *Interview Interview by Willow Williamson*.

Henry, C., Foss, L., & Ahl, H. (2015). Gender and Entrepreneurship Research: A Review of Methodological Approaches. *International Small Business Journal*, January. doi:https://doi.org/10.1177/0266242614549779.

Hervieux, C., & Voltan, A. (2018). Framing Social Problems in Social Entrepreneurship. *Journal of Business Ethics, 151*(2), 279–293.

Hjorth, D., & Steyaert, C. (2004). *Narrative and Discursive Approaches in Entrepreneurship: A Second Movements in Entrepreneurship Book*. SSRN Scholarly Paper ID 1496119. Social Science Research Network. http://papers.ssrn.com/abstract=1496119.

International Labor Organization. (2021). *Promoting Decent Work in Jordan*. Document. International Labor Organization. 2021. http://www.ilo.org/beirut/countries/jordan/WCMS_474549/lang%2D%2Den/index.htm

Maier, S., & Nair-Reichert, U. (2007). Empowering Women Through ICT-Based Business Initiatives: An Overview of Best Practices in E-Commerce/E-Retailing Projects. *Information Technologies and International Development, 4*(2), 43–60.

Martinez Dy, A., Marlow, S., & Martin, L. (2017). A Web of Opportunity or the Same Old Story? Women Digital Entrepreneurs and Intersectionality Theory. *Human Relations, 70*(3), 286–311. https://doi.org/10.1177/0018726716650730

Martinez Dy, A., Martin, L., & Marlow, S. (2018). Emancipation Through Digital Entrepreneurship? A Critical Realist Analysis. *Organization, 25*(5), 585–608. https://doi.org/10.1177/1350508418777891

Mathew, V. (2010). Women Entrepreneurship in Middle East: Understanding Barriers and Use of ICT for Entrepreneurship Development. *International Entrepreneurship and Management Journal, 6*(2), 163–181. https://doi.org/10.1007/s11365-010-0144-1

Ministry of Digital Economy and Entrepreneurship. (2021). *About MoDEE - Minister of Digital Economy and Entrepreneurship*. 2021. https://www.modee.gov.jo/EN/Pages/About_MoDEE.

Ministry of Foreign Affairs. (2021). *Kuwait Vision 2035 'New Kuwait'*. 2021. https://www.mofa.gov.kw/en.

Muna. (2016). *Interview Interview by Willow Williamson*.

Nicolopoulou, K., Kakabadse, N. K., Nikolopoulos, K. P., Alcaraz, J., & Sakellariou, K. (2016). Cosmopolitanism and Transnational Elite Entrepreneurial Practices: Manifesting the Cosmopolitan Disposition in a Cosmopolitan City. *Society and Business Review, 11*(3) http://www.emeraldinsight.com/doi/pdfplus/10.1108/SBR-01-2016-0001

Organization of the Petroleum Exporting Countries. (2021). *"OPEC: Kuwait"*. 2021. https://www.opec.org/opec_web/en/about_us/165.htm

Roberts, A., & Soederberg, S. (2012). Gender Equality as Smart Economics? A Critique of the 2012 World Development Report. *Third World Quarterly, 33*(5), 949–968. https://doi.org/10.1080/01436597.2012.677310

Schroeder, C. M. (2013). *Startup Rising: The Entrepreneurial Revolution Remaking the Middle East*. Palgrave Macmillan.

Shams. (2016). *Interview Interview by Willow Williamson*.

Sjoberg, L. (2013). *Gendering Global Conflict: Toward a Feminist Theory of War*. Columbia University Press.

State of Kuwait, Ministry of Home Affairs. (2021). *Building Kuwait's Future, One Small Enterprise at a Time*. Text/HTML. World Bank. 2021. https://www.worldbank.org/en/news/feature/2016/03/01/building-kuwait-future-one-small-enterprise-at-a-time

Tickner, J. A. (2006). Feminism Meets International Relations: Some Methodological Issues. In B. A. Ackerly, M. Stern, & J. True (Eds.), *Feminist Methodologies for International Relations* (1st ed., pp. 19–41). Cambridge University Press.

Wennberg, K., Pathak, S., & Autio, E. (2013). How Culture Moulds the Effects of Self-Efficacy and Fear of Failure on Entrepreneurship. *Entrepreneurship and Regional Development,* 25(9–10), 756–780. https://doi.org/10.1080/0898562 6.2013.862975

Yara. (2016). *Interview Interview by Willow Williamson.*

Zineddine, M., & Kindi, H. (2011). The Status of Emirati Women in the ICT Sector. *Proceedings of the International Conference on Technology and Business Management,* March 28.

CHAPTER 31

Disruptive Social Entrepreneurship from Bahrain: The Case of Esra'a Al Shafei

Loubna H. Skalli

This chapter focuses on the Bahraini native, Esra'a Al Shafei, and her *Majal.org* to discuss social entrepreneurship as it intersects with gender and digital technologies in authoritarian contexts. As the founder and executive director of *Majal.org*, Al Shafei has spearheaded since 2006 the creation of innovative online platforms including the award-winning aggregator *CrowdVoice* that documents protest movements and human rights abuses within MENA and beyond. Other online platforms were launched to "amplify underrepresented voices" of the young (*Mideast Youth*), the Arab LGBT community (*Ahwaa.org*), migrant workers in the Gulf countries (*Migrant-Rights.org*), and the region's underground and independent musicians (*Mideast Tunes*). Al Shafei was no more than 19 when she ventured into the world of social entrepreneurship.

This chapter approaches Al Shafei as a disruptive social entrepreneur who mobilizes digital technologies to engineer lasting social change. Al Shafei not only prevented gender hierarchical roles from constraining her work, but also refused to let the patriarchal and authoritarian institutions in Bahrain from interfering in her efforts to engineer social change across the region. Thus, the initial *Mideast Youth* platform soon developed into a more sophisticated non-profit organization that combines digital technologies with grassroots work that mobilize the creativity of young civic energies to advocate for the rights of the underrepresented.

L. H. Skalli (✉)
Washington Program, University of California, Washington, DC, USA

L. H. Skalli, N. Eltantawy (eds.), *The Palgrave Handbook of Gender, Media and Communication in the Middle East and North Africa*, https://doi.org/10.1007/978-3-031-11980-4_31

For her persistent efforts to protect and promote diversity and social justice, Al Shafei received numerous honors and awards from prestigious institutions. In 2008, she received the Berkman Award for Internet Innovation from Harvard Law School for her "outstanding contributions to the internet and its impact on society." The World Economic Forum listed her as one of "15 Women Changing the World in 2015." The same year, she won the "Most Courageous Media" Prize from Free Press Unlimited, and the Monaco Media Prize, which acknowledges innovative uses of media for the betterment of humanity.

Her list of accomplishments and leadership roles is impressively long for one so young. Yet, as this chapter argues, the title of human rights activist, which is often used to describe Al Shafei, rather fails to capture her unique contribution to broadening the meaning and implications of gender and social entrepreneurship as these intersect with digital technologies. While doing so was not her primary goal, her self-reflection on her work provides insights into how to best analyze her contributions:

> Most of my teammates are also hard-working women, and I've always felt encouraged being a part of a community or in a society (Bahrain) where women's contributions were always massive, enough to <u>generate a lot of entrepreneurship and entrepreneurial thinking</u> amongst women in the Gulf. If people question my capabilities for being a woman (especially in the field of technology), that's not really a problem I should be worried about, it's theirs. I've never really focused exclusively on women's rights or been a part of any feminist movements, primarily because I think that one of the best ways to fight for women's rights is to succeed as a woman. (Underlining added, interview with author in 2008)

It is precisely this brand of entrepreneurship and entrepreneurial thinking that this chapter examines to underscore its social and emancipatory potential. The growing literature on women's entrepreneurship in the Middle East and North Africa focuses largely on the business and economic dimensions of entrepreneurship. Without undermining the significance of this line of research, this chapter uses the case of Al Shafei to broaden our understanding and appreciation of women's social entrepreneurship in MENA.

The chapter draws on several sources of data collected over many years and analyzed by the author. The first is a series of personal interviews conducted with Al Shafei via emails (2008, 2010, 2012, and 2020). The questions that Al Shafei responded to are related to the rationale behind and goals set for each of her digital initiative, the role gender plays in her work, the constraints she faces and the successes she achieved despite them, and the nature of impact her work has. The next important data relied on is available by the platforms themselves and consists of a variety of materials including timelines for each initiative, infographics, feature articles, crowdsourced materials, and personal narratives and testimonies of the communities whose causes she advances (migrant workers, member of the LGBTQ communities, artists, activists). Although Al Shafei has so far maintained physical anonymity, she has accepted numerous speaking engagements and granted interviews to a variety of media sources and professional groups. This chapter draws on this body of information as well.

GENDER AND SOCIAL ENTREPRENEURSHIP

It has become a truism to start any discussion of social entrepreneurship with a reminder that the concept is nebulous or fuzzy. Rather than participate in the ongoing efforts to re-/define the concept, this section highlights, first, the core tenets of social entrepreneurship that scholars agree on despite their disciplinary differences. The section, then, engages with the gender perspective on social entrepreneurship to tease out the disruptive elements relevant to this chapter's focus.

As many scholars rightly contend, decades of broadening and deepening the meaning of social entrepreneurship have resulted in making the field "so inclusive that it now has an immense tent into which all manner of socially beneficial activities fit" (Martin and Osberg 2007). The consensus under this "tent" is that social entrepreneurship is both the *process* and the *outcome* of creating social change. It is this willful creation of social change and the relentless pursuit to make it permanent that are so central to any social entrepreneurship activity. G. Dees emphasizes this point in his widely quoted phrase that social entrepreneurship is about "innovation and impact, not income" (2003). What he means here is that the social entrepreneur, unlike the business entrepreneur, is driven by the "mission-related impact" rather than the accumulation of wealth.

This distinction between the business and social entrepreneur is critical for understanding *why* and *how* the social entrepreneur acts willfully to produce permanent "value in the form of large-scale, transformational benefit" targeting social groups (Martin and Osberg 2007). While benefit might accrue to the entire society, the social entrepreneur is primarily driven by justice and equity as well as a passion to leveling the field for the underserved social groups who have minimal to no financial or political capital with which to interrupt their marginalization. The social entrepreneurs' intimate knowledge of their environment, their alertness to social problems, and passion for problem solving are among the reasons why they are hailed as "reformers and revolutionaries" (as G. Dees reminds us, borrowing Schumpeter's phrase, 2001, 2). Their investment in change-making calls for a unique mindset, capabilities, and skill sets that allow them to leverage resources, networks, and capital to achieve their goal. The gender perspective on social entrepreneurship not only builds on and refines the above theoretical insights, but also nuances them by introducing such key concepts as power, authority, and emancipation that are so central to gender justice.

Reflections on gender and social entrepreneurship are fascinating even though research in this area is still in its infancy. This is surprising, however, since emerging studies suggest that there is a less prominent gender gap in social entrepreneurship than there is in the business sector (Nair, 2020). Scholars who have used the gender approach have pointed to the multiple ways that the entrepreneurial ecosystem (social-cultural, legal, political, and economic realities) typically interacts with the individual characteristics of the entrepreneur to shape the nature and scope of her entrepreneurial ventures (Brush et al., 2018; Bosma et al. 2016).

The work of Violina Rindova and her colleagues (2009) has been particularly pertinent in this context. These authors have introduced the notion of *emancipation* to our understanding of social entrepreneurship and refocused our attention on both its potential and implications. As Rindova and colleagues maintain, viewing "entrepreneurial projects as emancipatory efforts focuses on understanding the factors that cause individuals to seek to *disrupt* the status quo and change their position in the social order in which they are embedded—and, on occasion, the social order itself" (italics added 2009, 478). Importantly, the emancipatory approach to entrepreneurship invites us to examine the notion of power, autonomy, and freedom inherent in women's process of *entrepreneuring*. The refocusing of our attention makes the "pursuit of freedom and autonomy relative to an existing status quo the focal point of inquiry" (2009, 478).

This fresh perspective on *entrepreneuring* and emancipation is pertinent to understanding the disruptive potential of social entrepreneurship in the non-democratic context of MENA region, and Bahrain in particular. The emancipatory approach foregrounds the deliberate effort of the entrepreneur to challenge and disrupt the constraints set by the "conventional structures of authority" whether these are of "an intellectual, psychological, economic, social, institutional, or cultural nature" (Rindova et al., 2009, 479). The sections below demonstrate that in the case of Al Shafei's *Majal.org*, it is precisely these repressive structures of authority in the broader Middle East that her entrepreneuring efforts target, interrogate, defy, and seek to subvert. Further, the pursuit of autonomy and freedom, which Violina Rindova and colleagues emphasize as pillars of emancipatory entrepreneurship, is equally central to Al Shafei's projects of social innovation and change. Importantly, by focusing her entrepreneurial efforts on the marginalized individuals and communities in MENA, Al Shafei provides us with an interesting opportunity to study an area about which we know little: name, the intersection of gender, social entrepreneurship, and digital technologies in authoritarian settings.

Our knowledge about gender and social entrepreneurship in MENA remains extremely limited. In fact, the dearth of research in this area is very much consistent with dominant research trends around the world where significantly more attention has been given to women's business entrepreneurship. In the case of MENA, researchers have invariably foregrounded the normative, political, and economic constraints women business entrepreneurs typically face compared to their male counterparts (Aljuwaiber, 2021; Manzoor, 2017; Nair, 2020). While findings from this line of scholarship are insightful for understanding contextual constraints unique to the region, they do not explain how or why women venture into social entrepreneurship or which resources they mobilize to contribute to creating lasting social change. This chapter uses the case study of *Majal.com* to remedy this gap by exploring the disruptive and *emancipatory* potential of social entrepreneurship in MENA.

Contextualizing Esra'a Al Shafei's Entrepreneurship

As a native of Bahrain, Al Shafei' consciously launched her entrepreneurial journey with a focus on such high-risk issues as the promotion of the rights of communities typically marginalized because of their cultural and religious differences, sexual identities, or migration status. Al Shafei's focus has been willful, consistent, and unwavering despite the repressive institutional environment in which her efforts take place. The Kingdom of Bahrain is intolerant to free speech, political opposition, and dissent. Like most countries of the Gulf Cooperation Council (GCC), Bahrain is a perfect tale of contradictions with its heavy investment in a few modern economic institutions and aggressive protection of archaic cultural and social institutions. While the Kingdom has made remarkable strides in modernizing and advancing its economic development, infrastructure-building, and service provision (housing, health, and education), it has simultaneously heightened its restrictions on political freedom and religious and civil liberties. The Human Rights Reports document the extent to which political repression, detention, and censorship of free speech have considerably increased after the 2011 prodemocracy movements (HRW, 2020). Numerous reports also underscore the scope of state harassment and physical and sexual violence against women activists who are thrown in prison for challenging the status quo (Abdallah, 2019).

Today, censorship, erosion of human rights, and ban on independent media stand among some of the most glaring contrasts to the Kingdom's heavy investment in digital technologies. Bahrain is nearing its goal of becoming the region's digital hub. Its citizens enjoy one of the highest rates of cellular penetration in MENA (130 per 100 citizens), internet penetration (99% for both men and women), broadband satellite subscriptions (99%), and social media use (84%) (Global Digital Insights—Bahrain 2020).

Al Shafei's entrepreneuring ambitions have been shaped and informed by this unique context where her activities continue to expand against all odds. Entrepreneurship scholars agree that entrepreneurs have a unique capacity to identify social problems, capitalize on new opportunities, mobilize resources, and commit to pursuing their goals with an unflinching willingness despite the challenges and risks this entails (Oswald & Martin, 2007). Al Shafei identified the oppressive realities of the marginalized communities (youth, LGBT, migrants, and religious minorities), capitalized on advances in digital technologies and social media capabilities, and mobilized her social network and other resources to redress the wrongs she identified. Over the years, she forged a path for herself as a disruptive entrepreneur who is "primarily focused on reimagining social roles and motivating new behaviors" (Martin & Witter, 2011).

One of the social roles she challenges very early in her ventures is the limitations society put on gender roles, entrepreneurship, and digital technologies. As she put it in her 2008 interview with the author:

When I first started out [gender] was an issue, because I was 19 and not many people took me or my work seriously. Some people felt that because I am a young woman, I must be misinformed, or "brainwashed." So critics who disagreed with my work or my values would call me the "small one" in an attempt to mock my age. That just made me work harder and to keep launching new projects that I think helped highlight what youth are capable of. I never let my gender get in the way of anything I create. I always had other challenges to worry about, such as finding the right team and resources.

Although funding has remained a continued struggle, her entrepreneurial activities earned support in various forms. These include grants and paid fellowships from foundations, user donations, crowdfunding campaigns, income from research and consulting work on web development platform, as well as consultation with international organizations.

Yet, resistance to contextual pressures and continued search for resources to further innovative social-driven missions are the hallmarks of the social entrepreneur. Al Shafei's entrepreneurship is not only innovative but also disruptive in its deliberate engagement with the cultural, social, and political realities of her region. Her investment in social change sits at the intersection between human rights struggles, technological innovations, and the nonprofit sector. As the sections below detail, the change her entrepreneuring unleashes transcends the local and national to reach transnational contexts.

MAJAL.COM AND THE DISRUPTIVE SPACES OF SOCIAL ENTREPRENEURSHIP

Mideast Youth

When Al Shafei launched her first initiative, *Mideast Youth*, in 2006, inter-/national discourses about Muslim youth were largely shaped by the security logic of the post-9/11 terrorist attacks on New York City and Washington D.C. Specifically, young Muslim men were framed, by inter-/national media, the policy and security communities, and even academic experts, as a generation of disgruntled extremists attracted to nothing else but Jihadism and global terrorism (Fuller, 2004). Young Muslim women, by contrast, were confined to narratives of victimhood and vulnerability to violence from which they had to be protected and rescued (Skalli, 2013, 2015). These grossly simplistic narratives were convenient to the authoritarian regimes of MENA who further strengthened their control and surveillance of their young with the blessings and financial support of the international community. Like all mischaracterizations, however, the dominant narratives failed to capture the socioeconomic, political, cultural, and ethnic diversity of the young population.

This is the broader context in which Al Shafei launched her first online platform, *Mideast Youth*. Since its inception, *Mideast Youth* imposed itself as the voice of this Muslim young population which was much-talked about yet very little understood beyond the securitization framework. Unsurprisingly, the platform expressed the voice, concerns, as well as the consciousness of a young generation of Middle Easterners aware of not only their marginalities but also their potential as a force for positive change. The website's initial comic depiction of "what we're all about" (Fig. 31.1) captures visually and verbally this generational consciousness and the youth's intention to reframe the lenses through which the world presents it.

The first statements about "what we're all about" acknowledge young people's awareness of the post-9/11 reality, but also appropriate the negative frames of references applied to youth to subvert and disrupt the dominant narratives:

*We are Mideast Youth. We work against repression, discrimination, and persecution. We are **extremists** ... when it comes to conciliation! We believe in tolerance. We're completely fed up with divisiveness and hatred. We don't always agree ... but we listen and we learn. We grew up with 21st century culture and we see the foolishness of old barriers and grudges. We love our heritages but reject the us versus them attitude. Equality and free speech are a must and there's no way we'll shut up until everyone enjoys these basic human rights! Listen to us now because ours will soon be the generation in charge!*

The comic self-representation is striking for its inclusiveness and linguistic ingenuity. It makes references to "extremism" to express youth belief in tolerance, freedom, and human rights. It conveys the voice of a generation conscious of itself as a *generation* simultaneously anchored in its sociocultural and linguistic "heritages" as well as in the twenty-first-century culture where diversity and difference are celebrated above all divisiveness.

When *Mideast Youth* is contextualized within the larger environment within which it was launched, one cannot but see it as an innovative entrepreneurial effort fully engaged with a broad mission of social change that goes well beyond the local and national to include international scope. Reflecting on this early initiative, Al Shafei reminds us that in 2006, "We didn't have that influx of information we receive today ... This was important content, especially in places that historically experienced a lot of surveillance and censorship. Governments were still trying to work that out - technologies and channels to censor and surveil users, and how to trace their data" (2008 interview with author).

Aware of all these restrictions, Al Shafei capitalized on the opportunities that digital technology provided to "amplifying the voices of the underrepresented" by opening an alternative space for them to express themselves and exchange information. The website identifies itself as "a regional online network that supports freedoms, human rights, religious belief rights, minorities, and

Fig. 31.1 What we're all about

tolerance. It breaks the boundaries, both geographical and social, among the youth of the Middle East and North Africa and provides them with broad creative horizons to freely express their opinions, experiences, and exchange information with each other."

The calls for justice, diversity, tolerance, and self-representation launched on *Mideast Youth* were to be amplified in the subsequent platforms and project that Al Shafei has been spearheading since 2006.

INNOVATION AND ADAPTION: FROM *MIDEAST YOUTH* TO *MAJAL.COM*

Social entrepreneurs, according to scholars in the field, are seen to be directly and intimately involved in processes of innovation and change in their societies and beyond. Peter Drucker, for instance, considers this relationship to change as one of the distinguishing characteristics of the entrepreneur, since she/he "always searches for change, responds to it, and exploits it as an opportunity" (quoted in G. Dees 1998). Building on his assessment, G. Dees maintains that social entrepreneurs are unique because they "have a mind-set that sees the possibilities rather than the problems created by change" (1998). The point here is that what makes social entrepreneurs "agents of change" is precisely this constant search for smart ways to solve social problems through a relentless process of adaptation and innovation. Reflecting on the driving force behind her work, Al Shafei states that, in addition to giving voice and visibility to injustices, "I always knew that I wanted people to view the Middle East as a place where there's innovation, where people are actually creating things" (Vital Voices, 2018).

Innovation, adaptation, and adjustment are some of the key strategies that Al Shafei put in action under her *Mideast Youth*. The platform has been in a constant process of adaption by making it accessible to diverse linguistic communities (Arab, Farsi, English), religious communities (Christians, Jews, Baha'is, Hindus, Muslims, and members of the atheist communities), as well as marginalized ethnic communities (*Kurdish. Rights.org*). In 2006, Al Shafei turned her attention to one of the communities in the region whose plight had hitherto remained undocumented and unacknowledged: migrant workers.

With the launch of *Migrant-Rights.org*, the platform was designed to deliberately break the silence and expose the violence against migrants in the GCC countries: Bahrain, Kuwait, Oman, Qatar, Saudi Arabia, and the United Arab Emirates (UAE). Migrants make upwards of 50% of the GCC labor force. Yet, stories about their living and working conditions, the violations of their basic human rights, and the oppressive practices to which they are subjected daily remained quasi-absent from public discussion and debate. Outside of Western-based academic and human rights reports, migrant realities and voices were invisible in the region (Fernandez, 2014). Since its creation in 2007, *Migrant-Rights.org* set itself as the voice, eyes, and ears of the GCC migrant communities. The platform has provided a rare space for documenting and sharing their narratives of struggles as well as producing visual and statistical data to map out the scope of violation of their rights. The initiative mobilizes digital technologies in pertinent and innovative ways by providing interactive capabilities and infographics while protecting the anonymity of the storyteller. Further, *Migrant-Rights.org* combines its online platforms with on-ground projects, and grassroots mobilizing. Through this combination, the initiative has contributed to igniting open debates about migrants' lives among the public and carving out a path towards behavior change. Today, this organization has established itself as "one of the most credible, resource-rich, and rights-based initiatives that brings together diverse communities" (migrants, academics, media, citizens, employers, civil rights organizations) around the plight of the migrants (interview with author).

Adopting digital technologies and adapting them to the realities on the grounds are among the important strategies that stand out in Al Shafei's entrepreneurial work. Since 2006, the social entrepreneur has contextualized advances in digital technologies to make them relevant and meaningful within her largely undemocratic environment. As she put it: "There are a lot of cultural and political sensitivities to consider. People don't understand they are building technology for vulnerable populations. We knew that a lot of the tools we were using were not meant to be used by us" (McGivern Foundation, 2018). What she is referring to here is her awareness of the "limitless opportunities" that digital technologies offer to *both* the oppressors and to the oppressed. This awareness explains why privacy, security, and anonymity have been the three top priorities that have allowed Al Shafei to persevere, innovate, and expand her work. As she put it, "Privacy, security and anonymity are three things that were vastly underrated. These three things are not typically built-in when tools are exported to us, and if we didn't re-imagine such applications, it made no sense to use them in our context" (Shuttleworth Foundation, 2018).

Thus, although Al Shafei has given numerous interviews and been recognized by prestigious awards and fellowships, her identity remains anonymous. Although *Mideast Youth* has its physical base in the Middle East, its legal status as a formally registered nonprofit is granted from the Netherlands. The move was consciously made to protect the organization's finances from being frozen by regional governments. Again, it was only in 2015 that the Mideast Youth team met for the first time in The Hague after a decade of working together remotely. Privacy, security, and anonymity interact in a complex way especially in some of the groundbreaking work that intends to empower the most oppressed social group and communities. This is best illustrated through the following three award-winning initiatives launched prior to the 2011 democratic movements in MENA: *CrowdVoice*, *Ahwaa*, and *Mideast Tunes*.

CrowdVoice

The launch of *CrowdVoice* prior to the 2011 democratic uprising in MENA, and its adaptation to subsequent waves of social movements around the world, is probably one of the most powerful initiatives that captures Al Shafei's entrepreneurship mindset. The site was initially meant as an interactive aggregator of information *by* activists and *for* activists. The platform capitalized on advances in digital technologies, and specifically the power of crowdsourced media, to enable victims and witnesses of oppression to record and circulate images, videos, and links that document state violence against political dissent. Although initially started in the Middle East in response to the needs of local dissenting voices, its appeal and usefulness were immediate to political dissenters from Indonesia, Russia, India, and Pakistan to Uganda, North Korea, and Kyrgyzstan. This appeal can be explained by Al Shafei's ability to identify as well as respond to three interrelated needs hitherto unaddressed: a space for political activists to actively author and widely share their own narratives of dissent, an opportunity to disrupt and discredit the hegemonic narratives of authoritarian regimes, and a site for democratizing knowledge production and information sharing while informing global public opinion about the cost of dissent.

First, one of the key features of *CrowdVoice* is the opportunity it gives activists to author their own narratives of dissent. This is the case because this is a user-powered service that allows anyone to be content producer and contributors to information collection and distribution. Whether contributors are leaders, participants, or witnesses to social movements, the content they collect and share gives movements of social and political change both visibility and context. As a wise commentator put it, "watching protests or disasters happen across the world is virtually pointless without context. The genius of *CrowdVoice* was to help us all make sense of the data" (Shuttle Foundation, 2008). At the same time, the content (videos, images, personal accounts, and testimonies) is curated and contextualized by the community of users. *CrowdVoice*, according to Al Shafei, continues to grow and build a community of nearly 30,000 volunteers who actively moderate the content monthly (interview with author).

Second, and given the capabilities and built-in features of *CrowdVoice*, the site allows the users an opportunity to disrupt and discredit the hegemonic narratives of authoritarian regimes. This is inevitable when voices of dissent are able to instantly collect and disseminate information and when victims and witnesses of state violence are provided an outlet to recount their narratives of oppression. In fact, Al Shafei's initiative problematizes acts of witnessing and processes of documenting information. John Durham Peters' insights are relevant when he states that "[w]itnessing is an intricately tangled practice. It raises questions of truth and experience, presence and absence, death and pain, seeing and saying, and the trustworthiness of perception" (2001, 707). Regardless of their position of power(lessness), *CrowdVoice* approaches citizens around the world as meaning makers, content generators, and right bearers.

By elevating their acts of witnessing and personal narratives, the site raises questions about the truth and truthworthiness in the narratives produced by the authoritarian state's apparatuses of information and communication. That is, the diversity of authors, sources, and outlets of information available through *CrowdVoice* challenges the authoritative state in its monopoly over "facts" and "truths." Disruption in this monopoly allows oppressed and marginalized groups to bear witness to their own oppression despite their marginality. Since 2010, *CrowdVoice* has been actively engaged in giving voice to marginality by opening a space for producing counter-hegemonic discourses and creating hope for an alternative world based on justice.

It is the above features and possibilities that encourage us to consider *CrowdVoice* as a site for democratizing knowledge production and information sharing. This is done not only because citizens are content producers but also because one of the ambitions of initiative is to inform global public opinion about the cost of dissent. As Al Shafei states in one of her interviews:

> We wanted to raise awareness and deepen the insight into these forces of change … We had these interviews of activists that have since disappeared, media articles and blog posts and all this information, so we came up with the idea of infographics and timelines to make sure the platform followed the flow across the web of these ongoing conflicts.

Making information accessible, useable, and shareable among the largest public is one of the ambitions of the initiatives from the start. Responding to the question of Bahrain's censorship of online sites, Al Shafei responds "*CrowdVoice* still is censored in Bahrain to this day—but the rest of the world still has access. Sometimes that's enough for me, for people to see the information for themselves and to be able to use, repurpose it and adapt it." And the world has been turning to the site, from journalists and reporters to researchers, educators, and policy and advocacy groups who find educational value in the wide range of information *CrowdVoice* aggregates. The website points to ways in which its photo archives, aggregated articles, blogs, videos, educational materials, interactive timelines, and infographics have provided a textured understanding of topics for diverse users. The awards Al Shafei received for *CrowdVoice* recognize the public utility service of this initiative. Beyond being a clearing house of information to journalists around the world, the site according to Al Shafei "provides a lot of the legwork for anyone that doesn't have the time. For us, it meant things were getting reported, and it gave them that angle they previously didn't consider (Shuttle Foundation 2018).

Mideast Tunes

Social entrepreneurship and innovation, according to scholars, have the potential to "provide solutions to social needs that the current institutional status quo neglects or only partially attends to" (Jacobi et al., 2017, 265). Among the unattended needs that Al Shafei identified early in her career is a safe space for two marginalized and targeted social groups: independent musicians and LGBTQ communities in MENA. In the first case, Al Shafei launched *Mideast Tunes* in 2010 as a "platform for Middle Eastern musicians who use music as a tool for social change. It helps people discover and market these bands so that their voices and causes will always be heard" (interview with author, 2012). Music, like other cultural and artistic expressions, has always been part of the cultural histories of struggles in MENA, from earlier revolutions against colonial powers to ongoing struggles for citizens' rights, freedoms, and dignity. But politically conscious art and dissenting artistic voices have always been targeted by the authoritarian apparatuses of surveillance and punishment.

The cultural and artistic landscape prior to the 2011 democratic uprisings was vibrant with dissenting artistic voices who kept the circulation of their expressive art largely underground for understandable reasons. This is the "need" that Al Shafei identified and responded to. As she put it, "If you read the mainstream coverage on underground music during the revolutions and regional protests, it always brings across the idea that somehow, this is a new phenomenon here. But some musicians have been doing this for almost a decade, some much more than this. It's time they all get discovered." *Mideast Tunes* puts advances in digital technologies to the service of discovering the many facets of Middle Eastern music scene. Today, the prolific literature on the Middle East uprisings has confirmed the instrumental role that underground artists played prior to and during the recent uprisings (Skalli 2013). Artists were not only inspired by the regions' demands for social change but also invested in their artistic instruments to forge political consciousness around change. Since *Mideast Tunes* went live, the site continued to expand and diversify its applications and services. Today, *Mideast Tunes* provides weekly podcasts on the "intersection of alternative music and social change in the Arab world." The site has imposed itself within and outside the region as a major hub for recognizing and appreciating independent artists who have a space to "come out" of the underground to upload and share their music. The site boasts nearly 2000 artists with more than 11,000 tracks (including hip-hop, metal, folk, and other forms) all vetted and posted by Al Shafei and her team.

It is the same capacity to identify social needs, mobilize resources, and utilize digital technologies that drove Al Shafei to launch *Ahwaa*. Like all prior entrepreneurial innovations, this website provides a safe space for the LGBTQ community to connect and communicate. Virtually all members of the LGBTQ communities of MENA are underrepresented and subjected to systemic oppression, discrimination, and persecution. Incidents of violence against individuals from this social group are often sensationalized material for the region's newspapers and other popular media outlets. *Ahwaa* not only recognizes the marginalization and demonization of this community, but the lack of a space "to share their thoughts, fears, and concerns regarding their sexuality and identity … youth felt increasingly isolated, distant, and depressed."

But social entrepreneurs, as we have established, identify not only social problems and needs, but also opportunities and solutions. As Al Shafei states, "with so many young LGBT people across the Middle East and North Africa region embracing the web, we saw an opportunity to create an interactive platform that connected this community in an anonymous and supportive space" (interview with author). The three core principles of safety, anonymity, and privacy, discussed earlier in this chapter, are critical for this website as well. With these priorities in mind, the website deploys protective tools, such as data encryption, and numerous safety measures, to protect sensitive information of the users. Safety measures have allowed the website to survive censorship attempts and grow into a better organized, informed, and served community.

In addition to opening this space for interaction, Al Shafei reports how the website has created opportunities for support groups and rights groups to communicate, meet, and create synergies. LGBTQ organizations across the region, she maintains, use *Ahwaa* "to reach their target audiences more securely and efficiently. In turn, users have access to comprehensive educational resources regarding health, social, and legal issues from a regional perspective." In addition to this, *Ahwaa* has enabled users to connect for protests, build media campaigns against homophobia, and strategize for better communication with religious leaders and other power wielders in their societies. Finally, the platform also enables reporters and investigators to access members of the LGBTQ communities for interviews.

In the end, the numerous sites and services created under *Mideast Youth* since its creation in 2006 have grown well beyond their initial geographic locality and its specific needs. In 2016, M*ideast Youth* was officially rebranded and renamed *Majal.org*. The broad appeal of *CrowdVoice*, Migrants-Rights.com, *Mideast Tunes*, and *Ahwaa* all encouraged Al Shafei to engage in yet another process of adaptation and adjustment. She explains this best when she states in an interview with the author that "We changed the name from Mideast Youth because it no longer represented what we were working on: firstly our work impacts beyond youth, and secondly we expanded to include beyond the Mideast region. (*CrowdVoice*, for example, was a global project and its primary users were in Mexico and India.) *Majal* made a lot more sense because it also had a more local name, a local meaning, not just in Arabic but in Farsi with positive connotations in other languages like Hindi, Urdu, and Tagalog. We feel this name better represents our work, and how/why we do it."

Conclusion

This chapter has focused on the Bahraini-born Esra'a Al Shafei to discuss the emergence of a young generation of tech-savvy change-makers who deploy digital technologies in an innovative, relentless, and daring fashion to change the world around them. From the inception of her first digital platform, Al Shafei set the goals of promoting diversity, protecting human rights, and amplifying the voices of the underrepresented in MENA. Interviews with Al Shafei and analysis of her work over the last decade all point to the unique mindset and vision of a social entrepreneur who is deeply involved in the sociocultural, political, and economic challenges of her environment, yet determined to rise above them to effect change one platform at a time.

In addition to the contextual constraints, Al Shafei is aware that her entrepreneurial activities are taking place within an environment of entrenched hierarchical gendered roles and patriarchal cultural expectations. Rather than seeing these constraints, the entrepreneurial mindset creates opportunities to disrupt the status quo. *Majal.org*, as this chapter has argued, is a testament to the entrepreneur's capacity to turn problems into opportunities and challenges into possibilities to create lasting social change. Digital technologies here are instruments towards creating this desired change. Perhaps nothing captures better this drive for effecting change than the following statement from her: "For me to do all of this required an enormous amount of patience, persistence, loneliness. I mean, there were many times where I've felt I'm not communicating this idea enough because not enough people are getting behind it. I'm not getting the support, I'm not getting the funding. But, something in me just said, to keep going. And I had to teach myself how to develop websites at a very early stage, how to register a domain, how to start generating a community around an issue, how to reach people. And it really took a decade to get to where I am today. It was just a lot of challenges and obstacles. But really, the passion was always there" (interview with author).

Scholars see social entrepreneurs as change-makers who typically "propel" social change through a consistent, bold, and even stubborn pursuit of resources and tools to reach their goal. Yet, one of the main challenges in appreciating the contribution of social entrepreneurship is the difficulty in assessing the degree or scope of their social impact. G. Dees argues in this context that "It is inherently difficult to measure social value creation. How much social value is created by reducing pollution in a given stream, by saving the spotted owl, or by providing companionship to the elderly? The calculations are not only hard but also contentious" (1998, 3). Given the nature and focus of Al Shafei's work, one rightly wonders how to assess or measure value created by promoting the voices of the diverse youth population in the Middle East, giving visibility to the violations of migrants' rights, or providing a safe space for independent artists and LGBT individuals to interact and organize.

While it is challenging to capture the value of all these initiatives or "measure" their impact with any degree of accuracy, one is encouraged to turn to other "indicators" that can capture social change. In a recent interview with Al Shafei, she acknowledges precisely this measurement challenge and nuances how we should look at impact and reach. As she says:

> We know we're reaching the communities we're representing based on the analytics (local traffic) as well as the fact that we see many active engagements on platforms like *Ahwaa*. For Migrant Rights, many workers have been impacted by the advocacy work and you can follow @MigrantRights on Twitter to explore some of these direct campaigns that support workers in need, anything from urgent supplies to providing legal representation or assisting with tickets for workers to be able to go back home regardless of their debts in the countries they're stuck in. (Interview with author)

Al Shafei's statement problematizes the question of impact and encourages us to broaden its meaning by thinking of "proxy" measurements. These would include the growing number of the direct users of *Majal.org*, the expanding community of beneficiaries, the types of recognitions from awards and grants supporting her work, the acknowledgments from national/international communities of experts (academics, journalist, activists, and human rights organizations) who all use the platforms, as well as the growing army of volunteers who contribute to supporting the work. As a disruptive social entrepreneur, Al Shafei confirms that while social change might not be easily captured in numbers, entrepreneuring within restrictive environments, such as Bahrain, carries significant emancipatory potential for both the social entrepreneur and the marginalized communities she is targeting.

By focusing on the case of Al Shafei and *Majal.com*, this chapter makes two important claims. First, Al Shafei's innovative contributions call for rethinking activism beyond its classic definition to account for the emergence of new entrepreneurial possibilities and disruptive social innovation in the age of digital technologies. In his earliest and most influential piece on social entrepreneurship, Gregory Dees (1998) positions the entrepreneur as the problem solver in search for the "most effective methods" to generate lasting change. This chapter has discussed *Majal.com* as the work of a disruptive social innovator who deploys the most effective methods and strategies to promote social and cultural change despite the risks this entails.

The second claim this chapter makes is that the platforms launched by *Majal.com* complicate our understanding of knowledge production and the acts of witnessing, recording, documenting, and archiving human rights violations. In doing this, the numerous projects launched under *Majal.com* not only disrupt the direction and flow of state-controlled information but also interrupt the authoritarian state's hegemony over historical accounts of social movements, citizen participation, and the cultures of protest. Since 2006, the launch of the first platform, Al Shafei has structured the platforms around disruptive tactics based on fact finding and sharing, evidence-based claims, citizen reporting, acts of witnessing, and personal stories. Ultimately, analysis of Esra'a Al Shafei's work and accomplishments introduces us to the under-researched world of young disruptive social innovators who rise above political constraints and exclusionary social and political structures to engineer change one platform at a time. Future research should identify other types of social innovation in MENA to examine the unique characteristics and contributions that emerge from the intersection of gender and social entrepreneurship in this region.

REFERENCES

Abdallah, J. (2019). *Rights Groups Slam Bahrain over Detention of Female Activists*. Aljazeera. https://www.aljazeera.com/news/2019/10/29/rights-groups-slam-bahrain-over-detention-of-female-activists.

Aljuwaiber, A. (2021). Entrepreneurship Research in the Middle East and North Africa: Trends, Challenges, and Sustainability Issues. *Journal of Entrepreneurship in Emerging Economies, 13*(3), 380–426.

Bosma, N., Schøtt, T., Terjesen, S. A., & Kew, P. *Global Entrepreneurship Monitor 2015 to 2016. Special Topic Report on Social Entrepreneurship (May 31, 2016)*. SSRN: https://ssrn.com/abstract=2786949

Brush, C., Edelman, L. F., Manolova, T., et al. (2018). A Gendered Look at Entrepreneurial Ecosystems. *Small Business Economics, 53*, 393–408.

Dees, J. G. (1998). *The Meaning of "Social Entrepreneurship". The Kauffman Center for Entrepreneurial Leadership*. Kansas City, MO and Palo Alto, CA.

Dees, J. G. (2001). *The Meaning of "Social Entrepreneurship"*. Draft Paper. http://www.fuqua.duke.edu/centers/case/documents/dees_SE.

Dees, G. (2003). *Social Entrepreneurship Is About Innovation and Impact, Not Income*. Fuqua Duke Center. https://centers.fuqua.duke.edu/case/wp-content/uploads/sites/7/2015/02/Article_Dees_SEisAboutInnovationandImpactNotIncome_2003.pdf

Fernandez, B. (2014). *Essential Yet Invisible: Migrant Domestic Workers in the GCC*. Explanatory note, 4. Migration Policy Centre. http://hdl.handle.net/1814/32148

Fuller, G. (2004). *The Youth Crisis in Middle Eastern Society*. 4 Institute for Social Policy and Understanding. https://www.ispu.org/wp-content/uploads/2017/07/the-youth-crisis-in-middle-eastern-society-graham-fuller.pdf

Human Rights Watch. World Report. (2020). https://www.hrw.org/sites/default/files/world_report_download/hrw_world_report_2020_0.pdf

Manzoor, A. (2017) Womenpreneurs in MENA Region. In *Gender and Diversity: Concepts, Methodologies, Tools, and Applications* (pp. 1144–1158). IGI Global.

Martin, R., & Osberg, S. (2007). Social Entrepreneurship: The Case for Definition. *Stanford Social Innovation Review, 5*, 28.

Martin, C. E. & Witter, L. (2011). Social or Cultural Entrepreneurship: An Argument for a New Distinction. *Stanford Social Innovation Review*. Dec. 8, https://ssir.org/articles/entry/social_or_cultural_entrepreneurship_an_argument_for_a_new_distinction

McGivern, C. (2018). *Esra'a Al Shafei & CrowdVoice: Amplifying the Unheard*. Shuttleworth Foundation. https://shuttleworthfoundation.org/thinking/2018/12/27/thinking-esraa-crowdvoice/

Nair, S. R. (2020). To Examine Women Social Entrepreneurial Ecosystems: Opportunities and Challenges. *Handbook of Research on Smart Territories and Entrepreneurial Ecosystems for Social Innovation and Sustainable Growth* (pp. 326–345).

Peters, J. D. (2001). Witnessing. *Media, Culture and Society, 23*, 707–723.

Skalli, L. H. (2013). *Introduction, Middle East Journal of Culture and Communication, 6*(1), 5–14. https://doi.org/10.1163/18739865-00503001

Skalli, L. H. (2015). The Girl Factor and the (In)Security of Coloniality: *A View from the Middle East. Alternatives, 40*(2), 174–187. https://doi.org/10.1177/0304375415589433

Rindova, V., Barry, D., Ketchen, D. J., & JR. (2009). Entrepreneuring as Emancipation. *The Academy of Management Review, 34*(3), 477–491.

Vital Voices. (2018). *Global Leadership Award*. Esra'a Al Shafei. https://www.thefemword.world/her-story/esraa-al-shafei

von Jacobi, N., Nicholls, A., & Chiappero-Martinetti, E. (2017). Theorizing Social Innovation to Address Marginalization. *Journal of Social Entrepreneurship, 8*(3), 265–270.

Index[1]

[1] Note: Page numbers followed by 'n' refer to notes.